Charles Dickens

Dickens's Dictionary of the Thames

Charles Dickens

Dickens's Dictionary of the Thames

ISBN/EAN: 9783337509576

Printed in Europe, USA, Canada, Australia, Japan

Cover: Foto ©Thomas Meinert / pixelio.de

More available books at **www.hansebooks.com**

DICKENS'S

DICTIONARY

OF  THE THAMES

1885

MACMILLAN & CO.

3

DICKENS'S
DICTIONARY

THE THAMES,

FROM ITS SOURCE TO THE NORE.

1885.

AN UNCONVENTIONAL HANDBOOK.

London:
MACMILLAN & CO., BEDFORD STREET, STRAND.

PREFACE.

THE objects aimed at in this book, which follows naturally on the original Dictionary of London, have been to give practical information to oarsmen, anglers, yachtsmen, and others directly interested in the river; to serve as a guide to the numerous strangers who annually visit the principal places on its banks; to furnish a book of reference for residents; as well as to provide in a concise form a useful handbook for those connected with the port of London and its trade.

A Dictionary of the Thames which should include a Dictionary of London was obviously incompatible with the space at my disposal. From Kew to Woolwich, therefore, it has been necessary to omit all matters not immediately connected with the river itself.

The favourite excursion from Oxford to London will be found fully dealt with under the head, "Trip from Oxford," which includes full descriptions of locks, etc., and distances from place to place. The numerous maps already in existence vary so much as to the latter point, that I have thought it best to adopt the measurements kindly given to me by the Thames Conservancy, which are sufficiently accurate for all practical purposes. For convenience of reference the guide to Oxford is divided into two parts, Oxford City and Oxford University. Under the latter head will be found descriptions of the University buildings.

Since the book was first published, the trip from Cricklade to Oxford and a description of the principal places on the Thames above Oxford have also been added to its contents.

In conclusion, it is my pleasant duty to express my grateful thanks for the courteous readiness with which my applications for information and assistance have been responded to, both by the authorities of the Trinity House and Thames Conservancy, as well as by the very numerous correspondents who have afforded me valuable assistance.

CHARLES DICKENS.

ROPER FRÈRES & Cº.'S
CHAMPAGNES.

ROPER FRÈRES' First Quality Extra Dry or Medium Dry.
ROPER FRÈRES' Vin Brut or Natural Champagne.

ROPER FRÈRES & Co.'s Champagnes are most suitable for Yachting Matches, Boating Parties, Regattas, Picnics, &c., and can be obtained of all Wine Merchants and at all Hotels.

THURSTON'S

Established 1814.

By Appointment to H.M. The Queen and H.R.H. The Prince of Wales.

BILLIARD

TABLES.

First Class Prize Medal, London, 1851; Honourable Mention, London, 1862; Prize Medal, Sydney, 1879, "First Award"; First Class Certificate and Silver Medal, Calcutta, 1883; Diploma of Honour, "Highest Award," London, 1884.

Sole Makers of the "PERFECT" BILLIARD CUSHIONS as used by JOHN ROBERTS, Jun., and approved by the LEADING PROFESSIONAL PLAYERS (vide Testimonials), also of ROBERTS' CHAMPION CUE (registered).

The **NEW ELECTRIC CLOTH** can only be obtained of

THURSTON & CO.,

16, CATHERINE STREET, STRAND, LONDON, W.C.

DICKENS'S

DICTIONARY OF THE THAMES.

Abingdon, Berkshire, on the right bank, from London 103¾ miles, from Oxford 7¾ miles. A station on the Great Western Railway, from Paddington 60 miles. The time occupied by the trains varies from one hour and three-quarters upwards ; the station is about twelve minutes' walk from the river. Population, 6,506. Soil, gravel. Abingdon is situated at the junction of the Ock with the Thames, and can boast very considerable antiquity. It appears to have grown up round a great abbey which was founded here so far back as the 7th century, but it is probable that much of the early history of Abingdon is entirely of a legendary kind, and that little is known about it with absolute certainty until the time of the Conquest. The evidence of Domesday Book goes to show that the abbey at that time was rich in landed property. Desperate quarrels occurred between the monks and the citizens, and in 1327 a great part of the abbey was burnt in a riot, in which the Mayor of Oxford and certain disorderly students of that University took the part of the inhabitants of Abingdon. The town gradually grew into importance, principally through its extensive cloth trade, but received a severe blow when the abbey was abolished in 1538 and its large revenues diverted into other channels. Another reason for the importance of the town in ancient days was the building of its bridge by John Huchyns and Geoffrey Barbur in 1416. In the reign of Queen Mary, 1557, a Charter of Incorporation was granted to the town at the instigation of Sir John Mason, an influential inhabitant, and it has ever since been represented in Parliament, the original number of two members being now reduced to one. The borough is now represented by Mr. John C. Clarke, a Liberal. The number of voters on the register in 1878 was 890. The town is governed by a mayor, four aldermen, and twelve councillors. The principal business centre is the Market-place, in High-street, Stert-street, East St. Helen's-street, The Square, and Ock-street. It is a clean, quiet little place—quiet even to the point of dulness—with many good houses both modern and ancient. Among the latter may be instanced an excellent example of old timbering in a house in Stert-street. Notwithstanding its apparent quiet a fair amount of trade is carried on in Abingdon, and one of its principal industries is that of the manufacture of ready-made clothing, thus, oddly enough, carrying out the old traditions of the place, which, as Leland says, at one time, "stood by clothing." The market-house stands on an open arcade of stone pillars with a timbered roof, and is the work of Inigo Jones. Built in 1667, it was restored in 1853, and stands on the site of the famous old market cross which was destroyed by the Parliamentary General

Waller in 1644. A curious picture of the cross is on the outside of the south wall of Christ's Hospital, facing the river. The abbey gateway still stands to the eastward of the market-place, and a little beyond it, on the right, are some very interesting remains of the old abbey itself, now in the occupation of a brewer, but readily accessible to visitors. Here, at the extreme end of the yard, some crumbling steps with a time-worn wooden balustrade at the top lead to the abbot's apartments, now used as lofts, in which are the remains of a fine fireplace, said to be of the time of Henry III., with a capacious chimney, some good windows, and well-preserved pointed arches to the doorways. The roofs are lofty and the walls of immense thickness. Underneath this room is a remarkable crypt, also unusually lofty, which is at present used for the storage of bitter ale. The entrance to the crypt is close to the backwater of the Thames, and is shaded by some splendid chestnuts —for which indeed Abingdon is remarkable. The upper windows facing the river at this point are in good preservation, and, from a lane between the brewery and the abbey gateway, is a very picturesque view of the great chimney above mentioned.

The church of St. Nicholas adjoins the abbey gateway, and will well repay a visit. It contains a painted mural monument, with a carved stone base, reaching from the floor almost to the ceiling, dedicated to the memory of John Blacknall and Jane his wife, "who both of them finished an happy course upon earth, and ended their days in peace on the 21st day of August, 1625." They are represented by two figures in black kneeling on red and gilt cushions, she with her two children praying behind her ; and the epitaph runs as follows :

When once the liv'd on earth one bed did hold
Their bodies, which one minute turned to mould,
Being dead, one grave is trusted with that prize,
Until the trump doth sound, and all must rise;
Here death's stroke, even, did not part this pair,
But by this stroke they more vnited were :
And what left they behind you plainly see,
One only davghter, and their charity.
What thovgh the first by death's command did leave us,
The second, we are sure, will ne'er deceive us.

Blacknall was a great benefactor to the town, and among his charities is a dole of forty-seven loaves of bread, which are distributed from his tomb every Sunday. There is a small brass with an inscription to the Bostock family (1669), some curious old stained glass panes with an almost undecipherable inscription, and an old carved stone font. The registers date back to 1558, are in splendid order, and most carefully bound and preserved, and contain many curious entries ; among others, the records of several civil marriages, after publication of the names three times in the market, attested by John Bolton and others, mayors of the town in 1657. The church has a tower with a singular square turret attached, and a good Norman doorway.

A much finer church is St. Helen's, close to the river, the spire of which, with its flying buttresses, is a landmark to this portion of the Thames. This really handsome church has a nave and chancel of equal breadth, and side aisles, with timbered roof, good throughout and in the nave and chancel very elaborate. In the north aisle the roof is still decorated with curious paintings, many of which are gradually but surely fading. There is a new carved marble font and modern oak rood-screen, both of considerable beauty. Among the monuments is the stone memorial in the north aisle to John Roysse, the founder of the Abingdon Grammar School, who died in 1571, leaving express orders that the great stone in his arbour in his London garden should be the upper stone of his tomb at Abingdon, round about which four-and-twenty pensioners should for ever kneel on Sundays to receive alms ; and with further careful provision that "twelve pence in white bread, being good, sweet, and seasonable," should be distributed every Sunday at his tomb, to twelve old widows, "women or men," of whom every one at the receipt thereof should say, "The blessed Trinity upon JOHN ROYSSE'S soul have mercy !" Another stone monument, in the west of the north aisle, bears the following inscription : "This tombe is honord with the bones of our pious benefactour, Richard Curtaine, gent., a principall magistrate of this Corpá, hee was founded July ye 18, Ano Dominy 1643 ;" and elsewhere on the tomb are these lines, which at the time were no doubt considered to embody a quaint conceit :

> ... Our Cvrtaine in this lower press,
> Rests folded vp in natvre's dress.

At the foot of this tomb is a brass, with a half-length figure in action of prayer, Galfridus Barbur, 1417 ; and behind the organ is another brass, nearly obliterated, displaying a full-length female figure. In the east of the south aisle is a curious painting of the genealogical tree of W. Lee, 1637. Mr. Lee was five times Mayor of Abingdon, and "had in his lifetime issue from his loins two hundred lacking but three." The organ displays a quaint wood-carving of King David, with gilded harp and crown. The tomb of Mrs. Elizabeth Hawkins, 1780, is a capital example of what should be avoided in the way of monumental sculpture. It is crowded with busts of fat naked children, weeping tears of colossal size, and all the usual devices and properties of the most conventional stonemason. The perpetrator of this work of genius was, it appears, one Hickey, who was fortunate enough to receive for it £400 under the deceased lady's will.

In the churchyard of St. Helen's is a row of almshouses in memory of Charles Twitty, 1707, who gave £1,700 for building and endowing "an hospital for maintayning in meate, drinke, and apparrel, and all other necessarys of life 3 poor aged men, and the like number of poor aged women." Abutting on the churchyard also are the cloistered buildings of the charity of Christ's Hospital, which was refounded in 1553—having been dissolved by Henry VIII.—at the instance of Sir John Mason, who procured for it a charter from Edward VI. Over the central porch of the hospital are some curious old paintings, representing such subjects as the giving of alms, the story of the Good Samaritan, and other Scripture subjects, as well as a portrait of Edward VI. The picture of the old market cross has already been noticed. The oak-panelled hall, which is lighted by a lofty lantern, has several odd pictures, among them one representing the building of Abingdon Bridge, in memory of "Jefforye Barbur and John Howchion." On the frame is inscribed : "Frauncis Little, one of ye governors of this hospital, gave this table, An. Dni.

1607," and underneath the picture stands the table in question, a fine one of oak, with curiously carved legs. A portrait of Edward VI. hangs, with several others, in the hall ; and there is also preserved the original charter, which shows considerable signs of age. The later portion of the hospital buildings, which runs parallel to the river, dates from 1718, and it is just below this point that the waters of the Ock and of the Wilts and Berks Canal join the Thames.

At the north side of the town is the Albert Park, presented to the town by the trustees of Christ's Hospital in 1864. It is well laid out and planted, and in it stands a monument to the late Prince Consort, with his statue in the robes of the Garter. Adjoining the park are the new buildings of the grammar school, founded by John Roysse in 1563. The profligacy of John Roysse's son was the immediate cause of the foundation of Abingdon Grammar School. It is said that nothing but the universal estimation in which men held his father, "as well in the west country as also in Kent or otherwise," saved the criminal from the penalties of the law. Roysse disinherited him, and, after providing for his grandson and making certain other bequests, bequeathed the residue of his fortune, directing that as it was endowed A. D. 1563, and in the 63rd year of its founder's life, it should educate 63 boys for ever. Thomas Teesdale, the first scholar admitted into this school, endowed an ushership in the school, and left funds for purchasing lands for the maintenance of fellows and scholars from Abingdon school at Balliol College, Oxford. His trustees, however, combined with Richard Wightwick to found Pembroke College, Oxford, at which college the school possesses five of the incorporated scholarships. Of these one is filled up annually, and two boys who have been educated at the school for two years are nominated as candidates. Each scholarship is of the value of £50 per annum, with rooms rent free, and is tenable for five years. The fees for boarders under the age of 13 are £57 ; over 13, £63. Hard by Roysse's school is Sir Gilbert Scott's church of St. Michael, which serves as a chapel-of-ease to St. Helen's. The street leading to the park from Ock-street is by the side of the almshouses founded by Benjamin Tompkins in 1733.

The angler should not be afraid of fishing near the town, as there are some excellent swims close by. In Blake's Lockpool there are barbel, chub, perch, &c., and on the tow-path side, opposite Thrup, just past the overfall, there is a swim of considerable length, and full six feet deep, reachable from the bank.

BANKS.—Gillett & Co., The Square; London and County, Market-place.

FAIRS.—First Monday in Lent, May 6, June 20, July 1, September 19 and 30, December 11.

FIRE ENGINE.—Abbey-gateway.

HOTELS.—"Crown and Thistle" (landing-stage at the "Nag's Head"); "Lion," High-street; "Queen's," Market-place (landing-stage at the "Anchor").

MARKET DAY.—Monday.

PLACES OF WORSHIP.—St. Helen's, St. Michael's, and St. Nicholas; and the Roman Catholic Church of Our Lady and St. Edmund. There are also Baptist, Independent, Primitive Methodist, and Wesleyan Chapels in the town.

POLICE. — Borough, Abbey-gateway; County, Bridge-street, close to the bridge.

POSTAL ARRANGEMENTS.—Post Office (money order, savings bank, telegraph, and insurance), Market-place. Mails from London, 7, 10, and 11.30 a.m., 5 p.m.; Sunday, 7 a.m. Mails for London, 11.10 a.m., 1.55, 4.5, and 10 p.m.; Sunday, 10 p.m.

NEAREST *Bridge, Ferry, Lock,* and *Railway Station,* Abingdon. Nearest *Bridges,* up, Oxford, 7¾ miles; down, Sutton, 2 miles. *Locks,* up, Sandford, 5 miles; down, Culham, 2 miles.

FARES to Paddington: 1st, 10/10, 18/3; 2nd, 8/2, 13/9; 3rd, 5/1.

Albert Bridge, a handsome new suspension bridge, crossing the river from Albert-road, which skirts the west side of Battersea Park to Cadogan Pier, and the Chelsea Embankment. It affords the nearest means of communication between the district about Clapham and South Kensington.

Albert Bridge, Windsor Home Park. —An iron bridge of elegant design. Connects Berkshire and Buckinghamshire, crossing the river to the south of the park, about half a mile below Datchet.

Albert Embankment.—The Albert Embankment, London, S.E., on the right bank, from a point a little below Vauxhall Bridge to Westminster Bridge. The carriage way diverges to the right after leaving Lambeth Palace, and enters Westminster Bridge-road at the corner of Stangate; St. Thomas's Hospital, and a walk for foot passengers only, occupying the river frontage at this point.

NEAREST *Railway Stations,* Vauxhall and Westminster Bridge; *Omnibus Route,* Westminster Bridge-road; *Steamboat Pier,* Lambeth.

Alexandra Yacht Club, Southend-on-Sea. Club-house, Public Hall, Southend.—Election by ballot; five members form a quorum; one black ball in five excludes. Entrance fee for yacht owners, £1 1s.; non-yacht owners, £2 2s.; subscription, £2 2s. Members residing beyond two miles from the club pay only £1 1s. Officers: Commodore, vice-commodore, rear commodore, hon. secretary. The committee consists of the officers and 12 members, three to form a quorum. Red ensign; burgee blue, with the arms of the county of Essex.

Amateur Qualification.—At a meeting of the Stewards and Committee of Henley Regatta in April, 1879, the following definition of what constitutes an amateur was adopted: No person shall be considered an amateur oarsman or sculler—First, who has ever competed in any open competition for a stake, money, or entrance fee; secondly, who has ever competed with or against a professional for any prize; thirdly, who has ever taught, pursued, or assisted in the practice of athletic exercises of any kind as a means of gaining a livelihood; fourthly, who has been employed in or about boats for money or wages; fifthly, who is or has been, by trade or employment for wages, a mechanic, artisan, or labourer.

At a subsequent meeting it was resolved: That the entry of any crew out of the United Kingdom must be accompanied by a declaration, made before a notary public, with regard to the profession of each member of the crew, and to the effect that he is a member of a club duly established at least one year before the day of entry ; and that he has never competed with or against a professional for any prize ; has never taught, pursued, nor assisted in the practice of athletic exercises of any kind as a means of gaining a livelihood ; has never been employed in or about boats for money or wages ; and is not, nor ever has been, by trade or employment for wages, a mechanic, artisan, or labourer : and such declaration must be certified by the British Consul, or the mayor, or the chief authority of the locality.

Anglers' Tickets.—(See GREAT WESTERN RAILWAY and LONDON AND SOUTH WESTERN RAILWAY.)

Anglian Boat Club.—Established 1878. Subscriptions, rowing members, £1 10s.; coxswains, 10s.; honorary members, £1 1s. Entrance fee of £1 1s. may be remitted in certain cases. Election by ballot in general meeting ; one black ball in six excludes. Colours, marone, black, and light blue. Boathouse, Maynard's, Chiswick.

Angling Clubs.—The following list of London Angling Clubs has been kindly furnished by Mr. W. H. Brougham, Secretary of the Thames Angling Preservation Society.

EAST CENTRAL ASSOCIATION OF UNITED LONDON ANGLERS, "Bald-Faced Stag," Worship-square, Finsbury.—Secretary, Mr. R. Ghurney. Meet on the first Monday in each month.

WEST CENTRAL ASSOCIATION OF LONDON AND PROVINCIAL ANGLING SOCIETIES, "Portman Arms," Great Quebec-street, Baker-street.—Secretary, Mr. Tibbatts. Meet on the third Friday in each month at 9 o'clock.

CENTRAL ASSOCIATION OF LONDON ANGLING CLUBS, "Star and Garter Hotel," St. Martin's-lane, Charing-cross.—Secretary, Mr. S. Fitch, jun. Meet on the second Friday in each month at 9 o'clock.

ANGLERS' BENEVOLENT SOCIETY, New Foresters' Hall, Clerkenwell-road, E.C.—Secretary, Mr. R. Ghurney.

ACME, "Weavers' Arms," Drysdale-street, Kingsland-road.

ACT ON THE SQUARE, "The Ferry Boat," Tottenham.

ACTON, "George and Dragon," High-street, Acton.

ADMIRAL BROTHERS, "Admiral Hotel," Francis-street, Woolwich.

ALBERT, "The Crown Coffee-House," Coronet-street, Old-street.

ALBERT EDWARD, "The Tile Kiln," Tullerie-street, Hackney-road.

ALLIANCE, "Clerkenwell Tavern," Farringdon-road.

ALEXANDRA, "Crown and Anchor," Cheshire-street, Bethnal Green.

AMICABLE BROTHERS, "Bald-Faced Stag," Worship-square, Finsbury.

AMICABLE WALTONIANS, "White Horse," Fawn-street, City.

ANGLERS' PRIDE, "Five Bells," Bermondsey-square, S.E.

ANCHOR AND HOPE, "William the Fourth," Canal Bridge, Old Kent-road.

BARBICAN, "White Bear," St. John-street, Clerkenwell.

BATTERSEA FRIENDLY ANGLERS, "Queen's Hotel," Queen's-road.

BATTERSEA PISCATORIAL, "Queen's Head," York-road, Battersea.

BERESFORD, "Grove House Tavern," Camberwell Grove.

BERMONDSEY BROTHERS, "Alscot Arms," Alscot-road, George-road, Bermondsey.

BLOOMSBURY BROTHERS, "Rose and Crown," Broad-street, Bloomsbury.

BOSTONIAN, "Dalby Tavern," Dalby-street, Prince of Wales-road, Kentish Town.

BOW BELLS, "Bow Bells," Bow-road, E.

BROTHERS WELL MET, "Berkeley Castle," Rahere-street, Goswell-road.

BRIDGEWATER BROTHERS, "Three Tuns, Bridgewater-gardens, Barbican.

BRENTFORD, "Seven Stars," The Butts Brentford.

BRUNSWICK, "Brunswick Arms," Stamford-street, Blackfriars.

BUCKLAND ANGLING SOCIETY, "Middlesex Arms," Clerkenwell-green.

BURDETT, "Joiners' Arms," 118, Hackney-rd.

CAMBRIDGE FRIENDLY, "Rent Day," Cambridge-street, Hyde Park-square.

CADOGAN, "Prince of Wales," Exeter-street, Sloane-street, S.W.

CARLISLE, Hall of Science Club and Institute, Old-street.

CANONBURY, "Monmouth Arms," Haber-dasher-street, Hoxton.

CAVENDISH, "Duke of York," Wenlock-street, City-road.

CITY OF LONDON, Codger's Hall, Bride-lane, Fleet-street, E.C.

CLAPHAM JUNCTION, "Lord Ranelagh," Verona-street.

CLERKENWELL AMATEURS, "George and Dragon," St. John-street, Clerkenwell.

CLERKENWELL PISCATORIAL, "Horseshoe," Clerkenwell-close.

CONVIVIAL, "Bull and Bell," Ropemaker-street, Moorfields, City.

COBDEN, Cobden Club, Landseer-terrace, Westbourne-park.

CRITCHFIELD, "Myddleton Arms," Queen's-road, Dalston.

CRESCENT, "Giraffe Tavern," Kensington-crescent, Kensington Park-road, W.

CROWN, "Crown and Sceptre Tavern," Friendly-street, Deptford.

CROWN PISCATORIAL, "Crown Tavern," Clerkenwell-green.

DALSTON, "Hope," Holly-street, Dalston-lane.

DE BEAUVOIR, "Lord Raglan," Southgate-road, Islington.

DUKE OF NORFOLK, "Ledbury Arms," Ledbury-road, Bayswater.

DUKE OF CORNWALL, "Duke of Cornwall," Dissmore-circus, Haverstock-hill.

EALING DEAN CONVIVIAL, "Green Man," Ealing Dean.

EAST LONDON, "The Bell," Gracechurch-st.

EDEN PISCATORIALS, "Queen's Head," Amelia-street, Walworth-road.

EDMONTON AND TOTTENHAM, "Fountain," West Green-lane, Tottenham.

EUSTONIAN, "King's Head," Swinton-street, Gray's Inn-road.

EXCELSIOR, "Lord Palmerston," Well-street, Hackney.

FOXLEY ANGLERS, "Foxley Arms Tavern," Elliott-road, Brixton.

FRIENDLY ANGLERS, "Albion Tavern," Albion-street, Hyde Park.

FRIENDLY ANGLERS, "Jacob's Well," New Inn-yard, Shoreditch.

GLOBE, "George the Third," 111, Fonthill-road, Seven Sisters'-road.

GOLDEN BARBEL, "York Minster," Foley-street, Portland-road.

GOLDEN TENCH, "Somer's Town," Ossulton-street, Euston-road.

GOOD INTENT, "The Crown," Church-street, Shoreditch.

GRAFTON, "King's Arms," Strutton-ground, Westminster.

GRANGE, "Earl of Derby," Grange-road, Bermondsey.

GREAT NORTHERN BROTHERS, "Robin Hood," Southampton-street, Pentonville.

GRESHAM, "Mason's Hall Tavern," Basinghall-street, E.C.

HAMPSTEAD, "Cock and Crown," High-street, Hampstead.

HAMMERSMITH CLUB, "Grove House," Hammersmith Broadway.

HAMMERSMITH UNITED, "Builders' Arms," Bridge-road.

HAND-IN-HAND, "Queen's Head," Great Garden-street, Whitechapel, E.

HEARTS OF OAK, "The Dolphin," Church-street, Shoreditch.

HIGHBURY, "Plimsoll Arms," St. Thomas-road, Finsbury-park.

HOXTON BROTHERS, "Cherry Tree," Kingsland-road.

INDEPENDENT JOVIAL ANGLERS, "Waterman's Arms," Richmond.

ISLEDON PISCATORIALS, "Crown and Anchor," Cross-street, Islington.

IZAAK WALTON, "Old King John's Head," Mansfield-road, Kingsland-road.

JOLLY PISCATORIALS, "Sugar Loaf," Great Queen-street, W.

JOVIAL, "Jolly Anglers," Whitecross-row, Richmond.

JUNIOR PISCATORIALS, "Duke of Cornwall," South Island-place, Clapham-road.

KENNINGTONIANS, "Durham Arms," Hazleford-road, Kennington Oval.

KENTISH BROTHERS, "George and Dragon," Blackheath-hill.

KENTISH PERSEVERANCE, "Corner Pin," Cold Bath, Greenwich.

KENTON, "Lord Palmerston," Well-street, Hackney.

KINGFISHERS, "Oliver Arms," Westbourne-terrace, Harrow-road.

KINGSLAND BROTHERS, "Mortimer Arms," Mortimer-road, De Beauvoir-town, N.

KNIGHTS OF KNIGHTSBRIDGE, "Grove Tavern," Grove-place, Brompton, S.W.

LARKHALL, "The Larkhall," Larkhall-lane, Clapham.

LIMEHOUSE BROTHERS, "Dunlop Lodge," 70, Samuel-street, Limehouse.

LITTLE INDEPENDENT, "Russell Arms," Bedford-street, Ampthill-square.

LONDON AND SOUTH-WESTERN RAILWAY, "Brunswick House," Nine Elms.

MARYLEBONE, "Prince Albert," Sherborne-street, Blandford-square.

METROPOLITAN, "Rose Inn," Old Bailey.

MORTLAKE PISCATORIAL, "Queen's Head," Mortlake.

NAUTILUS, "British Lion," Central-street, St. Luke's.

NEVER FRETS, "Crown and Shuttle," High-street, Shoreditch.

NELSON, Nelson Working Men's Club, 90, Dean-street, Soho.

NEW GLOBE, "The Albion," Bridge-road, Stratford.

NEW WALTON AND COTTON, "Drapers' Arms," Upper Barnsbury-street, N.

NIL DESPERANDUM, "Pitt's Head," Tyssen-street, Bethnal Green-road.

NORFOLK, "Norfolk Arms," Burwood-place, Edgware-road.

NORTH-EASTERN, "Shepherd and Flock," Little Bell alley, Moorgate-street.

NORTH LONDON, "Prince Albert," Hollingsworth-street, Holloway.

NORTH-WESTERN, "Lord Southampton," Southampton-road, Haverstock-hill.

NORTON FOLGATE, "Rose and Crown," Fort-street, Spitalfields.

ODDS-AND-EVENS, "The Albion," East-road, Hoxton.

OLD ARTILLERY GROUND, "Alfred's Head," Brushfield-street, Bishopsgate.

ORIGINAL ALEXANDRA, "Duke of Wellington," Three Colt-lane, Bethnal Green.

ORIGINAL CLERKENWELL PISCATORIALS, "White Hart," Aylesbury-street, Clerkenwell.

PENGE, "Lord Palmerston," Maple-road, Penge.

PECKHAM BROTHERS, "Prince Albert," East Surrey-grove, Peckham.

PECKHAM PERSEVERANCE, "Eagles," 118, Trafalgar-road, Camberwell.

PERSEVERANCE, "The Perseverance," Pritchard's-row, Hackney-road.

PHŒNIX, "Tavistock Arms,"Wellington-street, Oakley-square.

PISCATORIAL, THE, "Ashley's Hotel," Henrietta-street, Covent Garden.

PICTORIAL, "King's Arms," Tottenham Court-road.

PIKE AND ANCHOR, "Pike and Anchor Tavern," Ponder's-end.

PRINCE OF WALES, "Victory," Newnham-street, John-street, Edgware-road.

PRINCE OF HESSE, "The Prince of Hesse," Field Gate-street, Whitechapel, E.

PRINCESS OF WALES, "Westmoreland Arms," George-street, Manchester-square.

QUEEN'S, "Black Bull," Silchester-road, Notting-hill.

REFORM, "Jolly Coopers," Clerkenwell-close.

RICHMOND PISCATORIAL, "Station Hotel," Richmond, Surrey.

RODNEY PISCATORIALS, "The Albion," Rodney-road, Walworth.

ROYAL GEORGE, "Hope Tavern," Tottenham Court-road.

SAVOY BROTHERS, "Green Man," St. Martin's-lane, Charing Cross.

SECOND SURREY, "Queen's Head," Brandon-street, Walworth.

SILVER TROUT, "Star and Garter," St. Martin's-lane, Charing-cross.

SIR HUGH MYDDELTON, "Empress of Russia," St. John-street-road, Clerkenwell.

SOCIETY OF CAXTONIANS, "Falcon Tavern," Gough-square.

SOCIABLE BROTHERS, "The Princess," 237, Cambridge-road, Mile End.

SOCIAL BROTHERS, "Prince Regent," Dulwich-road, Herne-hill.

SONS OF THE THAMES, "Green Man," Berwick-street, Oxford-street.

SOUTH BELGRAVIA, "Telegraph," Regency-street, Westminster.

SOUTH-EASTERN, "The George," George-street, Blackfriars-road, S.E.

SOUTH KENSINGTON PISCATORIAL, "Coleherne Hotel," Richmond-rd., S. Kensington.

SOUTH LONDON, "George and Dragon," 235, Camberwell-road.

SOUTH ESSEX, "The Elms," Leytonstone.

SOUTH ESSEX PISCATORIAL, "Victoria Dock Tavern," Canning Town.

SOUTH HACKNEY, "The Lamb," Wick-road, Hackney Wick.

SPORTSMAN, "Lady Owen's Arms," Goswell-road.

ST. ALBAN'S, "Royal George," Great New-street, Kennington-road.

ST. JOHN, "Fox and French Horn," Clerkenwell-square.

ST. JOHN'S WOOD, "British Stores," New-street, St. John's Wood.

ST. PANCRAS CLUB, 2, Crescent-place, Burton-crescent.

STANLEY ANGLERS, "The Lord Stanley," Camden Park-road.

STAR, "Champion Arms," Garnalt-place, near Sadler's Wells.

STOKE NEWINGTON, "Myddelton Arms," Mansfield-street, Kingsland.

STEPNEY, "Beehive," Rhodeswell-road, Stepney.

SUFFOLK, "Suffolk Arms," Boston-street, Hackney-road.

SURREY PISCATORIALS, "St. Paul's," Westmoreland-road, Walworth.

SUSSEX, "Sussex Arms," Grove-road, Holloway.

THREE PIGEONS, "Locomotive," Richmond.

TRUE WALTONIANS, "White Horse," 80, Liverpool-road, Islington.

UNITED ESSEX, "Dorset Arms," Leyton-road, Stratford New Town.

UNITED MARLBRO' BROTHERS, "Hercules Pillar," Greek-street, Soho.

UNITED SOCIETY OF ANGLERS, "Wellington," Shoreditch.

UNITED BROTHERS, "Druid's Head Tavern," Broadway, Deptford.

WALTHAMSTOW, "Common Gate," Mark House-lane, Walthamstow.

WALTON AND COTTON, "Crown and Woolpack," St. John-street, Clerkenwell.

WALTONIAN, "Jew's Harp," Redhill-street, Regent's Park.

WALWORTH WALTONIANS, "St. Paul's Tavern," Westmoreland-road, Walworth.

WELLINGTON, "Prince Regent," Beresford-street, Walworth.

WEST HAM BROTHERS, "Queen's Head," West Ham-lane, Stratford.

WEST CENTRAL, "Cross Keys," Theobald's-road, High Holborn.

WEST GREEN, "The Fountain," West Green-road, Tottenham.

WEST LONDON, "Windsor Castle," King-street, Hammersmith.

WESTBOURNE PARK PISCATORIAL, "Pelican," All Saints'-road, Westbourne-park.

WOOLWICH BROTHERS, "Prince Regent," King-street, Woolwich.

WOOLWICH INVICTA, "Golden Marine," Frances-street, Woolwich.

WOOLWICH PISCATORIALS, "Cricketers' Arms," Sand-street, Woolwich.

"Arethusa" and "Chichester," Office, 25, Great Queen-street, W.C. Two retired men-of-war, moored off Greenhithe ; are lent by the Government to the Committee of the National Refuges for homeless and destitute children, the President of which is the Earl of Shaftesbury. The *Chichester* was opened in 1866, and the *Arethusa* in 1874. The two ships are fitted to accommodate together 400 boys, who are entered from fourteen to seventeen years of age, and to train them for a sea life either in the Royal Navy or merchant service. The ships are entirely supported by voluntary contributions, and a visit to either of them will afford ample proof that the funds are administered carefully, and with eminently satisfactory results.

Ariadne Boat Club, Hammersmith. —Election by ballot in committee, one black ball in six excludes. Entrance fee, 10s. ; subscription, active members, £1 10s. ; honorary members, 10s. 6d. Boathouse, Biffen's, The Mall, Hammersmith. Motto, *Per ardua stabilis.* Colours, purple and white.

Art and the Thames.—Rivers have always been dear to the painters. From remote times intimate relations have subsisted between the Thames and the fine arts ; portrayers and illustrators of various kinds have long employed themselves in studying, transcribing, and picturing it, now from its banks, now while floating upon its waters. To Wenzel or Wenceslaus Hollar, that "Bohemian of gentle birth," who, abandoning law for engraving, acquired fame as the most accurate delineator and technically perfect etcher of his time, we owe certain of the earliest and most precious representations of our old city and its river. Hollar is the Pepys of etchers. His simple fidelity, zealous painstaking, and keen observation have preserved for us invaluable records and presentments of the past ; in his plates London of two centuries ago, with its streets and buildings, manners and customs, costumes and characters, comes vividly to life again. It was in 1637 that Hollar was first brought to England by his patron, the art-loving Earl of Arundel. Filling some indistinct office in his lordship's household, Hollar had liberty to work for the London publishers, who paid him but poor prices for his labours, however. His first view of the Thames appears in his panoramic view of Greenwich, which he accomplished in the year of his arrival in England, for Stent the publisher, for the small sum of thirty shillings. For other of his performances he is said to have been paid by time, at the miserable rate of 4d. per hour ; yet so conscientious was he in this matter, that he "carefully accounted for the shortest interruptions, and deducted the time so wasted." The Great Fire of 1666 brought him employment. He produced plans and views of London, showing the ravaged condition of the city. Among his plates connected with the Thames may be mentioned his view of London from the top of Arundel House ; his views of London Bridge, the Tower, Whitehall, Lambeth, Richmond, and Windsor. The industrious artist executed nearly three thousand plates in all. But he earned only a poor subsistence : his arduous labours were wretchedly remunerated. During his last illness the bailiffs took possession of his house and furniture. The dying man had to beg of them as a favour that they would wait until he was dead before they took away the bed on which he was lying. He was buried in St. Margaret's, Westminster, March 28th, 1677. His engravings are, of course, of various sizes. His Birdseye View of London before the Fire, a work of the year 1647, measures when put together over eight feet in length, and is certainly one of the largest works of its class in existence.

Hollar's view of London Bridge and the Thames is of the time of Charles I. ; but there is extant an earlier treatment of the subject by John Norden, with a representation of the Lord Mayor's procession of boats in 1603. Norden was patronised by Lord Burleigh and his son, Lord Salisbury, was a surveyor of the king's lands in 1614, and published an historical and chorographical description of Middlesex and Hertfordshire, with a frontispiece and maps. Other pictures of London Bridge and the Thames are by Vertue in 1747-8 ; by Boydell in 1751 ; and by William James about 1756, in the royal collection at Hampton Court. James was the pupil or assistant of Canaletto. Hogarth has introduced a glimpse of the tumble-down houses on Old London Bridge in the first scene of his picture drama of Marriage à la Mode. And Hogarth is otherwise associated with the Thames. Copies were first printed in 1782, on nine folio pages, of the tour or five days' peregrination accomplished by Hogarth and his four friends, Tothall, Scott, Thornhill, and Forrest, in the year 1732. The accompanying drawings were by Hogarth himself, by his brother-in-law Thornhill, and by Samuel Scott, a landscape and marine painter of some eminence, who had produced views of London Bridge, the Custom House Quay, &c., and was judged by Horace Walpole to be second only to Vandevelde in sea-pieces, while excelling him in variety of subjects and in the treatment of buildings. The tour of the five friends was from Billingsgate to Gravesend by boat, and then upon foot to Rochester and Chatham. The excursionists afterwards proceeded to Upnor, Sheerness, and Queenborough. Returning by water to Billingsgate, they quitted their boat for a wherry which carried them through bridge, and landed them at Somerset Water Gate, "whence," they relate, "we walked altogether, and arrived at the 'Bedford Arms,' Covent Garden, in the same good humour we left it to set out on this very pleasant expedition." Nor is this the only trace of the Thames to be found in Hogarth's productions. Two memorable points of the river obtain illustration in one of the series of twelve plates called, The Effects of Industry and Idleness. For the warning of Tom Idle, and as a hint at the likely end of his profligate career, the Thames waterman points out Executiondock on the left bank of the Thames at Wapping in the East, with the dead pirate hanging in chains. By way of retort the idle apprentice, with significant gestures, invites the waterman's attention to Cuckold's Point, formerly known as Cuckold's Haven. Hogarth was interred in Chiswick churchyard, upon the river bank. Close by is the grave of Loutherbourg, scene-painter and Royal Academician, for some years resident upon The Mall, Hammersmith.

Antonio Canal, better known as Canaletto, and often erroneously called Canaletti, came to England in 1746, when he was about fifty, obtained much patronage here and executed various views of London and the Thames. He had practised scene-painting, and was encouraged to visit England by the success of his countryman, Amiconi; "but I think he did not stay above two years," writes Walpole. Mr. Ruskin reckons Canaletto "a little and a bad painter;" his works, however, have always been popular, perhaps because of his frank literalness, his clear colouring, his firm design, his thorough intelligibility. Among his best pictures may be considered his large views of the Thames in the royal collection at Windsor, lent by Her Majesty for Exhibition at Burlington House in 1878. The one picture looks down stream towards St. Paul's, with the Temple Gardens on the left, and London Bridge in the distance. The other picture looks up stream towards Westminster, the Abbey and old Westminster Bridge visible in the centre,

and the gardens of Northumberland House in the foreground. These are very interesting records of the aspect of the Thames in the last century. In the British Museum is preserved a valuable drawing by Canaletto of York Stairs and surrounding buildings in 1745. The water gate by Inigo Jones, at the end of Buckingham-street, now buried to the waist in the Embankment-garden, is here shown at the river's edge, a genuine aid to embarking and disembarking. The tall wooden tower, once belonging to the York Buildings Water Company, is also presented, with the large mansion at the south-west corner of Buckingham-street inhabited by Pepys, wherein during his presidency of the Royal Society he entertained its members. In the house at the opposite corner sojourned Peter the Great when he visited England for instruction in shipbuilding.

At the top of the house replacing Pepys' mansion dwelt Etty the painter for many years; he had previously occupied a studio in Stangate-walk, Lambeth. He was wont to call his Buckingham-street chambers the York Hotel, for upon the site had once stood York House or Palace; moreover, the painter was a native of York, and was often visited by friends and relatives from that city. He was chiefly occupied in limning nude figures, "dances of nymphs in [and out of] red and yellow shawls;" but he exhibited a view of the Thames at Chelsea, at the British Institution in 1843, and often expressed warmly his sense of the beauty and picturesqueness of the river. He wrote of his corner house overlooking the Thames: "It is a peaceful spot to be so near the middle of the metropolis—quiet as the country without its distance." He wrote from Italy that he "could not bear to desert old father Thames; that he had an affection for him." He records Turner's judgment that there is "finer scenery on its banks than on any river in Italy." Etty continues: "I love to watch its ebb and flow. It has associations connected with life not unedifying. I like it, too, on another score. Looking from Lambeth to Westminster Abbey it is not unlike Venice." On Tuesdays Etty kept open house in Buckingham-street, regaling his friends with tea, muffins, and toast, "with perhaps a *petit verre* of maraschino" to finish the evening. He saw more than one generation of artists assemble in his rooms overlooking the river. To Fuseli, Flaxman, Stothard, Constable, Hilton, succeeded Maclise, Dyce, Herbert, &c., with Turner as the connecting link between the two eras. "I remember," writes Mr. Charles Collins, " his asking all of us students of the Life school in St. Martin's-lane to tea and supper. The impression of his rooms looking out over the river was delightful. We enjoyed ourselves exceedingly, examining his sketches and studies, and were made very welcome. This was very good-natured of him." And Etty avowed that he loved "every stick, hole, and corner" of London, and that he had enjoyed a quarter of a century's happiness and peace in the house at the south-west corner of Buckingham-street.

The name of Turner is specially connected with the Thames. His first picture exhibited at the Royal Academy in 1790 was a "View of the Archbishop's Palace, Lambeth." A few years later, his address being Hand-court, Maidenlane, his father's barber's-shop, he exhibited "Moonlight; a study at Millbank." "On the banks of the Thames,' writes his biographer, "Turner began his art, on the banks of the Thames he lay down to die." It was probably Girtin who taught him to love the river : Girtin whose earlier studies had been upon the picturesque shores of Lambeth and Westminster, and of whom Turner exclaimed, "If Tom Girtin had lived, I should have starved." Turner's most famous and poetic picture connected with the Thames is his "Fighting Téméraire"—the grand old line-of-battle ship tugged by a diminutive steamer to her last moorings at Deptford. But his studies, drawings, and paintings of the river are very numerous, such as "Flounder-fishing near Battersea," and "The Thames near Kingston," unpublished plates of the Liber Studiorum ; The Tower of London, Old London Bridge, Westminster Bridge, The Thames at Mortlake, Richmond-hill on the Prince Regent's Birthday, Hampton Court, Abingdon from the Thames, &c. He died on the 19th December, 1851, aged 79, at the humble little house at Chelsea, fronting the river, and within a few yards of Cremorne Pier, to which he had some time before retreated, morbidly concealing his movements, almost his existence, from his friends, and even assuming a

fictitious name. By the street-boys of Chelsea he was called "Puggy Booth;" more respectable neighbours believed him to be a retired admiral in reduced circumstances. He was the most famous painter of his age ; he acquired a fortune of £140,000, and was buried in St. Paul's ; but he chose to die away from his friends, the occupant of a mean, ill-furnished garret in the house of a stranger. He found genuine pleasure during his closing days in climbing to the flat roof of the little Chelsea cottage, and watching the movement of the river, the glories of the sky, the rising and setting of the sun. Even to his last illness he was wont to quit his bed at daybreak, wrapped in a dressing-gown or blanket, to gaze at the beauty of dawn, the flushing and paling of the morning sky. Pleasure, too, he found at night in contemplating from the same point of view the firework displays of Vauxhall Gardens. Looking east at the scenery of the river he called it the Dutch view ; looking up-stream, to the west, he called it the English view of the Thames. The weather was cloudy and dark during the last days of his last illness, and he pined to see the sun again. A little before his death, he was found prostrate on the floor ; he had tried to creep to the window, but his strength had completely failed him. The sun shone forth at last, filling the chamber of death with a glory of light. Mr. Thornbury writes : "The day he died, nay, I believe the very hour almost that he died, his landlady wheeled Turner's chair to the window that he might see the sunshine he had loved so much, mantling the river, and glowing on the sails of the passing boats." Mr. Trimmer, the many years' friend of the dead painter, relates how he had often enjoyed long drives with Turner upon the banks of the Thames, and had watched him happily sketching the river from various points of view.

At Somerset House in 1807, "Morning, a view near Millbank," and "A scene near Millbank," were the first pictures ever exhibited by William Collins, R.A., a delightful artist, famous for his rendering of natural effects, silvery lights, far horizons, and long stretches of sandy shore. Millbank was a more picturesque spot early in the century than it appears at present. Another Royal Academician who has painted the Thames is Sir

Augustus Wall Callcott. It was one of Callcott's finest views of the Thames—he had priced the picture at £200 only—that Turner observed in the presence of several patrons of the fine arts : ".Had I been deputed to set a value upon that picture, I should have awarded a thousand guineas.". To the Royal Academicians and scene-painters, Stanfield and Roberts, the Thames presented assured attractions. One of Stanfield's best pictures is his view of "Tilbury Fort, Wind against Tide," painted in 1849 for R. Stephenson, M.P., and engraved for the Art Union of London. Stanfield had been a sailor ; he had served in the same ship with Douglas Jerrold during the midshipman days of that dramatist and satirist, and his early apprenticeship to the sea induced the accuracy of detail, and the characteristic fidelity of his illustrations of nautical life, his studies of wind and wave and cloud. From 1861 to 1863, David Roberts was much employed in picturing the Thames. He had projected, indeed, a series of illustrations of London viewed from the river, but he did not live to complete his plan. He executed, however, very vigorous paintings of St. Paul's and the Houses of Parliament, &c. In later years another excellent scenic artist, Mr. O'Connor, has exhibited certain interesting studies of the river, its bridges, and the buildings upon its bank, notably of York Gate as it appeared before it was sacrificed to the needs of the Embankment. Other modern painters of the London aspects of the Thames are Mr. Wyllie and Mr. Arthur Severn. Mention should be made also of a representative of the famous Norwich school of art, George Vincent, whose "View of the Thames" reappeared in London at the exhibition of works of the old masters, Burlington House, 1878. George Chambers must also be numbered among the scene-painters who have portrayed the Thames. Like Stanfield, Chambers had been apprenticed to the sea; he served upon a brig trading in the Mediterranean and Baltic Seas. Afterwards he painted scenes at the Pavilion Theatre, and assisted in producing the once famous great panorama of London at the now departed Colosseum in the Regent's Park. The Thames tempts the painters now by its rural aspects above the London and suburban bridges, and now by the picturesqueness of its Pool, crowded with shipping, a very quickset hedge of masts and rigging, with ragged buildings upon the shore, overhanging tavern bay-windows, ship-builders' yards, steaming factories, smoking chimneys, soaring warehouses, &c. If the river has suggested to Mr. Whistler certain so-called "nocturnes" not easily understood of the multitude, or "harmonies of colour," with ghostly suspension bridges looming through fogs of blue-gray paint, it is to the river's influence upon the same artist we owe many most admirable works of the etching needle illustrative of Thames life, scenery, and character, at Wapping, Putney, &c. Mr. Seymour Haden and Mr. Propert have also accomplished exquisite etchings of the Thames, its busy shores, and crowded vessels below bridge ; and M. Tissot, with a Frenchman's keen appreciation of the picturesquely quaint, has also found excellent occasions for his *genre* painting in the Thames and the boats and buildings upon its banks : especially in the neighbourhood of Greenwich and Gravesend, where whitebait dinners are eaten, and open windows and balconies command grand views of the water and of nautical life. In its more rural aspects, when its banks narrow, and it runs through meadow and woodland, the Thames has been an object of study to numberless painters. The sketchers and portrayers of Windsor and Eton, Henley and Maidenhead, may not be counted. For Cookham and its neighbourhood the late Frederick Walker and his followers may be said to have rendered pictorial services such as Hook has accomplished on behalf of the coast of North Devon. Certain of the best pictures of Mr. George Leslie owe much of their charm to their backgrounds—thoughtful and artistic studies of Thames scenery, and the artist, in 1881, published a handsome illustrated volume, called "Our River." Mr. Vicat Cole and Mr. Keeley Halswelle are also conspicuous amongst the best of the painters who have sought much of their inspiration in the pleasant reaches of the upper Thames, and perhaps the varying beauties of the river, in storm as well as in calm, have never been more successfully caught than by the last-named artist.

Athens.—A bathing-place of the Eton boys, rather more than half-a-mile below

Boveney Lock, railed off and provided with ladders, &c. The high ground is known as Acropolis, and is used for the purpose of taking running headers, in which the Eton boys excel.

Ballastage.— The ballastage and last-age of the river, and all the profits they produced, belonged originally to the Lord High Admiral of England; and the monopoly, as is the nature of monopolies, simply resulted in the acquisition by its fortunate proprietor of as much money as possible, and so long as sufficient ballast could be economically and easily dredged, the effect upon the channels of the river was but little regarded. In 1594 Lord High Admiral Lord Howard surrendered the privilege, stipulating that the business should be entrusted to the Trinity House, and by an Act of Elizabeth that Corporation acquired the exclusive right of ballasting vessels in the Thames from London Bridge to the sea, and were empowered to devote the profits to such purposes as they might deem fit. Subsequent Acts confirmed the Trinity House in their position with regard to ballastage; but in 1853, when the Merchant Shipping Act was passed, the ballastage revenues became part of the Mercantile Marine Fund. At that time, at the instance of the late Prince Consort, then Master of the Corporation, the work of ballast-heaving was entrusted to it, and a heaver's office was established for the benefit of the men, where they could attend for employment, and where they could receive their wages without the intervention of the middle men by whom they had been previously robbed. The Ballast Act expired in 1866, and the privilege of raising ballast ceased to be the exclusive right of the Trinity House. The brethren, however, empowered by their various royal grants, still raise and supply it, and at present the supply of the river remains to a great extent in their hands. The surplus revenue is funded for charitable purposes.

Barbel (The), is so named from the barbs or feelers which hang about its mouth, although there are other fish— notably the gudgeon—which have these appendages. Barbel fishing is a special sport with many anglers; in pursuit of no other kind of fish; it is a powerful quarry to have at the end of fine tackle in a rapid stream, and to ensure success great pains and previous preparation are employed to ensnare it. The swims it frequents are baited with quantities of worms, greaves, carrion gentles, bran, and bread, sunk with clay for some days, nay, weeks previously; and then, when they have been drawn together, a punt is moored near the swim, and they are mostly angled for with the leger, the barbel being a grovelling bottom frequenter. They are very capricious in their feeding: sometimes a whole season or seasons will pass and very few be taken; at others it is not unusual for a single rod in a day to capture one hundredweight or more, amongst which may be individual fish up to 11 and 13 lbs. They are occasionally caught while fishing for roach, and if so, they try the patience and skill of the angler to the utmost, often an hour or more being employed in playing them before they succumb sufficiently to be reached and secured by the landing-net. The most simple mode of taking barbel is with the leger. This consists of a yard of salmon gut, having four inches of gimp between it and the running line, on which is placed a perforated bullet or heavy flat piece of lead, kept from slipping down by a fixed shot. The hook used should be a No. 1 to 3, with a long shank; the bait, a well-scoured lob-worm; the hook being entered at the head of the worm and threaded all the way down, care being taken not to pierce or break the skin. Throw the bait out somewhat beyond where your ground bait has been deposited, and draw it gently over it. Keep the line as taut as is possible without shifting the lead, and keep it over your forefinger of the hand that holds the rod, by which means a bite, or "knock," as it is termed, will become the more perceptible, and when this is felt a second time, strike immediately, and if quick enough, as the barbel has a leathery mouth, there is little chance of losing him other than by unskilfulness, or the fish fouling itself round snags or amid piles, which it will at once attempt to make for if near. If the water is clear and the fish are shy, surround the whole of the hook with a ball of stiff ground-bait, letting a portion of the worm hang out. A more elegant way of barbel fishing, practised on the Trent, and of late years adopted on the Thames, is with a "travelling float."

This float is fitted with a loop of wire at both ends, without any cap or attachment to the line, and is extremely useful where the depth of water exceeds the length of the rod. A small piece of india-rubber thread is tied into the line at the proper depth by the means of two half-hitches; this will easily pass through the rings on the rod and yet rest on the small brass loop fixed on the float, so that there is no hindrance to the latter working properly at any required depth, and yet it never interferes with the killing of a heavy fish. Sometimes a second piece of india-rubber thread is tied underneath the float to prevent its falling unnecessarily low. There is every advantage when striking with a float fitted in this manner at the end of a 'long swim, as the line slips through the loops without dragging the float along, consequently the blow is sharper, more direct, and therefore quicker. There is little doubt, however, that with roach or dace tackle the sport is far more exciting, for although you may lose two fish out of three, while you do have the fish captive they are not so handicapped and checked by the lead of the leger; and this should be done with a No. 8 or 9 hook and with a good round gut line. Single hair would prove useless, although it is on record that barbel have been killed by this fragile means.

It was thought until very recent years that it was waste of time to try for barbel while the river was in flood; but some of the heaviest takes are now made by legering during these periods. Indeed, during the summer floods of 1879, very large bags were thus made in the Windsor and Datchet district; but it is more comfortable to wait until the waters are just beginning to subside and getting clear. The barbel is held in profound contempt as an edible fish; but the Jews are said to possess the secret of dressing them so as to render them extremely acceptable. It is said that they either boil them in vinegar and water, or if for the pan, merely scald them first in this mixture, and then fry them in cutlets in boiling oil. The roe, however, should be carefully avoided, as it affects many people in a serious manner.

Barge Match.—Twenty-one years ago the late Mr. H. Dodd, of the City Wharf, New North-road, started a sailing-barge match which has ever since been one of

the institutions of the river, and has had great influence in bringing about many improvements in the build of barges and in the smartness of their crews. Mr. Dodd died April 27th, 1881, and left £5,000 to the Fishmongers' Company, in trust to invest the same and apply the income in providing silver and gold cups for prizes for sailing-barge races on the Thames, and for the support and comfort of poor barge or lightermen, so that the recipient has not less than 1s. a day.

Few of the yacht races in the lower reaches of the Thames excite so much interest in so many people as does the annual barge match, and when there happens to be wind enough to display the qualities of the boats, the barges can show very nearly, if not quite, as good sport as the yachtsmen.

The race in 1884 took place on the 3rd of July, but, as was the case last year, owing to the extreme lightness of the wind, it was evident that the usual course from Erith round the Nore and back could not be accomplished; and it was therefore decided that the distance should be limited to a point beyond the Chapman Light instead. The following was the list of prizes and entries :

For the Topsails, not exceeding 55 tons register, there were three prizes, consisting of a £21 silver cup, and £10 10s. for the crew of the winner; a £15 silver cup, and £5 5s. for the crew of the second barge; a £10 silver cup, and £3 3s. for the hands in the third boat; the crew of each losing barge, going the entire course, to receive 30s.; in addition to which the champion flag was presented to the winner by the committee :—*Whimbrel*, 49 tons, H. W. Martin, owner; S. Beadle, master. *Electric*, 54 tons, E. J. Goldsmith, junior, owner; W. Bannister, master. *Atlantic*, 54 tons, A. H. Keep, owner; J. Peartree, master. *Godwit*, 54 tons, H. W. Martin, owner; F. Beadle, master. *R. A. Gibbons*, 54 tons, Lighterage Company, Limited, owners; G. Lodge, master. *British Lion*, 49 tons, S. Burford & Son, owners; W. Hammond, master.

For the Spritsail barges, not exceeding 50 tons, first prize, a silver cup, worth £16, and £10 10s. to the hands; second, £10 silver cup, and £5 5s. to the hands; third, silver cup worth £7, and £3 3s. to the hands; the crew of each losing barge, going the entire course, to receive 30s.:—*Kalulu*, 35 tons, T. F. Wood, owner; H. Cory, master. *Shannon*, 39 tons, Grays Chalk Quarries Company, owners; G. Tyler, master. *Louisa*, 44 tons, Lighterage Company, Limited, owners; J. Cosey, master. *Bessie*, 43 tons, G. Featherby, owner; J. Talbott, master.

The start was made at about half-past ten o'clock; the timing at the finish being as follows:

TOPSAILS.

	H.	M.	S.
Godwit (winner) … … …	…	6	13	43
Whimbrel (2nd prize)	…	…	6	16	22
British Lion (3rd prize)	…	…	6	23	30
R. A. Gibbons … … …	…	6	34	1
Electric … … … … …	…	7	0	48

The *Atlantic* did not start, owing to an accident.

SPRITSAILS.

	H.	M.	S.
Bessie (winner) … … …	…	6	36	25
Louisa … … … … …	…	6	48	35
Kalulu … … … … …	…	7	18	30
Shannon … … … …		Not timed.

Barges.—Although the extension of railway facilities in the country through which runs the Upper Thames has very considerably reduced the number of up-river barges, there are still many engaged in the carrying trade. That they are useful, may be taken for granted; that they are possibly ornamental, may be a matter of opinion; that they are a decided nuisance when a string of them, under the convoy of a vicious steam-tug, monopolises a lock for an hour or so, admits of no doubt. And the steam-tugs themselves are an abomination. They are driven along with a sublime disregard of the interests of persons in punts and small boats —in this respect resembling their more distinguished relatives, the steam-launches—and raise a wash which, one would suppose, can be as little beneficial to the banks of the river as it is to the peace of mind of anglers and oarsmen. Nor are the manners and customs of their crews, or of their associates the bargees, such as to conduce to the comfort of riparian pro-

prietors or of pleasure-seekers. Practically, they seem to have things all their own way, and to do and say just what they like. All that can be done is to give them as wide a berth as possible, and to be thankful, at all events, that there are not more of them.

Down the river—from about Brentford downwards that is—the barges occupy a very different position; an immense amount of the enormous goods traffic of the Port of London being distributed by their medium, and their numbers appearing to be steadily on the increase. They are of two kinds, sailing and dumb barges. These latter are propelled by oars alone, and drift up and down apparently at the mercy of the tide. The only use of the long sweeps with which they are provided is, in fact, to keep the barge straight, and even this is difficult, if not impossible, in a high wind. They are quite incapable of getting out of the way, or of keeping any definite course, and as they bump about among the shipping and get across the bows of steamers, they are the very type of blundering obstructiveness, and an excellent example of how time is allowed to be wasted in this country. Crowds of them hang about the entrances of the docks and the piers where steamers are unloaded, and the traffic of the river, always excessive, is becoming absolutely congested with them. The books of the Watermen's Company, in which all barges solely engaged in the London traffic are registered, showed in 1879 a total of 7,000, and about 1,000 additions are made to the list every year. The number of barges leaving the London and St. Katharine's Docks, on an average, in 24 hours is 100. In the same time 165 leave the East and West India Docks, 100 the Victoria Docks, and 150 the Surrey Docks. To these must be added the great crowd of dumb barges which go from wharf to wharf, and from ship to ship, without entering the docks at all. The consideration of these facts; a trip down the river in a steamboat; and contemplation of the miles and miles of wharves along both banks, almost all of which are incessantly receiving and sending out goods by dumb barges; will satisfy any one that these barges are a very large factor in the difficult problem of satisfactorily regulating the traffic on the river. And it is not only that their numbers are enormous, and their mode of progression slow, uncertain, and even dangerous to other vessels. It is provided in the Conservancy byelaws that every dumb barge shall have one competent man on board, and that when they exceed 50 tons they shall carry at least two men. The competent men, as has been said, are in fact incapable of navigating their clumsy charges to any satisfactory result; but that is not all. The evidence of all sorts of river experts given before the Traffic Committee is exceedingly unfavourable to the men. Mr. A. C. Howard, district superintendent of metropolitan police, gives them a singularly bad character. " In navigating they are the most indifferent class of men on the river," he thinks. Mr. Spicer, Trinity House pilot, is decidedly of opinion that dumb barges are the greatest cause of obstruction, and that they will very seldom get out of the way, or even put themselves straight, when hailed to do so. A great number of witnesses are of even a more decided way of thinking. "I invariably find the men in dumb barges neither obliging nor civil;" "If they only took a little pains, they would do what was necessary ; but if you ask them to put their head round, they generally make some vulgar observation. . . . they are uncivilised men like Greeks"—why Greeks should be selected as the uncivilised type is not apparent—"A very turbulent class of men;" "A very bad lot altogether;" "A rough and reckless class . . . . rough and disorderly;" " The conduct of some of them is so bad, that it is enough to taint the character of the whole of the watermen as a community;" "The state of things as regards the licensed men could not be more unsatisfactory or worse than it is." Certainly the licensing monopoly of the Watermen's Company has not produced any affection between the great body of lightermen and the hands they are compelled to employ.

But graver charges even than churlishness or incompetency are brought against the dumb bargemen. It has been roundly stated that their character for honesty is not all that it should be ; that, in renewing licenses, the Watermen's Company concern themselves very little with a man's personal character ; that gross neglect of duty is rarely punished by suspension. The late chairman of the company, Mr. Elliott, directly contradicts these asser-

tions. If a man has been complained against, he says, and his license has been endorsed, it is not renewed ; if a man has committed a theft on the river his license is cancelled, and never renewed. Only one such case had come before the court, and in that case the license was "pointedly refused." A letter subsequently written to the committee by the solicitors for the Wharfingers' Association of the Port of London is at direct issue with Mr. Elliott. If these gentlemen are right, and there seems to be little or no doubt that they are, either the chairman of the Watermen's Company was speaking without book, or the company itself possesses a plentiful lack of information. Say the solicitors : "The association have in their possession a list of freemen now employed on the river Thames who are known to the police as having been convicted of felony, and from such list it appears that there are 42 watermen now employed upon the river who have been convicted, of whom seven have been previously convicted, and that seven are or have been under police supervision for long terms." Forty-two black sheep are not many in so large a flock, but it would be curious to know how they come to have licenses, nor would the further information (for which the same firm asked, in vain, on behalf of their clients) be wholly devoid of interest—how many licenses of lightermen had been suspended in consequence of the felonious proceedings of their owners. "No separate account," says Mr. Humpherus, sending some statistics from the Watermen's Company to the committee at an earlier date, "has been kept of licenses which have been suspended or endorsed, of which there are but a few cases." But the separate account might not be without its public use for all that.

The monopoly of navigating, if the term may be used in this connection, the dumb barges is in the hands of licensed freemen of the Watermen's Company, although the second hand need not be a freeman. Freedom of the company may be obtained by serving an apprenticeship of five years. But it by no means follows that because a lad is apprenticed to the water, he necessarily learns the business of a waterman or lighterman. It is said that the steward's boy on board the unfortunate *Princess Alice*, who was em-

ployed in the useful but not aquatic occupation of drawing corks, was a waterman's apprentice, and that two years'
cork-drawing would count towards the
number of years' service necessary to
qualify him as a lighterman, although it
would, perhaps, not help in getting his
license. However this may be, and the
point seems to be doubtful, great complaints are made of the present system.
Mr. A. C. Scovell, representing the
Wharfingers' Association of the Port of
London, explains its working by stating
that owners of lighters must employ a
freeman who is a licensed lighterman, or
a man who has served for two years, and
has obtained his license through that
service ; and thinks that this restriction
unduly limits owners, and that any man
who has good personal character and
competency should be able to obtain
a license, as a matter of course, without
any reference to freedom of, or apprenticeship to, the Watermen's Company—very
much in the same way that a cabman
obtains his license. Furthermore, he
thinks that the power of granting licenses
should be taken from the Watermen's
Company and handed over to the Conservancy. There seems to be a very
general agreement among barge-owners
on this head, and the fact that the lightermen are only under the jurisdiction of the
Watermen's Company is undoubtedly
unsatisfactory to the masters. The feeling that obtains in many quarters that
the authorities in Watermen's Hall are
inclined to be unduly tender to the men,
and to some extent prejudiced against
barge-owners, may or may not have
foundation in fact ; but one thing is clear
—that there is a very strong impression
that the granting of licenses should be in
the hands of a public body and not of a
self-elected court such as the Watermen's,
and that the present mode of dealing with
delinquent watermen is eminently unsatisfactory. Of course a good deal has
also been urged on the other side—there
never yet was a story that could not be
told both ways— but it is significant that
the Traffic Committee, an unusually
practical and competent body, after
hearing an immense mass of evidence,
entirely agree in their report with the
case urged against the present system.
They express their opinion that it was
proved "beyond reasonable doubt that

the monopoly of the Watermen's Company
has produced the evils usually due to
monopoly, and that it should be put an
end to," and adopt the most free-trade
line in dealing with lightermen's licenses.
Their recommendation is that the navigation of barges be thrown open altogether, without examination or other
preliminary ceremony, leaving owners of
barges, who will naturally have a wary
eye to their own interests, to employ
whom they will. Furthermore, they
recommend the abolition of the judicial
functions of the Watermen's Company,
and suggest—and it would seem to the
lay mind that the suggestion is one which,
having been made, carries with it a kind
of astonishment that any other system
should ever have survived any Parliamentary inquiry—that the ordinary police-
courts should have jurisdiction over all
offences on the river. Indeed, it is abundantly clear that the Watermen's Company
did not succeed, in the course of the
inquiry, in recommending themselves and
their system to the favourable consideration of the committee. It is remarked
that many of the bye-laws of the company
are on the same subjects, and cover the
same ground, as those of the Conservancy;
and that it has been complained that, in
several cases, the bye-laws of the two
bodies clash seriously. This being the
case, the committee add that they are of
opinion that there should be only one
body charged with the regulation of the
navigation of the river, and that that
body should be the Conservancy ; un-
kindly adding the expression of their
opinion that the self-elected Watermen's
Company, "so far as they represent any
interest, represent only a section of barge-
owners." It naturally follows that it is
further proposed to take the registration
of barges out of the hands of the company, and what there will be for the
company to do if all these changes are
made, except to fold the said hands and
fall into a tranquil slumber, it is not easy
to see. The proposed alterations would
bring some money into the coffers of the
Conservancy, where it is much wanted.
Under existing regulations dumb barges
pay nothing to the Conservancy. The
dues payable to the Watermen's Company
are : On first registration, if owned by a
freeman, 10s.; if owned by a non-freeman,
£1; and annually, if owned by a free-

man, 2s. 6d.; if owned by a non-freeman, 5s. It is proposed that the Conservancy should charge 10s. per annum per barge.

It is not necessary here to enter at length into the controversy whether it is desirable or practicable that the system of dumb barges should be abolished altogether, and steam towing be rendered compulsory, although it may be mentioned here that there are at present about 50 tugs engaged in the barge-towing trade, and that many coal-barges are already regularly towed. The Traffic Committee clearly lean to making steam-towing compulsory, but do not go so far as to recommend it, except between London Bridge and the uppermost dock entrances in Blackwall Reach. The evidence of experts on this head is unusually conflicting ; for instance, the harbour-master is against compulsory towing, while the deputy harbour-master is in its favour; and probably the question is hardly yet ripe for settlement. One objection made by the supporters of the present system may be set forth here, as it gives a very good idea of the sort of business which is undoubtedly facilitated by the existence of the dumb barges. It is said, and said with an appearance of great truth, that the greater part of the trade of the Port of London is carried on in a manner wholly inconsistent with any system of towing numbers or trains of barges together. Goods taken from or to any particular ship are not dealt with by the dumb barges *en bloc*. For export they are sent from all sorts of places, sometimes in barge loads, sometimes different parcels are sent to different ships in the same barge. From the home-coming ships parcels are sent in one barge to numerous places. The dumb barge is, in fact, the carrier's cart or Pickford's van of the river. No doubt it would be difficult, extremely difficult—impossible, many people say—to organise a system of running trains of barges. That it is impossible, anybody who knows the difficulty attending the career of a "pick-up" goods train and the elaborate system that has gradually grown up to make that institution not only useful but necessary, would be very slow to believe. That the traffic of the river must be somehow or other relieved is a fact that no traveller, however indifferent, can doubt ; nor is it open to question

that the duty of undertaking the task, which daily becomes more difficult,' must in the long run be undertaken by some public body, whose constitution is not a relic of obsolete usage, and whose work will be done in the full light of day, with the wholesome check of publicity, and with a real sense of responsibility.

It is a singular fact, not unnoticed by the committee, that whereas the men who work in the dumb barges are very ill spoken of in almost every quarter, an excellent character is given to the men who navigate the sailing barges lower down the river. These men have no monopoly, and are exposed to free and open competition. They are, according to the almost unanimous evidence of skilled witnesses, pilots and so forth, skilful and careful navigators, and have gradually got into a custom of "give and take" with the steamers, which greatly facilitates the working of navigation rules. Of course opinions differ here, too, and Captain Woolcott, of the Peninsular and Oriental service, complains that he has suffered great inconvenience from sailing barges—it must always be a trying business to get a steamer of 4,000 tons, like the *Pekin*, down the Thames, and no doubt bargee is sometimes cantankerous and cross-grained—and suggested that the sailing vessel, in such cases, as being better under control, should give way. As the result of this and similar suggestions it was recommended that if two vessels, one of which is a sailing vessel and the other a steam vessel, are proceeding in such directions as to involve risk of collision, the steam vessel shall, *if it is safe and practicable for her to do so*, keep out of the way of the sailing vessel.

The sailing barge fleet has of late years largely increased, and is still growing. It numbers now nearly 3,000, and it is stated that 100 such craft leave the Medway every 24 hours. They are fine, handy vessels, much improved in many respects latterly, and a rate of speed can be got out of them which would surprise most people whose only idea of a barge is derived from some of the old-fashioned tubs or the graceful dumb barge. Sailing barges of 45 tons register pay a small rate to the Conservancy, but the majority are smaller than this. A barge of 45 tons register will carry some 100 tons of goods, and is navigated by two men, who, if the vessel comes from Rochester or thereabouts, need not be freemen of the Watermen's Company. Anybody, in fact, may bring a barge from the Medway, but if the vessel start from Gravesend a freeman must be on board—an anomaly which appears absurd. Further, a barge coming up and going through the bridges is compelled, if it take a third hand, to take a waterman, although all the way from the Medway to London Bridge she may have been sailed by outsiders. Vested interests are indeed wonderful institutions, and singularly tenacious of life !

The interests of barge-owners, both sailing and dumb, are protected by the Barge-Owners' Protection Society, which was founded in the year 1865. The members pay an annual subscription of 30*s.* for ten dumb or five sailing barges, for which they receive legal advice from the solicitor on all matters of detail connected with the carriage and transhipment of goods, their detention claims are pressed, and their collision cases contested after they have been thoroughly sifted by a committee of practical men. The society numbers amongst its members the principal barge-owners of the Thames and Medway, and has for some years past averaged 350 cases of damage annually. The society is recognised as one of the institutions of the river, and was specially asked, through its secretary, to send representatives to give evidence before the Thames Traffic Committee. Its office is at 9c, Lower Thames-street (*and see* EAST AND WEST INDIA DOCKS).

Barking Reach.—(*See* TRIPCOCK REACH.)

Barnes, London, s. w.—On the right bank of the Thames between Putney and Mortlake, and a good place for a view of the Oxford and Cambridge Boat-race. Barnes-common, in actual extent 135 acres, 15 of which, however, are now absorbed by the railway, is open and airy, and villas are rising rapidly all round it. It is one of the best kept commons round London, and, moreover, marches with Wimbledon Common and Putney Heath, so that the extent of open ground immediately around is really very large. There is a capital terrace with good houses fronting the river, and at high water the view is pretty enough.

At certain states of the tide, however, there is somewhat more mud on view than is altogether desirable. From Waterloo (about 20 min.), 1st, -/9, 1/-; 2nd, -/7, -/10 ; 3rd, -/6, -/8. From Ludgate-hill (45 min.), 1st, 1/-, 1/6 ; 2nd, -/10, 1/3 ; 3rd, -/8, 1/-. NEAREST *Bridge,* Hammersmith.

Barnes and Mortlake Amateur Regatta was originally founded in 1852, and has been held every year since without intermission. The course is between Maynard's boat-house at Strand-on-the-green and Barnes railway - bridge, a distance of about one and a half mile, and races are rowed up or down according to the tide. About £100 worth of prizes is annually distributed, and for the senior four-oared race there is a challenge-cup, value £75.

WINNERS OF THE CHALLENGE CUP.

1862 London Rowing Club.
1863 London Rowing Club.
1864 Kingston Rowing Club.
1865 Kingston Rowing Club.
1866 London Rowing Club.
1867 London Rowing Club.
1868 London Rowing Club.
1869 London Rowing Club.
1870 London Rowing Club.
1871 London Rowing Club.
1872 Thames Rowing Club.
1873 Thames Rowing Club.
1874 London Rowing Club.
1875 Thames Rowing Club.
1876 Thames Rowing Club.
1877 Thames Rowing Club.
1878 London Rowing Club.
1879 Thames Rowing Club.
1880 Thames Rowing Club.
1881 Thames Rowing Club.
1882 Not rowed, owing to the committee having accepted the entry of the American Hillsdale Crew, and the Thames and London Clubs therefore declining to compete.
1883 London Rowing Club.
1884 Grove Park Rowing Club.

REGATTA, July 26, 1884.

JUNIOR SCULLS (rowed up).

First Heat.

A. B. Vaux, West London R.C. ... 1
C. W. Mapleton, Thames R.C. ... 0

Second Heat.

C. G. Poole, Anglian B.C. 1
W. B. Powell, Grove Park R.C. ... 0

Final Heat.

Surrey Station—Vaux **1**
Middlesex Station—Poole ... disq.

EIGHTS (rowed up).

Surrey Station No. 2—West London
R.C.: G. J. Huntley, W. D. Gilbert,
F. A. Knight, C. H. Hickman,
C. J. Scott, E. Bartlett, A. Lawless,
G. C. Vaux (stroke), W. R. Wheeler
(cox) **1**
Surrey Station—Grove Park R.C.: C.
F. Cross, F. Watts, G. E. P. Gaskell,
R. H. Lawrie, F. S. Watts, W. H.
Cummings, F. J. Browne, W. F. J.
Watts (stroke), H. B. Ducker (cox) **0**
Middlesex Station No. 2 — East
Sheen B.C.: J. F. G. Glossopp, H.
F. Highton, H. O. F. Luckie, H. R.
Parker, A. Hughes, R. R. H. Lock-
hart-Ross, D. M. Robertson-Mac-
donald, R. H. Barron (stroke), R.
W. Willis (cox) **0**
Middlesex Station—Anglian R.C.: C.
G. Poole, R. A. Brown, J. A. Hol-
land, J. Leahy, G. S. K. Dewhirst,
W. A. Piggott, J. T. Musgrave, P.
W. S. Ell (stroke), D. F. Rail (cox) **0**

JUNIOR FOURS (rowed up).

Middlesex Station—Thames R. C. :
F. W. Long, A. Sturgeon, B. A.
Moore, W. A. Walters (stroke), R.
Soden (cox) **1**
Surrey Station—Anglian R.C.: A. W.
Burton, J. Freer, W. R. Edwards,
J. Leahy (stroke), D. F. Rail (cox) **0**
Centre Station—East Sheen B.C.: E.
A. Highton, A. P. Parker, J. F. G.
Glossop, H. F. Highton (stroke),
R. E. D. Brown (cox) **0**

THE FITZGERALD CHALLENGE CUP FOR
PUBLIC SCHOOL FOURS (rowed down).

Surrey Station — Bedford Modern
School : W. Tudhall, H. A. Poole,
A. Long, M. J. Gordon (stroke),
H. W. Godfrey (cox) **1**
Bedford Grammar School and London
International College also started.

SENIOR PAIRS (rowed down).

Middlesex Station—Grove Park R.C.:
F. J. Browne and W. H. Cummings **1**
Surrey Station—Thames R.C.: W. H.
Eyre and C. W. Hughes **0**

LOCAL FOURS (FOR THE COMMITTEE
CHALLENGE CUP) (rowed down).

Surrey Station—East Sheen B.C.: H.
R. Parker, A. Hughes, H. R. Sadel,
R. H. Barron (stroke), R. W. Willis,
(cox) **1**
East Sheen B.C. and London Inter-
national College also started.

SENIOR SCULLS (rowed down).

Surrey Station — R. H. Smith,
Thames R.C. **1**
Middlesex Station—C. W. Hughes,
Thames R.C. **0**

SENIOR FOURS (BARNES CHALLENGE
CUP) (rowed down).

Middlesex Station—Grove Park R.C.:
W. F. J. Watts (steers), F. J.
Browne, F. S. Watt, W. H. Cum-
mings (stroke) **1**
Surrey Station—London R.C.: P. D.
Ullmann (steers), C. Wood, J. Herr,
F. W. Earnshaw (stroke) ... ...sank
Centre Station — Thames R.C. : C.
Mapleton (steers), C. Dangerfield,
W. H. Eyre, C.W. Hughes (stroke) disq.

Basildon, Berkshire, on the right
bank, a small village, nearly midway
between Streatley and Pangbourne, and
standing a little distance back from the
river. Population about 700. On the hill
above, and somewhat to the south-west,
is Basildon Park, with the mansion of
Charles Morrison, Esq., which contains
a fine collection of pictures and works
of art. On the river-side, just above the
railway bridge, is the house known as the
"Grotto." The church of St. Bartholomew, supposed to have been built in the
time of Edward II., consists of chancel
and nave, with a square tower and Gothic
porch.

POSTAL ARRANGEMENTS.—Letters *via*
Reading. (Nearest money order and
telegraph office, Goring.)

NEAREST *Railway Station*, Goring,
distant about 2 miles *(which see).*

Bathing.—Few things are pleasanter
on a hot day than a plunge into one of
the deep, quiet, shady pools in which the
Thames abounds. Few things are more
exhilarating than to rise after a scientific
header in the rushing waters below some
such weir as that at Marlow. And at
ordinary times, in ordinary seasons, and

with ordinary caution, the pleasure is one almost entirely unaccompanied, to a reasonably good swimmer, with any amount of danger. But it should always be remembered that any sudden flood, which involves the raising, perhaps some miles away, of sluices and weir paddles, may transform the usually safe bathing-place into what is practically nothing more nor less than a death trap. Furthermore, it is well to remember that some of the most deplorable bathing accidents on record have happened to men with experience on the river, and practised swimmers to boot. Many weirs fall into absolute pits, and in many cases contain the *débris* of old bridges, blocks of concrete, or stumps of sunken trees; and in many cases again the eddies and whirlpools in the rush of waters defy all calculation. In quieter places another kind of danger is presented by the weeds, whose clinging embrace has proved fatal to many a good swimmer. It must not be supposed from this recapitulation of the dangers of river bathing, that it is intended here to discourage so laudable, so health-giving a practice. What is aimed at is to insist, as strongly as possible, on the absolute necessity of caution, and the desirability, when possible, of consulting before the plunge some local expert as to the condition of the water. The melancholy fate of Mr. Argles, who lost his life in August, 1879, in one of the best known and most frequented bathing-places on the river—Odney Pool at Cookham—ought most strongly to point this moral. Canon Argles, after his son's death, writing to the *Times* on the subject, said that a guide-book, which his son had in his possession at the time of the fatal accident, stated that there was "splendid bathing in Odney Weir." And splendid bathing at Odney Weir, under ordinary circumstances, there undoubtedly is, as the writer, from many years' experience of its waters, can aver; but the season of 1879 was in all respects exceptional, and there can be no doubt that the suck of the stream, owing to the great rush of water which it is impossible accurately to guage from the appearance of the surface, developed some peculiar source of danger unknown at quieter times. It is notorious to all rowing men and *habitués* of the river that Sandford Lasher has almost yearly demanded its

tale of victims, and it is almost inconceivable that people will continue year after year to tempt fate in this and other equally dangerous places.

It was originally intended to add to the other information contained in this book, which it is hoped will be of use to rowing men, a list of the best and most convenient bathing-places between Oxford and Teddington. But a careful personal inspection of the river, undertaken specially for the purposes of this article—an inspection following a practical Thames experience of over twenty years—led, irresistibly, to the conclusion that so great a responsibility was not lightly to be undertaken. The idea of giving such a list was, therefore, reluctantly abandoned, and the Editor has thought it more judicious, and even more practical, simply to give the few words of caution which are here set forth.

It is hardly credible, even taking into consideration the difficulty of moving the constituted authorities, that nowadays, when the river is year by year growing in popularity and attracting more and more visitors, so little has ever been attempted in the way of establishing safe and convenient bathing-places. A few local clubs and private houses have their own bathing-waters and bathing conveniences, properly kept in order and attended to; but, for the general public, there is hardly one that offers any attraction to the swimmer, except the bathing sheds and ladders at Solomon's Hatch, between Marsh Mill and Henley. It is not as if any great outlay were required, or as if any serious expense would be entailed by the maintenance of the simple buildings required, or the provision of the needful attendance. Enclosed baths are, no doubt, here and there to be found, but in the bright summer weather the temptation to swim in comparatively open water is almost irresistible, and, danger or no danger, is sure to be yielded to. That a little care and public spirit on the part of the governing bodies of the small towns along the river, who reap in good seasons so large a harvest from the boating and excursion public, would not only be the means of giving healthful enjoyment to many and would save many valuable lives is certain. That, in the long run, it would entail no loss of money admits of little doubt.

)f view, the estab-
l public bathing-
valuable boon to
ery often largely
o throng the river
. It is too often
resent absence of
man to cast his
to plunge into the
ibus, oblivious or
t after the bath a
ig becomes neces-
uarantee that the
hing, which may
pty a few minutes
e with boats while
ng processes are
state. The estab-
eltered and recog-
would go far to
nising situations
ar the pleasures of
. No system, how-
the reckless and
which is too often
gentle and simple,
their way to the
l other places of
sance is, naturally,
rhood of the more
i cases where the
undoubtedly have
e too supine to
ent of summoning
: magistrates, the
least may be com-
a vigilance com-
ed residents took
vn hands, and by
ent of some of the
idacious offenders
i signal and per-
ierhaps, too much
mes Conservancy,
uch work on their
he present at all
their attention to
tant subject; but
t constituted, has
i, and has shown
ulting the interests
isure on the river,
are there on busi-
ied that from them
the desired reform

iinishing the num-
nually occur from

incautious bathing, the following notice
is, by order of the Royal Humane Society,
issued by the secretary, and distributed
throughout the United Kingdom: "Important to Bathers.—Avoid bathing within two hours after a meal. Avoid bathing
when exhausted by fatigue or from any
other cause. Avoid bathing when the
body is cooling after perspiration. Avoid
bathing altogether in the open air if,
after having been a short time in the
water, there is a sense of chilliness with
numbness of the hands and feet; but
bathe when the body is warm, provided
no time is lost in getting into the water.
Avoid chilling the body by sitting or
standing undressed on the banks or in
boats after having been in the water.
Avoid remaining too long in the water,
but leave the water immediately there is
the slightest feeling of chilliness. The
vigorous and strong may bathe early in
the morning on an empty stomach. The
young and those who are weak had
better bathe two or three hours after a
meal; the best time for such is from two
to three hours after breakfast."

The *Lancet* says: "It is very generally
believed that the proper way to bathe is
to take a header into the sea, or, at least,
to immerse the whole body immediately.
Theoretically this may be done so far as
the most vigorous organisms are concerned, but it must not be forgotten that
a man may be perfectly healthy, and yet
not endowed with sufficient latent energy
to recover quickly from the 'shock' which
must in all cases be inflicted on the nerve-
centres by suddenly plunging the whole
surface of the skin, with its terminal
nervous twigs, into a cold bath. For a
time, at least, the central activity must
be reduced in force, if not in form.
When, therefore, a man plunges, and
immediately afterwards strikes out to
swim, it is not only possible but probable
that he may become exhausted, and fail
from depression of energy, with cramp."

Battersea Bridge, an old decrepit
structure, almost as much out of date as
Putney Bridge, and about to be replaced
by a new and more commodious structure. It connects Battersea with Chelsea.

Battersea Park, London, is on the
Surrey side of the river, and in the S.W.
district. One of the youngest of the
London parks, it is certainly one of the

prettiest. The sub-tropical garden is emphatically one of the sights which no visitor should fail to see, especially in the latter part of the summer. The park contains excellent drives, and is encircled by a superior prepared ride. There is every accommodation for cricketers, and boating may be indulged in on the lake. The park gates are in Albert-road, Prince of Wales's-road, and Victoria-road, and the fine terrace-walk facing the river is directly approached from the steamboat-pier. The best way of approaching Battersea from the west is along the Grosvenor Road and over Chelsea Suspension Bridge. NEAREST *Bridges*, Chelsea and Albert; *Steamboat Pier* and *Railway Station*, Battersea Park.

Beaconsfield Rowing Club, in connection with the Greenwich Conservative Club. Subscription for working members, 10s.; members are elected by the executive. Boat-house, Conservative Club House, Greenwich. Colours, red and white.

"Bells of Ouseley."—A tavern on the Berks bank, at Old Windsor; about a mile below the lock, and close to Beaumont Catholic College. Good accommodation can be had, and the house is noted for its ale. The scenery here is very pretty. The nearest railway station across the river is Wraysbury, Bucks; and by road, Datchet; both on the South-Western line, about an hour from town. Fares from Wraysbury to Waterloo: 1st, 3/6, 5/6; 2nd, 2/6, 3/9; 3rd, 1/9, 3/3. Fares from Datchet: 1st, 3/9, 5/6; 2nd, 2/9, 4/-; 3rd, 1/9.

Bensington, commonly called Benson, a village on the left bank in Oxfordshire, 92 miles from London, 19½ miles from Oxford. Population, 1,259. Soil, loam and gravel. This village, which was originally called Besintone, appears at one time to have been of some importance, but at present differs but little from the numerous places of a similar character which are scattered about the valley of the Thames. The church of St. Helen is of considerable age, but has been extensively restored, and in parts, indeed, entirely rebuilt. With the exception of the fine arch which separates the nave and chancel, there is little to arrest the attention. The following curious epitaph will be found on a tablet on the south wall:

M: S:

To the pious memory of Ralph Quelch and Jane his wife, who slept together in 1 { bed by ye space of 40 yeares. { grave till Ct. shall awaken them.

He { slept } fell asleep Ano Dui. { 1629 } being aged { 63 } yeares.
Shee { now sleepe } { 1619 } { 59 }

For ye fruit of their { labours } they left { ye new im twice built at { bodies } { thr. owne charg.

Their son being liberally bred in ye University of Oxon, thought himselfe { one only son & two daughters. bound to erect this small monument of { their } piety towards { God. { his } { them.

Ano. Dni. 16 .

The rest of the date was apparently never completed. Close by is a stone whence brasses have been removed.

Heavy baskets of fish are often got near here.

INNS.—"Castle;" "White Hart."

PLACES OF WORSHIP.—St. Helen's; and Baptist, Methodist, and Wesleyan Chapels, and a Free Church.

POSTAL ARRANGEMENTS.—Post Office (money order, savings' bank, telegraph, and insurance). Mails from London, 7.10 a.m., 2.10 p.m.; Sunday, 7.10 a.m. Mails for London, 11.45 a.m., 6.55 p.m.; Sunday, 11.30 a.m.

NEAREST *Bridges*, up, Shillingford 1½ mile; down, Wallingford 1¼ mile. *Locks,* Bensington; up, Day's 4 miles; down, Wallingford 1¾ mile. *Ferry,* Mill Stream. *Railway Station,* Wallingford.

FARES, Wallingford to Paddington: 1st, 11/-, 16/-; 2nd, 7/, 12/-; 3rd, 4/7½. No Sunday trains.

Billingsgate Market, in Thames-street, is about 300 yards east of London Bridge, and adjoins the west side of the

Custom House. The derivation of its name is matter of dispute. All that is certainly known is that the appropriation of the site to the purpose of a fish-market took place in the year 1699 A.D., and that a fish-market it has remained ever since. On the 27th of October, 1874, the first stone was laid of the handsome building which was to supersede the "elegant Italian structure" of Mr. Bunning, which, with its tall campanile, had long been one of the most conspicuous shore marks of the river below bridge. The construction presented considerable difficulties, both from the necessity of carrying it out without disturbance of the daily business of the market, and from the nature of the ground on which it had to be built, and which required an immense amount of preparation in the way of a platform of solid concrete, 15 feet in thickness. In 1877, however, the building was completed, and on the 20th of July of that year formally opened for business. Its river façade still adheres more or less to the Italian Gothic legend, but the campanile has disappeared, and the building now presents a uniform frontage of two lofty storeys, the centre portion being thrown a little back. The wings, which are, perhaps, artistically speaking, somewhat small in proportion to the central block, are occupied by taverns, at each of which is a daily fish ordinary.

All along the front runs a broad floating stage, alongside of which come the smaller craft by which the water-borne fish are brought up the river, and which vary in size and rig from the specially built steamer of more than 200 tons register, whose cargo has been collected from the smacks of the North Sea, to the little open barge in which cod or salmon has been lightered from the big sea-going ships in the docks of Victoria or Millwall. The landing process begins every morning, summer and winter, at 5 a.m., when the tolling of the big bell announces the opening of the market, and a rush takes place to secure the earliest sales.

The great hall in which the sales take place, and which occupies the whole ground-floor of the centre building, is let off in 140 "stands" at a rate per week, which, by the bye-laws of the market, sanctioned by the Board of Trade, is not to exceed 9d. per superficial foot. The total weekly supply of the market aver-

ages by water 800 to 850 tons, and by land as nearly as possible double that amount, and the whole of this enormous mass has to be carried on men's shoulders from ship or machine to salesman's stall, there to be disposed of in some four hours or so, more or less. The market is at its height from 5 a.m. to about 9, by which time the greater part of the morning supply has been cleared off; but the market remains nominally open until 3 p.m.

Meanwhile, in the great dungeon-like basement below the market, a somewhat similar scene to that above is being enacted with the day's supply of shell-fish.

The staff of the market includes about eleven hundred licensed porters, besides constables, detectives, clerks, &c. ; and the business, rough and riotous as it is, is conducted, so far as the official *personnel* is concerned, with machine-like precision and punctuality. The utmost care, too, is taken to ensure the most scrupulous cleanliness throughout the building.

Birds of the Thames Valley.—(*See* ORNITHOLOGY.)

Bisham, Berkshire, on the right bank, within the Parliamentary borough of Marlow, from London 57½ miles, from Oxford 54 miles. Population, 652. Soil, gravel and chalk. Bisham is chiefly celebrated for its abbey, the seat of G. H. Vansittart, Esq., which dates from the time of King Stephen. In 1338 it became a priory. Subsequently it was given by Henry VIII. to Anne of Cleves. Queen Elizabeth once resided here, under the charge of the Hobys, and appears to have had a "good time." In the abbey were buried a great number of distinguished people—among them that Earl of Salisbury who fought at Poictiers, and Richard Nevile, the Kingmaker. The porch and great hall, which are portions of the oldest part of the building, are exceedingly fine ; and the drawing-room, which contains a bay-window built specially for the Princess Elizabeth, is remarkable for some very good old stained glass. There is a remarkable tapestry bedchamber, with an entrance to a peculiarly constructed secret room high up in the wall ; and on the ground-floor is a very satisfactory ghost-room, which is said to be haunted by the apparition of one of the Ladies Hoby, who beat her little boy to death for inking his copies, and is now condemned to continual vain attempts to wash her own hands in a ghostly basin, which goes before her as she walks. Unfortunately it is not clear whether anybody has actually seen the ghost, but it is said that, during a period of repairing, a number of blotted copy-books of the time to which the legend refers were found secreted in the room—evidence which, as ghost stories go, is quite enough for all practical purposes. In Bisham Abbey are several interesting portraits of the Hoby family, to whom the house belonged from the time of Henry VIII. to rather later than the middle of the eighteenth century, and, of these, one, which represents the Lady Hoby of the legend with a deathly white face and a head-dress very like that of the kneeling female figure in the church, which is described lower down, is a remarkably fine work. Also, in the dining-room is a very jovial portrait of a certain Rev. Peregrine Hoby, who appears from his complexion to have thoroughly enjoyed the good things of this life. This, and its companion portrait of the rev. gentleman's wife, both by Burslee, are capital pictures. A portrait of Sir Francis Walsingham, over one of the doors, will also repay inspection ; and the gem of the collection will be found over the mantelpiece in the shape of a brilliant portrait of Henrietta Maria, by Van Dyck.

The church, the original name of which is in doubt, is now called All Saints. Almost all architectural features of interest were utterly destroyed, with the exception of the Norman Tower, about the beginning of the century. The chancel and south burial chapel were restored in early decorated style in 1849 ; the north aisle was the gift of Colonel Owen Williams, of Temple House, in 1878. The church is most picturesquely situated immediately on the bank of the river, and should certainly be visited on account of its remarkable group of magnificent tombs. These are in the south aisle. The first and most elaborate is that of a noble countess, who kneels in the act of prayer, attired in ruff, stomacher, and a most extraordinary head-dress surmounted by a coronet. Opposite to her, kneeling on a lower stool, is another

female coroneted figure, and behind are five other kneeling figures, three female and two male ; the whole group is under a canopy, supported by pillars, and the monument is set forth with elaborate carving and coloured coats-of-arms. Beyond this is a less gorgeous, but much more artistic monument to the brothers Hoby. They lie upon an altar-tomb, two knightly figures with peaked beards and in full armour. They both recline upon their left arms, and the one nearest the spectator has his legs crossed crusader-wise. The date is 1566. On the tomb are several inscriptions. Of these may be quoted one which gives concisely the history of the Hobys.

Two worthie knightes and Hobies both by
  name
Enclosed within this marble stone do rest
Philip the fyrst in Cæsar's court hathe fame ;
Such as tofore fewe legates like possest
A diepe discovrsing heed a noble breast
A covrties passing and a cvrteis knight
Zelovs to God whose gospel he profest
When gretest stormes can dym the sacred
  light.
A happie man whom death hath nowe redeemd
From care to loye that can not be esteemd.
Thomas in Fraunce possest the Legate's place
And with svch wisdome grew to gvide the
  same,
As had increst great honovr to his race
Ye sodein fate had not envied his fame,
Firme in God's truth, gentle, a faithful frend
Wel lernd and langvaged natvre besyde
Gave comely shape which made ruful his end
Sins in his flovre in Paris towne he died
Leaving with child behind his woful wief,
In forein land opprest with heapes of grief.
From part of which when she discharged was
By fall of teares that faithful wieves do sheed
The corps with honovr brovght she to this
  place
Performing here all dve vnto the dead.
That doon this noble tombe she cavsed to
  make
And both thes brethren closed within the same
A memory left here for vertve's sake
In spite of death to honovr them with fame
Thus live they dead, and we lerne wel thereby
That ye and we and all the world must die.
                    T. B.

Beyond the brothers Hoby is the tomb of Margaret, wife of Sir Edward Hoby, who died in 1605, oddly surmounted by an obelisk with a swan at each of the base angles. The stained glass window, with coats-of-arms of the Hoby family, in the east of the south aisle is very curious. In the nave is a fine brass with three full-length figures to the memory of " John

Brinckhorst, sometime citizen and mercer of London, and marchavnt adventvrar," and his two wives ; only one date is given, that of the death of one of the ladies in 1581. A smaller brass has a single figure, and is dated 1517 ; and one with inscription only, and dated 1525, records the decease of one Gray "and Wylmott hys wyffe."

HOTEL.—"The Complete Angler," by Marlow Bridge.

PLACE OF WORSHIP.—All Saints.

POSTAL ARRANGEMENTS. — Nearest money order, telegraph, &c., office, Marlow. Letters through Marlow. Mails from London, 6.30 a.m., 12.30 p.m. Mails for London, 10.35 a.m., 3.15 and 7.15 p.m.

NEAREST *Bridges*, down, Marlow ½ mile ; up, Henley 7½ miles. *Locks*, down, Marlow ¾ mile ; up, Temple, 1 mile. *Ferry*, Temple. *Rail. Station*, Marlow.

FARES, Marlow to Paddington, 1st, 6/-, 9/11 ; 2nd, 4/6, 7/6 ; 3rd, 2/7½.

Blackfriars Bridge is one of the handsomest in London, and would have a still better effect were not its appearance so seriously marred by the proximity of its neighbour, the Alexandra (London Chatham & Dover Railway) bridge. It was built in 1864-9, at a cost of £265,000, from the designs of Mr. William Cubitt, although those of Mr. Page, architect of Westminster Bridge, had been selected in the first instance. It crosses the river in five spans, the centre span being 185 feet. The piers are of granite, surmounted by recesses resting on short pillars of polished red Aberdeen granite, and with ornamental stone parapets. The parapet of the bridge itself is very low, which, with the extreme shortness of the ornamental pillars at the pier ends, gives the whole structure rather a dwarfed and stunted look ; but the general outline is bold and the *ensemble* rich, if perhaps a trifle gaudy, especially when the gilding, of which there is an unusual proportion, has been freshly renewed.

Blackwall, on the left bank from Orchard Wharf to the Isle of Dogs.— Here are the East India Docks, where the principal sailing ships trading from the port of London load and discharge. The visitor may in these docks inspect long tiers of China tea-clippers—now almost run off the line by fast steamers— and the fine passenger ships trading to the Australasian ports. Adjoining the docks is the spacious ship-building yard of Messrs. Green, and farther down the river are the Trinity House head-quarters, beyond which again are the Royal Victoria and Albert Docks. There is a railway-station on the steamboat-pier (*and see* TRINITY BUOY WHARF). Fares from Fenchurch-street (17 min.), 1st, -/6, -/10 ; 2nd, -/4, -/6 ; trains run each way every 15 minutes. Steamers from Westminster, Charing-cross, Temple, and London Bridge every ½-hour. Fares, aft, -/6 ; forward, -/4. Omnibus from Bank of England.

Blackwall Reach runs for rather more than a mile from Greenwich to Blackwall. The East and West India Docks are at Blackwall. Bearings N. by E. and S. by W.

Bleak (The), or fresh-water sprat, is a surface fish, affording great amusement to young anglers ; but they are a perfect pest to the roach and dace fisher, as they will bite at almost anything, seldom permitting the bait to descend to its allotted depth without seizing it. When thus annoyed, a handful of bran thrown upon the surface of the water will cause them to follow it some way down the stream, and keep them engaged for a long while, when the same course may be repeated. They are one of the best baits for spinning, from their resplendent silvery hue flashing its transmitted light far through the water. They spawn in May or June, and multiply very rapidly. This fish differs from the small dace by being thinner and by a greenish hue on its back, and its scales are not so firmly set, coming off easily by handling, like the sprat ; the belly is of a most silvery whiteness, the fins white.

Boat Races.—A Conservancy bye-law of 1869 runs as follows : Any vessel being on the upper river on the occasion of any boat-race, regatta, public procession, or launch of any vessel, or any other occasion when large crowds assemble thereon, shall not pass thereon so as to impede or interfere with the boat-race, regatta, procession or launch, or endanger the safety of persons assembling on the river, or prevent the maintenance of order thereon ;

and the master of every such vessel, on any such occasion as aforesaid, shall observe the directions of the officer of the Conservators engaged in superintending the execution of this bye-law; and if any such master fails in any respect to comply with the requirements of this bye-law, or does anything in contravention thereof, he shall be deemed guilty of an offence against these bye-laws, and shall for every such offence be liable to a penalty not exceeding £5. Persons in charge of steamers, similarly offending, are liable to a penalty of £20.

Boat Racing, Laws of, as settled and approved by the Universities of Oxford and Cambridge, and the principal boat clubs in London, on the 20th March, 1872.

1. All boat races shall be started in the following manner: The starter, on being satisfied that the competitors are ready, shall give the signal to start.

2. If the starter considers the start false, he shall at once recall the boats to their stations; and any boat refusing to start again shall be disqualified.

3. Any boat not at its post at the time specified shall be liable to be disqualified by the umpire.

4. The umpire may act as starter, as he thinks fit; where he does not so act, the starter shall be subject to the control of the umpire.

5. Each boat shall keep its own water throughout the race, and any boat departing from its own water will do so at its peril.

6. A boat's own water is its straight course, parallel with those of the other competing boats, from the station assigned to it at starting to the finish.

7. The umpire shall be sole judge of a boat's own water and proper course during the race.

8. No fouling whatever shall be allowed; the boat committing a foul shall be disqualified.

9. It shall be considered a foul when, after the race has commenced, any competitor, by his oar, boat, or person, comes in contact with the oar, boat, or person of another competitor; unless, in the opinion of the umpire, such contact is so slight as not to influence the race.

10. The umpire may, during the race, caution any competitor when in danger of committing a foul.

11. The umpire, when appealed to, shall decide all questions as to a foul.

12. A claim of foul must be made to the judge or the umpire by the competitor himself before getting out of his boat.

13. In case of a foul the umpire shall have the power: (a) To place the boats—except the boat committing the foul, which is disqualified—in the order in which they come in; (b) to order the boats engaged in the race, other than the boat committing the foul, to row over again on the same or another day; (c) to re-start the qualified boats from the place where the foul was committed.

14. Every boat shall abide by its accidents.

15. No boat shall be allowed to accompany a competitor for the purpose of directing his course or affording him other assistance. The boat receiving such direction or assistance shall be disqualified at the discretion of the umpire.

16. The jurisdiction of the umpire extends over the race and all matters connected with it, from the time the race is specified to start until its final termination, and his decision in all cases shall be final and without appeal.

17. Any competitor refusing to abide by the decision, or to follow the directions of the umpire, shall be disqualified.

18. The umpire, if he thinks proper, may reserve his decision, provided that in every case such decision be given on the day of the race.

Boats and Boatbuilders.—A comparison of the rates of charges of some of the principal boatbuilders on the Thames shows the price of racing-boats, including oars, sliding-seats, &c., to average as follows: Eights, £60; fours, £35; pairs, £22; and scullers' boats, £15. The prices of the other kinds of boats vary considerably according to length, material, fittings required, &c.; but a pair-oared gig or skiff, built of deal and mahogany, 22 feet long, plainly fitted, and without any very high degree of finish, with one pair oars, one pair sculls, one boathook, two mats, cushion, backrail, &c., complete, may be taken at £23; if built of oak and mahogany, or mahogany alone, at £25. The charges for hiring vary so much according to the class of boat required, and many other circumstances, that no useful list of prices can be compiled. Among the principal yards for building or letting may be mentioned those of Messrs. Salter, Oxford; Clasper, Oxford, and "The Feathers," Wandsworth; Searle & Sons, Stangate, Lambeth, London, S. E.; Phelps, Peters & Co., Unity Boat-house, Putney; Biffen, Mall-road, Hammersmith; Messum, Richmond; Wheeler & Sons, Richmond; and Tagg, Moulsey.—(*For cost of railway carriage of boats and canoes see* RAILWAY ARRANGEMENTS.)

Botany.—The botany of the Thames is perhaps better known than that of any other English river. The counties through which it flows have been for the most part fully investigated from a botanical point of view, and the results of these investigations are familiar to those of scientific tastes who are well acquainted with the works in which these results are published. But a general sketch of the more characteristic features of Thames botany may be of interest to the general reader, and this can best be gathered if we take a glance at the plants to be found in certain districts which are to a great extent typical.

First of all, let us visit the Thames somewhere about the middle of its course, in the charming neighbourhood of Great Marlow; which we may take as a type of that large extent of river which is uninfluenced by tidal influx and beyond the range of the metropolitan area. Here the banks of the river are crowded with a wealth and variety and richness of vegetation which is rarely to be met with except in such situations. We may pass over such common though beautiful waterside plants as the spiked purple loosestrife (*Lythrum Salicaria*), the yellow loosestrife (*Lysimachia vulgaris*), the meadow-rue (*Thalictrum flavum*), the water-dropwort (*Œnanthe crocata*), the yellow iris (*Iris Pseudacorus*), and the elegant meadow-sweet (*Spiræa Ulmaria*); but others demand a somewhat more special notice. The water-parsnip (*Sium latifolium*), for example, is a striking plant, with its parsnip-like leaves and tall stems bearing umbels of white flowers, and this may be found at intervals along the banks as far as Richmond—in former days it got as far as Chelsea. The sweet-flag (*Acorus Calamus*) is a very abundant Thames plant, getting up as far as Twickenham, and frequent both by the side of the main stream and of its tribu-

taries; its flag-like leaves may be distinguished from the many somewhat similar ones among which they grow by their very generally wrinkled margins—an appearance due, we imagine, to the action of some insect, and by their peculiar but pleasant aromatic odour when broken: although so frequent, there seems good ground for believing that it is not a native plant. The flowering-rush (*Butomus Umbellatus*), with tall stems surmounted by an umbel of six-parted pink flowers, is another conspicuous ornament of the Thames banks; while in the early summer the white blossoms of the large-flowered bitter-cress (*Cardamine amara*), made more conspicuous by their purple stamens, arrest attention. In the still backwaters of the river itself, we shall find besides the ever beautiful white and yellow water-lilies, a plant which at first sight, from its habit and the shape of its leaves, might be taken for a near relation of the latter of these; but if we examine its numerous yellow flowers we shall see that they differ in being all in one piece, or what botanists call monopetalous, and that they are bordered with an elegant fringe. This is the fringed buckbean (*Villarsia nymphæoides*), and is a very characteristic Thames plant; it was recorded as such by Lobel in 1570, and was formerly found as low down as Richmond, though it does not now get below Walton. The meadows by the Thames produce many beautiful and rare plants; at the head of these we may place two forms of early summer: the snowflake (*Leucojum æstivum*), which looks like an enlarged snowdrop, bearing several flowers on one stem, and the fritillary (*Fritillaria Meleagris*). The former of these grows in various places along the river in Berkshire and Buckinghamshire, at Newlock, Sonning, Windsor, and about Reading, where it is very abundant in the meadows by the Loddon, and hence called "Loddon lilies." The fritillary is a well-known and conspicuous ornament of Christ Church Meadows, Oxford; it also occurs at Reading and in other places. In the mowing grass, before it is cut, we shall find such handsome plants as the meadow cranesbill (*Geranium pratense*), and the clustered bell-flowers (*Campanula glomerata*), with the curious adder's-tongue (*Ophioglossum vulgatum*), for which some little search is necessary: in damp places we shall come across the large red rattle (*Pedicularis palustris*) and the marsh-stitchwort (*Stellaria glauca*). The still ditches and shallow ponds near the river, such as those at Cock Marsh near Cookham, contain the pretty frogbit (*Hydrocharis Morsusranæ*), with its three-petalled white flowers, the beautiful water-violet (*Hottonia palustris*), and the bladderwort (*Utricularia vulgaris*), which escapes notice save in the flowering season when it puts up its stalks with their curiously-shaped yellow flowers; the bladders on its leaves are, however, as students of Darwin will remember, its most remarkable feature, forming, as they do, small insect-traps of most effectual construction. A ramble in Quarry Wood, opposite Marlow, will probably lead to the discovery of the curious bird's-nest (*Monotropa Hypopitys*), with wax-like leafless stems and inflorescence; the pretty winter-green (*Pyrola minor*), the flowers of which remind us of the lily of the valley; the deadly nightshade (*Atropa Belladonna*); the brown withered-looking bird's-nest orchis (*Neottia Nidus-avis*); and, best of all, the rare military orchis (*Orchis militaris*). When we remember that nearly all these and many more are to be found in the immediate neighbourhood of the Thames at Great Marlow, we shall see that the botany here is indeed full of interest.

We will now come to another part of the Thames within the tidal influence, and glance at the plants to be found from Teddington downwards, until London effectually puts a stop to all riverside vegetation. Many of the characteristic riverside plants hold their own, in a more or less satisfactory way, up to Putney and Wandsworth, such as marsh-marigold, meadow-sweet, purple loosestrife, meadow-rue, water-dropwort, and the like; but there is an absence of the great variety of vegetation which greeted us at our last peep at the Thames. But there are many plants to be met with which interest the botanist, although to an ordinary observer they may be less striking. One of these is the tawny balsam (*Impatiens fulva*), with thick green succulent stems and reddish-orange balsam-like flowers dangling from slender stalks. Like the well-known American water-weed, this is a present to us from Brother Jonathan, but is now so thoroughly at home with us that none would suspect its exotic origin. "It almost certainly originated from the gardens of Albury Park, Surrey. A small stream, the Tillingbourne, flows through these gardens and runs into the Wey above Guildford, and this in time flows into the Thames a little above Shepperton. In this way the seeds have been carried by the water-current and by barges, &c., throughout the Thames Valley district" ("Flora of Middlesex"). It was first seen near Albury in 1822, and has completely established itself in many places, while plants may be met with here and there any year between Putney and Richmond. It may be worth while remarking that a freshwater mussel (*Dreissena polymorpha*), which is supposed to have been originally introduced from Russia on logs of timber, has spread itself in England in a similarly rapid manner. It was first noticed by Mr. J. de C. Sowerby in 1822 in the Commercial Docks, and is said to have been found even in the supply-pipes of the London water companies. Another foreigner may be found occasionally by the Thames, but more abundantly in fields and by road-sides at Kew, Richmond, and Mortlake; it is readily known by its yellow disk with a few white ray florets, the size of each flowerhead scarcely exceeding that of the common groundsel. This is *Galinsoga parviflora*, a Peruvian annual, which is supposed in the first instance to have escaped from Kew Gardens, and is now about the commonest weed in the district. A form of the winter-cress, known to botanists as *Barbarea stricta*, by no means a common plant, may be found early in the season on both sides of the river between Richmond and Isleworth. Two rare bulrushes (*Scirpus triqueter* and *S. carinatus*) are abundant by the Thames about Putney; they formerly extended along the river at intervals as far as Limehouse and the Isle of Dogs. The white saxifrage (*Saxifraga granulata*) is very abundant by the Thames about Kew and Chiswick; and here too the pretty little ivy-leaved toad-flax (*Linaria Cymbalaria*) makes itself at home wherever it can find a footing on a wall near the river; it grows, or grew until lately, on one of the piles of Battersea Bridge. The bistort (*Polygonum Bistorta*) and white saxifrage still puts in an appearance in Battersea Park, where they were very abundant ten years or so since. The fritillary, which used to be very abundant in meadows between Mortlake and Kew, has gradually died out, although it lingered until quite lately. The Star of Bethlehem (*Ornithogalum umbellatum*) is abundant by the river between Kew and Richmond, and *Cardamine amara* may also be found there, as well as the balm (*Melissa officinalis*), which is quite established. Above Teddington we may notice the Alexanders (*Smyrnium Olusatrum*) at Hampton Court, under the wall by the side of the river; the vervain (*Verbena officinalis*) and wild sage (*Salvia Verbenaca*) also occur there; while the pretty little autumnal squill (*Scilla autumnalis*) grows on the sloping bank by the towing-path between Hampton Court and Ditton Ferry.

The walls, and wharves, and docks being passed, the riverside begins again to display something in the way of plants; but now a new and potent factor appears in the shape of the salt water, which makes its way up with each tide, and materially influences the flora. We may regard the neighbourhood of Purfleet as the district where marine vegetation first puts in a well-defined appearance; here we find thrift (*Armeria maritima*), sea-plantain (*Plantago maritima*), and such inconspicuous flowered, yet characteristic marine plants as *Suæda maritima*, *Salicornia herbacea*, *Obione portulacoides*, *Atriplex marina*, and the like; besides such more striking plants as two sea-lavenders (*Statice Limonium* and *S. Bahusiensis*), and the Michaelmas-daisy (*Aster Tripolium*), which gets considerably higher up, and is found about Woolwich and Greenwich. The Woolwich and Plumstead marshes afford many plants of interest: in the first rank of which must be placed the great marsh sowthistle (*Sonchus palustris*), one of the largest, as well as one of the rarest of British plants. The pretty snow-flake, already mentioned among the plants of the Upper Thames, is to be found in the same locality, with scurvy-grass (*Cochlearia anglica*), and such sea plants as the sea-milkwort (*Glaux maritima*), *Lactuca saligna*, and the like. One of the rarest of British plants, a vetchling (*Lathyrus hirsutus*), which is almost confined to the south of Essex, is, or was lately, to be found at Hadleigh; while

an equally rare and much handsomer species (*L. tuberosus*), with much handsomer rose-coloured pea-like flowers, occurs in Canvey Island, with several other interesting plants. At Southend, as might be expected, the maritime flora is in full force; and there is much to interest the botanist. Among the rarities to be met with there upon the shore, are various trefoils and medicks, *Vicia bithynica*, *Lathyrus Aphaca*, *Bupleurum tenuissimum*, *Inula crithmoides*, the horned poppy (*Glaucium maritimum*), the sea-kale (*Crambe maritima*), and many more.

A sketch like the above must of necessity be very incomplete; it may be well, therefore, in conclusion, to enumerate the principal works in which the botany of the Thames, for certain districts, is more or less exhaustively treated. Middlesex, Surrey, and Essex boast complete county floras; the first, by Messrs. Trimen and Dyer, contains much information as to the botany of the Thames in former times; the second and third, by Messrs. Brewer and G. S. Gibson respectively, if less exhaustive, are still very useful works. A flora of Kent, which is greatly wanted by British botanists, is in progress under the authorship of Mr. F. J. Hanbury. No complete floras exist of Berkshire or Buckinghamshire; a paper on the plants of the former county, bringing together what has been recorded about them by various authors, has been published in "Transactions of the Newbury District Field Club," by the writer of this notice. Dr. De Crespigny's "New London Flora," published in 1877, will be found to contain a good deal of information relating to Thames-side plants.

Bourne End, Bucks, on the left bank, from London 53½ miles, from Oxford 58 miles, one of the scattered villages making up the parish of Wooburn. The little river Wye, Wick, or Wyke, as it is variously written, enters the Thames here. Bourne End is a place of no importance, except that it is a station on a branch of the great Western Railway, 32 miles from London, trains averaging about an hour. It is the junction for Marlow.

INNS.—"Railway" and "Old Red Lion."

NEAREST *Bridges*, up, Marlow 3¼ miles; down, Cookham ¾ mile. *Locks*, up, Marlow 3 miles; down, Cookham 1¼ mile. *Ferry*, Spade Oak.

FARES to Paddington, 1st, 5/3, 8/9; 2nd, 4/-, 6/9; 3rd, 2/4½.

Bray, Berkshire, a small village on the right bank, about a mile from Maidenhead, 62¾ miles from Oxford, 48¾ miles from London. Population, 2,717. The most prominent object in the village from the river is the fine old church, close to which stands the vicarage, with trim gardens, and smooth shaven lawns running down to the river. A profusion of fine trees adds to the beauty of the view, and the place is very happily situated at a beautiful bend of the river. It is not surprising that the ancient vicar, so celebrated in song, should have persistently determined to live and die vicar of Bray. For a secluded and quietly beautiful place of residence few more agreeable spots can be found. Visitors from the river can land at the "George Inn," and travellers walking down the bank on the Bucks side can be ferried over to the same point on hailing the opposite shore. It would seem at first sight that there was not much for the visitor to see in the village of Bray, but in fact the church, which is as handsome within as it is without, will well repay careful inspection ; and Jesus Hospital is also well worthy a visit, though, as it lies a few minutes' walk inland, it is generally overlooked by boating parties. The church, dedicated to St. Michael, dates back to the time of the first Edward, and is a fine example of the early English perpendicular style, with a fine square flint tower. It was entirely restored about 1860, and the ancient monuments and brasses, in which it is unusually rich, have been treated with reverent care. Several of the new corbels in the nave and chancel are portraits: two very noticeable ones on the right and left of the chancel are those of the Rev. Austen Leigh, the late vicar, and the late Samuel Wilberforce, bishop of Winchester, the latter an excellent likeness. There are many curious tablets on the walls, and the floor of the church is almost entirely paved with similar memorials. One of the most curious monuments is that of William Goddard, founder of Jesus Hospital, of Philliberts who died 1609, and of Joyce Maunsell his wife, died 1622. This consists of two painted half-length figures under canopied

niches, showing very vividly the costumes of the period. William's hands are crossed upon the skull, which so frequently occurs in the monumental art of this part of Berkshire, and his epitaph is worth quoting. It runs thus :

If what I was thou seekst to knowe,
Theis lynes my character shal showe ;
Those benifitts that God me lent
With thanks I tooke and freely spent.
I scorned what playnesse covld not gett,
And next to treason hated debt ;
I loved not those thet stird vp strife ;
Trve to my freinde and to my wife:
The latter here by me I have ;
We had one bed and have one grave
My honesty was svch that I
When death came feard not to dye.

Another odd epitaph inscribed on the memorial brass of an old vicar of Bray and his wife, probably of the time of James I., runs :

When Oxford gave thee two degrees in art,
And love possest thee mester of my heart ;
Thy colledge fellowshipp thou lefst for mine,
And novght bvt deathe covld seprate me fro
  thine.
Thirty-five yeares we livd'e in wedlocke bands,
Conioyned in ovr hearts as well as handes ;
Bvt death the bodies of best friendes devides,
And in the earth's close wombe their relyckes
  hides ;
Yet here they are not lost bvt sowen, that they
May rise more gloriovs at the Ivdgment day.

Among the brasses are those of Arthur Page, died 1610, and his wife Sessely, died 1598 ; and that of William Laken, a judge, dated 1475, on the south wall, which was found obliterated by plaster when the church was last restored. There is a curious brass with coloured coat-of-arms of William Smithe, 1594 ; and on the floor of the south aisle is another, without date, on which are the figures of one Will. Smyth, and his wives Agneta and Matilda. It would seem from the similarity of the heraldic devices that, notwithstanding the difference of spelling, both these gentlemen belonged to the same branch of the great family of Smith. On the south wall is the brass of Clement Kelke, a cytycen of London, "a marchant ventver," 1593. The crowning glory of the Bray brasses is the well-known memorial of the Foxley family. This depicts Sir John Foxley and his two wives early in the 14th century. The figures are under a triple canopy, a great part of which has unfortunately disappeared. The knight is in armour, with his feet on a lion couchant, and the whole rests on a column issuing from the back of a fox. In its pristine perfection this must have been a singularly fine example, even now it is a somewhat unique specimen. Another curious tablet is that to William Norreys, of "Fifild in Bray," who died 1591. The brass represents Norreys, his wife, and numerous progeny, with his arms and motto, "Faithfully sarve"; and the inscription informs us that he was "Usher of the Parliament Howse and of the most noble Order of the Garter, controller of the works of Windsor Castle and parks there." A curious little altar-table is extant, used in the church in 1646, and the carved stone font is of about the same period. In the vestry is preserved a tattered, torn, and dog's-eared black letter copy of Foxe's Book of Martyrs, which was originally chained for public perusal to a pillar in the church about the time of Elizabeth, and was found when the tower was restored.

Jesus Hospital—almshouses for forty poor persons—with chapel and house for resident parson, is a queer red-brick quadrangle with yews and cypresses trimmed in ancient style along its road frontage, and surrounding an old-world well-kept garden and an ancient pump, which latter institution is apparently held in great veneration by the alms-people. Over the porch is a full-length statue of the pious founder, on either side of which are shields with the arms, on the left, of William Goddard; on the right, of the Fishmongers' Company, by whom the charity is administered. The erection of the hospital commenced in 1623, and it was completed in 1628. The curious alms-box, which stands in the porch, dates back to 1635.

HOTEL.—"The George," by the river.
PLACE OF WORSHIP.—St. Michael's.
POSTAL ARRANGEMENTS. — Money order office and savings bank. Nearest telegraph office, Maidenhead. Mails from London, 6.30 and 11.30 a.m.; Sunday, 6.30 a.m. Mails for London, 9.40 and 11.36 a.m. and 7.40 p.m.; Sunday, 11.40 a.m.

NEAREST *Bridges*, up, Maidenhead 1¼ mile; down, Windsor 5¾ miles. *Locks*, Bray; up, Boulter's 1¼ mile; down, Boveney 3¾ miles. *Ferry*, Bray. *Railway Station*, Maidenhead.

FARES, Maid. to Padd.: 1st, 4/4, 7/6; 2nd, 3/3, 5/9; 3rd, 2/0½.

Bream (The) is much more plentiful in the Thames during recent years than formerly. It is a flat, bony fish generally, repulsive from its sliminess, but yet has its admirers, who fish for little else. It is mostly taken by legering with a lob-worm, or the traveller in deep holes and in a gentle current. It spawns in May and is in season from June to March. There are two sorts of bream—the golden and the silver. The former is a far superior fish to the latter.

Brentford, Middlesex, on the left bank, from London 13 miles, from Oxford 98½ miles, nearly opposite Kew; a station on the London and South-Western Railway 10½ miles from Waterloo. Trains average 35 minutes. There are alternative routes to Ludgate (about 1 hour) and Paddington (about 45 minutes). Population, 11,091. Soil, London clay. Brentford has been described as a

tedious town
For dirty streets and white-legged
chickens known;

and although the chickens are no longer a specialty, the streets are still open to improvement. The place, now divided into Old and New Brentford, is in fact, a bustling, busy, metropolitan water-side district rather than a self-contained town, and has the untidiness characteristic of such places. The river Brent enters the Thames here, and at its mouth are the extensive docks of the Great Western Railway, where whole fleets of barges discharge and take in cargoes. Many important manufactures are carried on in both parts of the town. The town-hall, the post-office, and other public buildings are in New Brentford. The church of Old Brentford is dedicated to St. George, and is a plain brick building of no great antiquity, with an altar-piece by Zoffany, who lived at Strand-on-the-Green, just below Kew Bridge. It is in contemplation to build a new church, and to this end a site costing £2,200 has been secured. The church of New Brentford is dedicated to St. Lawrence, and, except the tower, which is of great antiquity, dates from about the middle of the last century. St. Paul's Church, Old Brentford, was built in 1868.

BANK.—London and County, High-street.

HOTELS.—"Star and Garter;" "Kew Bridge Castle;" "New Brentford."

B 2

MARKET.—Tuesday.

PLACES OF WORSHIP.—St. George's, St. Lawrence, St. Paul's, and the Roman Catholic Church of St. John the Evangelist.

POLICE.—Station (T division, Metropolitan), High-street.

POSTAL ARRANGEMENTS.—Post Office (money order, savings bank, telegraph, insurance). Mails from London, 7 and 8.45 a.m., 2.40, 6.45, and 8.20 p.m. Sunday, over counter, 8 to 10 a.m. Mails for London, 6.15 and 9.30 a.m., 12.40, 3, 5, 8.15, and 9.50 p.m. Sunday, 9 p.m.

NEAREST *Bridges*, up, Richmond 2½ miles; down, Kew ½ mile. *Lock*, up, Teddington, 5½ miles. *Ferry* and *Railway Station*, Brentford.

FARES to Waterloo or Ludgate: 1st, 1/-, 1/6; 2nd, -/10, 1/2; 3rd, -/8, 1/-. To Paddington: 1st, 1/6, 2/3; 2nd, 1/2, 1/9; 3rd, -/10.

Bridges—

CRICKLADE TO OXFORD.

Name.	Miles from Crick-lade.	Miles from Folly Bd. Oxford.
Eisey (foot)	1	42
Castle Eaton	4	39
Hannington	6	37
Lechlade	9½	33½
St. John's	10½	32½
Radcot	17	26
Old Man's (foot)	18	25
Tadpole	21	22
Ten Foot (foot)	22	21
New	28	15
Langley's (or Ridges) Weir	29	14
Eynsham	36	7
Godstow	40	3
Osney	42½	½

(*And see* TRIP FROM CRICKLADE.)

OXFORD TO PUTNEY.

Name.	Miles from London.	Miles from Oxford.
Folly	111½	—
Abingdon	103¾	7¾
Sutton	101¾	9¾
Clifton Hampden	98½	13
Day's Lock (foot)	96	15½
Shillingford	93¼	18¼
Wallingford	90¼	21¼
Streatley	84¾	26¾
Pangbourne	80¾	30¾
Caversham	74½	37
Sonning	71¼	40¾
Henley	65	46½
Marlow	57	54½
Cookham	53	58½
Maidenhead	50	61½
Windsor	43	68½
Victoria	41½	70
Albert	40¼	71¼
Staines	35½	76
Chertsey	31¼	79¾
Walton	27½	84
Hampton Court	23¼	88¼
Kingston	20½	91
Richmond	15½	96
Kew	12½	99
Hammersmith	8½	103
Putney	7	104½

(*And see* TRIP FROM OXFORD.)

Below PUTNEY.

Wandsworth, Battersea, Albert, Chelsea (or Victoria), Vauxhall, Lambeth, Westminster, Charing Cross (foot), Waterloo, Blackfriars, Southwark, London (*for particulars see under their respective headings*).

Bugsby's Reach, about one mile long, runs from Blackwall to the beginning of Woolwich Reach. The Lea enters the Thames on the left bank by Bow Creek. Bearings N.N.W. and S.S.E.

Buoys.—The following is a list of the buoys between Gravesend and the Nore. They are all under the management of the Trinity House, and will be found described under their respective headings: NORTH SIDE—Ovens, Gravesend Reach; River Middle, Sea Reach; East River Middle, Sea Reach; Spit (off Leigh), Sea Reach; West Shoebury, Sea Reach; Middle Shoebury, Sea Reach. SOUTH SIDE—West Blyth, Sea Reach; Middle Blyth, Sea Reach; East Blyth, Sea Reach; Yantlet, Sea Reach; Jenkin, Sea Reach; Nore Sand, Sea Reach; Sheerness Middle, entrance to Sheerness; Grain Spit, entrance to Sheerness. The Ovens, Blyth, and Yantlet Buoys were transferred to the Thames Conservancy in 1865, and were re-transferred to the Trinity House in 1879.

Burcott, Oxfordshire, on the left bank, rather more than a mile and half above Day's Lock, is a hamlet of Dorchester of no importance. It receives letters through Abingdon, Dorchester being the nearest money order office and telegraph station.

Buscot, a village in Berkshire on the right bank, about 31 miles from Oxford. Soil, clay; population, 500. Buscot is only a small agricultural village, and, with the exception of the fine estate of Buscot House, contains nothing of any interest but its old church of St. Mary, with its rather low, square, embattled tower. The interior of the church is plain, but a fine Norman arch divides the nave and chancel; and there is a piscina of apparently considerable antiquity. Buscot church is further adorned by a couple of mural monuments, dating from the end of the eighteenth century, quite in the taste of that period, and fitted with the customary angels, fat boys, and generally hideous emblematical devices. There is a lock at the village, the second from the source of the river, with a fall of rather more than four feet in ordinary seasons.

POSTAL ARRANGEMENTS. — Letters through Lechlade.

NEAREST *Bridges,* up, St. John's, about 2 miles ; down, Radcot about 5 miles ; *Locks,* up, St. John's about 2 miles ; down, Rushy 8½ miles. *Railway Station,* Lechlade, distant about 2 miles (*which see*).

Bushey Park.—*See* HAMPTON COURT PALACE.

Camping Out is a form of entertainment which has lately come into fashion, and is spoken of with much enthusiasm by its devotees, among whom may be numbered a proportion of ladies. It is a little difficult to see the great enjoyment of sleeping in a tent when you can get a bed, or of being exposed to the mists and fogs which are so plentiful on the river at night and in the early morning even in the summer. It is not necessary to give any detailed advice on this subject, as the enthusiast will probably have imbibed the taste for camping from an experienced friend, who will be able to "show him all the ropes." It may be suggested that a good deal of the land on the banks of the river is private property, and that trespassing in private paddocks and gardens, as is too often done, indiscriminate wood-cutting for fires, and similar practices, should be avoided. The owner of one well-known and extremely

comfortable camping-ground has been, we regret to say, compelled to close it against campers owing to the ill return so constantly made him for his courtesy. This gentleman is a man of the world, and not at all of a fidgety or touchy disposition; but when it came to cutting down valuable ornamental shrubs, climbing garden walls, stealing fruit and eggs, and surreptitiously milking cows at unholy hours, it was felt that the line must be drawn. A lock-island is generally a good place for a camp. Tents should be pitched a little distance from the water, on rising ground if possible, and upon no account under the shadow of overhanging trees. It is well to be provided with a sufficiency of reasonable comforts, but the example of a party who were once seen by the writer at Cookham, with a servant in livery laying the table for dinner, is not one to be followed. Half the fun of camping consists in doing everything for oneself, and in the perfect freedom from all conventional social trammels which such a mode of existence involves. For cooking utensils, the cooking stoves sold at 93, Wigmore-street, have been well spoken of. An iron tripod, with chain and hook to which to hang the kettle or the saucepan, is very useful. B. Edgington, of 2, Duke-street, London Bridge, can be recommended for tents of all kinds.

Canoe Club (Royal). Office, 11, Buckingham-street, Adelphi.—The Royal Canoe Club Boat-house is at Turk's, Kingston-on-Thames. T. G. F. Winser, Sec. The object of the club is to improve canoes, promote canoeing, and unite canoeists, by arranging and recording canoe voyages, by holding meetings annually for business and bivouac, for paddling and sailing, and for racing and chasing in canoes over land and water, Any gentleman nominated by two members is eligible. Election is by ballot, one black ball in five to exclude. Entrance fee, £2 ; subscription, £1. Life members, £10, without entrance fee. Ladies are also eligible for election. Each member on election is required to send a carte portrait of himself for insertion in the club album. The officers are commodore (H. R. H. the Prince of Wales), captain, two mates, purser, cook, and secretary. The club ribbon is black, with crown and club cipher embroidered in gold. The club burgee is blue, with crown and cipher in white.

The principal sailing races of the Royal Canoe Club take place on Hendon Lake and at Teddington. The regatta of 1884 was held on the Thames at Teddington, on the 28th of June.

Canvey Island (Essex) is situated on the Thames, about 12 miles below Gravesend, and is close to Hole Haven, or Holy Haven, and not far from Thames Haven. There is a very comfortable and unobtrusive inn, where boating men are frequently accommodated with bed and board. The population of the island, purely agricultural, is about 300. The very pretty little church is dedicated to St. Katherine. There is a coastguard station on the island, and Benfleet station is on the land side about three miles from the water. There is a fine shell bay and beach, which nearly at all times of the tide is a most pleasant walk close to the sea.

NEAREST *Railway Station*, Benfleet, on the London, Tilbury, and Southend Railway, about 1 hour 30 minutes from London; *Steamboat-piers*, Thames Haven and Southend. Railway fares, Benfleet to London, 1st, 3/9, 6/3; 2nd, 2/10, 4/9; 3rd, 1/11, 3/10.

Carp are occasionally taken in the Thames whilst angling for roach, and they are only specially fished for at Teddington, where they are sometimes caught in considerable numbers.

Castle Eaton.—A little village in Wiltshire, on the right bank, about 39 miles from Oxford, with the small church of St. Mary, chiefly noteworthy for a fine old bell turret. The river increases considerably in its volume and width about here, and is spanned by a bridge. Population about 320.

POSTAL ARRANGEMENTS. — Letters through Fairford (the nearest moneyorder and telegraph office).

NEAREST *Bridges*, up, Eisey 3 miles; down, Hannington. *Lock*, down, St. John's about 6½ miles. *Railway Station*, Fairford 3 miles.

FARES to Paddington, 1st, 18/6, 27/6; 2nd, 12/-, 20/-; 3rd, 8/5½.

Causeway Stakes, also known as Coway Stakes, in the bend of the river

half a mile above Walton Bridge; the reputed scene of a battle between Cæsar's legions and the Britons. The river was forded by the invader notwithstanding that Cassivelaunus had planted the bank and filled the river bed with sharp stakes. It is said that remains of these stakes were to be seen in the river until quite recently, but this tradition had better not be accepted as a fact. The venerable Bede notes that these stakes "are seen to this day about the thickness of a man's thigh, stuck immovable, being driven hard into the bottom of the river," but it does not appear that the venerable one himself had ocular demonstration of the fact.

Caversham, Oxfordshire, on the left bank; from London 74½ miles, from Oxford 37 miles. Population, 2,500. Soil, chalk. Caversham is, to all intents and purposes, a suburb of Reading, with which it is connected by an iron bridge. The village is unimportant, but there are many good houses in the neighbourhood. Among the principal mansions is Caversham Park. An omnibus runs to and from the "Elephant Inn," Reading, and the "Prince of Wales," Little End, *via* Grey Friar's-road, Caversham Bridge, and the New-road. The Church of St. Peter has lately undergone extensive repairs and restorations. It contains some fine Norman work. There is also a Wesleyan Church at Lower Caversham.

INNS.—"Crown," on the Oxfordshire side; "White Hart," on the Berkshire side, where boats can be left, as well as at Causton's under the bridge.

POLICE.—Station, Prospect-street.

POSTAL ARRANGEMENTS.—Post Office (money order, telegraph, and savings bank). Mails from London, 7 a.m., 12 noon and 5 p.m.; Sunday, 7 a.m. Mails for London, 8.25 a.m., 1.50 and 7.30 p.m.; Sunday, 1 p.m. There is a pillar letter-box in the wall facing the bridge.

NEAREST *Bridge*, Caversham; up, Pangbourne 6¼ miles; down, Sonning 3¼ miles. *Locks*, up, Mapledurham 4 miles; down, Caversham about ¾ mile. *Ferry*, at "Roebuck." *Railway Station*, Reading (*which see for* FARES).

Championship of the Thames (Amateur).—The possession of the

Wingfield Sculls, a challenge prize instituted in 1830, carries with it the amateur Championship of the Thames. The course was originally from Westminster to Putney. In 1849 the long course from Putney to Kew was selected. Twelve years later the University course between Putney and Mortlake was adopted, and the race has been rowed there ever since. In 1882 Mr. J. Lowndes, the previous year's winner, resigned, and on the 21st August, Mr. Alexander Payne, of the Moulsey Boat Club, beat Mr. W. R. Grove, London R.C., after a good race, in 27 min. 35 sec.

In 1884, the race fell to W. S. Unwin, of Magdalen College, Oxford, who easily beat his four opponents in the good time of 24 min. 12 secs.

WINNERS.

1830 J. H. Bayford
1831 C. Lewis
1832 A. A. Julius
1833 C. Lewis
1834 A. A. Julius
1835 A. A. Julius
1836 H. Wood
1837 P. Colquhoun
1838 H. Wood
1839 H. Chapman
1840 T. L. Jenkins
1841 T. L. Jenkins
1842 H. Chapman
1843 H. Chapman
1844 T. B. Bumpstead
1845 H. Chapman
1846 W. Russell
1847 J. R. L. Walmisley
1848 J. R. L. Walmisley
1849 F. Playford
1850 T. R. Bone
1851 T. R. Bone
1852 E. G. Peacock
1853 J. Paine
1854 H. H. Playford
1855 A. A. Casamajor
1856 A. A. Casamajor
1857 A. A. Casamajor
1858 A. A. Casamajor
1859 A. A. Casamajor
1860 A. A. Casamajor
1861 E. D. Brickwood
1862 W. B. Woodgate
1863 J. E. Parker
1864 W. B. Woodgate
1865 C. B. Lawes
1866 E. B. Michell
1867 W. B. Woodgate

1868 W. Stout
1869 A. de L. Long
1870 A. de L. Long
1871 W. Faucus
1872 C. C. Knollys
1873 A. C. Dicker
1874 A. C. Dicker
1875 F. L. Playford
1876 F. L. Playford
1877 F. L. Playford
1878 F. L. Playford
1879 F. L. Playford
1880 A. Payne
1881 J. Lowndes
1882 A. Payne
1883 J. Lowndes
1884 W. S. Unwin.

Championship of the Thames (Professional.)—The first race rowed for the Championship of the Thames was in 1831, C. Campbell being the first to bear the title of Champion. Up to 1865, races for the Championship of the Thames were very properly rowed on the Metropolitan water ; but in 1866, when Hamill came over and challenged Harry Kelley, the title of the race became the Championship of the World, and the matches took place indifferently at Putney and at Newcastle. In 1877 the race was actually rowed on the Paramatta River, New South Wales, and in the same year a Challenge Cup was given by the proprietor of the *Newcastle Daily Chronicle*, with the understanding that instead of there being distinct Championships of the Thames and Tyne, the two titles should be merged into that of Champion of England. In 1878 J. Higgins succeeded in winning this cup a sufficient number of times to enable him to claim it as his own property. In 1878, the *Sportsman* newspaper gave another cup, which was first won by W. Elliott, and in 1879 was taken to Canada by Hanlan, whose property it finally became after his defeat of Laycock at Putney, Feb. 14, 1881. In 1880 Hanlan beat Trickett very easily over the Putney course, and proved himself fully worthy to rank among the best of the Champions. In April, 1882, he beat R. W. Boyd on the Tyne, and a month after again defeated Trickett on the Thames, winning both races with the most ridiculous ease. No Championship race on the Thames or Tyne occurred in 1883 or 1884.—(*For Chart of Course see* UNIVERSITY BOAT RACE.)

Date.	Winner.	Loser.	Course.	Time.
1831. September 9	C. Campbell........	C. Williams	W. to P.	m. s.
1838. November 1	Ditto	R. Coombes	W. to P.	—
1846. August 19	R. Coombes	C. Campbell	P. to M.	26.15
1847. September 29......	Ditto	R. Newell..........	P. to M.	23.46
1851. May 7.............	Ditto	T. Mackinney	P. to M.	26.5
1852. May 24	T. Cole	R. Coombes	P. to M.	25.15
1852. October 14	Ditto	Ditto............	P. to M.	23.35
1854. November 20......	J. A. Messenger	T. Cole	P. to M.	24.30
1857. May 12	H. Kelley..........	J. A. Messenger	P. to M.	24.30
1859. September 29......	R. Chambers	H. Kelley	P. to M.	25.25
1860. September 18......	Ditto	T. White	P. to M.	23.15
1863. April 14	Ditto	G. W. Everson......	P. to M.	25.27
1863. June 16	Ditto	R. A. W. Green	P. to M.	25.25
1865. August 8..........	H. Kelley	R. Chambers	P. to M.	23.26
1866. July 4	Ditto	Hamill	Tyne	33.29
1866. July 5	Ditto	Hamill	Tyne	—
1866. November 22......	R. Chambers	J. H. Sadler........	P. to M.	25.4
1867. May 6	H. Kelley	R. Chambers	Tyne	31.41
1868. November 17	J. Renforth	H. Kelley	P. to M.	23.15
1874. April 16	J. H. Sadler........	R. Bagnall	P. to M.	24.15
1875. November 15	Ditto............	R. W. Boyd	P. to M.	29.2
1876. June 27	E. Trickett	J. Sadler	P. to M.	24.35
1876. A match was made between Trickett and Lumsden, but the latter forfeited.
1876. June 29. A match was made between Sadler and Higgins for the Championship, subject to the former beating Trickett ; but after being defeated, Sadler forfeited.
1877. May 28	R. W. Boyd	J. Higgins	P. to M.	29.0
1877. June 30. Trickett beat Michael Rush for the Championship of the World, on the Paramatta River, New South Wales.
1877. October 8	J. Higgins	R. W. Boyd	P. to M.	24.10
1878. January 14........	Ditto	J. Higgins	Tyne	foul.
1878. June 3	Ditto	W. Elliott..........	P. to M.	24.38
1878. September 17......	W. Elliott beat R. W. Boyd in final heat of race.
1879. February 17	W. Elliott..........	J. Higgins	Tyne	—
1879. June 16	Hanlan	W. Elliott..........	Tyne	—
1880. November 15......	Hanlan	Trickett............	P. to M.	26.11
1881. February 14	Hanlan	Laycock............	P. to M.	25.41
1882. April 3............	Hanlan	R. W. Boyd	Tyne	—
1882. May 1	Hanlan	Trickett	P. to M.	27.58

Chapman Lighthouse is an iron screw-pile structure, painted red, built on Chapman Head, in Sea Reach. It shows towards the eastward a red light over the sand called the River Middle, and a white light in the safe channel ; to the westward its light is wholly white, and is designed to lead vessels clear of a danger called the Scar. The piles have each a Mitchell's screw at the lower end, by means of which they were driven into the sand when the structure was built, in 1851. Above the wash of the water, a six-sided chamber contains the accommodation for the keepers, two in number, which is surmounted by a six-sided lantern, enclosing a Dioptric or Lenticular apparatus of the second order, in the centre of which is the source of light, a fountain lamp, with four concentric wicks burning colza oil. The light since January, 1881, is occulting, disappearing twice in quick succession every half minute. The total height of the building from base to vane is 74 feet, and the light is exhibited at an elevation of 40 feet above high water. Three keepers are employed : two on duty and one on shore, and the relief is effected once a month, by a steamer from the Trinity depôt at Blackwall, so that each man serves two months at the lighthouse, and has one month in three on shore.

Charing Cross (Foot) Bridge, runs along and forms a portion of the Charing-cross railway-bridge, and is approached on the north side from Villiers-street, and on the south side from Belvedere-road. It is the shortest way for foot passengers from Charing-cross and neighbourhood to Waterloo Station.

Chelsea, S.W., on the left bank, once a quiet village three miles from London, is now a densely populated locality, and lies between the Brompton-road and the Thames, Sloane-street being its eastern boundary, while its western boundary is indeterminate, as it is still growing. It gives its name to a parliamentary borough, which includes the Kensington and Hammersmith parishes, and is now represented by Sir Charles Dilke and Mr. J, B. Firth, Liberals. Chelsea contains a great population of the working class. Chelsea is Radical, while Kensington may be looked upon as Conservative ; Hammersmith being a mixed parish. The old parish church stands on the embankment close to the river, and is rich in associations ecclesiastical, historical, and literary. The river front of Chelsea has been greatly improved by the embanking of Cheyne-walk and the construction of the Chelsea Embankment ; and the admirably designed red brick houses in the Queen Anne style, lately completed on the Cadogan estate, are thoroughly in accordance with old Chelsea traditions and associations. The principal public buildings are the Barracks, Chelsea Hospital, and the Military Asylum. The Gardens of the Apothecaries' Company are also well worth inspection. NEAREST *Railway Stations,* Sloane-square, Grosvenor-road, and Chelsea ; *Omnibus Routes,* Sloane-street, King's-road, and Fulham-road ; *Steamboat Piers,* Cadogan Pier and Battersea Pier.

Chelsea Suspension Bridge is another work by the designer of Westminster Bridge, and leads from Victoria-road to the east of Battersea-park, to the Chelsea Embankment and its continuation, the Grosvenor-road. It was made in Edinburgh, and set up in its present position in 1858 at a cost of £80,000.

Chertsey, Surrey, on the right bank, from Oxford 79¾ miles, from London

31¾ miles. A station on the London and South Western Railway, about an hour from London. The station is ten minutes' walk from the Town Hall, and twenty-five minutes' from Chertsey Bridge. Flys meet the trains. Population, 7,760.

Chertsey is an old-fashioned country town with a number of good houses and a few shops of some importance in its two principal thoroughfares, Windsor-street and Guildford-street, which runs at right angles to Windsor-street, and leads from the town-hall to the station. There is not much to be said in favour of the architectural pretensions of the two principal public buildings—the town-hall and the church. The town generally may be described as quiet and dull, but to make amends it is rich in interesting historical associations. Some remains of Chertsey Abbey, in which the body of Henry VI. was for a short time buried, still exist, although it is harder every day to conceive that so magnificent a building as has been described could have so utterly disappeared. Near Chertsey is St. Anne's Hill, a favourite retreat of Charles James Fox ; and in the Porch House in Guildford-street died the poet Cowley. The room in which he died is said to be still in existence, although the porch which gave its name to the house was removed in 1786. Cowley's death here is recorded in an inscription on the wall of the house, which concludes with Pope's line :

Here the last accents flowed from Cowley's tongue.

St. Anne's Hill has other recommendations besides its connection with the great statesman, as the views from its summit on both sides are singularly beautiful. The country around, indeed, is almost universally picturesque, being for the most part hilly and well-wooded. The charming neighbourhoods of Virginia Water and Sunningdale are within easy reach, and these excursions may be recommended to visitors. Weybridge and the country surrounding are also worthy of exploration. Chertsey Bridge, which connects Surrey and Middlesex, is of stone, with seven arches, and near it, on the right bank, is one of the most interesting experimental establishments on the river. Here Mr. Forbes, so long and so favourably known as an enthusi-

*

astic devotee of pisciculture, has brought his arrangements for the hatching and rearing of salmon trout and other fish to a singular degree of completeness. Mr. Forbes occasionally grants permission to view these fish nurseries. Sir William Perkins's Endowed Schools were founded in 1725 for the education of twenty-five poor boys of the parish of Chertsey. In 1736 Sir William Perkins built a similar school for twenty-five poor girls. The original school buildings were in Windsor-street. At his death in 1741, Sir William left £3,000 for the support of the schools, and in 1819 the fund had increased to over £5,000. It was then decided to sell the old houses and buy a piece of land at the west end of Chertsey, and largely to extend the benefits of the schools. Subsequently the buildings were again enlarged; the clothing which was given to the children and certain special gifts were abolished; and the whole of the income is devoted to giving a sound elementary education to between 500 and 600 children of Chertsey and neighbourhood. The Chertsey District Horticultural Society, founded some fifteen years ago, has, from small beginnings, made rapid progress, and its shows are now among the best in the home counties. There is also a Chrysanthemum Society, founded in 1876. Among the other public institutions is the Literary and Scientific, the members of which have the use of a reading-room, recreation-room, and a good library of 2,000 volumes. The subscription is for non-members, £1 1s.; for general members, 10s. 6d. per annum, 3s. per quarter; library members, 2s. 6d. per annum. Of water-side features Chertsey has but few. The "Bridge House Hotel," the Chertsey Rowing Club boat-house, and Messrs. Des Vigne's torpedo-launch manufactory pretty well exhaust the list. There is a convenient landing-place at the "Bridge House Hotel." The coach from London to Virginia Water changes horses at Chertsey.

Roach swims in plenty; good angling from bank. From this to Shepperton is fine jack water.

BANKS.—Ashby & Co., Old Bank, and London and County, both in Guildford-st.

FIRE.—Station in the town.

HOTELS.—"The Bridge House," on the river; "Crown," London-street.

PLACES OF WORSHIP.—St. Peter's; and Baptist, Congregational, and Wesleyan Chapels.

POLICE - STATION.—East-street, some distance from the town.

POSTAL ARRANGEMENTS.—Post Office, Windsor-street, opposite the church (money, savings bank, telegraph, insurance office). Mails from London, 3.35 and 8.40 a.m., 4.49 p.m. Mails for London, 9.35 and 11.35 a.m., 3.20 and 8 p.m.

NEAREST *Bridge, Station,* and *Lock,* Chertsey. Nearest *Bridges,* up, Staines 3¾ miles; down, Walton 4½ miles. *Locks,* up, Penton Hook 2 miles; down, Shepperton 2 miles. *Ferry,* Laleham.

FARES to Waterloo: 1st, 4/-, 5/6; 2nd, 3/-, 4/-; 3rd, 1/10, 3/4.

Chertsey Rowing Club.—Election by ballot in general meeting; one black ball in five excludes. Subscription, 15s.; honorary members, £1 1s.; lads for coxswains, 5s. Colours, black and white vertical stripes. Boat-house, just below Chertsey Bridge, right bank.

"Chichester."—(*See* "ARETHUSA.")

Chiswick.—London, S.W., on the left bank.—A waterside suburb about 5 miles west of Hyde Park Corner, rapidly being swallowed up by the advancing tide of buildings. Hogarth died here, and is buried in the churchyard. Rousseau also lived here, boarding at a little grocer's shop. The gardens of the Horticultural Society lie on the Turnham-green side. Chiswick Church is situated at the west-end of the pleasant riverside walk known as The Mall; and just opposite lies Chiswick Eyot, a well-known landmark in champion and University boat-races. There is a ferry here from the bottom of Chiswick-lane, in Middlesex, to Ferry-lane, leading to Barnes Common, in Surrey. Chiswick may be reached by rail from Waterloo, Ludgate-hill, and Mansion House.

Chub (The) is a great favourite with many anglers. Leather-mouthed is he, and for a while strong withal, when first hooked. But he is a very wary fish, which sinks out of sight at even the distant flight of a bird over his head. From the fact of his desperate rush when first feeling the barb very strong tackle is requisite to secure him, and yet that tackle must be of the finest if you desire to deceive him. Chub spawn in April or May, and the best season for them is from October throughout the winter months. Indeed, they may be taken in great numbers, and mostly of the largest size, when the water is frozen, with only here and there an open spot for the introduction of the lure. In summer a fly is the best method of catching him, and a large black or red palmer thrown just under the overhanging boughs and near their submerged roots will be sure to be attended with success, as in these places the fish resort in waiting to seize the insects which fall from the branches. A cockchafer, grasshopper, small frog, or beetle is another favourite bait which may be introduced through an opening of the foliage, while the fisher is concealed from observation: the angler approaching the spot with muffled tread, as the slightest concussion on the bank is sufficient to give the fish the alarm and put him on his guard. As it is difficult when a fish is thus hooked to land him, the following plan may be resorted to : Take a number 8 or 9 hook whipped on to about a yard of gut, on this place a good-sized swan shot, twist this on the end of your top joint until none of the tackle hangs from it : now push your rod quietly through a gap in the foliage, unroll the portion of your line by a few turns of the rod, and then let the bait by the weight of the shot descend to the surface of the water : when there move it up and down to make a slight splash, and to imitate the attempt of the bait to escape from drowning. If there be any chub in the neighbourhood they will presently rise to the surface, and after taking a survey of the lure perhaps hesitate to take it. You will, however, from your station command a view of your victims, and if there be one chub larger than the others you covet, offer the bait, not to that one, but to the others, as if from the accidental struggles of the chaffer, &c., but do not let them take it. Thus, after a while the chief of the lot will get excited and suddenly make a dash for it, and you have him. You must hold him with a strong grasp, relying upon your tackle, or he will dart for the fastnesses of roots, &c., beneath the bank. When you have exhausted him, go as low as you can on your hands and knees, get the landing-net under him,

and draw him deftly out. Having done this you have but to untie the line from the gut hook and wind up your line, now free from incumbrance, through the bushes. Now try another place, leaving this alone for a while, and thus in the extent of a single meadow margined with willows or elders you may continue to take chub from sunrise until eve. A very deadly bait, introduced on the Thames from the Trent, is the pipe-like pith from the backbone of an ox, simply scalded and slightly cut open. Chub are brought together after this bait by a sprinkling of ox-brains which the fishermen chew and blow out on the surface of the water from their mouths. But there is no occasion to resort to this objectionable practice, as the brains may be cut up and separated on a piece of wood or plate, and filliped off into the water with the point of the knife. A double hook is needed for this mode, as the pith requires an extra security, and the travelling float should be used, as the fish are shy in coming too near the punt, although this decidedly novel treat is almost irresistible. Large chub are often taken while trolling or spinning with the gudgeon or minnow, and they will run at the small fry, such as minnows, with great avidity when well on the feed. Their teeth are very formidable, and are placed out of sight in their throats, as are those of others of their fresh-water congeners. The chub is of little value for the table, except in hard frosty weather, when its flesh becomes firm and ceases to be woolly and insipid. If there are no obstructions near the chub when first hooked you may permit him to make his one desperate rush ; after that a little will subdue him.

Cleopatra's Needle stands on the Victoria Embankment, left hand of the river. This famous monolith of red granite, from Alexandria, originally stood at Heliopolis, and was presented to this country by Mehemet Ali in 1819. No ministry was bold enough to face the difficulty and expense of transporting it across the Bay of Biscay, and for many years it lay half-buried by sand at Alexandria, at the foot of its still erect sister, which, according to some people, is the real original Cleopatra's Needle. In the Alexandrian sand the English obelisk would probably have remained until the end of time (unless, indeed, the

British tourist had carried it away piece-meal in the form of relics) but for the public spirit of the late Sir (then Mr.) Erasmus Wilson and Mr. John Dixon, the well-known civil engineer. Mr. Wilson put down £10,000 for the expenses of transport, and Mr. Dixon undertook to deliver the monument in the Thames for that sum on the principle of "no cure, no pay"—no obelisk, no £10,000. A cylinder boat was designed, in which the needle was encased, and justified Mr. Dixon's expectations by making good weather of it until it became unmanageable and untenantable in a heavy gale in the Bay of Biscay. Abandoned by the steamer which had it in tow, after the sacrifice of six lives in a last gallant attempt to save the Cleopatra, few people doubted that the needle would find its last resting-place at the bottom of the sea. Fortunately a passing steamer succeeded in securing it, and towed it into Ferrol, whence it was safely transferred to its present site. Much ingenuity was shown in the machinery designed for its erection, the difficulties of which will readily be understood when it is stated that the obelisk is over 68 feet in height, and weighs 180 tons. NEAREST *Steamboat Piers* and *Bridges*, Waterloo and Charing-cross ; *Railway Stations*, Charing-cross (Dist. & S.E.) ; *Omnibus Routes*, Waterloo Bridge and Strand.

Clewer, Berkshire, a village standing on a creek of the Thames, just above Windsor railway-bridge, and close to Windsor race-course, which is in the parish. Clewer is notable for the number of important mansions and seats in and about it, and for the religious institutions which have grown up around the churches, principally under the auspices of the Rev. T. T. Carter. The institutions attached to St. Andrew's, the parish church, are independent of the parish. They are the House of Mercy, in connection with the London Church Penitentiary Association (32, Sackville-street, W.), where about 80 female penitents are maintained under the care of sisters of mercy, headed by a warden. Under the charge of the sisters are also a Convalescent Hospital with nearly 100 beds ; an Orphanage ; and St. Andrew's Cottage, for ladies needing rest. Attached to St. Stephen's Church is the Ladies' College, &c. The parish church is interesting, some parts of it

being very old, and dating back to Saxon times. It has a tablet to the memory of Field Marshal Earl Harcourt. The churchyard is made unusually pleasant, great care being taken of the graves, Her Majesty the Queen setting an example in bringing flowers. PLACES OF WORSHIP.—St. Andrew's and St. Stephen's. POSTAL ARRANGEMENTS.—Mails from London, 7.10 a.m. and 12.30 p.m. For London, 10.15 a.m. and 5.45 p.m.

Clifton Hampden, Oxfordshire, on the left bank, 98½ miles from London, 13 miles from Oxford. Population, 377. Soil, chiefly gravel. This picturesque little village is situated at the foot of a bold bluff, which rises abruptly from the somewhat flat country around. The cliff is surmounted by the church and vicarage, and is clothed with luxuriant trees down to the water's edge. The village, a pretty collection of old-fashioned cottages, all of which are bright with flowers, does not call in itself for more than a passing notice. It derives some importance from the new red brick bridge with six pointed arches, built by the lord of the manor in place of the ferry which formerly existed here, the towing-path crossing the river at this point. The toll for horses not drawing vehicles is 1½d., and for foot passengers, 1d. The church, dedicated to St. Michael and All Angels, formerly a chapelry in connection with the Abbey of Dorchester, was entirely restored in 1844 by the late Mr. G. H. Gibbs, and is a very elaborate specimen of the work of Sir Gilbert Scott. It contains in the north of the chancel a tomb with a recumbent portrait figure of the late Mr. Gibbs, and a most elaborate brass screen with figures in bronze. The reredos is a somewhat bold work in mosaic, representing on either side the Prophets, Evangelists, and Latin Doctors, and in the centre the Last Supper. The churchyard, from which a charming view extends up and down the river, is, like the village, ablaze with flowers, and is entered through a handsome modern lych gate. On the Berkshire side, two or three minutes' walk from the bridge, is the "Barley Mow Inn," one of the thatched, sile built, old-fashioned resting-places which have been almost improved out of existence by the modern system of hotels. The parlour of the "Barley Mow" is a queer panelled

45 CLI—CON

room, more like the cabin of a ship than the coffee-room of an inn, and is of so low a pitch as to still further favour the illusion. But although the house is primitive, and the entertainment unpretending, it is a capital little inn of its class, and may be recommended to boating men.

INNS.—"The Barley Mow" (Berkshire side); "Plough."

PLACE OF WORSHIP.—St. Michael and All Angels.

POSTAL ARRANGEMENTS.—The nearest money order and telegraph offices are at Dorchester and Abingdon. Mails from London, 8 a.m., and on Sundays. Mails for London, 6 p.m.; Sunday, 10.55 a.m. Pillar-box at Burcott, cleared at 5.40 p.m.

NEAREST *Bridges*, Clifton Hampden; up, Sutton Bridges (Culham) 3¼ miles; down, Shillingford, 5¼ miles (a foot-bridge at Day's Lock 2½ miles). *Locks*, up, Clifton ½ mile; down, Day's 2½ miles. *Railway Station*, Culham.

FARES, Culham to Pad.: 1st, 10/-, 17/6; 2nd, 7/6, 13/-; 3rd, 5s.

Coaching.—Riverside towns have not been neglected in the recent revival of coaching, and many pleasant views of the river are afforded to travellers by "the road."

Thus, the Guildford coach passes through Kingston (fare, 4s. 6d.) and Thames Ditton (5s.). The route of the "Old Times," Virginia Water coach, is *via* Barnes, Richmond, Twickenham, Hampton Court, Moulsey, Walton, Oatlands Park, Weybridge, and Chertsey, thus taking in all the best views of the river; the return fare for the whole distance being 17s. 6d.; intermediate fares are also charged. The Windsor coach visits Barnes, Richmond, Twickenham, Teddington, Hampton Court, Hampton, and Staines, the return fare being 17s. 6d., with various intermediate fares.

All information respecting these and other coaches can at any time be obtained of Mr. Banks, at the booking office, Hatchett's Hotel, Piccadilly.

Coastguard.—The Thames which is in the Harwich district is shared between the two divisions of Southend and Sheerness, the greater portion being under the former, which extends from Shoeburyness

round by Tilbury and Gravesend to Cliffe Creek, beyond which the Sheerness division continues in the direction of the sea.

Cobbler (The).—(*See* ROMNEY ISLAND.)

Conservators of the Thames, 41, Trinity Square, London, E.C.—The Conservators are a body constituted in 1857 by the Act 20 & 21 Vict. cap. 147, which was the result of a compromise between the Crown and the Corporation of a suit arising out of conflicting claims to the bed of the river. Under this Act the Conservators consisted of twelve persons representing various interests, and their jurisdiction extended from Staines in Middlesex to Yantlet Creek in Kent. In 1864 considerable changes were made in the Act, and six elective Conservators were added; and by a further Act of 1866, the Conservancy of the Upper Thames as far as Cricklade, in Wiltshire, was vested in the Conservators, and five Conservators were added, viz.: one appointed by the Board of Trade, and four elected by persons on the upper river. Acts passed in 1867, 1870, and 1878, further extended the scope of the Conservancy's duties. Of the Conservators as at present constituted, seven—the Lord Mayor, two aldermen, and four common councillors—represent the City; the Admiralty and Board of Trade have each two nominations; the Trinity House is represented by its deputy-master and one nominee. The elected Conservators represent the following interests: Owners of shipping registered in London, two; owners of lighters and steam tugs, two; owners of river passenger steamers, one; dock-owners and wharfingers, one; and persons of the upper river, four. Under the Act of 1866 the remuneration of the Conservators is fixed at £1,800 per annum, with a further addition of £700 from the upper river fund.

The principal matters to which the rules and bye-laws of the Conservancy apply, are the navigation of the river; the lights to be carried by vessels; the regulation of the carriage of explosive substances, and of petroleum; the fisheries; the regulating of boat races. The bye-laws can always be had on application at the London office.—(*See* BOAT RACES, FISHING, LIGHTS, NAVIGATION.)

Cookham, Berkshire, on the right bank; from London 53 miles, from Oxford 58½ miles. A station on a branch line of the Great Western Railway, about an hour from Paddington. An omnibus meets the trains; the station is about eight minutes from the river. Population (of village), 872. Soil, chalk and gravel. Cookham stands at the end of what is popularly supposed to be the best part of the Thames, and, together with Maidenhead, is probably better known to picnickers and London excursionists than almost any other place on the river. It is immediately opposite the woods of Hedsor, the seat of Lord Boston, and just below the lock is the pretty Formosa island on the right; and the magnificent hanging woods of Cliveden on the left. In the neighbourhood are many noble mansions, Dropmore being immediately behind Hedsor; White Place, formerly the property of the Duke of Buckingham, is in the meadow opposite Cliveden; with many others still farther removed from the river. The grounds of both Hedsor and (during the absence of the family) of Cliveden are shown on application. The conifers at Dropmore are renowned, and the view from the ridge, on which stands "Cliveden's proud alcove," is superb. The church of Holy Trinity, an ancient building with chancel, nave, aisles, and a square tower (about 1500), contains some modern stained glass windows, and an alabaster monument of the 16th century to the memory of Arthor Babham and wife with a quaint inscription. There are also some good brasses. That to George Welder, dated 1616, is in the south aisle; there is one dated 1615 in the north aisle with a curious epitaph; another, mutilated, to Richard Babham and wife (1527) on the north wall of the north aisle; and under an altar tomb in the chancel are the figures of Robert Peck (an official of Henry VI.) and wife, 1510. In the north aisle a brass with three full-length figures has the inscription, "Pray for the souls of William Andrew and John Monkeden and Margaret; which William deceased 1506;" also in the north aisle is a brass with full-length figure of John Babham—the companion figure of his wife being missing—with date 1458. On the north wall is a very good mural tablet to Sir Isaac Pocock, by Flaxman (1808). The most interesting monument, however, to many visitors to Cookham Church will be that to the late lamented Frederick Walker, A.R.A. The marble mural monument which records his untimely death, and which is placed on the west wall of the south aisle, bears a medallion bust, a most admirable likeness.

Cookham Reach, when not searched by the wind, is a safe resort for roach, for which the swims are many about Spade Oak, Bourne End, Hedsor, Cliveden, &c.

FAIRS.—May 16 and October 11.

HOTELS.—"Bell and the Dragon;" the "Ferry," on the river; the "King's Arms."

PLACES OF WORSHIP.—Holy Trinity, and a Wesleyan chapel.

POSTAL ARRANGEMENTS.—Post Office (money order, savings bank, telegraph, insurance). Mails from London, 7 a.m., 12.30 p.m.; Sunday, 7 a.m. Mails to London, 12.30 and 7.30 p.m.; Sunday, 7.15 p.m.

NEAREST *Bridge, Lock, Ferry,* and *Railway Station,* Cookham. Nearest *Bridges,* up, Marlow 4 miles; down, Maidenhead 3 miles. *Locks,* up, Marlow 3½ miles; down, Boulter's 2½ miles.

FARES to Paddington: 1st, 5/-, 8/6; 2nd, 3/8, 6/3; 3rd, 2/3.

Cooper's Hill.—(*See also* EGHAM.)

Cooper's Hill Boat Club (Royal Indian Engineering College).—This boating club numbers between fifty and sixty members. In 1881 the club sent an eight to Henley to compete for the Ladies' Plate, an eight and a four to Kingston, and a four to Reading. In 1882 it was unrepresented at Henley and Kingston, but had a four at Reading. The colours are dark blue and yellow. The boathouse, three-quarters of a mile from the college, is on the left bank, opposite the upper end of Magna Charta Island, about 600 yards below the "Bells of Ouseley."

Cooper's Hill College.—The Royal Indian Engineering College has been established under the orders of the Secretary of State for India in Council, in view to the education of Civil Engineers for the service of Government in the Indian Public Works Department; but it is open, to the extent of the accommodation available, to all persons desirous of following the course of study pursued there. All particulars as to admission, course of study, appointments, etc., may be obtained of the Secretary at the College.

Corinthian Yacht Club. — Clubhouse, Erith. The primary object of the club is the encouragement of amateur yacht sailing. The election is by ballot in committee ; three adverse votes exclude. The affairs of the club are administered by a commodore, vice-commodore, rear-commodore, hon. treasurer, secretary, and a committee of fifteen other members, with power to increase their number to twenty. The club numbers over 500 members. In races of this club no professional or paid hands are allowed except in the largest class, *i.e,*, over 20 tons. None but members of the C.Y.C. are to act as helmsmen in any race. Entrance fee, £2 2s.; subscriptions, £1 1s. Burgee, blue, with laurel wreath in gold in the centre.

" Cornwall."—This reformatory training-ship of the School-Ship Society is anchored off Purfleet. As a general rule the committee do not admit boys unless the three following conditions are satisfied :

1. That the boy be sentenced to not less than three years' detention.

2. That he be not less than 13 years of age nor more than 15.

3. That he be certified as sound and healthy.

The comparative cost per head on ordinary maintenance and management is £23 5s. 8d. Funds are urgently needed, as "the amounts received on account of the Treasury allowance and the county and borough rates do little more than suffice for the maintenance of the boys and for the payments of the officers." Visitors are requested not to go on Saturday, which is cleaning day on board. The *Cornwall* was once the *Wellesley*, and was built in Bombay of teak in 1815, and was the flagship of Sir W. Parker and of Lord Dundonald.

Coway Stakes (*See* CAUSEWAY STAKES).

Cricklade, Wiltshire, on the right bank, distant from Oxford 43 miles. Soil, loam ; population, about 2,000. The nearest railway station is Purton, about 4 miles off, an omnibus plying between the station and the town. The fast trains from Paddington, distance 82 miles, perform the journey in two hours and a quarter, or thereabouts. This is a

straggling and fairly picturesque little place on the Thames and Severn and North Wilts Canals, and it is here that the Thames, at its junction with the Churn, begins to assume the appearance of a navigable river. Though in itself a small place, Cricklade is the centre of a number of other parishes which have for many years united in returning two Members to Parliament, the constituency at the last general election numbering 7,473. The present Members are Mr. M. H. N. Story Maskelyne (L.) and Sir Daniel Gooch (C.). Cricklade is a pleasant little town, clean and well-paved, but has not been the scene of any particularly remarkable events, since it shared the fate of so many of the other Thames towns and was plundered by the Danes in 1015, and now contains few objects of interest, except the church of St. Sampson, a very handsome building, with chancel, nave, and side aisles, and a remarkably good square embattled tower, with parapet and four pinnacles. This, which is said to date from 1400, was built of stone from the same quarries as supplied the materials for the construction of Cirencester and Gloucester cathedrals, and which are now exhausted. On the north side of the tower are carved a pair of reaping hooks and a pair of shears, and above them a wheel projects. A local legend says that these objects refer to the three men who were most concerned in building the tower— a farmer, a tailor, and a clock-maker. This, however, is more than doubtful, seeing that whatever meaning may be supposed to attach to the shears and the reaping hooks, the wheel is simply a Catherine wheel, and a very good one too. But the builders of the tower delighted in quaint and out-of-the-way decoration, as is instanced in the walls and beautifully groined roof of the interior. Here, in addition to numerous coats of arms—including, on the south side, that of the Hungerford family, by whom the tower was, in all probability, built—are sculptured the aces of the four suits of the pack of cards, the shears again, two pairs of ladies' stays, and a number of other quaint devices. The church, which contains some excellent Early English windows and a very good west window and door, was undoubtedly the work of different periods, of which three may distinctly be noted at the flying buttress outside the east end, and is both handsome and commodious. Among the tablets on the floor is one in memory of one Simon Wild, jun., 1710, who is oddly enough said to have been "in Jenis for singing, ringing, and writing," and the tomb of Robert Jenner informs the world that he "deceased this life" in 1651. There is an empty niche in the north aisle to which it is probable that a curious and much-defaced stone figure, which lies by the side of the path to the church, of right belongs ; although here again local tradition steps in, and declares that the effigy in question represents the mangled body of a man who fell from the tower during its construction. At the west end of the pretty churchyard is a good old farmhouse, and on the north-east side a picturesque building dating from 1652, which, having started in life as a school, afterwards became a workhouse, and is now a school again. In the churchyard there is also a fine old cross, which formerly stood in the marketplace. Another good cross stands in the churchyard of St. Mary's at the other end of the town. This church, though much smaller than St. Sampson's, is architecturally interesting, notably by reason of a Norman arch of the eleventh century. The town also contains Baptist, Congregational, Wesleyan, and Methodist places of worship, and a Town Hall capable of holding about 300 people.

BANK.—The Gloucestershire Banking Company.

FIRE ENGINE.—Church-street.

MARKET DAY.—Third Tuesday in the month.

HOTELS.—"White Hart" and "White Horse."

PLACES OF WORSHIP.—St. Sampson's and St. Mary's.

POLICE.—The station is the last house at the north end of the town, just across the bridge over the Thames.

POSTAL ARRANGEMENTS.—Post Office (money order, savings bank, telegraph, and insurance), High-street. Mails from London, 3 a.m. and 2.30 p.m. Mails for London, noon, and 9.45 p.m.

NEAREST *Bridges*, down, Eisey, for foot passengers, about a mile, and Castle Eaton, about 4 miles. *Lock*, St. John's, about 10½ miles. *Railway Station*, Purton, 4 miles. Omnibus, three times a day.

FARES to Paddington, 1st, 14/4, 25/- ; 2nd, 10/9, 18/9 ; 3rd, 6/9½.

Crimps may be said to be practically an extinct order of reptile. Jack's ship is now boarded on arrival at Gravesend by the officers of the Board of Trade, who provide him with a passage straight home if he wishes it, and he is next awaited in the dock by the *employés* of the Sailors' Home. If their *régime* does not suit him, the private lodging-houses he prefers are under the strictest sanitary and police surveillance ; and when his money is out and he wants a ship, the only means by which he can obtain one is through the Shipping Office. Finally, if in spite of these tender surroundings he contrives, as he still occasionally does contrive, to procure his own ultimate ejectment from some unlicensed den in the minimum of clothing, and without even the minimum of coin, he has still the refuge of the "Straw House." Thus while blood-suckers of various breeds still ply their trade with more or less success at Jack's expense—a fact for which Jack has assuredly nowadays no one to thank but himself—the "crimp," whose specialty it was, after having sucked the blood, to dispose of the carcase to some sea-going skipper in want of a crew, has no longer any *raison d'être*, and has therefore practically ceased to be.

Crowmarsh Giffard, sometimes called Long Crowmarsh, Oxfordshire, on the left bank opposite Wallingford, 90¾ miles from London, 20¾ miles from Oxford. Population about 350. Soil, upper greensand. Crowmarsh is a small village joined to Wallingford, Berks, by a stone bridge, and within the Parliamentary borough of Wallingford. The church, St. Mary Magdalene, of great antiquity, was built in the reign of King Stephen, and consists of nave, chancel, and north transept. The western doorway is a fine specimen of Norman work. The old west door of massive oak has been recently removed and fitted to the vestry ; it still bears marks of the bullet-holes which were made (it is said) during the siege of Wallingford Castle at the time of the Civil Wars. In this parish is Howbery Park ; the old mansion (formerly the seat of W. S. Blackstone, Esq., M.P.) was burnt down a century ago. It is now rebuilt on same site, and owned by H. B. Watkin Williams Wynn, Esq. The rents of two acres of land in the parish have from time immemorial been applied to the repair of the church.

FAIR.—Horse fair, August 2.

PLACE OF WORSHIP. — St. Mary Magdalene.

POSTAL ARRANGEMENTS. — Letters through Wallingford, which is the nearest money order, telegraph, and insurance office. Mails from London, 6.15 a.m. Mails for London, 7 p.m.

NEAREST Lock, Bridge, and Ferry, Wallingford. NEAREST Bridges, up, Shillingford 2½ miles ; down, Streatley 5¾ miles. Locks, up, Bensington 1¼ mile ; down, Cleeve 5¼ miles. Railway Station, Wallingford.

FARES, Wallingford to Paddington : 1st, 9/5, 16/- ; 2nd, 7/-, 12/- ; 3rd, 4/3.

Crow Stone (The).—An obelisk on the Essex bank, about a mile westward of Southend, marks the limit of the jurisdiction of the Thames Conservancy ; an imaginary line being drawn across the river here to Yantlet Creek in Kent,

Cuckoo Weir.—A bathing-place for the junior boys of Eton College, the water being of a convenient depth with but little stream. It leaves the river at Upper Hope, a little distance below Athens, and re-enters it again above the Great Western Railway-bridge opposite Clewer. During the vacation the Royal Humane Society of Eton and Windsor keep a waterman here for the safety of the bathing public.

Culham, Oxfordshire, on the left bank, a portion of the parish being in Berkshire. A station on the Great Western Railway, 56 miles from Paddington, trains take from 1½ hour upwards ; from London 101¾ miles, from Oxford 9¾ miles. Population, about 600. Soil, gravel. The station is 30 minutes' walk from the lock. A small village 2 miles below Abingdon. The green is a few minutes' walk from the lock, the road passing by Culham House and grounds, the wall of which encloses a fine belt of trees. The church is at the western end of the green, and is dedicated to St. Paul. Little remains of the original edifice, the church having been rebuilt some 25 years ago. The square tower, however, which dates from

the first year of the last century, is still standing ; the register dates from 1650. The sum of between £50 and £60 is distributed annually in coal to the inhabitants, arising from the sale of some common land on which the parish had the right of cutting gorse. The following entry occurs in the parish register : "Oct. 10th, 1666. Collected for the poore of London, disabled by a dismall and lamentable fire, £1 3s. 8d." The training college for schoolmasters, with school attached, is about a mile from the railway-station. This institution, capable of accommodating nearly 100 students, was founded by the late Right Rev. Samuel Wilberforce, when Bishop of Oxford, for the purpose of training young men as Church schoolmasters. Seventy-five per cent. of the expenditure is defrayed by Government grant.

Just below Culham Lock is a fine reach for pike. Sutton Mill-pool close by is one of the deepest on the river, and when a fish is laid hold of here it is generally worth the taking.

In the wall of Culham House, and immediately opposite the "Sow and Pigs" Inn on the green—a good specimen of modern reproduction of an old red-bricked and timbered building—is the Post Office letter box, which is cleared on week-days at 7.10 p.m.,| and on Sundays at noon. Letters arrive from Abingdon, the nearest money order and telegraph office, at 7 a.m.

INNS.—"Sow and Pigs," and "Railway Hotel" at the station.

PLACE OF WORSHIP.—St. Paul's Church.

NEAREST Bridge, Lock, and Railway Station, Culham. Nearest Bridges, up, Abingdon 2 miles ; down, Clifton Hampden 3¼ miles. Locks, up, Abingdon 2½ miles ; down, Clifton 3 miles.

FARES to Paddington : 1st, 9/11, 17/6 ; 2nd, 7/5, 13/- ; 3rd, 4/8.

Cumnor, a very picturesque village in Berkshire, on the right bank, about a mile and a half from Bablock Hithe Ferry, and distant from Oxford 4 miles by road. Population, about 1,000. The walk from Bablock Hithe to' Cumnor is very pretty, though rather steep—the path past the cottage, immediately opposite the ferry, should be taken—but except from its association with Sir Walter Scott's noble romance of "Kenilworth,' the village itself has little to recommend it to the notice of passing travellers. Cumnor House or Place has now entirely disappeared, and except the tomb of Sir Anthony Forster (Scott's Tony "Fire-the-Faggot") in the church, nothing associated with the sad story of Amy Robsart now remains in Cumnor. The Church of St. Michael (the keys of which can be obtained at the post-office) is charmingly situated, and consists of nave, chancel, north aisle, and south transept, with a plain square tower. Inside it has some handsome pointed arches, and on the north wall of the chancel is the sculptured stone altar-tomb of Sir Anthony Forster, with brass of himself, his wife, and his three children. This monument has a long and florid Latin inscription, eulogising Sir Anthony and his lady in the highest terms, and especially attributing to the gentleman the possession of the highest Christian virtues in a very unusual degree. From this it would seem to follow that, unless the writer of the epitaph had even less regard for truth than such gentry are usually credited with, Sir Walter Scott's account of the facts connected with the death of Amy Robsart cannot be considered as in the least degree historically correct. The church also contains an old chained Bible, and on the south wall, on a brass, is the following curious

EPITAPH UPON YE DEATH OF IAMES WELSH.
The body of Iames Welsh lyeth bvryed here,
Who left this mortal life at fovrscore yeare ;
One thovsand and six hvndred twelve he dyed,
And for the poore did Christianly provide.
According to the talent God had lent,
Five povndes he gave of zeale and good intent ;
The frvite makes knowne the natvre of the tree,
Good life the Christian, even so was hee ;
Whose tyme well spent vnto his sovl did gaine
The heavenly rest where holy saynts remayne.
This memory a loving wife vnto her hvsband gave,
To show her hart remembers him, thovgh death inclose his grave.
The gyfte he gave vnto the poore she hath inlarged the same,
With five povndes added to his five, vnto her Christian fame ;
Hath placed them both to ye churchmen here, nowise to be delay'd,
Bvt that yearly to the poor of Cvmner be a mark of silver pay'd ;
Which is the fvll apoynted rent of the whole beqveathed some,
And so for ever shall remayne vntill the day of dome.

In Cvmner, for the poore's releife, Margery Welsh doth will,
The charge of this, when she is deade, may be performed still.

The lady certainly got a thorough good advertisement for the money.

POSTAL ARRANGEMENTS.—Post Office in the village. Nearest money order, telegraph office, &c., Oxford. Letters through Oxford.

NEAREST *Railway Station*, Oxford ; distant 4 miles (*which see*).

Cups, Cocktails, and Grogs,— Water-parties and picnics at Nuneham, or under the shade of Cliveden or Quarry Woods, require at all times a good and sufficient lunch to make the day go off in a satisfactory manner, and the presence of somebody who knows how to combine ice, sugar, lemon, and "drinks" artistically, is an additional advantage. A judicious mixer is not at all out of place on board a yacht on a hot day in the lower reaches of the river, and the services of such a benefactor to his species have even been appreciated by stern and energetic members of rowing clubs during compulsory pauses from the day's work within the cool walls of a lock. Not much is wanted in the way of paraphernalia. A very big jug or half-gallon mug, and a lump of ice, are, in fact, all the extras required. The sugar and lemon and the needful bottles take up very little room, and may even be classed as necessaries, and the skilful concocter will want but little space and time to produce any of the following "coolers," which have borne the test of time and experience with eminently satisfactory results. The basis of all wholesome cups is a brew of sugar and lemon-peel with a little water—hot if you are ashore and can get it conveniently, cold if you are in a boat and far from a fire and kettle. Only if the water be cold the lemon-peel must soak a little longer than if hot water be used. The quantity of sugar must vary, of course, in proportion to the amount of sweetness in the wine or cider to be used, and will also depend to some extent on the taste and fancy of the mixer. Four lumps of sugar to a bottle of fair average claret will be about the mark, and for a cup on this scale the following should be the mode of procedure. Take four good-sized lumps of sugar and the peel of half a lemon cut very thin. Put these into your jug or mug, and add sufficient water (hot for choice) to cover the sugar. Let the sugar melt—if hot water be used, cover the top of the jug while the stewing is going on—and then add a glass of sherry and half a glass of brandy. Put in as large a lump of ice as circumstances will admit of, and immediately add a bottle of claret and a bottle and a half or two bottles of soda-water. Then take out the lemon-peel, insert a handful of borage, a sprig of fresh mint, and a couple of thin slices of lemon, stir and drink. Some artists have a weakness for adding a piece of cucumber rind, and the suggestion is not without merit. Other mixers add liqueur, but, with a reservation in favour of orange brandy, this course is not to be recommended. Good orange brandy may be safely used instead of brandy pure and simple, but curaçoa, maraschino, and above all chartreuse, give a certain sickliness and flavour of subsequent headache to the cup in which they find a place. A bottle of lemonade and one of soda instead of the two bottles of soda, have been occasionally used with success, and, especially if the party consist largely of ladies, is a pleasant change; but the best variation in the original theme is to leave out the brandy, decrease the quantity of sugar, and add a bottle of champagne. There are very few better cups than this. Cider, champagne, or Moselle cups are made on exactly the same principles as the original claret cup, but the first will generally require more sugar, while for the others a couple of lumps will, as a rule, be enough. Almost any wine may be made into a cup, as any vegetable can be converted to the purposes of the salad bowl, if the two cardinal principles of always stirring your lemon-peel and sugar first, and of always pouring your wine, &c., on to the ice, and of not adding your ice after the cup is mixed, be carefully kept in view. Drinks poured on to ice will keep their freshness for a much longer time than those to which ice is merely added.

Cocktails are easy to concoct with the assistance of two metal cups with a bevelled edge, to enable them to fit closely together when required, and are, though simple in principle, a very agreeable form of refreshment at times. Put into one of your cups a piece of thin lemon-peel

about two or three inches long, a little powdered white sugar, a dash of bitters (Boker's is to be recommended in this connection), and half a glass of gin, whisky, or brandy, or a glass of sherry or claret. Fill up with small pieces or shavings of ice. Then fix on your other cup and shake the mixture vigorously. Remove the top cup, add a good squeeze of lemon-juice, and rub the edge of your cup with the same. If you prefer it you may turn the mixture into a wine-glass, but it is better served, as Mr. Bob Sawyer remarked, "in its native pewter." Champagne makes a capital cocktail, but will not stand the shaking up process, so it is better, in this case, to shake up the rest of the ingredients, and add the champagne last. Lemon, sugar, bitters, ice, as aforesaid, a glass of good sherry, a spoonful of brandy, and the yolk of an egg, all shaken well up together, make an excellent restorative after a hard day's work. The addition to the ordinary cocktail of a few sprigs of fresh mint, and the imbibition of the drink—which in this case may be advantageously made of rather more liberal proportions—through a straw, may not make a genuine American mint-julep, but the result is refreshing if not orthodox. Two or three strawberries or raspberries, a slice of orange, or, indeed, a dash of any fresh fruit, give additional charms to either cocktail or julep.

Grogs are simple matters, and require no advice until they reach the higher branches, and become punches, at which point the judicious mixer again comes into play, to be a welcome guest of the yachtsman in the chilly spring and summer weather often to be enjoyed off the marshes of Kent and Essex. The following will be found a very good punch for a cold night, and if taken in sufficient quantities, will excite no painful reminiscences in the morning. Assuming that the jug—it must be a jug, a bowl is an abomination—is to contain four good-sized tumblers, it will be well to proceed as follows. First ascertain that the jug is perfectly clean and dry : yacht stewards are not to be trusted in such matters any more than parlour maids. Have the kettle on the fire before you— never to take boiling water on trust should be the first maxim of the careful punch-maker. Into your jug put five lumps of sugar and the peel of a lemon cut thin. Add a little boiling water, and cover your jug with a plate. While the stewing is going on strain the juice of a lemon through a piece of muslin, and in five minutes add to the original foundation. Then add of wineglasses full of gin or whisky as many as you think discreet, and fill up with boiling water on the same principle. Take out the lemon-peel. Swaddle your jug up in a piece of thick flannel, carefully covering the top, and let it stand before the fire, or better still, in an oven if possible, for half an hour. It is a pleasant nightcap. Some people add liqueur even here, but that is a mistake to be carefully avoided. The best jug for this punch is one of the old-fashioned brown Uncle Toby sort. If the drink be wanted cold, add a lump of ice after the stewing, and proceed afterwards as before, but with iced water, and omitting the baking. This recipe is occasionally used for mixed punch, but for that there is a much better plan. Take a common earthenware painter's pipkin, glazed inside, of about one large tumbler capacity. Put in three lumps of sugar, about a third of the peel of a lemon, a glass of old rum, and a glass of brandy. Set fire to the mixture, and let it burn well for about two minutes, carefully stirring the while. Then add the juice of half a lemon, strained through muslin, blow out the fire, and fill up with boiling water. Pour into a tumbler and drink as soon as you can. You will find it hot and eminently comforting. Prevention is better than cure, and this is said to be a first-rate companion for a cautious man in an aguish country such as is to be found among the marshes about the Lower Hope. The mixture is also agreeable as a cold refresher, iced water being poured on the burnt mixture, and a lump of ice being put in the tumbler before the punch is poured in.

It is, of course, impossible to give anything like an exhaustive list of the numberless recipes which exist for cup and punch making. Many books exist which afford information of more or less value on the subject, and to them the curious must be referred. But for ordinary purposes the above hints may not be without use. As has already been said, they have successfully passed the ordeal of practical experience.

Dace (The), although commonly associated with the roach, varies much in its habits and choice of food. It is seldom found in still waters, and delights in clear, sharp, lively streams and gravelly shoals, in the runs between weeds, or on the shallows which terminate the deep pools of mill-tails, weirs, or sluice gates. They swim in schools, spawn in February and March, and are in season from July to February. They usually go up to the spawning grounds above Teddington Weir in what are called shifts, and begin about the middle of February. The balls of the ground-bait may be made of pollard, only thrown in much smaller than for roach. A little greaves chopped very fine will add to the attraction; but beware of over ground-baiting, or you may surfeit the fish to the loss of your sport. Your hook may be rather larger than that for roach, and tied on drawn gut. The best bait is a small red-worm, gentles, caddis, paste, &c. Fly-fishing for dace is excellent practice. If the angler can take two out of three rises he must be an adept, as the fish come at the fly in a very mincing and touch-and-go manner. The natural house-fly is an attractive bait, but it requires care in throwing the line to prevent it being whipped off the hook. The small black palmer, the soldier, the black gnat, and indeed almost any fly of delicate make will be taken by the dace in summer.

Datchet, Buckinghamshire, on the left bank, from London $41\frac{1}{4}$ miles, from Oxford $70\frac{1}{4}$ miles; a station on the Windsor branch of the South Western Railway, 24 miles from Waterloo; trains take about an hour. Population, 1,100. Soil, chiefly gravel. A pleasantly and prettily situated village, with good houses, and agreeable neighbourhood, though sometimes uncomfortably liable to floods. It is sometimes called Datchet St. Helen's, from the fact of there having been here at one time a branch establishment of the nunnery of St. Helen's, Bishopsgate. The buildings themselves have entirely disappeared, but the garden walls are still standing.

Datchet Mead is a well-known place for anglers, and is known to all the world in connexion with certain disagreeable experiences of the immortal Sir John Falstaff.

The parish church is dedicated to

St. Mary the Virgin. It was originally built about 1350, but nothing of the old structure remains except the east wall window of the chancel. The present fine building consists of nave, aisles, transept, chancel, and organ chamber, and was erected in 1860. Nearly all the windows are filled with stained glass. Among the charities of the village is Barker's Bridge House Trust, which, under a scheme sanctioned by the Charity Commissioners, provides for the lighting of the village, the maintenance of the foot-paths, landing-places, and similar works. Ditton Park, the seat of the Duke of Buccleuch, is about half a mile from the church.

This is perhaps as good a reach as any on the river for roach-fishing. Anglers are not permitted on the tow-path of the Home Park. Off the " Bells of Ouseley" is a fine shallow for the fly, and is upon a warm day literally alive with handsome chub and dace. Trolling and spinning may be practised with success for jack and perch right away down to Bell Weir Lock, in the weir of which very handsome trout are taken every season.

INNS.—"Manor House" and " Royal Stag."

PLACES OF WORSHIP.—St. Mary the Virgin, and Baptist Chapel.

POSTAL ARRANGEMENTS.—Post Office (money order, savings bank, and telegraph). Mails from London, 7.20 a.m., 12.15 p.m. Mails for London, 10 a.m., 3.50 and 7.5 p.m. Sunday, 10 a.m.

Nearest *Bridges*, up, Victoria ¼ mile ; down, Albert ½ mile. *Locks*, up, Romney 1¼ mile ; down, Old Windsor 1¾ mile.

FARES to Waterloo, 1st, 3/9, 5/6 ; 2nd, 2/9, 4/-; 3rd, 1/11.

Deptford Reach, about a mile long, from the end of Limehouse Reach to Greenwich Ferry. Bearings S.S.E. and E.N.E.

Destitute Sailors' Asylum, 10, Well-street, E., known to mercantile Jack as "The Straw House," was originally established in the year 1827, since which period it has been the means of dispensing shelter, food, and partial clothing, together with medical advice when necessary, as also spiritual counsel to destitute sailors of all creeds and tongues. The public cannot do better than refer

any destitute sailor who may apply to them for relief—or any tramp or mendicant professing to be a destitute sailor —to the Destitute Sailors' Asylum, where, if he be really a sailor, and really destitute, he will be sure of receiving a fortnight's maintenance, with the gift of certain articles of clothing ; while every exertion will be made to get him a ship. The directors very justly point out that by communicating this fact to seamen in real want, a much greater boon will be conferred upon them than by pecuniary relief, while the great evil of money-giving to mere impostors will be avoided.

Distances (Index Table of).—(*See next page.*)

Doggett's Coat and Badge.—This wager for young watermen out of their time was instituted by Thomas Doggett, the well-known actor at Drury-lane Theatre, at the first anniversary of the accession to the throne of George I., August 1, 1715. Doggett's prize was an orange-coloured coat and silver badge, on which were emblazoned the horse of Hanover, and at his death he bequeathed a sum of money to be devoted to further prizes. At present the Fishmongers' Company, who administer Doggett's trust, give £6 6s. to the winner in addition to the coat and badge, the prizes for the fourth, fifth, and sixth men respectively, £2 2s., £1 11s. 6d., and £1 6s. The second man receives £5 5s., and the third £3 3s., derived from various sources. The original conditions of the wager were that the six competitors to whom it was limited should be chosen by lot from the whole body of men who should put down their names as desirous of rowing. This arrangement was, although not until the lapse of a very great number of years, deemed to be unfair, and would-be competitors now row three trial heats from Putney to Hammersmith, the first and second in each heat being entitled to row in the final, which takes place on August 1st when not on a Sunday.

The course is against tide, from the "Swan " at London Bridge, to the "Swan " at Chelsea, when the current is strongest, according to the original conditions, and when the race is really rowed under these circumstances it is a "stiffish pull "

INDEX TABLE OF DISTANCES between the principal places of interest on the Thames between Oxford and London Bridge.

Explanation.—The table to be read with the names on the top from the left as far as the blank, and from the right towards the left as far as the blank. The square in line with the upper and side names showing the distance *by river* between those two places.

	London Bdg	Richmond	Twickenham	Teddington	Kingston	Henley	Wargrave	Shiplake	Sonning	Caversham	Mapledurhm	Pangbourne Whitchurch	Streatley Goring	Moulsford	Wallingford	Benson	Clifton	Culham	Abingdon	Sandford	Oxford	
Oxford ..	111½	96	94	93	91	47	43¼	42¾	40¾	37	33	30¾	26¾	24¼	21	19½	13	9¾	7¼	2¾		
Sandford ..	108¾	93¼	91¼	90¼	88¼	44¼	40¼	40	37½	34¼	30½	28	24	21¾	18¼	16¾	10¼	7	5		48¾	Hambledon
Abingdon ..	103¾	88¼	86¼	85¼	83¼	39¼	35½	35	32½	29¼	25¼	23	19	16¾	13¼	11¾	5¼	2		49¾	52¾	Hurley
Culham ..	101¾	86¼	84¼	83¼	81¼	37½	33½	33	30½	27¼	23¼	21	17	14¾	11¼	9¾	3¼		46¾	51¾	54¼	Marlow
Clifton ..	98½	83	81	80	78	34	30¼	29¾	27¼	24	20	17¾	13¾	11½	8	6½		48¾	50¼	55¾	58½	Cookham
Benson ..	92	76½	74½	73½	71½	27½	23¾	23¼	20¾	17½	13½	11¼	7¼	5	1½		48½	51¾	53¾	58¾	61½	Maidenhead
Wallingford	90½	75	73	72	70	26	22¼	21¾	19¼	16	12	9¾	5¾	3½		43¼	49¾	53	55	60	62¾	Bray
Moulsford ..	87	71½	69½	68½	66½	22½	18¾	18¼	15¾	12½	8½	6¼	2¼		47½	49	55½	58¾	60¾	65¾	68½	Windsor
Streatley Goring	84¾	69¼	67¼	66¼	64¼	20¼	15½	16	13½	10¼	6¼	4		45¾	50¼	50¾	57¼	60½	62½	67½	70¼	Datchet
Pangbrne Whitchrch	80¾	65¼	63¼	62¼	60¼	16¼	12½	12	9½	6½	2¼		46	48¼	51¾	53¼	59¾	63	65	70	72¾	Old Windsor
Mapledurhm	78½	63	61	60	58	14	10¼	9¾	7¼	4		45¼	49¼	51½	55	56½	63	66½	68¼	73¼	76	Staines
Caversham	74½	59	57	56	54	10	6¼	5¾	3¼		45½	47¾	51¾	54	57½	59	65½	68¾	70¾	75¾	78½	Laleham
Sonning ..	71¼	55¾	53¾	52¾	50¾	6¾	3	2½		42¾	46¾	49	53	55¼	58¾	60¼	66¾	70	72	77	79¾	Chertsey
Shiplake ..	68¾	53¼	51¼	50¼	48½	4¼	½		41¼	44½	48½	50¾	54¾	57	60½	62	68½	71¾	73¾	78¾	81½	Shepperton
Wargrave ..	68¼	52¾	50¾	49¾	47¾	3¾		40½	43¼	46½	50½	52¾	56¾	59	62½	64	70½	73¾	75¾	80¾	83½	Walton
Henley ..	64½	49	47	46	44		41¾	42¼	44¾	48	52	54¼	58¼	60½	64	65½	72	75¼	77¼	82¼	85	Sunbury
Maidenhead	50	34½	32½	31½		40½	44	44½	47	50¼	54¼	56½	60½	62¾	66½	67¾	74¼	77½	79½	84½	87¼	Hampton

The race in 1884 resulted as follows :

Final Heat, August 1.

Charles Phelps, Putney 1
Alfred Thos. Redknap, Richmond 2
Charles Bowle, Richmond ... 3
Charles Bradshaw, Deptford ... 4
James Crick, Horsleydown ... 5
George Daniel Evans, Deptford ... 6

The following is a list of winners since the introduction of trial heats :

1870 R. Harding, Blackwall.
1871 T. J. Mackinney, Richmond.
1872 T. G. Green, Hammersmith.
1873 H. Messum, Richmond.
1874 R. W. Burwood, Wapping.
1875 W. Phelps, Putney.
1876 C. T. Bulman, Shadwell.
1877 J. Tarryer, Rotherhithe.
1878 T. E. Taylor, Hermitage Stairs.
1879 H Cordery, Putney.
1880 W. J. Cobb, Putney.
1881 G. Claridge, Richmond.
1882 H. A. Audsley, Waterloo.
1883 James Lloyd, Wandsworth.
1884 Charles Phelps, Putney.

Dorchester, Oxfordshire, on the Thame, about a mile from its junction with the Thames, which some people delight to call, up to this point, the Isis, fondly imagining that the name Tamesis is a compound of Thame and Isis. The quaint conceit of Warton that

Beauteous Isis and her husband Thame,
With mingled waves for ever flow the same,

is probably to some extent responsible for this delusion, a hallucination further encouraged by Drayton, who expresses the same idea in somewhat more high-flown language. The Thame is not a comfortable river for boats, and visitors to Dorchester from the river would do well to leave their boats in charge of the keeper of Day's Lock and to take the footpath across the fields, some twenty minutes' walk. The path passes by some interesting Roman remains called the Dyke Hills, evidently portions of an extensive fortified camp which rested upon the Thame at one extremity and the Thames at the other, and being protected by the rivers, then probably running through much marsh land, must have been of great natural as well as artificial strength.

Dorchester, an unimportant village on the Oxford coach road, is distant from

Oxford about eight miles, from London fifty. Population, 1,050. Soil, alluvial. It is somewhat surprising to find in so small a village so fine a church as that of St. Peter and St. Paul, Dorchester, but in truth the village has a very ancient ecclesiastical history. So far back as 630 it is recorded that Birinus here baptized Cynegils, the king of Wessex, of which Dorchester was once the capital, and the authority of the venerable Bede is adduced to prove that the city called Dorcinca was the seat of many fine churches. These are also mentioned by William of Malmesbury, but it would seem that shortly after his time the line of bishops of Dorchester came to an end, and that its ecclesiastical brilliance rapidly waned. In 1554 the abbey church was bought by Richard Bewforest for £140, and by him bequeathed to the parish. The present church is the building in question, and represents the work of many architects. The north wall of the nave and two arches in the interior are probably part of the old Saxon cathedral. The rest of the fabric has been built at subsequent periods, as may easily be seen from the different styles of architecture peculiar to the successive periods down to the late Tudor porch. It was last restored, although not completed, by Sir Gilbert Scott, and is a most remarkable building. Restoration is still in progress. A number of carved fragments of stone have been collected from a house under repair in the village, and are now in the church awaiting the time when they can be again incorporated in the fabric. A fine window in the west front, now bricked in, might advantageously be opened, but the fact of the nave being closed by the tower will always necessarily give a somewhat sombre, not to say grim, appearance to this part of the church. The church is entered on the south side from the handsome churchyard by a fine stone porch with timbered roof, outside which, on the left, is a mutilated cross, the head of which has been restored. The curious in such matters may compare this cross with that standing by the great yew in the churchyard at Iffley. At the south-west angle of the church opposite the cross is a buttress with two canopied niches for statues. On the right of the entrance from the porch is the font, a Norman work of lead, exhibiting the figures of the Apostles minus

Judas, in excellent preservation. On the south side is a chapel, or ante-church, in which some singular carvings round one of the pillars should be noticed, and which is now used for the Sunday morning celebration and occasionally for other services. From here a pointed arch leads into the south aisle, which contains at the east end a lady-chapel, the altar in which is a memorial to the late Bishop of Winchester. Here is a remarkably fine groined roof, lofty and of the most graceful proportions. The roof of the nave, which is also of magnificent proportions, is supported by beautiful clustered columns. In the lady-chapel will be found four recumbent life-size monumental figures, one of which represents a most truculent Crusader, lying in a singular attitude, with legs crossed and apparently in the act of drawing his sword. If this figure be a portrait it is certain that the sculptor did not flatter his model. The other three monuments are of great antiquity, and one, that of a knight in armour, said to be of the Segrave family, is especially worthy of careful inspection. A tablet on the floor of the lady-chapel in memory of Thomas Day, who died in 1693, has this curious epitaph :

> Sweet Death he Came in Hast
> & said his glass is run,
> Thou art ye. man i say
> See what thy God has done.

To the amateur of brasses it must be a source of lasting regret that so few remain of what must at one time have been among the most magnificent specimens in the country. The church may be said to be carpeted with their remains. In the lady-chapel is a small brass in fair preservation of Richard Bewforest and his wife, and in the chancel is one of a bishop in cope and with crozier with the inscription: " Here lyeth Sir Richard Bewfforeste. I pray thee give his sowl good rest." On the south side of the chancel is a stone which bears witness to the existence at one time of a very important brass of a full-length figure under a canopy with much elaborate ornamentation, which must have been fine indeed. One of the curious devices in this is reproduced on the end of a carved oak seat in front of the organ, also commemorating Sir Richard Bewforest. The sedilia and piscina in the chancel are elaborate in design, and opposite to them on the north side is the renowned Jesse window, which is surely unique of its kind. It is in the form of a genealogical tree springing from the body of Jesse himself, and bearing stone effigies of the line of David ; the crowning figure of our Lord has unfortunately been destroyed. The stained glass of the window itself works with the design. The window dates from the 14th century. Leaving the church by the west door the path to the village passes under a lych-gate, overshadowed by a glorious chestnut. Dorchester Church lies a little out of the way of any but enthusiastic sightseers, but should certainly be visited if for the Jesse window alone.

The old Grammar School, endowed by the Fettiplace family, no longer exists as such, but has been converted, with the approval of the Education Commissioners, into a National School for boys. The building is supposed to have been a part of the old monastery (probably the refectory), established by Alexander, Bishop of Lincoln, in 1140. The massive wall of the south side of the building, the rude but substantial beams and quaint, closed-up fire-places, bespeak its antiquity. There is a Cottagers' Horticultural Society in Dorchester, instituted in 1869, which offers many prizes for competition at its annual shows.

Day's Lock and Weir, as well as right away down past the entrance to the Thames, has in recent years risen in estimation for the yield of fish. Barbel, jack, and perch are plentiful. It is one of the few places on the Thames in which the angler is almost certain to get from one to half-a-dozen fine tench in a day's general fishing : this applies almost as low as Shillingford.

FAIR.—Easter Tuesday.

INNS.—" Fleur de Lis," opposite the church, and " White Hart," up the village.

PLACES OF WORSHIP.—St. Peter and St. Paul (Abbey Church), and Roman Catholic Church.

POST OFFICE ARRANGEMENTS.—Post Office (money order, savings bank, and telegraph), near the church. Mails from London, 7.30 a.m., 2.45 p.m. (to callers) ; Sundays, 7.30 a.m. Mails to London, 10.45 a.m., 6.35 p.m. ; Sunday, 11.35 a.m.

NEAREST *Bridges*, up, Clifton Hampden 2½ miles ; down, Shillingford 2¾ miles, *Locks*, Day's ; up, Clifton 2¾ miles ; down, Bensington 4 miles. *Ferries*, Shillingford and Day's Lock. *Railway Station*, Cullham (which see for fares).

"Dreadnought." — (*See* SEAMEN'S HOSPITAL SOCIETY.)

Drowning.—Methods of treatment recommended by the Royal Humane Society. Directions for restoring the apparently dead.

I. IF FROM DROWNING OR OTHER SUFFOCATION OR NARCOTIC POISONING. —Send immediately for medical assistance, blankets, and dry clothing, but proceed to treat the patient instantly, securing as much fresh air as possible. The points to be aimed at are : first, and immediately, the restoration of breathing ; and secondly, after breathing is restored, the promotion of warmth and circulation. The efforts to restore life must be persevered in until the arrival of medical assistance, or until the pulse and breathing have ceased for at least an hour.

Treatment to Restore Natural Breathing.

RULE 1.—*To maintain a Free Entrance of Air into the Windpipe.*—Cleanse the mouth and nostrils ; open the mouth ; draw forward the patient's tongue, and keep it forward ; an elastic band over the tongue and under the chin will answer this purpose. Remove all tight clothing from about the neck and chest.

RULE 2.—*To adjust the Patient's Position.*—Place the patient on his back on a flat surface, inclined a little from the feet upwards ; raise and support the head and shoulders on a small firm cushion or folded article of dress placed under the shoulder-blades.

RULE 3.—*To imitate the Movements of Breathing.*—Grasp the patient's arms just above the elbows, and draw the arms gently and steadily upwards, until they meet above the head (this is for the purpose of drawing air into the lungs), and keep the arms in that position for two seconds. Then turn down the patient's arms, and press them gently and firmly for two seconds against the sides of the chest (this is with the object of pressing air out of the lungs. Pressure on the breast-bone will aid this). Repeat these measures alternately, deliberately, perseveringly, fifteen times in a minute, until a spontaneous effort to respire is perceived, immediately upon which cease to imitate the movements of breathing, and proceed to induce circulation and warmth (*as below*). Should a warm bath be procurable, the body may be placed in it up to the neck, continuing to imitate the movements of breathing. Raise the body in twenty seconds in a sitting position, and dash cold water against the chest and face, and pass ammonia under the nose. The patient should not be kept in the warm bath longer than five or six minutes. But it is preferable that artificial respiration and friction of the limbs and body with dry flannel or cloths should be first had recourse to, and that the warm bath should not be employed till there is proof of respiration having been restored.

RULE 4.—*To excite Inspiration.*—During the employment of the above method excite the nostrils with smelling-salts, or tickle the throat with a feather. Rub the chest and face briskly, and dash cold and hot water alternately on them.

Treatment after Natural Breathing has been restored.

RULE 5.—*To induce Circulation and Warmth.*—Wrap the patient in dry blankets and commence rubbing the limbs upwards, firmly and energetically. The friction must be continued under the blankets or over the dry clothing. Promote the warmth of the body by the application of hot flannels, bottles or bladders of hot water, heated bricks, &c., to the pit of the stomach, the armpits, between the thighs, and to the soles of the feet. On the restoration of life, when the power of swallowing has returned, a teaspoonful of warm water, small quantities of wine, warm brandy and water, or coffee, should be given. The patient should be kept in bed, and a disposition to sleep encouraged. During reaction large mustard plasters to the chest and below the shoulders will greatly relieve the distressed breathing.

II. IF FROM INTENSE COLD.—Rub the body with snow, ice, or cold water. Restore warmth by slow degrees. In these accidents it is highly dangerous to apply heat too early.

III. IF FROM INTOXICATION. — Lay the individual on his side on a bed with his head raised. The patient should be induced to vomit. Stimulants should be avoided.

IV. IF FROM APOPLEXY OR FROM SUNSTROKE.—Cold should be applied to the head, which should be kept well raised. Tight clothing should be removed from the neck and chest. Stimulants should be avoided.

Appearances which generally indicate Death.—There is no breathing or heart's action ; the eyelids are generally half-closed ; the pupils dilated ; the jaws clenched ; the fingers semi-contracted ; the tongue appearing between the teeth, and the mouth and nostrils are covered with a frothy mucus. Colour and pallor of surface increases.

General Observations.—On the restoration of life, a teaspoonful of warm water should be given ; and then, if the power of swallowing be returned, small quantities of warm wine or weak brandy and water, warm ; the patient should be kept in bed, and a disposition to sleep encouraged, except in cases of apoplexy, intoxication, and coup-de-soleil. Great care is requisite to maintain the restored vital actions, and at the same time to prevent undue excitement. The treatment recommended by the society is to be persevered in for three or four hours. It is an erroneous opinion that persons are irrecoverable because life does not soon make its appearance, as cases have come under the notice of the society of a successful result even after five hours' perseverance ; and it is absurd to suppose that a body must not be meddled with or removed without permission of a coroner.

East and West India Docks are situated at Blackwall between the West India Dock and Blackwall stations of the London and Blackwall Railway. The former of these stations is the best for persons having business at the general, police, customs, wharfingers, or other offices, or on board of vessels lying in the greater part of the West India Import Dock, the West India Export Dock, or the South-West India Dock. For those at the eastern extremity of these docks,

the Millwall Junction station will be found nearer, as also for the North London Railway Companies' Docks, the Blackwall Basin, and the new dock in course of formation by the Midland Railway Company, but not forming part of the East and West India Dock Company's system, and the extreme western extremity of the East India Import Dock. For the South-West India Docks and Basin, passengers should change at Millwall Junction ; and, proceeding by tram-car, alight at South Dock station. For the East India Export Dock, the greater part of the East India Import Dock, and the East India Dock Basin, the best station is that of Blackwall.

East Blyth Buoy.—A 16-foot conical buoy, made of iron, and painted with black and white stripes. It is situated in Sea Reach, nearly opposite the Chapman Light, on the edge of the Blyth Sand, and marks a depth of water, at low water spring tide, of 21 feet. It is moored with 18 fathoms of chain.

East Molesey, in Surrey, on the right bank opposite Hampton Court, the Hampton Court railway-station being in the parish. The distance from London is 23¼ miles, from Oxford 88¼ miles. Population, 2,500. Soil, light and gravelly. The village of Molesey is practically part of Hampton Court, with which it is connected by an iron bridge, and is chiefly interesting to excursionists from the point of view of refreshments. Here the Mole empties itself into the Thames, and hard by to the north-west is Molesey Hurst, where Hampton Races take place. The old church of St. Mary, which was a curious specimen of an old riverside church, was partly destroyed by fire in 1863 ; the present church, consisting of chancel, nave, and north aisle, was built in 1865. A good brass in memory of Anthonie Standen, cupbearer to Lord Darnley, father of James I., has been preserved. Near the church is an old inn, "The Bell," which is said to have been in the "good old times" much patronised by highwaymen.

HOTELS.—"Castle" and "Prince of Wales."

PLACES OF WORSHIP.—St. Mary's, and Wesleyan Chapel.

POSTAL ARRANGEMENTS.—Post Office (money order, savings bank, and tele-

graph). Mails from London, 6.45 and
9.50 a.m., 2.30 and 8 p.m. Sunday, 6.45
a.m. Mails for London, 8.40 and 11.50
a.m., 3.25 and 8 p.m. Sunday, 10 a.m.
NEAREST.—(*See* HAMPTON COURT).
FARES.—(*See* HAMPTON COURT).

Eel-Pie Island.—An Island of seven
acres off Twickenham, once in high repute
with picnic parties, but now rather out of
vogue. The island is close to the Orleans
Club, and a fine view of Richmond Hill
is to be obtained from it. Opposite,
almost entirely concealed by trees, is
Ham House, the seat of the Earls of
Dysart. The river about here is inconveniently shallow at low tide, notwithstanding the persistent efforts of the
Conservators to maintain a channel by
dredging. NEAREST *Post* and *Telegraph
Offices* and *Railway Station*, Twickenham
(*which see*).

Eels have greatly fallen off in individual
size and collective numbers of late years
in the Thames, which is attributed to
the obstacles opposed to their carrying
out their natural habit of making for
the estuary to spawn, to gain which
they have to encounter the metropolitan sewage, concentrated by the
junction of the Crossness and Barking outfalls. There is little doubt but
that here they are poisoned in the bad
water, in company with other migratory
fish that seek the ocean, and add to the
polluted character of the stream. Formerly, when no such impediment re-
tarded their course, they performed their
functions, and their young made their
way up the river in myriads, to populate
every ditch and tributary of the river
proper, and were seen in a black line on
either side of the river, the procession
reaching for miles. Their appearance
was termed "eel-fair," and the inhabitants on the banks used to resort with
sieves and pails to bail them out without
interruption, and make a species of cake
of them by compression. It is a moot
question whether the parent eels ever
returned to their old quarters. Naturalists
aver that at the season of migration they
are endowed with a thicker skin than
common, probably to fit them for the
dangers they may have to encounter.
Dr. Günther and other celebrated ichthy-
ologists have long since determined the
eel to be oviparous—the apparent young

found occasionally in them having proved
to be parasitical worms. Thus the eel
fishery of the Thames has greatly fallen
off, and those that are now caught in
small quantities by "weels," and wicker
baskets termed "pots," are either much
smaller in size or the grig species—a
much less worthy description of the
genus. Lampreys and lamperns from
the same cause have almost entirely disappeared, and the same observation
applies to the smelt, which formerly came
up in vast shoals to spawn off Chiswick
and Strand-on-the-Green, driving by their
ravenous nature and their mouths full of
formidable teeth all other fish off the
grounds selected by them. Special leave
to net smelts was formerly granted by the
Conservancy, as it required nets of a
smaller mesh, but this concession is rarely
sought for now by the fishermen, on
account of the almost entire absence of
these fish. The supply of eels to the
metropolis and the hotels along the
Thames is mostly from Holland. The
Dutch "busses"—very picturesque vessels
from Holland—may be seen any day off
Billingsgate at anchor, waiting with their
wells of eels upon the requirements of
the market. The vitality of the eel is
proverbial, and the difficulty of depriving
it of life great ; but if the eel be struck
upon the tail, in which is concealed a
lymphatic gland or "second heart," he
dies immediately.

Egham, Surrey.—Though not actually
on the bank, the parish of Egham im-
pinges on the Thames, and is connected
with Middlesex by Staines Bridge ; but
from the river the nearest approach is
from Bell Weir Lock, which is distant
from the post-office and church about
10 minutes' walk across the fields, the
pathway leaving the towing-path a few
yards below the "Anglers' Rest Hotel."
From the post-office to the railway-station
is about seven minutes' walk. Flys meet
the trains. It is a station on the South
Western Railway, 21 miles from Waterloo.
The average time of the railway journey
is about an hour. Egham is a small
town in a pretty country, with many
large houses and parks surrounding it,
but offers in itself little special attraction.
It consists of a long street containing a
few decent shops. North of the town is
Runnymede, and a race-meeting is held
on it annually ; the course being an oval

flat, not quite two miles, with a straight mile. Egham Races have considerably declined in interest and popularity of late years.

At the back of the town is Cooper's Hill, so well known in connection with Sir John Denham's poem, which has been, perhaps, as frequently quoted as any copy of verses in the language, and has obtained a certain popularity far beyond its deserts. It would seem that Somerville was poking his fun when he described Denham as "a tuneful bard," and his song as being "sublimely sweet." Pope goes even farther, and speaking of Cooper's Hill, which, by-the-bye with rather a stretch of poetic license, he calls a mountain, says :

Here his first lays majestic Denham sung.

Whatever the merits of Sir John Denham's poem may be, however, there can be no doubt of the beauty of the view from Cooper's Hill, and the ascent of Pope's "mountain" may be recommended to all visitors to Egham. At the present time Cooper's Hill has become known as the seat of the Royal Indian Engineering College (*see* COOPER'S HILL). Among the numerous pleasant excursions in the neighbourhood is that to Virginia Water, which is in this parish.

The church is a very plain brick building, with a rather mean little belfry, and within is also very plain, with a small chancel, nave, with pews and galleries. Over the altar is a painting respecting Elijah raising the widow's son, a good work of R. Westall, R.A. On the right of the altar is a marble mural monument in memory of G. Gostling, who died 1820, by Flaxman, R.A. In this a classically draped mourning female figure leans against the pedestal, surmounted by an urn, and bearing a medallion bust of the deceased. On the other side of the chancel this is balanced by a corresponding monument to Lydia Gostling, with the difference that the female figure is represented with an anchor presumably intended for that of Hope. Above the monument to G. Gostling is a tablet, with three figures in alto relievo, to other members of the Gostling family, from the chisel of E. H. Baily, R.A. High on the east wall, under the south gallery, is a brass with four kneeling figures, and the inscription : "Anthonye Bond, gent.,

once cittezen and writer of the Court Letter of London, 1576 :

Christ is to me as lyef on earthe and death to me is gayne
Because I wish through him alone saluacione to obtayne
So bryttle is the state of man so soone yt dothe decaye
So all the glory of this world must pas and vade away.

Close by is a tablet to the memory of the Rev. T. Beighton, 45 years vicar of Egham, who died 1771, with an epitaph signed D. Garrick :

Near half an age, with every good man's praise,
Among his flock the shepherd pass'd his days ;
The friend, the comfort, of the sick and poor,
Want never knock'd unheeded at his door.
Oft when his duty call'd, disease and pain
Strove to confine him, but they strove in vain :
All mourn his death, his virtues long they try'd,
They knew not how they lov'd him till he dy'd ;
Peculiar blessings did his life attend,
He had no foe, and Camden was his friend.

The great little David's "Camden was his friend" has a considerable family resemblance to the oft-quoted epitaph which records how the deceased "was first cousin to Lady O'Looney and of such is the kingdom of Heaven." Dr. Johnson pronounced this to be the best epitaph in the English language, but then even Dr. Johnson was not always right. On the east wall, under the north gallery, is a curious painted marble bust of Thomas Foster, a justice of the Common Bench in the times of James I. and Charles I. and II., afterwards of the Queen's Bench. The learned judge wears a red tippet and a chain, and on his flowing locks is a flat cap, presumably the black cap. He died in 1663, aged 74. Hard by is a tablet to Richard Kellefet, 1595, "a most faithfvll servant to hir majestie, chief groome in hir removing Garderobe of beddes and yeoman also of her standing Garderobe of Richmount." On the wall of the stairs to the north gallery is a very good and interesting monument to the two wives of Sir John Denham, father of the poet : Cicile (formerly wife of Richard Kellefet), and Ellenor, who died in childbed of a daughter who was buried with her. The monument is of stone and marble, with two three-quarter length female figures in the centre. One of these, Cicile, no doubt, still wears widow's mourning ;

while Lady Ellenor, who was married to Sir John Denham when he was Chief Justice in Ireland, is represented with a child in her arms. Below is an odd little painted figure of a boy, possibly intended for the poet himself. In the churchyard is an elevated granite grave, where a Mrs. Pocock lies above ground, it is said to ensure to her survivors some property which was to be held by them ''so long as she should be above ground.'' On the left of the road to Stroude is a stone marking the old Roman road.

Strode's Charity, Egham, is an institution consisting of almshouses and school, founded by Henry Strode, Esq., in the year 1747, and liberally endowed by him with landed property, of which he made the Coopers' Company of London trustees. The institution includes almshouses, school, chapel, master's house, with spacious lawn and gardens, and, opening to the High-street, is one of the principal ornaments of the thriving town of Egham. The benefits of Strode's Charity are confined to the parish.

BANK.—Ashby & Co.

DISPENSARY.—High-street.

FAIR.—May 29.

HOSPITAL.—Cottage Hospital, Egham-hill (eight beds).

INNS.—"Angler's Rest," Bell Weir Lock; "Catherine Wheel," High-street.

PLACES OF WORSHIP.—St. John the Baptist and St. Jude's Chapel of Ease; and Congregational & Wesleyan Chapels.

POLICE.—Station, Egham-hill.

POSTAL ARRANGEMENTS.—Post Office (money order, savings bank, telegraph, and insurance), High-street, opposite church. Mails from London, 7 and 10.5 a.m. and 4.55 p.m.; Sunday, 7 a.m. Mails for London, 8.40 and 11 a.m., 3.10 and 7.15 p.m.; Sunday, 7.15 p.m.

NEAREST *Bridges* (from Bell Weir Lock), up, Albert 3½ miles; down, Staines about 1 mile. *Locks*, up, Old Windsor 3 miles: down, Penton Hook 2¾ miles. *Railway Station*, Egham.

FARES to Waterloo: 1st, 3/8, 5/6; 2nd, 2/6, 4/-; 3rd, 1/9, 3/3.

Embankments.—(*See* ALBERT EMBANKMENT, CHELSEA, *and* VICTORIA EMBANKMENT).

Erith, Kent, on the right bank. From London 16½ miles.—A station on the North Kent line 15½ miles from Charing Cross; trains take about an hour. The straight road from the station to the river is about 300 yards, and the pier is distant ten minutes' walk. A fly meets the trains. Population, 8,289. The soil is principally gravel and chalk. Erith is not a particularly interesting village, lying in the bight between Erith Reach and Erith Rands. It faces the flat marshes of Essex, but the country behind it is pretty and well wooded, affording many pretty walks in a pleasant part of Kent. There are few good houses in the old part of the village, but a good deal of building, principally of villas, has of late years been going on above the station, and this is the most desirable part of Erith for residential purposes. There is a small pier which is occasionally used by the steamboats, and an attempt at an esplanade and garden was at one time made, by private enterprise, along the river bank to the eastward, but it cannot be said that the effort was crowned with success. The principal importance of Erith, from the river point of view, is that it is a popular Thames yachting station, the headquarters of the Erith and Corinthian Yacht Clubs, and a favourite point for starting sailing matches.

There is a public hall in Pier-road, capable of seating over 600 persons, which can be hired for balls, concerts, dramatic and other entertainments, public meetings, &c.; terms for hire may be obtained of the secretary. The Avenue Hall is in connection with the Congregational Church, and is used for classes, lectures, &c., having sitting room for about 200 persons. There is also a Masonic Hall (in the Pier-road), seating 250, which is fully licensed for music, dancing, &c. The "Cornwallis" Lodge of Masons meets here.

The parish church (St. John the Baptist) is noteworthy for its ancient tower, now elaborately shored up, and for some interesting monuments and brasses. The most important of the former is the monument of Chantrey to Lord Eardley and the altar-tomb of the Countess of Shrewsbury (1568). The brasses of John Aylmer and his wife (1435), of John Mylner and "Margaret and Benet his wyves" (1511), and, earliest of all, that to the memory of Roger Sencler (1425), will interest the antiquary. The old steps to the rood-screen are curious. In the Norman chancel of this church took place the meeting between the Barons and the Commissioners of King John after the grant of Magna Charta.

BANK.—London and County.

FIRE.—The engine-house is in the Avenue-road, not far from the pier.

HOSPITAL.—Cottage Hospital, Crayford-road. 8 beds. With this is connected the Provident Dispensary, with 1,500 members.

HOTEL.—" Prince of Wales," Avenue-road.

PLACES OF WORSHIP.—St. John the Baptist, and Christ Church ; the Roman Catholic Church of St. Fidelis, and Congregational, Baptist, Primitive Methodist, and Wesleyan Chapels.

POLICE-STATION.—Bexley-road, near railway-station.

POSTAL ARRANGEMENTS.—Post Office (money order, savings bank, telegraph, insurance), High-street. Mails from London at 8 and 11.30 a.m., 3.30 and 7 p.m., and (Saturdays) 9.30 p.m. None on Sunday. Mails for London at 8.40 and 11.20 a.m., 4.55, 8.55, and 10.50 p.m. Sunday, 10.20 p.m.

FARES to London (Charing-cross): 1st, 2/6, 3/9 ; 2nd, 1/10, 2/9 ; 3rd, 1/3, 2/3.

Erith Rands, a mile and a half in length from Erith to Crayfordness at the top of Long Reach. There is a ferry from Erith to Cold Harbour Point opposite. The Rand Hill Shoal is in the middle of the reach. Bearings, E.S.E. and W.N.W.

Erith Reach runs for a mile and a half from Halfway Reach to Erith. Bearings, N.N.E. and S.S.W.

Erith Yacht Club, Headquarters, Club House, Yacht *Gypsy,* Erith.—The object of this club is the encouragement of amateur yacht sailing. It is managed by commodore, vice-commodore, rear-commodore, treasurer, secretary, and a committee of thirteen, all of whom are elected in February. Election is invested in the committee. Annual subscription, £1 1s.; entrance, £1 1s. Yachts of 10 tons entered for club races must have the Yacht Racing Association certificate of measurement. Yachts under 10 tons are measured according to the R.T.Y.C. rule. Burgee red, with red Maltese cross on white shield.

Eton, Bucks, on the left bank, from Oxford 68½ miles, from London 43 miles.

Population, 3,500. But for its connection with the greatest public school in England, Eton is a place of but little importance. In 1800, Mark Antony Porney bequeathed funds for the education of 45 boys and 45 girls. Porney's Institution is now combined with the National School for the children of the parish of Eton and Eton Wick. There is also a charity called the Eton Poor Estate, for apprenticing seven or eight boys from the Free School in each year. Eton College should by all means be seen. The oldest portion of the buildings dates from 1523, and comprises two quadrangles and the cloisters. What is known as Upper School is on the west, on an arcade by Sir Christopher Wren ; on the south is the chapel, a beautiful building in the perpendicular style, greatly resembling that at King's College, Cambridge, to which Eton College was affiliated by its founder, King Henry VI. The chapel and ante-chapel contain the tombs of many celebrated personages ; a marble statue of the founder, by Bacon ; and monuments to Provosts Goodall and Sir Thomas Murray. The glass in the east window is by Willement. There are two memorial windows to Etonians who perished in the Crimea. There are also a few brasses dating from 1489. The College Library contains over 20,000 volumes, and is strong in ancient MSS. North of the college are the extensive playing-fields divided by Poet's Walk, and bordered by the Thames. To describe the manners and customs of Eton boys properly would occupy much more space than could here be afforded. Any one desirous of knowing all about Eton College should turn to the pages of Mr. Maxwell Lyte's admirable history published by Messrs. Macmillan. A bright little book, called " A Day of My Life at Eton," will also be found amusing and instructive.

The following statement of fees, &c., is given on the authority of " Cassell's Educational Year Book," but with reference to collegers, it may be observed that, in answer to a question, one of the officials of the college writes : " The cost to the parent of a colleger would be for school expenses under £30. The other expenses are optional, and consist of tradesmen's accounts for clothing, washing, &c. At an average, these expenses amount to

about £30, making about £60 in all."
As modified by recent statutes, the College Foundation will consist of provost, head master, lower master, not under seventy scholars and two chaplains. The endowment is said to be over £20,000 a year. Foundationers or "Collegers :" about twelve have vacancies a year. Election on last Monday in July. Candidates must be between twelve and fifteen. For permission to compete apply to the clerk to the Governing Body. Competitive examination of candidates. A Foundation Scholarship is tenable till election next following scholar's nineteenth birthday. Foundation scholars are educated and lodged in college during term at the expense of the college ; other expenses are purely personal. Oppidans ("Town Boys"): admission, ten to fourteen. Entrance examination determining boys' places in school. By fifteen, an Oppidan must have reached the fourth form, and by sixteen and a half the fifth form, except for reasons satisfactory to the head master, and an Oppidan may remain in school after nineteen, except for similar special reasons. Board and Fees : Oppidans may live with parents or guardians ; or they may, with special permission of the Governing Body, obtained on written application to the head master, lodge with other persons. Otherwise, they are lodged and boarded in masters' houses, where each boy is provided with a separate room ; two brothers may, on request of parents or guardians, share the same room. Entrance fee (on admission to the school) £10 10s. Annual payment to the School Fund, £24. Board and lodging in most houses, 100 guineas ; in a few £90 or 90 guineas. Use of furniture, £2 a term. Private classical tuition, 20 guineas a year. These charges include books, stationery, and the usual subscriptions. Boys learning German or Italian before reaching mid-division of the fifth form pay £3 10s. a term extra. Other expenses are purely personal. Scholarships and Exhibition : I. Tenable at School. As soon as funds permit, exhibitions worth £50 a year will be offered to the competition of boys between fourteen and sixteen. Tenable till election to foundation or till nineteen. II. Tenable after leaving : "Newcastle" Scholarship, £50 for three years, tenable at either University. Two "Chamberlayne" Ex-

hibitions, £50 for four years. "Reynolds" Exhibitions, £48 for four years at Exeter College, Oxford. "Berriman" Exhibition, and several others, with two postmasterships at Merton College, Oxford, tenable for four years. Vacant scholarships and exhibitions are decided annually in July, by an examination of the hundred highest boys in the school. Three or four scholarships at King's College, Cambridge, are open yearly to competition of Foundationers and Oppidans alike.

HOTELS.—"Bridge House," "Christopher," and "Crown and Cushion."

PLACE OF WORSHIP.—St. John the Evangelist.

POSTAL ARRANGEMENTS.—Post Office (money order, savings bank, telegraph). Week-day mails from London, 7 and 10.30 a.m., 2.30 and 6 p.m. Mails for London, 8.35 and 10.50 a.m., 1.35, 3.50, 9.25 p.m. Sunday, 9.30 p.m.

NEAREST.—(See WINDSOR.)

FARES.—(See WINDSOR.)

Eton College Boat Club consists of 92 members. The Monarch, ten oar, Victory, and Prince of Wales, compose the Upper boats ; Britannia, Dreadnought, Thetis, Hibernia, St. George, Alexandra, and Defiance the Lower boats. The Eton eight is chosen from the best oars amongst these boats, and enters at Henley for the Ladies' Plate, and sometimes for the Grand Challenge Cup. Eton has won the Ladies' Plate eight times. The boating season commences with the 1st of March, and ends with the end of the summer half. Mr. C. Barclay. is Captain of the Eton College Boat Club for 1885. Boat-houses just above Windsor Bridge. Colours of the eight, light blue, white cap.

Eton Excelsior Boat Club.—Election is in general meeting ; three black balls in five exclude. Entrance fee, 5s. ; subscription, £1 10s., in three monthly instalments ; hon. members, 10s. 6d. Boat-house, Goodman's. Colours, dark blue and amber.

Ewelme, a village in Oxfordshire (excursion from Bensington 2 miles, or from Wallingford 4 miles). Population, about 750. The road to Ewelme from Wallingford passes through Crowmarsh and Bensington, and affords a pleasant drive or walk along leafy roads, and past many good houses. Ewelme itself is a very pretty little village in a hollow, and gives its name to the hundred in which it is situated, and is formed by the combination of two words, one Norman and the other Saxon, "Eau" and "whelm," meaning "the outgush of water," a beautifully clear stream of water taking its rise near the church. Chaucer, whose son owned the manor by his marriage with Maud *née* Burghersh, must frequently have been at Ewelme, and he seems to have had this stream of water in his mind, as also the name of the place when he thus describes a brook :

In world is none more clear of hewe,
Its waters ever fresh and newe,
That whelmeth up in waves bright,
Its mountenance three fingers height.

The church stands on a hill, and is approached from the road through an old brick gateway, and through the cloisters of the almshouses, picturesque with their timbered brick walls, high red roofs, and elaborate wood carvings. A flight of steep steps leads thence to the west door of the church.

The church is of the perpendicular period, and contains many monuments of great beauty and interest. Among these is the alabaster tomb of Alice, Duchess of Suffolk, widow of the un- fortunate Duke who was beheaded by a skipper with a rusty sword on Dover beach in Henry VI.'s reign. This is placed between the chancel and side chapel of St. John, and is surrounded by small full-length angels bearing heraldic shields. The effigy of the duchess re- clines under a canopy, and below, in a sort of crypt, is an ogglesome representa- tion of a mouldering human body. The curious stone carvings above the tomb are surmounted by pinnacles with angels —four on each side. The tomb of her father, Thomas Chaucer, and his wife Maud (whose sister Margaret was third wife of John of Gaunt, and therefore aunt by marriage of King Richard II., and by virtue of which alliance the royal arms are displayed in many of the quar- terings emblazoned upon the tomb) is on the north side. The two figures are on an inlaid brass in fine preservation, he in complete armour standing on a unicorn, she on a lion rampant à queue fourchée, the Burghersh device. The church is

dedicated to the Blessed Virgin, and the side chapel, with its beautiful carved walnut (or chestnut) roof, to St. John the Baptist. This south chapel and the south aisle belong to the thirteen alms- men who inhabit the hospital, and receive 10s. weekly with apartments. The hos- pital is a venerable cloistered building, adjoining the church, founded by the Duke and Duchess of Suffolk, and en- dowed with valuable estates in Wilts, Hants, and Bucks. It is intended that these shall form the basis of a grammar school, when the property shall have recovered from the improvident manage- ment of four centuries. The Regius Professor of Physic, Oxford, is, *ex officio*, master of the hospital, with a council of twelve other trustees, according to the provisions of a scheme framed by the Court of Chancery in 1860. The manor- house, when the Suffolk property was escheated to the Crown, became a royal residence in the reigns of Henry VIII. and of Elizabeth. A road overhanging the common is still known as Queen Elizabeth's Walk. On the attainder of Edmund, Earl of Suffolk, in the reign of Henry VIII., the advowson with the manor passed into the possession of the Crown. James I., famed for inexpensive acts of generosity, endowed the Regius Professorship of Divinity in the University of Oxford with the Rectory of Ewelme, and entailed upon the parishioners for two centuries and a half a series of digni- fied but non-resident rectors. In 1871 a short Act was passed in the House of Commons, whereby the Rectory was severed once more from the Professorship, and opened out for the acceptance of any Clergyman of the Church of England. But the House of Lords took a more restrictive view and made it tenable only by members of the Oxford Convocation. The church contains many brasses. Among these may be mentioned that in the St. John's Chapel, in front of the altar, to Anne, wife of John ffroste, 1585; that to Catherine Palmer, 1599, in the north of the chancel ; and that dedicated to "Rodolpho Speiro, qui obiit, 1580," which bears a coat of arms and Latin epitaph, and will be found just within the painted iron rood screen. Of older date still is one representing the figures of a knight (once pursuivant-at-arms to King Henry VIII.) and lady, dated 1518.

Fifteenth-century brasses are represented by that of William Branwhait, a half-length in cope, &c., dated 1498 ; and one in the extreme west of the south aisle, dated 1454. In the middle of the nave is a brass of Samuel Brayle with inscription only, dated 1469 ; and in the north aisle is another, with inscription to Thomas Vernon, 1471.

PLACE OF WORSHIP.—Church of the Blessed Virgin.

POSTAL ARRANGEMENTS.—Post Office (money order and savings bank) in the village. Mails, through Wallingford, arrive at 7.30 a.m. and 2.30 p.m. ; dispatched at 6.30 p.m.

NEAREST Bridge, Lock, and Railway Station, Wallingford, 4 miles (which see).

Excursions.—(See GREAT WESTERN RAILWAY and LONDON AND SOUTH WESTERN RAILWAY.)

Exmouth Training Ship. Grays Thurrock. Commander, Captain Bourchier, R.N., formerly Captain-Superintendent of the Goliath. (Office, 37, Norfolk Street, W.C.).—On the destruction by fire, in December, 1875, of the Goliath training ship, which had been founded and carried on by three out of the thirty London Unions for about six years, the managers of the Metropolitan Asylum Board, at the request of the Local Government Board, undertook to provide and manage a training ship, in the advantages of which the whole of the metropolitan unions and parishes were to be entitled to participate, and towards the expenses of which all now contribute. The object of the ship, which provides accommodation for 600 lads, is to take healthy and otherwise suitable boys, from the ages of 12 to 15, from the Metropolitan Poor Law schools, educate them, and train them for service in either the Royal Navy, Army, or mercantile marine.

Eynsham, Oxfordshire, on the left bank, distant from Oxford about 7 miles, a station on the Great Western Railway, 70 miles from Paddington, the time occupied by the fast trains being about 2¼ hours. Eynsham is a sufficiently uninteresting little town ; situated on a hill, about three-quarters of a mile from the river, which is here spanned by a handsome bridge ; and, except as a centre for excursions, headquarters for anglers, or a resting-place for oarsmen travelling

between Cricklade and Oxford, offers no attraction to the visitor. The church of St. Leonard is an old stone building of considerable size, with a square embattled tower, and presents many varieties of architecture to the examination of the student. The interior, which contains several mural monuments and a brass of 1632, is chiefly remarkable for the arches which divide the nave from the aisles. There are also Baptist and Methodist places of worship in the town. The soil is various, and the population about 2,200.

FIRE.—Engine opposite the church.

HOTELS.—"The Swan" and "Red Lion."

POSTAL ARRANGEMENTS.—Post Office (money order, savings' bank, and telegraph), opposite the church. Mails from London (via Oxford) 6.48 a.m., 12.30 p.m. Mails for London, 10.40 a.m., 9 p.m.

NEAREST Bridges, up, Langley's (or Ridge's Weir) foot, about 7 miles, and New Bridge, a mile farther; down, Godstow, 2½ miles. Locks, up, Pinkhill, rather more than a mile ; down, Godstow, near the bridge. Ferry, Bablock Hithe, 3½ miles.

FARES.—From Eynsham to Paddington, 1st, 12/8, 21/3; 2nd, 9/6, 16/-; 3rd, 5/10.

Falcon Rowing Club, Oxford.—Number of members not limited. Election by ballot of general meeting, one black ball in three excludes. Members proposed and seconded at one meeting and balloted for at the next, except in the boating season, when names of candidates are posted in the Barge for six clear days before the meeting for election. Headquarters, King's Arms Hotel. Entrance fee, 2s. 6d. ; subscription, £1 ; honorary members, 5s. Colours, black, blue, and yellow.

Fish Dinners.—The typical fish dinner of London is the extraordinary entertainment offered at Greenwich—perhaps the most curious repast ever invented by the ingenuity of the most imaginative hotel-keeper. Many courses of fish prepared in every conceivable way, followed by ducks and peas, beans and bacon, cutlets, and other viands, so arranged as to stimulate a pleasing, if somewhat expensive thirst, are washed down at these Gargantuan feeds by the choicest brands at the highest prices known to civilisation. The effect at the

C

moment is eminently delightful. The sensation experienced when the bill is produced is not so pleasurable, and it has been said that there is no "next morning headache" like that which follows a Greenwich dinner. But there is no doubt that a Greenwich dinner is a very excellent thing in its way—especially if you happen to be invited to dine by a liberal friend, who knows how to order it, and pay for it. Only two houses can be recommended for this kind of sport—the "Trafalgar" and the "Ship." It may be noted that when the labours of the session are over, the Ministers of the Crown dine at the "Ship," and congratulate each other on their continued existence in office. A fish dinner of quite a different class, at which eleven kinds of fish, and a selection of joints are included in the bill of fare, is served twice a day—at 1 and 4—at the "Three Tuns Tavern," Billingsgate, at 2s. But although the price is low, and the accommodation a little rough, the dinner is excellent. Saturday afternoon during the winter months, or in the very early spring, may be specially recommended for this excursion. The flavour of the old-fashioned tavern dinner and after-dinner entertainment still hangs about Billingsgate. A good fish dinner is also to be had at Purfleet during the season.

Fishermen.—The Editor of this DICTIONARY has been asked in so many quarters to insert a list of trustworthy fishermen at the various fishing-stations, that the following list is given. As the Editor could not accept the responsibility of himself recommending men, unless personally known to him, the list has been taken from the report of the Thames Angling Preservation Society, and has been kindly corrected by Mr. W. H. Brougham, the excellent secretary. The names marked with an asterisk are those of men employed as bailiffs and under-bailiffs by the Angling Associations of their respective districts.

BRAY: George Chapman.

CHERTSEY: W. Galloway, T. Taylor, jun., J. Poulter, Jas. Haslett, and Henry Purss.

DATCHET: George Keene, G. Bailey, and *James Hoar.

GORING AND STREATLEY: *J. Rush, Bartholomew, J. Saunders, and E. Miles.

HALLIFORD: T. Rosewell, T. Purdue, Edward Rosewell, and E. S. Rosewell.

HAMPTON: W. Benn and Son, J. Langshaw and Son.

HAMPTON CT. AND EAST MOLESEY: W. Milbourne, T. Davis, J. Smith, Thos. Watford, T. Wheeler, C. Stone, C. Davis, G. Martin, and T. Melbourne.

HENLEY: W. Parrott, Alfred Parrott, Edward Vaughan, E. Woodley, H. Allum, G. Jerome, F. Potter, and G. Hamilton.

ISLEWORTH: W. Clark.

KINGSTON: John Johnson, senior, John Johnson, junior, B. Pope, E. Stevens, and J. Wilkies.

LALEHAM AND PENTON HOOK: Alfred Harris, Frank Harris, William Harris, and G. Harris.

MAIDENHEAD AND TAPLOW: *H. Wilder, *J. Gill, and *G. Winn.

MARLOW: Jas. Hatch, George White, *R. Shaw, *T. White, W. Shaw, *Jas. White, *H. Rockell, W. Thorpe, J. Sparkes, George Coster, and T. Barnes.

MOULSFORD: Frank Strange, Dawson, Cox, and Swadling.

OXFORD: A. Beesley, P. Beesley, and D. Talboy.

PANGBOURNE: G. Ashley, W. Davidson, R. Albury, F. Albury, *T. Lovegrove, and J. Champ.

READING: *R. Mills, *W. Clarke, *H. Knight, Oldway, W. Moss, and J. P. Hall.

RICHMOND: G. Howard, J. Bushnell, H. Howard, C. Brown, J. Brown, H. Wheeler, Job Brain, H. Mansell, and T. Young.

SHEPPERTON: W. Rogerson, G. Rosewell, A. Purdue, F. Purdue, G. Purdue, and D. Hackett.

SONNING: *W. Hull, *E. S. Lockley, and J. James Bromley.

STAINES: T. Fletcher, J. Keene, senr., J. Keene, junr., Charles Hone, and J. Tims.

SUNBURY: Thomas Stroud, Alfred Stroud, J. Stroud, and Edward Clarke and Sons.

TEDDINGTON: Alexander Kemp, Francis Kemp, T. Sawyer, Joseph Baldwin, B. Stevens, W. Baldwin, J. Stevens, C. Baldwin, and E. Cripps.

THAMES DITTON AND LONG DITTON : E. Tagg, A. Tagg, B. Buttery, and H. C. Hammerton.

TWICKENHAM : G. Coxen, John Coxen, S. Cole, J. Brand, H. Chamberlain, E. Finch, W. Francis, R. Coxen, S. Mesley, F. Coxen, C. Hennessey, R. Moffatt, G. Chamberlain, and P. Hammerton.

WALLINGFORD : Joseph Gulston, Cloudesley, T. Turner, and Wm. Moody.

WALTON ; Geo. Hone, George Rogerson, Samuel Rosewell, G. Hone, jun., and R. Watford.

WARGRAVE : W. Wyatt, S. Crampton, F. Wyatt. T. King, and D. Brown.

WEYBRIDGE ; M. House, and H. Curr.

WINDSOR : George Holland (Nottingham George), *James Grey, James Bunce, John Maisey, junior, Charles Kempster, George Plumridge, Chas. Smith, Thomas Bunce, and George Smith.

Fishing.—It may be well for the sake of simplicity to divide the fisheries of the Thames into three divisions : 1. From Isleworth down the river to the Nore ; 2. From Isleworth upwards to the Staines Stone ; the termination westward of the jurisdiction (including the first division) of the Lord Mayor and Corporation of the City of London ; and, 3. From the Staines Stone to Oxford, familiarly known as the Upper Thames waters. The fisheries below Isleworth to the Nore are open to the operation of the net, regulated by certain rules and ordinances which are too long to quote here, and which may be obtained at the office of the Thames Conservatory.

These "rules, orders, and ordinances" were made law by Act of Parliament in the year 1785, and being still in force, will serve to show what was the condition of the fishery at that period, and to contrast it with that of its present state. Salmon have entirely ceased to enter its waters. Shad, once plentiful, are very rarely taken. Smelts, which used to come up to spawn as high as Chiswick and Mortlake, and give profitable employment to the fishermen, are no longer seen in sufficient numbers to pay for their capture. Flounders, common, and then considered the finest in England, are almost extinct ; and what are taken seldom

exceed two or three inches in length. Soles and plaice, with the banks covered with the deposit of sewage by the outfalls at Crossness and Barking, from thence far down towards the Nore, have left their once clean, gravelly beds and scowers ; and the fry of eels, which once margined the flow from the ocean far into the country with a wide and dark line on either side of the river, termed "eel fair," no longer attracts crowds down to the river's banks with sieves, small mesh nets, &c., to capture them in thousands to make a peculiar kind of fish cake.

Lobsters were formerly sufficiently numerous in the Thames to justify special enactments, a fact not recognised at the passing of the Cromer (Norfolk) and South Coast Crab and Lobster Fisheries Bills, which were supposed to be an innovation of a novel character in ocean legislation.

With regard to the then, and subsequent, presence of pike, jack, roach, perch, dace, barbel, and gudgeon, the following, from angling works, will be sufficient to prove the lamentable degeneracy of the sport of angling in the metropolitan district and its vicinity. Salter, dating 1841, says : "It was not unusual for an expert angler to carry away upwards of twenty dozen of fine smelts from the angling stations about Blackwall. I have often taken five or six dozen before eight o'clock in the morning." He likewise recommends the angler to fish under and about the starlings of Battersea, Westminster, and Blackfriars bridges. The writer of this has fished for perch, roach, and smelts from the starlings of the old London Bridge and from a boat for perch, following the tide, as low as Limehouse. So common was this practice, that a waterman in a boat in the Pool used to draw attention to the fact of his having live shrimps for sale as bait by the ringing of a bell. Crooked-lane was then thought to be about the centre of the London angling stations, which accounts for the congregation of fishing-tackle makers there, which at one period amounted to 13 in number. A favourite pitch for roach was "near the bed of rushes off Temple-gardens," another from Carey's floating-bath near Westminster Bridge, and a third was commanded by the low wall of Cumberland-gardens, at the mouth of

C 2

"the pretty river Ephra," now, alas! a ditch. In fact, little or nothing appears to now remain of the fishery of the tidal waters but that of whitebait and shrimps. But should the metropolitan sewage be carried to the Maplin Sands, or to any point free of contaminating the waters of the Thames, there is every reason to believe that its once abundance of fish will return to its then purer waters. With some, the constant passage of steamboats is assigned as an additional reason for the absence of the salmon and other fish, but as there are rivers equally frequented by these vessels in which there appears to be little, if any, falling off in the visits of the salmon, shad, bass, &c., this theory does not receive much attention. The East and West India Docks and the Commercial Docks near Deptford were, within a comparatively recent date, famous resorts for the anglers. Permission to fish in the two former were considered a great favour, and the tickets were signed by the governors and directors of those companies; the latter was, by payment, only granted by written application, after enquiries had been made in reference to the respectability of the applicant. The perch in these docks were particularly large and fine in flavour, they obtaining great quantities of acceptable and fattening food from the discharge of the various vessels. It is a question now whether a fish could survive for an hour in the waters, so foul and polluted are they.

Many of the fishermen have left the river for other more profitable pursuits, and there has scarcely been a youth apprenticed to the calling of a fisherman for the last few years. When, however, a flush of water has brought down the fish from the preserved districts above into the tidal way, unauthorised persons have entered into netting, apparently without the fear of the interference of the authorities. The result being that, in the absence of supervision, the young and fry of fish, particularly flounders, are taken of less size than a crown piece, and thus the chances of the revival of the stock of these fish is considerably lessened. During heavy and continuous floods, such as prevailed in the autumn and winter of 1878, and the spring and summer of 1879, dace are met with in shoals as low as Putney, and then, if they are not immediately swept out with the net, the angler from the tow-path, or the fly-fisher wading in the shallows at low water, often gets a dish of these fish (*see* WHITEBAIT *and* STURGEON).

The middle waters or lower angling districts of the Thames, which extend from Isleworth to Staines Stone, above Staines, and near Bell Weir, Egham, are presided over and protected by a very energetic body under the Conservancy jurisdiction, called the Thames Angling Preservation Society, with London offices at 7, Ironmonger Lane, E.C. The Committee, principally composed of practical and experienced anglers, meet on the first Tuesday in each month at three o'clock; and the secretary, Mr. W. H. Brougham, is in attendance every Tuesday and Friday morning between the hours of ten and twelve o'clock, and oftener when necessary. The society dates from the year 1838. Rules were drawn up which may be obtained of the secretary; water-bailiffs and watchers were appointed at various stations between Richmond and Staines; and fence months, during which angling was restricted, were ordained for trout, from the 10th September to the 31st March. The fence months for pike, jack, roach, dace, chub, barbel, gudgeon, &c., are, under the provisions of Mr. Mundella's Act, 41 & 42 Vict. chap. 39, from the 15th March to the 15th June inclusive. The regulations for sizable fish are as follows: pike or jack, 18 inches; trout, 16 inches; barbel, 13 inches; chub, 10 inches; bream, 10 inches; carp, 10 inches; perch, 8 inches; tench, 8 inches; grayling, 7 inches; roach, 7 inches; flounders, 7 inches; dace, 6 inches; rudd, 6 inches; gudgeon, 4 inches. The measurement is the extreme length of the fish. All persons taking fish of less size and weight than those given above are liable to a penalty of £5 for each offence. The powers given to the river-keepers are to the following effect : "To enter any boat, vessel, or craft of any fisherman or dredgerman, or other person or persons fishing or taking fish, or endeavouring to take fish; and there to search for, take, and seize all spawn, fry, brood of fish, and unsizable, unwholesome, or unseasonable fish; and also all unlawful nets, engines, and instruments for taking or destroying fish as shall then be in any such boat, vessel, or craft, in and upon the river; and to take and seize on the shore or shores adjoining to the said river all unlawful nets, engines, and instruments for taking and destroying fish as shall there be found."

The fish at present native to the waters above Teddington are trout, pike, and jack—the latter so named when pike are under 3lb.—perch, roach, dace, carp, chub, barbel, tench, gudgeon, bleak, bream, eels, minnows, pope, or ruff (*all of which see*).

To those who would enter more fully into the arcana of the art, we suggest the careful perusal of Mr. Francis Francis's "Book on Angling" (Longman & Co.), and for yet more minute topographical information regarding the swims, Greville Fennell's "Rail and Rod" (*Field* Office), and "Book of the Roach" (Longman & Co.).

Fishmongers' Company (The) have built their hall appropriately on the north bank of the Thames at London Bridge. The building is large and imposing, without being able to lay claim to actual beauty. Inside, solid comfort rather than elegance has been realised. The rooms are lofty and spacious, and the great hall is rich in wood-carving and armorial bearings. In one of the rooms is a capacious chair, made out of the first pile that was driven in the construction of Old London Bridge. The seat of the chair is stone, part of the stone in fact on which the pile rested, and, according to all accounts, these two interesting relics must have been under water for upwards of six hundred and fifty years. Another curiosity on which the Fishmongers set much store is the dagger with which Sir W. Walworth, Lord Mayor, slew Wat Tyler. There is the usual collection of portraits of kings and queens and benevolent liverymen, amongst which may be mentioned Beechey's portrait of Lord St. Vincent; Mr. Wells's full-length portrait of Lord Chancellor Hatherley in his robes of office; and an exceedingly fine bust in marble of General Garibaldi, who was a freeman of the Company. The bust is the work of Signor Spertini, a Milanese sculptor. The Fishmongers used in olden time to be the object of popular rancour. At one period they had to appeal to the king for protection, and in 1382 Parliament enacted that no Fishmonger should be elected Lord Mayor. Nowadays they are justly popular for their works of charity and excellent dinners. Eighteen Exhibitions at the Universities are in the hands of the Fishmongers, and six presentations to the Blue Coat School. As a body the Fishmongers profess Liberal opinions in politics.

Floods.—Many reasons have been assigned for the frequency of floods during late years, amongst these are the multiplication of locks and weirs and the inattention of those who have the management of these "stops" in not letting the inundations pass at proper times and seasons. There may be some truth in this, but anyone conversant with the Thames cannot fail to be impressed with the fact that the many mills on the natural outlets of the river's flow have much to answer for. The mechanism of these mills, particularly by the enlargement of their undershot wheels, permits of their working much longer during floods than formerly, and it is to the interest of the millers to keep the water as high as possible until it is nearly over the axle, and then, of course, the power becomes nil. Then they may be careless of consequences, as they can use steam power, the larger mills having now shaft and steam-engine room to resort to in such emergency.

The floods below the locks and mills have very greatly increased during recent years. But this was not so much the case while Old London Bridge stood. Our forefathers appear to have studied most carefully this subject of inundations, which we have evidenced in the building of Old London Bridge. This structure served the threefold purposes of weirs, mill-dams, and locks; the narrow arches on the Southwark side were capable of being closed by gates, and those on the City side were blocked by the waterworks, which extended far into the river. Thus the flow of water up-stream could be regulated, as the bridge served all the purposes for which it was designed. (*See* E. W. Cooke's etchings of Old London Bridge; Lyson's "London," &c.) This judicious obstruction to the flow occasioned a fall of from four to six feet of water on the Pool side, the presence of which at certain tides influenced the building of the present bridge with wide arches, to the consequent occasion of an influx of water, which, meeting an overflood of accumulates from above, causes the inundations which are now so frequent at Lambeth and other low-lying districts.

Fog Signals.—Under the Conservancy bye-laws every steam vessel when the steam is up, and well under way, shall in all cases of fog use as a signal a steam whistle, which shall be sounded at least every three minutes. (*a*) Sailing vessels when under way shall in like manner use a fog horn. (*b*) When at anchor all vessels shall in like manner use a bell. The penalty for breach of these bye-laws is a sum not exceeding £5.

Foreign Cattle Market, Deptford, for stock from infected countries, only allowed to be landed on condition of slaughter before removal. It occupies the site of the abandoned dockyard, and is very inconveniently situated for its present purpose, at an out-of-the-way spot on the wrong side of the river; its purchase by the Corporation in 1871 exciting a good deal of comment.

Formosa.—The largest island on the upper Thames, said to be about 50 acres in extent; beautifully situated just below Cookham Lock, opposite the Hedsor and Cliveden woods. On it stands a handsome house, built by the late Sir George Young, with well laid out gardens and pleasure grounds.

NEAREST *Railway Station, Lock*, and *Bridge* at Cookham.

Fortifications.—The first land defences above the Nore are at Sheerness, where forts and batteries of considerable power guard the entrance to the Medway, and where also further protection is given by men-of-war and floating batteries. At Cliffe, and on the Lower Hope, is Cliffe Fort; Coal-house Fort is a little higher up on the other side of the river; and nearly opposite again, on the Kentish side, Shorne Fort. The three last-mentioned are all important buildings, very strongly armed, and would probably prove quite equal to the task for which they are intended. There are batteries, earthworks, and other defences at Gravesend and Tilbury, the real strength of which is matter for conjecture.

Galleon's Reach runs nearly north and south, rather over a mile from Woolwich to Tripcock Point. At the Woolwich end is a ferry. Bearings N.E. ¼ E., and S.W. ¼ W.

General Steam Navigation Company, 80, Great Tower-street, E.C., and 14, Waterloo-place, S.W. The steamers of the General Steam Navigation Company start from and arrive at Irongate and St. Katharine's Wharf, close to the Tower. The Home Stations are Edinburgh, Hull, Yarmouth, Margate, and Ramsgate. The Foreign Stations are Hamburg, Tonning, Harlingen, Amsterdam, Rotterdam, Antwerp, Bordeaux, Ostend, Boulogne, Havre, Charence, Oporto, Genoa, Leghorn, Naples, Messina, and Palermo. Through passenger tickets are issued to Brussels, Liege, and Cologne, *via* Ostend or Antwerp, and to the Pyrenees and the south of France and Spain, *via* Bordeaux. The passenger service on the Hull, Yarmouth, Margate and Ramsgate, Boulogne, and Havre stations is suspended during the winter months. All information as to fares, times of starting, &c., can be obtained at the London Offices. Passengers for Oporto or Italian ports are advised by the company to take tickets at least 36 hours before the time of sailing. Tickets for inland Continental places, other than Paris, must be purchased in advance, at the chief office in Great Tower-street, City.

When vessels start at or before 8 a.m., or arrive very late at night, passengers can embark on the previous evening, or postpone their landing until a convenient hour in the morning. Stewards are not allowed to take fees. Passengers embarking or landing at London should note the number on the badge of the porter who carries the baggage. The legal charge for each package carried between cab and ship is 2d. The Company's Official Handbook says: "Comfortable waiting and refreshment rooms have been established, and placed under good and experienced management."

Passengers about to embark should proceed direct to Irongate and St. Katharine's Wharf, where the Company's steamers start from, or a steam tender conveys passengers and their luggage from the wharf to the ship free of charge. Vessels engaged in the Yarmouth, Margate, and Ramsgate special summer service start from London Bridge Wharf. The above paragraph does not, therefore, apply to passengers by those vessels. The tender leaves the wharf ten minutes before the advertised time of sailing of the ships. Passengers arriving in the Thames from Hamburg, Antwerp, and Havre, between 8 a.m. and 8 p.m., are landed at Irongate and St. Katharine's Wharf by a special tender, free of charge.

One hundredweight of personal luggage is allowed free of freight by the Company's steamers. Missing property should be applied for at the chief office. There is a left luggage office at Irongate and St. Katharine's Wharf.

The nearest *Railway Stations* to the London Bridge Wharf are Cannon-st and London Br (South Eastern), Fenchurch-st (Great Eastern and. North London), and Mansion House (District). The nearest *Stations* to Irongate and St. Katharine's Wharf are Fenchurch-st (Great Eastern and North Lon.) and Mark-lane (Met.).

Geology of the Valley of the Thames.—1. GENERAL REMARKS.— The Thames may be conveniently divided into three parts: the upper, where the various streams of the Oolitic districts of Gloster and Oxon combine to form the Thames proper; the middle, where the river thus formed flows through the Chalk and the Tertiary beds of the London Basin, receiving further affluents from those formations, until it reaches the third and final stage of a tidal stream, still of course, with tributaries.

The broad valley in which the river flows has also a triple character, fairly agreeing with the above divisions of the stream. In the higher part its course is cut through various beds of the Oolitic series, and as the dip of these is at a greater angle than the fall of the river, and generally in much the same direction, higher and higher beds are successively crossed in the downward course, until those beds of the Cretaceous series below the Chalk are in their turn cut through. The middle part, beginning with the narrower cut through the Chalk hills, extends thence eastward across the wide expanse of the Chalk, and of the overlying Lower Tertiary beds, to the neighbourhood of London, the water slope being still less than the dip. The tidal Thames crosses the same formation as

the last division, with some local differences; for owing to some gentle disturbances the Chalk is brought up in various places, again to sink beneath the surface.

Accepting the above threefold division of our chief river, we will notice the geology of its valley, beginning with the highest division, which, however, is geologically the lowest. It may be well in the first place to give a general notion of the formations that occur in the course of the valley (using that term in a broad sense) from its sources to its mouth, and this may be seen at a glance from the following table, in which the formations are arranged according to age, the newest at the top. The letters "U," "M," and "L," show in which of the three suggested divisions of the valley (Upper, Middle, and Lower) the various beds are represented, and it will be seen that only the alluvium and Drift occur throughout, all the other beds being limited to one or two of the divisions. It will be convenient, therefore, to leave the notice of these newer beds, which are separated by a great gap from the rest, to the last.

Alluvium.—Marshland: Mud, peat, &c. ; U. M. L.

Drift.—Valley Drift: Gravel, sand, and loam; U. M. L. *Glacial Drift:* Boulder clay, gravel, and sand (? U.) M. L.

Older Tertiaries.—Bagshot Beds: Sand, with more clayey beds in the middle part, and with local pebble-beds in the lower part ; M. L. *London Clay:* M. L. *Lower London Tertiaries:* 1. Oldhaven and Blackheath Beds ; pebble-beds and sand ; L.—2. Woolwich and Reading Beds ; clay, sand, and pebbles; M. L.— 3. Thanet Beds ; sand and loam ; L.

Cretaceous Series.—Chalk: White limestone, mostly soft, upper part with flints; M. L. *Upper Greensand:* Soft sandstone and sand ; U. *Gault:* Bluish clay; U. *Lower Greensand:* Sand, with occasional conglomerate, U.

Upper Oolites.—Portland Beds: Limestone and sand ; U. *Kimmeridge Clay:* U.

Middle Oolites. — Coralline Oolite: Limestone and sand; U. *Oxford Clay:* U. *Lower Oolites. — Cornbrash, Forest Marble,* and *Great* or *Bath Oolite:* Limestone ; U. *Inferior Oolite:* Limestone, with sand at the base.

*Lias.—*Clay, with "marlstone" above the middle.

2. UPPER THAMES. TO A LITTLE BELOW WALLINGFORD. — With the greater part of this division of the river we are not now concerned : our journey may begin at Oxford. It may be noted, however, that above this city all the streams that make up the Thames have their origin in, and their course over, the great Liassic and Oolitic series, excepting a few small streams from the Chalk hills south-west of Faringdon, forming the Cole. The so-called "Thames Head" is in the Great Oolite limestone, and thence the main stream flows westward through a broad vale of Oxford Clay, receiving many tributaries from the north, but only the exceptional streams above-noticed on the south. The great excess of affluents from the north is probably owing to the more or less southerly dip of the various divisions of the Oolitic series, which consists of alternations of clays and limestones (with occasional beds of a more sandy nature). This geological structure has brought about the well-known features of the district : the denudation, or wearing away, of the harder limestones having given rise to abrupt hills facing northwards, with gentle "dip-slopes" (or slopes in the same direction as the dip) southwards ; whilst the softer and thicker clays form open vales, through the chief of which the main stream runs. The northerly tributaries, flowing in the same direction as the beds dip, but at a less angle, cut through the series, some, as the Evenlode and the Cherwell, starting in the Lias.

At Oxford the river turns southward, and the valley is somewhat narrower, being bounded both east and west by prominent hills, formed of outlines of Lower Cretaceous and Upper Oolitic beds (Shotover and Cumnor hills), whilst the lower part is still in the Middle Oolites. The lowest formation of these last, the Oxford Clay, a deposit some hundreds of feet thick and (from its contained fossils) clearly of marine origin, soon dips underground, near Iffley. The overlying Coralline Oolite, in places 100 feet thick, is divisible into two ; the lower part, or Calcareous Grit, consisting of irregular beds of more or less calcareous sand with occasional limestone ; whilst the higher, or Coral Rag, is a limestone in great part made up of the remains of corals.

The Coralline Oolite in its turn dips underground below Sandford, and the river then crosses the vale formed by the next overlying deposit, the Kimmeridge Clay, but soon turns westward along the foot of the range of hill from Nuneham Courtney to Culham, marked by the beautiful wooded mass of Nuneham Park. This hill is the "escarpment" (or bounding ridge) of the Lower Greensand, which here rests on the Kimmeridge Clay ; the Portland Stone, which comes between those formations in the large outlier of Shotover and Cuddesdon, being absent, from an unconformity or irregularity of deposit.

At Culham the river turns south-eastward, the Kimmeridge Clay sinks, and on the left side is the Lower Greensand tract with a small patch of Gault, whilst the last alone occurs on the right side. The Lower Greensand is here a sand often ferruginous and coarse, with sometimes a fine conglomerate, as in the river-cliff at Clifton Hampden. A few fossils showing a marine origin have been found in it, whilst those of the Shotover outlier bear witness to local fresh-water conditions. At Culham, owing to the overlap of the Gault, the Lower Greensand is only a few feet thick, and the two similar clays of the Gault and Kimmeridge nearly come together.

Below Clifton Hampden the Lower Greensand sinks beneath the surface, when the river crosses the vale of the Gault, receiving the Thame at Dorchester, and runs at the foot of the Upper Greensand escarpment from Little Wittenham to Bensington. This formation consists here of two parts : the lower, a soft whitish and often calcareous sandstone, which forms a marked, though small feature in the landscape, rising sharply from above the Gault ; the upper, a more or less clayey and calcareous Greensand, some twenty feet thick. From Bensington the Thames runs south across the Upper Greensand for about three miles, when it enters the boundary of the Chalk.

3. MIDDLE THAMES. FROM NEAR WALLINGFORD TO RICHMOND. — The Chalk in this district is divisible into two main parts, the lower marked by an absence of flints, whilst in the upper these are generally common ; the junction of the two being marked by a hard,

pale, cream-coloured bed a few feet thick. The great escarpment, the most marked feature cut through by the Thames, consists chiefly of the Lower Chalk, the Upper Chalk coming on near the top ; but southwards nearly the whole of the gently sloping plateau (a dip-slope) is formed of the latter division, which is only cut through in some of the valleys. Thus, although the Lower Chalk is at least as thick as the Upper, yet it crops out over a much smaller area. The total thickness of the formation here may be from 700 to 800 feet, which decreases to 650 under London (as proved by the few deep wells that pass through it), and then increases again eastward. Of late years the Chalk has been subdivided into a number of zones, marked chiefly by the general occurrence of certain fossils, but partly also by their litho-logical characters.

Where the Thames cuts through the great escarpment, it runs in a deep and narrow valley, with sharp turfed slopes of great beauty ; and in its course through the Chalk district it is usual to find, on one side or other, a high sharp slope, with the river at the foot.

The Lower Chalk gradually sinks, from the dip being still at a greater angle than the slope of the ground, but occurs in the bottom of the valley nearly as far as Pangbourne, when the Upper Chalk only is to be seen, higher beds coming on in succession lower down the course of the river. Below Pangbourne the right side of the valley consists, in its upper part, of a large Tertiary outlier (London Clay and Reading Beds), separated only from the main mass of those formations in the town of Reading by the cutting out of the valley of the Kennet. Thence the river turns north-eastward, and for a few miles the escarpment of the above-named Tertiary beds forms the greater part of the right bank of the valley, the Chalk being cut into only along the lower part ; the left side, on the other hand, consists of a dip-slope of chalk, with some Tertiary outliers on the high ground.

Near Sonning the Thames leaves the direct course, along the foot of the Tertiary escarpment (towards Maiden-head), and makes a sharp northerly turn, somewhat against the direction of the dip, to beyond Henley, and in consequence of this the bottom part of the valley is

again cut down into the Lower Chalk. From Remenham the river makes a second sharp turn, when it flows east for some miles to beyond Little Marlow, and then a third, after which it flows south to Bray, where it for the first time runs over Tertiary beds. The above course, which may be roughly described as three sides of a square, seems really to follow the line of a former Tertiary escarpment ; for the two well-marked wooded hills between Wargrave and Maidenhead (the gently conical form of which can be clearly seen from so far as Richmond) are parts of a large outlier, now barely separated from the main mass of the Tertiary beds at Ruscomb, and there are also smaller outliers round about, all of these being proofs of the former extension of those beds over the Chalk. In this tract there are fine examples of river-cliffs, or slopes, notably on the right bank from Wargrave to Henley, and opposite Great Marlow, and on the left bank from Hedsor to Taplow, including the grand sweep of Cliveden. Clothed, sometimes only with evergreen turf, but more generally with mighty masses of beech, these great chalk-slopes form some of the finest scenery in the south of Eng-land, their sharpness being set off by the tranquil river at the base, and by the level tract of marshland or the nearly level spreads of gravel in the bottom of the valley.

Below Maidenhead the character of the valley changes : instead of the bold features so common hitherto, we find long gentle slopes, with broad tracts of gravel along the bottom, often, indeed, spreading some way up the less inclined side. The river has entered the Tertiary district, and therefore, instead of having cut a channel with high slopes, as in the firmer chalk, it has made a broad vale through the more yielding and more easily denuded clays and sands. At Windsor, however, there is an exception to this for nearly a mile, and an old river-cliff, on which the castle stands, rises sharply about 100 feet above the plain on the north. This is owing to an uprise of the beds, whereby the Chalk has been brought to a higher level than it would otherwise have had, and its denudation has resulted in the formation of the usual feature.

Hence the river turns south-east, and

for a few miles the right bank of the valley consists of the London Clay slope of Windsor Park, crowned at the highest part above Egham by Bagshot Sand. The valley then broadens still more, and is marked on the left side by the occurrence of a vast spread of gravel and loam, from beneath which the London Clay rises up northwards to the high ground of Harrow, with its small outliers of Bagshot Sand. On the right side the London Clay sinks, and that part of the valley is formed of the more picturesque, though often barren, slopes of the Bagshot Sand. At Chertsey the river takes a general easterly course, which it keeps to Thames Ditton, before reaching which place the London Clay again crops out ; and then it turns north, the right bank of the valley being formed by the fine wooded slope of London Clay (an old river-cliff) along the western edge of Richmond Park.

4. LOWER THAMES. BELOW RICHMOND.—We have now reached the point where the river becomes tidal, though for some way, of course, the rise and fall of the tide is but slight. From Richmond the Thames again takes an easterly course, which it then keeps throughout—that is to say, in its general direction : as a matter of detail the course is in a series of curves from north to south in the plain of gravel or of marsh, sometimes varied by a straighter cut. The higher parts of the flanks of the valley, on both sides from Richmond to London, are formed of London Clay, with cappings of Bagshot Sand at Hampstead and Highgate hills on the north, and of gravel on the south. The clay here reaches a thickness of about 400 feet, with marine fossils throughout.

The beds now rise slightly, until in the far east of London the Lower London Tertiaries crop out from beneath the London Clay. It is to be noted that this set of beds reappears with a different character from that shown in the neighbourhood of Reading, where the middle division alone seems to occur, and consists of mottled clays and sands, some fifty feet thick, and almost without a trace of fossils. Here on the other hand we have nearly a full development of this interesting triple series ; the fine compact Thanet Sand, forty feet and more thick, without fossils ; the sand, pebbles, and

highly fossiliferous clays of the Woolwich Beds, often crowded with well-preserved shells of estuarine kinds, as may be well seen in the large pits at Lewisham and Charlton ; and the sandy pebble beds of Blackheath, sometimes with shells of much the same kind as those of the Woolwich Beds. The Chalk, too, again crops out, though only over small areas, on the southern side from Deptford to Woolwich. This side has marked features from Greenwich to Erith, caused by the generally sharp denuded slope of the Lower London Tertiaries, especially of their highest division, the Blackheath Beds, the top of which on the other hand forms the plateau or terrace of Blackheath, Plumstead Common, &c., above which the London Clay rises to the mass of Shooter's Hill. Along the base of the Tertiary hills there runs a fault, of comparatively small throw on the west near Lewisham, but for the rest of its course to Erith with a downthrow south of 100 feet or more, so that the pebble beds which form the high plateau above-mentioned are found also in the bottom of the valley.

On the north from London the valley has a gentle slope, and along the lower part there is a broad spread of gravel, from between which the London Clay rises to the high ground of Epping and Hainault Forests and of Havering, at which last place that formation is capped by a small outlier of Bagshot Beds, which occur in greater force farther east at Brentwood, and consist in the lower part of sand and in the upper of pebble-beds just like those (older than the London Clay) at Blackheath, &c.

Below Erith the Thames leaves the Tertiary beds and the Chalk again rises to the surface. On the north it appears at Purfleet, and forms the hill thence to Grays Thurrock, with small but well-marked outliers of Thanet Sand on the top ; whilst, from a local northerly dip, the Tertiary beds come on above the Chalk in the small tributary valley to the north ; and they then spread over the hill eastward to Little Thurrock, just east of which place the Chalk sinks below the surface to appear again for the last time along the edge of the marsh at East Tilbury. Here the Lower London Tertiaries have an exceptionally broad outcrop (much hidden by gravel) to the higher ground of Orsett, and are finally lost sight of at Standford-le-Hope, beyond which this side of the valley consists of London Clay, capped by a mass of Bagshot Sand round Hadleigh, whence the ground slopes gently eastward until at Southend (where the river comes up to the clay cliffs at high tide) and beyond is a sheet of the gravel and brick-earth that sinks farther east to the flats of Shoebury.

On the south below Erith, where the Darent joins the Thames, the valley is in chalk with a large Tertiary outlier above, forming the wooded mass of Swanscomb Park Hill, besides smaller outliers, the most marked of which is Windmill Hill, Gravesend. In this neighbourhood there are huge chalk-pits near the edge of the marshes, as also on the opposite side at Purfleet and Grays.

Round Higham the Tertiary beds crop out from beneath the marsh, and at Cliffe the Chalk rises up northwards from beneath these, is cut off sharply (as a river-cliff) along the southern edge of the marsh, and then finally sinks eastward at Cooling. The Tertiary beds here, therefore, lie in a slight trough. The range of hill south of the last two places, which forms the boundary of the valley, is formed of London Clay, from beneath which crop out in succession, in the lower grounds to the north, the Oldhaven Beds, here thin and chiefly sand; the Woolwich Beds, still with estuarine shells, and the Thanet Sand. These three divisions all disappear beneath the surface on the north of High Halstow, when the London Clay hills with their patches of gravel alone divide the valley of the Thames from that of the Medway, the two joining round the Isle of Grain; and the combined rivers then flow into the sea, with the alluvial flats of Foulness, &c., on the north, and on the south the cliffs of Sheppey, which consist chiefly of London Clay, but at the highest parts have a capping of Bagshot Sand and gravel.

5. NEWER DEPOSITS. — Besides the formations already noticed through which the valley of the Thames has been cut, and which succeed each other in almost regular order, we find also a set of beds of a much more irregular kind, lying indifferently on any of the other formations, occurring at all levels in the valley, and often hard to classify. Of these beds those known as " Glacial Drift " are the

oldest, and they get their name from the fact that icy conditions must have prevailed during the time at which they were deposited.

On the high grounds near Oxford there are gravels of uncertain age, but certainly older than the gravels at lower levels in the valley, and it is possible that these (full of pebbles from rocks that are found in the north) may be of Glacial age, relics of a once wide-spread deposit now mostly destroyed by denudation. Again, on some of the chalk hills, as well as on the outliers and high grounds of the Tertiary beds, there are patches of gravel that may also be of this age; indeed, in the case of the pebble-gravel (of flint and quartz) that occurs in small patches on some of the Tertiary hills (Ashley, Bowsey, Hampstead, and Shooter's) it seems likely that we have a still older deposit, perhaps equivalent to that of like character which comes between the Drift and the Crag series in parts of Suffolk.

A large spread of gravel on the high ground north of Windsor has been classed as Glacial, what little evidence that there is as to age pointing in that direction; and it is possible that other masses at much the same level on the southern side of the river are of the same age.

Below London, on the Essex side of the river, the bed which is the marked characteristic of the Glacial Drift comes (from the north where it is in force) to the edge of some of the hill-tops. This bed is the well-known Boulder Clay: a bluish clay full of stones, sometimes large masses, but mostly small roughly-rounded pieces of all kinds of rock, but here chiefly of chalk, the surfaces of the stones scratched in the same way as those of the stones in the deposits of existing glaciers. It is clear from the nature of the Boulder Clay that it has been brought by ice from the north; but in what form the ice did this is a moot point amongst geologists: some of whom will hear of nothing but a vast mass of land ice, or great ice-sheet as it is called; whilst others invoke a fleet of countless bergs floating southwards from ice-capped northern lands; and a third party swear by coast-ice. It is to be noted that the Boulder Clay, the highest member of the Glacial Drift, does not occur on the southern side of the Thames, but ends off near the northern side from London eastward.

The most important division of the Drift, as far as the Thames Valley is concerned, is that known as Post-glacial, by which is meant a set of gravels and loams newer than the Glacial Drift of the district. Such deposits occur all along the course of the river, and are of great interest, from their yielding in places bones of huge animals, of genera now extinct in this country, such as elephant, hippopotamus, and rhinoceros, associated sometimes with flint implements made by man. From the shells of freshwater and land species found, and from the disposition of the gravels and brick-earths in the valley, it is clear that the beds have been formed by the river, though under different conditions from those we now see. The stream must have been more powerful to transport the coarser material of the gravel; and it is inferred that, at the time these beds were formed, our island was part of Europe, and the Thames a tributary of a larger Rhine. The land was then at a higher level and the climate colder, so that from the consequent greater condensation of vapour there was a greater rainfall, and therefore a greater waterflow and a more swiftly-running stream; sometimes, too, wide-spread floods occurred, resulting in the deposit of broad tracts of loam.

These gravels and loams are not confined to the present bottom of the valley, but also occur in terraces at various heights on its flanks. These terraces are old valley-bottoms; and after the deposition of the gravel of the highest (then the bottom of the valley), the river has cut its way deeper through its former bed, until, a second period of comparative rest having arrived, it has again deposited gravel at a lower level—to be in its turn cut through, and another still lower deposit formed. The succession of gravel-flats at various levels may be well seen on the right bank of the river between Cookham and Maidenhead, where the terraces are well marked.

It is not until the Thames enters the Tertiary district, near Maidenhead, that this Valley Drift occurs over any large area. Where the valley is narrow, as in the Chalk tract, there is small room for the river-gravel; but where it broadens out they spread far and wide, hiding the formations below almost completely in the lower grounds, and forming great flats, as is the way with gravels. Below London again, on the southern side, where the Chalk rises up, the gravel is less extensive.

The best places to see the loam, or brick earth, are at the great brick-yards of Erith, Crayford, and Ilford, noted for the number of bones and shells that have been found in them. The equally well-known pits at Grays are now for the most part abandoned.

All the old parts of London are built on these beds. Forming a dry soil, but with water easily accessible (flowing out, indeed, in old times, in the many springs whose names we still keep), these gravel-terraces gave our ancestors one of the finest of sites, free from floods, and yet close to a tidal stream, the water-way to the world.

After the period of the river-gravels, when the land had sunk somewhat, when our island was separated from the mainland, and when the conditions approximated to those of the present time, the smaller and more sluggish river became unable to transport great quantities of coarse material and to form gravel; its enfeebled power was equal only to meandering in the bottom of its valley, cutting a channel through the gravel thereof, and depositing the layers of mud and silt of the alluvial flats that fringe the stream in most parts of its course.

In the upper and middle divisions of the Thames, and in the higher part of the lower division, these level tracts of meadow and marsh are comparatively narrow, and it is remarkable that this is especially the case in the Tertiary district above London, where the alluvium is generally a mere narrow strip on one side of the stream.

Below London, however, it is very different, and on either side of the broad river there are wide flats of rich pastureland, all some feet below high-water mark, over which the water used to flow, until ages ago it was embanked and kept to its present channel. In this broad alluvial tract there is a most interesting bed, rarely, however, to be seen, forming the bottom of the alluvium. It is a layer of peat, with trunks and branches of trees, known generally as "the submerged forest," and it gives evidence that the last movement of the land was one of slight depression, as the trees could hardly have grown in their present position, many feet below high-water mark.

6. FORMATION OF THE VALLEY.—In common with the valleys of our other rivers, that of the Thames has been formed by *denudation*: it has been cut out by the slow, long-continued, ceaseless action of the river, ever tending to deepen and widen its channel, aided greatly by the action of rain on the slopes, and in the limestone districts by the solvent power of carbonated water. There is no great gap or open fissure formed by the giving way of the earth, no sign of disruption or sudden violent action. That disturbances of the beds have had some effect in the formation of the valley is not however questioned, but their effect has been merely to *direct* in some cases the course which the denuding agents should follow, by making a certain course easier than any other. Thus, where the Thames cuts through the great chalk range below Wallingford, there are signs of some disturbance, for the strike or general trend of the beds changes from a direction about west to east to one about south-west to north-east ; but none the less has the valley been formed by the cutting away of the chalk. Again, though from Greenwich to Erith a fault, or fracture, with the displacement of the beds occurs, and may have greatly aided the erosive action of the old river, yet none the less has that part of the valley been formed by the wearing and carrying away of a vast mass of beds, hundreds of feet thick.

When we look across the wide valley of our chief river, and realise the facts that all the material which once filled it has been slowly loosened and carried away by actions like in kind to those now going on around us, though to a large extent, perhaps, greater in power, and that this work has been done merely in the very latest of the many great geological periods, we may begin to have a glimmering of the immensity of time that must have been taken up by the never-ceasing processes of denudation and deposition that have built up the successive sedimentary formations which compose the greater part of our earth. The destruction of rocks in one part has yielded material for the formation of newer rocks elsewhere ; and these actions,

accompanied by upward and downward movements in slow succession, have gone on side by side for countless ages.

Godstow.—Of the " house of Nunnes beside Oxford," as Stow calls it, in which Fair Rosamond was buried, nothing now remains but some ivy-covered walls and its association with the story, or rather the legend, of the lady who was certainly no better than she should have been, but who almost as certainly never had that interview with Queen Eleanor and a bowl and a dagger which was for so many years accepted as an historical fact. Travellers who wish to inspect the ruins will find them on the Berkshire shore, while those who are more interested in refreshing the inner man will find a snug little house on the opposite side of the bridge. At Godstow, which is 3½ miles from Oxford, is a lock as well as a bridge.

Goring, Oxfordshire, on the left bank. A station on the Great Western Railway, 45 miles from Paddington ; trains take about 1½ hours. The station is a few minutes' walk from the river. From London 85 miles, from Oxford 26½ miles. Population, 926. Soil, light, on gravel and chalk. Goring is a village situated in a most picturesque part of the valley of the Thames. The scenery around is deservedly admired. It consists of gently rising hills which recede from the river, and are clothed with woods and cornfields. The banks of the river are divided into a succession of verdant meadows. The river, here crossed by a long wooden bridge (toll 1*d.*), is much resorted to in the summer for fishing, and for picnic parties. This part of the valley of the Thames, owing to the fertility of the soil and its attractive features, has been settled from the earliest times. Traces of Roman villas and utensils have been occasionally found in the neighbourhood. An old Roman road called " Icknild-street " is believed to have crossed the Thames near Goring. The church, which is almost on the banks of the river, and is dedicated to St. Thomas A'Becket, is a very interesting structure. It is supposed to have been built in the reign of Henry II., and to have been enlarged in that of King John. It contains some interesting specimens of Norman and Early English architecture. It was connected with an Augustinian nunnery, traces of which are found to the south and west of the church. There was a priory about two miles north-east of the village, the remains of which are built into a farmhouse called Elvingdon. There are some excellent brasses in the church. On the right of the altar will be found four with full-length male and female effigies attended by their three sons and five daughters. They are in excellent order, and are probably of the time of Mary, although they bear no date. A full-length of a lady under a canopy in the north-aisle is dated 1401, and an inscription on a brass to Henry de Aldryngton, between the nave and north aisle, bears date 1375. A charity school, maintained by Alnutt's Charity, is at the extreme east end of Goring parish, this part of the parish is called Goring Heath. Alnutt's Charity was founded by a gentleman of that name, and endowed by him in 1724. There are twelve houses or rooms for almsmen, a school for twenty-seven boys from the parishes of Goring, Checkenden, and South Stoke, and one for girls. The boys are clothed and apprenticed by the Charity at the age of fourteen. A few boys and girls are admitted into the schools on the payment of a weekly fee of 3*d*. There is also an almshouse in Goring village, founded by Richard Lybbe, of Hardwick, in the parish of Whitchurch, in the year 1714. It admits four old men, two from Goring, one from Checkenden, and one from Whitchurch. The range of the Chiltern Hills commences with Goring. There are several beautiful and extensive views in the parish, while the air is extremely fresh and bracing.

The angling in the reaches of the sister villages, Streatley and Goring, is at times all that can be desired. The fisher may make his choice of waters, from the sharp and swift to the slow and deep. Pike, perch, roach, dace, gudgeon, and eels are abundant.

INNS.—"The Miller of Mansfield," "The Queen's Arms," "The Sloane Hotel."

PLACES OF WORSHIP.—St. Thomas A'Becket, and Lady Huntingdon's Chapel.

POSTAL ARRANGEMENTS.—Post Office (money order, savings bank, telegraph). — Mails from London, week days and Sundays, 7.5 a.m. and 12.5 p.m. Mails for London, 9.50 a.m., 7.30 p.m.; Sundays, 5.40 p.m.

NEAREST *Bridges*, Goring ; up, Wallingford 6 miles. *Locks*, up, Cleeve ¾ mile; down, Whitchurch 4 miles. *Ferries*, up, Moulsford 2 miles ; down, Basildon 1½ mile. *Railway Station*, Goring.

FARES to Paddington : 1st, 7/10, 14/- ; 2nd, 5/11, 10/6 ; 3rd, 3/9.

Grain, Isle of.—A grazing district, bounded by the Thames and Medway, and opposite Sheerness, which is about a mile and a half distant. An important portion of the defences of the Thames and Medway is furnished by the forts and batteries on the island. Being very difficult of access, the Isle of Grain is very little visited, and, indeed, offers but scant attraction. The island is connected with the North Kent Railway at Higham, the terminus in the Isle of Grain being PORT VICTORIA (*which see*).

Grain Spit Buoy.—A 6-foot can-buoy, made of wood, and painted black. It is situated on the Grain Spit, on the Kentish side to the entrance to the Medway, and marks a depth of water, at low water, spring tide, of 8 feet. It is moored with 6 fathom of chain. The weight of the sinker is 8 cwt. The Grain Spit Buoy belongs to the Trinity House.

Gravesend, Kent, on the right bank, from London 27 miles. A station on the North Kent Railway, 24 miles from Charing Cross. Express trains take about an hour. The station is close to the centre of the town, and about 10 minutes' walk from the Town Pier. Flys meet the trains. There is another route from Tilbury to Fenchurch-street, by express about 45 minutes. Ferry steamers ply between Tilbury station and the wharf in West-street. Population, 20,413. Soil, chalky. Gravesend, anciently, according Domesday Book, Gravesham, is, owing to its position as the gateway of the port of London, one of the most important towns on the river. All foreign-going ships are compelled to stop here and take on board pilots, and, on homeward voyage, Custom House officers. The river here narrows to the width of about half a mile, and the narrow channel is day and night full of shipping of every class and description, from the stately ironclad to the fussy tug, from the clean-cut China clipper to the picturesque if clumsy Dutch galliot, and from the graceful schooner yacht to the ungainly hay-barge. The shipping in the reach brings many visitors to Gravesend, for although it is no longer the custom, as it was extensively some years ago, for emigrants and other travellers to embark and disembark at Gravesend, it is still a convenient place for the last God-speed on the outward voyage or the first welcome home. It is well to remark in this connection that the Gravesend waterman is a personage in any dealings with whom it is desirable to keep the weather-eye open. Fancy fares are almost invariably demanded, and the smallest opportunity of laying the blame of the overcharge on the state of the weather or of the water is taken the utmost advantage of. There is, however, no reason why there should be any real difficulty in regard to this matter. A table of fares, with special regulations for luggage, is issued by the Corporation of Gravesend, and to it watermen are bound to adhere. The list will be found at the end of this article. From the river Gravesend, unlike most riverside towns, presents an attractive appearance. The town rises rapidly from the riverside to the hill which is crowned with the well-known windmill ; and the cliffs towards Rosherville and Northfleet, and the well-wooded rising ground towards Chalk and Cobham, add greatly to the beauty of the view.

Gravesend has, since the days of Elizabeth, been incorporated as a municipal borough, and the town is governed by a mayor, six aldermen, and eighteen councillors. Courts of Quarter Session are held here ; the present Recorder is Standish Grove Grady, Esq. The Parliamentary borough was constituted by the Act of 1867, and includes the parishes of Gravesend and Milton and a portion of Northfleet. The number of voters on the register in 1880 was 3,286. The borough is at present represented by Sir Sydney Waterlow, a Liberal. The principal streets are High-street, Harmer-street, Windmill-street, and the Milton and New roads, some of which contain good shops. The most favourite residential portions of the town are along the Milton-road, on the cliffs about Rosherville, and at the streets at the back of the town, which cluster about Windmill Hill and lead into the open country.

The town-hall, where the business of the municipality is transacted, and where petty and quarter sessions are held, is a handsome building in the High-street, and behind it is the market-place extending to Queen-street.

There are four piers : the Rosherville, just below the well-known gardens—this is a landing-stage, and nothing more ; the ferryboat-pier in West-street ; the Town Pier, at the bottom of High-street (toll for promenade 1d.), which combines the business of a steamboat-pier and landing-stage, with a somewhat feeble effort in the direction of bazaar keeping. This pier is covered in, and is occasionally utilised for amusements, as is also the case with the Royal Terrace Pier, still lower down the river, which stands in well-arranged grounds of its own. (Toll, 2d.)

Gravesend belongs to the Chatham military district. There are extensive barracks in Wellington-street, Milton, and a rifle range in Denton Marsh, on the east of the town, which was for a time closed, but which, after many difficulties and some litigation, has been again restored to its original objects. The forts at Tilbury, New Tavern Fort at Gravesend, as well as Shorne Fort, are included in the Gravesend district. The 1st Administrative Brigade and the 1st corps of that brigade of Kent Artillery Volunteers have their headquarters in the town. The office of the Customs Department is close to the river at the bottom of Harmer-street. The pilot-station is at the Terrace Pier, and the harbour-master's office and that of the mercantile marine are in Whitehall-place, where also are the offices of the London and St. Katharine and Victoria Docks, that of the East and West India Docks being in Milton-place.

There is a theatre in the New-road, which does not appear to be overburdened with patronage, and the pretty and attractive gardens at Rosherville are mainly supported by excursionists—(see ROSHERVILLE GARDENS.) The public hall is in New-road, nearly opposite the theatre, and contains, besides reading-room, club-room, and refreshment department, a large hall, which is available for entertainments, lectures, &c. The assembly-room, in Harmer-street, can be hired for one night at £3 3s., and for two nights at £5 5s., including gas. There is also a lecture-hall at Milton. The free library and reading-room is in Church-street. The reading-room of the St. Andrew's Waterside Mission is at the foot of the Town Pier, and is open on week-days from 9 to 9, and on Sundays from 2 to 6. The Gravesend Club, which has its quarters at the Nelson Hotel, New-road, numbers about seventy members. Entrance, £1 1s.; subscription, £1 1s. Election is by ballot of members; one black ball in ten excludes.

Gravesend is well supplied with schools, and one of the handsomest buildings on the hill above Milton is Milton Mount College, an institution founded in 1870 by the Rev. Wm. Guest for the training of the daughters of Congregational ministers. The college is intended to give a high literary culture at low terms, especially to those young ladies who pur-pose becoming teachers. The school depends for its support on subscriptions as well as on the payments of pupils. In connection with the college is Milton Congregational Church and Lecture Hall, in which several societies in asso-ciation with the church hold their meetings.

At Gravesend are the headquarters of the Nore Yacht Club at the New Falcon Hotel; and of the New Thames Yacht Club, who have a club-house at Clifton Marine Parade; and most of the impor-tant races of the leading London yacht clubs finish in Gravesend Reach.

Masonic lodges are held at the Town Hall and at the Old Falcon Hotel.

Varchall's Charity. — This trust is shortly as follows : David Varchall, an old inhabitant of Gravesend, by his will dated 15th September, 1703, left certain property lying by the waterside in trust, after his wife's death, to raise out of the rents £20 yearly, to be paid quarterly to the master of the Free School (now the National School) for ever to teach twenty poor boys, of whom ten were to be sent from Gravesend and ten from Milton by the churchwardens and parishioners of each parish. Also to lay out a sum of money to buy clothes for these twenty poor boys, and to pay the surplus to buy clothes for so many other poor people in Gravesend and Milton, as the respective churchwardens and parishioners should think fit. The rents of the properties now yield a surplus

averaging about £100 per annum, which is divided equally between the parishes, and about Christmas the Vestries examine each applicant for clothes, and send a list of approved persons to the clerk, who gives them each a ticket authorising them to receive, at any shop in their own parish, useful clothing to the extent of so many shillings; these are collected and paid by the trustees. There is a notice appended to the ticket that if the ticket be used for any other goods except clothes (such as liquor, &c.) it will not be paid. By a decree in Chancery the number of trustees is fixed at fourteen— seven for each parish ; five to be a quorum. Vacancies are to be filled up by the trustees, but so that there be never less than five trustees.

Pinnock's Charity.—Henry Pinnock, of Milton next Gravesend, gentleman, by his will dated the 13th of August, 1624, gave and bequeathed unto the poor people of the parishes of Gravesend and Milton the sum of £3, to be distributed indifferently, at the discretion of the churchwardens and overseers of the said parishes, without any other dole. Like-wise he gave and bequeathed unto the churchwardens and overseers of the parishes of Gravesend and Milton afore-said, for ever, for the time being, certain messuages or tenements with gardens in Milton aforesaid ; so that the said church-wardens and overseers do term the said messuages for ever by the name of "Saint Thomas's Houses," and do for ever con-vert, take, employ, and keep the same houses, with their appurtenances, to and for the only use and behoof, and for the better relief and maintenance of such poor decayed people as shall from time to time be or dwell in the said parishes, and to no other use, intent, or purpose. He further bequeathed unto the said churchwardens and overseers two acres of marsh ground, and other hereditaments at Grays Thurrock, in Essex, to the only use and stock of the said poor of Milton and Gravesend, and to keep them at work ; and that the trustees shall, during their natural lives, have the placing and displacing of the ancient poor people, into and out of the said houses. There are now ten tenements called "Saint Thomas's Houses," and four more are in course of erection out of funds derived from charitable legacies. The present poor people who are occupants number 37. With a view of establishing a fund for the endowment of the charity and in memory of the late Prince Consort, a fund was established in 1863 called "The Albert Memorial Endowment Fund," which now consists of nearly £1,400 Consols, the income of which is divided equally between the inhabitants of the houses.

The Orphans' Home, South-street, West-square, London, and 35, Harmer-street, Gravesend, was opened in 1867 for 10 children. There are now 214 orphans within its shelter—65 in the Branch Home, Harmer-street, Graves-end, the rest in the Parent Home, West-square, London. The Gravesend family consists of the little ones and the delicate ones of the flock, with a few older and stronger girls to do the work of the house. There is no assured income, and no funded property belonging to the institution. There are no managing expenses; the services of the architect, the legal adviser, the medical attendants, the secretary, and superintendent, are all given gratuitously ; so that every penny which is contributed to the Home goes direct to the support of the children. The average cost of each child's main-tenance is £15 a year. More than a hundred orphans are awaiting their turn for admission.

The Children's Home, Milton, for the rescue and nurture of orphan and ne-glected children, is a certified industrial school, providing accommodation for 150 boys. In connection with the Children's Home, Bonner-road, London ; Edgworth, Lancashire ; and Hamilton, Canada.

Many pleasant excursions may be made from Gravesend, some of the prettiest country in the county lying within easy reach. The woods of Cob-ham should certainly be visited, especially in the season when the rhododendron thickets are in bloom. But at all times of the year the woods are beautiful. Cobham Hall, the seat of the Earl of Darnley, is an interesting Elizabethan building, containing a fine picture gallery and a very perfect gilded music-room attributed to Inigo Jones. Cobham church also presents many points of interest. Fine views are obtained on the road from Gravesend to Rochester (7 miles) over Gad's Hill. Maidstone is

about three-quarters of an hour from Gravesend by the North Kent Railway, and a little beyond Maidstone are the celebrated Farleigh and Wateringbury hop-gardens. In the summer the steamer can be taken to Southend or Sheerness, from which latter point steamers run up the Medway to Rochester and Chatham.

BANKS.—London and County, and London and Provincial, both in High-street.

FAIR.—October 24th.

FIRE.—The Volunteer Brigade consists of captain, superintendent, and ten mem-bers. Three manual engines, two hand, hose and reel. Hydrants are fixed throughout the town. Fire-engines, escapes, and fire-annihilators are kept at the Town Hall.

HOTELS. — "Clarendon," "Falcon," "Old Falcon," "Rosherville," all facing the river.

PLACES OF WORSHIP.—Christ Church, Milton next Gravesend ; Holy Trinity Church, Milton next Gravesend ; St. George's (parish church of Gravesend); St. James's Church, London-road ; St. Mark's, Rosherville ; St. Peter and St. Paul (parish church of Milton); the Roman Catholic Church of St. John's, Milton-road ; Waterside Mission, St. Andrew's ; Bethel (for sailors and water-men, Danes, Norwegians, and Swedes), West-street. Gravesend also contains Congregational, Free Church, Primitive Methodist, Baptist, Presbyterian, and Wesleyan Chapels, and a Jewish Syna-gogue.

POLICE.—The station is at the Town Hall in High-street.

POSTAL ARRANGEMENTS.—Post Office (money order, savings bank, telegraph, and insurance), 144 and 145, Milton-road. Mails from London, 8 a.m., 2.5, 5.10, and 10.45 p.m. Mails for London, 9.30 a.m., 1, 4, 8, and 12 p.m. Receiving offices, 80, High-street, 38, New-road, 27, Wrotham-road, and at Denton. There is also a telegraph-station at the Terrace Pier.

NEAREST *RailwayStation, Steamboat-pier* and *Ferry*, Gravesend.

FARES to Charing Cross : 1st, 3/6, 4/6 ; 2nd, 2/8, 3/6 ; 3rd, 2/1, 3/-. To Fenchurch-street (*via* Tilbury) : 1st, 2/6, 3/9 ; 2nd, 1/11, 2/10 ; 3rd, 1/4, 2/-.

GRAVESEND WATERMEN'S FARES, between Broadness Point and Gray's, and Lower Hope Point below Gravesend.— Over the water directly, and to and from any steamboat, ship, or vessel, opposite, or near to any public plying place between Broadness Point and Grays, and Lower Hope Point aforesaid, both inclusive, one person, 1s.; exceeding one, 6d. each. From the Town Quay to or from Gladdish's Wharf on the west, and to and from all steamboats, ships, vessels, and places lying and being between the same, and from the Town Quay to and from all steamboats, ships, vessels, and places lying and being between the same, one person, 1s.; exceeding one, 6d. each. From the Town Quay at Gravesend, westward, to or from any steamboat, ship, vessel, or place between it and

	For one person.		Exceeding one.	
	s.	d.	s.	d.
The Red Lion Wharf....	1	6	0	9 each
Northfleet Creek........	2	6	1	3 ,,
Broadness Point or Grays	3	6	1	9 ,,

From the Town Quay at Gravesend, eastward, to and from any steamboat, ship, vessel, or place between it and

	For one person.		Exceeding one.	
	s.	d.	s.	d.
Denton Mill............	1	6	0	9 each
Shorne Mead Battery ..	2	6	1	3 ,,
Coalhouse Point	3	6	1	9 ,,
Halfway Lower Hope ..	5	0	2	6 ,,
Lower Hope Point Battery	6	6	3	3 ,,

Watermen bringing the same passengers or any of them back from any steamboat, ship, vessel, or place, to be paid only one half the fare above stated by such person or persons for the back passage. The above fares in all cases to include passengers' luggage or baggage, not exceeding fifty-six pounds for each passenger. All beyond that weight to be paid for at or after the rate of 6d. for each fifty-six pounds. Watermen detained by passengers stopping at steamboats, ships, wharves, and other places, to be paid for time or distance, according to the rate herein set forth respectively, at the option of the waterman.

For a full boat-load of passengers' luggage or baggage, the same fare as for carrying eight passengers : for half a boat-load, the same fare as four passengers.

Time for a pair of oars.—For the first hour, 2s.; for the second hour, 1s.; and for each succeeding hour, 1s. For the day, the day to be computed from 7 o'clock in the morning to 5 o'clock in the evening from Michaelmas Day to Lady Day, and from 6 o'clock in the morning to 8 o'clock in the evening, from Lady Day to Michaelmas Day, 12s.

GRAVESEND HACKNEY COACH FARES, to be affixed in a conspicuous position in the interior of every carriage licensed by the Urban Sanitary authority.

By distance—From the Town Ter-

	s.	d.
race, or Commercial Piers, to the North Kent Railway Station, or vice versa	1	0
From the piers or railway station to Rosherville Gardens, or Pier, or Perry-street...	1	6
To Springhead	2	6
From the King-street stand to the Denton boundary, or any place between the west side of Windmill and High streets, and south of the old Dover-road; or to the Rosherville boundary, or any place between Windmill and High-streets, and south of the Old-road	1	6
From the piers or railway-station into Old Dover-road, Constitution-crescent, Leith Park; West Hill, Shrubbery, South Hill, White Hill roads, or Old Sun-lane ...	1	6

Except in the above cases, for any distance not exceeding one mile, 1s. : for every additional half-mile, 6d. Half back fare if the parties return in the same carriage. *By time*—Between 6 a.m. and 10 p.m.

| for every hour or any less time, from the time of hiring to the nearest stand after discharged ... | 2 | 6 |

Half-fare additional may be charged between 10 p.m. and 6 a.m. When more than two persons may be and are carried, 6d. to be paid for every additional person for the whole hiring. Two children under ten years of age to be counted as one adult ; a single child under ten free. No driver to carry more than six persons in a carriage drawn by horses, or more than two in one drawn by mules or asses.

Luggage free up to twenty-eight pounds ; over that weight, 2d. for every additional fourteen pounds, or fractional part thereof. Carriage drawn by a goat to carry only three children under six years.

Gravesend Reach is about three miles and a half in length, and runs from Northfleet to Coal House Point. The first lighthouse of the Trinity House is at Northfleet. Bearings E.S.E. and W.N.W.

Grays Thurrock, a small town on the left (Essex) bank, rather more than 23 miles from London Bridge ; a station on the London, Tilbury, and Southend Railway, 20½ miles from London ; the trains average about three-quarters of an hour. Population, exclusive of the training-ships, about 4,000. Light soil on chalk. The principal trade of Grays is in bricks, and, especially, lime and cement.

The cruciform church is dedicated to St. Peter and St. Paul. It contains a tablet to the memory of the schoolmaster and boys of the training ship *Goliath*, who were drowned during the fire which destroyed that ship in 1876. About a century ago, Wm. Palmer, Esq., left property in London, now amounting to about £900 per annum, for the purposes of education in Grays, and a few years ago, at the cost of about £7,000, schools were erected to accommodate 140 boys and 75 girls, who obtain their education at a small charge.

The training ships *Exmouth* and *Shaftesbury* (*which see*) are moored in the river off Grays. The former is under the Metropolitan Asylums Board, the latter under the London School Board. A new police-station was opened in 1880.

BANK.—London and Provincial.

HOTELS.—" The King's Arms " and " The Railway."

PLACES OF WORSHIP.—Church of St. Peter and St. Paul, Congregational Church, and Chapels of the Primitive and United Methodist.

POSTAL ARRANGEMENTS.—Post Office (money order, savings bank, telegraph, insurance). Mails from London, 6.50 and 7.15 a.m., 6 p.m. ; Sundays, 9 a.m. For London, 12.10 a.m., 4.45, and 9 p.m.; Sundays, 4.30 and 9 p.m.

NEAREST *Steamboat Pier*, Rosherville,

about 3 miles, and Tilbury, a little lower down on the Essex side ; *Railway Station,* Grays.

FARES to London : 1st, 2/3, 3/9 ; 2nd, 1/8, 2/10 ; 3rd, 1/1, 2/-.

Great Marlow (*see* MARLOW).

Great Western Railway.—HORSES AND CARRIAGES.—Horses and carriages are conveyed to or from Windsor, Taplow, Maidenhead, Bourne End, Great Marlow, Henley, Reading, Pangbourne, Goring, Wallingford, Abingdon, and Oxford, and horses only to and from Cookham. They are conveyed by certain trains only, for which see time-tables. In no cases are horses or carriages conveyed by trains which run to or from Bishop's-road Station, or to or from the Metropolitan line. The rates from Paddington to the stations on the river are as under :

FROM PADDINGTON STATION TO	HORSES.			CARRIAGES.	
	1	If property of one person		4 wheel.	2 wheel.
		2	3		
	s. d.	s. d.	s. d.	s. d.	s. d.
Windsor	8 6	13 6	20 0	11 0	11 0
Taplow......	9 0	14 0	21 0	12 0	9 0
Maidenhead..	9 6	14 6	21 9	12 6	9 6
Cookham	10 0	15 6	23 3	..	..
Bourne End..	11 0	16 6	24 9	14 0	14 0
Great Marlow	12 6	18 0	27 0	16 0	16 0
Henley	12 0	19 6	29 3	16 0	12 0
Reading	12 0	19 0	28 6	18 0	12 0
Pangbourne..	13 6	22 0	33 0	18 0	13 6
Goring	14 6	23 6	35 3	19 0	14 3
Wallingford..	16 6	27 6	41 3	22 0	17 0
Abingdon....	18 0	36 0	54 0	24 0	24 0
Oxford	18 9	37 6	56 3	25 0	25 0

Previous intimation should be given to the station-master when horses or carriages are about to be sent, so that the necessary vehicles may be obtained and put in readiness by the time the horses or carriages are brought to the station.

COMPARTMENTS RETAINED.— Compartments, in carriages of any class, are reserved for families or parties of friends who are desirous of travelling together. Application should be made beforehand to the superintendent of the line, or the station-master at Paddington, as passengers cannot depend upon getting an empty compartment after they arrive at the station, if no previous notice has been given. The number of the party should always be stated.

CLOAK ROOMS.—Passengers' luggage can be deposited in the cloak rooms at Paddington, Westbourne-park, and other stations on the line. The charge which the company makes for warehousing passengers' luggage, which has been, or is about to be conveyed on the railway, is 2*d*. for each package for any period not exceeding three days, and 1*d*. additional per package for every day or part of a day after three days.

CHEAP TICKETS FOR PICNIC AND OTHER PLEASURE PARTIES.—Between May 1 and October 31 of every year, 1st, 2nd, and 3rd class return tickets at reduced fares are issued from all London stations to *bonâ fide* pleasure or picnic parties. of not less than six 1st class, or ten 2nd or 3rd class passengers. The tickets are available for use on the day of issue only ; they are not issued *to* London in any case, nor from London to any place more than thirty miles distant. In order to obtain these tickets it is necessary that application should be made for them at least three clear days before the excursion is proposed to be made, and the letter of application must specifically state that the party is exclusively a pleasure party, and give the following information :

1. The probable number of the party.
2. The class of carriage for which the tickets are required.
3. The stations from and to which the party will travel.
4. The date of the proposed excursion, and the trains by which the party intend to go and return.

The application may be addressed either to the general manager, the superintendent of the line, the superintendent of the London division (Paddington), or the station-master at Paddington. The power of refusing any application is reserved ; but if it be granted, a letter of authority will be sent to the applicant, on production of which at the booking-office of the station from whence the party travels the necessary tickets will be issued. The fares are generally about a single fare and a quarter. From Paddington

to the undermentioned stations on the Thames they are as under :

PADDINGTON TO	1st Class.		2nd Class.		3rd Class.	
	s.	*d.*	*s.*	*d.*	*s.*	*d.*
Brentford.............	1	11	1	6	1	1
Windsor	4	9	3	7	2	3
Taplow................	5	0	3	9	2	5
Maidenhead	5	5	4	1	2	7
Cookham.............	6	3	4	7	2	10
Bourne End	6	7	5	0	3	0

ANGLERS' TICKETS.—Cheap 3rd class return tickets to the undermentioned stations are issued from all London stations by all 3rd class trains to anglers who are *bonâ fide* members of anglers' clubs, and who produce their cards of membership at the time of taking their tickets. The fares from Paddington are as under :

	s.	*d.*			*s.*	*d.*
Maidenhead ..	2	7	Cookham	..	2	10
Taplow..	2	5	Bourne End	..	3	0
Twyford	3	3	Pangbourne	..	4	4
Henley..	3	9	Goring ..	..	4	9
Great Marlow..	3	4				

Anglers' tickets are in all cases "return" tickets, and are available for three days.

OUTSIDE PORTERS FOR TRANSFER OF LUGGAGE.—Where two stations belonging to separate companies are adjacent to each other, out-porters are appointed to convey passengers' luggage from one station to the other at fixed charges.

The Bishop's-road and Praed-street Stations adjoin the Paddington Station, and the authorised charge for the conveyance of luggage from one to the other is 2*d*. per package.

At Reading the stations of the Great Western and South-Eastern Companies adjoin. The charges for the transfer of luggage are :

	s.	*d.*
Single packages	0	2
Two or more packages, not exceeding ½ cwt. each	0	1
Each package exceeding ½ cwt... ..	0	2
Large quantities, per ton	2	0

At Oxford transfer porters convey luggage between the Great Western and North Western Stations at fixed charges, under the control of the station-masters. The fares charged for through tickets do not in any case include the conveyance of luggage between the stations.

CHEAP SATURDAY TO MONDAY TICKETS.—On Saturdays and Sundays 1st and 2nd class return tickets to Windsor are issued at Paddington, Kensington, Uxbridge-road, Westbourne-park, Aldgate, Bishopsgate, Moorgate-street, King's Cross, and stations on the Metropolitan Railway between Aldgate and Edgware-road inclusive; also from Hammersmith, Shepherd's Bush, Latimer-road, and Notting-hill, available for the return journey till the Monday following inclusive. Fares from either of the above-mentioned stations: 1st class, 4s. 6d.; 2nd class, 3s. 6d. Similar tickets are also issued from Mansion House, Charing Cross, Victoria, and all Stations on the District Railway between Mansion House and Hammersmith inclusive, also from Kensington (High-street), West Brompton and Walham Green, via Ealing only, available for the same period and at the same fares.

Similar tickets are also issued on Saturdays only from Victoria, Battersea, Chelsea, and West Brompton, available for return during the same period and at the same fares.

On Saturdays and Sundays cheap 1st and 2nd class return tickets to Henley are issued at Paddington, Kensington, Uxbridge-road, Westbourne-park, Hammersmith, Shepherd's Bush, Latimer-road, and Notting-hill, available for the return journey till the following Monday inclusive. Fares: 1st class, 7s. 6d.; 3rd class, 5s. Also from Aldgate, Bishops-gate, Moorgate-street, King's Cross, and stations on the Metropolitan Railway between Aldgate and Edgware-road, inclusive; and from Mansion House, Blackfriars, Charing Cross, Victoria, and all stations on the District Railway, between Mansion House and Gloucester-road inclusive; via Earl's Court and Westbourne-park only. Fares: 1st class, 8s.; 2nd class, 5s. 6d.

Tickets are also issued on Saturdays only from Victoria, Battersea, Chelsea, and West Brompton, available for return during the same period. Fares: 1st class, 7s. 6d.; 2nd class, 5s.

These tickets must be used on the down journey on the date of issue, but are available for return journey by any train on Sunday or Monday.

BOATS AND CANOES are conveyed at the risk of the owner by passenger trains at rates which may be obtained of the station-masters. In cases, however, where the crew, not less than four in number, travel with the boat, the charge for the latter will be reduced one-third; but in order to obtain this reduction previous application must be made to the superintendent of the line.

The reduction is made only one way if the crew accompany the boat only one way; but is made both ways if they accompany the boat both going and returning.

SEASON TICKET RATES.

PADDINGTON TO	FIRST CLASS.						SECOND CLASS.					
	Twelve months.	Nine months.	Six months.	Three months.	Two months.	One month.	Twelve months.	Nine months.	Six months.	Three months.	Two mnths.	One month.
	£ s. d.	£ s. d.	£ s. d.	£ s. d.	£ s. d.	£ s. d.	£ s. d.	£ s. d.	£ s. d.	£ s. d.	£ s. d.	£ s. d.
Brentford ..	15 0 0	..	9 0 0	5 10 0	..	..	11 0 0	..	7 0 0	4 0 0	..	..
Windsor ..	24 0 0	20 0 0	14 0 0	7 10 0	5 .5 0	3 0 0	18 0 0	15 0 0	10 10 0	5 12 6	3 17 6	2 5 0
Taplow	25 10 0	22 0 0	14 15 0	8 10 0	6 10 0	3 15 0	19 5 0	16 10 0	11 0 0	6 7 6	4 17 6	2 5 0
Maidenhead	26 15 0	23 0 0	15 5 0	8 17 6	6 15 0	4 0 0	20 2 6	17 5 0	11 12 6	6 12 6	5 0 0	3 0 0
Cookham ..	29 15 0	25 10 0	17 0 0	9 15 0	7 10 0	4 7 6	22 5 0	19 5 0	12 15 0	7 5 0	5 12 6	3 5 0
Bourne End	30 10 0	26 5 0	17 10 0	10 0 0	7 15 0	4 10 0	22 15 0	19 15 0	13 2 6	7 10 0	5 15 0	3 7 6
Gt. Marlow	35 0 0	30 5 0	20 5 0	11 10 0	9 0 0	5 5 0	26 5 0	22 15 0	15 2 6	8 15 0	6 12 6	3 18 6
Shiplake ..	34 5 0	29 15 0	19 15 0	11 10 0	8 15 0	5 0 0	25 15 0	22 5 0	14 17 6	8 12 0	6 10 0	3 17 6
Henley .. ⎫ Reading.. ⎭	36 0 0	31 0 0	20 15 0	11 17 6	9 2 6	5 5 0	27 0 0	23 5 0	15 10 0	8 17 6	6 12 6	3 17 6
Pangbourne	39 5 0	32 10 0	24 0 0	14 10 0	10 15 0	5 10 0	29 10 0	24 10 0	19 10 0	10 0 0	7 10 0	4 2 6
Goring	41 10 0	34 5 0	25 10 0	15 5 0	11 5 0	5 15 0	31 5 0	26 0 0	20 10 0	10 10 0	7 15 0	4 5 0
Wallingford	47 5 0	..	29 0 0	17 10 0	..	..	35 10 0	..	23 10 0	12 0 0	..	..
Radley	52 0 0	..	32 0 0	19 5 0	..	..	39 5 0	..	25 15 0	13 5 0	..	..
Abingdon ..	53 10 0	..	33 0 0	19 15 0	..	..	40 5 0	..	26 10 0	13 10 0	..	..
Oxford	56 15 0	..	35 0 0	21 0 0	..	..	42 15 0	..	28 5 0	14 10 0	..	..
Government duty extra												

SEASON TICKET RATES.

FARRINGDON STREET TO	FIRST CLASS.						SECOND CLASS.					
	Twelve months.	Nine months.	Six months.	Three months.	Two months.	One month.	Twelve months.	Nine months.	Six months.	Three months.	Two mnths.	One month.
	£ s. d.	£ s. d.	£ s. d.	£ s. d.	£ s. d.	£ s. d.	£ s. d.	£ s. d.	£ s. d.	£ s. d.	£ s. d.	£ s. d.
Brentford ..	18 0 0	15 10 0	10 5 0	6 0 0	4 12 6	2 12 6	13 10 0	11 10 0	7 15 0	4 10 0	3 7 6	2 0 0
Windsor ..	26 10 0	21 17 6	15 5 0	8 2 6	5 15 0	3 5 0	20 0 0	16 10 0	11 10 0	6 2 6	4 5 0	2 10 0
Taplow	29 10 0	25 10 0	17 10 0	10 0 0	7 15 0	4 7 6	22 5 0	19 0 0	12 15 0	7 7 6	5 12 6	3 5 0
Maidenhead	30 15 0	26 5 0	17 12 6	10 2 6	7 17 6	4 12 6	22 17 6	19 15 0	13 7 6	7 12 6	5 17 6	3 7 6
Cookham ..	32 15 0	28 5 0	18 15 0	10 15 0	8 5 0	4 15 0	24 10 0	21 5 0	14 2 6	8 2 6	5 0 0	3 12 6
Bourne End	34 10 0	29 10 0	19 15 0	11 5 0	8 15 0	5 0 0	25 15 0	22 5 0	14 17 6	8 10 0	6 10 0	3 15 0
Gt. Marlow	39 0 0	33 10 0	22 10 0	12 15 0	10 0 0	5 15 0	29 5 0	25 5 0	16 17 6	9 15 0	7 7 6	4 6 0
Shiplake ..	38 10 0	33 0 0	22 0 0	12 15 0	9 15 0	5 12 6	28 15 0	24 15 0	16 10 0	9 10 0	7 5 0	4 5 0
Henley ..) Reading.. }	40 0 0	34 10 0	23 0 0	13 5 0	10 2 6	5 15 0	30 0 0	25 17 6	17 5 0	9 17 6	7 12 6	4 7 6

SEASON TICKET RATES.

MOORGATE STREET OR BISHOPS-GATE TO	FIRST CLASS.						SECOND CLASS.					
	Twelve months.	Nine months.	Six months.	Three months.	Two months.	One month.	Twelve months.	Nine months.	Six months.	Three months.	Two mnths.	One month.
	£ s. d.	£ s. d.	£ s. d.	£ s. d.	£ s. d.	£ s. d.	£ s. d.	£ s. d.	£ s. d.	£ s. d.	£ s. d.	£ s. d.
Brentford ..	19 0 0	16 7 0	10 17 0	6 7 0	4 17 6	2 16 0	14 5 0	12 3 0	8 4 0	4 15 0	3 11 6	2 2 6
Windsor ..	26 10 0	21 17 6	15 5 0	8 2 6	5 15 0	3 5 0	20 0 0	16 10 0	11 10 0	6 2 6	4 5 0	2 10 0
Taplow	30 10 0	26 7 0	18 2 0	10 7 0	8 0 0	4 11 0	23 0 0	19 13 0	13 4 0	7 12 6	5 16 6	3 7 6
Maidenhead	31 15 0	27 2 0	18 5 0	10 9 6	8 2 6	4 16 0	23 2 0	20 8 0	13 16 6	7 17 6	6 1 6	3 10 0
Cookham ..	33 15 0	29 2 0	19 7 0	11 2 0	8 10 0	4 18 6	25 5 0	21 18 0	14 11 6	8 7 6	6 9 0	3 15 0
Bourne End	35 10 0	30 7 0	20 7 0	11 12 0	9 0 0	5 3 6	26 10 0	22 18 0	15 6 6	8 15 0	6 14 0	3 17 6
Gt. Marlow	40 0 0	34 7 0	23 2 0	13 2 0	10 5 0	5 18 0	30 0 0	25 18 0	17 6 6	10 0 0	7 11 6	4 8 6
Shiplake ..	39 10 0	33 17 0	22 12 0	13 2 0	10 5 0	5 16 0	29 10 0	25 8 0	16 19 0	9 15 0	7 9 0	4 7 6
Henley ..) Reading.. }	41 0 0	35 7 0	23 12 0	13 12 0	10 7 6	5 18 6	30 15 0	26 10 6	17 14 0	10 2 6	7 16 6	4 10 0
Pangbourne	44 5 0	38 5 0	26 17 0	16 4 6	12 7 6	7 2 6	33 5 0	28 15 0	21 14 0	11 5 0	8 15 0	5 0 0

CHEAP DAY EXCURSIONS. — Cheap Day Excursion Tickets are issued by certain specified trains, from May 1 to October 31, to the following places from Paddington, Westbourne-park, Kensington (Addison-road), Uxbridge-road, West Brompton, Chelsea, and Battersea. Also from Aldgate, Bishopsgate, Moorgate-street, Farringdon-street, and stations on the Metropolitan Railway between Aldgate and Edgware-road inclusive ; and from Hammersmith, Shepherd's Bush, Latimer-road, and Notting-hill, there and back, in 3rd class carriages, at the following fares :

	s. d.		s. d.
Windsor	2 6	Bourne End ..	3 6
Maidenhead ..	3 0	Great Marlow..	3 6
Taplow..	3 0	Henley..	3 6
Cookham	3 6		

Cheap Day Excursion Tickets are also issued to Windsor, by through trains via Ealing, from Mansion House and all stations on the District Railway between Mansion House and Ealing Common inclusive, and from Kensington (High-street) and stations between Putney Bridge and West Brompton inclusive, at the following fares :

	s. d.
From all Stations except Acton Green, Mill Hill Park, and Ealing Common	2 6
From Acton Green..	2 3
From Mill Hill Park, and Ealing Common	2 0

Cheap Day Excursion Tickets to the following places are also issued from the Mansion House and all stations on the District Railway between Mansion House and Earl's Court inclusive, from Kensington (High-street) and stations between Putney Bridge and West Brompton inclusive (*via* Earl's Court and Westbourne-park) at the following fares:

	s.	*d.*		*s.*	*d.*
Maidenhead	3	0	Bourne End	3	6
Taplow	3	0	Great Marlow	3	6
Cookham	3	6	Henley	3	6

These tickets are only available by specified trains as shown on handbills, copies of which may be had at Paddington, at any of the Great Western Stations or Receiving Offices in London, and also at the Metropolitan and District Railway Stations. Passengers must be careful to note that if the cheap tickets are used by any other than the specified trains, or if the journey there and back be not completed in the one day, the full ordinary fares will be charged.

SALOON CARRIAGES.—Saloon carriages constructed to carry about twenty-four passengers (1st class only) may be retained for parties of not less than eight passengers. Application should be made to the superintendent of the line, Paddington Station, some days before the date on which the carriages will be required, as the number is limited, and in the summer there is often a great demand for them. These carriages are not retained for parties holding picnic or other tickets issued at reduced rates.

CHANGING TO AND FROM THE METROPOLITAN LINE.—Passengers between the Metropolitan line and the Great Western Railway change either at Bishop's-road, Praed-street, or Westbourne-park. Some of the main-line trains do not stop at Westbourne-park, and therefore persons not fully conversant with the time-table will do well to change at Bishop's-road. Westbourne-park is, however, more convenient for passengers coming from Hammersmith, Kensington, or the Western suburbs served by the Metropolitan trains running through that station, as the change is made by simply walking from one side of the platform to the other.

The Metropolitan and Metropolitan District Extension is now completed, and trains run round the Circle *via* Praed-street, Moorgate-street, Aldgate, Mansion House, and High-street, Kensington. Passengers for Paddington by those trains must change at Praed-street Station. Bishop's-road communicates with the Paddington Station by means of a covered way; but persons passing to and from the Praed-street Station must cross the street. The authorised charge for conveying luggage between Paddington and Bishop's-road or Praed-street is 2d. per package, irrespective of weight.

PRIVATE BROUGHAMS. — Broughams may be hired at the Paddington Station at a fixed charge of for the first hour, 3s.; after the first hour, 2s. 6d. per hour; or at 1s. 6d. per mile if according to distance. A note to the station-master will always secure the attendance of as many carriages as may be required on the arrival of the train.

PRIVATE OMNIBUSES can also be hired. For terms apply to the station-master.

Greenhithe, Kent, on the right bank at the junction of Long and Fiddler's Reaches, from London 21 miles. A station on the North Kent Railway 20 miles from Charing Cross; express trains take about 45 minutes. The station is 10 minutes' walk from the river at the Pier Hotel, where there is a jetty (toll 1d.) recently erected in place of the old pier. Population 1,452. Soil, gravel and chalk. The *Arethusa* and *Chichester* training-ships for boys, and the *Worcester*, the ship of the Thames Nautical Training College, are stationed here, and here also are the headquarters of the Junior Thames Yacht Club (*all of which see*). Some considerable business is done by the cement works in the neighbourhood, not altogether to the satisfaction of some of the inhabitants, and many river pilots and masters of vessels complain loudly of the nuisance arising from the smoke of the numerous chimneys. The principal mansion at Greenhithe is Ingress Abbey, facing the river, which was formerly the residence of Alderman Harmer, and was constructed in part of stones from Old London Bridge. There are some good houses at the back of the village on what is known as The Terrace and in its neighbourhood. A masonic lodge is held at the Pier Hotel. The church is a handsome modern building in the early decorated style, picturesquely situated on the London-road. A short distance from Greenhithe—approached either from the London-road or by a footpath immediately opposite the railway station, a few minutes' walk—is Stone Church, a well-known landmark. The church has been recently restored by Mr. Street, who is of opinion that it was built by the same architect as Westminster Abbey. They were certainly built at the same time, and there are many points of resemblance between them. The chancel is remarkable for the great beauty of the carving of the arch and of the arcade on marble pillars which runs round the walls, and which Mr. Street pronounces to be "among the very best sculpture of the age that we have in this country." Among other features of interest are some ancient brasses.

The view from the churchyard is extensive ; visitors should by no means overlook the remarkably fine yew-tree which stands near the west door of the church.

There is a village club. Subscription, for working-men, 5s. per annum, or 1s. 6d. per quarter ; honorary members, 10s. per annum, 3s. per quarter. Reading-room open from 6 to 10 p.m., except Monday. Smoking-room open daily from 8 a.m. to 10 p.m. Library of 1,000 volumes.

PLACES OF WORSHIP.—St. Mary the Virgin, and Stone Church ; the Roman Catholic Church of Our Lady of Mount Carmel ; and Congregational and Wesleyan Chapels.

FIRE.—Volunteer Brigade : 2 officers and 11 men.

HOTELS.—"The Pier," "The White Hart," both in High-street.

POLICE.—No station ; 2 constables live in the village.

POSTAL ARRANGEMENTS.—Post Office (money order, savings bank, telegraph, and insurance), High-st. Mails from London at 8 a.m., 12.40 and 6.30 p.m. Mails for London, 1.15 and 8.15 p.m. There is also a branch office on The Terrace.

NEAREST *Station* and *Ferry*, Greenhithe.

FARES to London (Charing Cross) : 1st, 3/3, 4/6 ; 2nd, 2/6, 3/6 ; 3rd, 1/8, 2/9.

Greenwich Hospital and Royal Naval College, Greenwich, S.E.— Greenwich Hospital was founded by William III. Immediately after the death of Queen Mary, his consort, and was intended as a memorial of her virtues, and of the great victory of La Hogue ; "a monument," as Macaulay says, " the most superb that was ever erected to any sovereign." The building, a grand specimen of classical architecture, and one of Sir Christopher Wren's finest designs, was originally intended as an asylum for wounded and disabled sailors, in whom Queen Mary was greatly interested. The first stone in the building was laid in 1695, and ten years later forty-two seamen were admitted to the benefits of the asylum. This number in course of time was increased to something like three thousand ; but in 1865 an Act of Parliament was passed offering advantageous terms to such of the pensioners as would leave, and in 1869 another Act finally disestablished King William's foundation. When the Hospital was occupied by the pensioners it became one of the sights·of London, and it is possible that a too liberal distribution of *baksheesh* on the part of the public may have had something to do with the deterioration which was observable in the manners and customs of the in-pensioners during the later days of their existence. Nowadays, although one of their chief attractions exists no longer, Greenwich Hospital and Park are still well worthy a visit. The Painted Hall contains some fine pictures of sea-fights, and there are some noteworthy statues of celebrated sailors. The most interesting of the Greenwich sights, however, are the relics of Nelson—notably the Trafalgar coat and waistcoat. The public are admitted free. From Cannon-street (17 min.), 1st, -/10, 1/3 ; 2nd, -/8, 1/- ; 3rd, -/5, -/8. Charing Cross, (27 min.), 1st, 1/-, 1/6 ; 2nd, -/9, 1/2 ; 3rd, -/6, -/9 ; also by steamboat from all piers.

Greenwich Reach runs between Greenwich and the Isle of Dogs. Bearings S.S.E. and E.N.E.

Grove Park Rowing Club, Chiswick. —Amateur. Election by ballot in committee, one "negative vote" in five to exclude. Entrance fee, a £1 share in the Grove Park Boat-house Company (Lim.). Subscription, £1 11s. 6d. ; honorary members, £1 1s. Colours, red, black, and yellow. Club-house, Grove-park, Chiswick.

Gudgeon (The).—It is doubtful whether this fish is so abundant in the river, or that it reaches anything like the individual size as formerly. A gudgeon of the present day of two ounces, or about seven inches in length, is a monster fish. They swim in large shoals always close to the bottom, and are taken with the same tackle as that used for dace, excepting that the hook should be almost of the smallest. The best bait is a small portion of red worm, sufficient to cover the hook and no more ; for if there is a portion hanging down, it will be seized and nipped off by this bold biter. Fifteen to twenty dozen may be caught by a single rod on a favourable day. The minnows here, however, as do the bleak in the roach and dace swims, prove a great annoyance, and as there appears to be no way to get rid of them, their presence must be put up with. The bait should drag on the ground, the float slightly kept in the rear, that the bait may tilt, advance, and present itself to the fish without the interference of the line. They will bite in the hottest weather and in the middle of the day, when all other fish are lazy and indisposed to feed. Gudgeon fishing is a favourite pursuit with ladies, who are often more skilful in the capture than the stronger sex.

Halfway Reach, nearly two miles from Crossness—the Southern outfall—to the top of Erith Reach. Dagenham Reach and Marsh are on the left (Essex) bank. On the other side are the extensive Erith Marshes. Bearings S.E. by E. and N.W. by W.

Halliford, Middlesex (*and see* CAUSE-WAY STAKES) on the left bank, between Shepperton and Walton ; from London 28¾ miles, from Oxford 82¾ miles. Halliford—generally known as Lower Halliford, there being a so-called Upper Halliford in the parish of Sunbury—is a hamlet much in favour with anglers, with a fine view, across the river, of Oatlands Park and the Surrey hills. An iron bridge connects the counties of Middlesex and Surrey at Halliford ; the old brick bridge, with its numerous arches, having succumbed some years ago in a disastrous flood. There is no particular point calling for remark at Halliford, except that it has a very comfortable and reasonable hotel in Stone's well-known "Ship," which is largely used by anglers and rowing men. Shepperton rai'way station is an easy fifteen minutes' walk from the "Ship."

Punts now begin to thicken, and as many may be counted in a mile as in

twenty above ; yet roach are taken by the five to twelve dozen in a day with a single rod, and all the persistent angling appears to have no appreciable effect upon their presence.

There is a Wesleyan Chapel in the village.

POSTAL ARRANGEMENTS.—Post Office (money order, telegraph, and savings bank), about six minutes' walk to the left from the river. Mails from London, 7 and 10.40 a.m., 6.20 p.m.; Sunday, 7 a.m. Mails for London, 9.10 a.m., 2.0, 7.30, and 8.40 p.m. ; Sunday, 10.10 p.m.

NEAREST *Bridges,* up, Chertsey, 2¾ miles ; down, Walton 1 mile. *Locks,* up, Shepperton 1¼ mile ; down, Sunbury, 2½ miles. *Railway Station,* Shepperton.

FARES, Shepperton to Waterloo, 1st, 3/-, 4/-; 2nd, 2/4, 3/-; 3rd, 1/6½, 2/6.

Hambleden, Bucks, on the left bank. Population, 1,550. Soil, chalky. The diminutive village of Hambleden stands some distance from the river, its waterside suburb, so to speak, being Mill End, close to Hambleden Lock ; from London 62¾ miles, from Oxford 48¾ miles. There is little inducement to walk the mile or so, which separates this retired hamlet from the river, although it is easy to understand the attraction that Hambleden and its neighbourhood have for the landscape painter. The handsome old church, approached through a good lych-gate with two dormers, contains in the north aisle an alabaster monument of Sir Cope and Lady D'Oyley and their ten children. They are all in the usual kneeling posture, elaborately painted and gilded, the sons with the father, the daughters with the mother. Some of the figures bear skulls in their hands, probably to intimate that they had died before the erection of the monument. Lady D'Oyley was the sister of Quarles, of the "Emblems," to whom probably the epitaph to his sister is to be attributed. It runs thus :

Would'st thou reader draw to life
The perfect copy of a wife,
Read on then redeeme from shame
That lost that honourable name.
This dust was once in spirit a Jael
Rebecca in grace in heart an Abigail ;
In works a Dorcas to ye Church a Hanna
And to her spouse Susanna
Prudently simple providently wary
To th' world a Martha and to Heaven a Mary.

The inscription to the memory of Sir Cope, who died in 1633, fifteen years after his wife, is still more gushing :

Cope D'Oyley, died 1633.
Ask not me who's buried here ;
Goe ask the Commons, ask ye Sheire,
Goe ask ye Church ; they'll tell thee who
As well as blubbered eyes can doe ;
Goe ask ye Heraulds ; Ask ye poore ;
Thine eares shall heare enough to ask no more
Then, if thine eye bedewe this sacred vrne
Each drop a pearle will turn
T' adorne his Tombe ; or, if thou canst not vent
Thou bringst more marble to his monument.

It is further recorded that "they lived together in inviolated bands of holy wedlocke 22 yeares and multiplied themselves into 5 sonnes and 5 daughters." Close by the D'Oyley tomb is a very old stone coffin of unusual size, and in the vestry is a magnificent—restored—old oak press very richly carved with coats-of-arms, dragons, figures, and devices innumerable. In Hambleden parish, a little distance up the river, and with lawns extending to its bank, is Greenlands, the seat of the Right Hon. W. H. Smith, M.P., concerning which Langley gives the following account :

"The earliest deeds relative to this estate are from George Chowne to Robert Shipwath, of an ancient family here, as appears from several memorials in the Church ; from them it passed to a younger branch of the Doyley family, who resided here many years, as appears from various evidences. It was the jointure of Lady Periam, wife of Sir Robert Doyley, afterwards married to Sir Henry Neville, and lastly to Sir William Periam, knights. She died May 3rd, 1621, and was buried at Henley. By her will it appears that the house was of great extent and richly furnished. Among many other charitable bequests, her ladyship left a farm called the Borough, in this parish, to Archbishop Laud, in trust, to be applied to some college in Oxford, at his discretion. His Grace in consequence founded a fellowship and two scholarships in Balliol College, but without any preference to the Grammar School at Henley, also endowed by Lady Periam, or to the county of Bucks, in which the estate is situated. After Lady Periam's decease the estate came to John, brother of Sir Robert Doyley, and descended to his son, Sir Cope Doyley, to whom there is a monument in Hambleden Church. His eldest son and heir, John Doyley, who resided at Greenlands during the commencement of the Great Rebellion, and was firmly attached to the royal cause, had the misfortune to have his house converted into a garrison." In 1644 the house underwent a long siege at the hands of the Parliamentary forces under Lord Essex. He was succeeded by General Brown, who planted batteries on the opposite side of the river, which "made many shot and much battered" the house, and almost "beat it about the ears of the garrison." The garrison eventually surrendered to General Brown, but marched out with all the honours of war. The present house bears little resemblance to the former one ; the situation is extremely beautiful. Thomas Chaucer, son of Geoffrey Chaucer, the poet, died at an estate here in 1434.

INNS.—"Flower Pot," Aston, across the river ; "Stag and Huntsman," in the village.

PLACES OF WORSHIP.—St. Mary's, and Congregational Chapel.

POSTAL ARRANGEMENTS.—Post Office (money order, savings bank, and telegraph office). Mails from London, 7.30 a.m. Mails for London, 6 p.m. ; Sunday, 10.45 a.m.

NEAREST Bridges, up, Henley 2¼ miles; down, Marlow, 6 miles. Locks, Hambleden ; up, Marsh 3¼ miles ; down, Hurley 3¾ miles. Ferry, Aston. Railway Station, Henley.

FARES from Henley to Paddington, 1st, 6/3, 10/9 ; 2nd, 4/8, 8/-; 3rd, 2/11½.

Hammersmith, London, S.W.—On the left bank, is chiefly remarkable on the river for The Mall, just above the bridge, which contains, besides some modern houses, a few remnants of the Anne and Georgian periods. Below bridge the bank is more commercial and less pleasing. A suspension bridge, with carriage road, spans the river at this point, and was for many years a favourite and cheap grand stand on the University Boat-race day. Regard for the public safety has induced the authorities to close it during the race. It is now (1885) being rebuilt. At Hammersmith are the headquarters of a number of rowing clubs, and Biffen's well-known boat-house is on the Mall-road.

NEAREST Railway Stations, District and Metropolitan, Broadway ; Omnibus

Routes, Hammersmith, and Hammersmith and Barnes ; *Steamboat Pier*, Hammersmith.

Hampton, Middlesex, on the left bank ; from London 24¼ miles, from Oxford 87¼ miles. A station on the Thames Valley Line of the London and South Western Railway, 14½ miles from Waterloo ; trains average about forty-five minutes. Flys meet the trains. The station is about five minutes' walk from the landing-stage. Population, 3,915. Soil, gravel. Hampton is a small town scattered over a considerable space ; a number of villas and houses of a similar class having from time to time been added to the original street or strand of Hampton. The Cockney appellation 'Appy 'Ampton arises from the Hampton races (which, in point of fact, do not take place at Hampton at all, but at Molesey Hurst on the other side of the river, and in another county), which occur twice in the year. "All the fun of the fair" is to be found at the June meeting, and the road has quite a miniature Derby Day appearance. The sport, however, is seldom brilliant, a circumstance which makes little difference to the holiday people, who come out more for a picnic and "a spree" than to enjoy the "sport of kings." The course is a flat oval, about a mile and a half. The T.Y.C. is a little over half a mile in length and quite straight.

Amongst the notabilia of Hampton is Garrick's Villa on the bank of the river, opposite the island just past the church. The house itself stands some little distance back, being separated from the lawn which abuts on the river by the high road, under which Garrick constructed a short tunnel. On the lawn is a summer-house, sometimes described as a temple, which at one time contained Roubiliac's statue to Shakespeare, afterwards removed to the hall of the British Museum.

The Hampton Grammar School was founded in 1556, reconstituted 1878, and the buildings now stand near the railway-station. The course of instruction includes all the usual branches of a liberal education. The fees are from 3½ to 4½ guineas per term, of which there are three in the year ; boys not resident in Hampton or Hampton Wick pay an entrance fee of £2. The head-master takes a

limited number of boarders at £60 per annum, exclusive of tuition fee. The assistant-masters also take boarders.

At Tangley Park, near Hampton, is the Female Orphans' Home, the object of which is to train children for domestic service. All children of the ages from four to ten, who have lost both parents, and have no relatives able to provide for them, are eligible for admission. There is no election, but candidates are received as vacancies occur. The present number is limited to 50. The institution is supported by subscriptions.

The register dates from 1512, but the church itself is a comparatively modern building, not by any means to be commended, having been built at a disastrous architectural period. Unpromising as is its exterior it is not undeserving a visit, there being some curious monuments and epitaphs. At the west end of the church is a large marble monument, unfortunately mutilated, representing in life-size a Miss Susannah Thomas and her mother. In the western vestibule is a very curious monument with a recumbent female figure, under a canopy, bearing a singular resemblance to one of the ladies in the children's Noah's arks. The lady in question was Sibel, daughter of John Hampden, wife to one of the Penns, of Penn House, and nurse to King Edward VI. The following inscription records her history :

For here is brovght to home the place of longe abode
Whose vertv gvided hath her shippe into the qvyet rode
A myrror of her tyme for vertves of the mynde
A matrone such as in her dayes the like was herd to find
No plante of servile stocke, a Hampden by descent
Vnto whose race 300 yeres hathe friendly fortvne lent
To cowrte she called was to foster vp a kinge
Whose helping hand long lingring sobes to speedie end did bring.
Twoo qvenes that scepter bare gave credyt to this dame
Full many yeres in cowrt she dwelt without disgrac or blame
No house ne worldly wealthe on earthe she did regarde
Before eche joye yea and her life her prince's health prefard
Whose long and loyall love with skilfvl care to serve
Was such as did throvgh heavenly help her prince's thanks deserve

Woolde God the grovnd were grafte with trees
of svche delight
That idell braines of fruitfull plantes might find
just cavs to write
As I have plied my pen to praise this pen with
all
Who lyeth entombed in this grave untill the
trompe her call
This restinge place beholde no svbject place to
bale
To which perforce ye lokers on your fleetinge
bodyes shall.

On the north-east wall is a table to Robert Terwhit, 1616, and in the north gallery is a tablet to David Garrick, nephew of the great "Davy," with a weak inscription by Hannah More; and another to the memory of Richard, son of George Cumberland the dramatist. On the east wall is the monument of Edmond Pigeon, yeoman of the jewel-house to King Henry VIII., "by whose speciall command he attended him at Bouloigne and continued in that office under K. Edw. 6, Qveene Mary and Q. Elizabeth, who made him also clerke of her robes and wardrobes, also of his son Nickolas who succeeded him in both offices." An epitaph on a child, who died at the age of 13 months, contains the following sweetly poetical thought :

Sweet Babe—she tasted of Life's bitter cup,
Refused to drink the potion up !
But turned her little head aside,
Disgusted with the taste and died.

The organ in the church was the gift of William IV.

The deeps here do not yield their roach as formerly; still very fair baskets are obtained in the swim opposite the church.

FIRE.—The engine is kept opposite the "Red Lion Hotel."

HOTELS.—The "Red Lion," close to the river ; "Tagg's Hotel," on the island, about half a mile down, with good boat-houses.

PLACES OF WORSHIP.—St. Mary's, and Wesleyan Chapel.

POLICE.—Metropolitan (T Division), Station, New-street.

POSTAL ARRANGEMENTS.—Post Office (money order, savings bank, telegraph, and insurance), corner of New-street. Mails from London, 6.30 and 9 a.m., 2.20 and 7.20 p.m. ; Sunday, 6.55 a.m. Mails for London, 9.50 a.m., 12.30, 3.30 and 8.10 p.m. ; Sunday, no dispatch.

NEAREST *Bridge*, up, Walton 3 miles ;

down, Molesey 1½ mile. *Locks*, up, Sunbury 2 miles ; down, Molesey 1 mile. *Ferry*, Hampton. *Railway Station*, Hampton.

FARES to Waterloo : 1st, 2/3, 2/9 ; 2nd, 1/9, 2/3 ; 3rd, 1/2, 2/-.

Hampton Court, Middlesex, on the left bank ; from London 23¼ miles, from Oxford 88¼ miles. A terminus on the Hampton Court branch of the London and South Western Railway, 15 miles from Waterloo ; the trains average about 45 minutes. Flys meets the trains. Hampton Court is a very small village, which may be described as consisting of a few good houses on and about the green, and a number of taverns and tea-houses for the refreshment of the numerous excursionists who are attracted to Hampton Court by the palace and park. An ugly iron bridge spans the river at this point. What is called the Hampton Court railway-station is in fact in East Molesey, on the Surrey side of the river. Hampton Court is a great meet for bicyclists, who gather here "in their thousands" on their great parade day in the spring.

Fifteen minutes' walk from the station on the Hampton Court-road, is Hope Cottage, Lady Bourchier's Convalescent Home. Here five inmates are received of the class of servants, needlewomen, or tradespeople. These pay 5s. per week in advance. Ladies sending invalids pay 7s. 6d. per week. Applications for beds are to be made to the Convalescent Committee of the Charity Organisation Society, 15, Buckingham-street, London, W.C. The chapel at Hampton Court Palace is intended for the use of the residents in the palace, but the public is also admitted to divine service. The services are : Sunday, 11 a.m., 3.30 p.m. Saints' Days, 11 a.m. Wednesday and Friday, 10.30 a.m. During Lent and Advent, daily at 10.30 a.m. Holy Communion : Sunday, 8.30 a.m., or after morning service ; on Saints' Days, after morning service. There is a good organ in the chapel by Father Smith.

There are many ways of access to Hampton Court. Besides its own railway-station, Teddington, Twickenham, Hampton, Kingston, and Richmond are all more or less convenient. Steamboats occasionally run up in the summer months

if there be sufficient water in the river.
The Thames Ditton, the Virginia Water,
and the Windsor coaches all pass through
Hampton Court.—(*See* COACHING.)

HOTELS.—"Castle." by the bridge,
Molesey side; "Greyhound" and "King's
Arms," by the park entrance and Lion
Gate; "Mitre," by the bridge, Mid-
dlesex side.

POSTAL ARRANGEMENTS.—Post Office
(money order, savings bank, and telegraph). Mails from London, 7 and 10
a.m., 2.30 and 8 p.m.; Sundays 7 a.m.
Mails for London, 8.45 and 11.55 a.m.,
3.30 and 8 p.m.: Sundays, 10 a.m,

NEAREST *Bridges*, up, Walton 4¾
miles; down, Kingston 3 miles. *Locks*,
up, Sunbury 3 miles; down, Teddington,
4½ miles. *Ferries*, up, Hampton 1 mile;
down, Thames Ditton 1 mile.

FARES to Waterloo; 1st 2/-, 2/9; 2nd,
1/6, 2/-; 3rd, 1/2½, 1/10.

Hampton Court Palace, originally
founded by Cardinal Wolsey in 1515,
and by him presented to Henry VIII.
in 1526, in the same manner in which a
sop is presented to Cerberus, or a tub to a
whale, was for many years a favourite
royal residence. Henry VIII., who added
considerably to Wolsey's buildings, passed
much of his time at Hampton Court.
Here Edward VI. was born and Jane
Seymour died, and here the king was
married to his sixth wife, Katharine Parr.
Edward VI. lived at Hampton Court
Palace, and Queen Mary and Philip of
Spain passed their honeymoon here, and
a grand Christmas supper in the Great
Hall is recorded as having taken place in
their reign. Queen Elizabeth held high
state at Hampton Court, and in James
I.'s time the Palace was the scene of the
great conference between the Presby-
terians and the Established Church. It
was a favourite residence of Charles I.,
and after his execution passed into the
possession of Cromwell. Charles II. and
James II. occasionally visited the Palace.
William III. and Mary made it almost
their permanent place of abode, and
greatly enlarged and improved it. Their
immediate successors also lived at Hampton Court; its last royal occupant having
been George II. Since that time a
portion of the building has been devoted
to the use of the public, and in other

portions suites of apartments are granted
to ladies and gentlemen favoured by the
Crown.

The Palace originally consisted of five
quadrangles and the Great Hall, which
was added by Henry VIII. Two of
Wolsey's courts and the Great Hall
remain; the third, or Fountain Court,
was added by Sir Christopher Wren, to
whom is also due the eastern frontage,
which overlooks the gardens. The Palace
has been well and completely restored,
and the Great Hall especially, which is
described below, has been very perfectly
done.

The state apartments are open to the
public free every day throughout the
year, except Fridays and Christmas Day.
The hours are 10 a.m. to 6 p.m. from
April 1 to September 30, and from 10
a.m. to 4 p.m. during the remainder of
the year. On Sundays they are not open
until 2 p.m. The gardens are open until
8 p.m. in summer, and at other times
till dusk. An average of about 200,000
persons passes through the state rooms
annually. In the two Exhibition years—
1851 and 1862—the numbers were 350,848
and 369,162 respectively.

The entrance to the building, coming
from the railway, is through barracks
immediately opposite the Mitre Hotel.
Passing out of the first court, a staircase
on the left, under the clock-tower (the
groined roof and Tudor rose of the gateway should be remarked), leads to the

GREAT HALL,

a building of magnificent proportions,
especially remarkable for the lofty pitch
of its richly carved and decorated roof,
which is studded with the arms and blazons
of King Henry VIII., and for its elaborate
stained glass windows. Of these the great
west window, which is over the minstrel
gallery, contains the arms, badges, and
cyphers of Henry VIII. and his wives,
whose pedigrees, with their arms, initials,
and badges, are set forth in alternate
windows. The first on the south, or
right, looking from the minstrel gallery, is dedicated to Katharine of Aragon,
the third to Ann Boleyn, the fifth to
Jane Seymour, the eighth, on the opposite side, to Anne of Cleves, the tenth to
Katharine Howard, and the twelfth to
Katharine Parr; the seven intermediate
windows contain the heraldic badges of

HAMPTON COURT.

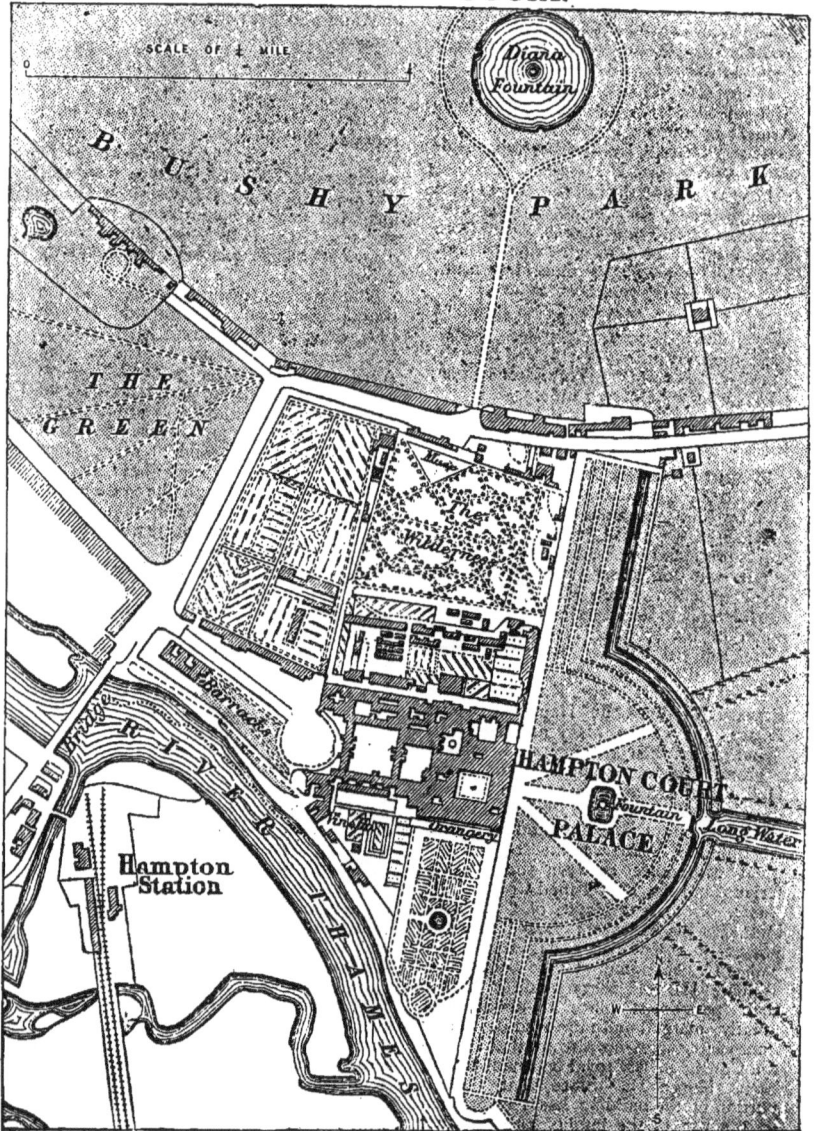

SCALE OF ¼ MILE

Diana Fountain

BUSHY PARK

THE GREEN

The Wilderness

RIVER

Barracks

Orangery

Hampton Station

HAMPTON COURT PALACE

Fountain

Long Water

N
W E
S

Stanford's Geog.ˡ Estab.ᵗ

HAMPTON COURT PALACE, STATE APARTMENTS.

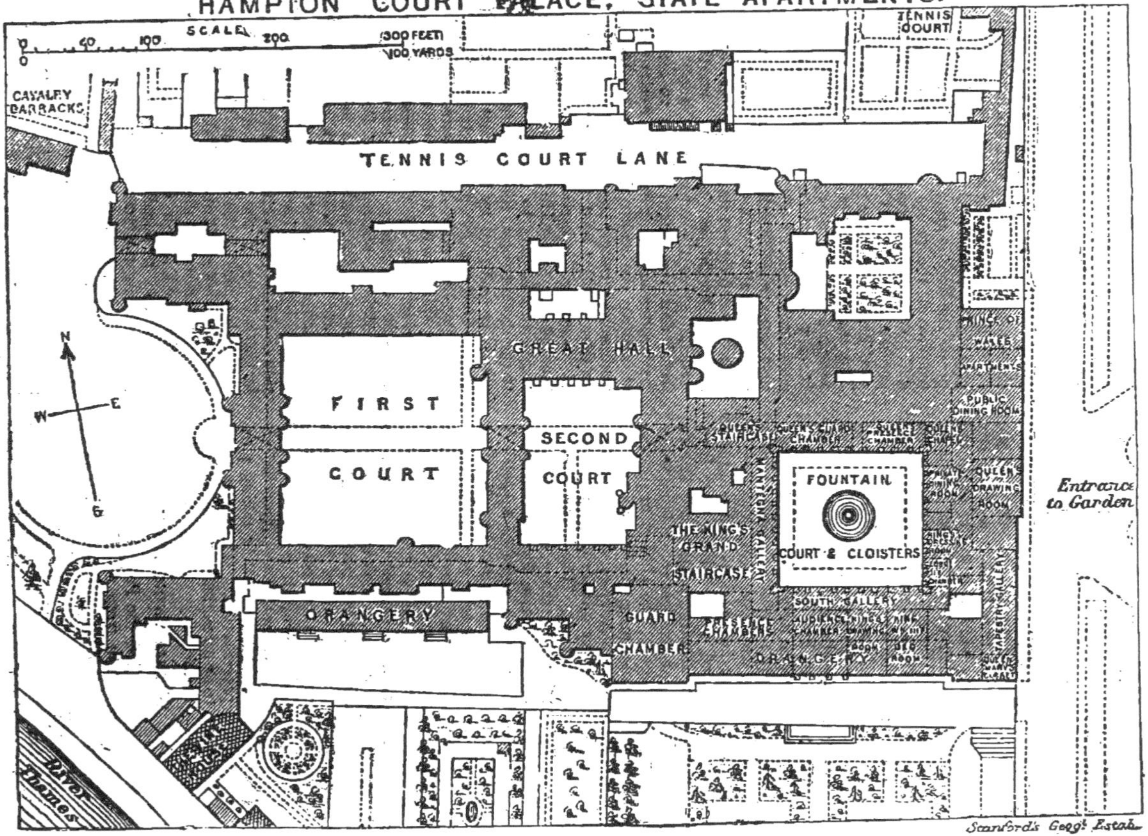

SCALE
0
60
100
200
300 FEET
100 YARDS
CAVALRY BARRACKS
TENNIS COURT
TENNIS COURT LANE
GREAT HALL
FIRST COURT
SECOND COURT
FOUNTAIN
COURT & CLOISTERS
THE KING'S GRAND STAIRCASE
GUARD CHAMBER
PRESENCE CHAMBERS
SOUTH GALLERY
ORANGERY
QUEEN'S STAIRCASE
QUEEN'S GUARD CHAMBER
PUBLIC DINING ROOM
QUEEN'S DRAWING ROOM
N
S
E
W
River Thames
Entrance to Garden
Stanford's Geog! Estab.

Henry VIII.: the lion, portcullis, fleur de lys, Tudor rose, red dragon of York, and the white greyhound of Lancaster. The great east window also contains numerous arms and other heraldic devices, such as those of Henry VII., Henry VIII., Edward III., Edward IV., &c. At the upper end of the Hall is a singularly beautiful bay window with the arms and cyphers of Henry VIII., Jane Seymour, and Cardinal Wolsey. From this end is the best place to take a general survey of the Hall, and hence the best idea is obtained of its great size and perfect symmetry of design. For the information of the accurate people who are never satisfied with general effects, but require to have everything reduced to figures, it may be noted that the length of Wolsey's Great Hall is 106 feet, its width 40 feet, and height 60 feet. The restorations and additions to the stained glass, which have been executed in admirable taste, are due to Mr. Williment, and were completed about forty years ago. The Hall is at present hung with some magnificent tapestry, representing the history of Abraham, bordered with many allegorical and other figures and devices. The series begins on the left of the entrance, and each subject bears a descriptive legend in Latin. The subject of each piece of tapestry is sufficiently apparent to render a detailed description unnecessary here. Under the minstrel gallery are several other pieces of tapestry of allegorical design, one of which represents the seven deadly sins riding on animals supposed by the artist to be appropriate. Before leaving the Hall it may be added that it has more than once been used for theatrical purposes, and tradition even says that Shakespeare's "King Henry VIII., or the Fall of Wolsey," was here acted before Queen Elizabeth, the author taking part in the representation. There appears, however, to be no evidence to support this legend. In the

WITHDRAWING ROOM,

sometimes called the Presence Chamber, which opens out from the Hall, is a further collection of tapestries, the designs of which are remarkable achievements in the way of allegory, thus :—Chastity attended by Lucretia, and Scipio Africanus (at least, so say the experts) drives his chariot over Sensuality ; The Fates

triumph ; Renown summons the illustrious dead, and in another place submits to the influence of Time, the signs of the Zodiac indulging in remarkable pranks the while ; and many similar eccentricities. Obscured and dimmed by time, these tapestries are still well worth careful inspection. Above the tapestries are some graceful cartoons by Carlo Cignani. Opposite the door is another handsome bay window, in the recess of which is an indifferent marble Venus. The ceiling is panelled and adorned with pendants and with badges of rose portcullis, &c., &c. The mantelpiece is of handsome carved oak, and bears a profile portrait of Wolsey. It is a good instance of the value of statistics in matters of this kind to record that considerable difference of opinion exists as to the dimensions of this room. One authority gives its length at 62 feet, and its height at 29 feet; another (official) gives the length as "about 70 feet," and the height "about 20 feet." As neither authority has any hesitation in setting the width down at 29 feet, visitors may congratulate themselves that on that point at least they are possessed of accurate information. Returning through the Great Hall, descending the stairs, and turning to the left, we come to the second court, the northern side of which is occupied by the length of the Hall. Over the gateway at the western end is the dial plate of an astronomical clock, which was, if the date (1540) be correct, one of the earliest public clocks in the country. The tower bears the medallion busts of the Cæsars in terra-cotta, which, with those in the first court, are the restored work of Lucca della Robbia, and were given to Cardinal Wolsey by Pope Leo X. The eastern side of the court was considerably restored in the middle of the last century, and this point marks the end of the principal remains of Wolsey's Palace. The eastern portion of the present building was designed by Sir Christopher Wren, who is also responsible for the Ionic colonnade in the southern side of the second court, a colonnade which might or might not be worth looking at elsewhere, but which here is as inappropriate as a modern chimney-pot hat would have been on the head of Wolsey himself. The visitor entering at the door in the south-east corner of the colonnade has

to deliver up stick and umbrella, parcel
and bag, preparatory to making the
passage of the picture - galleries — an
arduous undertaking, which, it were well
to remark, once begun must be gone
through with, from the first room to the
last—and there are a great many of them
—no turning back is permitted. None
of the attendants are allowed to receive a
fee. Any articles left with the custodian
at the entrance to the galleries, not
claimed by closing hours, will be forwarded if the ticket and address are sent
to the superintendent, at the Palace.
After the transaction of the necessary
business at the foot of the staircase comes
the ascent of the

KING'S STAIRCASE,

which is fine in itself, and would perhaps
be finer if it were not for the sprawling
monstrosities and garish colouring of
that arch impostor, Antonio Verrio. This
Neapolitan painter, whose introduction
to England is not the least of the merry
sins for which Charles II. has to answer,
is seen at his worst in Hampton Court
Palace, and perhaps the King's Staircase
gives as good a notion of his idea of art
as can anywhere be found. The first
room of the two dozen or so devoted to
pictures, which are approached by the
King's Staircase, is the

GUARD CHAMBER,

which is decorated with trophies of arms,
and contains two handsome wrought-iron
screens, the work of H. Shaw, of Nottingham, 1695. Before proceeding to give
any hints as to the pictures best worthy
inspection, it should be stated that in
almost every case the description of the
picture and the name of the artist is
affixed to it, and that there is, therefore,
no absolute necessity for a catalogue.
Painted on each canvas is a number.
This is distinct from that of the cata-
logues, and is the private number affixed
by the surveyor of pictures to identify the
work under any changes. It is here given
in brackets, after the wall number, as a
means of identification should the latter
be changed. Considerable uncertainty
prevails as to the authorship of many of
the Hampton Court pictures. The official
view is adopted here. Throughout the
rooms are many valuable specimens of
the carved woodwork of Grinling Gibbons,

and admirers of blue and white china,
whether Delft or Oriental, will find good
examples in almost every room. In the
Guard Chamber are 9 [15], a rather conventional view of the Colosseum at Rome,
Canaletto ; and a quaintly humorous
portrait, 20 [4], of Queen Elizabeth's
porter, 1580, by Zucchero. There are
also a number of battle - pieces and
portraits in keeping with the character
of the room.
Immediately on the left of the doorway,
in the

KING'S FIRST PRESENCE CHAMBER,

is a very weak picture of King William
III. landing at Torbay, 29 [25], in which
Sir G. Kneller has introduced Neptune
and other incongruous company. A pair
of curious Dutch pictures are 38 [34],
King William III. embarking from
Holland, and 51 [48], his landing at
Brixham. Number 62 [61] is an interesting picture full of detail, representing
King Charles II. taking leave of the
Dutch Court at the time of the Restora-
tion. Number 58 [241] is a very good
group of portraits of William, Duke of
Buckingham, and his family, by Hon-
thorst. Numbers 26 [22], 30 [26], 33 [29],
37 [33], 40 [37], 46 [43], 50 [47], and 53
[51] represent ladies of the Court of
William and Mary, by Kneller, known
as the Hampton Court beauties. Other
Knellers in the room are of very unequal
merit. The chandelier is of the time of
Queen Anne.

THE SECOND PRESENCE CHAMBER.

Here, 85 [87], are the fine equestrian
portraits of Charles I., by Vandyck, and
90 [91], Queen Christina, consort of
Philip IV., by Velasquez, a good example
in excellent preservation ; and also 72
[67], a Sculptor, by Leandro Bassano ;
84 [158], a Venetian Senator, Pordenone ;
91 [159], a Knight of Malta, an excellent
Tintoretto ; 98 [100], a large full-length
of Christian IV., King of Denmark, by
Van Somer ; 103 [128], portrait of
Giorgione, by himself ; and 73 [136],
a much-esteemed Diana and Actæon,
by Giorgione, in which Actæon wears
a pantomime stag's head and court suit,
and in which so many extraneous figures
are introduced that Diana could not have
bathed more publicly even at Margate.

D

THE AUDIENCE CHAMBER.

Number 108 [53], a Portrait of a Man, by Tintoretto ; 113 [111], a portra it by Titian, said to be, but probably not, that of Ignatius Loyola ; 117 [277], John de Bellini, attributed to himself ; 128 [125], a full-length of Elizabeth, Queen of Bohemia, daughter of James I., by Honthorst; 131 [130], the Woman taken in Adultery, Sebastiano Ricci ; 138 [74], a Warrior in Armour, ascribed to Savoldo ; 144 [554], a Concert, Lorenzo Lotto ; 147 [134], a Man's Head, Bassano ; and 149 [68], Alexander de Medicis, by Titian, are among the principal pictures on the walls of the Audience Chamber. In the middle of the room is a triptych for an altar, a work of the highest interest, attributed, perhaps doubtfully, to Lucas Van Leyden. Whatever doubt there may be as to the artist there can be none as to the merit of the pictures. The canopy of this room is that of the throne on which sat James II. when giving audience to the Pope's Nuncio. The furniture and chandelier date from William and Mary and Queen Anne.

THE KING'S DRAWING-ROOM

contains, among others, 154 [145], the Expulsion of Heresy, a portrait picture, by Paolo Veronese ; 155 [333], the Duke of Richmond, by Van Somer ; 158 [905], a good Giorgione, a portrait of a Venetian Gentleman ; 164 [569], a Venus, ascribed to Titian, stated to be a "replica" of the celebrated picture at Florence, but looking much more like an indifferent copy ; 174 [553], a Lady with Orrery and Dog, ascribed to Parmegiano ; 180 [498], a Venetian Gentleman, by Bassano ; and 182 [52], an Italian Lawyer, by Paris Bordone.

KING WILLIAM III.'S BED-ROOM.

In this room are the state bed of Queen Charlotte, and the portraits of the Beauties of Charles II.'s Court, by Sir Peter Lely, which were formerly at Windsor. The fine marble mantelpiece and glass, and the carving of the cornice and ornaments above the mantelpiece by Gibbons, should be specially noticed. Near the head of the bed is a clock which requires winding but once a year, a ceremony which appears to have been omitted on the last anniversary ; and in a corner is an odd old Tompion barometer. The ceiling, unhappily, has been painted by Verrio in a manner calculated to disturb the dreams of any but the stoutest heart.

Besides the Beauties is a delightful portrait, 186 [171], of the Princess Mary as Diana, also by Sir P. Lely, and much pleasanter to look upon than Charles's leering, simpering favourites. The numbers attached to the portraits of these ladies are 185 [170], 195 [189], 196 [190], 197 [191], 199 [193], 204 [198], 205 [199]. No. 194 [188], Louise de Querouaille, Duchess of Portsmouth, is by H. Gascar.

THE KING'S DRESSING-ROOM.

Here, again, Verrio has given reins to his allegorical nightmares. No. 210 [741] is a comic picture of men fighting with bears, by Bassano ; 212 [670], robbers, in a cave, dividing their spoils, is like many other Salvator Rosas.

THE KING'S WRITING CLOSET

contains a mirror so placed as to reflect the whole suite of rooms. Among the pictures may be noted 225 [222], and 243 [229], by Bogdane.

QUEEN MARY'S CLOSET,

containing 251 [247], a Holy Family after Raffaelo, by Giulio Romano ; and 267 [417], Sophonisba, or Fair Rosamond —the choice of subject is elastic—attributed to Gaetano. In

THE QUEEN'S GALLERY

will be found seven large and important pieces of tapestry, after paintings by Le Brun, 1690, representing incidents in the history of Alexander the Great. These have suffered somewhat at the hands of time, but deserve careful notice.

THE QUEEN'S BED-ROOM.

Here is the state bed of Queen Anne. The ceiling is the work of Sir James Thornhill, and among the pictures are, 273 [459], the Queen of James I., by Van Somer ; 275 [462], St. Francis with the Infant Jesus, Guido ; 283 [461], a Princess of Brunswick, the painter of which is not named ; 301 [230], Judith with the Head of Holofernes, by Guido ; 306 [76], a portrait of an Italian Lady with a singular taste in dress, by Parmegiano ; and 307 [456], by Francesco Francia, St. John baptizing Christ, a very fine example of the master.

THE QUEEN'S DRAWING-ROOM

is the centre of the eastern front of Wren's portion of Hampton Court Palace. From its windows is a beautiful view of the gardens with three long avenues of trees stretching away from the Palace towards the river, Kingston Church closing the vista on the left hand, and the canal and fountain lending agreeable variety to the centre. On the ceiling Verrio has depicted Queen Anne in the character of Justice. The walls are hung with the works of Sir Benjamin West.

THE QUEEN'S AUDIENCE CHAMBER.

The state canopy of Queen Mary still hangs in this room, and among the pictures may be mentioned 326 [506], the Duchess of Luneberg, Brunswick, Mytens; 327 [593], a portrait of Don Gusman, another fine Mytens ; 330 [457], Christian, Duke of Brunswick, Honthorst ; a doubtful Holbein, 331 [524], the Meeting of Henry VIII. and the Emperor Maximilian ; 335 [521], the Duke of Brunswick, Mytens ; 340 [510], portraits of Henry VIII. and his family, a work of unusual interest and importance, Holbein; 342 [520] the Field of the Cloth of Gold, also Holbein ; 343 [525], Isabella of Austria, Pourbus ; 346 [780], Anne, Queen of James I., Van Somer ; and 349 [299], a portrait of Queen Elizabeth, in a fancy dress with remarkably fancy blue and white shoes, crowning a stag with flowers. On the right of the picture are three mottoes, and a tablet on the left contains the following lines :

The restles swallow fits my restles minde,
In still revivinge, still renewinge wronges ;
Her just complaintes of cruelty unkinde
Are all the musique that my life prolonges.
With pensive thoughtes my weepinge stagg I crowne,
Whose melancholy tears my cares expresse ;
Hes teares in sylence, and my sighes unknowne,
Are all the physicke that my harmes redresse,
My onely hope was in this goodly tree,
Which I did plant in love, bringe up in care ;
But all in vaine, for now to late I see,
The shales be mine, the kernels others are.
My musique may be plaintes, my physique teares,
If this be all the fruite my love-tree beares.

In the official catalogue this picture is ascribed, hesitatingly, to L. de Heere. On the frame, however, there is the name of Zucchero.

THE PUBLIC DINING-ROOM

is principally remarkable for two excellent Gainsboroughs, 352 [747], Fisher the Composer, and 353 [733], Colonel St. Leger (Handsome Jack); 355 [961], 358 [950], and 359 [960], are good examples

of Hoppner. 360 [951] is a curious picture, by Home, of the King of Oude receiving tribute. Over the noble marble mantelpiece hangs 362 [155], the Nabob of Arcot, G. Willison. 363 [936] is a portrait of Friedrich von Gentz, by Sir Thomas Lawrence ; 395 [587], by Robert Walker, is a portrait of himself ; 369 [847], a capital picture by Michael Wright, represents John Lacy, a comedian of the time of Charles II., in three characters ; and 375 [944] is a portrait of Mrs. Delany, by Opie. In the left corner is the door leading to the Queen's Chapel, &c., but there are still three rooms approached by the door near the window.

THE PRINCE OF WALES'S PRESENCE CHAMBER, DRAWING-ROOM, AND BED-ROOM.

The principal pictures in these rooms are 382 [421] and 382 [432], respectively a Jewish Rabbi and Dutch Lady, both splendid Rembrandts ; 389 [285], Portrait of an Old Man, Quintin Matsys ; 390 [464], Dogs, Snyders ; 393 [249], Singing by Candlelight, Honthorst ; 397 [57], and 398 [437], Boys, Murillo ; 407 [580, not 581, as described in the official catalogue], Van Belchamp ; 413 [516], Louis XVI. of France, Greuze ; 417 [984], Mdlle. de Clermont, Greuze ; and 429 [986], a portrait of Mdme. de Pompadour, a very superior work by the same master. From these rooms visitors return through the Public Dining-room, and pass through the Queen's Private Chapel and Closet, in which the pictures, principally of flowers and birds, are of no great importance. The next apartment is

THE PRIVATE DINING-ROOM,

which looks out on to Fountain Court. The state beds, with crimson trappings, of William and the, which are preserved in this room, and the smaller bed used by George II., do not give a very lively idea of the comforts enjoyed by royal personages. There is some particularly good china here, and among other pictures, a portrait of the Duchess of Brunswick, sister to George III., 507 [603], by Angelica Kauffmann. In the adjoining closet is 507 [64], a curious picture, by Fialetti, representing senators of Venice in the Senate House. In the

QUEEN'S PRIVATE CHAMBER

are 512 [907], an unnamed Queen of Prussia, by an unnamed artist ; 518 [619],

D 2

Frederick, Prince of Wales, a smirking, highly-coloured portrait, by Vanloo ; and 524 [787], a Labyrinth, the eccentric production of Tintoretto.

THE KING'S PRIVATE DRESSING-ROOM has a fine marble bust of a negro, and portraits of four Doges of Venice, by Fialetti, 526 [791 to 794]. 531 [577], is a humorous picture of a barrack-room, by C. Troost.

GEORGE II.'s PRIVATE CHAMBER,

and the closet adjoining, lead to the

SOUTH GALLERY,

where formerly Raffaelle's cartoons, now at South Kensington, were exhibited. This is a very long gallery, divided into compartments, in the third of which is a finely carved marble mantelpiece. It contains many pictures of great value and merit. The following is a list of some of those to which the attention of visitors is especially directed : 559 [513], the Countess of Lennox, Holbein ; 560 [667], Mary Queen of Scots, Zucchero ; 563 [313], Henry VIII., Holbein ; 572 [343], Countess of Derby, L. de Heere : 573 [344], Sir Geo. Carew, Holbein ; 582 [908], La Belle Gabrielle, by an unnamed artist ; 589 [275], a portrait of a Youth, A. Durer ; 593 [1085], 594 [331], portraits of Erasmus, 597, [324], a similar subject, 598 [330], all by Holbein ; 600 [612], St. Christopher with Saints, L. Cranach ; 603 [323], Joannes Frobenius, printer ; 606 [326], King Henry VIII. ; 608 [336], the painter's father and mother, Holbein ; 609 [989], Lazarus Spinola, W. Kay ; 610 [325], "A sidefaced gentleman out of Cornwall," attributed to Holbein ; 611 [401], St. Jerome, after A. Durer ; 613 [290], Sir Francis Walsingham ; 615 [270], Sir P. Carew, both by an unnamed artist ; 616 [293], 619 [273], portraits of Queen Elizabeth, the former by Zucchero, the latter by Gerrard ; 622 [347], a charming portrait of a Lady, Sir A. More ; 632 [316], Francis II. when a boy, Janette ; 633 [291], Philip II. of Spain, Sir A. More ; 642 [345], a companion picture to 622, and an equally good work, by the same artist ; 644 [306], another portrait of a Lady, Sir A. More ; 657 [644], Windsor Castle, Verdussen ; 666 [329], an admirably humorous portrait of Henry

VIII.'s Jester, Will Somers, Holbein ; 676 [234], a small whole-length of a Man, F. Hals ; 684 [825], a flower piece with insects, Withoos ; 704 [959], a wild boar hunt, Snyders, full of life and vigour ; 707 [588], Villiers, Duke of Buckingham, C. Janssen ; 710 [278], a portrait of Raffaelle, attributed to himself ; 763 [514], James I., and 764 [591], his Queen, the companion picture to it, both by Van Somer ; 765 [650], Elizabeth, Queen of Bohemia, a daughter of James I., Derick ; and 707 [106], a Dutch Gentleman, Van der Halst.

THE ANTE ROOM,

adjoining the South Gallery—780 [846], a landscape, Oldenburg—leads to the

MANTEGNA GALLERY.

so called from a set of paintings in distemper, on linen, 9 feet high, by Andrea Mantegna. They are nine in number, 797 [873 to 881], and represent the triumphs of Julius Cæsar. Originally purchased by Charles I., they were sold by Parliament for £1,000, and subsequently repurchased by Charles II. They are in a faded and damaged condition, and it is difficult always to follow the artist's intention. In the same gallery is 798 [892], a quaint portrait of Sir Jeffrey Hudson, by Mytens, and three pictures by unnamed artists. Of these, 793 [901], is a portrait of Jane Shore, who is described on the canvas as "Baker's wife, mistris to a king ; " 808 [899] represents "Schachner of Austria ; " and 809 [958] is a Young Lady with a feather fan. On the

QUEEN'S STAIRCASE

is an immense painting 810 [932], Honthorst, whereof, as is not uncommon with allegorical works of the kind, the subject appears to be in doubt. According to Horace Walpole, it is intended to represent Charles I. and his Queen as Apollo and Diana receiving the Arts and Sciences, the ceremony of introduction being performed by the Duke of Buckingham, as Mercury. Another authority, also quoted in the official guide, is of opinion that the royal personages are the King and Queen of Bohemia in the clouds. The judicious visitor may select either of these interpretations, or indeed any other which may seem good to him, but Honthorst, in any

case, cannot be congratulated on his
work.

THE QUEEN'S GUARD CHAMBER,
like the South Gallery, is divided into
compartments, noticeable in the second of
which are two most singular terminal
figures of beefeaters which serve as supporters to the mantelpiece. Among the
pictures are 815 [967], 816 [966], 819
[970], 821 [965], portraits respectively of
Giulio Romano, Michael Angelo, Tintoretto, and P. del Vaga, by an unnamed
hand; 858 [902], is a portrait of a Man
with a watch in his hand, by Peter Van
Aelst. From this chamber an ante-room
leads to the

QUEEN'S PRESENCE CHAMBER,
in which are numerous pictures of sea-
fights, &c., and two portions of timbers
from Nelson's *Victory*. There are also a
series of views on the Thames, by James
and others, which should be interesting
to readers of this DICTIONARY. They
are 883 [1043], Fleet Ditch, &c.; 884
[1044], Old London Bridge; 885 [1045],
the Old Savoy Palace; 914 [1079], Greenwich Hospital, &c.; 918 [1016], a similar
subject; 920 [1024] the Tower; 921
[1023], old Somerset House and the
Temple; 922 [1026], the Temple again;
923 [1031], another view of the Savoy; and
925 [1032], Westminster Bridge, &c. &c.
This closes the list of apartments open to
the public. The chapel is not visible
except on Sunday, when it is open for
divine service.

Returning from the Queen's Presence
Chamber to the Queen's Staircase, the
visitor again emerges into the Middle
Court; and, after reclaiming any property
which he may have left at the King's
Staircase entrance, proceeds by the
Fountain Court to the gardens, which
extend along the whole east front of the
building. Should the visitor on leaving
the building wish to visit the famous
grape-vine, which is shown (admission,
1d.) as one of the great attractions of
Hampton Court, he will turn to the
right; should he, on the other hand,
prefer to make direct for the Wilderness and the Maze, he will turn to the
left, passing the tennis-court on his way.
The price of admission to the Maze is 1d.
Some writers in treating of Hampton
Court give precise directions how to
traverse the paths of the Maze; but, as

the greater part of the fun consists in
losing your way, and in observing the
idiosyncracies of your fellow-creatures
who are in the same predicament, rather
than getting to the centre and out again
in "the shortest time on record," no clue
to the mystery is given here. To many
people, perhaps, the greatest attraction
of Hampton Court will be found in its
beautiful gardens, which are unreservedly
thrown open to the public. They are
tastefully laid out, and every year considerable ingenuity and skill are displayed
in the carpet-bedding devices, and other
floral adornments of the gardens, by Mr.
Graham, the able superintendent. The
lawns are always in perfect order, there
is abundance of shade from the yews and
other trees with which they are studded,
and seats have been distributed about
with no niggard hand. There is not the
usual annoying restriction as to walking
on the grass, except as to the verge of
the flower beds, and it is pleasant to see
that the request, that the public will
protect what is intended for public enjoyment, is carefully respected.

The principal entrance on the north
is through the Lion Gates, opposite Bushey
Park. Visitors who propose to go through
the galleries are recommended to enter
the palace by the barrack gateway, near
the bridge, already described.

The restrictions imposed by the regulations are few, and are dictated by obvious
considerations for the general convenience
and comfort both of the visitors and
residents in the palace. The following
are the principal rules. No smoking is
permitted in any part of the palace or
grounds. No baskets or parcels are
allowed to be taken into the gardens.
No dogs are admitted. Bath-chairs and
perambulators are allowed to residents
only. Last, and not least, it is fortunately
provided that no public address may be
delivered.

The famous avenue of chestnuts in
Bushey Park leads from the Lion Gates of
Hampton Court Palace to Teddington,
and is one of the chief sights of the spring
season, when its grand old trees are
covered with their pyramids of blossom.
The fountain in the centre of the oval
pond, near the Hampton Court entrance,
is surmounted by a bronze statue of
Diana. The Park contains, besides its
chestnuts, many fine elms and oaks, and

the hawthorns are almost as celebrated as the chestnuts. A herd of deer roam in the park, adding greatly to its romantic character. It is a favourite place for picnics, and after inspection of Hampton Court Palace the contents of the reclaimed baskets and parcels are freely discussed under the shady glades of Bushey.

Hampton Wick, Middlesex, on the left bank, about a mile east of Hampton Court by road ; from London 22 miles, Oxford 89½ miles. A station on the Kingston branch of the London and South Western Railway, 14½ miles from Waterloo ; the trains average about 45 minutes. Population, 2,207. Soil, gravel. Hampton Wick is nowadays practically a suburb of Kingston, with which it is connected by Kingston Bridge, and consists to a large extent of pleasant villa residences.

PLACE OF WORSHIP.—St. Mary's.

POSTAL ARRANGEMENTS.—Post Office (money order and savings bank), High-street. Letters through Kingston. Mails from London 6.45 and 9.15 a.m. ; 2.15 and 7.30 p.m. Mails for London 9 a.m., 12.10, 3.45, and 8.20 p.m.

NEAREST (from Kingston Bridge) *Bridges*, up Hampton Court 3¼ miles : down, Richmond 5 miles. *Locks*, up, Molesey about 3½ miles ; down, Teddington 2 miles. *Railway Station*, Hampton Wick.

FARES to Waterloo (or Ludgate-hill) : 1st, 2/, 2/6 ; 2nd, 1/6, 2/-; 3rd, 1/-, 1/8.

Harbour Masters, for carrying out the bye-laws of the Thames Conservancy, are appointed by that body.—(*See* CONSERVATORS OF THE THAMES.)

Henley, Oxfordshire, on the left bank ; from London 64½ miles, from Oxford 47 miles. The terminus of a branch on the Great Western Railway, from an hour to an hour and a half from Paddington. Flys and omnibuses meet the trains. The station is close to the river, and about five minutes' walk from the bridge. Population, 4523. Henley, the Mecca of the rowing man and one of the most favourite places of pilgrimage for anglers, is a comfortable, prosperous-looking town, set down in a pleasant valley almost entirely surrounded by well-wooded heights, and is as good a place to stay at for the tourist who takes no interest either in

oars or rods, punts or wager-boats, as can well be desired. Both by river and by road there are almost innumerable excursions, and the walks either at the back of the town or on the road to Marlow across the river afford many charming glimpses of some of the prettiest of the Thames scenery. The town itself is well built with good broad streets, the principal business centres being Hart-street, the Market-place, and Bell-street, all of which contain good shops. The outskirts are noticeable for a number of handsome houses, especially towards the Fair Mile, a fine avenue of trees which leads into the north of the town. Henley is under the government of a high steward, a mayor, ten aldermen, and sixteen burgesses. The Town Hall is in the Market-place, and differs in no respect from the usual type of buildings of its class in the neighbourhood. It contains two good portraits, presented to the town by the widow of Sir Godfrey Kneller ; one of George I., by Sir Godfrey himself, and the other of the Earl of Macclesfield, the first high steward of the town. Lady Kneller is buried with her parents at Henley in the church. The church of St. Mary, whose lofty embattled tower is a prominent landmark, as well from the river as from the hills around, stands close to the bridge. It is a fine building, with chancel, north chancel aisle, nave, and aisles, and in the tower hangs a remarkably good peal of bells. A beautiful new west window and an entrance screen of carved oak have been added, and the space under the tower has been formed into a beautiful Baptistery. Under the tower is the monument of Lady Elizabeth Periam : a semi-recumbent figure reclining on its right elbow, and dressed in a ruff, stomacher, and hood. In the right hand is a Book of Hours. Lady Elizabeth died in 1621. Behind the organ is a mural monument, with a marble angel, in memory of certain members of the Elmes family from 1621 to 1720. In the south wall is a tablet with a long inscription to the memory of General Dumouriez, who died near Henley in 1823. In the churchyard is the grave of Richard Jennings, the master builder of St. Paul's Cathedral. Along the sides of the churchyard stand almshouses : four built by Mrs. Messenger, 1669, and rebuilt 1846 ; ten due to Humphrey Newberry, 1664, rebuilt 1846;

and twelve endowed by John Longland, Bishop of Lincoln (a native of Henley), in 1547 ; these were rebuilt in 1830. The church of Holy Trinity is on the south side of the town in the parish of Rother-field Grays. The living is a vicarage, and the patron for the next turn is the Bishop of Oxford.

The Congregational chapel here originated in 1662. The first preacher was the Rev. W. Brice, Fellow of Exeter College, Oxford, rector of St. Mary's, Henley, ejected by the Act of Uniformity. The first pastor was Rev. John Gyles, ejected from the vicarage of Lindridge. The tablet of Mr. Gyles has the following quaint inscription :

Heaven's Pilgrim, pause you here,
And with many drop a teare
O'er John Gyles, from Heaven sent
To preach to men Christ's commandment.
Whose learning, utterance, and parts
Meekness and grace did win all hearts.
Him now you see translated thus
A dying witness to Christ's truth.
Both taught and practis'd from his youth.
His race is run, he's glorified
This stone you see his dust doth hide.
         Deceased 26 Aprill, 1683.

Rev. Humphrey Gainsborough, brother of Gainsborough the painter, was a minister of the chapel for upwards of twenty-eight years. He was a very ingenious man ; is supposed to have been the discoverer of the separate condenser for steam engines ; constructed a weighing-machine for the corporation in 1776 ; made the road to the town over White Hill ; arranged and superintended the construction of the arch and ruins over Twyford-road, at the bottom of the Happy Valley ; constructed the locks on the river near New Mills ; and made many curious clocks, dials, &c. He was offered very good preferment in the Established Church, but nothing would induce him to leave his own people, by whom he was greatly esteemed. The Grammar School was founded in 1604 by James I., and is now managed under a scheme of the Endowed Schools Commissioners. It prepares for the Universities, professions, and public service. Day boys pay £11 per annum, no extras ; boarders, £40 to £50, according to age. The Blue Coat, or Lower Grammar School, was founded by Lady Elizabeth Periam in the reign of

James I., for the purpose of educating, free of all cost, twenty boys of the town. In the reign of George III. the school was united with the Upper Grammar School. Three years ago it came under a new scheme, and is now called the "English School ;" and although under the same governing body as the Upper, or Grammar School, is quite a separate establishment, under its own masters, &c. Twenty boys are still educated free of cost, together with about forty others, who pay a fee of £3 per annum each.

It was on a window at the "Red Lion" at Henley, that Shenstone wrote the now hackneyed lines :

Whoe'er has travelled life's dull round,
Where'er his stages may have been,
May sigh to think he still has found
The warmest welcome at an inn.

The counties of Oxfordshire and Berkshire are united at Henley by a handsome and convenient stone bridge of five arches with stone balustrades. The key-stones of the centre arch represent respectively Thames and Isis. The Thames, which looks down stream, is the conventional bearded old Father Thames crowned with bulrushes ; and the Isis, looking up stream, is, in allusion to the fabled marriage of Thame and Isis, a-female head adorned with water plants. These works of art were executed by the Hon. Mrs. Damer, the daughter of General Conway, who lived at Park Place, near Henley. They have, no doubt, considerable merit, but not so much as to warrant the excessive admiration they have sometimes evoked, and which probably would not have been expressed had it not been for the extravagant eulogium of Horace Walpole, the artist's cousin.

Among the notable houses in the neighbourhood of Henley is Park Place, on the summit of the hill on the Berkshire side. Stonor Park, Henley Park, Phyllis Court, Fawley Court, Greenlands, and many other county houses, are either in or near the parish.

Henley was once justly celebrated for its pike, but is now scarcely worth the trouble of fishing, except for roach and chub.

BANKS.—London and County, Market-place ; Simonds and Co., Market-place.

FAIRS.—March 7, Holy Thursday, Trinity Thursday, and the Thursday after September 21.

FIRE.—Volunteer Fire Brigade; captain-lieutenant, two firemen, engineer, and twenty pioneers; three manual engines and one fire-escape.

HOTELS.—"Angel," at the foot of the bridge; "Catherine Wheel," Hart-street; "Red Lion," foot of the bridge; "Royal," facing the river near the railway-station.

MARKET DAY.—Thursday.

PLACES OF WORSHIP.—Holy Trinity (Rutherford Greys) and St. Mary's; and Baptist, Congregational, and Wesleyan Chapels, and a Friends' Meeting House.

POLICE.—Station, West-street, by the side of the Town Hall.

POSTAL ARRANGEMENTS.—Post Office (money order, savings bank, telegraph, and insurance), Market-place. Mails from London, 7 and 11.30 a.m., 6.45 p.m.: Sunday, 7 a.m. Mails for London, 9.55 a.m.; 3.20, 7.50, and 8.15 p.m.; Sunday, 8.15 p.m.

NEAREST *Bridges*, up, Sonning 6¼ miles; down, Marlow 8 miles. *Locks*, up, Marsh 1 mile; down, Hambleden 2¼ miles. *Ferry*, just below Bolney Court, ½ mile above Marsh Lock. *Railway Station*, Henley.

FARES to Paddington: 1st, 6/3, 10/9; 2nd, 4/8, 8/-; 3rd, 2/11½.

Henley Rowing Club.—The usual amateur qualifications. Subscription, 10s. 6d. Election is by ballot in committee, unless the captain, on private notice being given by a member who objects to a candidate, shall direct the secretary to call a general meeting. If the committee proceed to election, one black ball in three excludes. The club was established in 1830. Colour, blue. Boathouse, near the bridge.

Henley Royal Regatta.—This, the most important gathering of amateur oarsmen in England, takes place usually about the beginning of July, and almost ranks with Ascot among the favourite fashionable meetings of the season. A grand stand is provided, but the accommodation for visitors is not of the best. One of the favourite points of view is the "Red Lion" lawn, where, at the conclusion of the regatta on the second day, the prizes are distributed, but by far the most popular resort is the river itself. Indeed, of late years, this has become so much the case, and the river is so inconveniently crowded with steam launches, house boats, skiffs, gigs, punts, dingeys, canoes, and every other conceivable and inconceivable variety of craft, that the racing boats have sometimes the greatest difficulty in threading a way through the crowd. In this connection some astonishment may be expressed at the supineness of the executive, in regard to the important matter of regulating this annually increasing picnic traffic. As it was years ago, so it seems to be now. The racing boats are always hampered to a more or less inconvenient degree—sometimes even to the point of disaster. No doubt it is extremely difficult to keep the course clear, but certainly much more might be done than at present. As in the case with all boat races, only a very small part of the struggle can properly be seen, except by the fortunate few in the umpire's boat, or by the enthusiastic friends of the competitors who run up the tow-path with the boats.

The course is a little over a mile and a quarter in length, and the races are rowed from Regatta Island, just below Remenham, against the stream, to a point opposite the "Red Lion," and just below the bridge. For the first mile the course is very fair, but the river taking a somewhat sharp turn at what is called Poplar Point, gives a great advantage to the boat with the inside or Berks station. The only chance of equalising the stations is when a high wind blows from the other bank. Under these circumstances men on the Bucks station have the advantage of being sheltered by the bushes, while their opponents out in the open are struggling with the full force of wind and wave. The lead that the Bucks boat is thus enabled to obtain, not unfrequently neutralises the effect of the dreaded corner. Many attempts have been made to improve matters by buoying and by staking out the river with the object of keeping the Berks boat well out in the stream, but hitherto these ingenious arrangements have met with but a very moderate means of success. It has even been suggested that the race should be started below the island, and that the finish should be at Poplar Point. But as this would disestablish the bridge and the lawn, its adoption is, to say the least of it, doubtful.

The principal races in the programme

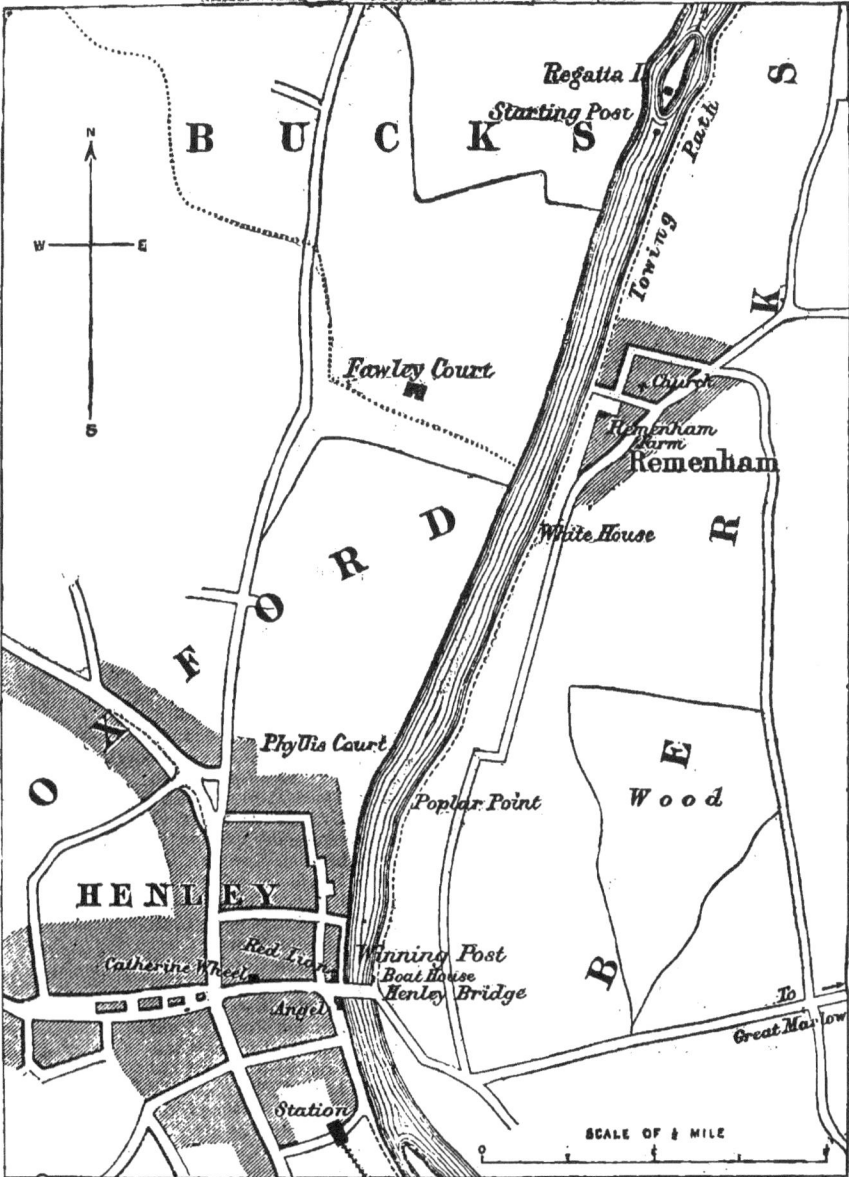

N
W   E
S

B U C K S

Regatta I.
Starting Post
Towing Path

K S

Fawley Court

Church
Remenham
Farm
Remenham

O R D

White House

R

F

Phyllis Court

E

O X

Poplar Point

W o o d

H E N L E Y

Catherine Wheel   Red Lion

Winning Post
Boat House
Henley Bridge

Angel

B

To
Great Marlow

Station

SCALE OF ¼ MILE
0

Stanford's Geog¹ Estab.

are the Grand Challenge Cup for eights, and the Stewards' Challenge Cup for fours, both of which, subject to the regulations of the Regatta Committee, are open to all amateurs, and up to twenty years ago, were frequently competed for by University crews. The Thames Challenge Cup for eights, the Wyfold Challenge Cup for fours,. the Silver Goblets for pairs, the Diamond Challenge Sculls for scullers (the latter the oldest race in the programme), are also open races. The Ladies' Challenge Plate for eights, and the Visitors' Challenge Cup for fours are confined to college and public school crews.

Subjoined is a list of winners of the above prizes from the commencement of the regatta to the present year :

GRAND CHALLENGE CUP FOR EIGHT OARS.

1839 First Trinity, Cambridge
1840 Leander Boat Club
1841 Cambridge Subscription Rooms
1842 Cambridge Subscription Rooms
1843 Oxford University Boat Club(7 oars)
1844 Etonian Club, Oxford
1845 Cambridge University Boat Club
1846 Thames Club, London
1847 Oxford University Boat Club
1848 Oxford University Boat Club
1849 Wadham College, Oxford
1850 Oxford University Boat Club
1851 Oxford University Boat Club
1852 Oxford University Boat Club
1853 Oxford University Boat Club
1854 First Trinity, Cambridge
1855 Cambridge University Boat Club
1856 Royal Chester Rowing Club
1857 London Rowing Club
1858 Cambridge University Boat Club
1859 London Rowing Club
1860 First Trinity, Cambridge
1861 First Trinity, Cambridge
1862 London Rowing Club
1863 University College, Oxford
1864 Kingston Rowing Club
1865 Kingston Rowing Club
1866 Etonian Club, Oxford
1867 Etonian Club, Oxford
1868 London Rowing Club
1869 Etonian Club, Oxford
1870 Etonian Club, Oxford
1871 Etonian Club, Oxford
1872 London Rowing Club
1873 London Rowing Club
1874 London Rowing Club

1875 Leander Boat Club
1876 Thames Rowing Club
1877 London Rowing Club
1878 Thames Rowing Club
1879 Jesus College, Cambridge
1880 Leander Rowing Club
1881 London Rowing Club
1882 Exeter College, Oxford
1883 London Rowing Club
1884 London Rowing Club

STEWARDS' CHALLENGE CUP FOR FOUR OARS.

1842 Oxford Club, London
1843 St. George's Club, London
1844 Oxford University Boat Club
1845 Oxford University Boat Club
1846 Oxford University Boat Club
1847 Christ Church, Oxford
1848 Christ Church, Oxford
1849 Leander Boat Club
1850 Oxford University Boat Club
1851 Cambridge University Boat Club
1852 Oxford University Boat Club
1853 Oxford University Boat Club
1854 Pembroke College, Oxford
1855 Royal Chester Rowing Club
1856 Argonauts Club, London
1857 London Rowing Club
1858 London Rowing Club
1859 Third Trinity, Cambridge
1860 First Trinity, Cambridge
1861 First Trinity, Cambridge
1862 Brasenose College, Oxford
1863 University College, Oxford
1864 London Rowing Club
1865 Third Trinity, Cambridge
1866 University College, Oxford
1867 University College, Oxford
1868 London Rowing Club
1869 London Rowing Club
1870 Etonian Club, Oxford
1871 London Rowing Club
1872 London Rowing Club
1873 London Rowing Club
1874 London Rowing Club
1875 London Rowing Club
1876 London Rowing Club
1877 London Rowing Club
1878 London Rowing Club
1879 Jesus College, Cambridge
1880 Thames Rowing Club
1881 Hertford College B.C., Oxford
1882 Hertford College B.C., Oxford
1883 Thames Rowing Club
1884 Kingston Rowing Club

THAMES CHALLENGE CLUB FOR EIGHT OARS.

1868 Pembroke College, Oxford
1869 Oscillators Boat Club, Surbiton
1870 Oscillators Boat Club, Surbiton
1871 Ino Rowing Club, London
1872 Thames Rowing Club.
1873 Thames Rowing Club
1874 Thames Rowing Club
1875 London Rowing Club
1876 West London Rowing Club
1877 London Rowing Club
1878 London Rowing Club
1879 Twickenham Rowing Club
1880 London Rowing Club
1881 Twickenham Rowing Club
1882 Royal Chester Rowing Club
1883 London Rowing Club
1884 Twickenham Rowing Club

WYFOLD CHALLENGE CUP FOR FOUR OARS.

1856 Argonauts Club, London
1857 Pembroke College, Oxford
1858 First Trinity, Cambridge
1859 First Trinity, Cambridge
1860 London Rowing Club
1861 Brasenose College, Oxford
1862 London Rowing Club
1863 Kingston Rowing Club
1864 Kingston Rowing Club
1865 Kingston Rowing Club
1866 Kingston Rowing Club
1867 Kingston Rowing Club
1868 Kingston Rowing Club
1869 Oscillators Boat Club, Surbiton
1870 Thames Rowing Club
1871 Thames Rowing Club
1872 Thames Rowing Club
1873 Kingstown Harbour Boat Club
1874 Newcastle Amateur Rowing Club
1875 Thames Rowing Club
1876 West London Rowing Club
1877 Kingston Rowing Club
1878 Kingston Rowing Club
1879 London Rowing Club
1880 London Rowing Club
1881 Dublin University R.C.
1882 Jesus College B.C., Cambridge
1883 Kingston Rowing Club
1884 Thames Rowing Club

SILVER GOBLETS FOR PAIR OARS.

1845 Arnold and Mann, Caius, Cambridge
1846 Milman and Haggard, C.C. Oxford
1847 Falls and Coulthard, St. George's, London

1848 Milman & Haggard, Christ Church, Oxford
1849 Peacock and H. Playford, London
1850 Chitty and Hornby, Balliol and B.N.C., Oxford
1851 Chitty and Aitken, Balliol and Exeter, Oxford
1852 Barker and Nind, Christ Church, Oxford
1853 Barlee and Gordon, Christ's, Cambs.
1854 Cadogan and Short, Christ Church and New, Oxford
1855 Nottidge and Casamajor, London
1856 Nottidge and Casamajor, London
1857 Warre and Lonsdale, Balliol, Oxford
1858 H. H. Playford and Casamajor, London Rowing Club
1859 Warre and Arkell, Oxford
1860 Casamajor and Woodbridge, London Rowing Club
1861 Woodgate and Champneys, Oxford
1862 Woodgate and Champneys, Oxford
1863 Woodgate and Shepherd, Oxford
1864 Selwyn and Kinglake, Cambridge
1865 May and Fenner, London R.C.
1866 Corrie and Woodgate, Kingston Rowing Club
1867 Corrie and Brown, Kingston R.C.
1868 Crofts and Woodgate, Brasenose
1869 Long and Stout, London Rowing Club
1870 Corrie and Hall, Kingston Rowing Club
1871 Long and Gulston, London R.C.
1872 Long and Gulston, London R.C.
1873 C. C. Knollys and A. Trower, Kingston Rowing Club
1874 Long and Gulston, London R.C.
1875 Chillingworth and Herbert
1876 Smith and Gulston, London R.C.
1877 Eyre and Hastie, Thames R.C.
1878 Ellison and Edwardes-Moss, Oxford
1879 Labat and Gulston, London R.C.
1880 Eyre and Hastie, Thames R.C.
1881 Eyre and Hastie, Thames R.C.
1882 D. E. Brown and J. Lowndes, Hertford College, Oxford
1883 G. Q. Roberts and D. E. Brown, Twickenham Rowing Club
1884 J. Lowndes and D. E. Brown, Twickenham Rowing Club

DIAMOND CHALLENGE SCULLS FOR SCULLERS.

1844 Bumpstead, Scullers' C., London
1845 Wallace, Leander B.C.

1846 Moon, Magdalen College, Oxford
1847 Maude, First Trinity, Cambridge
1848 Bagshawe,Third Trinity,Cambridge
1849 T. R. Bone, Meteor Club, London
1850 T. R. Bone, Meteor Club, London
1851 E. G. Peacock, Thames Club, London
1852 E. Macnaghten, First Trinity, Cambridge
1853 Rippingall, Peterhouse, Cambridge
1854 H. H. Playford, Wandle Club, London
1855 A. A. Casamajor, Argonauts Club, London
1856 A. A. Casamajor, Argonauts Club, London
1857 A. A. Casamajor, L.R.C.
1858 A. A. Casamajor, L.R.C.
1859 E. D. Brickwood, Richmond
1860 H. H. Playford, L.R.C.
1861 A. A. Casamajor, L.R.C.
1862 E. D. Brickwood, L.R.C. After a dead heat with W. B. Woodgate, Brasenose College
1863 C. B. Lawes, Third Trinity, Cambridge
1864 W. B. Woodgate, Brasenose College, Oxford
1865 E. B. Michell, Magdalen College, Oxford
1866 E. B. Michell, Magdalen College, Oxford
1867 W. C. Crofts, Brasenose College, Oxford
1868 W. Stout, L.R.C.
1869 W. C. Crofts, Brasenose College, Oxford
1870 John B. Close, First Trinity, Cambridge
1871 W. Faucus, Tynemouth R.C.
1872 C. C. Knollys, Magdalen College, Oxford
1873 A. C. Dicker, St. John's College, Cambridge
1874 A. C. Dicker, St. John's College, Cambridge
1875 A. C. Dicker, St. John's College, Cambridge
1876 F. L. Playford, L.R.C.
1877 T. C. Edwardes-Moss, Brasenose College, Oxford
1878 T. C. Edwardes-Moss, Brasenose College, Oxford
1879 J.Lowndes, Hertford College,Oxford
1880 J.Lowndes, Hertford College,Oxford
1881 J.Lowndes, Hertford College,Oxford
1882 J.Lowndes, Hertford College,Oxford
1883 J. Lowndes. Twickenham R.C.
1884 W. S. Unwin, Magd. Coll., Oxford

LADIES' CHALLENGE PLATE FOR EIGHT OARS.

1845 St. George's Club, London
1846 First Trinity, Cambridge
1847 Brasenose College, Oxford
1848 Christ Church, Oxford
1849 Wadham College, Oxford
1850 Lincoln College, Oxford, r. o.
1851 Brasenose College, Oxford
1852 Pembroke College, Oxford
1853 First Trinity, Cambridge
1854 First Trinity, Cambridge
1855 Balliol College, Oxford
1856 Royal Chester Rowing Club
1857 Exeter College, Oxford
1858 Balliol College, Oxford
1859 First Trinity, Cambridge
1860 First Trinity, Cambridge, r. o.
1861 First Trinity, Cambridge, r. o.
1862 University College, Oxford
1863 University College, Oxford
1864 Eton College Boat Club
1865 Third Trinity, Cambridge
1866 Eton College Boat Club
1867 Eton College Boat Club
1868 Eton College Boat Club
1869 Eton College Boat Club
1870 Eton College Boat Club
1871 Pembroke College, Oxford
1872 Jesus College, Cambridge
1873 Jesus College, Cambridge
1874 First Trinity, Cambridge
1875 Trinity College, Dublin
1876 Jesus College, Cambridge
1877 Jesus College, Cambridge
1878 Jesus College, Cambridge
1879 Lady Margaret BoatClub,Cambridge
1880 Trinity Hall Boat Club
1881 First Trinity Boat Club, Cambridge
1882 Eton College Boat Club
1883 Christ Church Boat Club, Oxford
1884 Eton College Boat Club

VISITORS' CHALLENGE CUP FOR FOUR OARS.

1847 Christ Church, Oxford
1848 Christ Church, Oxford
1849 Christ Church, Oxford
1850 Christ Church, Oxford
1851 Christ Church, Oxford
1852 Argonauts Club, London
1853 Argonauts Club, London
1854 St. John's, Cambridge
1855 St. John's, Cambridge
1856 St. John's, Cambridge
1857 Pembroke College, Oxford
1858 First Trinity, Cambridge
1859 Third Trinity, Cambridge
1860 First Trinity, Cambridge

1861 First Trinity, Cambridge
1862 Brasenose College, Oxford
1863 Brasenose College, Oxford
1864 University College, Oxford
1865 Third Trinity, Cambridge
1866 University College, Oxford
1867 University College, Oxford, r. o.
1868 University College, Oxford
1869 University College, Oxford
1870 Trinity College, Dublin
1871 First Trinity, Cambridge
1872 Pembroke College, Oxford
1873 Trinity College, Dublin
1874 Trinity College, Dublin
1875 University College, Oxford
1876 University College, Oxford
1877 Jesus College, Cambridge
1878 Columbia College
1879 Lady Margaret B.C., Cambridge
1880 Third Trinity, B.C., Cambridge
1881 First Trinity, B.C., Cambridge
1882 Brasenose College, Oxford.
1883 Christ Church B.C., Oxford
1884 Third Trinity B.C., Cambridge

PUBLIC SCHOOLS CUP.

1879 Cheltenham
1880 Bedford Grammar School
1881 Bedford Grammar School
1882 Magdalen College School, Oxford
1883 Hereford Cathedral School, B.C.
1884 Derby School B.C.

RACES IN 1884.

July 3 and 4.

GRAND CHALLENGE CUP.
First Heat.

Berks Station—London R.C. ... 1
Bucks Station—Thames R.C. ... 0
Centre Station—Royal Chester R.C. 0
London.—G. R. B. Earnshaw, C. Earn-shaw, W. Bergh, J. F. Stillwell, H. J. Hill, A. S. J. Hurrell, J. T. Crier, W. W. Hewett (stroke), W. F. Sheard (cox).
Thames.—B. E. Cole, G. H. Eyre, Gordon Smith, A. M. Hutchinson, S. Fairbairn, J. Hastie, H. J. Rust, J. A. Drake-Smith (stroke), E. A. Safford (cox).
Royal Chester.—C. A. Bean, T. G. Frost, J. P. Small, A. M. Robertson, E. R. Royston, F. Billington, J. J. Gardiner, J. G. Frost (stroke), J. F. Lowe (cox).

Second Heat.

Berks Station—Twickenham R.C. ... 1
Bucks Station—Leander R.C. ... 0
Centre Station—Kingston R.C. ... 0

Twickenham.—F. Leader, R. H. Chap-man, E. Hodgkin, J. Lowndes, Stuart-Green, J. Sharpe, D. E. Brown, L. Frere (stroke), D. Caddy (cox).
Leander.—H. S. Close, F. C. Meyrick, C. R. Carter, E. L. Puxley, D. H. M'Lean, A. R. Paterson, R. A. Pinckney, W. B. D. Curry (stroke), F. J. Humphreys (cox).
Kingston.—P. H. Champernowne, W. Bazalgette, H. S. Till, W. Graham, F. Cobb, H. Butler, R. H. Cobb, H. A. Harvey (stroke), P. Waterhouse (cox).

Final Heat.

Berks Station—London R.C. ... 1
Bucks Station—Twickenham R.C. ... 0

STEWARDS' CHALLENGE CUP.
First Heat.

Bucks Station—Kingston R.C. ... 1
Berks Station—London R.C. ... 0
Kingston.—F. Cobb, H. A. Harvey, H. S. Till, R. H. Cobb (stroke).
London.—J. Farrell, J. F. Stillwell, J. T. Crier, W. Hewett (stroke).

Second Heat.

Berks Station—Twickenham R.C. ... 1
Bucks Station—Thames R.C. ... 0
Twickenham.—F. Leader, J. Lowndes, D. E. Brown, L. Frere (stroke).
Thames.—G. H. Eyre, J. Hastie, H. J. Rust, J. A. Drake-Smith (stroke).

Final Heat.

Berks Station—Kingston R.C. ... 1
Bucks Station—Twickenham R.C. ... 0

THAMES CHALLENGE CUP.
First Heat.

Berks Station—Thames R.C. ... 1
Centre Station—London R.C. ... 0
Bucks Station—Albion R.C. 0
Thames.—W. S. Warlters, F. W. Long, W. Theobald, S. M. Cooke, W. Liddle, B. W. Looker, J. Hughes, H. Atkinson (stroke), E. A. Safford (cox).
London.—G. B. James, W. Wells, P. D. Ullman, E. S. M'Ewen, W. R. Lyne, F. Earnshaw, J. Kerr, C. Wood (stroke), W. F. Sheard (cox).
Albion.—J. W. Macqueen, S. E. Carlin, G. H. Capper, C. R. Sutherland, W. W. Butler, A. Edwards, C. F. Munro, E. Christian (stroke), A. Barnard (cox).

Second Heat.

Berks Station—Twickenham R.C. ... 1
Bucks Station—West London R.C. 0
Centre Station—Grove Park R.C. ... 0
Twickenham.—A. F. Gardiner, C. F.
Russell, S. Hodgkin, J. M. Haslip, W.
Williams, G. A. Bonner, G. Vertue, H.
Blackmore (stroke), G. Haslip (cox).
West London.—W. H. Bone, A. B.
Vaux, J. H. Welch, E. H. Bartlett, A. S.
Lawless, C. E. Brown, A. Huntley, G.
C. Vaux (stroke), W. Rupert-Wheeler
(cox).
Grove Park.—H. Summerhayes, F.
Watts, A. P. Firminger, R. H. Laurie,
F. S. Watts, W. H. Cumming, F. J.
Browne, W. F. Watts (stroke), H. B.
Ducker (cox).

Final Heat.

Twickenham 1
Thames 0

WYFOLD CHALLENGE CUP.

First Heat.

Berks Station—London R.C. ... 1
Bucks Station—Reading R.C. ... 0
London.—P. D. Ullman, W. Bergh,
H. J. Hill, C. Wood (stroke).
Reading.—H. G. Lovejoy, W. J. Brown,
H. E. Cottrell, T. H. Clarke (stroke).

Second Heat.

Bucks Station—Thames R.C. ... 1
Centre Station—Royal Chester R.C. 0
Berks Station—Clare College B.C.,
Cambridge 0
Thames.—B. W. Looker, W. Liddle,
S. Fairbairn, A. M. Hutchinson (stroke).
Royal Chester.—R. Royston, F. Bil-
lington, J. J. Gardiner, J. G. Frost
(stroke).
Clare College.—J. R. Fuller, E. K.
Man, A. D. Flower, R. G. Wilde (stroke).

Third Heat.

Berks Station—Marlow R.C. ... 1
Bucks Station—Twickenham R.C. ... 0
Marlow.—W. T. Shaw, W. T. Porter,
C. H. Yates, J. S. Kirkpatrick (stroke).
Twickenham.—C. F. Russell, G. A.
Bonner, E. Hodgkin, H. Blackmore
(stroke).

Final Heat.

Berks Station—Thames R.C. ... 1
Bucks Station—Marlow R.C. ... 0
Centre Station—London R.C. ... 0

DIAMOND CHALLENGE SCULLS.

First Heat.

Berks Station—J. Farrell, London
R.C. 1
Bucks Station—E. St. J. Christophers,
Thames R.C. 0
Centre Station—Jean Bungert, Mann-
heimer Ruder Club 0

Second Heat.

Berks Station—W. S. Unwin, Mag-
dalen College B.C., Oxford. ... 1
Centre Station—W. R. Patton, Kölner
Club, Cologne 0

Third Heat.

Berks Station—R. H. Smith, Thames
R.C. 1
Centre Station—J. Lowndes, Twick-
enham R.C. 0
Bucks Station—E. C. Kendall, Royal
Chester R.C. 0

Final Heat.

Bucks Station—W. S. Unwin ... 1
Berks Station—R. H. Smith 0
Centre Station—J. Farrell 0

LADIES' CHALLENGE PLATE.

First Heat.

Berks Station—Radley College B.C. 1
Bucks Station—Christ Church B.C.,
Oxford... 0
Radley College.—J. Richards, C. V.
Gresley, R. H. Cooper, L. W. North,
R. G. Harding, H. R. Fort, O. Stock,
L. Hannen (stroke), R. E. Watt (cox).
Christ Church.—A. J. Newsome, R. H.
Williams, E. P. Wethered, C. K. Bowes,
Lord Packenham, E. H. Kempson, A. G.
Shortt, A. B. Shaw (stroke), R. E. Raw-
storne (cox).

Second Heat.

Bucks Station—Eton College B.C. ... 1
Berks Station—Caius College B.C.,
Cambridge 0
Eton College.—M. E. Bradford, C. T.
Barclay, W. P. Mellor, S. D. Muttlebury,
H. M'Lean, S. R. Fothergill, G. E. Hale,
C. Barclay (stroke), F. P. Barnett (cox).
Caius College.—R. W. Mitchell, E. L.
Burd, R. F. E. Cook, E. J. D. Mitchell,
M. Pemberton, T. W. Scott, W. P. G.
Graham, J. E. A. Lewis (stroke), A. A.
Hare (cox).

Final Heat.

Berks Station—Eton College B.C. ... 1
Bucks Station—Radley College B.C.   0

VISITORS' CHALLENGE CUP.

First Heat.

Bucks Station—Christ Church B.C.,
Oxford...   1
Berks Station—Caius College B.C.,
Cambridge 0
Christ Church.—A. J. Newsome, C. K.
Bowes, A. G. Shortt, A. B. Shaw (stroke).
Caius College—W. P. Gore-Graham,
T. W. Scott, M. Pemberton, E. L. Burd
(stroke).

Second Heat.

Bucks Station—Third Trinity B.C.,
Cambridge 1
Berks Station—Clare College B.C.,
Cambridge 0
Third Trinity.—St. C. Donaldson, E.
W. Haig, F. E. Churchill, F. J. Pitman
(stroke).
Clare College.—J. R. Fuller, E. K. Man,
A. D. Flower, R. G. Wilde (stroke).

Final Heat.

Berks Station—Third Trinity B.C.,
Cambridge 1
Bucks Station—Christ Church B.C.,
Oxford...   0

PUBLIC SCHOOLS' CHALLENGE CUP.

First Heat.

Berks Station — Magdalen College
School B.C., Oxford   1
Centre Station—London International
College B.C. 0
Bucks Station — Merchant Taylors'
School B.C. 0
Magdalen School.—H. W. Mence, J.
W. Bickerton, J. M. Bailey, L. S. Par-
tridge (stroke), C. A. S. Jones (cox).
London International College.—A. W.
Barton, A. Allport, L. Pharazyn, A. O.
Trechman (stroke), S. Donkin (cox).
Merchant Taylors' School. — H. Ed-
munds, J. S. Richards, A. H. Green, H.
Dobb (stroke), J. E. V. Oldham (cox).

Second Heat.

Berks Station — Hereford Cathedral
School B.C. 1
Bucks Station — Bedford Modern
School B.C. 0

Hereford Cathedral School. — R. H.
Palmer, R. H. T. Symonds, A. T.
Nicholson, F. C. Palmer (stroke), B.
Norton (cox).
Bedford Modern School.—W. Tudball,
H. A. Block, T. E. Hart-Smith, A. Long
(stroke), H. W. Godfrey (cox).

Third Heat.

Centre Station—Derby School B.C. ... 1
Berks Station — Bedford Grammar
School B.C. 0
Bucks Station — St. Mark's School
B.C., Windsor   0
Derby School.—G. Moss, F. Sargeant,
C. M'Dakin Clench, H. L. F. Scalthorpe
(stroke), R. A. Vargas (cox).
Bedford Grammar School. — J. M.
Glubb, G. Cary Elwes, H. Cross, G.
Verey (stroke), C. Dalton (cox).
St. Mark's School.—W. G. Price, F.
H. Watson, H. W. G. Crofton, H. V.
Cobbold (stroke), F. C. Vignoles (cox).

Final Heat.

Berks Station—Derby School B.C. ... 1
Centre Station—Hereford Cathedral
School B.C. 0
Bucks Station — Magdalen College
School B.C., Oxford   0

Hope (The), or **Lower Hope,** runs
about three nautical miles, almost due
north and south, from Coal House Point,
about two miles below Gravesend, to the
Mucking Light at the beginning of Sea
Reach. Both banks are here very flat
and marshy, the Mucking Flats being on
the left (Essex) and Cliffe Marsh on the
right (Kent). Just beyond Coal House
Point is the Oven Spit and Ovens Buoy.
Bearings N.E. and S.W.

Humane Society.—The Royal
Humane Society, 4, Trafalgar Square,
London, was founded about a century
ago, to provide against the loss of life
arising from the many casualties annually
recurring with water, also for the purpose
of collecting and circulating the best
methods for the recovery of the apparently drowned or dead, for providing
suitable apparatus for the recovery of
those apparently drowned, and the be-
stowal of rewards on those persons who,
by their courage, activity, and presence of
mind, assist in preserving and restoring
life. (*See* DROWNING.)

Hurley, Berkshire, on the right bank; from London 59 miles, from Oxford 52½ miles. Population, 193. Soil, chalk and gravel. A small village beautifully situated in a charming country, but retiring so coyly from the river as to afford little or no indication of its existence to the casual passer-by. But the famous Lady Place at Hurley made for itself a name in history; and, although but little of the building now remains it is not likely to be forgotten so long as the graphic description of Macaulay remains in evidence.

The church, dedicated to St. Mary the Virgin, was consecrated in 1086, by Osmund "the Good," Bishop of Sarum. It was once the chapel of a Benedictine monastery. The old refectory of the monastery still exists on the north side of the church, and the monastic quadrangle is on the same side. There are several plates on the north wall of the quadrangle behind the church. One runs as follows: "The priory of St. Mary, Hurley, founded in the reign of William the Conqueror by Geoffrey de Mandeville and his wife Lecelina, A.D. 1086. A cell to Westminster Abbey." On another: "King Edward the Confessor, principal founder of Westminster Abbey, after the times of King Sebert and King Offa." The church contains an antique stone font, and in the vestry are two half-length stone figures. Above the one is a scutcheon, under which is an inscription: "Richard Lovelace, sone of John Lovelace, Esqvire, 1601." Under the scutcheon which surmounts the other is the inscription: "Sir Richd. Lovelace, Knighted in ye Warrs." No date is filled in. There are also in the vestry paintings of Moses and Aaron. On the floor of the nave are the remains of some early brasses.

The principal fish at Hurley are pike and chub, and there are perch in the deep weir pool.

PLACES OF WORSHIP.—St. Mary the Virgin, and a school-chapel at Birchet's Green.

POSTAL ARRANGEMENTS. — Letters through Marlow. Pillar letter-box cleared 10 a.m., 6.30 p.m. Sunday 9.30 a.m, Nearest money order, telegraph, &c., office, Marlow.

NEAREST *Bridges*, up, Henley about 5¾ miles; down, Marlow 2¼ miles. *Locks*, up, Hambleden 3¾ miles; down, Temple about ½ mile. *Ferry*, Temple. *Railway*

Station, Marlow; but as Marlow is on a branch line, Maidenhead is generally preferred.

FARES from Marlow to Paddington 1st, 6/-; 9/11; 2nd, 4/6, 7/6; 3rd, 2/7½. From Maidenhead to Paddington: 1st, 4/4, 7/6; 2nd, 3/3, 5/9; 3rd, 2/-½.

Hurlingham Club, on the left bank' a short distance below Putney Bridge. The club is instituted for the purpose of providing a ground for pigeon-shooting, polo, lawn-tennis, &c., surrounded with such accessories and so situated as to render it an agreeable country resort, not alone to those who take part in pigeon-shooting and polo, but also to their families and friends. The club consists, at the time of revising this description of it, of shooting, polo, and non-shooting members. Elected members pay an entrance fee of £15 15s., and an annual subscription of £5 5s. They are entitled to all the privileges of the club, and to admit two ladies without payment, and may give orders of admission to as many friends as they please, on payment. The non-shooting members, who are not elected, pay an annual subscription of £2 2s. each, and are entitled to admit two ladies without payment and to all the privileges of the club, except shooting and polo-playing. They may give orders of admission to as many friends as they may please, on payment only. Every member is entitled, by the payment of £1 1s. extra per annum, to give one additional order for ladies only for free admission daily. No person is eligible for admission who is not received in general society. The committee elect by ballot, and the candidate balloted for shall be put up not sooner than one week after he is proposed. Five members must be present; if there be one black ball he shall be considered as not elected.

Iffley, called in Domesday Book Giftelei, Oxfordshire, on the left bank, 110 miles from London, 1½ miles from Oxford. Population about 1,000. Soil, loam. Iffley is noticeable chiefly for its old mill on the river, and for its church, which is one of the best specimens of Anglo-Norman architecture now left to us in a building of this size. It is hardly necessary to visit Iffley to see the mill. It has been painted in every kind of medium, and photographed in every sort of camera, till it must be as familiar to most people as Windsor Castle itself. Rarely, indeed, is there an exhibition of the Academy, or the Dudley, or of any of the water-colour societies, without at least one bit from Iffley. From the lock, the village is approached by a bridge over the weir, passing through a gate at the mill. This is kept locked, and a toll is required from each person of 1d. About five minutes' walk from the lock is the post-office, and about 200 yards to the right is the church, dedicated to St. Mary, which is known to have been built prior to 1189, so that a tablet on the outer north wall, dated 1659, which elsewhere might lay claim to a decent antiquity, here appears to be even absurdly juvenile. The fine embattled tower rises between the chancel and the nave, and is in common with the rest of the church, in singularly fine preservation. Perhaps the best point about the exterior is the west front, which has a grand doorway with a noble arch, enriched with carving, about which there is even something Saracenic, as is indeed the case with some of the carved and fretted work of the interior. The east bay of the chancel is as built by Robert de Efteley, a prior of Kenilworth, about 1270. The ornamented piers and capitals of the south and north doorways and the chevron and sunflowers of the tower arches in the interior, are very noteworthy. The vaulted chancel roof is boldly groined. The building appears to be unusually narrow in proportion to its length. Above the doorway at the west end is a characteristic circular window. The font is large and massive, and is said to be coeval with the church itself. The windows are of stained glass of no great interest, except in so far that the west window commemorates the author of "*The Crescent and the Cross.*" The churchyard is famous for its yew, certainly one of the finest old trees of that class in the country, and which it requires no great stretch of imagination to believe might have been planted at a date not very much later than the foundation of the church itself. Near it stands a monumental cross of ancient date, which has recently been restored by Mr. G. Street, R.A. The rectory house, which abuts on the churchyard, harmonises well with its venerable neighbours. The west side contains some excellent perpendicular work, and with the old Norman tower

behind it, and its garden sloping to the river, forms one of the prettiest pictures on the Thames. The Manor House (which overlooks the lock), though perhaps older by a century than the rectory, has been altered and patched until scarcely any traces of what it was remain. Dr. Johnson visited this house with Boswell on 11th June, 1784, when Dr. Nowell resided there. Boswell says : " We were well entertained and very happy at Dr. Nowell's, where was a very agreeable company, and we drank ' Church and King' after dinner with true Tory cordiality." The name of the village has, it is said, been found spelt in eighty different ways during the last 1,000 years. Iffley lock is on the right bank of the lasher, immediately on passing which the lock comes into view, leaving the river a little distance up stream. The weir, on which is the mill, has a very rapid stream, and has a somewhat evil reputation for accidents. Some care, therefore, should be exercised when waiting for the lock to open. The lock is of stone, in good repair except as to the gates. A roller slip has been recently added. The fall is from 2½ to 3 feet. Excellent dace-fishing with the fly on the scowers and shallows from Iffley Mid-tail to Rose Island, Kennington.

INNS.—" Isis " (Grandpont on the river); " The Trees," in the village.

PLACE OF WORSHIP.—St. Mary's.

POSTAL ARRANGEMENTS.—Mails from London, 6.23 a.m., 2.5 p.m.; Sundays, 6.23 a.m. Mails for London, 6.20 p.m.; Sundays, 3.19 p.m. Nearest money order and telegraph office, Cowley.

NEAREST *Bridges*, up, Oxford ; down, Abingdon about 7 miles. *Locks*, Iffley ; down, Sandford 1¾ miles. *Railway Stations*, Oxford and Littlemore.

FARES, Oxford to Paddington : 1st, 11/-, 18/6 ; 2nd, 8/4, 14/- ; 3rd, 5/7. From Littlemore the fares are a trifle lower.

Ilex Swimming Club.—This club was founded in 1871, its members being drawn from the ranks of amateur rowing, yachting, canoe, cruising, athletic, and football clubs. It is managed by a president, vice-president, captain, secretary, and twelve committee men. These officers are all elective, with the exception of the captaincy, which is annually swum for in

Thames. Members are elected by ballot, one black ball in five excluding. The subscription for active members is 10s. per annum, or £2 2s. for life; non-active members pay 5s. per annum, or £1 1s. for life. The headquarters of the club are at the Lambeth Baths, where most of its races take place; colours, black and crimson.

Isis.—A name frequently given to the Thames until it is joined by the Thame a mile below Day's Lock, near Dorchester. Camden thus derives the word Tamesis, or Thames, from the junction of the names of the two rivers. This fanciful derivation appears to have no foundation in actual fact, but has been perpetuated by the poets who have sung of the nuptials of Thame and Isis; "Beautiful Isis and her husband Thame," Warton calls them. In Julius Cæsar's time the river was known as Tamesis, and the Anglo-Saxon name was Temese; very like the "Tamise ripe" of other days. Whether Camden considered that he had sufficient evidence to justify Isis, or whether, misled by the other river Thame, he merely invented the derivation as the shortest way out of a difficulty, is not quite clear.

Probably he followed Leland, as other chroniclers in their turn followed him: a sheep-like practice much in favour in such cases, and productive of considerable confusion. But as there can be no good reason why a river for a portion of its course should bear one name, and presently change it for something quite different, it seems desirable that, except as a poetical conceit, the Isis legend should be abandoned, and the river throughout be called the Thames.

Isle of Dogs, on the left bank opposite Greenwich.—An uninviting title euphemistically derived from "Isle of Ducks," and applied to what was till lately about the best imitation on a small scale of the Great Dismal Swamp to be found in England. The place, it may be observed *en passant,* was not until late years an island at all, but simply a peninsula jutting out into the river between Limehouse and Blackwall.

Just at the beginning of the present century, however, the Corporation, which had long been exercised by the demands of enterprising engineers for permission to put the river straight and take possession of its old Scamandering bed for docks, took heart of grace, and cut a canal through the neck of the "unlucky Isle of Doggs," as Master Pepys hath it, and so opened a short cut for ships bound up or down the river. Apparently, however, the new road was not found satisfactory, for it has been long since closed and sold to the West India Dock Company, who now use it as a timber dock.

NEAREST *Steamboat Piers.* Millwall (west) and Cubitt Town (east); *Ferries,* Ferry-street to Greenwich Pier, and north-east corner of Commercial Docks; *Railway Station,* West India Dock; *Omnibus Route,* Blackwall.

Isle of Grain.—(*See* GRAIN, ISLE OF).

Isleworth, Middlesex, on the left bank; from London 15 miles, from Oxford 96½ miles. A station on the South Western Railway 12 miles from Waterloo. Trains average about 40 minutes, or from Ludgate-hill about an hour and a half. Population, about 12,000. Soil, light. Isleworth, known to Doomsday Book as Ghistelworde, and called in Elizabeth's time Thistleworth, is a place of some antiquity; but is now generally known in consequence of its market gardens, which are very numerous and prolific. Here, also, are extensive flour mills, cement works, &c. Close to the little town is Syon House, the seat of the Duke of Northumberland. It is a large, plain mansion facing the river, and stands on the site of a nunnery founded in the time of Henry V. In the natural course of events the nunnery was dissolved by Henry VIII. It was given by Edward VI. to Seymour, Duke of Somerset, and after several confiscations was finally granted, in 1604, to the Earl of Northumberland, who built the present house. The well-known Lion from Northumberland House, Strand, having retired from public life, now takes his ease at Syon. Half a mile above Syon House is the Church Ferry, and another ferry is above the eyots, half a mile nearer Richmond.

Among the local institutions are the Isleworth and St. John's Working Men's Clubs, and the Public Reading-room and Library. The subscription to the latter is 5s. annually, 1s. 6d. quarterly. The Reading-room is in South-street. Opposite the Church Ferry is the Green School, a red brick building, erected in 1861 by the late Duchess of Northumberland. This school is endowed to clothe and educate 40 girls between the ages of seven and fourteen. The Blue Schools are for girls and boys. In addition to various places of worship is a Roman Catholic convent. The list of charities and alms-houses is very extensive.

The parish church, All Saints, was rebuilt in 1705, and restored in 1866. It is a fine building, with a remarkably beautiful ivy-covered tower. In it are some good brasses, one of the 15th century, and one in front of the Duke of Northumberland's pew to the memory of Margaret Dely, who died 1561, having been a nun at Syon when it was restored to its original purposes by Queen Mary.

FIRE.—Volunteer Fire Brigade, Station-house-square.

INNS.—"London Apprentice," Church-street ; "Northumberland Arms," Brent-ford End ; "Orange Tree," Mill Bridge.

PLACES OF WORSHIP.—All Saints (pa-rish), St. John the Baptist, and St. Mary's. The Roman Catholic Church of St. Mary Immaculate and St. Bridget, and the Con-vent Chapels ; also Congregational and Wesleyan Chapels, and Friends' Meeting House.

POLICE.—Metropolitan (T Division), Station, Worple-road.

POSTAL ARRANGEMENTS.—Post Office (money order, savings bank, telegraph, and insurance). Mails from London, 7 and 9 a.m., 2.30 and 6.45 p.m. (Satur-days, 8.30 p.m.) No Sunday delivery. Mails for London, 6.15 and 9.45 a.m., 12.45, 5.15, and 9.30 p.m. Sundays, 9 p.m.

NEAREST *Bridges*, up, Richmond about ½ mile ; down, Kew about 2 miles. *Lock*, up, Teddington, 3½ miles. *Ferries*, Isle-worth and Brentford. *Railway Station*, Isleworth.

FARES to Waterloo and Ludgate-hill : 1st, 1/2, 1/9 ; 2nd, 1/-, 1/6 ; 3rd, -/10, 1/4.

Jenkin Buoy.—An 8-foot cylinder buoy, made of iron, and painted with black and white chequers. It is situated in Sea Reach, to the westward of the Nore Sand, and marks a depth of water, at low-water spring tide, of 21 feet. It is moored with 12 fathoms of chain. The Jenkin buoy belongs to the Trinity House.

Junior Kingston Rowing Club, Sun Hotel, Kingston.—Election by ballot ;

one black ball in three excludes. Entrance fee, 5s. ; subscriptions, £1 1s. Boathouse, High-street, Kingston. Colours, black and gold.

Junior Thames Yacht Club, White Hart Hotel, Greenhithe, and Royal Oak Hotel, Ramsgate.—The object of the club is the encouragement of practical amateur yachtsmen. For this purpose the crews of yachts in all sailing matches must be amateurs, with the exception of one paid hand in the 5-ton class, two in the 10-ton class, and three in the 20-ton class, such hands not to touch the tiller. Yachts limited to 20 tons only are allowed to take part in the club matches. The officers are commodore, vice commodore, rear commodore, hon. treasurer, secre-tary, and two auditors. The committee consists of twenty members, the flag-officers being *ex-officio* members. Elec-tion by ballot of the club ; one black ball in three excludes. Entrance fee, £1 1s. ; subscription, £1 1s. Burgee, white, with blue cross running through. Ensign red.

Kempsford.—A village in Gloucester-shire on the Thames and Severn Canal, and not far from the Thames at Castle Eaton, situated about 4½ miles from Lech-lade and 6 from Cricklade. Kempsford is of no particular importance, but is worth visiting for the very fine square tower, with two noble windows, which rises from the centre of the church of St. Mary the Virgin. The interior of the church, though possessing many features of architectural interest, is rather plain, except for the roof of the tower, which is very rich in colour, and for some good stained glass. In the chancel is a stone altar tomb with figures considerably muti-lated ; and in the vestry, which is notable for a good Norman arch, is a curious old picture which apparently represents King David, and was "the gift of Robert Pope, London." The population is about 1,000.

POSTAL ARRANGEMENTS.—Post Office in the village. Letters through Fairford. Mails arrive at 7.30 a.m., and are des-patched at 6.10 p.m.

NEAREST *Railway Station*, Fairford, distant about 3 miles.

FARES to Paddington, 1st, 18/6, 27/6 ; 2nd, 12/-, 20/-; 3rd, 8/5½.

Kempton Park.—(*See* SUNBURY.)

Kensington Island, sometimes called Rose Island, opposite the little village of

Kennington in Berkshire, about 2½ miles from Oxford. Here is a good little inn, " The Swan," to which is attached some private fishing. From the railway bridge, just above, is a pleasant view of the distant spires of Oxford.

NEAREST *Bridges*, up, Oxford about 2½ miles; down, Abingdon about 5½ miles. *Locks*, up, Iffley ¼ mile; down, Sandford 1½ mile. *Railway Station*, Littlemore.

FARES, Littlemore to Paddington : 1st, 10/9, 18/-; 2nd, 7/6, 12/6 ; 3rd, 5/2.

FARES, from Paddington : 1st, 10/9, 18/-; 2nd, 7/6, 12/6 ; 5rd, 5/2.

Kensington Rowing Club.—Headquarters, Biffen's, Hammersmith. Election by ballot, either at general or committee meeting; two adverse votes at a committee, or four at a general meeting, excluding. Entrance fee, 10s. 6d. Subscription, 30s. acting members, 21s. honorary members. Boathouse, Biffen's, Hammersmith. Colours, pink and black.

Kew, Surrey, on the right bank ; from London 12½ miles, from Oxford 99 miles. Kew Bridge is a station on the South Western Railway, 9¼ miles from Waterloo; trains take about half an hour. There is another route to Ludgate-hill, trains, average 1¼ hour. The Kew Gardens station is on the Surrey side, and is in connection with most of the Metropolitan Railway stations, *via* District, &c. The Kew Bridge station is on the Middlesex side, the two counties being here connected by a stone bridge, where there is also a steamboat pier. Population, 1033. Soil, gravel.

Like most villages near London, Kew is losing most of its distinctive features, and but for the quaint old green with its picturesque surroundings, there is little to remind of the Kew of even twenty years ago. By the side of Kew Green is Cambridge Cottage, and near it an entrance to the magnificent Botanical Gardens, among the finest in the world.

Kew Gardens are not only among the most favourite resorts of the London holiday-maker, but have special value to the botanist and horticulturist. The judicious expenditure of public money has made the gardens and houses at Kew almost unique among public institutions of the kind. Here are to be seen flourishing in an atmosphere of their own,

though in an uncongenial climate, the most beautiful tropical palms, plants, ferns, fern-trees, and cacti ; and the pleasure-grounds and arboretum contain in endless and exhaustive profusion specimens of the flowers, shrubs, and trees indigenous to Great Britain. Attached to the gardens is a valuable museum of useful vegetable products. The Gardens are at present open free to the public every day in the week, Sundays included, in the afternoon ; the morning hours being reserved for the necessary work of the gardeners, curators, and a few favoured students. On Bank Holidays, however, the Gardens are opened at 10 a.m.

Kew Palace was built by Sir Hugh Portman during the reign of James I., and is close to the gardens. It is a plain building of red brick, and, like many other plain things and people, was high in favour with George III. and Queen Charlotte.

The Church of St. Anne was built in 1714, and enlarged in 1840. It is chiefly noteworthy for its graveyard, which contains the tombs of many celebrated men, amongst them being Gainsborough and Zoffany, the latter having been a resident of Strand-on-the-Green just across the river. Gainsborough was not a resident in the neighbourhood, but was buried here by his own desire. A brief inscription on the stone records Gainsborough's death, and in the church is a tablet to his memory, erected by E. M. Ward, R.A. In Kew churchyard also lie Meyer the painter, and Sir William Hooker, the late director of the Botanic Gardens. To the east of the church is the mausoleum of the late Duke of Cambridge. The following curious epitaph is inscribed on a slab at the entrance to the church :

Here lyeth the bodys of Robert and Ann Plaistow, late of Tyso, near Edy Hill, died August the 28, 1728.
> At Tyso they were born and bred,
> And in the same good lives they led
> Until they came to marriage state,
> Which was to them most fortunate.
> Near sixty years of mortal life
> They were a happy man and wife ;
> And being so by nature ty'd,
> When one fell sick the other dy'd,
> And both together laid in dust
> To wait the rising of the just.
> They had six children, born and bred,
> And five before them being dead,
> Their only one surviving son
> Hath caus'd this stone for to be done.

The foundation stone of the Queen's Free School for boys and girls was laid by William IV.; the Queen and Royal Family, especially the Cambridge branch. are liberal benefactors.

INNS.—"Star and Garter," Middlesex side; "Coach and Horses," "Greyhound," "Cumberland Arms," Kew-road; "King's Arms," "Rose and Crown," the Green.

PLACE OF WORSHIP.—St. Anne's.

POSTAL ARRANGEMENTS.—Post Office (money order, savings bank, and telegraph). Mails from London, 7 and 8.30 a.m., 2.20, 6.30, and 8.40 p.m.; Sunday, 7.30 a.m. Mails to London, 6.15, 9.40 a.m., 12.50, 5.10, and 9.5 p.m.; Sunday, 9.15 p.m.

NEAREST*Bridge*, Kew; nearest *Bridges*, up, Richmond 3 miles; down, Hammersmith 4 miles. *Lock*, up, Teddington about 6 miles. *Ferry*, Kew, above the Eyots. *Railway Station*, Kew.

FARES TO WATERLOO: 1st, 1/-, 1/6; 2nd, -/9, 1/2; 3rd, -/8, 1/-. Kew Gardens to Mansion House: 1st, 1/2, 1/9; 2nd, 1/-, 1/4; 3rd, -/9, 1/2.

Kingston, Surrey, on the right bank, from London 20½ miles, from Oxford 91 miles. A station (at Surbiton) on the main line of the London and South Western Railway, 12 miles from Waterloo; trains take about 25 minutes. Kingston station is connected, *via* Twickenham, with the Windsor branch of the same railway, and is also in communication with the Metropolitan and North London systems. Flys meet the trains. The Guildford Coach (*see* COACHING) passes through Kingston. Population, about 17,000. The town is divided into four wards, and is governed by a high steward, mayor, eight aldermen, and twenty-four councillors. It is an assize town; the present Recorder being William Hardman, Esq. It is the headquarters of the 47th Infantry Brigade Depôt, and the barracks are in King's-road; the district includes the 1st and 3rd regiments Surrey Militia, the 1st and 2nd Administrative Battalions, and the 1st, 7th, and 12th corps of Surrey Volunteers, the latter being the Kingston corps, with headquarters in Orchard-road. The rifle range —600 yards—is near the cemetery.

Kingston, once called Kyningestun, was a place of considerable importance in the very early times of English history, having been intimately connected with the Saxon kings so far back as the ninth century The ubiquitous Cæsar had, of course, already left his mark in the neighbourhood. Many Roman remains and fragments of camps have been found all about Kingston and Wimbledon, and some writers prefer to believe that the Romans, when in pursuit of Cassivelaunus, crossed the Thames at Kingston, and not at Causeway or Coway Stakes. In 838, Kingston was selected as the seat of the Great Council or Wittenagemot, convened by King Egbert, which his son Athelwolf, and many bishops and nobles attended, the president being Ceolnothus, Archbishop of Canterbury. The fact that the records of this meeting, describing the town as Kyningestun *famosa illa locus* does away with the legend that the town derived its name from the subsequent coronation of Saxon kings on the stone in the marketplace. There is, however, no doubt that such coronations did take place here, and perhaps on the stone which is still preserved. Leland says "the townisch men have certen knowledge of a few kinges crownid there afore the Conqueste." The names and dates of these "kinges," as recorded on the pedestal of the stone, are:

Eadweard	.. 901	Eadwig ..	.. 955
Adelstan	.. 923	Eadweard	.. 975
Eadmund	.. 943	Ædelred	.. 978
Eadred ..	.. 946		

A picturesque account of the crowning of Adelstan will be found in Dean Hook's "Lives of the Archbishops of Canterbury." The coronation of these kings at Kingston appears to be sufficiently established. Whether young Edwy, who married his cousin Elgiva, and became, with his unfortunate queen, the victim of the cruelty and brutality of "Saint" Dunstan and his friend Odo, Archbishop of Canterbury—*par nobile fratrum*—was crowned at Kingston is less certain. The story goes that the king withdrew early from the rough coronation feast to seek the society of Elgiva, and greatly excited the wrath of the nobles. Dunstan and Odo were sent to bring the king back, and forcibly dragged him from his apartments, assailing the queen with foul and opprobrious epithets. Unfortunately for poor Elgiva, she had her revenge on Dunstan, who was finally banished from the kingdom, and whose fall was bitterly avenged by his friend Odo. First branded with hot irons to destroy the beauty which had so much power over the young king, she fell, at a later period, again into the hands of Odo, and was cruelly put to death, the king dying of a broken heart shortly afterwards. In Domesday Book the town is called Chingestune. The townsmen received their first and second municipal charters from King John ; that of 1209 is still preserved. Another charter in the possession of the corporation is one granted by Henry III., in 1256, and subsequent charters of Henry VI., 1441, James I., 1603, Charles I., 1629, and finally, James II., 1685, conferred various privileges on the municipality and burgesses. In 1264, Henry III. took and destroyed Kingston Castle, at that time the property of the Earl of Gloucester. For about sixty years from the beginning of the fourteenth century the town was represented ir Parliament. During the great civil war, Kingston was frequently occupied by one or other of the contending parties, and in 1648 Lord Francis Villiers was killed here in a skirmish.

There is little in the present thriving and busy town of Kingston to recall its ancient history, unless it be the coronation stone, which has been set up and fenced in by a gorgeous railing, close to the Assize Courts. The principal business centre is the Market-place, in the middle of which stands the Town Hall, a modern building supported on arches and columns, and displaying over the southern entrance the inevitable statue of Queen Anne, which formerly adorned the old building. The Council Chamber, a handsome apartment, contains a full-length portrait of Queen Anne, by Sir Godfrey Kneller ; a drawing of Kingston Bridge, by Edward Lapidge, the architect ; and some other pictures of inferior merit. The middle window has eight very curious panes of painted and stained glass, displaying armorial bearings and mottoes, which are well worth careful examination. In the justices' room is some good old oak carving, formerly in the old Town Hall. The bridge which connects Surrey and Middlesex, is close to the Market-place. It is a handsome stone structure of five arches, was opened in 1828, and freed in 1870. It affords very pleasant views both up and down stream. A little below

it is the railway-bridge, Kingston station being close to the river.

Kingston has largely increased in importance, owing to the growth of its suburbs, Norbiton, Surbiton, and New Malden ; the convenience of access from London, and the pleasant surroundings of the neighbourhood, having attracted a large residential population. Along the riverside road the authorities of Surbiton have constructed and laid out public walks and gardens, which extend as far as the Water-works and Raven Eyot and Boat-houses. From Raven Eyot to Surbiton railway-station is by Grove-road, nearly opposite the Ferry, about ten minutes' walk.

The Grammar School has been rebuilt, and was opened January 30, 1878, for one hundred boys, including boarders. The building, and master's house adjoining, form a handsome block of buildings, facing London-street. The old school-room is the only part of the old buildings left standing. It was built as a chapel (chantry), and dedicated to St. Mary Magdalene, by Edward Lovekyn, A.D. 1305. John Lovekyn, his heir, rebuilt the chapel and house contiguous thereto, and improved the foundation by the addition of another chaplain ; he gave to the new foundation considerable property in Kingston, and houses in St. Michael's, Crooked-lane, London, where he resided. Leland says : "He was a native of Kingston . . . and was Lord Mayer in 1347, 1357, 1364, and 1365. He was buried in St. Michael's Church, under a large raised tomb, having the figures of himself and his wife in alabaster—but this was destroyed by the Great Fire of London." The famous William Walworth was an apprentice of John Lovekyn, and he added another chaplain to the foundation. The chapel was seized by Henry VIII., and Queen Elizabeth converted it into a school, A.D. 1561. In March, 1873, a new scheme for the management of the school, in combination with several other charities, was issued by the Endowed Schools Commissioners, giving 10-24ths to the Upper Grammar School, and 7-24ths to Tiffins's School for Boys, and 7-24ths to Tiffins's School for Girls, for lower middle-class children. The buildings for Tiffins's School stand in the Fair-field. The fees for the Upper or Grammar School are 10 guineas per annum, and

than £3 nor more
:rs for Mid-Surrey,
Sir T. Lawrence,
holarsbip for five
ees. Scholarships
ns's for boys from
nd at the Grammar
om Tiffins's, and,
·om the Grammar
ies.
:on, Surbiton, and
ber of institutions
c character. Some
inder their proper
iongst the others
The Society for
Relief and Repress-
:h the Rev. F. M.
leave's Almhouses,
eave, 1665, for the
ien and six poor
nts of Kingston,
of age—the Cleave
augmented by the
Three Per Cents.
Tilsey in the reign
: Children's Con-
connection with
ition at Walton-on-
i Hill, and contains
n's Reading Room,
Kitchen, in con-
arity Organisation
rkmen's Club; and
i. There are also
iurbiton Horticul-
ium Societies.
is dedicated to All
)se to the Market-
)rick building, with
ipally of flint and
:en very lately re-
e old church once
St. Mary, which is
scene of the coro-
e Saxon kings, and
s were preserved.
'ell, and the sexton
: killed. The sex-
was working in a
saved by the falling
column across the
The piece of stone,
rved, 1731," is still
irch. The present
iave, chancel, and
the latter disfigured
/er contains a good

peal of ten bells. There are numerous monuments. Near the chancel is a statue in white marble, by Chantrey: a seated figure of the Countess of Liverpool, who died in June, 1821. Close by, under a canopy on the south wall, is the altar tomb of Sir Anthony Benn, once recorder of Kingston, who died in 1618. Under the canopy lies the alabaster effigy of the deceased, in his official robes. Also against the south wall are several monuments of the Davidson family, one being a white marble figure, and another a somewhat conventional mourning figure, with urn and drapery. There are signs of numerous brasses, and a few still remain. The best is that to the memory of Robert Skern, and Joan his wife, which is on the south wall. It represents two figures, some three feet in length, is elaborately executed, and is of the fifteenth century. Another brass, with two kneeling figures, is on a column near the north entrance, and records the deaths of John and Katherine Hertcombe, who died respectively 1488 and 1487. The brass to Dr. Edmund Staunton's ten children has the following curious inscription:

Here ly ye Bodies

Children which ye Lord gave to EDMUND STAVNTON,
Dr. of D., late Minister of Kingston-vpon-Thames,
now Presidt. of Corpus Christi Colledge, Oxon;
by Mary, his Wife, Davghtr. of Rich. Balthrop,
Servant to ye late Qveene Elizab.

1653.

Francis | Richard
Richard | Edmvnd
Mary | Edmvnd
Mathew | Sarah
Mary | Richard

Ten Children in one grave! A dreadful sight
Seven Sons and Daughters three, Job's number a right
Childhood b and Youth are vaine, Death reigns ouer all;
Even those who never sin'd like Adams c fall:
But why over all? In the first d Man every one
Sin'd and fell, not he himself alone.

Our hope's e in Christ. The second Adam: He

Who saves f the Elect from Sin and Misery.
What's that to Vs poore children? This our Creed,
God is g a God to th'faithfull, and their seed.
Sleepe h on deare Children, never that you wake
Till Christ doth raise i you and to glory take.

a Iob 1. 2.
b Eccl. 11. 10.
c Rom. 5. 14.
d Rom. 5. 12.
e 1 Cor. 15. 22.
f 1 Tim. 1. 1.
f Mat. 1. 21.
Rom. 5. 9. 10.
g Gen. 17. 7.
h 1 Thes. 4. 14.
i Rev. 20. 12.

Another curious epitaph is that on a memorial stone of Thos. Hayward, 1665:

Earth to earth
Ashes on Ashes lye, on Ashes tread
Ashes engrav'd these words which Ashes read
Then what poore thing is Man when any gust
Can blow his Ashes to their elder dust?
More was intended but a wind did rise
And filled with Ashes both my Mouth and Eyes.

There are a vast number of other tablets, some curious, in the church. The other churches in Kingston are St. John the Evangelist, and St. John the Baptist. The Congregational Church, Eden-street, was founded in 1662, by the Rev. Richard Mayo, Vicar of Kingston, who seceded from the Established Church on the passing of the Act of Uniformity.

CAB STANDS.—Kingston and Surbiton Railway stations, and Market-place. *Cab Fares.*—If by distance: Not exceeding one mile, 1s.; exceeding one mile—for each mile or part of a mile, 1s. If by time: For one hour or less, 2s. 6d.; above one hour, for every 15 minutes, 8d.; for any less period, 8d. Extra payments, whether hired by distance or by time: For each package carried outside, 2d.; for each person above two, 6d.; for each child under 10 years, 3d.; by distance—waiting, for every 15 minutes complete, 8d.

BANKS.—London and County, Market-place; Shrubsole and Co., 11, Market-place.

FAIR.—Nov. 13.

FIRE. — Borough Fire and Escape Brigade, Church-street (steam-engine, escape, &c.); Volunteer Steam Fire Brigade, London-street (steam-engine, &c.).

HOTELS.—"Griffin," "Sun," "Wheat-sheaf," all in Market-place.

MARKETS.—Thursday and Saturday.

PLACES OF WORSHIP. — All Saints (parish church); St. John the Evangelist, Springfield-road; St. Paul's, Kingston-hill; and Baptist, Congregational, Presbyterian, Primitive Methodist, and Wesleyan Chapels, and Friends' Meeting-house.

POLICE.—Station, London-street.

POSTAL ARRANGEMENTS.—Post Office (money order, savings bank, telegraph, and insurance), Eden-street. Mails from London, 6.30 and 9 a.m., 4.30 and 7.30 p.m. Sunday, 6.30 a.m., by letter-carrier; delivery over the counter, 8 to 10 a.m. Mails for London, 7.20 and 10 a.m., 12.30, 3, 4, 4.50, 8.30, and 10 p.m.; Sunday, 10 p.m.

NEAREST *Bridges,* Kingston; up, Hampton Court about 3 miles; down, Richmond 5 miles. *Locks,* up, Molesey, 3½ miles; down, Teddington 1¾ mile. *Ferry,* Surbiton. *Railway Station,* Surbiton and Kingston.

FARES, Kingston and Surbiton to Waterloo: 1st, 2/-, 2/6; 2nd, 1/6, 2/-; 3rd, 1/-, 1/8.

Kingston Amateur Regatta—

RACES IN 1884.

July 19.

JUNIOR SCULLS.

First Heat.

Station 3 — G. R. B. Earnshaw, London R.C. 1
Station 1—B. W. Looker, Thames R.C. 0
Station 2—H. Blackmore, Twickenham R.C. 0

Second Heat.

Station 3—G. A. S. Buckley, Kingston R.C. 1
Station 1—W. Stevenson, Kingston R.C. 0

Final Heat.

Station 1—Earnshaw 1
Station 2—Buckley 0

JUNIOR FOURS.

Station 1—Kingston R.C. 1
Station 2—London R.C. 0
Kingston.—A. Spurling, F. Butler, C. L. Fyfe, S. G. Lushington (stroke), F. J. Bell (cox).
London.—C. F. Schlotel, A. S. Bryden, E. S. M'Ewen, W. J. Leeman (stroke), W. F. Sheard (cox).

SENIOR PAIRS.

First Heat.

Station 1—Twickenham R.C. ... 1
Station 2—London R.C. 0
Twickenham.— E. Hodgkin and L. Frere.
London.—P. Ullman and J. F. Stillwell.

Second Heat.

Station 2—Kingston R.C. ... ...r.o.
F. Cobb and R. H. Cobb.

Final Heat.

Station 2—Kingston 1
Station 1—Twickenham 0

JUNIOR EIGHTS.

First Heat.

Station 3—Thames R.C. 1
Station 2—West London R.C. ... 0
Station 1—Kingston R.C. 0
Thames.—C. E. Smith, F. Bolt, G. A.
Herdman, W. Andrews, F. W. Guerrier,
C. S. Sowerby, W. Theobald, H. Atkinson (stroke), E. A. Safford (cox).
West London. — L. Thierry, W. D.
Gilbert, J. R. Withers, G. S. Herschell,
A. C. Ellis, C. J. Scott, F. A. Knight,
C. H. Hickman (stroke), W. R. Wheeler
(cox).
Kingston.—A. Spurling, W. Butler, C.
L. Fyfe, W. Stevenson, M. W. Wadham,
F. Butler, S. G. Lushington, E. Bazalgette (stroke), F. G. Bull (cox).

Second Heat.

Station 3—London R.C. 1
Station 2—East Sheen... 0
London.— C. F. Schlotel, P. A. N.
Thorn, W. R. Bishop, A. B. Coutts, A.
Silversparre, A. S. Bryden, E. S. M'Ewen,
W. J. Leeman (stroke), W. F. Sheard
(cox).
East Sheen.—H. F. Highton, A. P.
Parker, F. B. Lewis, H. O. F. Luckie,
H. R. Parker, R. H. Barron, J. F. C.
Glossop, A. Hughes (stroke), H. M.
Ripley (cox).

Final Heat.

Station 2—Thames 1
Station 1—London 0

KINGSTON GRAND CHALLENGE CUP
FOR EIGHT OARS.

Station 1—Thames R.C. 1
Station 2—London R.C. 0
Station 3—Twickenham R.C. ... 0
Thames.—B. W. Looker, B. E. Cole,
Gordon Smith, A. M. Hutchinson, W.
Liddle, J. Hastie, H. J. Rust, J. A. Drake-Smith (stroke), E. A. Safford (cox).
London.—G. R. B. Earnshaw, C. Earnshaw, W. Bergh, J. F. Stillwell, H. J.
Hill, A. S. J. Hurrell, J. T. Crier, W. W.
Hewett (stroke), W. F. Sheard (cox).

Twickenham.—G. G. Vertue, H. Blackmore, S. Hodgkin, E. Hodgkin, Stuart
Green, G. A. Bonnor, F. D. Leader,
L. Frere (stroke), D. Caddy (cox).

SENIOR SCULLS.

First Heat.

Station 2 — C. J. Standen Batt,
Thames R.C.... ... ...r.o.

Second Heat.

Station 1—E. F. Grün, London R.C. 1
Station 2—F. J. Browne, Grove Park
R.C. 0

Final Heat.

Station 2—Grün 1
Station 1—Batt... ... ... disq.

SENIOR FOURS.

Station 3—Kingston R.C. 1
Station 1—Thames R.C. 0
Kingston.—F. Cobb, H. A. Harvey,
H. S. Till, R. H. Cobb (stroke).
Thames.—B. W. Looker, J. Hastie,
H. J. Rust, J. A. Drake-Smith (stroke).

Kingston Rowing Club.—This club
consists of ordinary members and three
classes of life members. Full members
are those who live within a radius of six
miles from the club boat-house, for any
period not less than one month during
the rowing season, or who row in any
races in club boats. Half members are
those who live beyond a radius of six
miles from the club boat-house, or resident
members of the Universities of Oxford and
Cambridge and public schools. Honorary
members shall be entitled to the use of
the club-room only. Entrance fee for
full and half members, £1 1s.; subscriptions, full members, £2 2s.; half and
honorary members, £1 1s.; life full members, £15 15s.; half, £8 8s.; honorary,
£5 5s. Election is by ballot in general
meeting: one black ball in six excludes.
Boat-house, The Island, Surbiton. The
Raven's Ait Company (Limited) are now
the proprietors of the island. Colours,
scarlet and white, horizontal.

Laleham, Middlesex, on the left bank;
from London 33 miles; from Oxford 78¾
miles. Population, 566. Soil, gravel
and brick earth. A village rather more

than two miles from Staines, and about a mile and a half from Chertsey, well known for its ferry, where there is a long shallow for the fly. On the south side of the river near the ferry-house is a Roman camp, evidently intended to guard the ford; while on the north side, about half a mile from the river, there are still traditions of another Cæsar's camp. The tract of meadow land on the south side of the river, known as the Burway, used to belong and pay rates to Laleham parish, but on the occasion of Laleham parish refusing to pay for the burial of the body of a drowned man cast on shore on the Burway, Chertsey parish buried the corpse and claimed the rates, which it has retained ever since. The Earl of Lucan owns a considerable quantity of land in the neighbourhood, and claims as his property a chapel on the north side of the church. The church, dedicated to All Saints, contains some fine old Norman pillars and arches, some of which are built in the south wall, showing that in the old Norman time there was a south aisle to the church. This was cut off in the decorated Gothic period, and windows of that date inserted in the arches. This seems to point to the much greater comparative importance of villages on a great waterway when the uplying parts were heavily clothed with forest than when, 200 years later, the forests were to a large extent cut down. The tower is a brick structure of George I.'s time. In the chancel is a large altar-piece of Our Saviour and St. Peter on the sea, painted by Harlowe during a stay in the village; and on the south of the chancel is a mural monument to Mrs. Hartwell, by Chantrey, not a very favourable specimen of the master. In the churchyard at the foot of the tower is an epitaph, date 1789, which offers a variation on the old-fashioned "Affliction sore long time I bore":

Pain was my portion, physic was my food,
Groans my devotion, drugs did me no good,
Christ my physician knew which way was best
To ease my pain and set my soul at rest.

INNS. — The "Feathers," and the "Horse Shoes."

PLACE OF WORSHIP.—All Saints.

POSTAL ARRANGEMENTS.—Post Office near the church (money order and telegraph office). Mails from London, 7 a.m. and 12 noon; Sunday, 7 a.m. Mails for London, 10.10 a.m. and 6.40 p.m.; Sunday, 10 a.m.

NEAREST *Bridges*, up, Staines 2½ miles; down, Chertsey 1 mile. *Locks*, up, Penton Hook ½ mile; down, Chertsey 1¼ mile. *Ferry*, Laleham. *Railway Stations*, Staines and Chertsey.

FARES from Staines: 1st, 3/3, 5/-; 2nd, 2/3, 3/6; 3rd, 1/7, 3/-. From Chertsey, 1st, 4/-, 5/6; 2nd, 3/-, 4/-; 3rd, 1/10, 3/4.

Lambeth Bridge is perhaps, on the whole, the ugliest ever built. It was also, when it was built, supposed to be the cheapest. It is a suspension bridge of three spans, and one great economy in its construction consists in the use of wire cables in place of the usual chains. It connects Westminster with Lambeth, where it lands close to the Archbishop's Palace.

Leander Club.—This old-established rowing club (sometimes called the "Brilliants") consists of members and honorary members; the subscription for the former is £2 2s., for the latter £1 1s. Members of the Universities of Oxford and Cambridge are only liable to a subscription of 10s. 6d. per annum so long as they are resident undergraduates. The election of members is entrusted to the committee. Colours, red. Boathouse, Biffen's, Hammersmith.

Lechlade, Gloucestershire, on the left bank, distant from Oxford 33 miles. A station on the Great Western Railway, 86 miles from Paddington, the time occupied by the fast trains being about 2¾ hours. The station is some little distance from the town, but an omnibus meets the trains. Population about 1,300. Soil, loam; subsoil, gravel. Lechlade is situated a short distance below the junction of the Thames with the Thames and Severn Canal. The river Lech here falls into the Thames, which at Lechlade first becomes navigable for practical purposes, and runs, except in very dry seasons, in a goodly stream under the handsome arch of the bridge. Lechlade is a pretty little place, with a sheep and cattle market on the last Tuesday in each month, but, except for its position on the river, is not of any importance. The ideas of its inhabitants on the subject of paving are, it may be remarked, open to considerable excep.

tion. Its church of St. Lawrence, which was built by one Conrad Ney, the then vicar, in the time of King Edward IV., is, with its tower and spire, a conspicuous object in the landscape for many miles round, and is a rather plain but handsome building in the Gothic style. It appears, however, to have been somewhat severely restored. The most pretentious monument it contains is on the south wall of the chancel, and consists of a medallion of Mrs. Anne Simons (1769), to which one of the fat and ugly naked boys, who were so popular with the sculptors of that period, is pointing ; and in the east of the south nave is a mural tablet with coats of arms and two fat marble children, the whole being dedicated to the memory of certain members of the Coxeter family. Nearly under this is an imperfect brass and in the north nave are two more, one of a male and another of a female figure, in good preservation.

Lechlade is the point at which boats may be taken for the trip down the river (see Trip from Lechlade to Oxford), and boats may either be sent from Salter's at Oxford by van or by the Great Western Railway Company, who make arrangements for conveying them from the station to the river. There is a good hotel in the town (the " New Inn "), but boating parties occasionally prefer to put up at the " Trout Inn," at St. John's Bridge, about half a mile down the stream, which is also favourably spoken of, but of which the Editor has no personal experience.

BANKS.—County of Gloucester Banking Company and Gloucestershire Banking Company.

FIRE ENGINE.—In the town.

HOTELS.—" New Inn," in the town ; " Trout," St. John's Bridge, about half a mile off.

MARKET DAY.—Last Tuesday in each month.

POSTAL ARRANGEMENTS.—Post Office (money order, telegraph, savings bank, and insurance) near the " New Inn." Mails from London, 4.50 a.m. and 1 p.m. ; mails for London, 10 a.m. and 8.45 p.m.

NEAREST Bridges, up, Hannington, 3 miles ; down, St. John's, about half a mile. Lock, down, St. John's, about half a mile, the first lock on the Thames.

FARES, from Lechlade to Paddington, 1st, 15/9, 26/3 ; 2nd, 11/7, 19/6 ; 3rd, 7/11½.

Legal Quays and Sufferance Wharves are the places licensed for the landing of goods in the Port of London ; the term " Sufferance " being taken from the phraseology of the old writs, which ran : " Suffer such and such persons " to land or warehouse such and such articles. The licences vary in respect of the particular articles which may be landed at each place.

Leigh, Essex, on the left bank, from London about 42 miles. A station on the London, Tilbury, and Southend Railway, about one hour and a half from Fenchurch-street. Population, 1,688. Soil, loam, clay, and gravel. Leigh is a picturesque fishing village situated on a creek of the Thames, and of but little importance. Behind the village, which is built close on to the river, rises a somewhat steep hill, on which are the church, the post-office, and some few houses. The church, which is dedicated to St. Clement, is a large building in the perpendicular style, with a handsome and lofty tower, which is a well-known landmark, and commands an extensive prospect. It contains a few brasses, notably that to Richard Hadock and wives (1453) in the north aisle. In the chancel is a bust of Robert Salmon (died 1641), curiously painted, and with an inscription in Latin and English setting forth the fact that he had restored the ancient art of navigation, which had been almost lost. The church also contains an ancient alms-box, with three massive locks, inscribed, " I pray you the pore remember." Just below the church, on the way to the river, are the school buildings.

PLACES OF WORSHIP.—St. Clement's, and Wesleyan Chapel.

POSTAL ARRANGEMENTS.—Post Office (money order, savings bank, telegraph, and insurance), half-way down the hill, between the church and the village. Mails from London 10.45 a.m. Mails for London, 11.20 a.m. and 7 p.m.

NEAREST Railway Station, Leigh ; Steamboat Pier and Ferry, Southend.

FARES to London : 1st, 4/1, 6/10 ; 2nd, 3/-, 5/-; 3rd, 2/1.

Lights to be carried by vessels under the Conservancy bye-laws.—Every steam-vessel navigating the River Thames (except as hereinafter provided) shall, between sunset and sunrise, while under way, exhibit the three following lights of sufficient power to be distinctly visible with a clear atmosphere on a dark night at a distance of at least one mile, namely : (a) At the foremast, or, if there be no foremast, at the funnel, a bright white light suspended at the height of not less than ten feet from the deck, and so fixed as to throw the light from right ahead to two points abaft the beam on either side. (b) On the starboard side, a green light so fixed and fitted with an inboard screen as to throw the light from direct ahead to two points abaft the beam on the starboard side. (c) On the port side, a red light so fixed and fitted with an inboard screen as to throw the light from direct ahead to two points abaft the beam on the port side. (d) Provided, however, that no passenger steam vessel whilst navigating the said river above London Bridge, and when under way, shall be bound to exhibit between sunset and sunrise any other lights than two bright white lights, one at her mast-head, and one at her stem. Steamers towing vessels shall, between sunset and sunrise, exhibit, in addition to the above-mentioned three lights, a white light on the foremast or funnel not less than four feet vertically above the first-mentioned white light, of the like power and similar to it in every respect. Every steam dredger moored in the River Thames shall, between sunset and sunrise, exhibit three bright lights from globular lanterns of not less than eight inches in diameter, the said three lights to be placed in a triangular form, and to be of sufficient power to be distinctly visible with a clear atmosphere on a dark night at a distance of at least one mile, and to be placed not less than six feet apart on the highest part of the framework athwart ships. All barges on the River Thames above Putney Bridge, whether navigated by sail, towed by steam or horses, shall between sunset and sunrise, while under way, exhibit in their bows or on their masts a red light of sufficient power to be distinctly visible with a clear atmosphere on a dark night at a distance of at least one mile. (The report of the committee appointed by the Board of Trade to inquire into the navigation of the Thames, which was presented to both Houses in the summer of 1879, recommended the abolition of this clause, which the committee stated "appears never to have been obeyed.") All vessels under sail east of London Bridge shall exhibit between sunset and sunrise two lights, viz., a green light on the starboard and a red light on the port side, such lights to be visible on a dark night with a clear atmosphere at a distance of at least one mile. Every person in charge of a dumb-barge when under way and not in tow shall, between sunset and sunrise, when below or to the eastward of a line drawn from the upper part of Silvertown, in the county of Essex, to Charlton Pier, in the county of Kent, have a white light always ready, and exhibit the same on the approach of any vessel. The person in charge of the sternmost or last of a line of barges, when being towed, shall exhibit, between sunset and sunrise, a white light from the stern of his barge. All vessels and barges, when at anchor in the fairway of the river, shall exhibit the usual riding light. All vessels, when employed to mark the position of wrecks or other obstructions, shall exhibit two bright lights placed horizontally not less than six feet apart. The penalty for breach of any of these bye-laws is a sum not exceeding £5.— (And see RULE OF THE ROAD, AND STEAM LAUNCHES.)

Limehouse Reach extends from the Lower Pool to the beginning of Deptford Reach. On the right bank are the Commercial Docks. At the top of the Reach are Limehouse and Shadwell churches. Bearings N. N. E. and S.S.W.

Little Stoke.—A ferry between Oxfordshire and Berkshire, nearly opposite the Berks county lunatic asylum, in the parish of Cholsey, and about one mile from Moulsford.

Locks :

ABOVE OXFORD.

Name.			Miles from Cricklade.		Miles from Oxford.
St. John's...	...	...	10½	...	32½
Buscot	...	...	12½	...	30½
Rushy	...	...	20	...	23
Pinkhill	...	...	34½	...	8½
Godstow ...	...	...	39½	...	3½
Osney	...	...	42½	...	½

BELOW OXFORD.

Name.	Miles from London.	Miles from Oxford.
Iffley	110½	1
Sandford	108¾	2¾
Abingdon	104¼	7¼
Culham	101¾	9¾
Clifton	98¾	12¾
Day's	96	15½
Bensington	92	19½
Cleeve	85½	26
Goring	84¾	26¾
Whitchurch	80¾	30¾
Mapledurham	78½	33
Caversham	74¼	37½
Sonning	71½	40
Shiplake	68¾	42¾
Marsh	66	45½
Hambleden	62¾	48¾
Hurley	59	52½
Temple	58½	53
Marlow	56¾	54¾
Cookham	52½	59
Boulter's	50½	61
Bray	48¼	63¼
Boveney	45	66½
Romney	42¾	68¾
Old Windsor	39¾	71¾
Bell Weir	36¾	74¾
Penton Hook	34	77½
Chertsey	32	79½
Shepperton	30	81½
Sunbury	26½	85
Molesey	23½	88
Teddington	18½	93

The length of the locks is about 130 feet, and a vessel of 16-feet beam can pass through them as far as Oxford.

(*And see* TRIP FROM CRICKLADE, TRIP FROM OXFORD, and, for tolls, etc., NAVIGATION, UPPER THAMES.)

London and South Western Railway. — HORSES AND CARRIAGES. — Horses and carriages are conveyed to or from Richmond, Twickenham, Teddington, Kingston, Shepperton, Staines, Windsor, Virginia Water, Reading, Surbiton, Hampton Court, Walton, and Chertsey. They are conveyed by certain trains only, for which see time-tables. The rates from Waterloo to the station on the river are as under:

FROM WATERLOO STATION TO	HORSES.	If property of one person.		CARRIAGES.	
	1	2	3	4 wheel.	2 wheel.
	s. d.	s. d.	s. d.	s. d.	s. d.
Richmond	6 0	9 0	12 0	7 6	
Twickenham	6 0	9 0	12 0	8 6	
Teddington	6 0	9 0	12 0	8 6	
Kingston	6 0	9 0	12 0	9 0	
Shepperton	7 6	10 6	15 0	10 6	
Staines	7 6	10 6	15 0	10 6	
Windsor	8 6	13 6	20 0	11 0	
Reading	12 0	19 0	28 6	18 0	12 0
Surbiton	6 0	8 6	10 6	8 0	
Hampton Crt.	6 0	9 0	11 0	8 6	
Walton	7 0	10 0	12 6	10 0	
Chertsey	8 0	12 0	15 0	12 0	

COMPARTMENTS RETAINED.—Compartments, in carriages of any class, are reserved for families or parties of friends who are desirous of travelling together. Application should be made beforehand to the Traffic Superintendent, Waterloo Station, as passengers cannot depend upon getting an empty compartment after they arrive at the station if no previous notice has been given. The number of the party should always be stated.

CLOAK ROOMS.—Passengers' luggage may be deposited in the cloak rooms at all stations. The charge which the company makes for warehousing passengers' luggage, which has been, or is about to be conveyed on the railway is *2d.* for each package for any period not exceeding two days, and *1d.* per package for every day or part of a day after two days.

PICNIC OR PLEASURE PARTIES.—During the summer months first, second, and third class return tickets, at a reduced fare, are issued, with certain limitations, at all the principal stations to parties of not less than six first class, or ten second or third class passengers desirous of making pleasure excursions to places on or adjacent to this railway. The tickets will be available for return the same day only, and parties can only proceed and return by the trains which stop at the stations where they wish to join and leave the railway, and having that class of carriage attached for which they have taken tickets. All persons forming this party must travel by the same train in both directions. To obtain these tickets application must be made at any of the stations not less than three clear days before the excursion, stating the following particulars, viz. : That it is exclusively a pleasure party ; the station from and to which tickets are required ; for what class of carriage ; the date of the proposed excursion ; and the probable number of the party. The power of refusing any application is reserved. These tickets will not be issued by the London and South Western Railway Company from or to London.

ANGLERS' TICKETS.—Cheap second and third class return tickets to the undermentioned stations are issued from all London Stations to anglers who are *bona fide* members of anglers' clubs, and who produce their cards of membership at the time of taking their tickets. The fares from Waterloo are as under ;

	2nd Class. s. d.	3rd Class. s. d.
Fulwell	2 0	1 4
Hampton Wick and Kingston	2 0	1 3
Esher	2 3	1 6
Hampton	2 3	1 6
Sunbury	2 6	1 8
Walton	2 6	1 10
Shepperton	3 0	2 0
Weybridge	3 2	2 0
Staines	2 10	2 0
Egham	3 2	2 3
Wraysbury	3 2	2 3
Addlestone	3 6	2 2
Datchet	3 6	2 3
Windsor	3 9	2 6
Virginia Water	3 9	2 6
Chertsey	3 9	2 4
Woking	4 6	2 6

These are "return" tickets, available for three days.

OUTSIDE PORTERS FOR TRANSFER OF LUGGAGE.—Where two stations belonging to separate companies are adjacent to each other, out-porters are appointed to convey luggage from one station to the other at fixed charges.

The fares charged for through tickets do not in any case include the conveyance of luggage between the stations.

The men appointed to the duty are in uniform, and the companies cannot control the charges made by any other persons whom passengers may employ to convey their luggage.

CHEAP SATURDAY TO MONDAY TICKETS.—On Saturdays and Sundays 1st and 2nd class return tickets to Windsor are issued at Waterloo, Vauxhall, Clapham Junction, Chelsea, and Kensington, available for the return journey till the Monday following inclusive. These tickets are also available to or from Datchet. Fares, from either of the above-named stations : 1st class, 4s. 6d. ; 2nd class, 3s. 6d.

BOATS AND CANOES.—These are conveyed in the guard's van or on the roof of a carriage at the rate of 2d. per mile, with a minimum charge of 5s. If a carriage truck is required, the same charge is made as for a private carriage ; if two trucks are required, a charge is made for one private carriage with 50 per cent. added. In cases, however, where the crew, not less than four in number, travel with the boat, the charge for the latter will be reduced one half ; but in order to obtain this reduction, previous application must be made to the superintendent of the traffic, Waterloo Station, who will send a written authority to the applicant, to be produced when the tickets are taken.

CHEAP DAY EXCURSIONS. —Cheap Day Excursion Tickets are issued by certain specified trains from May 1 to October 31, to the following places, from Waterloo, Vauxhall, Clapham Junction, Chelsea, Kensington (Addison-road), and from Hammersmith, there and back, in 3rd class carriages, at the following fares— :

	s. d.
Windsor	2 6
Twickenham	1 6
Kingston	1 6
Teddington	1 6
Kew Bridge	1 0

Also to Virginia Water and back : 1st class, 4s. ; 2nd, 3s.

Passengers holding Windsor tickets can return from Virginia Water on payment of 6d. each.

The trains by which these tickets are available are published month by month in the South Western Company's Book of Time Tables. Passengers must be careful to note that if the cheap tickets are used by any other than the specified trains, or if the journey there and back be not completed in the one day, the full ordinary fares will be charged.

SALOON CARRIAGES.—Saloon carriages constructed to carry about 10 passengers (1st class only) may be retained for parties of not less than seven passengsrs. Application should be made to the superintendent of the traffic, Waterloo, some days before the date on which the carriages will be required, as the number is limited, and in the summer there is often a great demand for them. These,

carriages are not retained for parties holding picnic or other tickets issued at reduced rates.

PRIVATE BROUGHAMS. — Broughams and private omnibuses may be hired at the Waterloo Station at moderate charges. A note to the station-master will always secure the attendance of as many carriages as may be required on the arrival of the train.

SCALE OF CHARGES FOR RESIDENTIAL OR SEASON TICKETS.

WATERLOO BRIDGE OR KENSINGTON. To or From	FIRST CLASS.			SECOND CLASS.		
	Twelve Months.	Six Months.	Three Months.	Twelve Months.	Six Months.	Three Months.
	£ s. d.	£ s. d.	£ s. d.	£ s. d.	£ s. d.	£ s. d.
Wandsworth	10 0 0	6 0 0	3 5 0	7 10 0	4 10 0	2 7 6
Putney	10 10 0	6 5 0	3 10 0	7 17 6	4 15 0	2 12 6
Barnes	12 0 0	7 0 0	4 0 0	9 0 0	5 5 0	3 0 0
Mortlake	14 0 0	8 10 0	4 15 0	10 10 0	6 7 6	3 10 0
Richmond	16 0 0	9 10 0	5 10 0	12 0 0	7 2 6	4 0 0
St. Margaret's	16 10 0	10 0 0	5 10 0	12 7 6	7 10 0	4 0 0
Twickenham	17 0 0	10 10 0	5 15 0	12 15 0	7 17 6	4 0 0
Feltham / Ashford	20 0 0	12 0 0	6 15 0	15 0 0	9 0 0	5 2 6
Staines / Wraysbury	22 0 0	13 5 0	7 10 0	16 10 0	10 0 0	5 12 6
Datchet / Windsor	24 0 0	14 0 0	7 10 0	18 0 0	10 10 0	5 12 6
Chiswick	13 0 0	8 0 0	4 10 0	9 15 0	6 0 0	3 7 6
Kew Bridge	15 0 0	9 0 0	5 0 0	10 0 0	6 7 6	3 10 0
Brentford	15 0 0	9 0 0	5 0 0	11 5 0	6 15 0	3 15 0
Isleworth	16 0 0	9 10 0	5 10 0	12 0 0	7 2 6	4 2 6
Hounslow	17 0 0	10 10 0	5 15 0	12 15 0	7 17 6	4 5 0
Strawberry Hill / Teddington / Hampton Wick / Kingston / Fulwell	18 0 0	11 0 0	6 0 0	13 10 0	8 0 0	4 0 0
Sunbury	20 0 0	12 0 0	6 15 0	15 0 0	9 0 0	5 2 6
Shepperton	22 0 0	13 5 0	7 10 0	16 10 0	10 0 0	5 12 6
Hampton	19 0 0	11 10 0	6 7 6	14 0 0	8 10 0	4 15 0
urbiton / orbiton / ingston	18 0 0	11 0 0	6 0 0	13 10 0	8 0 0	4 0 0
hames Ditton / ampton Court / sher	20 0 0	12 0 0	6 15 0	15 0 0	9 0 0	5 2 6
alton / eybridge	21 0 0	12 10 0	7 0 0	15 15 0	9 7 6	5 5 0
ddlestone / hertsey	22 0 0	13 5 0	7 10 0	16 10 0	10 0 0	5 12 6

Left margin group labels: Richmond and Windsor Line; via Barnes; Loop Line, via Barnes; Thames Valley Lines, via Barnes.

WINDSOR AND DATCHET.—Nine Months: 1st, £20; 2nd, £15. Two months: 1st, £5 5s.; 2nd, £3 17s. 6d. ne month: 1st, £3; 2nd, £2 5s.
STATIONS.—Strawberry Hill to Fulwell: Nine months, 2nd, £11.
READING.—Nine months: 1st, £31; 2nd, £23 5s.

SEASON TICKETS. — Season Tickets may be obtained at the Season Ticket Office, No. 114, Waterloo-road, S.E. ; or by letter to Mr. C. Harvey, Season Ticket Office.

A reduction is made of 10 per cent. when two tickets, and of 15 per cent., when three or more tickets are taken by the same family residing in the same house for the same period, but not as lodgers (that is, commencing and expiring on the same dates), and between the same stations.

CHILDREN under three years of age, accompanying adult passengers, no charge ; above three years and under twelve, half-price by all trains.

London Bridge—built in 1824-27 from the designs of John Rennie, architect of Southwark and Waterloo Bridges, partly by himself, partly on his death by his son, Mr. J. Rennie. Altogether some eight or nine designs for London Bridge were prepared by members of the Rennie family. The cost, from various causes, was enormous, and a good deal of mis-apprehension seems to exist upon this point ; some authorities placing it at a little under a million and a half, while others give it at over two and a half millions. It is built of granite in five arches ; the centre arch being 152 ft., the two next 140 ft., and the two shore arches 130 ft. each in span. In order to facilitate traffic, police-constables are stationed along the middle of the roadway, and all vehicles travelling at a walking pace only are compelled to keep close to the curb. There are still, however, frequent blocks. and the bridge should be avoided as much as possible, especially between 9 and 10 a.m. and 4 and 6 p.m. Seen from the river, it is the handsomest bridge in London.

NEAREST *Railway Stations*, Cannon-street and London Bridge; *Omnibus Routes*, Cannon-street, King William-street, London Bridge, and Southwark-street.

London Docks.—The London Docks belong to the same company as the St. Katharine and Victoria Docks (*which see*), and lie immediately to the eastward of the former, from which they are divided by Nightingale-lane, running from Upper East Smithfield to Wapping High-street.

The best means of approach is, from the west, by way of Aldgate and the Minories to East Smithfield, or from the east, by way of the Leman-street Station. The entrance is at the corner of Nightingale-lane, where East Smithfield and Upper East Smithfield join.

London Hospital Rowing Club, Hammersmith. — Subscription : Effective members, 10s. 6d. ; hon. members, "not less than 10s. 6d." Candidates for membership shall become members on giving in their names and subscriptions to the secretary. Boat-house, Biffen's, Hammersmith. Colours, red and black stripe. Badge, red and black oar, serpent and garter. Motto, *Celer et certus.*

London Rowing Club, Putney.— Was founded in 1856. In 1869, for the purpose of borrowing funds for the erection of a new boat-house, the members formed themselves into the London Boat-house Co., Limited, which was duly incorporated in January, 1870. The new house was opened in January, 1871, and some additions were made to it in 1875. The sum expended was nearly £3,000, and the money was raised by debentures, some of which are drawn by lot for payment in each year. The number of members is upwards of 500.

The election of members is by ballot in general meeting : one black ball in five excludes. Entrance £2, being the cost of a share in the Boat-house Co., on which there is no further liability. Subscription, £2 2s. A payment of £15 15s. at the time of election, or of £7 17s. 6d. after five years' membership, constitutes a life-membership. The share reverts to the company on resignation, forfeiture, or expulsion of a member. Sons, brothers, or nephews of members may be elected by ballot in general meeting under certain restrictions as cadet members, but the cadet member at the time of his election must not be less than ten years of age, and not more than sixteen ; he must be able to swim, and cadet membership ceases at the age of eighteen. Cadets pay no subscriptions or entrance fee. Boat-house, Putney. Colours, blue and white vertical stripes. Members who have passed an examination, and have qualified as "oarsmen," are also entitled to wear a silver badge.

London Sailing Club.—Club-house, The Rutland Hotel, the Mall, Hammersmith. The officers are commodore, vice and rear-commodores, treasurer, and hon. secretary, who with eight members constitute the committee both for sailing and general purposes. Election is by ballot in general meeting : one black ball in four excludes. Entrance fee, 10s. 6d. Subscription : owners of boats, £1 1s.; non-owners, or honorary members, 10s. 6d. Burgee, blue with yellow dolphin.

Long Reach extends from Crayford-ness to Greenhithe, 3 miles. Purfleet, with its powder magazines, the training-ship *Cornwall*, and its hotel, so well known for fish dinners, is at the west of the left (Essex) bank. A ferry crosses here to "Long Reach Tavern," a little to the westward of which is Dartford Creek, on the right (Kent) bank, at the eastern extremity of the reach. Stone Church is a prominent object just before arriving at Greenhithe. Bearings, S.E. by S. and N.W. by W.

Long Wittenham.—A village in Berkshire, on the right bank, 4 miles, S.E. from Abingdon. Population, 629. Soil, gravel on gault clay, with upper green-sand.

The parish church, dedicated to St. Mary the Virgin, is of mixed age, as shown by the variety of its architecture. The earliest portions are Norman and Early English (decorated) of several periods, and late perpendicular. The chancel, which is of the same period, is divided from the nave by a good Norman arch. The chancel was originally Norman, as shown by a small round-headed window and a piscina of the same date. The remainder of the chancel is Early English, as shown by one-light lancet-windows ; others are of the decorated period. The north and south aisles are divided from the nave by piers and arches of very Early English. The font, standing in the north aisle, is of lead, resting on a base of stone. It bears on it a row of figures of a mitred bishop under an arcade, holding a cross, and in the act of blessing. In a chapel to the south is a small piscina with the effigy of a cross-legged knight in full armour treading on a serpent, with the figures of two angels sculptured on the arch above him. The

figure is only two feet in length, and is thought to be of unique design. The tower is late perpendicular. The south porch is of the decorated period ; the barge board of elegant design.

INNS.—"Plough," "Vine Cottage," "Three Poplars," "Machine Man's Inn."

PLACE OF WORSHIP.—St. Mary the Virgin.

POLICE.—A constable lives in the village.

POSTAL ARRANGEMENTS. — Nearest money order and telegraph offices, Abingdon and Dorchester. Mail from London, 8 a.m. Mail to London, 5.35 p.m. Sunday, 10 a.m.

NEAREST *Bridge*, Clifton Hampden ; *Lock*, Clifton ; *Railway Station*, Culham (*which see* for FARES).

Magna Charta Island, a mile and a half from Old Windsor Lock, near the Middlesex bank, one of the most charming islands on the river, and of historical interest as the scene of the little arrangement between King John and his barons, which, as "every schoolboy knows," was the foundation of the freedom of England. In a cottage which stands on the island is a stone on which it is said that Magna Charta was signed. The usual uncertainty and vagueness which characterise all history step in even at what ought to be so very simple a matter as this. Tradition undoubtedly assigns the honour of being the scene of signature to the island, but in the charter itself it is said to be given at Runningmede, so that it would seem to be doubtful whether the finishing stroke was given to the palladium of English liberties on this island itself, or on Runnymede on the Surrey bank. Mr. and Mrs. S. C. Hall. who give an excellent account of Magna Charta in their delightful "Book of the Thames," express a regret "that no monument marks the spot at Runnymede where the rights and liberties of the people of England were maintained and secured, although several attempts have been made to raise one here." The same page gives us the inscription on the stone on which the parchment is said to have been signed : "Be it remembered that on this island, in June,

E

1215, King John of England signed the Magna Charta, and in the year 1834 this building was erected in commemoration of that great event by George Simon Harcourt, Esq., lord of the manor, and then high sheriff of the county."

Maidenhead, Berkshire, on the right bank ; from London 50 miles, from Oxford 61½ miles ; a station on the Great Western Railway 25 miles from Paddington ; trains take from 35 to 80 minutes. The station is twenty minutes' walk from Bond's boat-house at the bridge, and about five minutes from the town-hall. Flys and omnibuses meet the trains. For boating purposes or for visitors to the Orkney Arms Hotel, Taplow station is somewhat nearer and more convenient than Maidenhead. The counties of Berks and Bucks are here connected by a stone bridge of thirteen arches, and the Great Western Railway crosses the river a little below on a brick bridge of two arches, designed by the late Sir Isambard Brunel, and being remarkable as exhibiting the greatest span of brick extant, as also for its acoustic peculiarities. Population, 6,473. Maidenhead is a corporate town, governed by a high steward, mayor, four aldermen, and twelve councillors. It consists mainly of two streets, High-street and Queen-street, and is not very important or in itself attractive. There are, however, many good houses in the outskirts, more particularly along the bank of the river between Maidenhead Bridge and the Great Western Railway-bridge, and between the bridge and Boulter's Lock, in which direction a little inland, a new suburb of Maidenhead, known as Ray Park, has sprung into existence. The Town Hall is in the High-street, as is also the post-office. The Church of Saints Andrew and Mary is in the High-street, occupying the site of two older churches, dates from 1826, and was finished in 1878. It affords in itself no points of attraction. Part of the vicar's income is a Crown payment of "seven marks (£4 13s. 4d.), dating from the time of Philip and Mary, in compliance with the prayer of the inhabitants, who base their application on the fact that their chapel is distant from the mother churches "too myles or nere thereaboutes, to which yr. sede subjects cannot at sundry tymes in the yere, cum and make ther

repaire, to here the dyvyne seruice of Allmyghty God, and to serue God there, as of duty they are bounde to doe, bycause manie tymes thereof letted through vysytacyon of sycknesse, women labrynge and travelynge in childbedd ; and also bycause the seid toune of Maydenhedd is scituat in a loo contree, and very nere adjoynynge to the ryver Thamys, so that the seid contre is, dyvers tymes in the yere, so surrounded and overflowen wyth water that yr. Highnes seid subjects cannot passe goe nor travell to their seid churches ; by reson whereof the dutie of yr. seid subjects towards Allmyghtye God hath byn many tymes, agenst ther wyll, left undon." Allusion is then made to the endowment, by John Husbonde, "in the tyme of Kynge Edward the Thirde, oon of yr. Grace's noble progenitors, and of whose worthie stock and most noble lineage yr. Maiesties bothe are dyscended and lynyally comen," and to the loss of this revenue by "ye dyssolucyon of ye Pryorye of Hurley," the petitioners plaintively adding, "Sithen wyche dyssolucyon the pore inh'itants of the toune of Maydenhedd haue not hadd ther dyvyne seruice celebrated in the seyd chapell, as accustomably heretofore they haue hadd, bycause they be not able to fynde and mayntayn a convenyent prest to say dyvyne seruice in the seid chapell, to the greete decay and hyndraunce of Godd's seruice and to the discoragement of yr. faythfull subjects dwelling in the seid toune." Finally, coming to the point, they implore their majesties "to graunt an ordynarye pencyon and lyvynge to on honest and secular prest, to celebrate dyvyne seruice in the seid chapell of Maydenhedd, for the ease of ye pore inh'itants." This petition is thought by the Rev. C. G. Gorham (whose full and learned account of this church will be found in Vol. VI. of the "Collectanea Typographica et Genealogica") to have been written in 1557. The patronage of the church was in the hands of the prior of Hurley until the dissolution of the monasteries, when it seems to have been assumed by the inhabitants of the town, until the Charter of Incorporation, granted by Queen Elizabeth in 1582, when the corporation assumed the right. The advowson was sold by the corporation under the compulsory clause of the

Act for municipal reform, and purchased by Mr. Fuller Maitland in 1838. Mr. Gorham's opinion as to the etymology of the name of the town is very clear. He derives it from " Maiden Hythe," " the New Wharf," rejecting as absurd all connection with the head of " one of St. Ursula's virgins," or any other holy person. The present name first appears about A.D. 1300, previous to which date the place is called Elington, Elyngton, or South Elington. The Sacrament plate dates chiefly from 1657. There are a number of charitable funds in connection with the church. On the road to the river are the almshouses, founded in 1659 by James Smyth, citizen and salter. The Hambletonian Hall seats 2,000, and may be hired at a cost of £2 2s. per night, including gas, piano, &c. There is a large swimming-bath attached.

Although Maidenhead itself has few charms for the visitor, the country about it, more particularly the woods of Cliveden and Hedsor, a short distance up the river on the Bucks side, is charming indeed. Between Maidenhead and Marlow is, perhaps, the best known and the most popular part of the river. And its popularity is well deserved; for whether for the angler, the artist, the oarsman, or the simple tourist ; whether for fishing, picnicking, and it has been even whispered " spooning," to say nothing of camping-out, there are few places in England to beat the Cliveden Reach at Maidenhead or Quarry Woods at Marlow.

The interests of anglers in Maidenhead, Cookham, and Bray waters are attended to by the Maidenhead, Cookham, and Bray Angling Association (*which see*).

There are many and pleasant walks and drives about Maidenhead to supplement the river excursions. Among them may be mentioned Burnham Beeches (4 miles), one of the grandest collection of trees in England, and remarkably interesting for the varied growth of ferns and mosses. The Corporation of the City of London has recently saved Burnham Beeches from the hands of the brick and mortar spoilers,continuing here the good work commenced at Epping Forest. Hurley and Bisham are each about 4½ miles from Maidenhead by road, and Great Marlow is about 6 miles. In the other direction Windsor is also

about 6 miles distant. From Winter Hill, near Cookham Dene, a distance of about 4 miles, a grand view may be obtained on a clear day. Shorter walks are those to Maidenhead Thicket, Cookham, and Bray.

BANKS.—London and County, High-street ; Stephens, Blandy, and Co., High-street.

FAIRS.—Whit Wednesday, September 29, November 30.

FIRE.—Volunteer Brigade. Strength: Captain, deputy-captain, 3 first lieutenants, 3 second lieutenants, 2 engineers, 1 deputy-engineer, 18 pioneers, secretary, foreman of fire-escape, 3 manual-engines.

HOTELS.—The " Bear," High-street ; the " Ray Mead," near the river, above bridge ; " Skindle's," across the Bridge, in Bucks ; the " Thames," Ray Park ; the " White Hart," High-street.

MARKET DAY.—Wednesday.

PLACES OF WORSHIP.—All Saints, Boyn Hill ; St. Andrew and St. Mary, High-street ; St. Luke's ; The Roman Catholic Church of St. Mary the Immaculate; and Baptist, Congregational, Primitive Methodist, and Wesleyan Chapels.

POLICE.— Borough police - station, Queen-street : county police - station, South-street.

POSTAL ARRANGEMENTS.—Post Office (money order, savings bank, telegraph, and insurance), High-street. Mails from London, 7 and 10.30 a.m., 6.30 p.m. ; Sunday, 7 a.m. Mails to London, 10.30 a.m., 12.45, 4.30, and 9.45 p.m.; Sunday, 9.30 p.m.

NEAREST *Bridges*, Maidenhead ; up, Cookham 3 miles ; down, Windsor 7 miles. *Locks*, up, Boulter's ½ mile ; down, Bray 1¾ mile. *Railway Station*, Maidenhead.

FARES to Paddington : 1st, 4/4, 7/6 ; 2nd, 3/3, 5/9 ; 3rd, 2/0½.

Maidenhead, Cookham, and Bray Thames Angling Association.—The object of this association is the improvement of the fishery from the Shrubbery to Monkey Island. The annual subscription is £1 1s. Water-bailiffs and watchers are appointed at the discretion of the committee. A large number of fish, more especially trout, have been turned into the river by the association.

The water-bailiffs are required to keep live baits for the accommodation of members free of charge (lob worms and other baits to be paid for). A reward of 10s. is offered to anyone who shall give sufficient information to any member of the committee of any illegal fishing, or of being in unlawful possession of fish during the close season, provided that it be considered by the committee a fit case for prosecution, and that if the persons so prosecuted be convicted by the magistrates, the amount shall be doubled. A reward of £1 is offered to anyone capturing an otter in the waters under the supervision of the association.

Maidenhead Rowing Club.—Election by committee of thirteen : three black balls exclude. Subscription, 10s. 6d. Members subscribing £1 1s. and upwards may introduce a friend to the privileges of the club, free for one week, and for one month on payment of 5s. ; such friend not being resident in or within five miles of Maidenhead. There is a challenge cup for monthly competition. Colours, dark blue and primrose.

Mapledurham, Oxfordshire, on the left bank ; from London 78½ miles, from Oxford 33 miles. Population, 479. Soil, chalk. The chief glory of this village is the grand old Elizabethan Mapledurham House, belonging to the Blount family, of which Pope's Martha Blount was a member. The house, from the river, has a somewhat conventual or monastic appearance, and the principal front, facing the park and not the river, is approached by a magnificent avenue of ancient elms. A great old-fashioned pair of iron gates afford access from Mapledurham House to the churchyard, in which, nestling amongst noble trees, is the church of St. Margaret, which has been extensively restored, and exhibits some remarkable combinations of colour, which might, perhaps, be described as the barber's-pole style of decoration. The greater part of the church, as well as the roof of the chancel, is curiously picked out with every variety of brilliant colour, and the idea is still further carried out by the font, which is painted red, white, blue, and gold, and further exhibits the real barber's pole blue and gilt stripes. There is a handsome reredos, and

between the south aisle and the nave is a grand monument of Sir Richard Blount and his wife Elizabeth, with two recumbent life-sized figures, the one in armour, the other in rough and farthingale. A close inspection of this is difficult, as it is jealously enclosed with spiked iron railings. Indeed, the whole of the south aisle presents the curious anomaly of being walled and railed off from the rest of the church. It is claimed by the Blount family as a private mortuary chapel, and is kept rigidly locked and strictly private. It is understood that the opinion of ecclesiastical lawyers has been found favourable to this exercise of power.

Just above Mapledurham is another singularly fine mansion — Hardwick House—where it is said that Charles I. frequently indulged in his favourite pastime of bowls, and if the royal martyr had been as judicious in all matters as he undoubtedly was when he selected Hardwick for a playground, the course of English history might have been considerably changed.

Mapledurham Reach is celebrated for its jack and perch, for the latter particularly. The Caversham and Reading fishermen generally make for this district.

INN.—"The Roebuck," on the Berkshire bank, about a mile below the lock. There is a ferry here.

PLACES OF WORSHIP.—St. Margaret ; Catholic, attached to Mapledurham House.

POSTAL ARRANGEMENTS. — Letters through Reading. Letter-box in Vicarage-wall cleared 6.30 p.m. week-days, and noon on Sundays. Nearest money order, telegraph, &c., offices, Caversham and Pangbourne.

NEAREST *Bridges*, up, Whitchurch about 2 miles ; down, Caversham 4 miles. *Locks*, up, Whitchurch 2¼ miles; down, Caversham 4¼ miles. *Ferry*, Purley. *Railway Station*, Pangbourne.

FARES, Pangbourne to Paddington : 1st, 7/4, 13/-; 2nd, 5/6, 9/6 ; 3rd, 3/5½.

Maplin Sands begin just to the eastward of Southend and extend to beyond the Maplin Light. They are on the north side, and are well buoyed.

Maps:

Margaret Ness.—(*See* TRIPCOCK REACH.)

Marine Board, Local.—Office for examination of masters and mates, St. Katharine Dock House, Tower-hill.—NEAREST *Railway Station*, Cannon-street; *Omnibus Route*, Fenchurch-street.

Marine Society, Office, Bishopsgate-street-within. Training ship, *Warspite*, off Charlton Pier, Woolwich.—The report of the society for 1881 gives the following complete account of its history and progress. The Marine Society owes its origin to the sentiments of humanity and benevolence exerted on behalf of a number of wretched and distressed boys, who were in the spring of the year 1756 collected together by that active magistrate, Sir John Fielding, clothed at the expense of the Duke of Bolton, and sent to serve on board His Majesty's ship *Barfleur*, then under His Grace's command. The utility of this humane design, in rescuing from misery and reclaiming as many as possible of this class of neglected youths from the paths of idleness, and too probably of infamy and perdition, was so obvious, that the plan was immediately followed up with the most active philanthropy by a private gentleman (Mr. Walker, of Lincoln's-inn), who had accidentally met with those lads on their way to join the *Barfleur*. By subscription, which he promoted, from three to four hundred boys were in a short time clothed and provided for in a profession most likely

to make them useful and creditable members of the community. At a subsequent meeting of merchants and shipowners in June, 1756, Mr. Jonas Hanway, a merchant totally unconnected with the nobleman and both the gentlemen beforementioned, proposed that they should form themselves into a society to give clothing to boys for the sea-service. The proposal being readily adopted, the Marine Society was instituted; and eventually, in the year 1772, incorporated by Act of Parliament. The boys selected for the sea service are taken from the labouring classes, the utterly destitute being the first to be admitted. No dishonest boys are received. Parish boys may be received to fill vacancies on board the society's ship, on payment of £4 4s. No boys are received whose friends appear to be in a capacity to fit them out for sea at their own charge. Various plans were at different times brought under the contemplation of the society for a more beneficial arrangement as to some receptace for the objects of the charity, in which they might be taken care of, and receive the benefit of instruction, both religious and professional, until such time as they could be properly provided for. In the year 1786, a proposition, originating with Alderman Brook Watson, M.P., was adopted by the society. They first procured a merchant vessel, named the *Beatty;* this ship having become decayed and worn out in 1799, application was made to the Admiralty for the loan of a Government ship. The application was complied with, and from that time the Lords Commissioners, in order to promote the views of the Marine Society, have accommodated them with one of Her Majesty's ships as a training vessel for boys. The *Warspite*, a noble two-decker, formerly the *Conqueror*, is the ship now lent to the society. The society holds in trust the following special funds, devoted solely to the purposes for which they were given or bequeathed:— 1. Consols, £17,045 9s., under the will of William Hickes, Esq., of Hamburg, for apprenticing poor boys and girls. In time of war the income of this fund is appropriated, with the general funds of the society, in clothing and fitting out boys for sea, rendering them thereby fit for service in the Royal Navy. 2. Consols, £14,333 6s. 8d., ten thousand pounds of this amount being the gift of the late

Isaac Hawkins, Esq. The annual interest of this trust fund produces £430, which is appropriated every year in the month of June, in donations of £10 each to forty-three widows of captains and lieutenants in the Royal Navy. The Marine Society is also entrusted with the payments of certain annuities to the widows of the sufferers in the engagement of the 11th October, 1797, under Admiral Lord Duncan, under rules and regulations transmitted by the Chairman of the Committee of Lloyd's Coffee House, on the 15th of October, 1802.

Marlow, Great, Buckinghamshire, on the left bank of the river, is a terminus of the Bourne End and Marlow branch of the Great Western Railway, 35½ miles from Paddington, the trains averaging a little over an hour. The station is about five minutes' walk from the bridge. Fly and omnibus meet the trains. The distance from London is 57 miles, from Oxford 54½ miles. Population, 4,701. Soil : flint, chalk, gravel, and loam. The name Marlow, or, as it is called in Domesday Book, Merelaw, is derived by Camden from "the chalk commonly called marle," which he asserts to be very plentiful here ; a piece of etymology derided by Langley in his Hundred of Desborough, who derives the name from a mere, or piece of standing water, which he supposes to have been here in ancient times. Langley, who has strong and usually common-sense views on these matters, derives the name of Desborough Hundred from *duo burgi*—Wycomb and Marlow—quite repudiating Danesborough. Marlow is a very ancient manor, and appears from its earliest history to have been connected with royalty. Before the Conquest it was held by Algar, Earl of Mercia, from whose son it was taken by William the Conqueror, and bestowed upon Queen Matilda. Later on it became, through his wife, the property of Richard Nevil, Earl of Warwick, the king-maker, who was slain at Barnet, and is buried in Bisham Abbey ; later still it was granted by Philip and Mary to Lord Paget of Beaudesert, an extraordinary statesman, who enjoyed the confidence of four succeeding sovereigns : an unusual tenure he possibly owed to the practice of the

following precepts discovered in his commonplace book :

Fly the courte,
Speke little,
Care less.
Devise nothing.
Never earnest,
In answer cold.
Lerne to spare ;
Spend with measure,
Care for home.
Pray often.
Live better.
And dye well.

Court Garden, which is on the left just above the bridge, the last part of the estate remaining in the Paget family, was sold by Lord Uxbridge in 1758. Marlow is a parliamentary constituency, and returns one member to Parliament, the present member being Major-Gen. Owen Williams, of Temple, a Conservative. The borough was first summoned to return burgesses by Edward I. in 1299, the first two burgesses whose names are recorded being Richard le Mouner and Richard le Veel ; but from 1308 until 1622, when the privilege was restored by Parliament, no members were returned on "account of the expence."

Since the time the Knight Templars were at Bisham, the counties of Berks and Bucks have been here united by various bridges, the present suspension bridge, which cost £20,000, having been erected in 1835. There is still in existence a writ for the repairs of the bridge, dated 27 Edward III., 1352, directed *probis hominibus villæ de Merlawe.* The bridge in more modern times has acquired a certain notoriety in connection with a "puppy pie," concerning which succulent pastry there are various traditions : and "Who ate the puppy pie under Marlow Bridge ?" is popularly supposed to be a crushing retort to any bargee impertinence. From Marlow Bridge, the view up or down the river is hardly to be surpassed on the Thames.

Indeed, whether for fishing, boating, holiday, or sketching purposes, there is no more fascinating spot on the river than Marlow. From Bourne End to New Lock — the backwater by Harleford Manor House—the river teems at various points with trout, pike, barbel, roach, chub, perch, and gudgeon, a result greatly attributable to the constant care of the Marlow Angling Association, and the liberality of some of its individual members, who have at their own expense turned large numbers of trout and other fish into the river. For boating purposes, the reaches from Cookham to Marlow and from Marlow to Temple Hurley and Medmenham, are excellently adapted, and for camping-out purposes there is no more favourite spot on the river than the Quarry Woods below Marlow. As to its attractions for the artist, the numerous pictures that yearly appear on the walls of the Academy and the Water Colour Societies abundantly testify. Boats are taken care of by Haynes and R. Shaw, under the bridge, and the numerous hotels in the town afford excellent accommodation for tourists of all classes. Ordinary boating parties will do well to remember that it is unwise to rely upon obtaining quarters at the well-known "Complete Angler," near the bridge, without considerable previous notice; but great improvement has recently taken place in the management here, and much more space than of old has been made available for dinners, etc. The "Crown," at the end of the main street, and five minutes' walk from the river, is a comfortable, old-fashioned house, with a first-rate billiard-room.

In the town itself there is little of interest; the old quaint houses have nearly all given place to staring brick or vulgar stucco erections; the only really ancient remains being a portion of a house in St. Peter's-street, known as the Deanery, with fine old mullioned windows. There are two principal streets: High-street, leading up from the river; and West-street, at right angles to it. In the latter is the house, on which is now a tablet, in which Shelley lived and was visited by Lord Byron. Of this period Mrs. Shelley says: "During the year 1817 we were established at Marlow, in Buckinghamshire. Shelley's choice of abode was fixed chiefly by this town being at no great distance from London, and its neighbourhood of the Thames. The poem, 'The Revolt of Islam,' was written in his boat, as it floated under the beech groves of Bisham, or during wanderings in the neighbouring country." At Remnantz, a house nearly opposite to Shelley's, was for thirteen or fourteen years the Royal Military College,

before it was removed to Sandhurst. Seymour Court, Mr. Wethered's residence, is asserted to have been the birthplace of Henry VIII.'s Jane Seymour, but the honour is disputed by the family seat of the Seymours in Wiltshire. Harleyford House, the seat of Sir William Clayton, is about two miles up the river.

The church, a modern structure of a style of architecture variously described as Late English or Modern Gothic, is ugly without and bald within, although it must at one time have been rich in brasses and monuments, some of the former dating from the latter end of the fourteenth century. Langley records several curious entries in the church books, commencing with one in 1592: "Paid for mendynge the bells when the queen came to Bysham, 1s." The loyalty of the bellringers appears to have outrun their discretion. There are many entries for payments to bellringers when the kings passed through the town, in 1604, 1605, 1612, 1617, and 1647. In 1608, among the church goods are catalogued:

Fyve pair of garters and bells,
Fyve coats and a fool's coat.

In 1650 appears the significant entry, "For defacing of the king's arms, 1s.;" and in 1651, "Paid to the painter for setting up the State's arms, 16s." The Catholic church, in St. Peter's-street, one of the elder Pugin's last works, was opened in 1846; but, together with Holy Trinity, a chapel of ease to the parish church, will scarcely repay a visit. Marlow has a literary and scientific institution, with a library and reading-room, well supplied with books and newspapers. Subscription: 1st class members, £1 1s. per annum; 2nd, 10s.; 3rd, 5s. It also possesses a Lawn-Tennis Club, a Choral Society, and Cricket and Football Clubs. A Cottager's Horticultural Show is held every year, and there is a Lecture or Music Room in St. Peter's-street. The Maidenhead and Marlow Regatta is held alternately at Marlow and Maidenhead, and there is in addition an annual town regatta. The town is also privileged to possess a Constitutional Association, established for the modest purpose of securing on an income of £76 per annum, "the proper registration, as voters, of all persons within the several parishes of the borough who hold constitutional principles; of resisting any movement directed against the institutions of the country; of defending the rights and privileges of the people; and of promoting beneficial legislation in the spirit of the Constitution."

The walks and excursions from Marlow are varied and numerous. Within easy walking distance are Henley, Maidenhead, and the quaint and interesting towns of High or Chipping Wycombe, and Cookham. Hurley and Medmenham are, as it were, next door. Wycombe is well worth a visit, and its church, All Saints, which dates from 1273, restored by Mr. Street at a cost of £10,000, is one of the finest in the county, and contains many brasses and memorials. The Quarry Woods are within a ten minutes' saunter of Marlow Bridge, and offer in every direction the pleasantest and most picturesque walks by the riverside, or across the hill to Cookham Dene. From Winter Hill, the extremity of the woods in the Cookham direction, a view as magnificent as it is extensive is to be obtained, and includes the course of the Thames from Henley to Maidenhead. Bisham Abbey and Church are close at hand, and Mr. Borgnis's grounds at Highfield are a short mile from the town on the Henley road.

Borlase's School, or, as it is more generally denominated, the Blue Coat School, was founded by Sir William Borlase in 1624 for the education of twenty-four boys —of whom three are chosen from Medenham, three from Little Marlow, and eighteen from Great Marlow. They are each allowed £2 to apprentice them, but this at the present day being insufficient for the purpose is generally added to by contribution of £8 or £12—from Loftin's Charity—bequeathed by Benjamin Loftin in 1759. The education comprised reading, writing, and casting accounts. Sir William Borlase also made bequests for founding a school for teaching twenty-four girls to knit, spin, or make bone lace, and for establishing a house of correction. The income being found insufficient for its purpose the girls' school was some years ago merged in the National and Infants' Schools. In order to increase the public usefulness of Borlase's boys' school, negotiations have been opened by the feoffees with the Charity Commissioners, who propounded a scheme on the following lines : Tuition fees are to be not less than £3 or more than £5 per year. School to be unsectarian. Education to comprise reading, writing, arithmetic, geography, history, English grammar, composition, and literature, mathematics, Latin, at least one foreign European language, natural science, drawing, drill, and vocal music. This scheme has since been elaborated, and the school is of considerable importance as a middle-class Grammar School.

BANK.—Stephens, Blandy, & Co.

FAIR.—October 29.

FIRE.—Volunteer Brigade: Superintendent, foreman, engineer, sub-engineer, hon. treasurer, 9 firemen, and 5 reserve. Manual engine. Next the "Crown."

HOTELS AND INNS. — "Complete Angler" (by the river, in Bisham parish); "Crown," up the town; "Fisherman's Retreat," "George and Dragon," "Railway."

PLACES OF WORSHIP.—All Saints, and Holy Trinity; the Roman Catholic Church of St. Peter's; and Congregational, Baptist, and Primitive Methodist Chapels.

POLICE.—Station in the town.

POSTAL ARRANGEMENTS.—Post Office (money order, savings bank, telegraph, and insurance), West-street. Mails from London, 7.30 and 10.45 a.m., 6.45 p.m. Sunday, 7.30 a.m. Mails for London, 9.40 a.m., noon, and 3.40 and 7.50 p.m.; Sunday, 7.50 p.m. Wall letter-box opposite the church, cleared 10.50 a.m., 3.30 and 7.40 p.m. ; Sunday, 7.40 p.m. Station wall box cleared 10.40 a.m. and 7.40 p.m. Thames Lawn wall box cleared 8.25 a.m., 10.45 a.m., and 7.35 p.m.

NEAREST *Bridges,* up, Henley 8 miles ; down, Cookham 3¾ miles. *Locks,* up, Temple 1½ mile ; down, Cookham 4 miles. *Ferry,* Temple. *Railway Station,* Marlow.

FARES to Paddington : 1st, 6/-, 9/11 ; 2nd, 4/6, 7/6 ; 3rd, 2/7½.

Marlow (Great) Amateur Rowing Club.—Usual amateur qualification. Donors of £10 10s. and upwards are life members, and all life members and annual subscribers of £2 2s. and upwards are vice-presidents. No subscription is less than 10s. 6d. Election by ballot in committee, two black balls in five to exclude. The monthly challenge cup is competed for the last Wednesday in every month. The club, established in 1871, now numbers about ninety members. Boat-house, Haynes's, Marlow Bridge. Club colours, cardinal.

Marlow (Great) Regatta—

Saturday, July 5, 1884.

JUNIOR SCULLS.

Bucks Station—A. V. H. Bone, West London R.C. 1
Centre Station—R. E. Cole, Thames R.C. 0

SENIOR SCULLS.

First Heat.

Berks Station- -E. St. J. Christophers, Thames R.C. 1
Bucks Station—E. C. Kendall, Chester R.C. 0

Second Heat.

R. H. Smith, Thames R.C. ... ...r.o.

Final Heat.

Bucks Station—Christophers... ... 1
Berks Station—Smith 0

JUNIOR FOURS.

Bucks Station—Reading R.C. ... 1
Berks Station—Clare College B.C. ... 0
Centre Station—Cookham R.C. ... 0
Reading.—J. H. Cooper, D. F. Cooksey, J. H. Tyrell, F. Cuttrill (stroke), T. Rose (cox).
Clare College.—E. E. Dorling, J. R. Fuller, A. D. Flower, R. G. Wilde (stroke), J. Frome (cox).
Cookham.—E. Ford, F. T. Ford, A. C. Bloomfield, F. Speller (stroke), F. Hyde (cox).

GRAND CHALLENGE CUP (for eight oars).

First Heat.

Centre Station—Abney R.C. 1
Berks Station—London R.C. ... 0
Bucks Station—Thames R.C. ... disq.
Abney.—H. S. Close, A. H. Knox, R. C. Lehman, E. W. Haig, F. E. Churchill, A. R. Patterson, D. H. Maclean, F. J. Pitman (stroke), Humphreys (cox).
London.—B. James, W. H. Wells, P. D. Ullman, E. S. M'Ewan, W. R. Lyne, F. Earnshaw, J. Kerr, C. Wood (stroke), W. F. Sheard (cox).

Thames.—C. N. Hughes, B. E. Cole, Gordon Smith, B. Looker, W. Liddle, A. M. Hutchinson, S. Fairbairn, H. Atkinson (stroke), E. A. Safford (cox).

Second Heat.

Centre Station—Royal Chester R.C. 1
Bucks Station—West London R.C. 0
Royal Chester.—C. A. Beam, T. G. Royston, P. Small, A. M. Robertson, E. R. F. G. Frost, Billington, J. J. Gardiner, *West London.*—ke), J. J. Lowe (cox).
Vaux, J. H. Welch, H. Bowen, A. B. less, C. E. Brown, A. Tilett, A. Law-Vaux (stroke), W. R. Wheeler, G. C.

Third Heat.

Centre Station—Twickenham R.C. ... 1
Bucks Station—Albion R.C. ... 0
Twickenham.—E. Vertue, H. Blackmore, S. Hodgkin, Stuart Green, G. J. Bonner, J. Lowndes, F. Leader, L. Frere (stroke), B. Caddy (cox).
Albion.—J. W. Macqueen, S. E. Carlin, G. H. Capper, C. R. Sutherland, W. W. Butler, A. Edwards, C. F. Munro, E. Christian (stroke), A. Barnard (cox).

Final Heat.

Bucks Station—Twickenham R.C. ... 1
Berks Station—Chester R.C. 0
Centre Station—Abney R.C. 0

SENIOR FOURS.

First Heat.

Bucks Station—Marlow R.C. ... 1
Centre Station—London R.C. ... 0
Berks Station—Royal Chester R.C. ... 0
Marlow.—W. T. Shaw, W. T. Porter, C. H. Yates, J. S. Kirkpatrick (stroke).
London.—P. D. Ullmann, W. Bergh, H. J. Hill, C. Wood (stroke).
Royal Chester.—C. R. Royston, J. Billington, J. J. Gardiner, J. G. Frost (stroke).

Second Heat.

Bucks Station—Thames R.C. ... 1
Centre Station—Clare College B.C. ... 0
Thames.—B. Looker, W. Liddle, S. Fairbairn, A. M. Hutchinson (stroke).
Clare College.—J. R. Fuller, E. K. Mead, A. D. Flower, R. G. Wilde (stroke).

Final Heat.

Centre Station—Thames R.C. ... 1
Bucks Station—Marlow R.C. ... 0

SENIOR PAIRS.

Kingston R.C.—R. H. Cobb and F. Cobb ... ...r.o.

TOWN CHALLENGE CUP.

Centre Station—Marlow R.C.   ...   I
Bucks Station—Reading R.C.   ...   o

Marlow.—W. T. Shaw, W. T. Porter, C. H. Yates, J. S. Kirkpatrick (stroke), N. Shaw (cox).

Reading.—H. G. Lovejoy, W. J. Brown, H. E. Cottrell, T. H. Clark (stroke), T. Rose (cox).

Marlow (Great) Thames Angling Association.—The water held by the association reaches from Temple Mills to the "Shrubbery." The annual subscription is £1 1s. A head water-bailiff, assistant bailiffs, and sub-assistant bailiffs are appointed by the committee, who are required to provide live bait for the members free of charge. A reward of 10s. is offered to any one who shall give information of any poaching or illegal fishing to the water-bailiff, provided that it be considered by the committee a fit case for prosecution ; if the person prosecuted be convicted the reward is doubled. A reward of 10s. is offered for every dead otter proved to have been caught between the top of the reach immediately above Temple Lock and the "Shrubbery." The association has turned a very large number of fish, more especially trout, into the river, and to it Marlow owes much of the enhanced reputation it now enjoys among anglers.

Medmenham, Buckinghamshire, on the left bank ; a small village of about 350 inhabitants, from London 60½ miles, from Oxford 51 miles, from Marlow, the nearest railway-station, 3 miles by road ; chiefly notorious from its connection with the Medmenham Monks of Francis Dashwood and John Wilkes. There seems to be no doubt that considerable "high jinks" were indulged in by this fraternity, and that they were not altogether what is generally known as respectable society. But it is probable that exaggeration has had much to do with the records, or rather legends, of its proceedings, as is always the case where an affectation of mystery and secrecy is maintained. The monks of Medmenham, sometimes politely called the Hell Fire Club, lived at a time when drunkenness and profanity were considered to be amongst the gentlemanly virtues, and probably, as a matter of fact, they were not very much worse than other people. The audacious

motto of the club may, perhaps, have had something to do with the holy horror which it excited. "*Fay ce que voudras*" was not a good motto at a time when doing as you pleased was about the last thing that good old-fashioned Toryism was likely to tolerate ; and when amongst the people who were to do as they liked was the hated Wilkes, the prejudices of respectability were certain to be even further outraged. "*Fay ce que voudras,*" as it appears over a doorway at the abbey, has in these times quite a hospitable look, and the invitation is readily accepted by the scores and scores of picnic parties who resort to Medmenham in the summer, and whose innocent merrymaking is, at all events, an improvement on Wilkes and his monks, however much they may have been libelled. Medmenham Abbey, as it stands at present, is, architecturally, but a bogus affair, and, except an ancient archway and a single pillar of the church, there is little of the ancient abbey to be found in the present edifice, but it stands in so beautiful a position, and commands such lovely views, that its artificial appearance will be readily forgiven. Once upon a time there was indeed a very important monastery here, founded by Hugh de Bolebec, to whom a charter was given by King John in 1201. The monastery was originally colonised from the Cistercian Abbey of Woburn in 1204, but the Woburn monks did not seem able to make much of it, and very shortly afterwards returned whence they had come. In 1212 a second colonisation was effected by Cistercian monks from Cisteaux in the bishopric of Chalons, in France. Their rules certainly would not have suited Wilkes and his friends. "They neither wore skins, nor shirts, nor even eat flesh, except in sickness ; and abstained from fish, eggs, milk, and cheese ; they lay upon straw beds in tunics and cowls ; they rose at midnight to prayers ; they spent the day in labour, reading, and prayer ; and in all their exercises observed a continual silence." This cheerful community held possession of the abbey for several hundred years. In the beginning of the 16th century it was annexed to the Abbey of Bristleham or Bisham, on the opposite side of the river, and so remained until the suppression of the monasteries by Henry VIII. ; and from the report of the commissioners at that time, the institution seems to have fallen upon very evil days. The clear value was returned at £20 6s. 2d. "Monks," continues the report, "there are two; and both desyring to go to houses of religion; servants, none; bells, &c., worth £2 6s. 8d.; the house wholly in ruin; the value of the moveable goods, £1 3s. 8d.; woods, none.; debts, none." Whether the last item is due to the care of the monks or to the caution of the local tradespeople, may remain an open question. The most distinguished of the real monks of Medmenham was John, who was elected Abbot of Chertsey in 1261, and of whom there is an interesting memorial in the British Museum in the shape of his seal. At one time the Abbot of Medmenham was, *ex officio*, epistolar of the Order of the Garter, and it was his duty to read the epistle in the morning service on St. George's Day at Windsor.

The church has been considerably restored, but still presents traces of its Norman origin. There are more considerable portions Early English, but the church must have been nearly rebuilt in the days of the perpendicular style. It has chancel, nave, and square embattled tower, and a good old carved oak pulpit. There are not many ancient monuments in the church, but a brass remains in memory of Richard Levyng and Alicia his wife, bearing dates 1415 and 1419. The church and post-office are five or six minutes' walk from the river.

The principal mansion in the neighbourhood is Danesfield, the seat of C. R. Scott-Murray, Esq., which owes its name to the time when the Danes, after seizing and fortifying Shoebury, marched along the river until they came to Boddington in Gloucestershire. The encampment called the "Danes' Ditches" and the "Horse-shoe Entrenchment," date, no doubt, from this campaign. Attached to the house is a fine chapel built by the Pugins, containing some good pictures. There are fine roach swims all the way up this reach.

HOTEL.—The "Ferry Boat," adjoining the abbey.

PLACE OF WORSHIP.—St. Peter's.

POSTAL ARRANGEMENTS.—Letters through Marlow. Nearest savings bank, telegraph office, &c., Marlow. Mails from London, 7.40 a.m. week-days and

Sundays; mails to London, 6.15 p.m.; Sunday, 9.25 a.m.

NEAREST *Bridges*, up, Henley 4½ miles; down, Marlow 2½ miles. *Locks*, up, Hambleden 2 miles; down, Hurley 1½ mile. *Ferry*, Medmenham. *Railway Station*, Marlow.

FARES, Marlow to Paddington: 1st, 6/-, 9/11; 2nd, 4/6, 7/6; 3rd, 2/7½.

Mercantile Marine Offices.—*See* SHIPPING OFFICE.

Metropolitan Amateur Regatta, Putney. This regatta, which was founded in 1866, arose out of a challenge given by the West London Rowing Club to the London Rowing Club in the previous year for a junior eight-oared match. Other clubs connected with the then existing Amateur Rowing Clubs Association joined in, and several crews started, with the result that the final heat from Putney to Chiswick Church was won by the London Rowing Club Crew, the Thames being second, and the West London third. The event was so successful that it was decided to establish an annual regatta on the Putney water, and a large amount being collected amongst the members of the associated clubs and others, valuable—perhaps even too valuable—challenge prizes were bought, and the regatta was duly started under the management of the association. That body, however, experienced the fate that has befallen so many attempts at combination amongst amateur clubs, and was in a short time dissolved. Since then the management of the regatta has been in the hands of the London Rowing Club, the members of which subscribe and collect among their friends by far the greater portion of the money required to carry on the regatta, which takes place on the first available tide after Henley, when it is high water at about 5 p.m., that is to say.

The course—about a mile and three-quarters—is from Putney to Hammersmith, or *vice versâ*, according to the state of the tide. The winners of the challenge cups are as follows:

METROPOLITAN CHAMPION CUP FOR
EIGHTS.

1866 London Rowing Club
1867 London Rowing Club
1868 London Rowing Club

1869 London Rowing Club
1870 Kingston Rowing Club
1871 Kingston Rowing Club
1872 London Rowing Club
1873 Thames Rowing Club
1874 Thames Rowing Club
1875 Molesey Boat Club
1876 Thames Rowing Club
1877 London Rowing Club
1878 London Rowing Club
1879 London Rowing Club
1880 Thames Rowing Club
1881 London Rowing Club
1882 London Rowing Club
1883 Twickenham Rowing Club
1884 London Rowing Club

THE THAMES CUP FOR FOURS.

1866 London Rowing Club
1867 London Rowing Club
1868 London Rowing Club
1869 London Rowing Club
1870 Kingston Rowing Club
1871 London Rowing Club
1872 London Rowing Club
1873 London Rowing Club
1874 London Rowing Club
1875 Thames Rowing Club
1876 London Rowing Club
1877 London Rowing Club
1878 London Rowing Club
1879 Bath Avon Rowing Club
1880 Thames Rowing Club
1881 London Rowing Club
1882 Thames Rowing Club
1883 Thames Rowing Club
1884 Thames Rowing Club

METROPOLITAN CHALLENGE CUP FOR JUNIOR EIGHTS.

1866 Thames Rowing Club
1867 London Rowing Club
1868 North London Rowing Club
1869 West London Rowing Club
1870 Ino Rowing Club
1871 London Rowing Club
1872 Ino Rowing Club
1873 West London Rowing Club
1874 Thames Rowing Club
1875 Ino Rowing Club
1876 Thames Rowing Club
1877 London Rowing Club
1878 London Rowing Club
1879 Thames Rowing Club
1880 Thames Rowing Club
1881 West London Rowing Club
1882 London Rowing Club
1883 Thames Rowing Club
1884 Anglian Boat Club

THE LONDON CUP FOR SCULLERS.

1866 George Ryan, London R.C.
1867 W. B. Woodgate, O.U.B.C.
1868 W. Stout, London R.C.
1869 A. de L. Long, London R.C.
1870 W. L. Slater, West L.R.C.
1871 W. Faucus, Tynemouth R.C.
1872 C. C. Knollys, O.U.B.C.
1873 C. C. Knollys, O.U.B.C.
1874 H. S. Freeman, Thames R.C.
1875 F. L. Playford, London R.C.
1876 F. L. Playford, London R.C.
1877 A. H. Grove, London R.C.
1878 A. Payne, Molesey R.C.
1879 C. G. White, London R.C.
1880 W. A. D. Evanson, London R.C.
1881 J. Lowndes, Hertford Coll. Oxford.
1882 W. R. Grove, London R.C.
1883 J. Lowndes, Twickenham R.C.
1884 R. H. Smith, Thames R.C.

RACES IN 1884.

Thursday, July 10.

Course between Putney and Hammersmith. The first five races were rowed up, and the remainder down, the stations counting from the Surrey shore.

METROPOLITAN PAIRS (rowed up).

F. W. Long and J. Hastie, Thames R.C. ... ...r.o.

JUNIOR SCULLS (rowed up).

Fifth Station—C. J. S. Batt, Thames R.C. 1
Fourth Station—W. H. Bone, West London R.C.... 0
Second Station—G. R. B. Earnshaw, London R.C.... 0
First Station—B. W. Looker, Thames R.C. 0

METROPOLITAN CHALLENGE CUP.

First Heat (rowed up).

First Station—Anglian B.C. 1
Second Station—London R.C. ... 0
Third Station—Kensington R.C. ... 0

Anglian—C. G. Poole, R. A. Brown, A. W. Piggott, A. E. Edwards, G. S. K. Dewhirst, C. Humble, J. T. Musgrave, P. W. S. Ell (stroke), D. F. Rait (cox).

London—C. F. Schlotel, P. A. N. Thorn, W. J. Leeman, A. S. Bryden, A. M. Evanson, F. W. Danter, W. F. Shillito, J. E. Molson (stroke), W. F. Sheard (cox).

Kensington—W. A. Spencer, W. E. Neville, T. G. Jeffery, W. E. Beckett, M. Clarke, H. Venn, jun., F. W. Upton, J. B. S. Hickman (stroke), J. W. Staples (cox).

Second Heat (rowed up).

Third Station—West London R.C. ... 1
Second Station—Thames R.C.   ... 0
First Station—East Sheen B.C.   ... 0

West London—A. Gray, W. D. Gilbert, A. C. Ellis, G. S. Herschell, C. J. Scott, W. E. Wallis, F. A. Knight, C. H. Hickman (stroke), E. P. Owens (cox).

Thames—C. Smith, F. W. Guerrier, G. A. Herdman, W. Andrewes, M. C. Gie, C. S. Sowerby, W. Theobald, H. Atkinson (stroke), E. A. Safford (cox).

East Sheen—J. G. F. Glossop, A. P. Parker, F. B. Lewis, F. Chattaway, H. R. Parker, R. H. Barron, H. O. F. Luckie, A. Hughes (stroke), H. M. Ripley (cox).

Final Heat (rowed down).

First Station—Anglian B.C. 1
Second Station—West London R.C.   0

THAMES CUP (rowed up).

Third Station—Thames R.C.   ... 1
Second Station—Kingston R.C.   ... 0
First Station—London R.C. 0

Thames—G. H. Eyre, J. Hastie, H. J. Rust, J. A. Drake-Smith (stroke).

Kingston—F. H. Cobb, H. A. Harvey, H. S. Till, R. H. Cobb (stroke).

London—L. Maclean, J. F. Stillwell, J. T. Crier, W. W. Hewett (stroke).

METROPOLITAN CHAMPION CUP (rowed down).

First Station—London R.C.

Second Station—Thames R.C.

Dead heat.

London—G. R. B. Earnshaw, C. Earnshaw, W. Bergh, J. F. Stillwell, H. J. Hill, A. S. J. Hurrell, J. T. Crier, W. W. Hewett (stroke), W. F. Sheard (cox).

Thames — B. E. Cole, G. H. Eyre, Gordon Smith, A. M. Hutchinson, S. Fairbairn, J. Hastie, H. J. Rust, J. A. Drake-Smith (stroke), E. A. Safford (cox).

LONDON CUP—SENIOR SCULLS (rowed down).

Fourth Station—R. H. Smith, Thames R.C. 1

Second Station—E. F. Grün, London R.C. 0

First Station—E. St. J. Christophers, Thames R.C. 0

SENIOR FOURS (with coxswains, rowed down).

Second Station—Twickenham R.C. ... 1
First Station—London R.C. 0

Twickenham—H. Blackmore, G. A. Bonner, E. Hodgkin, Stuart Green (stroke), D. Caddy (cox).

London—P. D. Ullman, W. Bergh, H. J. Hill, C. Wood (stroke), W. F. Sheard (cox).

CHAMPION PAIRS (rowed down).

First Station — G. R. B. Earnshaw and C. Earnshaw, London R.C. ... 1

Second Station—R. H. Cobb and F. Cobb, Kingston R.C.   0

Metropolitan Railway Rowing Club, Hammersmith.—Election : Either majority at the general meeting on election of officers, or afterwards by the officers. Boat-house, Biffen's, Hammersmith. Colours, blue and violet.

Middle Blyth Buoy.—A 16-ft. can buoy, made of iron, and painted with black and white stripes. It is situated in Sea Reach, a short distance below Thames Haven, on the edge of the Blyth Sand, and marks a depth of water, at low-water spring tide, of 20 ft. It is moored with 18 fathom of chain.

Millwall Docks (Office, 1, Railway-place, Fenchurch-street, E.C.) are situate on the Isle of Dogs, just south of the West India Docks, the access being by the Millwall Extension branch of the Blackwall Railway.

Minnows, stickleback, loach, and miller's thumb, are all found in the Thames, and each used in turn for bait ; but they are rarely purposely fished for, even by tyros, as there is such an abundance of choicer game. When wanted in quantities the cast-net is thrown, and they are taken in great numbers on the shallows and in the tributaries of the main river.

Missions to Seamen, 11, Buckingham-street, Strand, London.—The following are the objects and regulations of the society : The object of the society is the spiritual welfare of the seafaring classes at home and abroad. In pursuance of this object, the society uses every means consistent with the principles and received practice of the Church of England. The operations of the society are, for the most part, carried on afloat, and for this purpose its chaplains and scripture readers are, as far as possible, provided with vessels and boats for visiting the ships in roadsteads, rivers, and harbours.

Molesey.—*See* EAST MOLESEY.

Molesey Hurst.—*See* HAMPTON.

Molesey Regatta.—The course is about a mile, from a little above the cherry-orchard to a flag-boat below Garrick's Villa.

RACES IN 1884.

Saturday, July 26.

JUNIOR SCULLS.

First Heat.

G. E. B. Kennedy, Moulsey B.C. ...	1
G. A. S. Buckley, Kingston R.C. ...	0
B. W. Looker, Thames R.C. ...	disq.

Second Heat.

H. Blackmore, Twickenham R.C. ...r.o.

Final Heat.

Blackmore	...	..	...	...	1
Kennedy...	...	...	...	...	0

GARRICK PAIRS.

Kingston R.C.—C. L. Fyfe and R. H. Cobb	1
Moulsey B.C.—R. Milner and R. G. Till	0
London R.C.—J. F. Stillwell and W. Bazalgette	0

JUNIOR FOURS.

Kingston R.C. ...	...	...	...	1
Moulsey B.C. ...	...	...	...	0
London R.C. ...	...	...	...	0

Kingston.—W. Bazalgette, E. Bazalgette, P. H. Champernowne, S. S. Lushington (stroke), C. Fyfe (cox).

Moulsey.—A. Piper, C. Piper, R. G. Till, G. E. B. Kennedy (stroke), H. O. Milner (cox).

London.—C. F. Schlotel, A. S. Bryden, E. S. M'Ewen, W. J. Leeman (stroke), W. F. Sheard (cox).

SENIOR PAIRS.

London R.C.—G. R. B. Earnshaw and C. Earnshaw	1
Twickenham R.C.—E. Hodgkin and L. Frere	0
Kingston R.C.—F. Cobb and R. H. Cobb	0

JUNIOR EIGHTS.

First Heat.

London R.C. 1

Kingston R.C. 0

London.—C. F. Schlotel, P. A. N. Thorn, H. H. Winterbottom, A. Silversparre, F. W. Daunter, A. S. Bryden, E. S. M'Ewen, W. J. Leeman (stroke), W. F. Sheard (cox).

Kingston.—W. Stevenson, F. Butler, W. Bazalgette, J. Stevenson, C. L. Fyfe, E. Bazalgette, P. H. Champernowne, S. S. Lushington (stroke), F. J. Bell (cox).

Second Heat.

Thames R.C. 1

Cooper's Hill College B.C. 0

Thames.—C. E. Smith, F. W. Guerrier, G. A. Herdman, W. Andrews, M. C. Gie, C. S. Sowerby, W. Theobald, H. Atkinson (stroke), E. A. Safford (cox).

Cooper's Hill College.—O. Burne, J. S. Fowler, H. S. Wildeblood, N. Kirby, C. F. A. Egerton, C. F. Sykes, J. H. Burton, J. C. Tyle (stroke), E. J. Reeves (cox).

Final Heat.

Thames 1

London 0

SENIOR SCULLS.

W. H. Bone, West London R.C. ... 1

Stuart Green, Twickenham R.C. ... 0

G. R. B. Earnshaw, London R.C. ... 0

MOULSEY GRAND CHALLENGE CUP (for Eights).

Thames R.C. 1

London R.C. 0

Thames.—B. W. Looker, S. M. Cooke, Gordon Smith, B. E. Cole, W. Liddle, J. Hastie, H. Rust, J. A. Drake-Smith (stroke), E. A. Safford (cox).

London.—G. R. B. Earnshaw, C. Earnshaw, W. Bergh, J. F. Stillwell, H. J. Hill, A. S. J. Hurrell, J. T. Crier, W. W. Hewett (stroke), W. F. Sheard (cox).

MOULSEY CHALLENGE CUP—SENIOR FOURS.

Thames R.C. 1

Kingston R.C. 0

Thames.—B. W. Looker, J. Hastie (steers), H. J. Rust, J. A. Drake-Smith (stroke).

Kingston.—F. Cobb, H. A. Harvey, H. S. Till (steers), R. H. Cobb (stroke).

WINNERS OF CHALLENGE CUPS.

EIGHTS.

1867 Molesey Boat Club
1873 Molesey Boat Club
1874 Thames Rowing Club
1875 Molesey Boat Club
1876 Thames Rowing Club
1879 Molesey Boat Club
1880 Thames Rowing Club
1881 Thames Rowing Club
1882 Thames Rowing Club
1883 Twickenham Rowing Club
1884 Thames Rowing Club

FOURS.

1875 Molesey Boat Club
1876 Molesey Boat Club
1879 Molesey Boat Club
1880 London Rowing Club
1881 Thames Rowing Club
1882 London Rowing Club
1883 Kingston Rowing Club
1884 Thames Rowing Club.

Mongewell, Oxfordshire, on the left bank, about a mile from Wallingford, from London 82½ miles, from Oxford 22 miles. Population, 106. Soil, chalk. A small village, with church dedicated to St. John the Baptist. Mongewell Park, which stands on the bank of the river here, is one of the most charming residences on the river.

PLACE OF WORSHIP.—St. John the Baptist.

POSTAL ARRANGEMENTS. — Letters through Wallingford, which is the nearest money order office, &c.

NEAREST *Bridges*, up, Wallingford ¾ mile ; down, Streatley 5 miles. *Locks,* up, Wallingford ¼ mile ; down, Cleeve 4½ miles. *Ferry,* Wallingford. *Railway Station,* Wallingford.

FARES, Wallingford to Paddington, 1st, 9/5, 16/- ; 2nd, 7/-, 12/- ; 3rd, 4/3. No Sunday trains.

Monkey Island is about half a mile below Bray Lock, and owes its name to a number of pictures of monkeys, engaged in various human occupations, with which the third Duke of Marlborough adorned a fishing-lodge which he built upon the island. The pictures are sometimes attributed to a French artist named Clermont, but in truth they are not sufficiently remarkable to make the question of their authorship a matter of any importance. Mrs. S. C. Hall's "Book of the Thames" thus describes them : "Although clever in design they are of no great merit in execution. One of the best of these groups represents two of the animals awkwardly carrying home fish, the eels escaping from the basket. The most ludicrous scene occupies the centre of the ceiling, and is a burlesque on the triumph of Galatea ; even the Cupid attending her is represented as a winged monkey with fluttering drapery, strewing flowers on the nymph, who, with her attendant Tritons and sea-nymphs, are also represented as monkeys." The house is now converted into an inn, which is considerably used by anglers, oarsmen, and camping parties. An outbuilding —a sort of pavilion—which is sometimes used as a billiard-room, has a carved ceiling, which it is to be regretted is being allowed to fall into decay. The accommodation is primitive and cheap. There is excellent fishing all about this neighbourhood, and an extremely rapid stream runs past the island at all times. There is a ferry from the island to the Bucks bank.

NEAREST *Post Office,* Bray (*which see*); *Telegraph Office,* Taplow Station ; *Railway Station,* Taplow.

FARES from Taplow to Paddington : 1st, 4/1, 7/- ; 2nd, 3/1, 5/3 ; 3rd, 2/-.

Mortlake, London, S.W.—On the right bank from a river point of view, is chiefly noticeable as being the terminus of the championship and University boat-races. From Waterloo (about 25 min.). 1st, 1/-, 1/6 ; 2nd, -/10, 1/3 ; 3rd, -/8, 1/-. NEAREST *Bridge,* Kew.

Moulsey Boat Club.—Election by committee, who "have exclusive powers." Subscription : Honorary members, £1 1s. per annum ; ordinary members, £2 2s. per annum. Boat-house, the Island. Colours, black and white vertical stripes.

Moulsford, Berkshire, on the right bank, 87 miles from London, 24½ miles from Oxford ; a station on the Great Western Railway, 47½ miles from Paddington ; trains take 2 or 2½ hours. Flys can be hired at the Railway Tavern. Population, 180. Soil, chalk. A village on the right bank, about 3½ miles from Wallingford, principally known to boating men and anglers for the "Beetle and Wedge Inn," and for the fact that the trial eights of the Oxford University Boat Club are rowed on the splendid stretch of water which here affords, perhaps, the best course on the river. There is excellent perch fishing between the islands near the bridge. Moulsford station and the Berks lunatic asylum are in the adjoining parish of Cholsey. The church, St. John the Baptist, is of the 14th century, and was restored by Sir Gilbert Scott in 1847. It stands immediately on the bank of the river.

INNS.—"Beetle and Wedge," on the river at the ferry ; Railway Tavern, close to the station.

PLACE OF WORSHIP.—St. John's.

POSTAL ARRANGEMENTS. — Letters through Wallingford. Nearest money order office, Cholsey ; telegraph station, Moulsford.

NEAREST *Bridges,* up, Wallingford 3¾ miles ; down, Streatley 2¼ miles. *Locks,* up, Wallingford 3¼ miles ; down, Cleeve 2 miles. *Ferries,* Moulsford and Little Stoke. *Railway Station,* Moulsford.

FARES to Paddington, 1st, 8/5, 14/6 ; 2nd, 6/3, 11/- ; 3rd, 3/11.

Mucking Flat Lighthouse, Sea Reach.—Built of iron upon a hollow pile foundation. A temporary light was first exhibited from this position in October, 1849, and the present structure was built in 1851. It is painted black and white in alternate horizontal bands, and is connected with the shore by a long footbridge, also built on piles and coloured white. The height of the light tower from base to vane is 66 feet, and its central lamp burns at 40 feet above high water. The light is under occultation once in every half minute, and the apparatus used is lenticular, giving forth a white beam with red sectors. A fog bell is sounded during foggy weather. There are two keepers employed in tending the station, who, having their dwellings at hand, with coals, light, and furniture provided for them, and living with their families, have a much more comfortable billet than their neighbours at the Chapman lower down.

Naval Volunteers, Royal.—Headquarters for drill, H.M.S. *President,* West India Docks. Armoury and boat-station, H.M.S. *Rainbow,* off Somerset House. Office, 35, Great George Street, Westminster.

Navigation, LOWER THAMES.

REGULATIONS FOR PREVENTING COLLISIONS AT SEA.

Published in the London Gazette of August 19, 1884.

Art. 1. In the following rules every steam ship which is under sail and not under steam is to be considered a sailing ship ; and every steam ship which is under steam, whether under sail or not, is to be considered a ship under steam.

Rules concerning Lights.

Art. 2. The lights mentioned in the following Articles, numbered 3, 4, 5, 6, 7, 8, 9, 10, and 11, and no others, shall be carried in all weathers from sunset to sunrise.

Art. 3. A sea-going steam ship, when under way shall carry : (*a*) On or in front of the foremast, at a height above the hull of not less than 20 feet, and if the breadth of the ship exceeds 20 feet then at a height above the hull not less than such breadth, a bright white light, so constructed as to show a uniform and unbroken light over an arc of the horizon of twenty points of the compass ; so fixed as to throw the light ten points on each side of the ship, viz. from right ahead to two points abaft the beam on either side ; and of such a character as to be visible on a dark night, with a clear atmosphere, at a distance of at least five miles. (*b*) On the starboard side, a green light so constructed as to show a uniform and unbroken light over an arc of the horizon of ten points of the compass ; so fixed as to throw the light from right ahead to two points abaft the beam on the starboard side ; and of such a character as to be visible on a dark night, with a clear atmosphere, at a distance of at least two miles. (*c*) On the port side, a red light, so constructed as to show a uniform and unbroken light over an arc of the horizon of ten points of the compass ; so fixed as to throw the light from right ahead to two points abaft the beam on the port side ; and of such a character as to be visible on a dark night, with a clear atmosphere, at a distance of at least two miles. (*d*) The said green and red side lights shall be fitted with inboard screens projecting at least 3 feet forward from the light, so as to prevent these lights from being seen across the bow.

Art. 4. A steam ship, when towing another ship shall, in addition to her side lights, carry two bright white lights in a vertical line one over the other, not less than 3 feet apart, so as to distinguish her from other steam ships. Each of these lights shall be of the same construction and character, and shall be carried in the same position as the white light which other steam ships are required to carry.

Art. 5. (*a*) A ship, whether a steamship or a sailing ship, which from any accident is not under command, shall at night carry, in the same position as the white light which steamships are required to carry, and, if a steamship, in place of that light, three red lights in globular lanterns, each not less than 10 inches in diameter, in a vertical line one over the other, not less than 3 feet apart, and of such a character as to be visible on a dark night, with a clear atmosphere, at a distance of at least-two miles ; and shall by day carry, in a vertical line one over the other, not less than 3 feet apart, in front of but not lower than her foremast head, three black balls or shapes, each two feet in diameter.

(*b*) A ship, whether a steamship or a sailing ship, employed in laying or in picking up a telegraph cable, shall at night carry in the same position as the white light, which steamships are required to carry, and, if a steamship, in place of that light, three lights in globular lanterns each not less than 10 inches in diameter, in a vertical line over one another, not less than 6 feet apart ; the highest and lowest of these lights shall be red, and the middle light shall be white, and they shall be of such a character that the red lights shall be visible at the same distance as the white light. By day she shall carry, in a vertical line one over the other, not less than 6 feet apart, in front of but not lower than her foremast head, three shapes not less than two feet in diameter, of which the top and bottom shall be globular in shape and red in colour, and the middle one diamond in shape and white.

(*c*) The ships referred to in this Article, when not making any way through the water, shall not carry the side lights, but when making way shall carry them.

(*d*) The lights and shapes required to be shown by this Article are to be taken by other ships as signals that the ship showing them is not under command, and cannot, therefore, get out of the way. The signals to. be made by ships in distress and requiring assistance are contained in Article 27.

Art. 6. A sailing ship under way, or being towed, shall carry the same lights as are provided by Article 3 for a steam ship under way, with the exception of the white light, which she shall never carry.

Art. 7. Whenever, as in the case of small vessels during bad weather, the green and red side lights cannot be fixed, these lights shall be kept on deck, on their respective sides of the vessel, ready for use : and shall, on the approach of or to other vessels, be exhibited on their respective sides in sufficient time to prevent collision, in such a manner as to make them most visible, and so that the green light shall not be seen on the port side nor the red light on the starboard side. To make the use of these portable lights more certain and easy, the lanterns containing them shall each be painted outside with the colour of the light they respectively contain, and shall be provided with proper screens.

Art. 8. A ship, whether a steam ship or a sailing ship, when at anchor, shall carry, where it can best be seen, but at a height not exceeding 20 feet above the hull, a white light, in a globular lantern of not less than 8 inches in diameter, and so constructed as to show a clear uniform and unbroken light visible all round the horizon, at a distance of at least one mile.

Art. 9. A pilot vessel, when engaged on her station on pilotage duty, shall not carry the lights required for other vessels, but shall carry a white light at the masthead, visible all round the horizon, and shall also exhibit a flare-up light or flare-up lights at short intervals, which shall never exceed fifteen minutes. A pilot vessel, when not engaged on her station on pilotage duty, shall carry lights similar to those of other ships.

Art. 10. Open boats and fishing vessels of less than 20 tons net registered tonnage, when under way and when not having their nets, trawls, dredges, or lines in the water, shall not be obliged to carry the coloured side lights ; but every such boat and vessel shall in lieu thereof have ready at hand a lantern with a green glass on the one side and a red glass on the other side, and on approaching to or being approached by another vessel such lantern shall be exhibited in sufficient time to prevent collision, so that the green light shall not be seen on the port side nor the red light on the starboard side.

Art. 11. A ship which is being overtaken by another shall show from her stern to such last-mentioned ship a white light or a flare-up light.

Sound Signals for Fog, &c.

Art. 12. A steam ship shall be provided with a steam whistle or other efficient steam sound signal, so placed that the sound may not be intercepted by any obstructions, and with an efficient fog-horn to be sounded by a bellows or other mechanical means, and also with an efficient bell. In all cases where the regulations require a bell to be used, a drum will be substituted on board Turkish vessels. A sailing ship shall be provided with a similar fog-horn and bell. In fog, mist, or falling snow, whether by day or night, the signals described in this Article shall be used as follows : that is to say, (a) A steam ship under way shall make with her steam whistle, or other steam sound signal, at intervals of not more than two minutes, a prolonged blast. (b) A sailing ship under way shall make with her fog-horn, at intervals of not more than two minutes, when on the starboard tack one blast, when on the port tack two blasts in succession, and when with the wind abaft the beam three blasts in succession. (c) A steam ship and a sailing ship when not under way shall, at intervals of not more than two minutes, ring the bell.

Speed of Ships to be moderate in Fog, &c.

Art. 13. Every ship, whether a sailing ship or steam ship, shall in a fog, mist, or falling snow, go at a moderate speed.

Steering and Sailing Rules.

Art. 14. When two sailing ships are approaching one another, so as to involve risk of collision, one of them shall keep out of the way of the other as follows, viz.: (a) A ship which is running free shall keep out of the way of a ship which is close-hauled. (b) A ship which is close-hauled on the port tack shall keep out of the way of a ship which is close-hauled on the starboard tack. (c) When both are running free with the wind on different sides, the ship which has the wind on the port side shall keep out of the way of the other. (d) When both are running free with the wind on the same side, the ship which is to windward shall keep out of the way of the ship which is to leeward. (e) A ship which has the wind aft shall keep out of the way of the other ship.

Art. 15. If two ships under steam are meeting end on, or nearly end on, so as to involve risk of collision, each shall

alter her course to starboard, so that each may pass on the port side of the other. [This Article only applies to cases where ships are meeting end on, or nearly end on, in such a manner as to involve risk of collision, and does not apply to two ships which must, if both keep on their respective courses, pass clear of each other. The only cases to which it does apply are, when each of the two ships is end on, or nearly end on, to the other ; in other words, to cases in which, by day, each ship sees the masts of the other in a line, or nearly in a line, with her own ; and by night, to cases in which each ship is in such a position as to see both the side lights of the other. It does not apply by day to cases in which a ship sees another ahead crossing her own course ; or by night, to cases where the red light of one ship is opposed to the red light of the other, or where the green light of one ship is opposed to the green light of the other, or where a red light without a green light, or a green light without a red light, is seen ahead, or where both green and red lights are seen anywhere but ahead.]

Art. 16. If two ships under steam are crossing, so as to involve risk of collision, the ship which has the other on her own starboard side shall keep out of the way of the other.

Art. 17. If two ships, one of which is a sailing ship, and the other a steam ship, are proceeding in such directions as to involve risk of collision, the steam ship shall keep out of the way of the sailing ship.

Art 18. Every steam ship when approaching another ship, so as to involve risk of collision, shall slacken her speed or stop and reverse, if necessary.

Art. 19. In taking any course authorised or required by these regulations, a steam ship under way may indicate that course to any other ship which she has in sight by the following signals on her steam whistle, viz.: One short blast to mean "I am directing my course to starboard." Two short blasts to mean "I am directing my course to port." Three short blasts to mean "I am going full speed astern." The use of these signals is optional ; but if they are used, the course of the ship must be in accordance with the signal made.

Art. 20. Notwithstanding anything contained in any preceding Article, every ship, whether a sailing ship or a steam ship, overtaking any other, shall keep out of the way of the overtaken ship.

Art. 21. In narrow channels every steam ship shall, when it is safe and practicable, keep to that side of the fairway or midchannel which lies on the starboard side of such ship.

Art. 22. Where by the above rules one of two ships is to keep out of the way, the other shall keep her course.

Art. 23. In obeying and construing these rules due regard shall be had to all dangers of navigation ; and to any special circumstances which may render a departure from the above rules necessary in order to avoid immediate danger.

No Ship under any Circumstances to neglect proper Precautions.

Art. 24. Nothing in these rules shall exonerate any ship, or the owner, or master, or crew thereof, from the consequences of any neglect to carry lights or signals, or of any neglect to keep a proper look-out, or of the neglect of any precaution which may be required by the ordinary practice of seamen, or by the special circumstances of the case.

Reservation of Rules for Harbours and Inland Navigation.

Art. 25. Nothing in these rules shall interfere with the operation of a special rule, duly made by local authority, relative to the navigation of any harbour, river, or inland navigation.

Special Lights for Squadrons and Convoys.

Art. 26. Nothing in these rules shall interfere with the operation of any special rules made by the Government of any nation with respect to additional station and signal lights for two or more ships of war or for ships sailing under convoy.

Art. : 7. When a ship is in distress and requires assistance from other ships or from the shore, the following shall be the signals to be used or displayed by her, either together or separately, that is to say: In the daytime—(1) A gun fired at intervals of about a minute ; (2) the International Code signal of distress indicated by N C ; (3) the distant signal, consisting of a square flag, having either above or below it a ball. or anything resembling a ball.

At night—(1) A gun fired at intervals of about a minute ; (2) flames on the ship (as from a burning tar barrel, oil barrel, &c.) ; (3) rockets or shells throwing stars of any colour or description, fired one at a time, at short intervals.

All vessels navigating Gravesend **Reach** are to keep to the northward of a line defined by a skeleton beacon erected upon the India Arms Wharf end on with the high chimney of the Cement Works at Northfleet ; and all vessels intending to anchor in the reach are to bring up to the southward of that line. A lantern is placed on the above beacon which shows (at night) a bright light to the northward of the same line, and a red light to the southward of it, over the anchorage ground. All vessels so anchoring and remaining beyond a period of twenty-four hours are to be moored.

All barges, boats, lighters, and other like craft navigating the river shall, when under way, have at least one competent man constantly on board for the navigation and management thereof, and all such craft of above 50 tons burden shall, when under way, have one man, in addition, on board, to assist in the navigation and management of the same, with the following exceptions : When being towed by a steam vessel, or when being moved to and fro between any vessels or places a distance not exceeding 200 yards ; and in case of non-compliance with this present bye-law, the harbour-master may take charge of and remove such craft to such place as to such harbour-master may seem fit, and the amount of the charges and expenses of taking charge thereof, and of such removal, shall be recoverable from the owner or owners, or master thereof, to the use of the Conservators, as provided by the Thames Conservancy Act, 1857. Any person committing any breach of, or in any way infringing any of these bye-laws, is liable to a penalty of £5.

UPPER THAMES.—On the Upper Thames no steamer is allowed, between Teddington Lock and Cricklade, to run at such a speed as to endanger any other boat or injure the river bank. No one is allowed to ride or drive on the towing path, to unload anything upon it, to place any vessel on the shore in front of it, or to take any stones, &c., from the banks.

No vessel must remain in any lock longer than time enough to pass through, and if she pass without paying toll, the amount due can be demanded at any other lock before admitting her. No vessel—unless in case of necessity, through strength of current—is to be towed from the bank otherwise than from a mast of sufficient height to protect the banks, gates, &c., from injury. There are very strict regulations against the pollution of the river by sewage matter. Tolls for cargo boats are levied under the following regulations :

The following tolls, rates, or duties shall be taken by the Conservators from the owners, coast-bearers, or chief boatmen of and for every vessel carrying a cargo, and passing through any lock or locks between Cricklade and Staines, or vice versa, for the use of such lock or locks according to the burthen or tonnage of such vessel, the measurement of such burthen or tonnage to be limited as in the 6th clause of the said Act 28th George III. chap. 51, that is to say :

The sum of 2d. per ton at every lock, subject to such provisions as to the aggregate of tolls as hereinafter mentioned.

If the vessel in the downward voyage shall pass through all the locks between the undermentioned places, the aggregate of such tolls per ton shall be as follows:

For all locks between—		Per ton.
		s. d.
Oxford and Abingdon inclusive	..	0 6
Oxford and Wallingford inclusive	..	1 0
Oxford and Pangbourne	,,	1 6
Oxford and Reading	,,	1 9
Oxford and Henley	,,	2 0
Oxford and Marlow	,,	2 6
Oxford and Maidenhead	,,	2 9
Oxford and Windsor	,,	3 0
Oxford and Staines	,,	3 6

If the vessel, in the upward voyage, shall pass through all the locks between the undermentioned places, the aggregate of such tolls, per ton, shall be as follows :

To all locks between—		Per ton.
		s. d.
Staines and Windsor inclusive	..	0 3
Staines and Maidenhead inclusive	..	0 6
Staines and Marlow	,,	0 9
Staines and Henley	,,	1 3
Staines and Reading	,,	1 9
Staines and Pangbourne	,,	2 0
Staines and Wallingford	,,	2 6
Staines and Abingdon	,,	3 0
Staines and Oxford	,,	3 6

Oxford and Cricklade 2d. per ton for each lock.

For timber in rafts—

The same rate per ton as is charged if conveyed in vessels, there being 50 cubic feet in one ton.

The tolls for pleasure-boats are :

	s. d.
For every steam pleasure-boat and passenger-steamer	1 6
Class 1.—For every sculling-boat, pair-oared row-boat and skiff, and for every randan, canoe, punt, and dingey	0 3
Class 2.—For every four-oared row-boat (other than boats enumerated in Class 1) and sailing-boat ..	0 6
Class 3.—For every row-boat shallop over four oars (other than boats enumerated in Classes 1 and 2) ..	1 0
For every house-boat under 50 feet in length	1 6
For every house-boat over 50 feet in length	2 6

The above charges to be for passing once through, by, or over a lock, and returning on the same day.

In lieu of the above tolls, pleasure steamers or rowboats may be registered on the payment to the Conservators of the undermentioned sums, and shall, in consideration of such payment, pass the several locks free of any other charge, from the 1st day of January to the 31st day of December in each year.

	£ s. d.
For every steam pleasure-boat and steam passenger-boat, not exceeding 35 feet in length..	5 0 0
Ditto above 35 feet in length, and not exceeding 45	7 10 0
Ditto exceeding 45 feet in length ..	10 0 0
For every row-boat of Class 1 ..	2 0 0
For every row-boat or yacht of Class 2	2 10 0
For every row-boat of Class 3 ..	3 0 0
For every house-boat not exceeding 30 feet in length	3 0 0
Ditto above 30 and not exceeding 50 feet in length..	5 0 0
Ditto exceeding 50 feet in length ..	7 10 0

In computing the tolls, every number less than the entire numbers above stated is to be charged as the entire number.

The above rates on Classes 1, 2, and 3 to be doubled if towed by horse or any other animal.

The plate with the registered number thereon is to be fastened on to the boat for which it is issued, and is not transferable from one boat to another.

Any person committing any breach of, or in any way infringing any of these bye-laws, is liable to a penalty of £5.

The tolls for the Conservators' ferry-boats above Teddington-lock are :

For every horse not engaged in towing, taken across by ferry-boat, the sum of..	3d.
For every carriage, waggon, cart, or other vehicle, in addition to the toll on the horse	3d.
For every foot passenger	1d.

There is a long list of penalties for infringements of these bye-laws, ranging from £2 for bargemen stealing goods on board to £100 for infraction of the laws relating to sewage (*and see* STEAM LAUNCHES.)

Neptune Rowing Club, Oxford.—The object of this club, which consists of effective members, members, and honorary members, is to encourage amateur rowing. Effective members pay a subscription of £1, members one of 10s., and honorary members not less than 5s. The members elect ; one black ball in four excludes. Colours, orange, black and red. Headquarters, "Three Cups" Hotel, Queen Street, Oxford.

Newnham Murren, Oxfordshire, on the left bank, about one mile from Wallingford Bridge, from London 89½ miles, from Oxford 22 miles. Population, 170. Soil, gravel. The little church has a curiously carved oak pulpit, and a small brass tablet representing Letitia Barnarde and her four children, dated 1593.

PLACE OF WORSHIP.—St. Mary's.

POSTAL ARRANGEMENTS. — Letters through Wallingford, which is the nearest money order office, &c.

NEAREST *Bridges*, up, Wallingford 1 mile ; down, Goring 5 miles. *Locks*, up, Wallingford ¼ mile ; down, Cleeve 4¾ miles. *Ferry*, Wallingford. *Railway Station*, Wallingford.

FARES, Wallingford to Paddington : 1st, 9/5, 16/- ; 2nd, 7/-, 12/- ; 3rd, 4/3. No Sunday trains.

New Thames Yacht Club, Club-houses, Caledonian Hotel, Adelphi, W.C., and Gravesend.—The object of the club is the encouragement of yacht building and sailing on the river Thames ; and the funds of the club are appropriated, after payment of the necessary expenses, to the providing of prizes in money or otherwise to be sailed for by yachts on the river Thames. The members elect, and one black ball in five excludes. The club is managed by commodore, vice-commodore, rear-commodore, and treasurer, who are ex-officio members of every committee, with a sailing committee of fourteen, and a house committee of six. The entrance fee is £5 5s., and the subscription £3 3s. The club burgee is blue with gold phœnix ; ensign, blue with gold phœnix in fly.

Norbiton, a suburb of Kingston, to the north-east, rapidly extending its rows of villas and cottages towards the open country in the neighbourhood of Wimbledon Common and Richmond Park, where Jerry Abershaw and other knights of the road once took toll from travellers. It is a railway station on the South Western, and may also be reached by the Metropolitan line. The walks about Norbiton are numerous, and the scenery is very pretty ; the open commons being agreeably diversified with finely-timbered woods. At Norbiton is the Royal Cambridge Asylum for soldiers' widows, established in 1851, under the patronage of the royal family, in memory of the late Duke of Cambridge. Widows of non-commissioned officers and privates of the Army, not under 50 years of age, are eligible. Each widow has a furnished room and 7s. weekly, besides a monthly allowance of coals. The funded income of the charity is a little over £600, and the estimated expenditure £2,300, the balance being raised by subscriptions. The Children's Convalescent Institution is at Kingston Hill, and contains 150 beds. The institution is open for inspection every day except Sunday. The Children's Home for 22 girls is at 4, Park-road-villas, Park-road. Visitors can inspect the Home on Tuesday, Wednesday, Thursday, and Friday afternoons, between 3 and 5.—(*And see* KINGSTON.)

PLACES OF WORSHIP.—St. John the Baptist, Kingston Vale ; St. Peter's ; and Baptist Primitive Methodist, and Wesleyan Chapels.

POSTAL ARRANGEMENTS.—Post Office (money order, savings bank, telegraph). Mails from London, 7 and 9.30 a.m., 2.35 and 7.30 p.m. Sun., 7 a.m. Mails for London, 8.20 and 11.50 a.m., 3.30, 4.55, 7.30, and 9 p.m. No London mail out on Sunday.

FARES to Waterloo : 2/-, 2/6 ; 2nd, 1/6, 2/-; 3rd, -/11, 1/8.

Nore Light, about 50 miles from London Bridge. The Nore light-ship is the first sea light to be passed on leaving the port of London. It is the first in order of seniority among its kind, for at this station the first light-ship set afloat on the coast of England was permanently laid in the year 1730.

The original hull was that of a sloop, with a large lantern at each end of a yard laid across the mast. An improvement in the method of illumination in 1825 rendered one lantern sufficient, incorporate with the mast, and showing a "fixed" light. In 1855 for purposes of distinction, the light was made "revolving." After seven years' service in one commission, the ships are brought into port for a thorough overhaul. The Nore lightship was built of wood at Limehouse 40 years ago, and is 96 feet long by 21 broad; her tonnage, 156; hull, mast-head, and globe painted red, and the name "Nore" in large white letters on each broadside. The hollow globe at the mast-head, 6 feet in diameter, made of bent laths, is characteristic of such craft by day; it is never removed unless when the ships are driven from their stations. About 10 feet below it hangs the lantern, an octagonal glass case, framed in copper, and fitting round the mast like a great gem ring, housed on deck by day, and hoisted as high up the mast as the shrouds will permit by night.

On deck forward is a powerful windlass—a necessary provision for managing the heavy cable, which is composed of very short links; the iron 1⅜ in. thick, and of sufficient length to veer out 100 fathoms if required. On a netting attached to the bumpkin (an apology for a bowsprit) is a sail neatly stowed ready for use if required; and at the stern, furled close to a jigger mast, is another sail. These are used in ordinary times to steady the ship when it is blowing hard, or in case of breaking adrift and being driven to sea (which has never yet happened) they would enable her to run to an anchorage.

Around the mast and fitting on to the deck is a circular wooden chamber into which the lantern is lowered in the daytime, affording convenience for cleaning it and trimming the lamps.

Passing down to the lower deck is a companion ladder, serving both for officers and crew. The latter are lodged forward, and occupy all the 'tween deck space from the mast to the bows of the ship. Their hammocks, chests, and lockers are along the sides of the berth, and a good broad table down the middle, with a bench seat at each side of it. Amidships, near the mast, is the cooking stove, a large grate whose warmth must be particularly acceptable in hard weather. Close against the mast is a clockwork machine, set in motion by a descending weight, whose office is to turn an iron spindle-rod laid against the mast, and so contrived that when the lantern is hoisted into its place it sets the light revolving in the manner to be presently described.

Immediately behind the mast, after passing the companion ladder, a small passage-way leads to the captain's cabin and the store-rooms. On the right, in large lockers breast-high, the bread and provisions are kept; on the left is the principal store, where the oil, cotton wicks, and spare lamps are deposited. Here are four or five cylindrical cisterns, each containing 100 gallons of colza oil, a bench, and a set of bright copper measures, and a black-board ruled into suitable spaces for a record in chalk of the quantities drawn off. Two or three spare lamps and reflectors hang from the beams, all ready for use; and a trimming-tray, with scissors, holders for wicks, and glass cylinders, and other appliances used by the lamp-trimmer when performing his daily task, lies here in the place provided for it.

From the passage a door opens into the stern cabin, a snug little den for the use of the officer in command, neatly but plainly furnished, with a library for the use of the crew, the books of which circulate throughout the service.

Below this deck is the hold, in which water tanks, spare cables, and some few tons of ballast, keep the vessel steady.

The principal function for which a lightvessel is placed is, as the name implies, the exhibition of a warning or a guiding light at night. To prevent confusion with lamps or fires on shore or on board other vessels, a distinguishing character is given to the light, which, in the case of the "Nore," is called the revolving halfminute character. The effect to be produced is that a brilliant flash shall pass before the eye of the observer every 30 seconds, which is accomplished in the following manner :

Argand lamps, fitted each within a paraboloidal reflector, and slung upon gimbal work to counteract the vessel's rolling, are arranged in three groups of three lamps each on a frame within the lantern, and surrounding the mast. The property of this kind of reflector is that it gathers all, or nearly all, the rays into a parallel beam of light, and when in position this beam is thrown towards the horizon. The three in a group are cornered together with their rims in one plane, like a triple-barrelled opera glass, so that the blended beams of three lamps reach the observer at the same time. The framework which carries the three groups runs on wheels on a circular rail, and its inner ring which encircles the mast is cogged upon one edge. When the lantern is hoisted these cogs come into connection with the cogged head of the iron spindle laid beside the mast, which is kept turning by machinery below the deck, as before explained, and sets the frame in motion. If there were only one group of lamps the frame must revolve very fast to bring the beam round in half a minute, and the lamps would flare; but by placing three groups the speed is reduced to one-third. To put this description into a homely shape: the sea-gull flying over the lantern sees three bright spokes of a wheel going slowly round and round, while he drops down on to the water he will get a spoke in his eye every half-minute from sunset to sunrise.

From stem to stern, deck, lantern, lamps, cabin, and utensils, are all kept scrupulously clean and bright. The crew who are charged with this duty number eleven in all, but only seven are on board at one time, the master or mate, two lamplighters, and four seamen. Once a month the relief steamer comes down from Blackwall, brings the shoremen back, and takes others away. The master and mate take month about, the rest have two months on board to one on shore. Provisions and water are renewed monthly by this vessel, and stores are kept up to service requirements. There is plenty of work in keeping a look-out, keeping all clean, especially the lantern, lantern-glass, lamps, and reflectors, and in keeping very neat and careful records of the state of wind and weather, barometer, &c., and of the daily and nightly expenditure of oil and stores. The men

have, nevertheless, a good deal of leisure, which some of them employ in mat-making, some in shoe-making, some in a kind of cabinet work or in toy-making. They live as a rule to a good age, and are entitled to a pension when past work. The cost of this vessel with apparatus complete was £5000, and its maintenance may be stated at £1200 a year.

Nore Sand Buoy.—A 7-ft. can-buoy, made of wood, and painted with black and white stripes. It is situated in Sea Reach, on the northern edge of the Nore Sand, and marks a depth of water, at low-water spring tide, of 16 feet. It is moored with 10 fathom of chain. The Nore Sand Buoy belongs to the Trinity House.

Nore Yacht Club, New Falcon Hotel, Gravesend.—Object : To promote yacht and naval architecture ; to encourage amateur seamanship and yacht racing in classes of 40 tons and under ; and to establish yachting accommodation on metropolitan waters. Officers : commodore, vice-commodore, rear-commodore, and honorary treasurer and secretary, who, with twenty members, form the committee. Election by ballot in committee ; nine votes must be recorded : one black ball in eight excludes. Burgee, light blue, dark blue cross through it, gold anchor in centre, red ensign.

Northern Outfall.—The Abbey Mills Pumping Station, one of the curiosities of modern civilisation, lies on the London, Tilbury, and Southend Railway, between Bromley-by-Bow and Plaistow. For permission to view, apply to the Engineers' Department, Metropolitan Board of Works, Spring Gardens, S.W.

Northfleet, Kent, on the right bank, between Northfleet Hope and Gravesend Reach, 25 miles from London. A station on the North Kent Railway, about an hour and a quarter from Charing Cross. The station is close to the lower part of the village. Population, 6,416. Soil, chalk. Northfleet is a straggling village on the side of a hill, on the summit of which are the church and a quaint, old-fashioned, open, triangular space—probably once the village green—which is known by the name of The Hill. The principal trade of Northfleet is in cement, and some shipbuilding and repairing are carried on by the river. A pro-

minent object both from the railway
and from the river is the college, built
and endowed in 1847 by John Huggens,
Esq., of Sittingbourne, for the benefit
of ladies and gentlemen in reduced
circumstances. It consists of 50 superior almshouses, each of the inmates
receiving £1 per week. A handsome
chapel forms part of the building. In
addition to the 50 inmates, there are 40
out-pensioners who also receive £1 per
week. Perhaps the most prominent object
in Northfleet is the Factory Club, a handsome building erected at the sole cost of
Mr. Bevan, of the firm of Knight, Bevan,
and Sturge, for the benefit of the working-
men of the village. It is a large hall,
with galleries at either end, in which
1,000 persons can be accommodated, and
a number of rooms in the basement, with
wings at the back, one of which contains
the kitchen, offices, lavatories, &c., and
the other a billiard-room. The building
itself is mainly erected of red and white
bricks, but relieved by columns in cement
of apparently mixed Italian and Corinthian
styles, in addition to which there are
facings and cornices of a similar material.
At each end of the building is a lofty
slated tower, with a flag-staff, and margined with handsome ironwork. The
internal finishings of the large hall are
executed in pitch pine; underneath one
of the galleries is a bar, fitted up for the
supply of refreshments; and the whole
of the fittings, seats, and tables are also
of pitch pine. From the towers a splendid view may be obtained, embracing
Southend and about twenty miles of
beautiful scenery. The entrance fee is
1s. 3d. for Messrs. Knight's men, and
2s. 9d. for those not belonging to that
firm. The subscription is 4d. per month.
The church of St. Botolph, approached
from the Hill, stands in a churchyard
full of weatherbeaten old tombstones of
all shapes and sizes. Many crumbling
carvings and half-obliterated corbels on the
porch and older walls of the church attest
the antiquity of the structure, and on the
right-hand side of the porch the curious
may still discover the Rose of York or
Lancaster. The tower, which was originally built to serve the purpose of a stronghold against the incursions of pirates
and river thieves, has been partly rebuilt. The external flight of stairs leading to the tower is part of the original

building. According to Mr. E. W.
Godwin, F.S.A., the church in Norman
times belonged to the Archbishop of
Canterbury, until it was given to the
Priory of St. Andrew, Rochester, when it
was in some measure rebuilt. The original Norman church has entirely disappeared, but traces of the re-building
are visible in the three westernmost arches
of the nave. These probably belong to
the close of the 12th century. The
present chancel would seem to have been
built about the middle of the 14th century.
The restoration of the chancel, under
Mr. Godwin's superintendence, was
finished in 1864. The chancel possesses
one of the architectural rarities of England,
a 14th century rood screen beautifully
carved in oak, on which are heads of
Christ and his Apostles, much mutilated
by the Puritans. There are some fine
brasses, notably one of Peter de Lacy,
rector in 1375, whose body lies in the
centre of the chancel, and others of
William Lye (1391), and of William
Rikhill and wife (1433). The sedilia in
the chancel have been beautifully restored
and decorated; another set of sedilia
and piscina have been partially restored,
and will be found at the east end of the
south aisle. The roof is of oak and has
been partly renovated; that in the chancel
was new in 1864. The registers date
back to 1539. The old parish church
iron-bound chest, with six locks, is evidently of great antiquity. In the north
aisle is a curious canopied monument
displaying the bewigged marble effigies,
nearly if not quite life-size, of Richard
Crich and Esther his wife, "erected by
his sole executor." Also in the north
aisle is the monument of Dr. Edward
Brown. The doctor's will is sculptured
on the marble, and by it he leaves to his
"dear and loving wife sundry fields in
Northfleet, and the rent of the chalk, and
the profits of the cherries." In the south
aisle is a monument tablet to Walter, son
of Robert, Lord Viscount Molesworth,
who died in 1773, his wife (1763), and his
daughters (1766 and 1772). On the
general question of epitaphs it is said of
this Walter, son of Robert, in the inscription on the tablet to his memory:
"Never fond of monumental compli-
ments he forbade any use of them in
regard to the carcases below."
PLACES OF WORSHIP.—All Saints

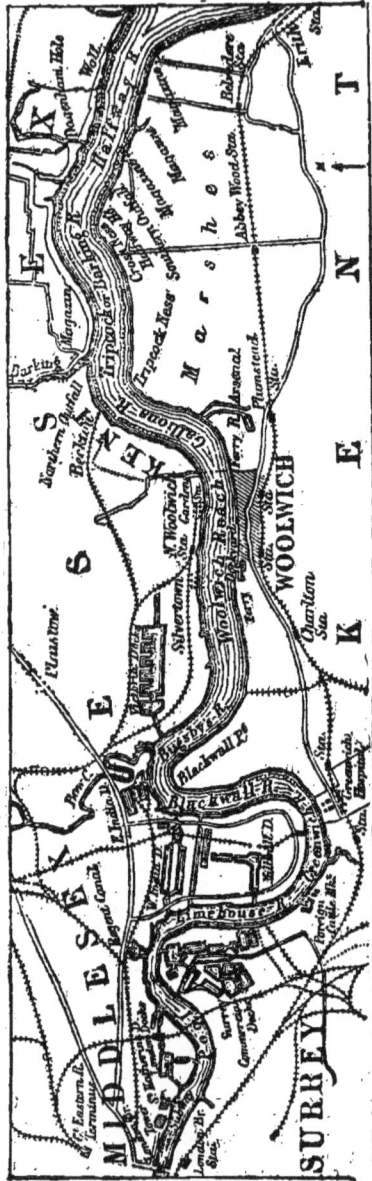

LONDON TO ERITH.

ERITH TO GRAVESEND.

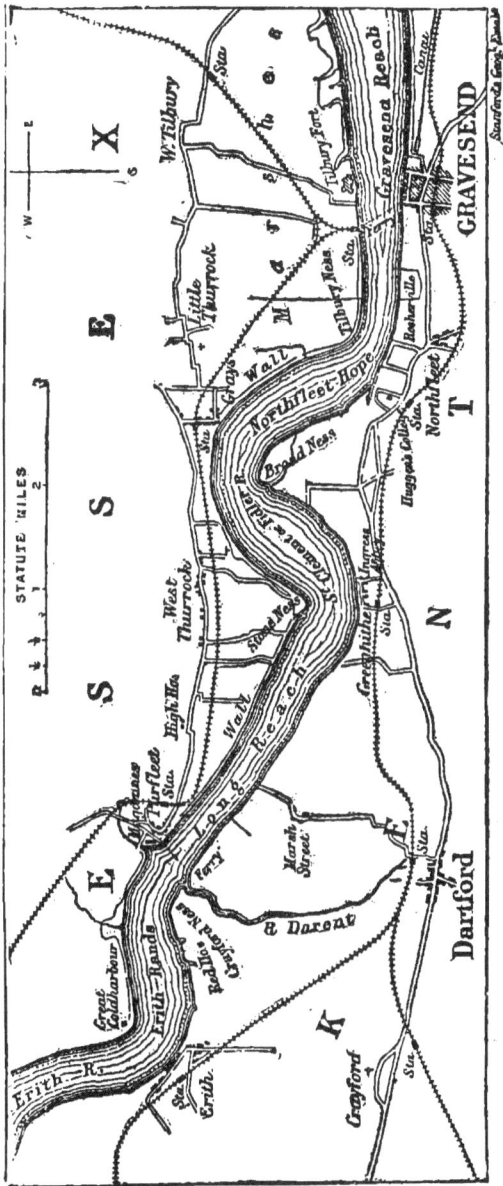

STATUTE MILES

E S S E X

K E N T

Erith R.
Great Coalharbour
Erith Reach
Erith Sta.
Slade Green
Crayford
Crayford Sta.
West Thurrock
Purfleet Sta.
High Ho.
Wall
Long Reach
Marsh Street
Ferry
& Darent
Dartford
Dartford Sta.
Stone Ness
Grays
Wall
Fiddler's R.
Northfleet Hope
Broad Ness
Greenhithe
Greenhithe Sta.
Ingress Abbey
Huggens College
Northfleet
Northfleet Sta.
Rosherville
Tilbury Ness
Tilbury Sta.
Little Thurrock
W. Tilbury
W. Tilbury Sta.
Tilbury Fort
Gravesend Reach
Canal
GRAVESEND

GRAVESEND TO CANVEY I.

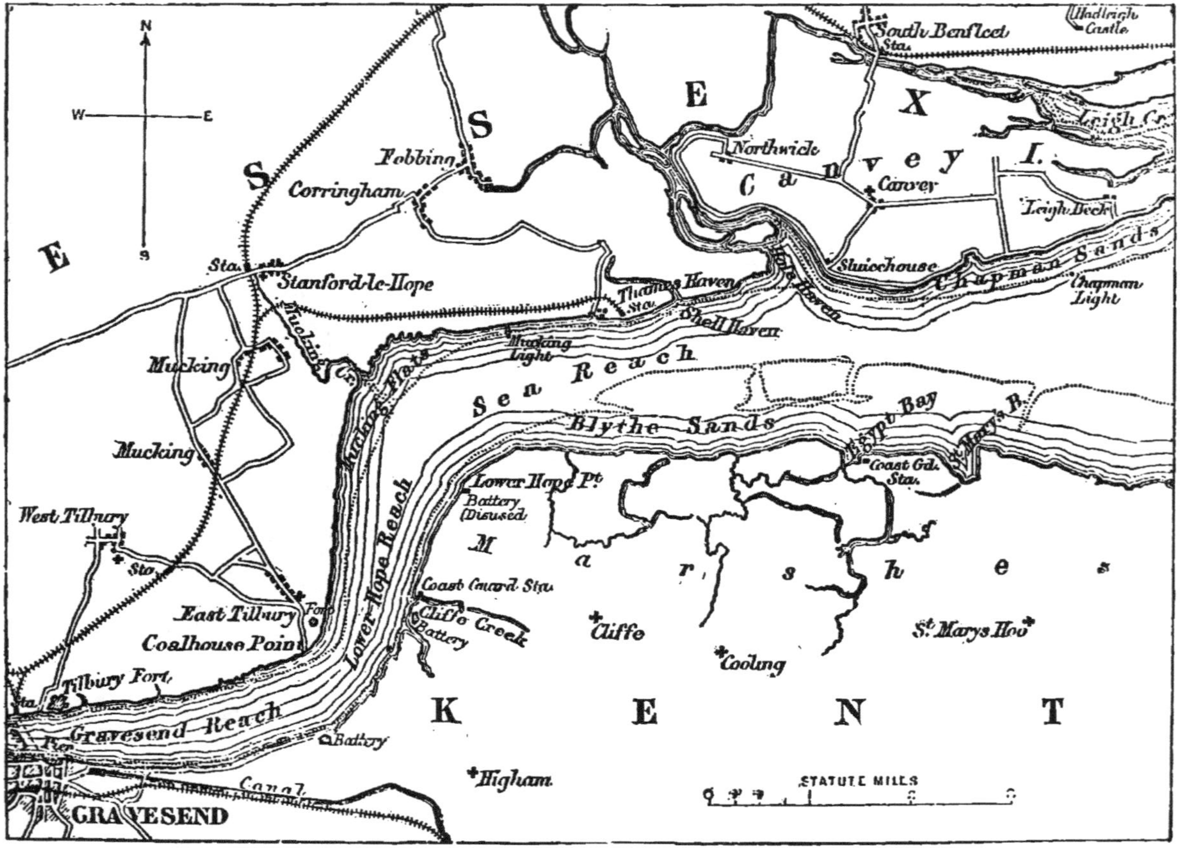

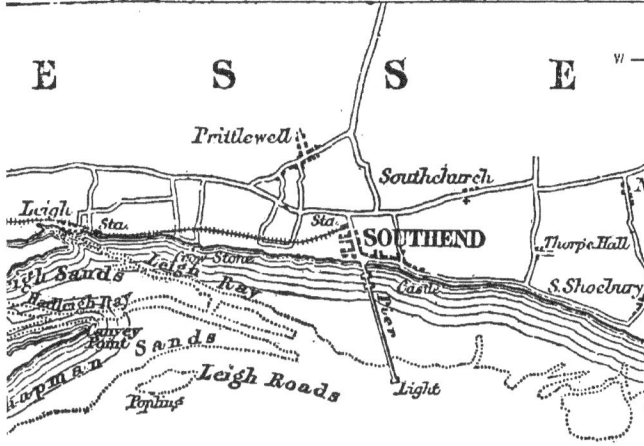

Perry-street and St. Botolph's (parish church); the Roman Catholic Church of Our Immaculate Mother and St. Joseph ; and Congregational, Primitive Methodist, Wesleyan, and Wycliffe Congregational Chapels.

POLICE.—Station, High-street.

POSTAL ARRANGEMENTS.—Post Office (money order, telegraph, savings bank, and insurance), The Hill. Branch in High-street. Mails from London, 7.15 and 11.30 a.m., 6.45 p.m. Mails to London, 10.30 and 11.30 a.m., 2.15 and 8 p.m. Sundays 6.30 p.m.

NEAREST *Railway Station*, Northfleet; *Ferries*, Greenhithe and Gravesend.

FARES to London : 1st, 3/6, 4/6 ; 2nd, 2/8, 3/6, 3rd, 1/10, 3/-.

Northfleet Hope runs from Grays Thurrock to Northfleet, nearly north and south, about a mile and a half. There is at the west side of the Hope a shoal with as little as three feet of water in places at low tide. At Grays Thurrock and at Northfleet there are very extensive cement works, and at the former place is moored the *Exmouth* training-ship. Bearings N. and S.

Northfleet Light.—This, the first of the Trinity House lighthouses, is an iron pillar-light illuminated by gas. It was transferred to the care of the Trinity House by the Thames Conservancy in 1870.

North London Rowing Club, Hammersmith. — Election is by ballot in general meeting : one black ball in five excludes. Entrance fee, £1 1s.; subscription, £1 10s. Colours, dark blue and light blue vertical. Boat-house, Biffen's, Hammersmith.

North Stoke, Oxfordshire, on the left bank, 2 miles from Wallingford (a station on the Great Western Railway 51 miles from Paddington), from London 88 miles, from Oxford 23½ miles. Population 187. Soil, chalk. The church of St. Mary has a good pointed arch between the nave and chancel and another good arch at the west end, filled up and spoiled by a gallery. Unlike most of its neighbours, the church has not been touched by the hand of the restorer, but it is high time that it should be taken in hand. At present it has an almost pitiably bare and barn-like look. It is understood that the delay in the restoration of the church is a matter of finance.

PLACE OF WORSHIP.—St. Mary's.

POSTAL ARRANGEMENTS. — Letters through Wallingford. Mail from London, 6.55 a.m. Mail to London, 7.10 p.m. No delivery or collection on Sunday. Nearest money-order office, &c., Wallingford.

NEAREST *Bridges*, up, Wallingford 2½ miles down, Streatley 3¾ miles. *Locks*, up, Wallingford 2 miles ; down, Cleeve 3 miles. *Ferry*, Little Stoke. *Railway Stations*, Wallingford and Moulsford, G.W.R.

FARES from Wallingford to Paddington : 1st, 9/5, 16/-; 2nd, 7/-, 12/-; 3rd, 4/3. No Sunday trains. From Moulsford to Paddington : 1st, 8/5, 14/6 ; 2nd, 6/3, 11/- ; 3rd, 3/11½.

North Woolwich Gardens.—On the left bank of the river, adjacent to the North Woolwich Station of the Great Eastern Railway, about half an hour from Fenchurch-street. Almost the only survivors of the open-air places of amusement which were once so numerous, are now Rosherville and North Woolwich. The latter, though by no means so picturesque as the lofty and tree-crowned crags of Rosherville, are prettily laid out, and in the summer-time are a pleasant enough place of resort. A variety of entertainments of the usual class are given here during the season : in fine weather the gardens are generally thronged. The price of admission is 6d., and the fares from Fenchurch-st. are : 1st, 1/1, 1/7 ; 2nd, -/10, 1/3 ; 3rd, -/7, -/11.

Nuneham Courteney (Oxfordshire), a seat of the Harcourt family, is one of the most delightful residences on the Thames. The house, which is fortunately free from the inconvenience of over magnificence, is large and roomy, and gardens and park are second to none on the river's banks. The property was purchased in 1710 by Simon, first Viscount Harcourt and Lord Chancellor, it is said for £17,000. The house was built by him from designs by Leadbetter. It consists of a central block, united to its two wings by curved corridors, and from almost all its windows commands beautiful views. It is a perfect storehouse of curiosities and relics, with a fine library and many excellent pictures, and with literary associations of special value,

Mason, Pope, Prior, Horace Walpole, and many others having been frequent visitors at Nuneham. The library contains a most interesting and valuable collection of autograph letters and family documents; among the former being a very curious letter from Lord Salisbury after the Gunpowder Plot, which completely upsets the theory that the King behaved with courage and presence of mind on hearing of the threatened danger, as it expressly states that James was not told of the plot until all was safely over. There is a strange and melancholy interest about a collection of letters of George III., from his schoolboy days to the time when his brain failed him, in which the progressive steps of the fatal malady can be clearly traced. George III. was on very intimate terms with General Harcourt, and among the pictures now at Nuneham are drawings by the King, Queen Charlotte, and the Duke of York— not very successful, it may be added, as works of art. Among the most remarkable pictures in the extensive collection may be mentioned Sir J. Reynolds, by himself, æt. 17; Michael Harcourt, by Velasquez; a portrait of Sir Simon Harcourt, said to have been the first man killed in the conflict between Charles I. and the Parliament (fortunately for the family, Sir Simon's widow married General Waller, and so saved Stanton Harcourt from confiscation); a portrait of Lady Anne Finch, by Van Dyck; portraits of Rousseau (from a bust taken after death) and John Evelyn; a fine Sir Joshua (in the drawing-room) of the Earl and Countess and Hon. W. Harcourt. In the same room hangs a very noteworthy Rubens, "The Two Lights," and another laudscape by the same master; good specimens of Ruysdael, Van der Neer, and Van der Velde, and another beautiful Reynolds, a portrait of a Duchess of Gloucester. In the octagon drawing-room, from the windows of which the views are specially delightful, are a portrait of Pope, by Kneller; another of Mary Countess Harcourt, by Opie; and a good Velasquez. The dining-room contains a boy with an asp, by Murillo; a landscape by Ruysdael, with figures by Wouvermans; and a portrait of Georgiana Poyntz, Countess Spencer, by Gainsborough. This lady was the mother of the beautiful

Duchess of Devonshire, and alludes to her daughter, in a letter now at Nuneham, as a lanky girl, with no pretensions to good looks, but who hopes to have something of a figure. The family portraits in this room are very interesting; one of Lady Harcourt, the wife of Sir Robert Harcourt, is specially odd, from its extraordinary costume. Near it hangs a portrait of Sir Robert himself, one of Raleigh's men, who parted with hundreds of broad acres to fit out an expedition to Guiana, with no result but the subsequent publication of a little book. There is a good portrait of Lady Anne Harcourt, by Jackson, and a large picture of Simon, Earl of Harcourt (the earldom was granted by George II.), with his little dog, by Hunter. To this a curious bit of family history is attached. Lady Nuneham, the earl's daughter, who was staying in the house, was one night much disturbed by a dream, in which she saw her father lying dead in the kitchen at four o'clock in the afternoon—Lord Harcourt being at the time in perfect health. Lady Nuneham was so impressed with the vividness with which the dream presented itself to her, that she was unable to persuade herself that some disaster was not impending, and confided her fears to her husband, and subsequently at breakfast to the rest of the family. After breakfast the earl went out into the park, for the purpose of marking trees, and nothing further was seen or heard of him until a labourer was attracted by the violent barking of a dog to a well in the grounds. There he found the body of the earl head downwards in the mud at the bottom of the well, having, it was supposed, overbalanced himself in an attempt to rescue his little dog, who had fallen in. A stretcher was brought, and the body taken into the house. The nearest room was the kitchen, and on the dresser the corpse was laid—strange to say, at exactly four o'clock in the afternoon! The coincidence is, to say the least of it, very remarkable, and the story is undoubtedly well authenticated.

In the small dining-room is a portrait of Aubrey Vere, twentieth Earl of Oxford, by Walker; a Salvator Rosa, "Ulysses and Nausicaa;" and two portraits by Reynolds of Simon Lord Harcourt and his son, respecting which the family accounts have the following curious entry:

"£24 10s. paid Mr. Reynolds, the painter." The library contains many portraits valuable in themselves and for their associations. There are portraits of Horace Walpole, Prior, Mason, and Pope, all presented by themselves ; a portrait of Rowe ; a good specimen of Kneller ; and a very fine portrait of Milton as a youth, by Van der Gucht, probably the earliest portrait of the poet in existence. The curiosities and relics, whose name is legion, comprise the service of Sèvres made for the great fête at Ranelagh Gardens on the occasion of the king's recovery in 1789, and given by Marquis del Campo to Earl and Countess Harcourt ; a locket which once contained a portion of the heart of Louis Quatorze, brought from Paris, in 1793, by Lord Harcourt ; Rousseau's Tasso and pocket-book, with numerous papers and memoranda, given by his widow to Lord Harcourt ; a piece of glass from Stanton Harcourt, on which Pope scratched, "Finished here the Fifth Book of Homer ;" Queen Charlotte's snuff-box, still containing a little high-dried ; her majesty's box of rouge, &c. ; a tiny watch, given by the Queen of Bohemia, daughter of James I., to Frederick Harcourt ; a piece of Charles II.'s oak ; and a box said to be made from the tree against which Sir Walter Tyrrell's arrow glanced. Strict belief in the latter article is not considered absolutely necessary at Nuneham. There is also a curious piece of 14th century needlework, and some tapestry worked by Mary Queen of Scots.

The gardens on the right of the house were laid out by Mason in rather a formal style, and abound in monuments and tablets with somewhat pompous inscriptions, grottoes, and high hedges. The present owner has made great improvements, which have had the effect of opening up fine views which were formerly shut out. Beyond the gardens is the old church (now closed), dedicated to All Saints, which was built in 1764 by the second Lord Harcourt, and is modelled on the design of an Early Christian church. On the left of the house run for some distance along the river's bank, and amidst most beautiful trees, the walks constructed by Capability Brown, where artfully-devised vistas, cut through the foliage, afford lovely and unexpected peeps of Oxford, Abingdon, and Radley. At what is known as Whitehead's Oak, there is a particularly fine view of Oxford, although it must be confessed, from a landscape-painter's point of view, Sandford Mill, with its ugly chimney, is decidedly in the way. On a knoll in this part of the park stands Carfax Conduit, which was built by Otho Nicholson in 1590, and being taken down in 1787 to enlarge the High-street, Oxford, was presented by the University to George Simon Earl Harcourt.

The village, which formerly stood near the house, was removed to some distance down the road by Earl Harcourt, who at one time had an odd idea of improving the villagers by the institution of orders of merit, prizes of virtue, &c. &c. It is scarcely necessary to add that the attempt did not answer the sanguine expectations of its promoter. The population of the village is 304. The nearest railway-station is Culham, a station on the Great Western Railway, 56 miles from Paddington. Divine Service is celebrated in the new church, close to the village (which was consecrated on May 18th, 1880) on Sundays, Holy Days, Wednesdays, and Fridays. The house is not shown to casual visitors, but the park is, owing to the kindness of Mr. E. W. Harcourt, M.P., its present owner, a famous place for picnics and water-parties. The regulations for admission to the park are as follows : The season for admission commences on the 1st of May and ends on the 1st of September. The days of admission are Tuesdays and Thursdays only, by ticket. Each ticket admits ten persons to the lock and Carfax. Tickets for private parties, giving admission to the gardens between the hours of 2 and 5, are granted for Tuesdays only. Members of Oxford University and their friends are admitted on Tuesdays and Thursdays without tickets, but are required to inscribe their names in a book kept for that purpose at the lock. Tickets can be had on application by letter from F. Mair, Esq., Nuneham Courteney, Oxfordshire. Dogs are not admitted, and it is particularly requested that all broken glass and other *débris* of picnic parties may be carefully removed. Accommodation for small parties can be had at the lock cottages.

FARES to Paddington, *see* CULHAM.

Occidental Rowing Club, Hammersmith.—Election by ballot of members, not less than fifteen to vote, one black ball in five to exclude. Entrance fee, 10*s.* 6*d.* ; subscription, £1 10*s.* Headquarters, Biffen's, The Mall, Hammersmith. Colours, blue, black, and gold diagonals.

Ornithology.—When the eye grows weary of wood and water-meadow, of lofty poplar and lowly pollard, it is pleasant to turn one's mind to the varied incidents of bird-life which present themselves along the Thames, and which provide a fund of entertainment at all seasons for lovers of nature.

Go where you will, and when you will, to any spot upon the river bank, you will hardly fail to discover some representative of the feathered tribe, whose actions attract notice, whose habits are worth observing.

To the naturalist, however, who would attempt a sketch of the bird-life of the Thames, two difficulties present themselves at the outset. In the first place, the district to be examined has no natural boundaries ; and in the second, a bird has such perfect freedom of action, that its presence or absence in any particular spot may be a matter of the merest chance ; while the advent of an ornithologist to observe and record that of the bird is a still greater uncertainty.

Nevertheless, there are certain birds which are characteristic of the river. Some are found only in summer, others only in winter ; while not a few of the rarer kinds, although their visits to particular spots at irregular intervals can only be regarded as accidental, deserve at least a passing notice whenever and wherever their occurrence has been satisfactorily ascertained. Upon some such basis as this, a tolerably long list of the birds of the Thames Valley might be made out.

Foremost amongst the species which at once attract attention are the Swans. Although scarcely to be called wild birds, they can yet hardly be termed domesticated. It is true they have owners, but they are never fed by them, nor are they ever driven home. Their home is the river, where they have to forage for themselves, and where, from their appearance, it would seem that they do not fare badly. Aquatic plants, particularly the *Anacharis alsinastrum*, mollusca, and fish ova, form their principal food, while at certain

favoured spots they pick up many a morsel thrown to them by the passers-by. Each family of swans on the river has its own district, and if the limits of that district are encroached upon by other swans, a pursuit immediately takes place, and the intruders are driven away. Except in this instance, they appear to live in a state of the most perfect harmony. The male is very attentive to the female, assists in making the nest, and when a sudden rising of the river takes place, joins her with great assiduity in raising the nest sufficiently high to prevent the eggs from being chilled by the action of the water, though sometimes its rise is so rapid that the whole nest is washed away and destroyed. Swans generally breed in their third year. Six or seven eggs are laid, and incubation lasts six weeks, during which time the male is in constant attendance upon the female, occasionally taking her place upon the eggs, or guarding her with jealous care, giving chase and battle if necessary to every intruder.

The young when hatched, which is generally about the end of May, are conducted to the water by their parents, and are even said to be carried there ; it is certain that the cygnets are frequently carried on the back of the female when she is sailing about on the water, and by raising one leg she assists them in getting upon her back. This habit has been not unnoticed by Shakespeare, who wrote :

So doth the swan her downy cygnets save,
Keeping them prisoner underneath her wings.
Henry VI. Part I. Act v. sc. 3.

By the expression "underneath her wings," we may understand under shelter of her wings, which she arches over her back whereon the young are seated.

A full-grown male bird (technically termed "cobb") would weigh about 40 lb., and a female ("pen") 5 lb. or 6 lb. less, while a cygnet will run to 28 lb. or so, and it is about this weight, when properly fattened, they are killed for table. Her Majesty usually has a score or so fattening every year.—(*See* SWAN-UPPING.)

When the river is frozen, the swans sometimes fare badly. A waterman at Kingston informed us that he once found fourteen of these birds in a backwater, with their feet frozen in the ice, and so firmly held that they must have perished

F

from starvation if he had not rescued them. He took them all home and fed them, for some days, for which, in due course, he was properly rewarded.

During severe winters, Wild Swans, or Whoopers, occasionally visit the Thames, but seldom make any stay, for their conspicuous size and colour at once attract attention, and all the guns within reach are directed towards them. A wild swan may always be known from a tame one when within shot by the colour of its bill. In the domesticated bird, the base of the bill is black, with a large horny protuberance on the forehead, while the tip of the bill is yellow; in the wild bird these colours are reversed.

Wherever a thick bed of osiers, often fringed with the foliage of the purple loosestrife, affords concealment and a convenient nesting-place, we are sure to find a few Moorhens, their white flank feathers contrasting prettily with their dark bodies and green legs, as, scuttling in from mid-stream at our approach, they seek shelter amongst the dense undergrowth. Dabchicks, or Little Grebes, are occasionally to be met with, but they are so uncommonly wary, and dive so quickly at the approach of an intruder, that we seldom get more than a momentary glimpse of them.

Nor do we often get very near to a Heron, whose long neck and long legs enable him to see over the tall rank herbage in which he stands; and at the first sign of danger he is off. Early morning, or twilight, is the time at which to find herons by the riverside—that is, on the Upper Thames. Lower down, about Barking or Rainham, these birds may be met with at all times of the day in the marshes adjoining the river, as well as in the creeks and on the mud-flats around Canvey Island. There are several heronries in proximity to the Thames, from which these birds come to fish. In Oxfordshire there is a small colony in Far Wood, Southleigh, the seat of Colonel Harcourt. A pair or two used to breed about Henley, but nowhere in sufficient numbers to be worthy the name of a heronry. In Berkshire there used to be two colonies in Windsor Great Park, but we are not sure whether they are still preserved. At Coley Park, near Reading, the seat of Mr. J. B. Monck, a pair of herons, about the year

1834, built their nest on the top of a fine lime in the park, growing on a small island close to the Holybrook, and not far from the Kennet. This pair having brought off their young in safety, departed with them the following autumn; but in January of the succeeding year they all returned, and during the next month they actively commenced founding the colony, which has gone on gradually increasing to the present time. Mr. Monck was so well pleased with these new visitors locating themselves in view of the house, that he not only ordered his servants to leave them unmolested, but also inserted a clause to the same effect in the lease of a neighbouring tenant. So numerous are the nests on these trees from successive repairs and additions during each succeeding year, that many of them touch one another; and such is the quantity of sticks heaped together, that many of them are actually a yard in height. These nests remain throughout the winter, and at a distance look like a gigantic rookery. Notwithstanding the contiguity of the two branch railways to Newbury and Basingstoke from Reading, which run within a short distance of the heronry, the birds do not seem to be in the least disturbed by the change which has taken place in the former quietude and seclusion of this once retired spot. About the year 1845 a few emigrants from the original stock established themselves in some large beech-trees in a wood about three miles distant, and within half a mile of the Thames.

In Buckinghamshire Sir W. Clayton can boast of a heronry at Harleyford, and a few years ago a pair of herons nested in an oak at Fawley Court, not far from Henley; but the young were taken, and they deserted the spot.

In the metropolitan county there were formerly two heronries—one at Uxbridge, and another at Osterly Park, the seat of Lord Jersey. The last-named, however, has ceased to exist, and, we believe, also the former.

In Surrey there are, at least, two heronries at no great distance from the Thames. In Ashley Park, Walton-on-Thames, the seat of Sir Henry Fletcher, the nests are built in some of the finest fir-trees in the kingdom. Mr. Jesse relates that a young bird from this heronry, having fallen out of the nest, was taken away in the evening by a gentleman, who carried it to his house at some miles' distance, and turned it into a walled garden that night. The next morning one of the old birds was seen to feed it, and continued to do so until the young one made its escape. The parent bird must have gone over a considerable extent of ground in search of it. There is a second heronry in this county at Cobham Park, the residence of Mr. Harvey Coombe; and there was formerly another at Oatlands, near Weybridge.

A large assemblage of herons takes place at certain times of the year in Richmond Park, where as many as 50 or 60 have been counted at one time. Sometimes they may be seen on the tops of trees, and at others on the ground at a distance from the ponds, appearing perfectly motionless till they are disturbed. This assemblage is very curious. There seems to be no reason why they should congregate and remain for so long a time in the listless manner observed. It is seldom that one sees more than two or three herons together in one place, except at a heronry, and then only when they are watching for their prey.

In Kent, at Cobham Hall, near Gravesend, the Earl of Darnley has an old-established heronry, which we visited not long since. Here about thirty nests are built, chiefly on ash-trees, and the birds always depart in the autumn, to return again the following spring. In the same county there are heronries at Penshurst Park, and Chilham Park, near Canterbury, the residence of Mr. Charles Hardy. At the last-named place as many as eighty nests have been counted in close proximity. On the opposite side of the river, in Essex, there is a colony of these birds at Wanstead Park, the seat of Lord Cowley. Five-and-twenty years ago the herons here tenanted some trees at a different spot in the park. They now occupy some tall elms and wych-elms upon an island in the largest sheet of water. When we last visited the spot we estimated that there were about thirty pairs nesting here. Farther inland, near Chelmsford, is a heronry belonging to Sir John Tyrell. Although 13 or 14 miles from the river in a direct line, it is probable that most of the herons which are seen about Canvey Island, at the mouth of the Thames,

come from this heronry, as well as from Wanstead and from Cobham Hall. These birds travel great distances to and from their feeding-grounds. We have met with them at times more than 20 miles away from home. Several instances have come to our knowledge of herons having been caught with trimmers set for pike, and the head-keeper at Hampton Court Park once found one which was caught by the beak in a vermin-trap.

Another fisher on the Thames, although a much smaller one, is the King-fisher, one of the handsomest of British birds, quite tropical, indeed, in his bright blue and orange plumage. These birds frequent the backwaters of the Thames, where the water is shallow and still, and where they can easily see their tiny prey. Occasionally, however, as we push our boat noiselessly round a bend of the river, we may see one sitting on an overhanging bough or a drooping osier. But he does not stay long. A flash of bright blue, and away he speeds in a line so straight, and at a pace so swift, that the eye can scarcely follow him.

On some parts of the river, during the summer months, kingfishers are not uncommon, especially after the nesting season, when the young are on their wing. They then keep together in little family parties; but later on, in autumn, they migrate, and numbers go down to the coast, where they may be seen fishing in the creeks and tidal harbours, as well as in the numerous dykes which intersect the marshes at the mouth of the river.

We once picked up a dead kingfisher, which on examination we found to have been choked by a stickleback, a spine of which was firmly fixed across its gullet. A similar accident not unfrequently happens to the dabchick or little grebe. We have seen many of these birds which had died in their efforts to swallow a good-sized river bull-head, or "miller's thumb" (*Cottus gobio*).

Where the ground is flat and soft by the margin, Rooks and Peewits love to feed; and during hard weather, especially, these birds may sometimes be seen congregating in large numbers in the early morning, before the traffic on the river has commenced to disturb them. Peewits are much attached to their old haunts. A large plantation was made in a part of Richmond Park where these birds had for

F 2

many years been in the habit of breeding. They continued to do so until the young plants had attained sufficient height and thickness, to exclude them from the ground. They have since continued to lay their eggs near the same spot. The situation is a low-lying moist one, and probably selected in consequence of the grass being stronger there, and the young in consequence more easily concealed. As soon, however, as the young birds are able to accompany them, the old birds take them to higher grounds. They run as soon as they are hatched, but cannot fly till they are nearly full-grown.

Although we have never observed the Jackdaws come down to the river's brink to feed with rooks, they may often be seen with these birds in the meadows adjoining. They build in the holes of pollards and old trees in the parks, and with very little attempt either at concealment or security. At the time of year when the fallow deer is doffing his winter coat to assume a new one, the jackdaw finds it convenient to appropriate the rejected materials, as the best he can find, in sufficient quantity for the lining of his nest, and his proceedings on the occasion are characterised—in some individuals, at least—by a singular absence of ceremony. Not content with the scattered tufts, which with a little industry he might collect from the trunks of trees, the fences, or any other object against which the deer has been rubbing himself, he actually has the effrontery to tear off fragments of the worn-out coat from the person of the owner, the latter meanwhile calmly watching the process of denudation as if it really ministered to his comfort.

The same old trees that are tenanted by jackdaws often give shelter to owls of two species—the White or Barn Owl, and the Tawny Owl. When pulling up the river during the still twilight of a summer evening, we have not unfrequently observed a White Owl skimming low, with noiseless flight, over the mead, now and then dropping out of sight, and anon reappearing as if unsuccessful in its stoop. At times the first indication we have had of its proximity has been the utterance of its unearthly "screech," which has earned for it, amongst the superstitious, the title of a bird of ill-omen. When passing the overhanging woods on various parts of the river, we

have heard the very different cry of the Brown Owl. This is a loud melancholy "hoot," not always in the same key, and taken up and answered by other individuals of the same species that happen to be within call. The effect is very fine on a still summer evening, when the swallows are dipping to roost amongst the osier-beds, when most other birds are at rest, and the great bats emerge from their hiding-places, and dash wildly up and down in pursuit of the late-flying gnats. As the boat drifts gently down with the stream, a sudden splash, and a widening circle, reveals the spot where a moorhen or a dabchick has disappeared. A low twittering of swallows is heard from the osiers, as flock after flock settles down for the night, while the hurried, startling song of the reed-warbler bursts forth at intervals from the gloom. Then the deep note of the brown owl chimes in as a bass, and strikes the attentive listener with a feeling akin to melancholy, but a feeling, withal, of intense enjoyment. Cowper has truly said:

There is in souls a sympathy with sounds,
And as the mind is pitch'd the ear is pleas'd.

At such times, during the summer evenings, another and a stranger bird may be seen upon the wing. This is the Nightjar, a summer visitor. At a little distance, when flying away, it looks not unlike a hawk or a cuckoo, its long wings and tail, and slim figure, giving it this resemblance. But mark the character of its flight. It does not go far in a straight line, like either of the birds we have named. It wheels and drops suddenly with half-closed wings, recovers itself, flies on, wheels and drops again; at every stoop, we may be sure, catching some incautious moth or beetle. Its evolutions are very curious, while its monotonous jarring note, generally uttered while the bird is perched, is so remarkable as not to be forgotten when once identified.

A "companion-in-arms" is the Spotted Flycatcher, for he also wages war against winged insects. A small gray bird he is —the young are spotted—generally to be seen sitting upon a park fence or paling, a low bough, or even a post along the towing-path. Motionless he sits for some seconds on his post of observation, then suddenly sallying forth into the air, he makes a raid upon the passing prey, and, returning to the same resting-place, there is one gnat less in his immediate neighbourhood.

Not unlike this little bird in size and general appearance when seen at a little distance is the Garden Warbler, another summer visitant. Its actions, however, are very different. It hunts about the tree-tops for *aphides*, and may often be seen upon overhanging boughs by the riverside. Its general colour is gray above, silvery-white beneath. It has a sweet song, and a loud one for so small a throat.

But in the matter of song, by common consent, no bird can vie with the Nightingale, whose clear, liquid notes and inimitable trills have furnished a theme time out of mind to poets and naturalists. Wherever a wood or copse comes down to the river, as at Nuneham, Whitchurch, Shiplake, Marlow, Cliveden, and Datchet, the song of the nightingale may be heard during the months of April and May, not only in the evening, but during the greater part of the day, as the birds sit in some leafy bower, shaded from the sun's rays. The male birds arrive first, generally about the 7th of April, and on the arrival of the hens they pair and assist in building, during which time, and during the time the hens are sitting, they are in full song. When the young are hatched, the males leave off singing, and feed them. Their song usually ceases before the end of the first week in June, but we have occasionally heard a nightingale sing on throughout June, a circumstance which we accounted for by supposing that the nest had been robbed, and that the cock was singing while the hen hatched a second brood.

We have alluded to the song of the Reed-Warbler, a very characteristic bird of the Thames in summer-time. It may be distinguished from its congener the Sedge-Warbler, which visits us at the same period of the year, and is very common along the Thames, by its being a longer and slimmer bird, by the uniform colour of its head and back, and by its note and different flight. In the sedge-warbler the most conspicuous characters are a white line over the eye, a darker back, and dark centres to the wing feathers, with lighter margins. The note of the reed-warbler, as distinguished from that of the sedge-warbler, may be

described as more of a song and less of a chatter ; clearer, less harsh, and more sustained. The nests and eggs of the two species differ considerably. The nest of the sedge-warbler is placed on the ground, formed of dry grass, and lined with hair. The eggs are yellowish-brown. The nest of the reed-warbler is supported on reed stems, formed of the seed branches of the reeds and long grass coiled horizontally round with a little wool, including the upright reeds in the substance. The eggs are greenish-white, freckled with dark green and brown. It is in the nest of the latter bird that the Cuckoo often deposits its egg, and perhaps no bird along the Thames more frequently acts the part of foster parent to the young cuckoo, unless, perhaps, the titlark. Mr. Jesse states in his interesting "Gleanings" that young cuckoos used frequently to be found in the titlarks' nests in Richmond Park, both birds abounding there.

We have repeatedly seen cuckoos visiting the reed-beds on the Thames, in search apparently of a "procreant cradle."

About the time that the cuckoo sings all day, the voice of the Turtle is heard in the land, and a pleasant soft murmur it is. This bird may often be seen crossing the river, generally in pairs, on its way to and from the woods, where it builds its shallow flimsy nest, and lays its two pearl-white eggs. In the autumn it frequents the stubbles and turnips in little parties, and manifests unusual cleverness in keeping out of gunshot. During the month of May the meadows by the riverside resound with the note of the Landrail, or Corncrake, which is heard not only all day, but often far into the night. The nest, with its prettily blotched eggs, is not unfrequently cut out by the mowers in the grass fields. The Water-Rail is far less obtrusive, and its retired habits and stealthy gait cause it frequently to pass unobserved.

Wherever the bank shelves, and a margin of soft ooze offers a tempting spot whereon to rest and feed, we naturally look for the Common Sandpiper, or "Summer Snipe," as it is frequently called. So closely does the colour of its back resemble the mud on which it walks, that when perfectly still it is almost invisible. Sometimes it will suffer a tolerably near approach, and then with a shrill "Weet, weet, weet," will be off, skimming low over the water, with a jerky, pulsating beat of wing, which distinguishes it from all others of its kind. Another species of sandpiper visits us twice a year—namely, at the periods of migration in spring and autumn. This is the Green Sandpiper (*Totanus ochropus*). It generally arrives during the third or fourth week of April, stays a few weeks, and then passes on towards the north-east to breed in Norway, Sweden, and Lapland. Towards the middle of July it appears with its fully-fledged young, and remains about creeks, ditches, and quiet, out-of-the-way ponds, until far into the autumn, occasionally even being met with here in winter. It particularly affects the salt marshes at the mouth of the river, frequenting the dykes and mud-flats, where at ebb tide it seems to get plenty of food. This sandpiper may be known from the last-named by its larger size and darker colour, its white rump, and different flight and note. In the marshes at the mouth of the river, and along shore at ebb-tide, may be seen many other kinds of wading birds, each of which has its characteristic flight and actions, and its own peculiar note. Amongst these may be named the Dunlin, or Ox-bird, sometimes also called Sand-lark, and, erroneously, Stint—this last name belonging properly to two of our least sandpipers (*Tringa minuta* and *Tringa Temminckii*). Then there is the Redshank, whose musical yet melancholy call may often be heard from the marshes in spring ; the Greenshank, a rarer visitant in spring and autumn ; and the Curlew. A flock of Knots (*Tringa canutus*) may sometimes be seen in company with the dunlins on the mud-flats, and occasionally the rarer Curlew Sandpiper (*Tringa subarquata*).

But of all the river birds to force themselves upon your notice in summer-time, there are none like the Swallows, Martins, and Sand-Martins. At certain favoured spots they positively swarm, and filling the air with life and motion, seem to vie with one another in trying how near they can approach without touching you. The swallows build under the arches of many of the bridges ; the sand-martins here and there in the banks, where these are high enough, and the soil favourable for mining operations.

The latter birds, however, seem more partial to sand-pits and to the artificial banks formed by railway-cuttings. A sand-martin's nest, taken from a bank of the Thames, was composed of a layer of grasses, above which was a second layer of swan's breast-feathers, so placed as to curl over the eggs ; the appearance forcibly reminding one of the calyx of a tulip, or a white water-lily. Although the hole was damp, the platform of grass and feathers formed a warm and dry receptacle for the eggs, which were of a pearly white, and six in number.

In August and September sand-martins congregate in vast numbers on many parts of the Thames. We have seen them perching in hundreds on the telegraph wires over the railway bridge at Taplow.

In the second volume of his beautifully illustrated work on the birds of Great Britain, Mr. Gould has given a very pleasing picture of a flight of sand-martins over the Thames, in referring to which he says : "Those who have not seen these vast assemblages, can form but a faint conception of the sight ; it must be seen, and the myriads of their twittering voices heard, to be understood. I have frequently observed masses of these birds collect high up in the air, and having performed certain circular flights and other evolutions, descend with a loud rushing sound to the willow-beds like a shower of stones—the willows upon which they settle being completely covered and bowed down by the united weight of these little birds, which sit side by side for the sake of warmth, and the occupation of the least possible space. If the night be cold, and the morning ushered in by frost, these little creatures suffer severely, and hundreds may be found benumbed by the sudden lowering of the temperature ; in this case many of them die, while others take warning, and with wonderful instinct wing their way southward to the more congenial climates of Spain and Africa."

Swifts, although not so numerous as the last-mentioned birds, breed at several places along the river, as at Maidenhead, where Mr. Gould has taken the young between June 28th and July 12th. They are late comers, and leave, as a rule, long before the swallows and martins do. The swift was one of the birds particularly noticed by Gilbert White during his visits to London. In his twenty-first letter to Daines Barrington, he writes ; "In London, a party of Swifts frequents the tower, playing and feeding over the river just below the bridge ; others haunt some of the churches of the Borough next the fields, but do not venture, like the House-martin, into the close, crowded part of the town." During the spring and autumn migration, several species of Terns, or "Sea Swallows," as they are popularly termed, come up the river from its mouth, and often wander a considerable distance inland. We have identified at various times, and at different places, the Common Tern, the Arctic Tern, the Lesser Tern, and the Black Tern ; and in June, 1869, we saw a very beautiful specimen of the Sooty Tern (*Sterna fuliginosa*), which had just been shot on the Thames at Wallingford. The first flock of terns generally arrive during the first week in May, and consist almost entirely of old birds. In August, young as well as old birds are seen. At night we have seen them roosting upon boats and upon posts projecting above the water below high-water mark. The flight of all the terns is exceedingly graceful, and there can hardly be a prettier sight, or one more interesting to the ornithologist, than a flock of these birds fishing in undisturbed enjoyment.

With the terns, also, come Gulls in twos and threes; the commonest species on the Thames above London being the Black-headed Gull (oftener seen without than with its dark hood) and the Kittiwake. Below London may be seen the Common Gull, the Herring Gull, in all stages of plumage, and the Great Black-backed Gull, which used formerly to breed in the marshes at the mouth of the Thames ; but all these birds ascend the river for some distance during hard weather, or after a gale. The common gull has been seen and shot at Hampton, and a great black-backed gull was killed as high up as Putney during a frost. Sir Humphrey Davy says in his "Salmonia" (p. 193): "I believe that the reason of this migration of sea-gulls and other sea-birds to the land, is their security of finding food. They may be observed at this time feeding greedily on the earth-worms and larvæ driven out of the ground by severe floods, and the fish on which they prey in severe weather

in the sea leave the surface when storms prevail and go deeper."

Occasionally the rarer Little Gull (*Larus minutus*) pays a visit to the Thames, but the specimens which have been procured have generally been immature birds. It is worthy of remark that the little gull was first noticed as a British bird by Colonel Montagu, who described a specimen which had been shot on the Thames, near Chelsea. Within the last twenty years, we have noted the occurrence of eight or nine individuals of this species in Blackwall Reach. at Rainham, Grays, and Gravesend, besides two others that were shot at Kingsbury Reservoir in August, 1871. In September, 1862, we received an immature example of the still rarer Sabine's Gull, which was shot on the Thames at Blackwall.

So far, we have attempted to give some idea of the characteristic birds which may be met with on the river, both as residents and summer visitants. In winter, the avifauna changes. It is true that the residents may then still be met with, although with some of these even (as for instance the kingfisher) a partial migration takes place. The Heron, the Moorhen, the Dabchick, are still there, and, of course, our old friends the Swans. But we miss the Swallows and the Reed-Warblers, the Flycatchers and Nightjars. The Cuckoo is gone, and the song of the Nightingale, Titlark, Blackcap, and Garden Warbler are all hushed. The Grey Wagtail has come to take the place of the pretty yellow one, whose canary-coloured breast was so conspicuous as it ran amongst the cattle by the river in summertime ; and the former more sombre, though no less elegant little bird may be seen about the weirs in incessant motion, with ever undulating tail. Fieldfares and Redwings in flocks pass over with noisy twitterings, and in hard weather alight upon the oozy margin of the river at low water, to seek a sustenance which is elsewhere denied them. The Hooded Crow, too, arrives as a winter visitant, and at that season is sometimes common in the marshes on both sides of the river below London. In November, 1874, a hooded crow was observed feeding on the lawn of the Inner Temple Gardens. Flocks of Linnets and Lesser Redpolls may be seen careering along the banks, and dropping down amongst the weeds in search of food, which consists chiefly of seeds and minute beetles. In company with them, at times, are found Bramblings and Mealy Redpolls ; the last-named, however (known to the London birdcatchers as the Stony Redpoll), is comparatively a rare bird, and seldom more than four or five are seen together at the same time. Wherever any alders fringe the river bank, the Siskin in winter may often be found ; and the pretty "Snow-flake," or Snow-bunting, arriving in flocks, contrives to pick up a living in the riverside marshes until the spring, when it disappears. In company with the last-named, the rarer Lapland-bunting is occasionally met with, but the examples obtained from time to time have almost invariably proved to be immature birds. Snipe, Duck, and Teal, although regular winter visitants, and often to be seen upon the wing at that season, are never found in any number along the Thames, in consequence of its being too much disturbed by constant traffic. They undoubtedly visit the river by night, but, as a rule, betake themselves during the day to some quieter retreat, either in the marshes, or in some preserve often at considerable distance from the river, where they can rest undisturbed until twilight. Woodcocks are comparatively scarce, that is, in the immediate vicinity of the river, although a score of places might be named in the neighbourhood of London, even in the metropolis itself, where woodcocks have been killed or caught. A few pairs occasionally remain to breed in the metropolitan county. Both eggs and young have been found in the Hampstead and Highgate Woods. The last nest we remember to have heard of was discovered in a wood at Englefield Green, near Staines.

Amongst the wild fowl which visit the Thames in winter, beside Duck and Teal, may be mentioned the Widgeon, the Golden-eye, and the Pochard, and occasionally the Tufted Duck. Geese are seen passing over in hard weather, but seldom alight. On Christmas Day, 1860, however, a flock of about fifty White-fronted Geese alighted in a large field at Friar's Place, Acton, and remained all day, when some took their departure, about twenty remaining for two or three days longer. On the 28th one was shot,

and the species then identified. Meyer, in his "Illustrations of British Birds and their Eggs," mentions a white-fronted goose which he shot on the Thames near London, in February, 1846. In January, 1867, a small flock of white-fronted geese visited the Thames at Surly, and during the last fifteen years several specimens have been procured near Eton, Windsor, and Datchet. The Grey-leg Goose has been killed on the river at Cookham, and a Bernicle Goose was shot some years since at Datchet. The Red-throated Diver occasionally appears on the river in winter. We once saw one which had been shot between Richmond and Twickenham, nearly opposite Eel-pie Island. Several instances have been recorded of the occurrence of the Great Northern Diver on the Thames in winter, examples having been procured at King's Weir, near Oxford, at Pangbourne, and at Maidenhead. An immature bird of this species, which was found in a garden on Headington Hill, near Oxford, after a remarkably stormy night in October, was kept alive at the Anatomy School for six weeks, and is now preserved there.

Considering the number of observers at Oxford, it is not surprising that we should be made acquainted, not only with all the commoner birds to be found in that neighbourhood, but also with many of the rarer ones. Nor, for the same reason, can it be wondered at that a large proportion of rare species have from time to time been detected in that vicinity.

Some years ago a Honey Buzzard was captured near Oxford in a singular manner. This bird, which preys on wild bees, wasps, and their larvæ, had forced its head into a hole in the ground after a wasp's nest, and getting wedged in was seized by a countryman before it could extricate itself. Amongst other birds of prey, Montagu's Harrier and the Eagle Owl are both recorded to have been met with in the neighbourhood. Amongst the smaller perching birds, perhaps the Pied Fly-catcher is one of the rarest which has occurred at Oxford. A Rose-coloured Pastor, however, has been preserved, which was shot near Oxford so far back as the spring of 1837. Ravens at one time used to nest at no great distance from the city, but we have not heard of any young birds being found in that neighbourhood since the year 1834, when four were taken from one nest. Amongst the rarer shore birds may be noted the Little Stint (*Tringa minuta*), and Temminck's Stint, both of which have been observed near Oxford. A pair of the latter were shot on Port Meadow some years back.

The Grey Phalarope does not usually make its appearance until late in the year, when it has assumed its winter plumage. A specimen, however, in partial summer dress was killed near Oxford, and brought to one of the local bird-stuffers for preservation. Amongst the rarer wild-fowl killed in this locality may be noticed Bewick's Swan, the Ferruginous Duck, Smew (three of which, all males, were on one occasion, in the month of January, killed at one shot), and the Common and Velvet Scoters. The two last-named are usually seen only in severe winters. One Christmas Eve a Scaup Duck was caught in the basin in the quadrangle of Christ Church, where it had settled in company with two others; and some years later, in the month of November, a Little Auk was picked up in an exhausted state, after a storm, in Christ Church Meadow. The Sandwich Tern, rarely met with so far inland, has once been shot near Oxford in the month of August.

The Grebes, as already stated, are generally met with on the river in winter. A specimen of the Eared Grebe, however, procured near Sandford in the month of June, proved to be in full summer plumage. At this point of the river a Guillemot was once shot in October—an out-of-the-way place for so sea-loving a species. Fifty years ago the Kite was not an uncommon bird in Oxfordshire and Berkshire, and might be seen almost any day by persons taking a country walk; indeed, it used to be observed sailing over the streets of Oxford. The last we remember to have heard of in that direction was shot at Abingdon in 1855.

A specimen of that very curious bird, the Hoopoe, was killed at Wallingford about the 18th June, 1867, a time of year which indicates that the bird might have remained to breed in the neighbourhood if unmolested. At this same spot, in June, 1869, was shot one of the rarest of British sea-birds,—the Sooty Tern (*Sterna fuliginosa*). It was brought to us for

inspection the following morning preparatory to its being skinned and preserved for the owner, Mr. Franklyn of Wallingford. In appearance it was intermediate in size between the Common and Sandwich Terns; the bill, legs, and toes black; the head, nape, and all the upper surface of the body, sooty black; the chin, breast, and under-parts pure white; the tail long and considerably forked.

At Pangbourne the Osprey has been several times observed, and specimens have been procured at Oxford, Nuneham, Maidenhead, Cookham, Surly Hall, and Laleham. In September, 1866, a Grey Phalarope was shot by a fisherman between Pangbourne and Whitchurch. It was in a plumage intermediate between that of summer and winter, and was found on examination to have its mouth full of small flies and gnats. Others have been procured at Maidenhead and Windsor.

In the fine collection of British birds belonging to Mr. Frederick Bond, of Staines, is a specimen of the White-bellied or Alpine Swift, which was shot many years ago at Reading, near which place a short time previously a Glossy Ibis was procured. The latter bird was one of a pair, and was preserved for the late Dr. Lamb, of Newbury, whose collection was subsequently passed to Dr. Tomkins, of Abingdon. In this same collection were two Red-breasted Mergansers, killed on the river near Reading, together with a Whimbrel procured close by at Sonning, where half-a-dozen specimens of that beautiful bird, the Avocet (*Recurvirostra avocetta*), were killed at one shot while feeding at a small pond in the neighbourhood. During a severe frost an Eider Duck once came up the river as far as Sonning, where it was killed.

The White-tailed Eagle has occurred at Henley, where also have been procured at various time, an immature Gyr-falcon, a Black-winged Stilt, one of the rarest of marsh birds, and a Fork-tailed Petrel. At Fawley Court, some years back, another White-tailed Eagle was taken, as recorded by Yarrell in his "History of British Birds;" and an Osprey, seen here for several days in the autumn of 1858, was subsequently shot at no great distance. In January, 1864, a fine Bittern was shot here, and another at Medmenham. After a storm at sea many diving birds, such as Guillemots, Razorbills, Puffins, and Cormorants, are found cast ashore dead, or in a dying condition, from exhaustion and inability to procure food. Others, driven inland by the gale, wander sometimes a considerable distance from the coast in search of a quiet resting-place and food. In this way only can we account for the occasional appearance of such birds on the river, often at a great distance from the sea. Some years ago (1857) a fine cormorant, shot near Marlow railway-bridge, was preserved for the collection of Lord Boston, at Hedsor ; and others have been seen and killed at different times at Pangbourne and Wraysbury.

In James I.'s time cormorants on the Thames furnished a not uncommon sight, but these were tame birds belonging to the king, who went to considerable expense in procuring them, and having them trained to fish, as in China. His Majesty took great delight in seeing them at work, as he did also in watching his otters, which were trained for a similar purpose. A "Master of the Cormorant" was appointed, one John Wood, who, in April, 1611, was paid £30 for his trouble in "bringing up and training of certain fowls called cormorants, and making of them fit for the use of fishing." In May of the following year he was appointed "to travel into some of the furthest parts of this realm for young cormorants, which afterwards are to be made fit for His Majesty's sport and recreation," and for which he received another £30. In 1618 the king had become so fascinated with the sport, that he decided to build a house and make some ponds for his cormorants, ospreys, and otters at Westminster ; and for this purpose he leased off Lord Danvers a piece of meadow ground, about an acre and a quarter, lying in the Vine Garden, near Westminster Abbey, at the yearly rent of £7. A brick building was erected on this ground at a cost of £100, and nine fish-ponds were dug, costing altogether another £40. These ponds were stored with carp, tench, barbel, roach, and dace (100 of each), and a sluice of elm planking was made to bring the water from the Thames. The total outlay incurred upon this, the first Westminster Aquarium, was £286, for which amount, in August, 1618, the king gave an order upon the Treasury. A

copy of this order, with the bill annexed, will be found in the Appendix to the Issues of the Exchequer temp. Jac. I., preserved in the Pell Office, and commonly called the Pell Records. We should be very curious to know what success attended the efforts of Master Wood to train the osprey. We know, from the relation of eye-witnesses, what the cormorants could do (and still do in the hands of a few amateurs to this day), but we have not been able to find any proof that ospreys may be trained to take fish as are falcons to take game and wild-fowl.

Although we can no longer say with Goldsmith,

Along the glades a solitary guest
The hollow sounding bittern guards its nest,

we are enabled to include this fine species amongst the rarer birds of the Thames Valley, in consequence of its having been met with occasionally, as at Fawley Court, Medmenham, Maidenhead, Cookham, and Windsor. The Little Bittern, also, has occurred at Maidenhead, Monkey Island, and Surly Hall. In severe winters that beautiful little black and white duck, the Smew, has been met with at Maidenhead, Monkey Island, Surly Hall, and Boveney. Occasionally this bird is captured in the nets of fishermen in the Thames. Two were taken alive in this way in Bow Creek, but although abundantly supplied with food, refused all sustenance, and died. They had attained the full adult plumage, but one of them was without the elegant pendent crest.

At Cookham, some very interesting birds have been met with from time to time, amongst which may be mentioned, besides those already noticed, the Great Grey Shrike, Black Redstart, Cirl Bunting, Ortolan, Reeve, Great Snipe, Sheldrake, and Velvet Scoter.

That singular bird, the Night Heron, has once been found upon the Upper Thames, an immature example having been captured many years ago at Cliveden.

One of the rarest birds obtained in the neighbourhood of Boveney is the Spur-winged Goose, which was shot during the winter of 1858-59, by an Eton waterman named John Haverly, near Boveney Weir, and fell at Clewer Point. It was preserved by an Eton bird-stuffer; and ten years later was still in the possession of Haverly, who set great value upon it. In the winter of 1861 an Eared Grebe (the rarest of the British grebes) was shot while swimming on the Thames, close to Boveney Lock. Mr. Vidler, of Clewer, has a stuffed specimen of the Polish Swan, which he shot on the river by Clewer Mill, during the winter of 1854-55. About the same time and place, a Storm Petrel was killed after several days' prevalence of high winds.

Windsor is particularly noticeable in the annals of Ornithology for the number of large birds of prey which have been met with in the neighbourhood, a circumstance no doubt to be accounted for by the attractions of the great quantity of game preserved in the royal parks and warrens. A White-tailed Eagle, shot there in February, 1851, and exhibited in the Great Exhibition of that year, was afterwards presented by H. R. H. the late Prince Consort to the collection which was formed, principally by the late Provost at Eton College. Another of these fine birds was shot in the Great Park in December, 1856, and two others (immature birds) near the same spot in the autumn of 1865. One of these being only wounded on the wing was taken alive, and lived for some time in confinement, under the care of Mr. Cole, at the Sandpit Gate in the Park.

The Osprey, Peregrine, Buzzard, and Honey Buzzard have all been shot and trapped at various times in Windsor Great Park, and a rarer visitor in the shape of Tengmalm's Owl has twice been shot by gamekeepers in Windsor Forest.

A Great Grey Shrike was killed close to the river at Windsor in the winter of 1865-66, and a Hoopoe was seen in the Great Park. Two or three of the last-named birds have been procured near Eton.

At White Waltham, not far from Windsor, the rare Purple Heron, a native of Southern Europe and Africa, was obtained in September, 1861. During the summer of 1860, a pair of Pied Flycatchers nested at Eton, where, some years later (1865), two of those tiny little birds, the Fire-crested Wrens, were procured. One evening, during a strong gale of wind, a strange-looking bird was seen fluttering against a lamp at the corner of Brocas-lane, Eton, and on being captured proved to be a Fork-tailed Petrel. We may notice

Staines Moor as a good place formerly for Snipe, and occasionally Woodcock. At Penton Hook, just below, the Great Crested Grebe has been shot in winter ; the river is now too much disturbed to admit of its remaining here in summer to breed as formerly.

The Burgh-way, a tract of rough meadow land at Laleham belonging to the Earl of Lucan, in severe weather is often the resort of Snipe and other migratory marsh birds. Here, in the autumn of 1858, two Spotted Crakes were shot.

The Oyster-catcher is not often found far from the coast, but Yarrell states that he has known this bird killed as high up the Thames as Oatlands, near Shepperton, which is at least fifty miles from the mouth of the river. At Sunbury one of the rarest birds observed is the Little Owl ("The Birds of Middlesex," p. 21). At this spot we have observed the Black Tern in autumn, and have seen two Water-Rails which were shot there by Mr. J. H. Belfrage, in November, 1870. Mr. Jesse has recorded the occurrence of that singular marsh bird, the Ruff, in Bushey Park ("Gleanings," 2nd series, p. 281); and close by, at Hampton, the Redshank, the Bittern, and the Common Gull have at different times been obtained. At Thames Ditton, in September, 1863, an Osprey was shot by the lodge-keeper at Ditton Park ; and lower down, at Kingston, in January, 1869, a female Smew was shot and brought to us for identification. Another seen at the same time was equally the male.

In Richmond Park some pairs of Stock Doves build in the holes of old oak-pollards every year. The keepers always take the young, which they say are excellent eating. The Jackdaw, Cuckoo, and Tawny Owl have been noticed as haunting in their proper season this fine domain. Mr. Jesse, in his entertaining "Gleanings," has recorded the appearance of the Bittern here.

At Chiswick we may note the occurrence of the Spotted Crake in the autumn of 1862, and a Red-breasted Merganser, which was killed on the river in the winter of 1855.

During the summer of 1879 a pair of Nightjars nested on Barnes Common. At Hammersmith, in January, 1854, two Red-breasted Mergansers were shot, one of which we saw preserved some time afterwards. Another was killed during severe weather just above Putney Bridge. The Lesser-spotted Woodpecker has been found nesting at Fulham. In May, 1873, a pair built in an old poplar at Mulgrave House, the residence of Viscount Ranelagh. A Hoopoe, too, was observed in the grounds of Mr. Sullivan, at Fulham.

The description of the Ash-coloured Harrier, given by Graves in the third volume of his "British Ornithology," was taken from a pair which were killed in Battersea fields, about the middle of May, 1812. "The person who shot them," he says, "was not able to find their nest, though from their manner there seemed no doubt of its being near the spot."

The same author states that in his day the Hen Harrier was not uncommon about the marshes of Kent and Essex bordering on London. He often observed them skimming over the fields on the side of the Kent-road, called Rolls Meadows. In 1821 a pair of Marsh Harriers, he says, built their nest in an osier ground near the Grand Surrey Canal, on the Deptford-road. It was placed on a small hillock, just above the water's edge, and contained five dusky-white eggs, two of which were splashed with rust-coloured spots at the larger end. The hen bird was shot from the nest, and being but slightly wounded, lived in confinement for some months. In the "Zoological Journal" for 1825, the late Mr. Yarrell recorded the fact that in November, 1824, a Grey Phalarope was shot while swimming on the Thames near Battersea, where, some years later, the same naturalist noticed the occurrence of an immature specimen of Richardson's Skua. Graves mentions a Golden Oriole, which, at the date of the publication of his work, "was seen in the neighbourhood of Little Chelsea for some weeks, but eluded all attempts at capture."

Amongst other rare birds seen and obtained in the neighbourhood of Chelsea may be mentioned the Little Crake, mentioned by Yarrell; the Eared Grebe, which was found nesting in a pond on Chelsea Common ("British Miscellany," p. 19); and the Puffin, a specimen of which was caught by a fisherman in Chelsea Reach, and kept alive for some days.

In Edwards's "Gleanings in Natural History" (vol. i. p. 228), mention is made of a Little Owl (*Athene noctua*), which came down the chimney of a house in Lambeth: and Yarrell had in his collection a Ring Ouzel, which was caught in a trap in a garden at South Lambeth.

Some years ago we remember seeing in the shop of Messrs. Buffon and Wilson, taxidermists, in the Strand, a live Water Rail, which a boy had caught some days previously in a half-starved condition on the bank of the Thames, just opposite Surrey-street. This was before the Embankment was built. In September, 1866 (a year noted for an extraordinary immigration of Grey Phalaropes), we saw one of these birds which had been shot on the Thames near Waterloo Bridge, and another killed off Blackwall, where we have already noted the occurrence of the rare Sabine's Gull. In the autumn of 1862, an immature specimen of Richardson's Skua was brought to us, which had been shot in Greenwich Reach. In Bow Creek, the Smew and the Fork-tailed Petrel have been procured; and at Barking, the Great Snipe, and a curious cream-coloured variety of the Common Snipe. At Rainham we have noted the appearance and capture of the Waxwing, the Wood Sandpiper, and the Little Gull.

Dartford is celebrated in the annals of ornithology as the locality where, in April, 1773, Dr. Latham first discovered the Dartford Warbler, till then unrecognised as a British bird. Having communicated his discovery to Pennant, the bird was described and figured by the latter naturalist in the fourth edition of his "British Zoology," in 1776. Since that time it has been found on many of the commons and heaths of the southern counties in England.

At Greenhithe the Common Skua has been noted, and at Grays the Little Stint. The Skua has also been seen off the Chapman Light, where, in November, 1876, a fine pair of Avocets were shot.

In concluding this sketch of bird life on the Thames, we cannot refrain from noticing a beautiful little bird, which, once characteristic of the river and its great reed-beds, is now, it is feared, extinct there. We refer to the Bearded Titmouse, of which Mr. Stevenson, in his "Birds of Norfolk," has given so graphic an account from observation of its habits in that county. When Graves published the second edition of his "British Ornithology," in 1821, he wrote : "The Bearded Titmouse is found in considerable abundance in the extensive tracts of reed-land from Woolwich to Erith in Kent, and is occasionally seen in the like situation in various places adjacent to London. We have found it on the side of the Surrey Canal, on Sydenham Common, also on the roadside leading from Bermondsey to Deptford, called Blue Anchor-lane, and have seen it in numbers about Erith." There can be little doubt that the cutting down of the reed-beds, its favourite haunts, and the reclamation and cultivation of the marshes, has gradually led to its decrease, and, as it is feared, its final extinction ; no specimens of this bird having been observed on the river for many years past.

Oven Buoy.—A 20-foot conical buoy, made of iron, and painted black. It is situated in Gravesend Reach, three miles below Gravesend, at the edge of the Oven Spit on the Essex (left) bank, and marks a depth of water, at low-water spring tide, of 9 feet. It is moored with 15 fathoms of chain. This buoy has only been re-transferred to the Trinity House recently, having, in 1865, been transferred to the Thames Conservancy.

Oxford City.—From London 111½ miles. By rail from Paddington, 63 miles, Population, 32,000. Mr. John Richard Green, in his "Stray Studies from England and Italy," is hard upon the city of Oxford: "To most Oxford men—indeed, to the common visitor of Oxford—the town seems a mere offshoot of the University; its appearance is altogether modern . . . . In all outer seeming, Oxford appears a mere assemblage of indifferent streets that have grown out of the needs of the University, and the impression is heightened by its commercial unimportance . . . . as a municipality it seems to exist only by grace or usurpation of prior University privileges . . . . the peace of the town is still but partially in the hands of its magistrates, and the riotous student is amenable only to University jurisdiction." Mr. Green goes on to show, that so far from the above being the fact, Oxford had been a prosperous city hundreds of years before the foundation of the University, and opines that its con-

nection with the University "has probably been its commercial ruin . . . . The University found Oxford a busy, prosperous borough, and reduced it to a cluster of lodging-houses." It is certainly not given to the casual visitor to see anything of the commercial ruin of which Mr. Green speaks. The town has a thriving and money-making air ; even out of term the streets, especially about Corn-market-street and Carfax, are thronged, and although the business done may be of a retail sort, there is no doubt plenty of it. Its modern appearance, however, cannot be denied ; and although its history is surpassed in importance and romantic associations by that of few cities in the empire, it is for its University surroundings that it presents the most attractive features for the tourist and sightseer. Only a few ruins of the castle, which was built by Robert D'Oilly after the Conquest, and of the massive city walls remain. Oxford City is only old in its annals.

Oxford is governed by a high steward, mayor, recorder—W. H. Cooke, Esq., Q.C.—sheriff, ten aldermen, and thirty councillors. It is a Parliamentary borough, constituency, 6,134, and has returned members to Parliament since the time of Edward I., but is at present unrepresented. It is the capital of the episcopal see of Oxford ; the original abbey at Osney, which was at one time the cathedral, has long been destroyed, and the present cathedral is Christ Church. Oxford is an infantry brigade depot, is the headquarters of the Oxfordshire Militia and of the 1st (University) and 2nd Administrative Battalions Oxfordshire Rifle Volunteers.

The University boat-races attract many visitors, especially in the spring, and the great event of the year, which should be attended by all who wish to see Oxford from its best and brightest—but it must be owned most expensive, is the Encœnia or Commemoration of Founders —Commem. as it is generally abbreviated. The festivities of this function are spread over almost a week, and include public orations and recitations of prize exercises in the Sheldonian, which is annually filled by a crowd of ladies who, one would think, must find the proceedings dull ; balls, garden parties, processions of boats, picnics to Nuneham, excursions to Blenheim, Godstow, and Woodstock,

flower-shows, interspersed with little din
ners and breakfasts, the engineering of
which your Oxford Don well understands.
As the capital of an important agricultural district, Oxford is naturally selected
as the headquarters of many county
institutions. Among them are the Oxfordshire Agricultural Society, established in
1811 to encourage the rearing and breeding of live stock, &c., and for organising
shows in various parts of the county; the
Oxfordshire Horticultural Society, established 1830, a flourishing institution whose
objects are indicated by its name; the Charity Organisation Association, established
1844; and to take another point of view,
the Labourers' Union, an offshoot of
that which had its origin at Leamington.
The charities are numerous, the most
interesting and ancient being Cutler
Boulter's Charity; Stone's Hospital,
founded 1700 by the Rev. W. Stone,
Principal of New Inn Hall; and Richard
Wooten's Charity for 14 pensioners.
The Radcliffe Infirmary, founded by that
Dr. Radcliffe whose name occurs so often
in the annals of the University, opened
in 1770, has a weekly average of 112 beds
occupied, and treats, besides, a large
number of out-patients. A Provident
Dispensary has been established within
the last two or three years with satisfactory results. The Boys' and Girls'
Blue Coat Schools date respectively from
1710 and 1756, and educate about 110
children. Naturally Oxford is the home
of numerous educational establishments,
of which the Diocesan Training College
for schoolmistresses deserves notice.

Very important and significant are the
Colleges for Ladies, founded under the
auspices of the Association for Promoting
the Higher Education of Women. Following the example of Girton and Newnham at Cambridge, the Lady Margaret
Hall and Somerville Hall provide for
ladies such educational opportunities as
would qualify them for taking the University degree, if Alma Mater took as
much interest in the girls as she does in
the boys. At Lady Margaret, or Lady's
Hall, the expense is about £75 per
annum, in addition to about £15 per
annum fees for instruction. At Somerville Hall, the expenses are rather less. The
terms correspond generally with those of
the University. Full particulars in regard
to these novel and useful institutions may

be obtained, as to Lady Margaret Hall,
from Miss Wordsworth, the principal,
the Hon. Mrs. Talbot, Keble College, or
Mrs. A. H. Johnson, 22, Norham Gardens, Oxford; and as to Somerville Hall,
from the secretaries, the Hon. Mrs. Harcourt, Cowley Grange, Oxford, and Mrs.
T. H. Ward, 5, Bradmore-road, Oxford,
or the Principal, Miss M. Shaw Lefevre.

The City Public Library of about 9,000
volumes is at present located in inconvenient quarters under the Town Hall.
The Masonic body musters strongly;
and there are two Masonic Halls, one in
Alfred-street, High-street, where three
lodges meet, and the other, that of the
Apollo University Lodge, in Frewen-
court, Cornmarket-street. Two political
clubs, the Conservative and the Reform
(entrance fee, £1 1s., subscription, £1 1s.)
keep the fire of party politics alive and
there is also the Clarendon Club with
social and literary objects (entrance-fee,
£2 2s., subscription, £2 2s.), admission
being by ballot, excluding black balls
being calculated in proportion to number
of voters. There is also St. Catherine's
Club, Broad-street, founded in 1874 for
the benefit of the *scholares non ascripti*
of the University, and conducted by the
undergraduates themselves. The ordinary
subscription is 15s. per term. A dinner
at a very reasonable price is served every
evening, and co-operative stores, etc.,
are connected with the club.

There is an extensive corn exchange,
county hall, and courts where the assizes
are held, and the county gaol, the city
prison having been lately dismantled.
The Town Hall in St. Aldate-street is a
spacious chamber, and has at the back
of the daïs a quaint carving of the city
arms, dating from 1577. In the council
chamber will be found numerous portraits, the most important being one of
the third Duke of Marlborough by Gainsborough. Among others are portraits of
Queen Anne; Alderman Nixon, 1638, and
Joan his wife, principally noticeable for
her curious conical hat; Richard Hawkins,
Alderman, 1638; Sir Thomas White,
Alderman of London, "a worthy benefactor who gave unto the Cite of Oxford
and xxiii other cities and townes everie
23rd year one hvndred and fyve poundes
for ever."

St. Mary the Virgin, the University
church in the High-street, is, with curious

twisted pillars, elaborately-decorated façade, and beautiful spire, one of the most prominent buildings in the city. It was built under the superintendence of Adam de Brome, almoner to Eleanor of Castile, whose tomb is in the north chantry. On the south wall, under the tower, is a brass, apparently to Edmund Crofton, 1507, and over the door are some very curious carvings. The chancel and nave are separated by an organ-screen and loft. The Lenten University Sermon and Bampton Lectures are delivered here. In the south part of the nave is a brass inscription to William Tillyard, 1587, Peter Pory, 1610, and Elizabeth their wife, 1621. The stained glass on the south side of the nave is exceedingly good. By the reading-desk in the chancel, covered by a mat, is a marble slab let into the pavement, bearing the following inscription : " In a vault of brick, at the upper end of this quire, was buried Amy Robsart, wife of Lord Robert Dudley, K.G., on Sunday. 22nd September, A.D. 1560." St. Aldate's is dedicated to a British Saint, who lived about 450, and is supposed to have been originally founded by the Britons. Speed says it was founded or restored about 1004. It subsequently belonged to the Priory of St. Frideswide and to the Abbey of Abingdon. The present building is of various dates and styles. The oldest remains—an arcade of five small circular-headed arches, apparently of Norman work—were removed at the enlargement in 1862 from the chancel to the east end of the north chancel aisle. A recess in the north wall of the chancel, with a flat pointed arch of later date, probably once used as an Easter sepulchre, now contains a good alabaster altar tomb to the memory of John Noble, Principal of Broadgates Hall (the original of Pembroke College), who died 1522. The north aisle, originally called St. Saviour's Chapel, was built in 1455 by Philip Polton, Archdeacon of Gloucester. The south aisle was built early in the reign of Edward III. by Sir John de Docklington, several times Mayor of Oxford, and in its original state must have been a fine specimen of decorated work. The old tower and spire were of about the same date, but being in a dangerous state were taken down and rebuilt 1873-74. During the incumbency of the present rector more

than £6,000 have been expended under the superintendence of Mr. J. T. Christopher, of Bloomsbury-square, London, in the enlargement and restoration of the church. A number of brasses are in the church, but, as is unfortunately the case in too many of the Oxford churches, the interior is so dark as to preclude the possibility of deciphering the inscriptions. The church possesses a fine old carved font, supported at the foot by carved monsters. Hearne states that it was the custom for the people of this parish to eat sugar sops out of the font on Holy Thursday. The present sexton has a lively recollection of hot rolls and butter in his youth at Pembroke on the same date.

St. Mary Magdalen, between Balliol and Cornmarket-street, is a very ancient church, the original edifice dating from before the Conquest, but has been rebuilt, repaired, and restored from time to time down to 1875, when the tower arch was opened up. It has a perpendicular battlemented tower, partly built from materials taken from Osney Abbey, on the Cornmarket side of which will be observed in a niche a small cunningly-wrought stone effigy of St. Mary. The north, or martyr's aisle, was added by Sir Gilbert Scott in 1841. Here is the old oak door, surmounted by carvings of Ridley, Latimer, and Cranmer, which formerly stood in the old city gaol, the Bocardo, at the entrance to the cell in which the martyrs were confined. On the wall facing the old font are one or two old brasses : one to Jane Fitzherbert, 1574 ; another with a kneeling figure to General Smithers, 1580. Against the west wall of the south aisle is a slab (1735) to the memory of Francis Seely, late of the University of Oxford, Barber and Periwig Maker, " who, in the relation of a husband, a father, or a friend, was equalled by few, excelled by none." A slab in the vestry records in peculiar language the virtues of Mrs. Elizabeth Baylie, " niece to yt glorious Martyr and Asserter of the Church of England, Dr. William Lavd, Arch-Bpp. of Cant." Under the west window by the organ is a finely-carved old oak-chest, called The Jewel Chest, formerly used as a receptacle for the old Catholic communion-plate.

St. Michael, in Cornmarket-street, was restored by Mr. Street in 1855, and has a coloured marble altar-piece, his gift. In

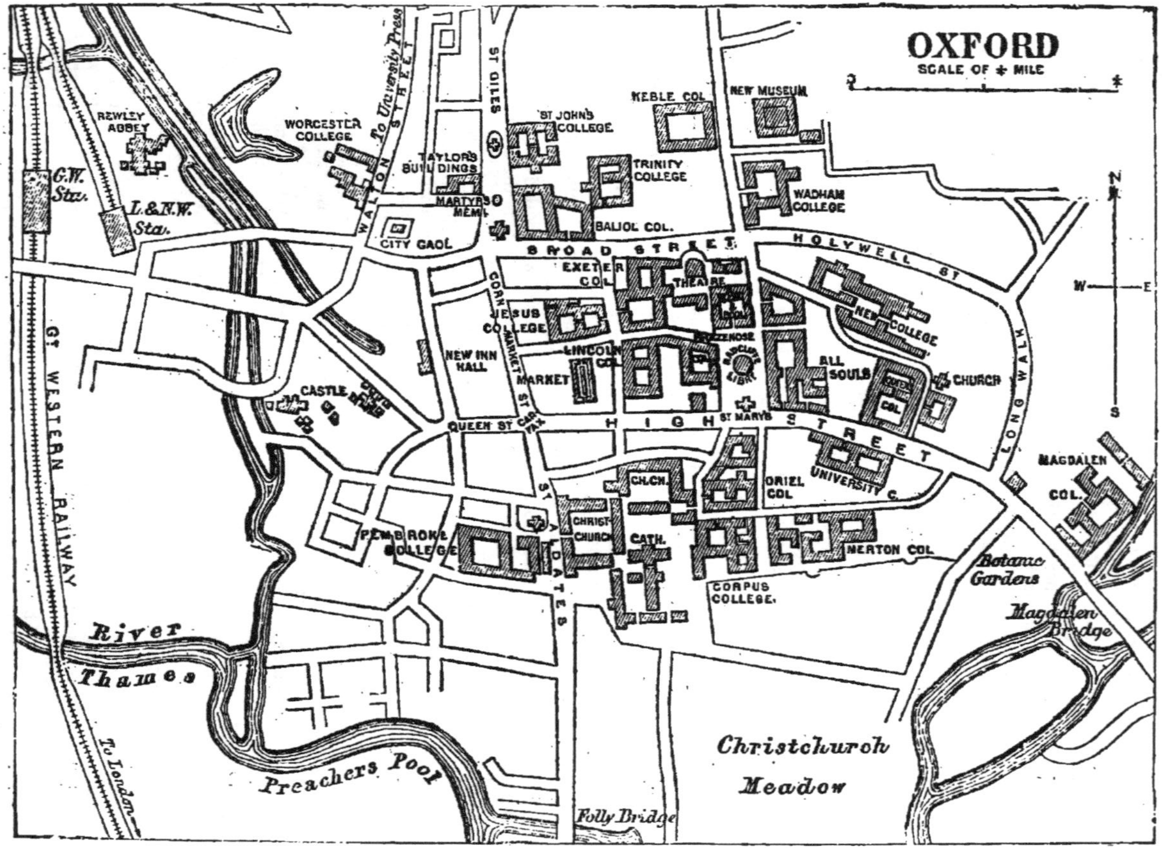

OXFORD
SCALE OF ¼ MILE
N
S
E
W
NEW MUSEUM
KEBLE COL
ST JOHN'S COLLEGE
TRINITY COLLEGE
WADHAM COLLEGE
BALIOL COL.
WORCESTER COLLEGE
To University Press
WALTON STREET
ST GILES
TAYLORS BUILDINGS
MARTYRS MEML
REWLEY ABBEY
G.W. Sta.
L.&N.W. Sta.
CITY GAOL
BROAD STREET
HOLYWELL ST
EXETER COL
THEATRE
JESUS COLLEGE
CORN MARKET ST
NEW INN HALL
LINCOLN COL
MARKET
BRAZENOSE
RADCLIFFE LIBY
NEW COLLEGE
ALL SOULS
CHURCH
COL.
LONG WALK
CASTLE
QUEEN ST
CARFAX
ST MARYS
HIGH STREET
MAGDALEN COL.
CH.CH.
ORIEL COL
UNIVERSITY C.
CHRIST CHURCH
CATH.
PEMBROKE COLLEGE
ST ALDATES
MERTON COL
CORPUS COLLEGE.
Botanic Gardens
Magdalen Bridge
GT WESTERN RAILWAY
River Thames
To London
Preachers Pool
Folly Bridge
Christchurch Meadow

the lady-chapel on the north is an elaborately-painted brass with kneeling figures of Alderman Randolphus Flexney and Catarina his wife, who died respectively in 1578 and 1567 ; close to which will be found an extraordinary stone carving of a man and a woman, apparently having high jinks with a skeleton. Here also is a brass, "Joannis Pendarves," 1617, and a stone with an incised portrait, dated 1603, of Walter Dotyn. St. Peter's-in-the-East, by St. Edmund Hall, the back of which runs along the churchyard, is a very ancient church, dating probably from the 12th century. The crypt, sometimes called Grymbald's with its rows of squat columns, is probably the oldest part of the building. A door is here pointed out, in connection with which is a Fair Rosamond legend. The south door, which is a unique specimen of Norman work, and the groined roof of the chancel with its appropriate chain ornaments, should be noted. The Petworth marble tomb to the memory of Sir R. Atkinson, 1574, four times Mayor of Oxford, is in the choir-room ; but as it is covered with a deal bookcase it is quite impossible to say more of it. On the right of the entrance to the crypt is a small but fine window. The Catholic church of St. Aloysius, St. Giles's-road-west, was opened in 1875, and is a lofty, though rather bare and cold building, with a fine reredos and altar, the gift of the Marquis of Bute.

BANKS.—Gillett and Co., 54, Corn-market-street ; London and County, 121, High-street ; Oxford University and City, 119, St. Aldate-street ; Parsons, Thomson, and Co., High-street.

FAIRS.—May 3 ; Monday and Tuesday after St. Giles ; Thursday before September 29.

FIRE.—Volunteer : Engine-house, New Inn Hall-street.

HOTELS.—" Clarendon," Cornmarket-street ; " Mitre," High-street : " Randolph," corner of Beaumont - street ; " Roebuck," Cornmarket-street.

INFIRMARY.—Radcliffe.

MARKETS.—Every second Wednesday (cattle) ; Saturday (corn).

PLACES OF WORSHIP.—Christ Church Cathedral, All Saints, Cowley St. John, Holy Trinity St. Ebbe's, Magdalen

College Chapel, New College Chapel, St. Aldate's, St. Barnabas, St. Clement's, St. Cross or Holywell, St. Ebbe's, St. Frideswides, St. George the Martyr, St. Giles's, St. John the Baptist, St. John the Baptist (Summertown), St. Mary Magdalene, St. Martin's (Carfax), St. Mary the Virgin, St. Michael's, St. Paul's, St. Peter's-in-the-East, St. Peter-le-Bailey, St. Philip and St. James, and St. Thomas the Martyr. The Roman Catholic Church of St. Aloysius, and numerous chapels belonging to the Baptist, Congregational, Independent, Methodist, Primitive Methodist, and Wesleyan bodies.

POLICE.—Station, High-street ; County Police Station, New-road.

POSTAL ARRANGEMENTS.—Post Office (money order, savings bank, telegraph, and insurance), St. Aldate-street. Mails from London, delivered at 6.30 and 9.30 a.m. and 12.30 and 6.45 p.m. ; Sunday, 6.30 a.m. Mails for London, 8.25 and 11.15 a.m., 3.20, 6.45, and 12 p.m. ; Sunday, 12 p.m.

NEAREST *Bridges*, Folly ; down, Abingdon 7¾ miles. *Lock*, down, Iffley about a mile. *Railway Station*, Oxford.

Fares to Paddington or Euston-square, 1st, 11/-, 18/6 ; 2nd, 8/4, 14/- ; 3rd, 5/3½.

CAB FARES, DISTANCE.—   *s. d.*
Not exceeding a mile and a quarter,
  one person 1 0
For every additional person...   ...   0 6
For each succeeding half-mile   ...   0 6
For every additional person...   ...   0 6
For every fifteen minutes' detention   0 6
  Persons hiring by distance may return to the place of hiring, or any portion of the distance, on payment of one-half the proper fare.

TIME.—   *s. d.*
One or two persons, one hour   ...   2 6
For every additional person...   ...   0 6
For every additional fifteen minutes   0 6
For every additional person...   ...   0 3

If a carriage be hired by time, and the driver cannot return to the nearest cab-stand within the hour, half-hour, or such other time for which he shall receive payment, he shall in such case be entitled to charge one-half the proper fare for so much time as may be necessary to enable him to return to the nearest cab-stand.

CHILDREN BEING PASSENGERS.—Infants carried in the arms or on the lap, or one child not so carried, but under seven years of age, and accompanied by an adult, shall not be charged for as passengers ; but every two children under seven years of age, not so carried, shall be charged for as one adult passenger.

NIGHT FARES.—An additional half fare, both by distance and time, shall be paid for every fare or so much of every fare as may be performed by any carriage after twelve o'clock at night and before six o'clock in the morning.

LUGGAGE.—Luggage allowed not to exceed 112 lbs. in weight ; 9d. to be paid for every 112 lbs. weight carried in excess of the weight allowed.

COMPUTATION OF DISTANCE.—The distance travelled shall be computed from the stand or place where the carriage may be engaged or hired, and shall extend to any distance not exceeding five miles within the district to be computed from the General Post Office aforesaid.

DISTANCES (as given in the "Oxford Chronicle Railway Guide").

From the Great Western Railway Station (down platform) to the following places is one mile and a quarter :
To the south end of Magdalen Bridge.
To the Banbury-road, opposite Shrublands (north of Bevington-road).
To Plantation-road, Woodstock-road.
To Kingston-road, midway between Tackley-place and Farndon-road.
To Abingdon-road, near Whitehouse-lane.

From Oxford Post Office (St. Aldate-street) to the following places is one mile and a quarter :

To Iffley-road, midway between Henley-street and Stanley-street.
To Cowley-road, about 20 yards short of Divinity-walk (Local Board boundary).
To Woodstock-road, at the Small-Pox Hospital, about 230 yards north of Rackham-lane.
To Abingdon-road, at Cold Harbour.
To Botley-road, 60 yards short of Seven Arches Bridge.

Oxford Royal Regatta, 1884.

Monday, August 4.

GRAND CHALLENGE CUP FOR EIGHT OARS—from Iffley.

First Heat.

Long Vacation Club	...	...	...	1
Neptune R.C.	...	...	...	0

Long Vacation Club.—F. P. Bulley, H. Balfour, C. de Coetlongen, H. S. Salter, J. G. Legg, R. S. De Havilland, P. A. Underhill, W. S. Unwin (stroke), P. Watson (cox).
Neptune.—H. L. Charlwood, A. Melville, C. Tymms, W. Haithwaite, G. R. Beesley, E. Bates, A. E. Hunt, F. F. Hunt (stroke), G. Castle (cox).

Second Heat.

Lily R.C.	...	...	...	1
Falcon R.C.	...	...	...	0

Lily.—F. Burborough, H. Broughton, T. A. Cook, A. Veale, A. Ackland, W. Charlton, J. Robinson, R. S. Dingle (stroke), W. Taylor (cox).
Falcon.—C. W. Eyles, W. Annis, F. Shepherd, A. J. Taylor, W. J. Howell, W. J. Clinton, F. Taylor, E. H. Bellamy (stroke), H. W. Franklin (cox).

Final Heat.

Vacation	...	...	...	1
Lily	...	...	...	0

PRINCE OF WALES'S CHALLENGE CUP FOR PAIR OARS—without coxswains, from Iffley.

First Heat.

Long Vacation Club	...	...	r.o.

Long Vacation Club.—F. P. Bulley, H. Balfour (stroke).

Second Heat.

Falcon	...	...	...	1
Neptune	...	...	...	0

Won on a foul.
Falcon.—A. Taylor, F. Taylor (stroke).
Neptune.—A. E. Hunt, E. Bates (stroke).

Third Heat.

Vacation	...	...	...	1
Wave	...	...	...	0

Wave.—F. E. Gibbons, C. W. Gibbons (stroke).

Final Heat.

Vacation	...	...	...	1
Falcon R.C.	...	...	...	0

CHALLENGE CUP FOR FOUR-OARED GIGS (from the Long Bridges), for those who have never won a prize.

First Heat.

Bellerophon R.C.	1
Lily R.C.	0

Bellerophon.—F. Plummer, P. Horser, R. Adams, G. Elstone (stroke), J. Hounslow (cox).

Lily.—H. Bishop, W. Court, W. Monk, J. W. Heavens (stroke), J. Beachey (cox).

Final Heat.

Bellerophon	1
Neptune	0

Neptune.—W. J. Basson, C. Symonds, J. C. Hewett, E. Simmons (stroke), W. Kendrick (cox).

TOWN JUNIOR CHALLENGE CUP FOR FOUR OARS—from Iffley.

First Heat.

Lily	1
Vacation	0

Lily.—J. Robinson, W. Heavens, A. Ackland, R. S. Dingle (stroke), W. Taylor (cox).

Vacation.—W. S. Hatch, W. Salter, L. F. Packer, W. Kirkby (stroke), C. A. Sturges Jones (cox).

Final Heat.

Lily	1
Falcon	0

Falcon.—A. J. Taylor, W. J. Clifton, F. Taylor, E. H. Bellamy (stroke), H. J. Eyles (cox).

SILVER CHALLENGE SCULLS—from Iffley.

E. Bates	1
G. W. Gibbons	0

SILVER CHALLENGE PRIZE FOR WHIFFS —from the Long Bridges.

First Heat.

R. Adams	1
R. G. Westmacott	0
C. W. Eyles	0

Second Heat.

A. E. Hunt	1
C. Symonds	0
P. Horser	0

Final Heat.

Hunt	1
Adams	0

JUNIOR SCULLING RACE—from Iffley.

First Heat.

H. S. Salter ... ...r.o.	

Second Heat.

E. Bates	1
A. E. Hunt	0

Final Heat.

E. Bates ... ... , ...r.o.	

SILVER CHALLENGE OARS FOR PAIR-OARED GIGS—from the Long Bridges.

First Heat.

Neptune	1
Vacation	0

Neptune.—G. R. Beesley, F. F. Hunt (stroke), G. Castle (cox).

Vacation.—R. G. Westmacott, W. Kirkby (stroke), P. D. Kirkby (cox).

Second Heat.

Magdalen ... ...r.o.	

Magdalen.—F. P. Bulley, L. S. Partridge (stroke), C. A. Sturges Jones (cox).

Final Heat.

Neptune	1
Magdalen	0

Oxford University.—The following is a brief account of the sights of Oxford from the University point of view, and with its assistance, and that of the accompanying map, it is hoped that visitors will be able to see all there is to be seen with the least expenditure of time and labour. Where chapels, &c., are not open for public inspection at stated hours, application should be made at the porter's lodge of the college. A small fee is expected, which will generally frank the visitor to the hall, chapel, and library. There are plenty of guides always hanging about the streets, especially in the neighbourhood of the Sheldonian Theatre, whose charge is 1s. per hour; but except to point out the localities of buildings, they are of little use.

ALL SOULS' COLLEGE, High-street, was founded in 1437 by Archbishop Chichele, its beginning having been as a chantry where prayers might be said for the souls of soldiers slain in the French wars. Above the entrance are statues of Henry VI. and the founder, and a group of figures in relief, variously said to represent the delivery of souls from purgatory, and the resurrection of the dead. The first quadrangle is in much the same condition as it was in the founder's time. The second quadrangle was built by Hawksmoor, and is noticeable for its twin towers, 'and a rather incongruous sun-dial, said to be designed by Wren. The chapel, which faces the visitor on entering the first quadrangle from the High-street, is open free daily from 12 to 1 and 2 to 4, except on Good Friday and All Souls' Day. It is approached by a gateway with fine vaulted roof with fan tracery, and is deservedly one of the sights of Oxford. The principal feature is the reredos, which consists of a number of statues and statuettes (for the most part representing personages who fought at the battle of Agincourt), some 135 in all, in elaborate canopied niches, and a group of the Crucifixion. The principal figures comprise a number of very dissimilar personages, such as, besides a large collection of saints, the Duke of York ; John Talbot of Shrewsbury, planting his flag under the walls of Rouen; Humphrey, Duke of Gloucester; Catherine of France ; Thomas, Duke of Clarence ; John 'o' Gaunt ; Margaret of Anjou ; Henry V ; Cardinal Beaufort ; and Earl Bathurst, the donor of reredos, and senior fellow of All Souls'. The reredos is the work of Mr. E. E. Geflowski. The floor of the chancel is of great beauty. In the ante-chapel are the tomb and bust of Thomas Hoveden, 1614, and a few brasses, one dated 1490, another 1461. Eastward of the chapel is the hall, containing several busts, among others one of Bishop Heber by Chantrey, and one of the founder by Roubiliac, as well as several portraits. Among the curiosities in the college is a very ancient salt-cellar of silver-gilt, supported by an armed figure, presented to the college by the founder or one of his descendants. The north side of the second quadrangle is occupied by the library, built with money left by Colonel Codrington in the early part of the last century. In it is a planetarium, a statue of Colonel Codrington, and a fine collection of books, more especially of a legal character. Sir Christopher Wren's original designs for the building of St. Paul's are also here. One of the curious old customs, which are one by one disappearing from the Oxford of to-day, was annually celebrated at All Souls'. It was a tradition that when the foundations of the college were being prepared, a very large mallard flew from one of the drains, and that this circumstance gave rise to the adoption of a mallard as the college crest. On the gaudy day or annual festival, a song and chorus in honour of the mallard was sung by the fellows ; a verse of this song, quoted by Shrimpton's local guide, is not calculated to inspire one with much idea of the versification of its author, or with much regret at the custom of singing it having fallen into desuetude. The first verse runs thus :

Griffin, bustard, turkey, capon,
Let other hungry mortals gape on :
And on the bones their stomach fall hard.
But let All Souls' men have their mallard.

CHORUS.

Oh, by the blood of King Edward !
Oh, by the blood of King Edward !
It was a swapping, swapping mallard.

ASHMOLEAN MUSEUM, at the back of the Sheldonian Theatre, and hard by Exeter College in Broad-street, was founded by Elias Ashmole in 1679, from which period the present edifice dates. The collections here, although not large, are of their kind good, and consist of Chinese and Japanese curiosities, flint implements, ancient pottery, arms, daggers, Polynesian weapons, Esquimaux and North American Indian objects, and a variety of relics interesting no less from their rarity than for their historical associations. Among the most notable objects may be mentioned—starting from the right on entering—some Burmese and Malabar MSS., written on talipot leaves ; a fine old carved powder-flask ; Charles I.'s spurs ; a mosaic portrait in shells of Pope Leo. XII. ; the sword sent by Leo. X. to Henry VIII. with the title of Defender of the Faith, with a crystal handle highly wrought ; King Alfred's jewel, enamelled in gold, and bearing the inscription in Saxon, "Alfred ordered me to be made ;" Queen Elizabeth's watch and riding-boots ; Charles II.'s bellows ; a glove which belonged to Mary Queen of Scots ; Henry VIII.'s hawking-glove ; and Oliver Cromwell's watch. The "Oxford Collection" comprises a variety of implements, and of pieces of pottery discovered in the town during the process of excavations. Descending the staircase to the left there will be found a number of clubs, arrows, patu patus, and other implements of war from Tongataboo, Fiji, New Zealand, and various parts of Polynesia, and on the basement are the celebrated Arundel Marbles. In the museum is a portrait of Ashmole, in a frame carved by Grinling Gibbons. The collection can be seen daily.

BALLIOL COLLEGE is in Broad-street and Magdalen-street. The date of the foundation of Balliol by Sir John Balliol, of Barnard Castle, Durham, the father of John Balliol, King of Scotland, is somewhat obscure. The year was perhaps 1268. The college has been practically entirely rebuilt, a small portion only of the older buildings now remaining, no part of the college being older than 1431. The south front, with the massive tower, was built about 1870 by Waterhouse, and ten years earlier the chapel was built from designs by Butterfield, who here employed the red and white Gothic, which he afterwards developed more fully at Keble. The library and hall, which have been enlarged, are of older date than most of the remainder of the college ; on the west of the Broad-street entrance is a very beautiful oriel window. In the hall are some portraits, and the library has a good collection of illuminated MSS. Opposite the door of the master's lodging in Broad-street are four small stones set crosswise, and it is supposed that it was here that Cranmer, Ridley, and Latimer suffered martyrdom. It is scarcely necessary to add that other authorities are quite certain that the stones do not exactly mark the actual scene of the auto-da-fé.

BODLEIAN LIBRARY. — This famous library, now one of the most important in existence, was founded in 1598 by Sir Thomas Bodley, at one time British Minister to the Hague and elsewhere, who died in 1612. The library existing before Bodley's time was founded by Humphrey Duke of Gloucester, son of Henry IV. But few remains of this existed when the Bodleian was founded. The library now numbers over 400,000 volumes, and as it can claim a copy of every work printed in this country, and is constantly increased by purchase, it is rapidly outgrowing the space originally assigned to it, and is overflowing into the neighbouring buildings. That portion of the library which is accessible to the public is situated over

the schools, which are between the Radcliffe and the Sheldonian Theatre. The entrance is in the south-west corner of the quad. It is open from 9 a.m. to 5 p.m. in April, May, June, July, and August ; from 9 a.m. to 4 p.m. in February, March, September, and October ; from 9 a.m. to 3 p.m. in January, November, and December. The statutes require that intending readers must bring a recommendation from a Master of Arts. The librarians, however, must necessarily have taken the M.A. degree, and are always glad to grant admissions to bona fide students who can satisfactorily show that they are so. If the sight-seeing visitor be not accompanied by a member of the University in academic dress an admission fee of 3d. is charged. Some of the curiosities of the Bodleian are always exhibited under glass cases, and are changed from time to time. It is not, therefore, certain that any of those here mentioned will be on view at any given time. Among them are the first book printed in the English language by Caxton at Bruges, circa 1472 ; a Block Book, the Apocalypse, to which the date 1440 is probably erroneously assigned ; the declaration made by the Duke of Monmouth on the morning of his execution, with his signature and those of six bishops ; a MS. book in the handwriting of Queen Elizabeth, a New Year's gift to her brother Edward ; gloves worn by the Maiden Queen when she visited the University in 1566 ; Wycliff's Bible, 1380 ; Gutenberg's first Bible ; Edward VI.'s exercise-book ; a psalter, with beautiful miniatures, 1340 ; some fine ivory carvings of the 9th century ; and a list of illuminated missals, MSS., Korans, autographs, &c., &c., to enumerate which would be too long. The PICTURE GALLERY, which also serves the purpose of a minor museum, is approached by the stairs on the left of the entrance to the library, and contains books, portraits, medals, models, seals, casts, ivories, busts, and curiosities of every kind. Some of the most notable of the latter are Sir Thomas Bodley's chest, with most intricate arrangement of locks ; Queen Elizabeth's fruit trenchers ; a chair made from the timbers of Sir Francis Drake's ship ; the chair of Fortesque, Chancellor of the University in the time of Queen Elizabeth ; and Guy Fawkes's lantern, as to the authenticity of which perhaps it is not unreasonable to express a doubt. On one of the walls is the following humorous admonition : "Touch what you like with your eyes, but do not see with your fingers."

BOTANIC GARDENS, opposite Magdalen College, formerly the Jews' cemetery, and, when first opened, called the Physic Gardens. Founded by Earl Danby, early in the 17th century, for the improvement of the faculty of medicine. The gardens are entered by a characteristic gateway, designed by Inigo Jones, ornamented with statues of Charles I. and II. They are of considerable extent, and are a pleasant lounge, though perhaps more generally interesting to the botanist than to the mere pleasure-seeker. There is a remarkably pleasant walk along the Cherwell. The buildings on the right of the entrance contain the herbarium, lecture-room, &c. The collection of dried plants is remarkably complete. On the left of the gateway are the Professors' dwellings, in which there is an excellent library, particularly rich in books of the 16th and 17th centuries. The greenhouses are not impressive, but contain a fine collection of aquatic and succulent plants. Entrance is free.

BRASENOSE COLLEGE, to the westward of the square in which stands the Radcliffe Library, was founded by Bishop Smith, of Lincoln, and Sir Richard Sutton of Prestbury, 1512. Over the entrance gateway are statues of the Virgin and Child and two saints, and just above the door is the immense brazen nose from which the college is sometimes erroneously supposed to take its name. The real derivation is said to have been a corruption of Brasenhas or Brewery of King Alfred, but it may fairly be supposed that there is not much more reason in this derivation than in the other. The first quadrangle contains the hall with a few portraits. In the middle of it is a group of sculpture, respecting which the authorities are at variance; some asserting that it was intended for Cain killing Abel, while the other side avers that the group represents Samson slaying a Philistine. One thing is very certain, that the sculpture itself is entirely devoid of merit. The passage to the left leads into the second quad, where is the chapel, chiefly remarkable for its roof.

There is also a good lectern. Two clergymen of curiously different temperaments and literary style were trained at Brasenose, Bishop Heber and the Rev. R. H. Barham of the "Ingoldsby Legends."

CHRIST CHURCH, the largest of all the Oxford colleges, but known as "The House," was founded by Cardinal Wolsey in 1525, and was originally intended to be called Cardinal's College. On the fall of Wolsey the college was seized, and the foundation suspended by King Henry VIII., who re-established it in 1532. In 1546 the see of Oxford was removed from Osney, and the church of St. Frideswide, in connection with the college, became the cathedral, and to the whole was given the name Christ Church. The principal entrance is in Aldate-street, under the gateway of the tower in which hangs the bell known as Great Tom. The tower was part of Wolsey's design, but was left unfinished by him, and was completed by Sir Christopher Wren in 1682. "Tom" originally came from Osney Abbey, and has been more than once re-cast. He is one of the largest bells in England, and weighs 17,000 lbs. Every night at closing time, ten minutes past nine, Tom tolls 101 times, that having been the original number of the students. The great quadrangle is generally known as Tom Quad, and is of imposing dimensions, although the effect is a little bare. Should the contemplated cloisters (part of the original design) ever be built, the effect of the quad will be greatly enhanced. In the north-east corner are the dean's apartments, and in the south-east a gateway, under a statue of Wolsey, in the tower leads to a staircase with a beautiful fan roof springing from a single pillar—a noticeable architectural triumph, even in a city so rich in such matters as Oxford. This staircase leads to the hall, the finest refectory in Oxford, and perhaps in the world. It has a grandly-carved oak roof, with pendants, &c., and at the upper end two splendid bay windows, somewhat similar in character to those at Hampton Court Palace. The walls are adorned with a number of interesting portraits by Holbein, Zucchero, Lely, Lawrence, Janssen, Hoppner, Van Dyck, Kneller, Hogarth, Reynolds, Gainsborough, and other masters. All the pictures bear labels with the names of the originals and of the painters. The hall was used on the occasions of several royal visits to theatrical performances, and in it King Charles I. held a parliament. At the bottom of the hall stairs is the great kitchen, which is said to be the oldest part of the building.

Nearly opposite the principal entrance to Tom Quad is the entrance to the cathedral, which is also the chapel of the college. It was founded on the remains of the church of the convent of St. Frideswide, a more or less mythical heroine of the middle of the eighth century. It was consecrated in 1180. The tower contained ten bells from Osney Abbey, which, in consequence of some doubts as to the safety of the cathedral spire, now hang in the tower over the hall. It is said by Warton that Dr. Johnson was moved to very Johnsonian wrath on viewing some of the Osney remains which had been moved to Christ Church. The verger will be found in the cathedral from 11 to 1 and from 2.30 to 4.30, except on Sunday, and at other times at Meadow Gate. No fees are permitted. The cathedral consists of choir, nave, aisles, and transepts, and is generally Norman in character. The roof of the choir, with its elaborate fan tracery and groining, which is particularly noticeable; the oak pulpit; the carved wood and iron-work in the choir, and its inlaid pavements; together with its new bishop's throne of carved walnut with a medallion portrait of the late Bishop Wilberforce, are all well worth careful inspection. There are a few brasses in the church, one in the north-west dated 1602, one in the south-east with the date 1587. North of the choir are two aisles, the first the Lady or Latin Chapel, and the second the Dean's or St. Frideswide's Chapel. The Latin chapel was built 1346 by Lady Montacute, the donor to the college of Christ Church Meadows. Her tomb is between the two chapels to the eastward. On it reposes a full-length figure of the lady, the costume, especially the head-dress, being very interesting. In niches around the tomb are figures of her children. Next to Lady Montacute, and to the westward, is the tomb of Prior Guymand, said to be of the middle of the 12th century, with effigy of the prior under a highly ornamented canopy. Farther still to the westward is

the tomb of Sir George Nowers, who died in 1425. The figure of Sir George is clothed in armour. At the foot of this tomb is the tablet to the memory of Burton, the author of the "Anatomy of Melancholy." The inscription, written by himself, says :

Paucis notus, paucioribus ignotus
Hic jacet
Democritus junior
Cvi vitam dedit et mortem
Melancholia
Obiit VIII ID JAN A.C MDCXXXIX.

To the extreme east, beyond the tomb of Lady Montacute, is what is called the shrine of St. Frideswide. It dates from 1480, and is a richly ornamented wooden structure, raised upon a tomb. It is supposed to have been in fact the chamber of the keeper of the shrine, which was at one time in high repute with the gift-bearing faithful. In St. Frideswide's Chapel will be found some good carved oakwork, and some old stained glass windows. In the south aisle is a curious mural monument in memory of Sir W. Brouncker and wife, 1645-1649. They are represented sitting with their elbows leaning on a table, on which stands a skull; the prolonged contemplation of which, no doubt, has produced the dejected appearance for which the faces of the figures are remarkable. In the south transept is a window made up of fragments of old stained glass. In the centre of it is a representation of the murder of A'Becket, the hole which will be observed in the glass is where the head of the martyr was punched out by an unappreciative Cromwellite. In the north-west is a remarkable window, signed Abraham Linge, dated 163-, the last figure undecipherable. There is a vast number of slabs and mural tablets, amongst which may be mentioned those of Dean Aldrich and Bishop Tanner.

In the north corner of Tom Quad is a gateway and passage leading to Peckwater Quad, so-called from its having been built on the site of the inn kept by certain Peckweather, once Mayor of Oxford. It was rebuilt from designs by Dean Aldrich, except as regards the library side in 1795. The library is on the south side. The entrance hall contains a fine statue of Dean Cyril Jackson, by Chantrey, and several busts of Christ

Church worthies and others. The lower storey is used as a picture gallery, and contains a collection of unequal merit. The pictures, all of which are labelled with subject and name of painter, contain examples of Tintoretto, Holbein, Titian, Paolo Veronese, Botticelli, Parmegiano, Van Eyck, Velasquez, Carlo Maratti, Spagnoletto, and others. There is a sketch for a fan-mount by Guido, and a singular picture of a butcher's shop by A. Caracci, the butcher and his assistants being caricatures of the artist and of some members of his family against whom he had a grudge. The visitor, descending the stairs to the library, is faced by a marble bust of Proserpina, by Hiram Power, and in a niche on the right is a full-length statue of John Locke, by Rysbrach. From the window on the landing is a splendid view of the cathedral. The library is a fine room, with curious plaster decorations on the walls and ceiling ; the woodwork is of Norwegian oak. The library contains many treasures, including a letter from Charles II., signed Sunderland, expelling John Locke from his studentship at Christ Church for misdemeanour ; and an illuminated lectionary for the use of Wolsey, said to be the last in this style executed in England. On the right, leaving the library, is Canterbury Quad, in which noble undergraduates are usually quartered, and where a large gateway in the classic style leads to Oriel, Corpus, and Merton. The new buildings of Christ Church are in the south, facing the meadows and the river.

CLARENDON BUILDING, at the back of the schools, was originally built for the printing-office of the University in 1713, from the profits of the sale of Lord Clarendon's "History of the Rebellion." It is at present used for various offices by the governing body of the University. The present printing-office stands to the northward of Worcester College.

CORPUS CHRISTI COLLEGE is at the back of Christ Church, at the corner of King-street. It was founded in 1516 by Richard Fox, Bishop of Winchester. The quadrangle, which is approached through a gateway with good vaulted roof, contains a curious cylindrical sundial with perpetual calendar, bearing on the summit the arms of the University, of Henry VII., as well as of the founder, and his friend, Bishop Oldham. The pelican over the college gateway, and its companion owl, also commemorate the founder and his friend. A description of the sun-dial is in the library, which contains also Fox's set of the Aldine Classics, and many other ancient books and MSS. Here also is the University chest or cista, an iron chest only accessible by several keys, kept by the Vice-Chancellor, the Dean of Christ Church, the President of Corpus, and other heads of houses. The founder is commemorated by some fine plate and a crozier preserved in the college. The hall is a fine room adorned with portraits, and in the chapel is an altar-piece by Rubens.

DIVINITY SCHOOL, in the same quadrangle as the entrance to the Bodleian, is particularly noticeable for the extreme beauty of its stone roof, with elaborate groining, tracery, and pendants. The arms of Duke Humphrey of Gloucester are in the centre of the roof, and those of other benefactors are interspersed with scriptural monograms. The ancient disputation pulpits are still preserved, and stand in either side of the school. The Divinity School has historical interest. It was here in 1555 that Bishops Ridley and Latimer were tried a fortnight before their martyrdom ; and when Parliament sat at Oxford in 1625 to avoid the Plague, the Divinity School was assigned to the use of the House of Commons. It afterwards fell upon evil days, and was for some time used as a storehouse for corn, but even this was not so bad as the fate that had befallen it at the time of Edward VI., when it was used as a pig-market. In the Convocation House, which leads from the school, is a good roof, and pictures of Lords Eldon and Stowell, by Owen. The oak panelling in the building is attributed to Wren.

EXETER COLLEGE, Turl-street, founded in 1314 by Walter de Stapleton, Bishop of Exeter and Lord High Treasurer, is entered by a fine tower gateway with heavy bosses, and has been almost entirely rebuilt at one period or another. The first quadrangle contains both the hall and the chapel. The hall possesses a fine open timber roof, and portraits of the founder, Charles I., Archbishops Secker and Selden, and one of Dr. Prideaux; who from a scullion in the college rose to be rector of it, Bishop of Worcester, and—greater dignity of all, perhaps, in University esteem—Regius Professor of Divinity. The elaborate oak screen appears to have been painted and varnished, and spoiled, by some spick-and-span paint-loving Goth. The chapel, rebuilt about twenty years ago from designs by Sir Gilbert Scott, has an apse, with fine Salviati mosaics, and some good modern stained glass windows. On the floor of the nave are three brasses, dated 1624, 1627, and 1636, to the memory of three children of the Dr. Prideaux above-mentioned. The chapel, with its high pitched roof and small but graceful spire, is considered to be a masterpiece of Gothic architecture. The library fronts towards the Fellows' Garden, and is a modern Gothic building also by Scott. Here will be found Henry VII.'s fine illuminated Mass-book, and a number of other rare and interesting works. At the bottom of the garden is a large chestnut tree, overshadowing Brasenose-lane and Heber's rooms in that college, whence it is called Heber's tree; and another curiosity is Dr. Kennicot's fig-tree, concerning which some curious stories may be gleaned by the inquisitive visitor.

HERTFORD COLLEGE, facing the Bodleian and New College-lane, has only recently acquired its present name. The college was first founded as Hart Hall at the end of the 13th century. In 1740, Hart Hall was transformed into Hertford College, by Dr. Newton, of Christ Church. The college did not flourish, and some few years after the death of Dr. Newton it was found impossible to induce any qualified person to become principal. In 1822 Magdalen Hall was transferred to the buildings of Hertford College after the old Magdalen Hall had been destroyed by fire, and in 1874 the foundation was incorporated under the name of Hertford College. From the sightseer's point of view, the college calls for no comment.

JESUS COLLEGE, Turl-street, opposite Exeter, was founded in 1571 by Dr. Price, treasurer of St. David's, though Queen Elizabeth, who contributed to the expense, is more generally recognised in that capacity. Jesus was originally intended for Welshmen, a rule that has been departed from, but is commemorated in

some quaint lines in an old pamphlet, two of which run :

Hugo Preesh built this Collesh for Jesus Creesh, and the Welsh geesh, Who love a peesch of toasted cheesh—here it ish.

In the first quadrangle are the chapel, hall, and library. The chapel, which was restored in 1864, is on the right. Over the entrance door, carved in stone, is the motto "Ascendat oratio, descendat gratia." Beyond a good east window the chapel has little to detain the visitor. In the hall is a fine Jacobean screen and a good bay window. On the walls are some portraits : Charles I. by Vandyck ; Charles II.; Sir Leoline Jenkins, a slab to whose memory is on the floor of the chancel in the chapel ; Nash, the architect, by Sir Thomas Lawrence ; and Queen Elizabeth, a bust of whom will be found over the mantelpiece. The library contains some curious Welsh MSS., and in the bursary is an enormous punch-bowl, holding ten gallons, while the ladle carries half a pint.

KEBLE COLLEGE, nearly opposite the new University Museum in the parks and in Keble-road, which runs out of St. Giles's. This, the youngest, and in many respects the most remarkable, of the Oxford colleges, was erected in 1868-70, in memory of the Rev. John Keble, the author of "The Christian Year." A sum of £50,000 was subscribed for the site and collegiate buildings, and the execution of the work was entrusted to Mr. Butterfield. The general intention of the foundation is to provide university education for young men whose means do not enable them to prosecute their studies at the older and more expensive colleges, and is supposed to be especially adapted to the requirements of divinity students, although it is not confined to them. At the same time it is stated in a somewhat deprecatory manner, that "it is not to be in any invidious sense a poor man's college, though it will be possible to live there on a smaller income than elsewhere." The present buildings are only a portion of the scheme intended to be carried out, and as Keble has already become very popular, it is probable that the proposed extensions will not be long delayed. The style of architecture adopted is that decorated Gothic of the

13th century. which involves lavish use of many coloured bricks and stone dressings, which has been by 19th century Goths playfully but irreverently described as the striped and mottled or " Zebra " order. Opinions vary greatly as to the general effects attained, but there can be no doubt that a certain restless and uneasy feeling is produced upon the spectator by the want of repose and tone inseparable from this peculiar style of colouring. And if this feeling is produced by the exterior of the buildings, it is intensified a thousandfold in the interior of the chapel. In this magnificent building, which was erected at the cost of W. Gibbs, Esq., of Tynesfield, and is crowded with mosaic and other decorations of the most elaborate kind, there is actually—it is not too much to say—no single point to which the eye can turn for relief or calm. The design and execution of the mosaics are both, no doubt, admirable, and under other circumstances their effect would probably be very pleasing; but it is impossible in Keble Chapel to get away from a certain feverish sense of unrest, and a consciousness that the place is overloaded with ornament, and decoration and colour. The mosaics, according to the explanation on a tablet in the vestibule, are intended to illustrate "after the manner of the ' Christian Year,'" the successive dealings of God with His Church, patriarchal, Jewish, and Christian. The chapel is open from 10 to noon, and from 2 to 4 in winter, and from 2 to 5.30 in summer. It is always closed between noon and 2 o'clock. The chapel attendant is strictly forbidden to receive gratuities. The hall is a handsomely proportioned building, in strict consonance with the rest of the college, and in the library hangs Holman Hunt's famous picture, "The Light of the World," which curiously symbolises many of the ways of thought and peculiarities of doctrine of the more enthusiastic admirers of Keble and of Keble College,

LINCOLN COLLEGE, Turl-street, next to Exeter and opposite to Jesus, founded in 1427 by Richard Flemyng, Bishop of Lincoln. The south quadrangle was added by Bishop Rotherham in 1479. The entrance from Turl-street is by a tower gateway with groined roof, and to the east of the first quadrangle is the hall, the exterior of which remains nearly

in its pristine state ; the interior was remodelled in 1701. It is a plain room with varnished screen and panelling, and contains a few pictures. The chapel was built in 1629 by Archbishop Williams. It is wainscoted with cedar, and the heavy roof and screen are of the same wood. The seats are surmounted by a number of carved figures which are said to be the work of Grinling Gibbons. There is some remarkable stained glass in the windows, of which that in the east is particularly fine. The glass was brought from Italy by Archbishop Williams, and is said to be at least 500 years old. It appears from the date (1631) on the glass itself to have been placed in the chapel at that date. In the inner quadrangle is a luxuriant vine, said to be cultivated in consequence of the heart of Bishop Rotherham having been so touched by a sermon preached by Dr. Tristoppe, the rector, from the text, "Behold and visit this vine," that he was moved to build the second quadrangle. One of the principal names associated with Lincoln is that of John Wesley, who was a fellow of Lincoln in 1726.

MAGDALEN COLLEGE, at the end of High-street, was founded in 1457 by William of Waynflete, Bishop of Winchester, on the site of an ancient hospital of St. John the Baptist, which afforded rest and refreshment to the pilgrims to the shrine of St. Frideswide. The pilgrims' wicket is still recognisable by persons who possess faith and a lively imagination. The foundation-stone of the new college was laid in 1474. If any one thing can be said to be the best in such a wonderful collection of combined architectural and natural beauties as is presented by Oxford, Magdalen College has certainly the right to the first place. Its situation is perfect, its buildings are most beautiful and interesting, and among all the spires of Oxford there is not one so graceful as the tower of Magdalen. The college is entered by a small door at the right of a gateway, designed by Pugin as late as 1844, and the condition to which the stone has been reduced in 35 years is conclusive proof, if proof were needed, of the unfitness for its purpose of the material generally selected for the buildings in the University. Opposite the entrance is the west window of the chapel; and in the south-west corner is a stone

pulpit, from which, on St. John the
Baptist's Day, a sermon was preached,
the court being decorated with boughs
and rushes to represent the wilderness.
On the opposite side of the court, in the
gate-house, is the grand oriel window of
what is known as the Founder's Chamber.
On the left of the court are the president's
apartments. From the small court near
the stone pulpit is a very good view of the
tower. The principal quadrangle is of the
time of the founder, and is one of the few
cloistered quads in Oxford. Above the
cloisters are a number of grotesque
figures of sandstone, which were erected
in honour of a visit of James I., and are
in the maddest style of emblematical art.
Some idea of the peculiar notions of the
sculptor may be gleaned from the fact
that the figure of a hippopotamus, carrying his young upon his shoulders, is supposed to be the "emblem of a good tutor
or fellow of a college, who is set to watch
over the youth of a society, and by whose
prudence they are to be led through the
dangers of their first entrance into the
world." The strange wild fowl, by which
the artist has endeavoured to represent
sins and vices, defy description. To the
north of the great quadrangle is the new
building erected in 1733, and remarkable
for the ingenuity of the architect in design-
ing a building which should be in all
respects out of keeping with the ancient
and beautiful portions of the college.
There is some compensation in the gardens, and the water-walk along the
Cherwell, just beyond the gardens, is
most beautiful. The walk to the left is
named after Addison. The hall is remarkable for its oak wainscot, and contains portraits of many distinguished
men, alumni or benefactors of Magdalen,
among others the founder; Cardinal
Wolsey, who built the tower; Cardinal
Pole; Dean Colet; Prince Rupert; Dr.
Sacheverell; Dr. Hammond; and Addison. The chapel has an entrance in the
first court, and in the archway leading to
the first quadrangle. It is open daily
from 11 to 12.30. The ante-chapel contains some brasses, one of W. Grey, 1605;
above this is a tomb with bust of W.
Langton, 1626; and on the opposite side
is a similar monument, with the date 1589.
It is, however, owing to the dark colouring of the great west window, difficult to
discern objects in the ante-chapel with

any degree of accuracy. The chapel
itself is remarkable for its elaborate carved
stalls and sconces. The altar and the
stone screen of the organ should be observed. Before the altar is a modern
brass to the memory of Dr. Routh, the
late president, who died in his 100th year.
On the north of the altar is a small oratory,
with groined roof, in which is the tomb
of the founder's father, Richard Patten,
removed from Waynflete. It is an altar
tomb with recumbent figure, at the head
of which sits the diminutive effigy supposed to be that of the founder himself.
At 5 o'clock on May morning the choristers
of the college ascend the tower and sing
a Latin hymn.

Attached to the college is Magdalen
School, also founded by William of
Waynflete. Boys, not being choristers
of the college, are admitted between the
ages of nine and fifteen after passing a
preliminary examination. The total
ordinary fixed payment for day boys is
£21 4s. 6d. per annum, or £7 1s. 6d. per
term. Extra subjects are not obligatory.
There are sixteen choristers of Magdalen
College educated at the school, with
free board, lodging, and instruction in
ordinary subjects. Their school subscriptions and weekly allowance are fixed
at £3 3s. a year. The charge for boarders,
with the head and other masters, is fixed
at £94 10s. per annum, exclusive of
tuition fee, but including weekly allowance and general subscriptions, such as
cricket, boating, &c. There is a Head
Master's Exhibition of £30 per annum
for three years, tenable at either University
if the holder obtain an open scholarship
or exhibition. Ten exhibitions of £22 1s.
a year each are given in the school.

MARTYRS' MEMORIAL, St. Giles's,
opposite Balliol College and Beaumont-
street, was designed by Sir Gilbert Scott
on the lines of the Eleanor crosses, and
erected at a cost of £5,000. It is 73
feet in height. The statues of Bishops
Latimer, Ridley, and Cranmer are by
Weekes.

MERTON COLLEGE, King-street, was
founded by Walter de Merton, Lord
Chancellor and Bishop of Rochester,
1264, and was originally established at
Malden and Merton, in Surrey. It was
subsequently removed to Oxford as an endowment for scholars "*qui non religiosi*

viverent." The principal quadrangle is entered through a gateway, over which are figures of the founder and Henry III., and a singular piece of sculpture representing the founder in full canonicals presenting a book to the Lamb in the wilderness. Apes, unicorns, and other unusual animals figure in the composition, in which also is St. John the Baptist. One of the entrances to the library quadrangle is under the treasury, with its high-pitched fire-proof ashlar roof. The library will well repay a visit, and its oak screen, ancient settles and tables, and tiled floor, give a good idea of the old-fashioned homes of learning ; and the illusion is all the more perfect, as specimens of the old style of attaching books to their shelves by chains are still exhibited. The library is rich in curious books and MSS., including a magnificent copy of Caxton's Chaucer, with richly illuminated borders. The principal features of the chapel, which is the parish church of St. John the Baptist, are its massive tower and great east window, with Catherine wheel and rich tracery. The gurgoyles and corbels are remarkably quaint. The ante-chapel and tower date from the beginning of the 15th century. The tower has been recently restored, and the floor of the bellringers' chamber has been removed to an open gallery constructed for them, so that the whole of the arches and fine oak roof are fully exposed to view from below. In the ante-chapel is the mural monument of Sir Henry Savile, a former warden and provost of Eton (died 1621), which is ornamented with odd devices emblematic of his fame as a traveller, and views of Merton and Eton. On the other side of the organ is the monument of Sir Thomas Bodley, the founder of the Bodleian Library, who died 1612 ; and on the opposite wall is the monument to Bishop Patteson, by T. Woolner, R.A. The ante-chapel contains the remains of ancient brasses, one 1310, and in the south is a fine piscina. In the chapel itself are two superb brasses ; one on the south of the choir of Henry Sever, warden in 1471, in cope and full canonicals ; that in the north bearing the effigies of John Bloxham, warden, 1387, and John Whytton, his friend, 1420, side by side under a Gothic canopy. The fine brass lectern is inscribed *"Orate pro anima magistri Johannis Martok,"* and is of the

15th century. The altar-piece is attributed to Tintoretto. The very fine sedilia formed part of the original building. The glass in the great east window is modern, but there is some very old stained glass in the side and west windows.

MUSIC SCHOOL.—In the same quadrangle as the Divinity School is the scene of examination for musical degrees. Here will be found portraits of Dr. Croft, Henry Lawes, Lord Crewe, Dr. Child, Thomas Blegrave, Dr. Boyce, Dr. Burney, Handel, and John Bull. Round the latter is painted the following legend ·

> The Bull by force
> In field doth Raigne,
> But Bull by skill
> Good will doth Gayne.

NEW COLLEGE, New College-lane, founded, and for the most part built, by William of Wykeham, the first stone having been laid 1380. The entrance to the college is not very promising ; but the quadrangle, which is approached through a gateway surmounted by statues of the Virgin, the founder, and an angel, is most striking. On the left is the chapel, the restoration of which was completed in October, 1879. One of the principal features is Sir Gilbert Scott's fine roof, the carved angels being especially remarkable. The west window is from the design of Sir Joshua Reynolds. The ante-chapel, with its two beautiful pillars, is separated from the chapel by the carved oak organ-loft and splendid organ. The stalls and reredos are new. Among the objects of interest in the chapel are the sedilia on the south side, and the founder's crozier in a niche in the north wall. The cloisters and gardens of New are singularly fine, and the ironwork between the garden and the second quad is well worth attention.

ORIEL COLLEGE, opposite Corpus and the Canterbury Quadrangle entrance to Christ Church, was founded by Adam de Brome and Edward II. in 1326. The origin of the name Oriel is very doubtful. It is said that the building which originally stood here was a monastery of Le Oriole, but it does not seem that the authority for this statement is to be relied on. The buildings of Oriel are not so remarkable as those of many other colleges, but are very picturesque, and present an appearance of greater age than they can in fact lay claim to. Entering from Oriel-street, the chapel and hall are on the opposite side of the quadrangle. In the centre of the block of buildings stand three statues, of Edward II., Edward III., and the Virgin Mary. The chapel is plain, and there is little of interest in the hall except its excellent roof and a few portraits. The college possesses, among other rare plate, a cup of Edward II., and one of Bishop Carpenter, 1476. The common room contains a picture by Vasari, but is most interesting from its associations connected with the days of the early activity of such men as John Henry Newman, Keble, Arnold, Wilberforce, and Pusey. The library has been rebuilt, and is of comparatively modern date (1788). Indeed, none of the buildings are older than 1620.

PEMBROKE COLLEGE, founded in 1624 by Thomas Tesdale and named after the then Chancellor of the University, in St. Aldate-street, is entered by a very fine gateway, with a handsome oriel. It consists of two quadrangles. The hall, which was built in 1848, has a good roof. The founder's arms decorate the windows, and on the walls are a few portraits, including Charles I. and the inevitable Queen Anne, and one of Dr. Johnson, who was a servitor of the college, by Sir Joshua. Pembroke appears not to despise conviviality, for in the hall is the strange apparition of a piano, and it is whispered that the social glee is occasionally here indulged in. The chapel is a plain, unpretentious building of no interest, architectural or otherwise. In the library is a bust of Johnson by Bacon, and a few of his college exercises are here treasured. The college possesses a small collection of plate, including some 17th century cups and a handsome chalice.

QUEEN'S COLLEGE, High-street, was founded in 1431 by Robert de Eglesfield, Chaplain to Queen Philippa. The present buildings are comparatively modern, being the work of Wren and Hawksmoor, and dating from 1714. The first quadrangle is entered under a cupola containing the statue of Caroline, the consort of George II. The buildings are plain, and of no particular interest. The chapel is chiefly remarkable for its

windows and marble pillars. The hall, like all Christopher Wren's rooms, is of fine proportions, and has a lofty arched roof. On the walls are portraits and armorial bearings of the founder and benefactors to the college, including several kings and queens. The procession of the Boar's Head is an annual custom at Queen's on Christmas Day, and is carried out with much pomp and antique ceremony. There is another odd custom on New Year's Day, when the Bursar presents to each guest a needle and thread with the words : "Take this and be thrifty." With that love of far-fetched derivation, which appears to be indigenous to Oxford, this custom is said to be a punning allusion to the name of the founder. But the most abandoned writer of burlesques, the most case-hardened perpetrator of japes, would scarcely be bold enough to derive Eglesfield from *aiguille* and *fil*. In the library, which is close to the hall, and was first started in 1691, Queen's College has an excellent collection of standard works in almost all departments of literature. Among the curiosities of Queen's are the ancient drinking horn, presented by Queen Philippa ; the cocoa-nut cup of Provost Bost (1503) ; and the brasses of Robert de Eglesfield and Dr. Langton (1518).

RADCLIFFE LIBRARY is the circular building at the back of St. Mary's Church and in the centre of the square in which are the schools of Brasenose and All Souls' Colleges. The fine building, now known as the Camera Bodleiana, was formerly the home of the Radcliffe Library, and was founded by Dr. Radcliffe, a great benefactor of the University, who left a sum of £40,000 for the erection of the building, and certain annuities for the purchase of books and the payment of a librarian. The domed hall is now used as a supplementary reading-room of the Bodleian, and is appropriated to periodicals and books of the last four years. It is open from 10 a.m. to 10 p.m, for those who have the *entrée*.

ST. EDMUND HALL, New College-lane, opposite Queen's, consists of one small quadrangle, and is not particularly attractive to sightseers, except for its magnificent wistaria, which covers the outside of the walls, and is the finest in England.

ST. JOHN'S COLLEGE, St. Giles's-street, was grafted in 1555 on to the previous foundation of Archbishop Chichele, by Sir Thomas White, Lord Mayor of London, as the outcome, or so it is said, of a dream, in which he was warned to build a college for the education of youth in religion and learning. The college is fronted by a row of elms and terrace-walk. The front and a portion of the first quadrangle are parts of Archbishop Chichele's original structure, St. Bernard's; but the hall in the latter is a plain modernised structure, which it is proposed to replace by a new building. It contains an elaborate mantelpiece and a number of portraits, including that of the founder; Archbishop Laud, a benefactor to the college; Archbishop Juxon; Sir Walter Raleigh; George III., in his coronation robes; Sir William Paddy, surgeon to James I.; and many others of inferior interest. The chapel, built in 1630, and restored by Blore, in 1843, contains some monuments of importance. The founder and Archbishop Laud are buried beneath the altar. Under the east window of the ante-chapel, the roof of which is worthy of notice, is an altar tomb, with recumbent figure, to Dr. Baylie, president of the college in the time of Charles I. There is a monumental urn, said to contain the heart of Dr. Rawlinson, with the inscription, "*Ubi thesaurus ibi cor*," and a monument, with the laconic epitaph "*Præivit*," and in the wall, left of the entrance, are some old brasses, dated 1571, 1577, and 1578; many old mural monuments; and a stone figure, kneeling, of Richard Latewan, 1603. Through a fine vaulted passage, with richly-traced roof, we reach the inner quadrangle, partly designed by Inigo Jones, and built at the expense of Archbishop Laud. The gate towers are ornamented with bronze statues by Fanelli of Charles I. and Henrietta Maria. The southern and eastern sides of this court are taken up by the library, which contains much to occupy the visitor, and deserves a lengthened inspection. Here Laud entertained his royal master, and a play, written and acted by members of St. John's, was presented for His Majesty's entertainment. In the library will be found the red skull-cap in which Laud was executed, his MS. diary, and a crozier, found, built in the wall, in re-

pairing the President's lodgings, which is presumed to have belonged to that prelate. There is a splendid copy of Caxton's Chaucer, some fine old Bibles and Psalters, a fine 13th century MS. *Bestiarium*, and, peculiarly interesting to ladies, some magnificent 15th century embroidered vestments, banners, and an altar-cloth, unique specimens of ancient needlework. The eastern wing of the library, Laud's wing, affords fine views of the extensive gardens (five acres), which are perhaps the most beautiful in Oxford. From the gardens, Laud's wing of the library presents a most picturesque appearance, with its gables and oriels, King Charles I.'s window being a prominent feature.

SHELDONIAN THEATRE, between the schools and Broad-street, was built by Gilbert Sheldon, Archbishop of Canterbury, and opened in 1669. The architect was Sir Christopher Wren. This handsome hall is used for the Encænia, or annual commemoration of founders, when prize competitions are recited and honorary degrees conferred amidst the freely expressed comments of the undergraduates who occupy the upper gallery. The ceiling is the work of one Streater, sergeant-painter to Charles I., whose artistic views and execution are very much on a par with those of Verrio. From the top of the building an excellent view of Oxford is obtained. A small fee is expected by the custodian, who will take visitors to the upper regions.

TRINITY COLLEGE, standing a little back from Broad-street, next to Balliol, was originally founded by the Priors of Durham at the end of the 13th century. Sir Thomas Pope founded a new college on the ruins of the old college of Durham in 1554. The entrance is under the tower, which adjoins the chapel. These buildings were erected by Dr. Bathurst in the last years of the 17th century, and are in the classical styles. The chapel contains a fine alabaster tomb with recumbent figures of the founder and his wife. It is particularly noteworthy for the extremely beautiful carved screen and altar-piece in cedar and lime, unusually fine specimens of the work of Grinling Gibbons. The plain panels are of oak. The library contains many rare works, and some ancient stained glass. Among the curiosities of Trinity is a large chalice brought from St. Alban's Abbey. The library possesses a few portraits. The library and hall are not shown to casual visitors, an introduction from a Fellow being necessary. The gardens are extensive, and celebrated for a beautiful lime-tree avenue.

UNIVERSITY COLLEGE, the oldest in Oxford, on the south side of the High-street, nearly opposite All Souls', was not founded by King Alfred, as has been frequently asserted. The real founder appears to have been William of Durham, and the period the early part of the 13th century. The first statutes date from 1280. The present buildings extend along the street a distance of 260 feet, with two courts and two towered gate-ways. The first stone was laid in 1634. Over the gateway leading into the west quad is, on the outside, a statue of Queen Anne, and on the inside one of James II.; the statues over the eastern gateway are those of Queen Mary and Dr. Radcliffe. The hall contains an ex-tensive fire-place, designed from a tomb in Ely Cathedral, in the centre of which is a medallion marble bust of King Alfred. The walls are hung with portraits of Archbishop Potter; Bishop Bancroft; Dr. Radcliffe; Sir Roger Newdigate; Lord Eldon; and Lord Stowell, by Hoppner; Sir Thomas Lawrence, and others. The hall has been several times altered and restored, and was lengthened in 1860, and has been provided with new oak doors. The library dates from about the same period as the last alteration to the hall, and was designed by Sir Gilbert Scott. It contains two colossal statues, exhibited in the Exhibition of 1862, of Lords Eldon and Stowell. These were intended for Westminster Abbey, but were rejected on account of their size. The chapel was remodelled in 1862 by Sir Gilbert Scott, when the roof and east window were added. There is some fine stained glass by Van Linge: A carved altar-piece by Grinling Gibbons, that formerly stood in the chapel, is now to be found in the bursary. In the ante-chapel, on the north wall, is a monument by Flaxman to Nathan Wetherell, formerly master, who died in 1807. Here is also another monument by Flaxman repre-senting Sir W. Jones, once a fellow, engaged in the study of the Indian Vedas,

which two Brahmins expound to him. There is also a stained-glass window given by Dr. Radcliffe.

UNIVERSITY GALLERIES, in Taylor's Buildings, corner of St. Giles's and Beau-mont-street. The University Galleries were erected partly from a legacy be-queathed by Dr. Francis Randolph. They comprise galleries for ancient and modern sculpture, including the original models for the works of Sir Francis Chantrey, which are on the ground floor; rooms for collections of drawings by Michael Angelo and Raffaelle; and a large gallery for paintings. The entrance is from Beau-mont-street. The galleries are open daily from 12 to 4, except at intervals, of which due notice is given. Application for per-mission to copy must be made to the keeper of the galleries. The Ruskin School of Drawing is open during term. Visitors can see it on Monday and Thurs-day from 2 to 4, and on Wednesday and Saturday from 12 to 4, and during class hours on personal application to Mr. Macdonald. In the ante-room is a por-trait of Lady Betty Paulet, wife of Sir Thomas Pope, founder of Trinity College, attributed to Mytens; some sketches by Professor Ruskin; and a view of Sheer-ness by J. M. W. Turner. In the room to the right are ten drawings by Turner, executed for the Oxford University Almanack; a number of sketches pre-sented by Professor Ruskin; and the Eldon Art Library. In the gallery which contains the Raffaelle and Michael Angelo drawings, which are of the greatest art value, is a copy, supposed to be by Giulio Romano, of the School of Athens fresco, by Raffaelle, in the Vatican. The picture gallery contains a number of works of varying merit. Among them will be found some curious specimens of the earlier masters of the Florentine school; scenes from the life of Cæsar Aretino; an up-right landscape with cattle, Gainsborough; horses with figures hunting, G. Morland; landscape, R. Wilson; a small landscape, John Constable; two fine Sir Joshuas, one a portrait of Mrs. Meyrick, the other James Paine, architect, and his son; Hogarth's sketch for the Enraged Musi-cian; the Flute Player, Caraveggio; a Sea-shore, Willarts; the Village Surgeon, Teniers; Pilgrimage of Roman Virgins, Fillipo Lippi. There are also examples of, or attributed to, Van Dyck, Fra Angelico,

Opie, Snyders, Zoffany, Canaletto, Andrea del Sarto, and Paolo Veronese. Among the pictures attributed to Canaletto are views of Chelsea, Greenwich, Lambeth, and the Temple Gardens.

WADHAM COLLEGE, Park-road, opposite the gardens of Trinity College, was founded in 1613 by Nicholas Wadham, on the site of a monastery of the Austin or Augustine Friars. Wadham did not live to see the completion of his work, which was eventually carried out by his widow Dorothy. The buildings are Gothic. The entrance gate is under a square tower with a handsome window, and in the quadrangle on the eastern side are the chapel and hall. The hall has a fine though rather heavy open timber roof, and a good oak screen of curious design. The portraits of Nicholas and Dorothy Wadham hang with others on the walls, amongst them being a portrait of Dr. Wright, the first warden. Tradition has it that it was the foundress's intention to marry Dr. Wright, and to take up her quarters with him in the warden's lodge. Whether or no Dr. Wright was a consenting party to this arrangement, and obtained the office of warden under condition that he took the lady as one of the fixtures, does not very clearly appear. After his appointment he certainly preferred to remain single. Whether it was a case of breach of promise, or only of misplaced confidence, the *spretæ injuria formæ* asserted itself, and it was made a condition that the warden should be henceforth a bachelor. It was not until the beginning of the present century that this restriction was abolished; although it is on record that Oliver Cromwell, who had a way of his own of dealing with pious founders and statutes which were not to his liking, granted a special dispensation to Dr. Wilkins, one of the founders of the Royal Society, the warden in his time, whose portrait will be found in the hall. The chapel is a remarkably fine building, and is particularly noticeable for its old stained glass, the work of Bernard van Ling in the year 1622, as is shown by the date on the great east window. The glass for this and other windows in the chapel, was made in the precincts of the college, and the ovens, &c., used in its manufacture were destroyed but a few years ago. In the ante-chapel is the

good marble tomb of Sir John Portman, with date 1624. The garden of Wadham, though not so extensive as the pleasaunces of many other colleges, is very prettily designed and laid out, and contains numerous fine trees, among which the cedars are prominent.

WORCESTER COLLEGE, facing the end of Beaumont-street, was founded in 1714 by Sir Thomas Cookes, on the site of Gloucester Hall, a Benedictine establishment dating from 1283. The principal attraction to visitors at Worcester will undoubtedly be the gardens, which are of considerable size, and contain a fine sheet of water apparently well stocked with fish, including, according to local tradition, pike of that abnormal size only obtained in waters where fishing is prohibited. Here during Commemoration is the Flower Show. The hall is a fine room, and is surrounded by oak panelling with the armorial bearings and names of members who subscribed towards its erection. The mantelpiece is of an elaborate character. The chapel is gorgeously decorated with mediæval groups on dead-gold ground, and the roof is richly ornamented in similar style, the whole after a design by Mr. Burges. The fine tesselated marble pavement contains portraits of King Alfred, Bede, and many saints, including St. Oswald, St. Boniface, St. Gregory, &c. In the language of an ecclesiological critic, Worcester Chapel is one of the richest interiors in the University, and one of the finest examples of the Renaissance in England.

Pangbourne, Berkshire, on the right bank. A station on the Great Western Railway 41½ miles from Paddington ; fast trains take about 85 minutes. The station is three minutes' walk from the river at the Swan Hotel ; from London 80¾ miles, from Oxford 30¾ miles. Population, 757. Soil, gravel and chalk. Pangbourne is a small village not particularly noticeable in itself but charmingly situated, and one of the most favourite angling resorts on the river. The view from the path below the "Swan" along the weir is very characteristic, vying even with the peculiarly Thames-like scenery at Streatley, and the reaches both above and below are full of tranquil beauty. A long wooden bridge of much the same character as that which connects Goring , and

Streatley crosses the river just below Pangbourne to Whitchurch, and hence again the pleasant up-river scenery is seen at its best. Pangbourne has something of a history of its own, although there is now little in the way of antiquities as evidence of it. It is mentioned in Domesday Book as having been held by one Miles Crispin, and the manor and church subsequently came into the possession of the Abbey of Reading. After passing through several hands it was granted by Queen Elizabeth to the cofferer of her household. Bere Court, the manor-house of Pangbourne, is mentioned by Leland as "a fair manor place" that had belonged to the abbots of Reading. It is now the property of the Breedon family, many of whose monuments are to be seen in the parish church, which is dedicated to St. James the Less. In 1865 the old church was in so sad a state of dilapidation that it was taken down, and the present church erected on its site. The red brick tower, of date 1718, which contains six first-rate bells, was left standing. The present building is of some architectural pretensions, and is remarkable for a fine arch, springing from clustered columns which divides the nave and chancel, and for an extremely good oak pulpit carved in arabesques, and said to be of the time of Elizabeth. In the south aisle is a mural monument, date 1658, to three sisters, the daughters of Sir John Suckling, controller to the household of Charles I. The finest monument in the church will be found near the organ, and is that of Sir John Davis, at one time the occupant of Bere Court, who was knighted at the taking of Cales, in Spain, in the reign of Queen Elizabeth, and who died in 1625. The monument is of considerable size, and exhibits the full-length recumbent figure of the knight with his two wives beneath an elaborate canopy surmounted by a skull. In niches below are too odd little kneeling figures. The effigies of Sir John and the two ladies are in good preservation, but the rest of the monument, which is of chalk, is, unfortunately, in a somewhat cracked and chippy state. The registers date from the middle of the 16th century, and in the tower room hangs a decaying parchment, apparently a will of one of the early benefactors of the parish.

In 1685, John Breedon bequeathed

"for the encouragement of the inhabitants of the parish Pangbourne aforesaid, especially those of a poorer sort of them to bring up and educate their children in good learning," half an acre of land and a building "100 feet in length and 15 feet in breadth" for a school-house and habitation for schoolmaster. A sum of £40 per annum was also left as an endowment, of which £25 per annum were to be paid "for the livelihood and support of a good schoolmaster to live and inhabit in the said house . . . . which schoolmaster shall, from time to time be obliged diligently to teach and instruct freely and without charge the youth, male children or boys of the parish of Pangbourne, especially of the poorer sort of them, not exceeding 12 in number at one time." The remaining £15 per annum were ordered to be employed towards apprenticing "once in every two or three years such and so many of the said youth or boys so taught as aforesaid."

The pools at Pangbourne used to be famous for their trout, supposed to be bred in the little river Pang close by; but this is of the past. There are shoals of other freshwater fish.

HOTELS.—"Elephant and Castle" and "George," both in village; "Swan," by the river.

PLACES OF WORSHIP.—St. James the Great, and a Congregational Church.

POSTAL ARRANGEMENTS.—Post Office in village, six minutes from river (money order, savings bank, telegraph, and insurance). Mails from London, 7 a.m., 12 noon, 5.10 p.m.; Sunday, 7 a.m. Mails for London, 9.50 a.m., 3 and 7 p.m.; Sunday, 7 p.m.

NEAREST *Bridges*, Whitchurch; up, Streatley 4 miles; down, Caversham 6¼ miles. *Locks*, Whitchurch; up, Goring about 4 miles; down, Mapledurham 2¼ miles. *Ferry*, Basildon. *Railway Station*, Pangbourne. G.W.R. Parly. 3/5½.

FARES to Paddington: 1st, 7/4, 13/-; 2nd, 5/6, 9/6; 3rd, 3/5½.

Parliamentary Constituencies.

Counties.

BERKS   8,601
    Col. Loyd-Lindsay, V.C., *C.*
    P. Wroughton, *C.*
    J. Walter, *L.*

G

BUCKS 8,114
Sir R. B. Harvey, *C.*
Hon. R. Carington, *L.*
Hon. T. Fremantle, *C.*

ESSEX, SOUTH 11,950
T. C. Baring, *C.*
W. T. Makins, *C.*

GLOUCESTERSHIRE, EAST ... 8,579
Rt. Hon. Sir M. Hicks-Beach, *C.*
J. R. Yorke, *C.*

KENT, EAST 13,169
A. Douglas, *C.*
E. L. Pemberton, *C.*

KENT, MID 8,763
Sir W. Hart Dyke, *C.*
Hon. J. S. G.-Hardy, *C.*

KENT, WEST 14,873
Sir C. H. Mills, *C.*
Viscount Lewisham, *C.*

MIDDLESEX 30,707
Rt. Hon. Lord G. Hamilton, *C.*
O. E. Coope, *C.*

OXFORDSHIRE 7,495
Lieut.-Col. J. S. North, *C.*
W. C. Cartwright, *L.*
Col. E. W. Harcourt, *C.*

SURREY, MID 20,433
Sir T. Lawrence, *C.*
Sir J. W. Ellis, Bart., *C.*

SURREY, WEST 7,779
Right Hon. G. Cubitt, *C.*
Hon. W. S. F. Brodrick, *C.*

OXFORD UNIVERSITY 5,033
Rt. Hon. J. R. Mowbray, *C.*
J. G. Talbot, *C.*

WILTS, NORTH 7,249
W. H. Long, *C.*
G. T. S. Estcourt, *C.*

· *Boroughs.*

ABINGDON 890
J. C. Clarke, *L.*

CHELSEA 30,951
Sir C. Dilke, *L.*
J. B. Firth, *L.*

CRICKLADE 7,473
N. S. Maskelyne, *L.*
Sir Daniel Gooch, *C.*

GRAVESEND 3,256
Sir S. H. Waterlow, *L.*

GREENWICH 22,161
T. W. Boord, *C.*
Baron de Worms, *C.*

LAMBETH 50,541
Ald. Sir J. C. Lawrence, Bt., *L.*
Ald. W. M'Arthur, *L.*

LONDON, CITY 20,042
Ald. Cotton, *C.*
R. N. Fowler, *C.*
Rt. Hon. J. G. Hubbard, *C.*
Ald. W. Lawrence, *L.*

MARLOW... 941
Col. O. Williams, *C.*

OXFORD CITY 6,193
(*Vacant.*)

READING 5,107
Rt. Hon. G. J. Shaw Lefevre, *L.*
G. Palmer, *L.*

SOUTHWARK 23,472
Arthur Cohen, Q.C., *L.*
Professor Thorold Rogers, *L.*

TOWER HAMLETS... 41,042
Professor Bryce, *L.*
C. T. Ritchie, *C.*

WALLINGFORD 1,226
P. Ralli, *L.*

WESTMINSTER 21,081
Rt. Hon. W. H. Smith, *C.*
Lord Algernon Percy, *C.*

WINDSOR, NEW 2,122
R. Richardson-Gardner, *C.*

Perch.—The perch, which is *par excellence* a "breakfast fish," is almost equal to the pike in boldness and voracity, and bites at some periods at almost every kind of bait ; indeed, anything moving in the water will attract its attention if it does not satisfy its appetite. It has been known to seize leaden plummets, naked hooks, and even the eyes of its fellows, and indeed its own, and is taken with the most primitive tackle. Its hogback and formidable array of spines render no other description necessary. They spawn in April, and are in season from May till March, but they are more than usually gamesome and on the feed from September till February. They swim in shoals, several dozen being often taken from the same spot. The morning and evening are the best times. The rod should be rather stiff, the line of almost any kind if strong enough, the hook about No. 5, and the bottom gut full a yard in length ; a float is necessary when still-fishing. Minnows, live fresh or salt water shrimps, brandling, and red worms, small gudgeon or dace, and many other baits have their attractions in turn, for perch are at times most capricious in this respect. On one day they will refect on worms, the next take nothing but minnows, and so on. When you have a bite, avoid striking violently, as the fish has a tender mouth, which necessitates your giving it a little time, but not too much, as it will swallow the hook and cause trouble and needless cruelty in extracting it. It may be well here to say that all fish intended to be retained should be killed immediately, as it not only greatly improves the firmness and flavour of the flesh, but prevents giving needless pain. A few pieces of worm thrown in occasionally will help to keep them together.

In fishing for perch with a worm, a No. 5 or 6 hook tied on single gut may be used, and the bait allowed to swim within an inch or two of the bottom, drawing it here and there and gently up and down occasionally. This action will make the perch, not sufficiently eager for bait, fancy that they are about to lose it ; and often the largest of the school will dart at it even when it is near the top of the water and take it. If you bait with a minnow or small gudgeon, the hook, a No. 4, should be placed through the root of the back fin, or through the lip, unless the presence of small jack are suspected, in which case the former snap plan is better, as it gives a chance of striking the fish before the hook has passed down its mouth sufficiently far to jeopardise the gut, and, as a sportsman, the life of the jack being spared it may be returned to the water.

The paternoster is most resorted to by professed perch fishers. It is made by taking a yard of stout gut, with a perforated bullet or pear-shaped lead at the bottom end. On to this line, at about 18 inches apart, are threaded two or three conical pieces of ivory or perforated shot, with their sides flattened to permit of a hog's bristle of three inches long being

looped tightly round them ; to the end of these bristles hooks are whipped. The shots are kept in their place by a small fixed shot on the line below and above them, but are not so close as to prevent the perforated ones from rotating round the line, with the hooks baited with numerous small gudgeon, stone loach, or worms. Some use gut instead of hogs' bristles, but the latter have a decided advantage, as no length of time will soak them and make them bag, and consequently hang on to the main line. With this line no float is required, as the lead is either permitted to be on the bottom while the line is kept tight between it and the rod, or it is used to sink and rise amongst weeds and such places as the perch are known to frequent. In this way as many perch as you have hooks may be on the line at the same time. But beware of losing a fish, for the instant one escapes he makes a dash for other districts, and the whole of his companions generally rush after him. If a float is used with a paternoster, a hook should be substituted for the lead, and the line shotted elsewhere. Very many large perch are taken by spinning either the spoon or the dead bait, and the trailing a lob-worm at the bottom, weighted with a small bullet, in some waters and seasons is a very killing mode.

The late Mr. Jesse, who was prolific in expedients, used to practise a novel method of ground-baiting for perch. His receipt was : Procure a large glass bottle, such as may be seen in the windows of chemists' shops : the clearer the glass the better. Fill this bottle with river water, and put into it a quantity of live minnows ; cover the top with a piece of gauze or perforated parchment, tie a strong cord round the neck of the bottle so prepared, and sink it near a pile in the river, or in a deep hole near the bank. This should be done early in the morning or late in the evening, when no one is about to witness the operation ; conceal the cord, and leave the bottle for two days ; at the end of that time drop a paternoster baited with live minnows by the side of the bottle, and the angler may be sure of excellent sport, as the sight of the minnows in the bottle will have attracted numerous perch to the spot. Thames perch of late years seldom exceed 2 lb. in weight, but occasionally one of

3 lb. or 3½ lb. will fall to the rod. Maidenhead, Cookham, Mapledurham, Walton, Egham Weir, and indeed all the quiet portions of mill pools in which old timber is present, are the certain haunts of perch ; this fish being passionately fond of the fresh-water shrimp and other insects which breed in the vegetation growing on rotting wood.

Petersham, Surrey, on the right bank, a small village at the foot of Richmond Hill. Population, 683. Soil, sand and gravel. Here was once Petersham Lodge, which was some years ago pulled down and the grounds thrown into Richmond Park, including the Mount, where, according to some chroniclers, Henry VIII. stood to see the signal for the execution of Anne Boleyn. There must be some mistake as to this matter, for other lovers of tradition assert that the king awaited the signal at Ankerwycke ; while we have it on the unimpeachable authority of Mr. Harrison Ainsworth that the king waited the firing of the signal gun in company with Herne the Hunter in Windsor Forest.

At Petersham is Ham House, the property of the Earl of Dysart, a rather gloomy mansion jealously surrounded by trees. It contains many rare and valuable portraits and pictures, and is in itself curious.

The church is a very small red-brick building with brick tower, and is said to date from 1505, though almost the only portion bearing any signs of age is the diminutive chancel. This was originally a chapel attached to the priory of Merton. In it were discovered by the late Sir Gilbert Scott a window of the 13th century and an oak roof, the remains of the church as remodelled in 1505. In the chancel is a fine marble tomb, reaching from the floor to the ceiling, to the memory of some members of the Cole family. There are three recumbent lifesize figures each leaning on its right elbow. Mrs. Cole wears a ruff and curious poke head-dress of the period, which appears to be 1624. Over George Cole and his wife Francisca is an arch with carved cherubs smiling down upon them and upon the child which reposes underneath them, and which may be either a boy or a girl, according to fancy. Opposite to this interesting monument is a marble mural tablet, with the chronic

skull at the base, and with the usual accompanying cherubs and a profuse display of armorial bearings to Sir Thomas Jenner, who married Anne Poe, only daughter and heiress of James Poe, whose father, Leonard Poe, Doctor of Physicke, was physician to Queen Elizabeth, King James, and Charles I. Sir Thomas Jenner was Recorder of London, and afterwards Baron of the Exchequer and Justice of "ye Comon Pleas." He died in 1706-1707. Facing the pulpit on the right is a marble tablet erected by the Hudson's Bay Company to Captain Vancouver, the North Pacific explorer, who is buried in the churchyard, which also contains the tomb of the Duchess of Lauderdale. The picturesque almshouses for the reception of six inmates were built with money left by a lady who desired her name to remain unknown. A handsome school for the children of the village was built in Richmond Park by the late Earl Russell. At Petersham is Sudbrook Park, the well-known hydropathic establishment of Dr. Lane.

INN.—"The Dysart Arms," opposite Richmond Park Gate.

PLACES OF WORSHIP.—St. Peter's, and a Wesleyan Chapel.

POSTAL ARRANGEMENTS.—Post Office (money order, savings bank, telegraph, and insurance). Mails from London, 7 and 9 a.m., 2.30 and 7.25 p.m. For London, 8.30 and 11.25 a.m., 4.20 and 8.20 p.m.

NEAREST *Bridges,* Richmond; up, Kingston 4½ miles ; down, Kew 2¼ miles. *Lock,* up, Teddington 3 miles. *Ferries,* Petersham and Isleworth.

NEAREST *Railway Station,* Richmond (*which see for* FARES).

Petroleum.—The carriage of petroleum on the Thames is subject to the following bye-laws, under the Petroleum Act, 1871: 1. No ship or vessel laden either wholly or in part with petroleum, rock oil, Rangoon oil, Burmah oil, or oil made from petroleum, coal, schist, shale, peat, or other bituminous substance, or any products of petroleum, or of any of the above-mentioned oils, which said oils, or products of oils, when tested in manner set forth in Schedule I. to "The Petroleum Act, 1871," give off an inflammable vapour at a temperature of less than 100 degrees of Fahrenheit's thermometer, shall, for any purpose whatever, be navigated, lie in, or be moored, and no part of the cargo shall be discharged from any such ship or vessel in any part of the River Thames above or westward of Thames Haven ; and all such ships or vessels, whilst laden as aforesaid, shall, when moored or anchored, lie singly and apart from each other, with a clear space of not less than 100 feet of water separating them. 2. The cargoes of such ships or vessels may be discharged below Thames Haven into covered barges constructed of iron, and licensed for the purpose by the Conservators of the River Thames, but whilst so employed the barges shall be towed during daylight only to their places of destination, and no fires or lights shall be used on board them.

Picnic and Pleasure-Party Tickets.—(*See* GREAT WESTERN RAILWAY *and* LONDON AND SOUTH WESTERN RAILWAY.)

Picnic (The).—The favourite resort of pleasure-seekers near Ankerwycke House, just below Magna Charta Island (*which see*). In the grounds of Ankerwycke are a small portion of the ruins of the old priory, in the pleasure-grounds of which Henry VIII. used to meet Anne Boleyn, and some splendid timber, particularly a yew near the old ruins, computed by Dr. Lardner in the "Arboretum Britannicum" to be 2000 years old.—(*For railway fares to* WRAYSBURY, *the nearest station, see* "BELLS OF OUSELEY.")

On the general subject of pleasure excursions it may be suggested that it is only courteous to ask permission, even for a picnic. A riparian proprietor writes to us : "I never refuse such permission. But it is no uncommon thing to have twelve to twenty parties in a day, who land without ceremony, intrude into the most private parts of the grounds, light fires, destroy trees, and leave the place littered all over with paper, boxes, straw, bottles, empty tins, and *débris.* People trespass from the river in a way that they would never think of doing off the highway."

Pike.—Although pike fishing is permitted as early as June, the legitimate anglers leave their pursuit until October and quit it at the end of January. In June these fish are seldom in good condition, give little sport, and the number thus deducts very considerably from the sport which would be had later in the season when their flesh is firm and they are full of dash and pluck. The best bait for pike is a large gudgeon, either alive or dead, but it will at times take almost anything ; perch with the back fin removed, roach, dace, frogs, birds, eels, &c. If you fish for pike with a live-bait, snap tackle, or spinning, it should always be with the hooks attached to gimp, in consequence of the several rows of sharp teeth with which the pike is armed, and which enable it to bite gut in two. The whipping of the hooks should likewise be bound round with fine wire, as the teeth of the fish are likely to fray the silk whipping and thus many a good fish is lost.

Live-baiting, if from the bank, requires the addition of a kettle of gudgeon, with a few roach and dace, a heavier rod and line than those used for spinning, and a good-sized float with a hole down the middle, through which the running line is passed and fastened with a wooden peg. A swivel on the line will permit the bait to swim here and there without incessantly twisting the float. The bait may be either attached by the lip with a No. 3, 4, or 5 hook ; in which case, after the bait has been seized, the pike must be allowed to run as far as he will and have time to gorge the bait, so that the hook may find some better attachment than its bony jaws, and every care must be taken not to check him, for which purpose the line should be paid out freely ; or the hook may be inserted in the back fin of the bait, and you may then strike at once, as the pike invariably takes the bait crosswise in its mouth before turning its head downwards to gorge it. The lip method has its advantages when the pike are ravenous, as the bait lives longer ; but the snap plan must be resorted to when the fish are fastidious, and only take, play with, and drop the bait. There are many descriptions of snap and live-bait hooks which may be seen at any tackle makers. One, however, of the most simple kind, which is used partly by spinning and partly by trolling, is merely composed of a triangle hook, the gimp being passed through the vent of a dead fish and out of the mouth ; one of the three hooks being inserted near the tail to give it a slight turning motion when the bait is sunk and drawn up again. This method is very deadly, and the prey seldom escapes after laying hold of the bait. The old and still common style of trolling for pike is what is termed the dead gorge, and most effective when the water is encumbered by weeds. The gorge is a double hook on twisted brass wire, loaded above the shanks with lead. The hooks are set with their barbs at right angles, more or less rank, according to the size of the pike you are in pursuit of. This is affixed to a foot of gimp, with a loop at the extreme end. This loop is taken up by your baiting needle, the point inserted in the mouth of the bait, and brought out at the extreme end of the fish, exactly in the centre of the fork of the tail, and drawn up until the hooks are on either side of the fish's mouth ; a piece of silk should be then tied round the tail to keep the wire firm and in its place. Some anglers supplement a length of gimp with swivels between the line and the gorge hook, but this is not needed. The rod for trolling may be the same as for live-baiting. Much time may be saved by previously preparing both spinning and gorge baits, and keeping them in a tin box with bran ; but if the bait is gudgeon they cannot be used too fresh, their flesh being somewhat tender, and they are liable to burst, in which condition no pike will touch them unless extremely ravenous.

Pilot Station, Gravesend. — The pilot-station at Gravesend is the chief rendezvous of all the various classes of men licensed to conduct ships into and out of the River Thames. This station represents the point of division between the functions of river and sea pilotage. The outward-bounder, after being brought from the docks under the care of a river-licensed man, lands him, and comes under the charge of a man whose license qualifies him to take her to sea. The inward-bound reverse the process. The pilotage of the River Thames is now wholly under the management of the Trinity House of London. Until 1853 their authority as respects vessels hailing to or from the southward was divided with the fellowship of the Cinque Ports, but now the two bodies are consolidated.

The Trinity House licenses pilots from Gravesend outwards to the northward, who give up charge at Orfordness, or southward as far as Dungeness, and *vice versa*, besides certifying special qualifications for particular coasts, British or foreign, towards which a Thames pilot may have occasion to go.

To obtain a sea-license a candidate must not be more than thirty-five years of age, and must have served at sea three years as mate or master in a square-rigged ship. Applicants thus far approved are put upon the register, and as vacancies occur come forward for examination as to their knowledge of the coast and channels, the depths of water, tides, dangers, sea-marks, &c. The Elder Brethren of the Trinity House are the examiners, the nature of whose duties in buoyage and beaconage, and marine surveying, affords exactly the kind of experience required for such a task. The examination passed, the license under seal of that corporation is granted, and the newly-made pilot, having first paid his fee of admission, goes to Gravesend and takes his turn as a Channel or sea pilot.

A license for the river is obtained in a manner somewhat similar, except that there are several classes of qualifications, each securing a particular kind of license. The highest class enables the holder to insist on the acceptance of his services, to the exclusion of one of an inferior grade, in any vessel not exempted from compulsory pilotage. Another class has authority to conduct passenger steam-ships passing inward or outward on coasting or on short foreign voyages ; while a third class is employed solely in ships which, though not compelled by law to employ a pilot, prefer to do so.

The remuneration of the pilots, whether above or below Gravesend, is dependent upon the distance piloted, and the draft of water in feet of the vessel, subject to a deduction when steam has been employed. The sea-pilots may not take less than the legal rate, but some of the river-pilots may make their own bargain. They work in rotation according to turn, but if a pilot is chosen by any shipowner for a particular ship, his name is taken off the turn list until he has fulfilled his selective engagement, when he comes on turn again at the bottom of the roll. There are two waiting-rooms on the Terrace Pier, and two steam-launches in attendance, the one on the sea, the other on the river division, the expenses of which are defrayed by a fund to which the men subscribe. Those who go seaward have to be landed from their ships by local boatmen.

The whole number of pilots holding licenses for the River Thames is about 500, of whom 200 are exclusively for service above Gravesend.

Piscatorial Society, The, established 1836, the largest and most influential society of the kind in London. Headquarters, Ashley's Hotel, Henrietta-street, Covent Garden, London, W.C.— "The objects of this society being to meet their friends and associates in social conversation and harmony (religion and politics being totally excluded), and to encourage fair angling." Part of the funds are appropriated in giving prizes, and in forming a museum and a collection of works on angling. "The election shall depend on the decision of the society by ballot, one black ball in four to exclude." The name of the candidate must first be submitted to the committee for approval. Entrance fee, 10s. 6d.; subscription, £1 1s. A sum of money is voted annually, to be divided into prizes by the committee, as they may think advisable. Ten competitions for various fish also take place at various intervals during the year for the greatest weight, subject to the rules for size of fish. It is the secretary's duty fairly to insert the names and weights of all fish taken, with full particulars, in a book kept for that purpose, and every Monday evening to read the weight of fish caught by each member, and to lay the book of the same on the table. Any member refusing to give the locale where the fish were taken, and the name and address of the fisherman, if required by the committee, shall not be allowed to take any prize for the same. Members are only permitted to weigh fish caught by themselves with rod and line. Only two rods are allowed. The attendant is not to angle for, strike, or play the fish, but merely land the same. The museum contains many specimens of large and rare fish. The Society's exhibit of specimens at the Norwich Fisheries Exhibition gained the 1st prize of £15 and silver medal. The library is well stocked with books, both ancient and

modern, and the members have the privilege of borrowing a volume any Monday evening and retaining the same a week. The total value of prizes offered in 1881 was as follows : Given by the club, £14 ; private prizes, £76 2s. 6d.

Poets and Poetry of the Thames (The).—Perhaps the finest poetical mention of the Thames is in Spenser's "Prothalamion," in which the poet records how he

Walked forth to ease my payne
Along the shoare of silver streaming Temmes;
Whose rutty Bancke the which his River nemmes
Was paynted all with variable flowers ;
And all the meades adorned with daintie gemmes
Fit to deck maydens' bowres
And crown their paramours
Against the Bridall day which is not long :
Sweete Temmes! runne softly, till I end my song !

But let us begin at the beginning. The poetical memories of the Thames commence with the Tower. All the tragic pathos of mediæval English history is concentrated within the precincts of this gloomy pile : alike a palace, a prison, and a place of martyrdom, where the gay, the brave, the noble, and the innocent, as well as the guilty, have paid the penalty of pre-eminence, in a time when pre-eminence was always dangerous and too often fatal.

In close contiguity are three spots of classic ground, hallowed by association with the lives and labours of three great poets, one of them the greatest that the world ever saw. The first is the Custom House, the second the church of St. Saviour's, Southwark, and the third Bankside.

The Custom House may seem in our day a very prosaic place. But this locality, unromantic, dull, tame, and eminently statistical as it may appear to the unliterary mind, is sacred to literature and to the name of Geoffrey Chaucer, the father of English poetry, the author of the "Canterbury Tales" and the "Romaunt of the Rose," who was the first that ever filled the office of Controller of Customs in England. Let it not be supposed, however, that Chaucer received the lucrative post of controller because he was a great poet. In those days as in ours great poets did not receive honours or rewards from the State on account of their poetic genius, and it is highly probable—inasmuch as his works were unprinted—that his contemporaries knew nothing about them, not even the king who showed him favour. Chaucer was not a struggling man of genius, for if he had been he might have struggled and died, unlamented and unknown, but he had the good fortune to be royally connected. He married the sister of the wife of John of Gaunt, the "time-honoured Lancaster" of Shakespeare, and mounted into office from the vantage-ground of his family relationship.

Nearly opposite, on the Surrey side of the river, the handsome tower of St. Saviour's suggests the memory of John Gower, another poet of that early period, the author of the "Confessio Amantis." He erected the tower, and some say the church, at his own expense in the reign of Edward III. It is not known that any other poet, unless it were Voltaire three centuries later, ever built or endowed a church, or had the means to do so. The circumstances led to the following epigram:

This church was rebuilt by Gower the rhymer,
Who in Richard's gay court was a fortunate climber;
Should anyone start 'tis but right he should know it,
This wight was a lawyer as well as a poet!

Gower was very successful in his profession, and became Attorney-General, and afterwards a Judge of the Court of King's Bench. He amassed a considerable fortune, which he invested profitably in land, and was, according to tradition, the ancestor of the noble family of the Gowers, Earls and Marquises of Stafford.

Bankside, overshadowed by the world-renowned brewery of Barclay & Perkins, and occupied on the river front by warehouses and receptacles of old iron, is as dingy, mean, unromantic, and squalid a spot as London affords, but is, nevertheless, sacred to the memories of Shakespeare and his contemporaries. Here stood the Globe Theatre, where his immortal works were produced, and in the management of which he gained not only fame, of which he was singularly careless, but fortune, which he certainly prized, and which enabled him to end his days as a prosperous and respected gentle-

man in his native Warwickshire. The Thames at that time was a pure and limpid river, the haunt of salmon and other edible fish, unpolluted to any appreciable extent by the abominations of the town, and bearing on the pleasant summer afternoons upon its clear bosom the pleasure-barges and wherries of the young, the rich, the noble, the fashionable, and the beautiful, bound for the Globe. And not alone the memories of Shakespeare, but of Ben Jonson, Beaumont and Fletcher, Massinger, Marlow, and other scarcely inferior dramatists cling to the hallowed ground. To these great spirits of the past may be added William Herbert, Earl of Pembroke, poet himself and the associate of poets, and the gay and gallant Lord Southampton, Shakespeare's best and most liberal friend.

Auguste Barbier, a modern French poet, describes the Thames as seen from London Bridge in the gloomiest colours.

Un fleuve tout houleux
Roulant sa vase noire en détours sinueux
Et rappelant l'effroi des ondes infernales ;
De gigantesque pont aux piles colossales.
.   .   .   .   .
Une marée infecte, et toujours avec l'onde
Apportant, remportant les richesses du monde.
.   .   .   .   .
Puis un ciel tourmenté, nuage sur nuage
Le soleil comme un mort, le drap sur le visage.
Ou parfois dans les flots d'un air empoisonné
Montrant comme un miroir sur front tout charbonné.

This powerful description, if it does not owe its inspiration to indigestion, must have been due to the mingled influences of rain and fog and wintry weather. If the poet had stood upon London Bridge in the early hours of a clear summer morning he would have beheld a panorama of surpassing loveliness, and have dipped his descriptive pen in light instead of in darkness, and acknowledged the reality, opposed though it be to French tradition, that London, if not quite so beautiful as Paris, has attractions of its own, independent of its vastness, that in some respects not even Paris can surpass.

It is impossible to pass under Waterloo Bridge—an edifice that the great sculptor, Canova, so admired that he declared it was worth making a voyage from the Antipodes only to look at it—without remembering the poetical halo that Thomas

Hood has thrown around it by his immortal poem, "The Bridge of Sighs."

Richmond, and beautiful Richmond Park, one of the favourite resorts of Londoners when they make holiday, are closely associated with the life and labours of James Thomson, author of the almost forgotten series of poems, "The Seasons," and the national anthem of "Rule Britannia," not heard in our day so frequently as in the last generation. Here he lived and died, a prosperous and contented gentleman, and here he was buried. The latter fact is celebrated by some beautiful lines of his brother poet Collins, the author of the famous "Ode to the Passions."

An American poet, traveller, and diplomatist, the late Bayard Taylor, was taken on his first visit to England to dine at the "Star and Garter" (the old original "Star and Garter," the retreat of King Louis Philippe and his family after his flight from Paris in 1848, since destroyed by fire), and from all he had heard and read expected to find the view from Richmond Hill surpassingly beautiful. He admired the silvery winding and meanderings of the Thames, as seen from the gardens of the hotel, but on the whole he experienced a feeling of disappointment with the over-vaunted charm of the landscape. "It is fine, no doubt, but it sadly wants *clearing!*" He spoke in this respect not as a poet, but as a backwoodsman, whose first thought in America when he sees a vast expanse of what he calls "timber", is to cut it down, to facilitate the operations of the plough.

The popular song, "The Lass of Richmond Hill," which has been a favourite of the English people for three-quarters of a century, is supposed to have been inspired by admiration of some fair unknown who resided on the Terrace. It has been ascribed to the Prince of Wales, afterwards George IV., who, however, was quite innocent of its perpetration. The music was the composition of Hook, the father of Theodore Hook, the celebrated novelist ; and the poetry, which scarcely deserves the name, except in a country where unfortunately any doggrel passes muster for a song, was written, according to the authority of Sir Henry Bishop, by one Upton, who wrote many scores of similar effusions for the once popular open-air concerts at Vauxhall Gardens. There have been many controversies to determine, if possible, whether Richmond in Surrey or Richmond in Yorkshire were the abode of the real or possibly fabulous beauty of the song ; but the probability is that there was no such person except in the fancy of Mr. Upton.

The genius loci of Twickenham, on the opposite side of the river, is Alexander Pope. In this village he lived and died, and constructed at his villa—which has long since disappeared—the grotto, still existing, which goes by his name.

The original "Pope's Villa," which the poet Rogers in after times desired to purchase and to occupy, was demolished by Lady Howe, who erected a more commodious villa on its site, which in its turn disappeared to make room for the present structure. Many comments were made on the occasion, and many accusations of Vandalism and want of reverence were hurled at the head of Lady Howe ; but as she spared the grotto, the removal of the house was in due time forgiven her. A willow once overhung the Thames from Pope's garden, but the relic-hunters in the course of time so chipped and cut and lopped the tree—in admiration, not of the tree, but of the poet—that its vitality was destroyed. It was cut down, and converted most probably into snuff-boxes—in the not very remote days when the use of snuff was almost universal. The grotto was erected about the year 1715. "Being," as Dr. Johnson says in his "Lives of the Poets," "under the necessity of making a subterranean passage to a garden on the other side of the road, he adorned it with fossils, and dignified it with the name of a grotto ; a place of silence and retreat, from which he endeavoured to persuade himself and his friends that cares and passions could be excluded." His principal friends at this time were Lords Bolingbroke and Marchmont, who, like Pope himself, were by far too sensible to imagine that cares and passions could be excluded from a spot on earth, except •

The pleasant fosse, six feet by twain,
Impervious to all grief,

which, until cremation becomes the law of sepulture, must be the final dwelling-place of all humanity.

Pope intended to inscribe on the walls

of his grotto the following lines which he wrote for the purpose. Though included in his works they do not appear to have ever been set forth in the place for which they were intended.

Thou who shalt stop where Thames' trans-
    lucent wave
Shines, a broad mirror, through the shady cave,
Where lingering drops from mineral roofs
    distil,
And pointed crystals break the sparkling rill !
Unpolish'd gems no ray of pride bestow,
And latent metals innocently glow.
Approach ! great Nature studiously behold,
And eye the mint, without a wish for gold !
Approach ! but awful. Lo ! the Egerian grot
Where, nobly pensive, St. John sat and thought,
Where British sighs from dying Wyndham stole,
And the bright flame was shot through March-
    mont's soul,
Let such, such only, tread this sacred floor,
Who dare to love their country and be poor.

Strawberry Hill, the abode of Horace Walpole, author of "The Castle of Otranto," and in our day the favourite residence of the late Countess of Walde-grave, daughter of John Braham, one of the most celebrated of English vocalists, must be mentioned among the places on the banks of the Thames that recall plea-sant memories of literature and song.

Hampton Court, so closely associated with the history of England during the reigns of Henry VIII. and his successors up to the time of William and Mary, belongs also to the history of English poetry, if it were only for the episode of the Earl of Surrey and the fair Geraldine. Surrey's romantic love for the beautiful Geraldine was a tradition, founded on his poetry, until the supposed facts on which it rested were for the first time investi-gated by the author of "The Thames and its Tributaries," and found to be mythical.

Chertsey was long the residence of Abraham Cowley, a poet very celebrated in the time of Charles II., who called himself "the melancholy," and who was called by his contemporaries the "divine" and the "incomparable." An inscription on a house in the little town records the fact that here he lived and died. His popularity was great in his lifetime, his name was upon everybody's lips, and it was predicted by his fond admirers that his fame would last as long as the English language. Cow-ley's poems, though seldom read in our

day, and scarcely known except to literary antiquaries, contain many epigrammatic lines and expressions, which speakers and writers in search of apt but un-familiar and unhackneyed quotations would do well to study. The late Sir Robert Peel, in one of his greatest speeches on the subject of Free Trade and the Repeal of the Corn Laws, un-earthed from the obscurity in which it lay hidden in Cowley's works, a magnifi-cent passage in deprecation of civil war. By this passage Cowley is best known at the present time.

Come the eleventh plague rather than this
    should be ;
Come rather sink us in the sea.
Come pestilence and mow us down ;
Come God's sword rather than our own.
In all the pangs we felt before
We groaned, we sighed, we wept—we never
    blushed before.

Charles II., true to the character so well bestowed upon him of "never doing a wise thing, nor ever saying a foolish one," neglected Cowley, and broke his repeated promises to him during his life, but said, on the news of his death reach-ing him, "that Mr. Cowley had not left a better man behind him in England." And this was the poet's reward — not worth having even had it not been posthumous !

Cooper's Hill, near Egham, has been celebrated in verse by Sir John Denham, in a poem which received the praise of Alexander Pope.

The sequestered scenes,
The bow'ry mazes and surrounding greens
On Thames's banks, while fragrant breezes fill,
And where the Muses sport on Cooper's Hill.
On Cooper's Hill eternal wreaths shall grow,
While lasts the mountain or while Thames
    shall flow !
Here his first lays majestic Denham sung.

Sir John Denham, the author of this once well-known poem, resided in the parish of Egham, and was made sheriff of Surrey in 1642. He was afterwards governor of Farnham Castle for the Royalists in the time of the Civil Wars. A devoted adherent of the House of Stuart, he retired with the Royal Family into France after the execution of Charles I., and at the Restoration, more fortunate than many who ruined themselves for the king, he obtained honours, with profits attached to them, as a reward for his fidelity.

Denham's poem was written at Oxford in 1643, whither he had retired after he resigned the governorship of Farnham Castle. Its success was so great, that the cynics of the time spread abroad a report that the author had not written it himself, but had bought it of some nameless curate for £40. He outlived the calumny by many years, disproving it, moreover, by his other writings.

Until Pope took up the pen, no poem produced in England excited so much immediate popularity as "Cooper's Hill." But fame in literature was easily obtained in those days, when authors were few. Even the critics who maligned the man for political reasons lauded the work as one of the happiest efforts of the natural, even while affecting to believe that its nominal was not its real author. Denham's description of the Thames is still popular :

My eye, descending from this hill, surveys,
Where Thames among the wanton valleys strays,
Thames, the most lov'd of all the ocean's sons
By his old sire to his embraces runs,
Hasting to pay his tribute to the sea
Like mortal life to meet eternity.
Though with those streams he no resemblance hold,
Whose form is amber and their gravel gold,
His genuine and less guilty wealth t' explore,
Search not his bottom but survey his shore,
O'er which he kindly spreads his spacious wing,
And hatches plenty for th' ensuing spring ;
Nor then destroys it with too fond a stay
Like mothers who their infants overlay :
Nor with a sudden and impetuous wave,
Like profuse kings, resumes the wealth he gave.
No unexpected inundations spoil
The mower's hopes, nor mock the ploughman's toil ;
But godlike his unwearied bounty flows ;
First loves to do, then loves the good he does.
Nor are his blessings to his banks confined,
But free and common as the sea or wind ;
When he, to boast or to dispense his stores
Full of the tributes of his grateful shores,
Visits the world, and in his flying towers
Brings home to us, and makes both Indies ours ;
Finds wealth where 'tis, and bestows it where it wants,
Cities in deserts, woods in cities plants ;
So that to us no thing, no place is strange,
While his fair bosom is the world's exchange.

Datchet, Eton, and Windsor are as redolent of poetry and romance as they are famous in history. Datchet Mead, which is known by name at least wherever Shakespeare is read as the scene where the "Merry Wives of Windsor" played their scurvy trick, and inflicted the well-deserved punishment upon the too fat, too amorous, too confident, too villainous, and too agreeable Sir John Falstaff, thrown "hissing hot" into the cool surge from the buck-basket, where he was coiled up amid the dirty linen, "like a piece of butcher's offal in a barrow." Eton suggests the beautiful lines of the poet Gray, one of the few Englishmen of letters who have written too little, "On a Distant View of Eton College." This poem has found its way into every collection of the "Beauties of English Poetry," and suggested to Thomas Hood a parody—à propos of a Clapham school —which is scarcely less admirable in its own peculiar vein than its unsurpassable original.

Windsor Castle, so closely associated with the lives and fortunes, the loves, the sorrows, and the deaths of the sovereigns of England, was the scene of a romantic incident, not recorded in English history, in the career of a King of Scotland, the first of the Stuart line who bore the name of James, who was not only an enlightened sovereign, but an amiable and accomplished man, and a poet of no mean order.

His history in connection with Windsor Castle is a romance of true love—and of a true love, whose course ran smoothly to its close—a contradiction, possibly rare, to the authoritative judgment of Shakespeare in a contrary sense. His old and sorrow-stricken father, King Robert III., grieving for the loss of one son, the Duke of Rothsay, whose sad fate is so finely told by Sir Walter Scott in his "Fair Maid of Perth," and dreading that his youngest darling, and only surviving son, James, then eleven years old, might share a similar fate, thought it advisable to send him out of Scotland. A governor being provided, the young prince was sent to finish his education in France ; but the vessel in which the heir of Scotland was embarked had sailed no farther than Flamborough Head when it was attacked by an English cruiser, and all on board were taken prisoners. Some say that the capture was made when the young prince and suite landed to refresh themselves at Flamborough, where they had been driven by stress of weather. However this may be, Henry IV. of England, although a truce subsisted at the time between England and Scotland, resolved to detain the royal child as a hostage for the future good behaviour of his troublesome neighbour. So overjoyed was that grim warrior at his good fortune, that he relaxed so far as to give utterance to a pleasantry. "His father was sending him to learn French," quoth he; "by my troth he might as well have sent him to me! I am an excellent French scholar myself, and will see to his instruction." And he kept his word. The young prince was provided with the best masters and made rapid progress in every polite accomplishment; but his loss broke his father's heart. It needed not that last calamity to embitter the days of King Robert: he never held up his head again, but pined away and died about a year afterwards. But the captive himself, with the exception of the loss of liberty, had nothing to complain of. Every luxury was his, and every indulgence. He became well versed in all the literature of his age, and grew up an excellent musician, a sweet poet, and expert in all the manly accomplishments that befitted a prince. He studied Chaucer, then recently deceased, and made him his model, and produced poems little inferior to those of his master. In the "Quair," or "book," written shortly before his return to Scotland, he informs the world in elegant rhymes how he passed his time in captivity, and how he fell in love with the beautiful Lady Jane Beaufort as she was walking with her maid in the gardens of Windsor Castle. The royal poet, after pathetically lamenting that he was doomed to be a captive while the birds were free, continues:

And therewith cast I down my eyes again
  Whereas I saw, walking under the tower
Full secretly, new coning her to pleyne
  The fairest and the freshest younge flower
That ever I saw, methought, before that hour,
At which sudden abate, anon astart,
The blood of all my body to my heart!

.   .   .   .
    .   .   .   My wittis all
Were so o'ercome with pleasure and delight;
  And then eft soon I leaned it out again,
And saw her walk, that very womanlie
  With no wight more, but only women twaine,
  Then 'gan I study in myself and sayn,
" Ah, sweet! are ye a worldly creature,
Or heavenly thing in likeness of our nature?"

He then describes, in elegant, though partly obsolete, language, her golden hair and rich attire, adorned with fretwork of "perlis white" with many a diamond, emerald, and sapphire:

And on her head a chaplet fresh of hue,
With plumes partly red and white and blue.

And above all,

.   .   .   as well he wot
Beauty enough to make a world to doat!

This fair creature was the daughter of John, Earl of Somerset, and granddaughter of John of Gaunt; and although we have no record of their courtship, there is every reason to believe that she looked with a favourable eye upon the handsome and accomplished prince, then doubly a captive. In the year 1428 negotiations were commenced by Murdoch, Regent of Scotland, for the liberation of the king, and Henry V. agreed with but little difficulty. The sum of £40,000 was stipulated to be paid by Scotland, not as a ransom—it was a disagreeable word—but as compensation for the maintenance and education of the prince; and it was further agreed that he should marry some lady of the royal blood of England, as a bond of peace and goodwill between the two countries. The heart of James must have leaped for joy within him at the latter proposal. He accepted it with eagerness, and named the Lady Jane Beaufort as the object of his choice. The lady on her part was quite as willing, and their nuptials were celebrated with great pomp, first at Windsor, and afterwards at London, the bride receiving for her portion a sum of £10,000. She was a most faithful and attached wife, and during the many cares, anxieties, and troubles that beset the path of her royal partner on his return into his own disturbed dominions, was always the affectionate friend, the kind adviser, and chief comfort of her lord. The king was himself murdered by a conspiracy of noblemen—noble by title, but not by nature. Overwhelmed by superior numbers he took refuge with his wife in an inner apartment of the palace, and when the assailants, thirsting for his blood, battered at the closed door, she placed her arm in the place of the bolt which had snapped under their heavy blows, and with that beautiful weak limb managed to keep them at bay for a few moments. Her heroism was in vain : the tender and loving arm was shattered, and her husband and lover was slaughtered at her feet.

Windsor Park has one great poetical association, that of Herne the Hunter, in " The Merry Wives of Windsor ;" and the old tree, still standing and cared for in its decrepitude, and which is known by the name of Herne's Oak, is the supposed scene of one of the tricks played off on Sir John Falstaff in Shakespeare's immortal comedy.

Binfield, within the bounds of the forest, was once very generally supposed to have been the birthplace of Pope ; but Mr. Lysons stated on the authority of Dr. Wilson, rector of the parish, that the young poet was in his sixth year when he first came to reside there with his parents, and it has been ascertained beyond doubt that he was born in London. It was at Binfield, however, that he composed his "Windsor Forest." Upon one of the trees in a neighbouring enclosure, under which it is supposed he was fond of musing, is cut into the bark the inscription, '' Here Pope sung."

In the immediate neighbourhood of Windsor are two villages, celebrated in English poetry and song—Stoke Pogis and Bray. Stoke Pogis is considered on sufficient authority to be the scene of Gray's beautiful and renowned " Elegy in a Country Churchyard," than which no poem in the language has been more generally admired and more frequently quoted, and which will never lose its place in English anthology. Bray— though the distinction has been questioned on behalf of another Bray near Dublin—is generally believed to have been the abode of the renowned Vicar, who changed his religion from the Roman Catholic to the Protestant, and from the Protestant back again to the Catholic, and was prepared to do so any number of times upon the sole condition, that, come what might, and do what he might, he should continue to be Vicar of Bray ; or, in the words of the well-known chorus :

> And this is law I will maintain
> Unto my dying day, sir,
> That whatsoever king shall reign
> I'll still be Vicar of Bray, sir.

Only doubtful tradition has preserved the name of the time-serving ecclesiastic, who loved his revenue so much better than his convictions ; but the fine-stirring old English melody to which the shameless confession is sung, and which has since been wedded to many other songs more worthy of its beauty, will preserve his reputation, though his name has long since sunk into hopeless oblivion.

Among the poets whose names and works are associated with the scenery and traditions of the Thames may be mentioned Dr. Johnson, the lexicographer, and hero of Boswell's inimitable biography ; Charles Dibdin, the author of the best sea-songs in the English language ; Taylor, known as the '' Water Poet," whose contributions to literature have sunk into deserved oblivion ; and Drayton, author of the '' Polyolbion," a rhymed discourse on all the rivers of England. Johnson had such a reverence for Queen Elizabeth, that he expressed in his poem on London a vehement desire to disembark at Greenwich, in order that he might "kiss the sacred earth " where the great queen was born. Dibdin's allusions to the Thames watermen and sailors are frequent and well known. Drayton's works are no longer read except by poetical antiquaries.

Police.—Except in respect of carrying out their patrolling work in boats instead of on foot, the Thames Police, or more correctly speaking under the present arrangement, the Thames Division of the Metropolitan Police, differs but little from the other divisions of the force. Its headquarter station is at Wapping, a little above the entrance of the old Thames Tunnel, now a station of the East London Railway, and has a pleasant look-out over the river, just at the junction between the Upper and Lower Pool. It is at present under the command of Superintendent George Steed, who has under him 44 inspectors, 4 sergeants, and 124 constables ; the latter being of a somewhat amphibious type, as is designated by their uniform, wherein the tight blue tunic is superseded by a blue double-breasted jacket, and the helmet by a hard glazed hat such as, were it not carried on the nape of the neck, might impart an additional polish to the forehead of Captain Cuttle himself. Both night and day several boats patrol the river in different parts ; a fresh boat starting from the station-hard every two hours to relieve the one whose watch is up. Each boat contains an inspector and two men, the latter of whom do the rowing, and a careful system of supervision is maintained by which the passing of each boat is checked at varying points. Two steam launches are also employed.

An important portion of the duties of the Thames division consists in searching for and dealing with the bodies of suicides, murdered persons, and persons accidentally drowned. The dragging process is only carried on for one tide, after which it is considered that the missing body will pretty certainly have been carried out of reach, and it occasionally happens that a corpse will drift into a hole and be covered over before it becomes sufficiently buoyant to rise. Should it be eventually recovered, it is first photographed and then preserved as long as possible for identification, not at the station, but at the parish dead-house, following in these respects the regular course pursued with respect to all corpses found by the police in any part of the town, as well as the bodies of all insensible persons so found who may die before identification. When ultimately buried on the coroner's order, the clothes are preserved by the parish authorities, but are only shown to those who bring with them a police order to that effect.

The return of the number of persons arrested and convictions obtained by detectives attached to this division is rather curious. Up to 1875 there appear to have been no detectives attached to the division. In that year three were allotted to it, increased in 1877 to four; the number of arrests, however, which began in 1875 with 107, dropped in 1876 to 88, and fell again, notwithstanding the addition of the fourth detective, to 73 in 1877, whilst the convictions obtained fell from 70 to 57, and thence to 48. This does not appear to have arisen from any general decrease of crime in the neighbourhood; the K division which holds the bank of the river at Stepney, the L and M which patrol the southern bank at Lambeth and Southwark, and the R which performs the waterside duties of Greenwich, exhibiting for the most part rather an increase than otherwise, and in no case a similar continuous decrease. The apparent discrepancy, however, is no doubt susceptible of explanation. The division is one of the most hardly worked, and by far the most exposed to privation of any in the force, the night-guard rowing, especially in the storms and fogs of winter, being exceedingly trying.

Pool (The), the most striking and characteristic feature of the river, extends from below London Bridge to a little above the Regent's Canal. It is divided into the Upper and the Lower Pool, the point of division being the headquarter station of the Thames Police at Wapping, a few hundred yards above the old Thames Tunnel, now part of the East London Railway. By the bye-laws of the Thames Conservancy Board the minimum free navigable passage to be kept "as far as practicable" for vessels passing up and down the river through that portion of the Upper Pool which extends from London Bridge to Irongate Stairs, on the lower side of the Tower, is 200 feet. At this point commence the premises of the General Steam Navigation Company, which occupy the whole of Irongate and the adjoining St. Katharine's Wharf, and the large sea-going steamers starting from which constitute one of the most important features of the home traffic of the river. The minimum navigable passage is therefore extended here to 300 feet, at which width it continues as far as Barking Creek, about three miles and a half below Woolwich, on the opposite side of the river. The average number of vessels lying in the Upper Pool is about 55, with an average registered tonnage of about 200 tons; in the Lower Pool about 70, with an average registered tonnage of about 150 tons. These numbers apply only to vessels discharging in the river. There are a great many ships that discharge in the river below the Pool; the average is about 32, with an average registered tonnage of about 150 tons, besides all the coal-laden vessels that discharge in Cory's hulks in Bugsby's Reach.

Pope or **Ruff (The)** differs very little in its shape, food, and haunts from the perch, except that the bands are absent which characterise the latter. It is likewise of a more yellowish hue, and while partaking of the contour and spinal dorsal fin of the perch has somewhat the appearance in the body of the gudgeon. For this reason many have supposed it to be a cross or hybrid of those fish. It is very prevalent at times in the Thames; and while its presence and voraciousness is looked upon as a perfect nuisance by the scientific sportsman, it is a great favourite from the same cause with the youths who first essay their powers of fish capture. The greediness of the pope is proverbial, and it is seldom that one is caught without the necessity of an operation to extract the hook from far down in its intestines. It is said, likewise, and experience appears to warrant the impression, that when the pope is on the feed it is very difficult to get perch or other fish to take the hook. This may arise from a restless pugnaciousness on its part when food is present to be contested for. The flesh is sapid and wholesome, and a fry is not to be despised, although it is not so firm a fish as the perch.

Port Victoria.—Almost unnoticed except by Kentish men, and by those chiefly who inhabit the district of the Isle of Grain, the Hundred of Hoo, and the country generally in the neighbourhood of the Medway estuary, a railway branching from the South-Eastern line, or rather from its tributary, the North Kent, at Higham, five miles east of Gravesend, has been made to the southern side of the Yantlet Creek, nearly opposite Queenborough, including a maritime station and wharf, which, by permission of Her Majesty the Queen, has been named Port Victoria, was in 1884 celebrated by a visit from London; a large party of gentlemen interested in the development of the new and important scheme having started for that purpose from Cannon-street. The distance is thirty-eight miles, the new line being thirteen miles long, and its terminus less than two miles from the mouth of the Medway. At Port Victoria, as the terminus is called, will be established, by the South-Eastern Railway, a port which will open a new and shortened route to the Continent, and which will greatly assist the American traffic of such vessels as those belonging to the Monarch line of the Royal Exchange Steam Shipping Company, the National line, and other great steamship companies requiring deep-water anchorage.

FARES to Charing Cross: 1st, 7/3, 10/9; 2nd, 5/2, 7/9; 3rd, 3/-, 5/6.

Punting.—It is needless to describe a punt beyond the fact that it has at one end an acclivity with cross-bars of wood resembling steps; a well to hold fish alive, about one third from the other end; the bottom perfectly flat, and the sides bevelled slightly outwards. The punt is worked by a pole, of a length according to the depth of water met with, and heavier at the bottom than the top. The puntsman starts generally from the head of the punt, taking the pole about its middle, and, poising it upright, permits it to slip through his hands until it touches the bottom of the stream. He then walks or runs back towards the well, giving a final push, which imparts an impetus to the punt which allows of the puntsman again taking his place at the head of the punt without losing way. One great necessity for good punting is that the pole should never touch the side of the punt unless it is required to give it a turn or new direction. If it is to be turned to the right (the man being at work on the left side) he need not quit the head of the punt, but simply incline the pole to a more obtuse angle and direct the head towards the course he desires. Suppose, however, he wishes to go to the left, he, instead of lifting his pole over the heads of the occupants to the jeopardy of their hats, walks down to the well, and pressing the pole close to the bevelled side of the punt turns the head of it towards the left. A good puntsman starts on one side and keeps there, and it is marvellous how, even against the force of a heavy mill or weir stream, they can stem the current and never deviate from a straight line. It should be borne in mind by amateurs who trust themselves in weir pools without a practised hand that the back surface stream will draw a punt under the fall, and if presence of mind deserts its occupiers, but a few seconds is sufficient to fill and swamp the punt, an accident that may be attended with fatal consequences. Punting matches are occasionally held upon the Thames, prizes awarded, and the winner holds the honourable distinction of champion.

Purfleet, on the left bank, in Essex, about 18½ miles from London Bridge. Population, exclusive of the garrison and of the training-ship *Cornwall,* 150. Soil, light and sandy on chalk. Purfleet, a hamlet of West Thurrock, is a station on the London, Tilbury, and Southend Railway; the average time of the trains is about three-quarters of an hour. It is a pretty village, with some picturesque chalk hills pleasantly wooded, and with a fine view down Long Reach towards Greenhithe and the Kentish hills. Opposite is Dartford Creek, and there is a ferry from Purfleet to "Long Reach Tavern" on the opposite bank. A large stock of gunpowder is stored in the Government magazines here. Below the village is moored the training-ship *Cornwall*. The principal attraction which Purfleet has to offer to visitors is the "Royal Hotel," which has of late years acquired a considerable reputation for fish-dinners.

HOTEL.—"The Royal."

NEAREST *Steamboat Piers*, Rosherville, about 8 miles, and Tilbury, a little farther on ; *Ferry*, Purfleet ; *Railway Station*, Purfleet.

POSTAL ARRANGEMENTS.—Post Office (money order, savings bank, and telegraph). Mails from London, 7 and 8.30 a.m., and 7 p.m. Mails for London, 12.35 and 9.50 p.m.

FARES to London : 1st, 1/11, 3/2 ; 2nd, 1/5, 2/4 ; 3rd, -/11, 1/10.

Purley, Berkshire, stands about half a mile from the river ; the church, close to which is a ferry, being on the right bank ; from London 78 miles, from Oxford 33½ miles, and most delightfully situated in a clearing among the fine trees of Purley Park, with a pretty avenue leading to the village. Population, about 200. Soil, gravelly. The church is modern, with the exception of the tower, and contains some good Norman remains. The scutcheon on the south of the tower, with the date 1626, bears the arms of the Bolingbroke family.

PLACE OF WORSHIP.—St. Mary's.

POSTAL ARRANGEMENTS. — Letters through Reading. Mails from London, 6.15 a.m. Mails for London, 7.30 p.m. Pangbourne is the nearest money-order office and telegraph station.

NEAREST *Bridges*, up, Pangbourne 2½ miles ; down, Caversham 3¾ miles. *Locks*, up, Mapledurham ½ mile ; down, Caversham 4 miles. *Ferry*, Purley. *Railway Station*, Pangbourne, G.W.R.

FARES, Pangbourne to Paddington : 1st : 7/4, 13/-; 2nd, 5/6, 9/6 ; 3rd, 3/5½.

Putney, on the right bank, rather more than 7 miles from London, is a considerable suburb grafted on to an old-fashioned High-street and water frontage. It is the headquarters of London rowing, and during the fortnight before the University Boat-race and the period of the Volunteer encampment at Wimbledon is a very lively and bustling place. At other times there is little to attract any but rowing men. A most inconvenient, and even dangerous, bridge (now being rebuilt) connects Putney with Fulham, and a little above is an aqueduct of singularly unprepossessing exterior. Putney is a station on the London and South Western Railway, about twenty minutes from London, and is a stopping place for steamers in the summer. Omnibuses run from the City, *via* the Strand and Piccadilly, to the Fulham end of Putney Bridge.

FARES : 1st, -/9, 1/-; 2nd, -/7, -/10; 3rd, -/5, -/8.

Radley (ST. PETER'S COLLEGE), near Abingdon, in the county of Berks, was opened by the Rev. Dr. Sewell, of Exeter College, Oxford, on June 9, 1847. It is situated on rising ground within easy distance of the Thames, 4½ miles from Oxford, and about a mile from the Radley station on the Great Western Railway. The design of the college is to give a thorough public school education to boys of the upper classes on the principles of the Church of England, and boys are admitted between the ages of 10 and 15. Each boy is assigned to the special care of one of the masters, who is called his social tutor, and who is entrusted with a general supervision over his progress and welfare. The gymnasium is made a special feature. The Sewell Scholarships were founded in memory of the late Dr. Sewell, value £55 per annum. Scholars are elected every second or third year. Four Entrance Scholarships (value £50, £30, and £20 respectively) are filled up each year, and are open to boys who were under 14 on the 1st of January preceding the examination. The entrance scholarships are tenable for four years. The other scholarships are : one founded by Sir Walter C. James, Bart., for boys under

18, value £30; two in memory of the late Rev. W. Beedon Heathcote, formerly warden, for boys under 17 and 18 respectively, value £20 each (one for classics and one for mathematics); one, founded by the late W. Gibbs, Esq., for boys under 16, value £20. All these scholarships are tenable for one year only. There is an entrance fee (for boys over 12) of £10 10s., and the college fees vary from about £105 to £126 per annum.

Railway Station, Radley. Fares to Paddington: 1st, 10/4, 18/-; 2nd, 7/9, 13/6 ; 3rd, 4/10½.

Radley Boat Club is composed of students at St. Peter's College, Radley, in Berkshire, and is consequently a private club. Its training course is from Abingdon Lasher to Nuneham Island, and the club annually puts on an eight for the Ladies' Plate at Henley Regatta. Boathouse at Sandford Lock. Colours, red and white. Flag, white with red Maltese cross.

Ranelagh Club, Barn Elms, on the right bank.—On much the same principles as the Hurlingham. Entrance fee, £10 10s., and annual subscription, £5 5s. Members are entitled to admit two ladies with free passes, and may give vouchers of admission on payment to as many friends as they please. The price of admission to members' friends is 10s., except on such day as the committee may appoint, when it is raised to 20s. No person is eligible for membership who is not received in general society. The election is in the hands of the committee. At least five members must vote, and one black ball in five excludes.

Reading, Berkshire, a short distance from right bank of the Thames at its junction with the Kennet ; a station on the Great Western Railway, main line, the junction of the Hungerford and Basingstoke branches of the Great Western Railway, and a terminus of the South Eastern (Reigate branch), and also of the South Western (Staines, Wokingham, and Reading branch). The stations are about ten minutes' walk from the river at Caversham Bridge, and about five minutes' walk from the market-place. Flys and omnibuses from the hotels meet the trains. Distance from London 74½ miles, from Oxford 37 miles. The trains

on the Great Western Railway average about an hour from Paddington ; from Waterloo about an hour and three-quarters ; and from Charing Cross three hours or more. Population, 38,400. Death rate, 18 per 1,000. Soil, chalk and gravel. There is a good and constant supply of water from the waterworks, and a system of main drainage with an irrigation farm about two miles from the borough. Reading can lay claim to great antiquity, and is the most important and flourishing town in the county of Berkshire. It is a parliamentary municipal borough returning two members—at present Mr. Shaw-Lefevre and Mr. George Palmer, both Liberals. It is a well-built town with fine broad streets and many excellent shops, and is evidently well cared for, although it is understood that the various improvements which have been carried out by the corporation, and the general cost of local government, have raised the burdens on the ratepayers to an inconvenient if not excessive amount. There are some very good houses in the Bath-road and near Coley-avenue. Many descriptions of business flourish in Reading besides that which naturally arises from its being the chief town of a large agricultural district, and for the accommodation of which the town is provided with a spacious corn exchange connected by an arcade with the market-place. There are extensive iron foundries and engine works, breweries, &c., but perhaps the staples of the town —Reading, it may be added, is said to have manufactured 140 clothiers in the 15th century—which are now best known are biscuits and seeds : the manufactory of Messrs. Huntley & Palmer, and the seed nurseries, &c., of Messrs. Sutton & Sons, being known all over the world. The corporation consists of a high steward, mayor, six aldermen, and eighteen town councillors. It is an assize town ; the present recorder is J. O. Griffits, Esq., Q.C. The municipal buildings face the east end of Friar-street, and date from 1875 ; a portion of the old building, renovated in 1780, is still standing. Besides the offices of the town clerk, medical officer of health, public analyst, inspector of nuisances, &c., the building contains a public hall capable of seating 700, which can be hired for balls, concerts, &c., and a spacious and convenient council-chamber adorned with several curious and interesting portraits, amongst which the most noteworthy are those of Sir Thomas White, Lord Mayor of London (1566); John Kendrick, a well-known benefactor of Reading (1624) ; Richard Aldworth, founder of the Blue Coat School here (1646) ; Gustavus Adolphus, King of Sweden, a very fine head ; Archbishop Laud, a native of the town, presented by Archdeacon Mews (1667) ; and an admirable full-length of Queen Elizabeth, which is hung above the mantelpiece over a shield in stone sculptured with the arms of the borough ; the heads of good Queen Bess herself and of four of her maids of honour. There is also a posthumous portrait of one of the most distinguished sons of Reading, Sir Thomas Noon Talfourd, in his judicial robes.

The town (which figured in Domesday Book as Readings) has been the scene of many memorable historical events. So far back as 871 the Danes managed to bring their war-ships up the Thames as far as the Kennet, and made Reading their base of operations for their campaign in Wessex. Parliament, driven from London by plague, down to Queen Elizabeth's time frequently sat at Reading, and the same cause drove the lawyers to the town in 1625, when all the law courts came here from Westminster. Some of the most important events in its records occurred in 1643, when it suffered severely during the siege by the Parliamentary troops under the Earl of Essex, and later, in 1688, when the Prince of Orange defeated the king's troops. Among the buildings which suffered most at the hands of the Roundheads was St. Giles's Church, but the chief sufferer was the famous old Benedictine Abbey, founded in 1121 by Henry I. What was begun by Cromwell's cannon was completed by the ravages of time and of depredators, who carried away wholesale stone and other material to be used for building purposes elsewhere, until nothing now remains of this once magnificent building but a few half-ruined arches and enormous walls of flint and rubble. There is no monument in or near the ruins to show that King Henry I. was buried there, or that Maude, daughter of Henry I., wife of Henry IV., Emperor of Germany, and mother of our Henry II., was also buried in the abbey grounds

with great pomp. Royal marriages of great importance took place in the abbey, John of Gaunt being there married to Blanche of the Plantagenets, and here also the marriage of Henry IV. to Lady Grey was announced. Some part of the walls, which are said to have been eight feet thick, were used nearly a century ago by General Conway and employed in building a bridge between Henley and Wargrave, near the general's residence at Park Place. The old gateway has been rebuilt, and serves as the headquarters of the Royal Berks Volunteers. The abbey ruins are best approached from the prettily-laid-out Forbury Gardens, adjacent to which are the extensive assize courts, the county gaol being beyond the abbey ruins to the eastward. A handsome esplanade, planted with trees, runs from the foot of the abbey along one face of the gaol wall which overlooks the Kennet.

Among the many churches in Reading, two at least are well worth a visit : those of St. Lawrence, corner of Friar-street, near the market-place, and of St. Mary, Minster-street. The former is of the flint and stone so common in the architecture of this part of the country, and has a square tower with turrets, and is a handsome building in the perpendicular style. Among the brasses are those of Edward Butler and his wife (1585), of John Kent and his wife, and of W. Barton (1538). In the south aisle is a curious painted monument of John Blagrave, dressed in cloak and ruff, and holding a quadrant and globe. Two skulls support the monument, and on each side of the tablet is a plump gilt cherub. The inscription runs, " *Johannes Blagravus totus mathematicus cum matre sepultus.*" A figure in marble, kneeling at a *prie-dieu*, commemorates the death in 1636 of Martha, wife of Charles Hamley, and the ruff and extraordinarily large hat of the figure challenge attention. Another interesting memorial is the stained-glass window in three compartments, situated in the south side of the chancel, and inscribed : " Memorial to Charles Lamb : Henry and Rachel, children of T. N. Talfourd : erected 1848." The handsome church of St. Mary is remarkable for its curious chequered tower (1551), surmounted with pinnacles added in 1624 by John Kendrick, whose name occurs so fre-

READING

SCALE OF ¼ MILE.

quently in the annals of Reading. The church, which is said to have been originally built with portions of the abbey ruins, was carefully restored fifteen years ago. It has a fine old oak roof, and contains many objects of interest. Of these may be mentioned a black and gold monument to William Kendrick and his wife (1635), with a strange profusion of gilded skulls by way of ornament. The ancient alms-box (1627) inscribed " Remember the poore, and God will bless thee and thy store," and a smaller box at the entrance to the vestry, are curious. In the vestry itself are some 15th-century brasses of no very great importance, and an odd list of charitable gifts to the parish, beginning with a benefaction of alms-houses and money from "John of the Larder." In the choir-room is an oil picture which, before the restoration of the church, hung over the altar, and which is attributed to one of the Caracci. In the chancel hang the tattered colours of the 66th (Berkshire) Regiment. The ancient screen of carved wood over the western entrance should not be overlooked. One of the handsomest churches in Reading, recently restored, is that of St. Giles, Horn-street, which, however, contains now no brasses or monuments calling for special notice. A curious epitaph which exists in the churchyard runs as follows :

He was—
But words are wanting to say what:
Say what is kind !
And he was that.

The parish registers date from 1564, the churchwardens' accounts from 1518. Grey Friars' Church, Friar-street, is a stately 15th-century edifice with some fine windows. It was originally built by the Grey Friars on the site granted by the Abbot of Reading. Falling into decay, it stood roofless for 200 years, the side aisles being used as cells of the town Bridewell. In 1861 it was restored by the late Archdeacon Phelps.

Reading is the headquarters of the 41st Infantry Brigade Depôt, of the Royal Berks Militia, and of the 1st Berkshire Rifle Volunteers.

In Friar-street there is a theatre and an Athenæum Institution, with reading-room and library (subscription, £1 1s. per annum ; less for shorter periods). The free library and reading-rooms, with subscription reading-room and library attached, and with an evening college in connection, are in West-street. The terms for the subscription library are 2s. 6d. per quarter, for the subscription reading-room a like amount ; for the two combined, 4s. The Government School of Art and Science, in connection with South Kensington, is situated in Castle-street. The classes meet morning and evening, and full particulars can be obtained of the honorary secretary. The Victoria Hall seats 400 to 500 people, and may be hired for lectures, &c. The Charity Organisation Society, established to investigate and report upon alleged cases of want, to dispense charity, and to repress mendicity and fraud, has its offices in Carey-street. There is a Servants' Training Institution intended for girls of good character, who are admitted between the ages of 13 and 15, the payment for each being £10 per annum. The School of Industry was founded 1802 by Lady Cadogan for the education of 32 poor girls, who are partly clothed at the expense of the school. Among the charitable institutions may be mentioned St. Mary's Home for Girls, Baker-street, a penitentiary receiving 20 inmates.

Two lodges of craft masons (Union 414, Grey Friars 1101), and one of mark master masons (Leopold 235), as well as a Royal Arch Chapter, are held in the Masonic Hall, which is used solely for masonic purposes.

There are numerous schools in Reading, the most important of which is that known as the Reading School, which has succeeded the old grammar school, formerly so well known in connection with Dr. Valpy, and the buildings of which were opened in 1871. The subjects of instruction are divided into the classical and modern sides. The school-fees are, for boys under fourteen, £10 per annum ; between fourteen and sixteen, £15 per annum ; above sixteen, £20 per annum. An inclusive fee of £4 4s. for instruction in French, German, and drawing, and for the use of gymnasium and library, is paid by all boys. Boarders are received by the head master, and by two other masters ; boys under fourteen pay £67 4s.; above fourteen, £78 15s., including board, laundress, and the school-fees above set forth. There are certain entrance scholarships both for day pupils and boarders, and three Appleton Scholarships for day pupils. Ten scholarships at St. John's College, Oxford, each of the value of £100 per annum, and tenable for five years, will, as soon as vacated by the present holders of fellowships into which they have for the time been converted, be awarded to boys from Reading School.

The Blue Coat School, Reading, was founded by Richard Aldworth, late of the parish of St. Mary Magdalen, in Milk-street, London, Esquire, and a native of Reading. By his will dated 1646 he bequeathed money and other property in trust, the income from which was to be spent yearly for certain pious and charitable uses, one of which was to pay for the education and bringing up of twenty poor male children, being the children of honest, religious poor men of the town of Reading, to and for their meat, drink, and clothing. These twenty children were to be boarded and lodged in the master's dwelling-house, and to be dieted and clothed similarly to the children in Christ's Hospital in London. Since the above date several other bequests have been made for the purpose of increasing the number of boys to be maintained in Mr. Aldworth's School. The number of boys at present maintained in the school is forty-four. The boys are elected by the trustees every year in the month of January ; the successful candidates remain in the school about three years. The education is such as is given in English commercial schools. The boys, on leaving the school, are generally apprenticed. The school appears to be greatly valued, and the candidates for election every year far exceed the number of vacancies. The present school premises were purchased about the year 1852, and are situated in one of the most healthy parts of the town.

An omnibus runs at intervals to Caversham, fare 2d. The tramway starts from the barracks, Oxford-road, and runs through Broad-street, King-street, and King's-road, to the cemetery at Erleigh ; distance about 2¼ miles ; fare, any distance, 2d. Cars run about every twelve minutes.

Being situated on so many lines of rail, as well as on the river, Reading affords excellent headquarters for the excursionist. It is surrounded in all directions

by a beautiful country. Down the river are Sonning, 3½ miles, and Henley, 9½ miles, the latter of which also is easily reached by railway ; and up stream are the delightful reaches of Mapledurham, 3½ miles, and Pangbourne, 5½ miles (also on the Great Western Railway). Inland, within easy reach, are Bradfield ; Whiteknights ; Strathfieldsaye ; Englefield ; Three Mile Cross, on the Basingstoke-road—the " Our Village " of Miss Mitford —near Swallowfield, the seat of Sir George Russell ; Shinfield ; Aldermaston ; and, in another direction, Windsor.

BANKS.—London and County, Market-place ; J. and C. Simmonds & Co., King-street, and Market-place ; Stephens, Blandy, & Co., Market-place.

FAIRS.—February 2, May 1, July 25, September 21, October 21.

FIRE. — (Volunteer) Engine - house, Friar-street ; (Police) Star-lane ; (County) Mill-lane.

HOSPITAL.—Royal Berkshire Hospital, London-road.

HOTELS. — " Great Western," close to station ; " Queen's," Friar-street ; " Ship," Duke-street.

MARKET DAY.—Saturday. Monday for cattle.

PLACES OF WORSHIP.—All Saints ; Christ Church, Whitley ; Grey Friars, Friar-street ; Grey Friars, North-street ; St. Giles's, Southampton-street ; St. John's ; St. Lawrence, Market-place ; St. Luke's, Erleigh-road ; St. Mary's, Minster-street ; St. Saviour's ; and St. Stephen's. The Roman Catholic Church of St. James, Abbey Ruins ; the Episcopalian Church of St. Mary; Friends' Meeting House ; numerous chapels of the Baptist, Congregational, Independent, Methodist, and Wesleyan Bodies ; the Unitarian (Free) Church, London-road, and Presbyterian (Church of England) ; Church of St. Andrew, London-road.

POLICE. — Borough Police-station, High-bridge, London-street ; County Police-station, Abbey-street.

POSTAL ARRANGEMENTS. — Post Office (money order, savings bank, telegraph, insurance), 99, Broad-street. Town receiving offices : Brunswick-hill, Castle-street, Duke-street, London-road, London-street, New-town, Oxford-road,

Queen's-road, Redlands, Spring-gardens, the Barracks. These are all insurance offices, and there is a telegraph office at the London-street branch. Mails from London, 7 and 8.30 a.m., 3 and 6.45 p.m.; Sundays, 7 a.m. Mails for London, 2, 9.30, and 10.30 a.m., 12.45, 2.30, 3.30, 4, 7.30, and 8.30 p.m.; Sundays, 2 a.m.

NEAREST *Bridges*, Caversham; up, Pangbourne 6¼ miles; down, Sonning 3¾ miles. *Locks*, Caversham: up, Whitchurch, 6¼ miles; down, Sonning 3½ miles. *Railway Station*, Reading.

FARES to Paddington, Waterloo, or Charing Cross: 1st, 6/3, 11/8; 2nd, 4/8, 8/3; 3rd, 3/1½.

Reading Amateur Regatta takes place usually about the end of July, over the excellent course from the Fisheries, down stream to a point above Caversham Bridge, a distance of about a mile and one furlong.

RACES IN 1884.

REGATTA, Wednesday, July 23.
(On Caversham Reach.)

JUNIOR SCULLS.

Centre Station—G. R. B. Earnshaw, London R.C. 1
Berks Station—F. Cutbill, Reading R.C. 0
Oxon Station—G. P. M. Pridham, Reading R.C. 0

SENIOR PAIRS.

F. Cobb and R. H. Cobb, Kingston R.C. ... ...r.o.

MAIDEN ERLEIGH CHALLENGE CUP
(FOUR OARS).

First Heat.

Berks Station—Oxford Vacation B.C. 1
Oxon Station—Marlow R.C. 0
Oxford Vacation.—F. P. Bulley, H. S. Salter, P. A. Underhill, H. Balfour (stroke), P. Watson (cox).
Marlow.—B. Heath, W. Millward, V. Audrey, E. K. Mann (stroke), A. Shaw (cox).

Second Heat.

Oxon Station—Abney House R.C. ... 1
Centre Station—Reading R.C. ... 0
Berks Station—Avon R.C. 0

Abney House.—A. H. Knox, D. H. M'Lean, F. E. Churchill, H. S. Close (stroke), F. S. Humphreys (cox).
Reading.—F. Cutbill, W. E. P. Austin, H. E. Cottrell, G. M. P. Pridham (stroke), T. Rose (cox).
Avon.—Bond, F. Barking, F. Soane, A. H. West (stroke), R. Bagnall Wild (cox).

Final Heat.

Oxon Station—Abney House R.C. ... 1
Berks Station—Oxford Vacation B.C. 0

THE READING CHALLENGE BOWL FOR SENIOR SCULLS.

Berks Station—G. R. B. Earnshaw, London R.C. 1
Oxon Station—C. G. S. Batt, Thames R.C. ... ... disq.

THE SANDEMAN CHALLENGE CUP FOR EIGHTS.

First Heat.

Berks Station—Reading R.C. ... ...r.o.
Reading.—F. Cutbill, W. J. Brown, J. H. Tyrrell, R. H. Jones, H. E. Cottrell, W. E. P. Austin, G. M. P. Pridham, H. G. Lovejoy (stroke), T. Rose (cox).

Second Heat.

Oxon Station—West London R.C. ... 1
Berks Station—Marlow R.C. 0
West London.—A. B. Vaux, J. H. Welsh, A. Lawless, E. Bartlett, C. J. Scott, C. E. Brown, A. Huntley, G. C. Vaux (stroke), W. R. Wheeler (cox).
Marlow.—B. Heath, W. Milward, W. T. Shaw, W. T. Porter, V. Audrey, E. K. Mann, C. H. Yates, J. S. Kirkpatrick (stroke), A. Shaw (cox).

Final Heat.

Oxon Station—West London R.C. ... 1
Berks Station—Reading R.C. ... 0

THE READING GRAND CHALLENGE CUP FOR EIGHTS.

Berks Station—London R.C. ...r.o.
London.—G. R. B. Earnshaw, C. Earnshaw, W. Bergh, P. Cooke, H. J. Hill, A. S. J. Hurrell, J. T. Crier, W. W. Hewett (stroke), W. F. Sheard (cox).

THE READING CHALLENGE VASE FOR
SENIOR FOURS.

Oxon Station—Kingston R. C.   ... 1
Berks Station—Marlow R.C....   ... 0
Kingston.—F. Cobb, H. A. Harvey,
H . S. Till, R. H. Cobb (stroke).
Marlow.—W. J. Shaw, W. T. Porter,
C. H. Yates, J. S. Kirkpatrick (stroke).

Reading Abbey Boating Club.—
A branch of a large club for young men,
founded in Reading in 1872. Subscription, 10s. ; for honorary members, 5s.
Boat-house at Caversham. Colours, red
and blue, with arms of Reading Abbey.

**Reading and District Angling
Association,** for the protection and improvement of that portion of the Thames
between Goring Lock and Shiplake Lock.
Annual subscription not less than 10s. 6d.
A reward of £1 is offered to any person
who shall give information to any member
of the committee, or bailiff, of any illegal
netting or night poaching, provided that
it be considered by the committee a fit
case for prosecution ; and that the
person prosecuted be convicted by the
magistrates. A reward of £1 is offered
for infringement of the " Upper Thames
(Fishery) Bye-laws of 1869," or the Fresh-
water Fisheries Act of 1878, provided it
lead to the conviction of the offender ;
and a similar reward for killing an otter
within the district protected by the Association, or on the Kennet or Loddon
within ten miles of the Thames.

Reading Rowing Club, Upper Ship
Hotel. Election by committee. Entrance
fee, 5s. ; subscription, rowing members,
£1 1s. ; honorary members, 10s. 6d.
Boat-house at Caversham Bridge. Colours, dark blue and white diagonal.

Remenham, Berkshire, on the right
bank, is connected with Oxfordshire by
Henley Bridge. Population, 533. Soil,
loam ; sub-soil, gravel and chalk. Remenham extends for some distance along
the river. Park Place, which is so conspicuous a feature in the scenery above
Henley, is in the parish of Remenham
Hill, and the church is almost opposite
Fawley Court, about a mile down the
river from Henley. Remenham Farm,
close to the church, is one of the first land-

marks in the Henley Regatta course. The
church, which is close to the river, has
been recently restored ; but the chancel
apse, which is both ancient and curious,
remains in very much its pristine state.
The windows are all of stained glass, and
are mostly memorials of recent date, and
two good brasses are preserved on the
west wall : the one of Thomas Maryet,
of " Remneham," 1591, has the figure of
a man in armour, the face of which has
been destroyed, and the other of John
Newman, " *hujus ecclesiæ quondam pas-
torus,*" who died in 1622, represents the
reverend gentleman in full canonicals.
A niche in the vestry contains an antique
decapitated stone statuette.
Lord Palmerston resided during many
of his early days at Woodlands in this
parish.

PLACE OF WORSHIP.—St. Nicholas.

POSTAL ARRANGEMENTS. — Letters
through Henley at 7 a.m. Letters for
London, through Henley, at 6.30 p.m.;
Sundays at noon. The nearest money-
order, telegraph, &c., office, is Henley.

NEAREST *Bridges* from Remenham
Farm—up, Henley about 1 mile ; down,
Marlow 7 miles. *Locks*—up, Marsh 2
miles ; down, Hambledon 1¼ mile. *Ferry,*
Aston. *Railway Station,* Henley, G. W. R.

FARES, Henley to Paddington : 1st,
6/3, 10/9 ; 2nd, 4/8, 8/-; 3rd, 2/11½.

Richmond, Surrey, on the right bank
from London 15½ miles, from Oxford 96
miles. A station on the Windsor branch
of the London and South Western Railway, 9¾ miles from Waterloo ; average
duration of journey rather less than ½ hour.
Richmond is also in communication with
Ludgate-hill (from 1 hour to 1½ hour);
Mansion House (about ¾ hour); Broad-
street (about 1 hour) ; and Aldgate (1
hour). Steamboats occasionally run to
Richmond in the summer. Population,
15,110. Soil : clay, sand, and gravel.
Richmond, one of the most favourite
excursions of Londoners of all classes,
received its present name from Henry
VII., having been previously called
Sheen, which name still survives at East
Sheen, one of the entrances to Richmond
Park. For a long period Sheen was
a royal residence. The first three
Edwards resided there. The third, unable to bear the associations of the

place after it had been the scene of the death of his wife, dismantled it, but Henry V. restored it, and also founded a great monastery of Carthusians, and a grand tournament at Henry VII.'s manor of Richmond is now on record. Henry VIII. also occasionally visited the Surrey palace, and at one time lent it to Wolsey. Queen Elizabeth was imprisoned at Richmond, where she afterwards frequently resided, and where she died. Part of Charles I.'s troubled life was passed here. The palace stood on the spot now known as the Green, and has long since disappeared.

From a small village Richmond has rapidly grown into a considerable town, and building is still actively carried on. Its convenient distance from London, beautiful and healthy situation, and pleasant neighbourhood, all combine to make it attractive to those who have daily business in town, and still want a certain amount of fresh air, while the railway facilities have been greatly increased and improved of late years. Houses, therefore, of all classes, from the mansion to the cottage, have been lately springing up in all directions. The principal business streets are George-street and Hill-street; the principal residential portion of the town being about the hill. Nothing in the neighbourhood of London is better known or more delightful than the view from Richmond Hill and Terrace, and when Sir Walter Scott described it as an unrivalled landscape, he was hardly saying too much. At the top of the hill is the Great Park, some eight miles in circumference, and affording an infinite variety of delightful walks and drives. There are entrances from Richmond Hill, East Sheen, Roehampton, Wimbledon, and Kingston. Cabs are not admitted. Angling in the Pen Ponds only by special permission. The view of Richmond Hill and town from the river, here crossed by a stone bridge of five arches, is extremely good.

The Richmond Theatre, once very popular and associated with many great names—notably with that of Edmund Kean—is on the Green; but in regard to public amusements generally Richmond is practically a London suburb, and the Waterloo Station is too near the great theatrical district about the Strand to give the Richmond Theatre a very brilliant chance. There is a parochial library of about 3,000 volumes and reading-room at 2, The Quadrant. The subscription is 6s. per annum, or 2s. per quarter, with 6d. entrance fee. Entertainments and lectures are given in the winter months. The Richmond Piscatorial Society has been recently established, with headquarters at the "Station Hotel." The Associated Home Company has been started at Richmond with the object of providing "a private home, freed by a joint system of board and service from the burdens and troubles of isolated housekeeping." A handsome mansion on Richmond Hill has been secured, and board with service is charged £2 2s. per week. Rooms are from 10s. 6d. to £2 2s. per week.

The church is of the hideous red brick usual hereabouts, but unpromising as it appears from a cursory view, it contains many monuments of note. Here was buried Edmund Kean, and a tablet to his memory, with a medallion portrait, has been erected. Here also the poet Thomson was interred, and a brass in the west of the north aisle tells us : " The Earl of Buchan, unwilling that so good a man and sweet a poet should be without a memorial, has denoted the place of his interment for the satisfaction of his admirers in the year of our Lord 1792." In the chancel on the right is a mural monument, with two principal and seven subsidiary kneeling figures in stone or alabaster, to Lady Dorothie Wright, 1631, and an early brass to Robert Cotton, " officer of the remooving wardroppe of ye beddes to Queene Marie." On the left is a monument with kneeling figures to Lady Margaret Chudleigh, 1628 ; and a tablet with two marble full-length angels, by E. H. Baily, R.A., to Samuel Paynter, who died in 1844. In the south aisle is a monument by Flaxman, a full-length marble figure of a female, apparently leaning on a pillar letter-box, to Mrs. Barbara Lowther, 1805. This was erected by the Duchess of Bolton, Mrs. Lowther's sister. In the south gallery is a mural monument, surmounted by a bust, to Robert Lewes, who appears to have been a barrister. This bears an odd Latin epitaph, commencing "*Eheu viator siste gradum paulisper,*" and ending "*Abi viator et cave ne posthac Litiges.*" As Cook's local guide observes, Robert Lewes "was such a great lover of peace and quietness, that when a contention arose in his body between life and death, he immediately gave up the ghost to end the dispute." The remaining churches are modern erections of no special attractiveness. On Richmond Hill is the Wesleyan Theological Institution for the training of ministers. There are almshouses for over seventy poor people, of which Hickey's Almshouses are said to have an income of more than £1,000 a year.

Many celebrated names besides those connected with the church of St. Mary Magdalen are associated with Richmond. Dean Swift lived in a house on the site of the old monastery, and Thomson, the poet, lived and died in the house now used as the Richmond Hospital. The matron's sitting-room was occupied by him, and is still called Thomson's Room.

BANKS.—London and County, George-street ; London and Provincial, Hill-street.

FIRE.—Engine-station, The Square.

HOSPITAL.—The Richmond Hospital.

HOTELS AND INNS.—"Greyhound," "King's Head," "Star and Garter," "Station," "Talbot," "Three Pigeons."

PLACES OF WORSHIP.—Hickey's Almshouses Chapel ; Holy Trinity Church ; St. John's ; St. Mary Magdalen (parish); and St. Matthias ; the Roman Catholic Church of St. Elizabeth ; and Baptist, Congregational, Independent, Presbyterian, Primitive Methodist, and Wesleyan Chapels.

POLICE.—Metropolitan (V Division) : Station, George-street.

POSTAL ARRANGEMENTS.—Post Office (money order, savings' bank, telegraph, insurance), George-street. Mails from London, 6.30 and 8.30 a.m., 1.50, 3.50, 6.50, and 9 p.m. No delivery on Sunday, but letters are delivered on Saturday at 9 p.m. Mails for London, 6.15 and 9.35 a.m., 12.50, 3.5, 5.15, 9.15, and 10 p.m.; Sunday, 8.30 p.m.

NEAREST *Bridges*, Richmond ; up, Kingston 5 miles ; down, Kew 3 miles. *Lock*, up, Teddington, 3 miles. *Ferries*, Petersham and Isleworth.

FARES to Waterloo, 1st, 1/3, 2/-; 2nd, 1/-, 1/6 ; 3rd, -/9, 1/3. To Broad-street, 1st, 1/6, 2/3 ; 2nd, 1/2, 1/8 ; 3rd, 1/-, 1/6.

To Ludgate-hill or Mansion House, 1st, 1/6, 2/3 ; 2nd, 1/3, 1/9 ; 3rd, 1/-, 1/6. To the Tower, 1st, 1/8, 2/6 ; 2nd, 1/4, 1/11 ; 3rd, -/11, 1/8.

River Middle Buoy.—An 8-foot can-buoy, made of wood, and painted black. It is situated in Sea Reach, on the Leigh Middle Sand, to the westward of South-end Light, and marks fourteen feet of water at low-water spring tide. It is moored with twelve fathoms of chain. This buoy belongs to the Trinity House.

River Middle Buoy, East.—An 8-foot convex-bottomed conical buoy, surmounted by staff and diamond, made of iron, and painted black with white rings. It is situated in Sea Reach, to the eastward of the Leigh Middle Sand, and marks twenty-three feet of water at low-water spring tide. It is moored with twelve fathom of chain. This buoy belongs to the Trinity House.

Rivers Purification Association, Limited, 232, Gresham House, E.C.—The objects of this association are to assist towns and sanitary authorities to comply with the requirements of the Rivers Pollution Prevention Act, and to undertake the work of sewage purification for town and sanitary authorities.

Roach (The) " is a deserved favourite with the London angler, and when in season a plucky fish, and with fine tackle affords very exciting sport. Great skill is necessary in their capture, although a notion exists among many that it is an easy fish to hook, if not to land. Yet this idea probably arises from a limited experience of some small and confined pond in which food is scarce, and those who entertain it have but to try their skill in a large river to prove how false is the assumption. Roach spawn about the middle of May, but the period varies greatly in different localities, and even in the same river, as that of the Thames. Its prime season is in October and November, beginning to feed well in September, when their vegetable food fails them by the weeds turning sour." ("Book of the Roach," Longman and Co.) The rod should be light and somewhat pliant, and of bamboo ; the line, either gut or single hair ; hook No. 11 or 12 ; baits (if float-fishing with tight line), pastes, gentles, or red worms ; when the water is coloured the float should be suited to the water you are fishing. If you can well command the swim there should not be more than eighteen inches between the float and the top of the rod, the latter being always kept over the float if possible. With a tight line the bait may be within an inch of the bottom, but if with running or travelling it should just touch it, tripping over the pebbly bottom as is natural to substances carried along by the current. Ground bait for roach is necessary. This is made by the crumb of bread dipped in warm water and then kneaded up with coarse bran or pollard, and sunk in the swim in balls squeezed hard with a stone in them, or clay mixed with them to sink them. If a good swim is once found the angler should never desert it, as his constant visits and baiting will eventually bring the fish to the spot in expectation of a repetition of the refection. In the autumn roach retire to the deeps, in the summer they are found in about three feet of water. A light hand is necessary in striking the roach. Their individual weight in our river seldom exceeds 1½ lb. or 2 lb., although very exceptionable individual fish up to 3lb. were caught during the autumn of 1879. Very many handsome trays of roach were got in the lower districts as far down as Putney during the season of 1879. The fish ran very large for the Thames, 1lb. and 1½lb. fish not being uncommon. These fish travel down stream with the up-country water and floods ; as soon as these subside, and the " bad water " from below assumes its supremacy of volume, the fish head back again into the Richmond and Twickenham districts out of reach of the nets, which are unceasingly at work to the east of Isleworth.

Romney Island, a narrow island rather more than half a mile long, just below Windsor Bridge, and extending to the playing fields of Eton College. At its upper extremity is The Cobbler, a long point projecting into the stream. The cut to Romney Lock is on the right ; the weir, where there is a bathing place of the Eton masters, is on the left.

Rosherville Gardens,—These popular and well-conducted gardens are on the high road to the west of Gravesend, and can be reached direct from the steamboat pier. The admission is 6d.,

and there is a constant succession of amusement throughout the day ; dancing on the circular platform from 2 o'clock to 11 being a special and favourite feature. Besides the tea and shrimps so dear to the heart of the Gravesend excursionist, other refreshments of a more substantial and stimulating character can be obtained at very reasonable rates. The extent of the grounds, which are tastefully laid out and produce abundance of flowers, is about 20 acres. There is a conservatory about 200 feet long, a bijou theatre, a maze, museum, " baronial hall," occasionally used for dancing, but more often for purposes of refreshment. There is a very good fernery and a bear-pit, and some 10 miles of walks are held out as additional inducements to the excursion public. The peculiar situation of Rosherville—it being an old chalk quarry—has lent itself admirably to the landscape gardener's art, and the result is a really pretty and remarkable diversified garden, in which it is quite feasible to pass that " Happy Day " which in the advertisements is always coupled with the name of Rosherville. For railway and steamboat arrangements, *see* GRAVESEND *and* STEAMBOATS.

Rowing Clubs. (*See next page.*)

Royal Harwich Yacht Club.—Headquarters, Harwich. Entrance fee, £1 1s. ; subscription, £1 1s. Burgee blue, with lion rampant or ; ensign blue, with lion rampant or.

Royal London Yacht Club, 22, Regent-street, London, S.W.—The object of this club is the improvement of yacht building and the encouragement of yacht sailing. The election is by ballot of the committee; one black ball in four excludes. The officers are commodore, vice-commodore, rear-commodore, and cup-bearer. The general affairs of the club are managed by a committee consisting of the flag-officers, cup-bearer, and not exceeding twenty-four members, of whom three shall form a quorum. A branch of the club has been established at Cowes. Entrance fee, £5 5s. ; subscription, £4 4s., to either house of the club, and £6 6s. to both. Burgee blue, with crown over City arms ; ensign blue, with crown over City arms in the fly.

Royal Thames Yacht Club, 7, Albemarle-street.—The object of the club

Rowing Clubs.

The following are the principal Rowing Clubs on the river, with their headquarters and colours, information as to which has been received from the various officers. They will be found described under their respective headings :

Name of Club.	Headquarters.	Colours.
ANGLIAN BOAT CLUB	Chiswick	Marone, black, and light blue.
ARIADNE BOAT CLUB	Hammersmith ..	Purple and white.
CHERTSEY ROWING CLUB ..	Chertsey	Black, white vertical stripes.
COOPER'S HILL BOAT CLUB ..	.. ..	Dark blue and yellow.
ETON COLLEGE BOAT CLUB (the eight)..	Eton	Light blue, white cap.
ETON EXCELSIOR ROWING CLUB..	Eton	Dark blue and amber.
FALCON BOAT CLUB	Oxford	Black, blue, and yellow.
GROVE PARK ROWING CLUB ..	Chiswick	Red, black, and yellow.
HENLEY BOAT CLUB	Henley..	Blue.
KENSINGTON ROWING CLUB ..	Hammersmith ..	Pink and black.
KINGSTON ROWING CLUB	Kingston	Scarlet and white horizontal.
KINGSTON JUNIOR ROWING CLUB.	Kingston	Black, gold vertical stripes.
LEANDER CLUB	Hammersmith ..	Red.
LONDON ROWING CLUB	Putney..	Blue, white vertical stripes.
LONDON HOSPITAL ROWING CLUB	Hammersmith ..	Red and black stripe.
LOWER THAMES ROWING CLUB ..	Greenwich	Black and light blue.
MAIDENHEAD ROWING CLUB ..	Maidenhead	Dark blue and primrose.
MARLOW ROWING CLUB	Marlow	Cardinal.
METROPOLITAN RAILWAY ROWING CLUB	Hammersmith ..	Blue and violet.
MOULSEY BOAT CLUB	Molesey	Black, white vertical stripes.
NEPTUNE ROWING CLUB	Oxford	Orange, black, and red.
NORTH LONDON ROWING CLUB ..	Hammersmith ..	Dark blue and light blue vertical.
OCCIDENTAL ROWING CLUB ..	Hammersmith ..	Blue, black, and gold diagonals.
OXFORD UNIVERSITY BOAT CLUB (the eight)	Oxford	Dark blue.
RADLEY BOAT CLUB	Radley..	Red and white.
READING ABBEY BOAT CLUB ..	.. ..	Red and blue, with arms of Reading Abbey.
READING ROWING CLUB	Reading	Dark blue, white diagonals.
STAINES ROWING CLUB	.. ..	Red and black.
THAMES ROWING CLUB	Putney..	Red, white, and black.
TWICKENHAM ROWING CLUB ..	.. ..	Dark blue, crimson horizontal stripe.
VESTA ROWING CLUB	.. ..	Crimson, black stripes oblique.
WALDEGRAVE ROWING CLUB ..	Twickenham	Black and gold.
WEST LONDON ROWING CLUB ..	.. ..	Scarlet and white stripes.

is the encouragement of yacht building and sailing on the River Thames, and the funds are appropriated, after payment of necessary current expenses, to the purchase of prizes to be sailed for. The officers are a commodore, vice-commodore, rear-commodore, three trustees, secretary, cup-bearer, and three auditors; the commodore, vice-commodore, rear-commodore, and trustees are *ex-officio* members of all committees. The secretary is a paid officer. The subscriptions are, for members who have joined the club prior to the 1st May, 1874, £5 5s.; for members admitted after the above date, £7 7s., except in the case of a candidate owning, on being elected a member, a yacht of or exceeding the lowest tonnage classed in the club matches, whose subscription shall be £5 5s. The entrance fee is £21, except in the case of yacht owners, who only pay £15 15s. The election is by ballot in committee, eight members form a quorum, and one black ball in four excludes. The general committee of management consists of twenty-one members, exclusive of the *ex-officio* members, five to form a quorum. The ensign and burgee of the club are thus defined by Rule 21 : The club flag shall be the blue ensign of Her Majesty's fleet agreeably to a warrant dated 24th July, 1848, granted to the club by the Lords Commissioners of the Admiralty ; the burgee shall be blue with a white cross, and a red crown in the centre ; the hoist of the ensign to be two-thirds of the length, the burgee to be always hoisted with the club ensign.

Sailors' Home, Well-street, E., was originally founded in 1828 by Captain R. J. Elliott, R.N., Admiral G. C. Gambier, and Lieut. R. Justice, R.N., who, in the previous year, had successfully started the Destitute Sailors' Asylum.

St. Clement's Reach, sometimes called Fiddler's Reach, runs from Greenhithe to Grays Thurrock, about a mile and three-quarters. Opposite Greenhithe on the Essex bank is Stoneness Beacon, and opposite the so-called Black Shelf, west of Grays Thurrock, is Broadness. The tide runs very strongly round this point. On the north of the reach is West Thurrock. Bearings E.N.E. and W.S.W.

St. Katharine Docks, belonging to the same company as the London and Victoria Docks, adjoin the east side of the Tower, from which they are separated only by Little Tower-hill, running from the Minories to Irongate Stairs. They are best reached from the west from Aldgate Station down the Minories to the entrance in Upper East Smithfield, or from the east by the Leman-street Station of the Blackwall Railway.

Salmon.—There may be more causes than one to which the entire absence of salmon from the Thames are attributable, but pollutions alone would sufficiently account for their absence. Mr. Buckland, in his "Familiar History of British Fisheries," says : "I feel more and more certain every day that purity of water is the principal element of a good salmon fishery ; if, therefore, stinking water is allowed to go into the river, the fish will perceive the fact when he may be possibly miles down the river. A foxhound can smell the scent of the fox on the ground, even although the fox may have passed over the ground a considerable time before. We ourselves can smell weeds being burnt in a field at a very great distance. Just so the salmon may receive cognisance of a town sewer, or tar water, or the dirty water from sheep washing, for a long distance down the river. His instinct will teach him there is danger ahead, and he is very likely to fall back again, and small blame to him." Yet, strange to say, Mr. Buckland has introduced countless numbers of the young of salmon during the last twenty years past, and that at a period when the Thames during its history was never so before polluted. Abominations which have existed since the suppression of the cesspool system are in themselves sufficient to have occasioned this change, and to have caused so susceptible a fish as the salmon to turn from the waters as a fitting breeding-ground ; and when it is considered that the filth of the entire metropolitan area, so enormously increased in extent of late years, now forms a concentrated flow at Barking and Crossness, any expectation that the salmon fisheries will ever revive is in the highest degree problematical, if not altogether beyond reason. Indeed, long before pollutions did not exist, and weirs (one cause assigned by many) did not prevail, and the water at Old London Bridge was considered sufficiently pure for the requirements of domestic purposes, the takes of salmon were few and far between. In confirmation of this statement it may be of interest to refer back to the time when salmon and salmon-fry were taken in the Thames, and their gradual exodus from the river. There is an allusion in a work in the British Museum to a stew or fish-pond then still existing (time 1655) in the residence of one Sir Richard Constable, a mercer, on old London Bridge. The house had originally been a chapel dedicated to St. Thomas A'Becket, and the stew—a large square-grated opening in the starling of the bridge—was reached by a long winding stair leading to a dark vaulted chamber. The writer says : "Whatever luxuries in the salmon way the monks used to have, there is but one caught now and then; they have for the most part gone long ago, poisoned out by the sad nuisances the people throw into the river. It is well known that salmon will not pass through any water in the slightest degree impregnated with blood, and that malicious persons have succeeded in turning shoals of spawning fish back to the sea by the mere act of throwing the entrails of a sheep into a pool *en route* to the upper waters of a river."

In *The British Spy*, September 27th, 1735: "On Saturday afternoon, in the reach between Limehouse and Deptford, a fisherman caught in a common net a large salmon, which he immediately sold to a gentleman passing for two guineas. When the buyer landed at Deptford it was alive, and 34 in. long and 15½ in. round. The fisherman that rowed, seeing so large a fish in the net, had the presence of mind to jump over, and holding by the boat's gunnel, with one hand, threw the fish in with the other, fearing the net would break."

In 1784 *The London Chronicle* of April 13 says : "A salmon which weighed near 30 lb. was taken off one of the starlings of London Bridge by two watermen, who saw it leap out of the water at low-water mark, and immediately put off in their boat." In the same journal on May 26, 1766: "Yesterday was caught in the Thames a salmon of a most extraordinary size ; it weighed 51½ lb., measured from eye to fork 4 ft. 5 in., and round the middle 2 ft. 4 in."

Faulkner, in his "History of Fulham," 1813, writes : "The salmon caught here are highly esteemed, and sell from 5s. to 12s. per pound. Only one was caught here during the last season. They have abandoned the Thames since the opening of the docks." The price here would tend to show their scarcity.

From observations taken at Boulter's Lock and Pool, above Maidenhead, until comparatively recent years the first lock and weir then on the Thames, by the Rev. George Venables, from 1794 to 1821, a period of twenty-eight years, there were 483 salmon only, of an aggregate weight of 7,346 lb., or about an individual average of 12 lb. weight, taken in the nets.

Before, however, the notion of coaxing these fish again up the Thames was looked upon as chimerical, fish passes were erected at Teddington and Sunbury Weirs. But it is true these helps to migration were built in such a way that no fish whatever, such as dace that congregated in the breeding season, and were trying to surmount the barriers to their progress up stream, were ever seen to take advantage of the help thus afforded to them.

There is no record extant which alludes to the taking of salmon by the fly as in other salmon rivers where they were and are still plentiful. But the fry or young of salmon, called "skeggers," were caught in vast numbers in this way, more particularly on the shallows between Laleham and Staines. One of the Harris family of fishermen, who worked the ferry at Laleham, used to put his rod in a hole in the stern of his boat with two artificial flies on his line with a small gentle, and thus allowed his tackle to fish for itself as he rowed to and fro from either side, taking off his fish upon landing. In this way he was known to catch many dozen of these fish throughout the day; as at that period little was known of the startling changes salmon undergo from their babyhood to maturity, and these skeggers have since been proved indubitably to be the youthful produce of the parent salmon.

Sandford, Oxfordshire, on the left bank, 108¾ miles from London, 2¾ miles from Oxford. Population, 348. Soil, heavy clay. Sandford is a village nestling in a well-wooded country, its most picturesque portion lying in a dip at the back of the churchyard, where is an old farm-house, dating from the beginning of the 17th century, which deserves attention. A walk of about seven minutes from the river leads to the church, which was originally founded in the time of William the Norman, and which has been twice extensively restored within the last thirty years, the last time in 1864. A memorial of a former restorer exists in the shape of a tablet over the porch, bearing the following inscription : "Condidit me Dnina Eliza Isham Anno Gratiæ 1652. Porticus patronæ.

Thanks to thy charitie religiose dame,
Wch. found mee old, and made mee new againe."

Within the church is a mural monument to one William Powell, dated 1661, and adorned with the cherubs and skull so dear to the monumental designer of that period. On the east wall is an elaborate carving in a somewhat defaced condition, which is said to represent the Assumption of the Virgin. This interesting specimen of 16th-century art was found buried in the churchyard, where it had probably been concealed from the spoiler. The church stands in a quaint little walled churchyard, containing very ancient grave-stones, and made bright and cheerful with standard roses along the main pathway. From one side of it is a view of the old farm-house and of some fine trees, which, together, make a picture such as Creswick delighted to paint, Abutting on the churchyard at the west end are the schools, built in 1860 and 1868 ; and opposite are the village shop and post-office.

A Preceptory of Knights Templars was founded in Sandford by Queen Maud, which latterly fell into the possession of the Knights Hospitallers.

The pool here is good for pike and perch, and where the water is quiet, heavy bags of roach may be made in the season, particularly during September and October, when the aquatic vegetation upon which the fish feed becomes sour and unpalatable. All the way down below Nuneham good swims may be found for roach and gudgeon, while under the overhanging trees of Nuneham Park very handsome chub lie in wait for the insects that breed and fall from the foliage.

INN.—The " King's Arms."

PLACE OF WORSHIP.—St. Andrew's.

POSTAL ARRANGEMENTS.—Mails from London, from 6.45 to 9 ; same on Sunday. Mails for London, 5.45 p.m. ; Sunday, 2.45 p.m. Nearest telegraph office, Cowley.

NEAREST *Bridges*, up, Folly Bridge, Oxford 2¾ miles ; down, Abingdon 5 miles. *Locks*, up, Iffley 1¾ mile ; down, Abingdon 4½ miles. *Railway Station*, Littlemore, near Oxford.

FARES, from Littlemore to Paddington : 1st, 10/9, 18/- ; 2nd, 7/6, 12/6 ; 3rd, 5/-.

Seamen's Christian Friend Society. Office, 237, Commercial-road, E. ; Institution, 215 and 216, St. George-street.

Seamen's Hospital Society (late *Dreadnought*), Greenwich.—This excellent institution owed its origin to the funds subscribed in 1817 and 1818 for the temporary relief of distressed seamen. In 1821 the hospital was established on board the *Grampus*, a 50-gun ship, at Greenwich. More accommodation being required, the *Grampus*, in 1830, was exchanged for the *Dreadnought*, 104 guns. In 1857, this vessel having become very unhealthy, was replaced by the *Caledonia*, 120 guns, which then took the name of the old *Dreadnought*. Although much good was done in these floating hospitals, the drawbacks inseparable from ship-life were found to be serious. Questions of ventilation, of light, of quiet, and of access, became, at last, so pressing that the committee of the society were only too glad to take the opportunity of the vacation of Greenwich Hospital by the pensioners and to move their patients ashore in April, 1870. The Seamen's Hospital Dispensary, near the London Docks, was opened in October, 1880, as an out-patient department of the hospital, and is free to *bona-fide* sailors of all nations.

Sea Reach runs east and west from the Mucking to the Nore, being about 12 nautical miles. The banks are, for the most part, flat and shoaly, with hills rising behind, and the river here rapidly widens. On the north (Essex) side of Sea Reach, approaching the Nore, are Canvey Island ; the Chapman Light ; the Leigh Middle, with its two buoys ;

Southend; and the West and Middle Shoebury buoys, at the edge of the Maplin Sands. On the South (Kent) is the Blyth Sand, extending some six nautical miles, with three buoys; the Yantlet Middle with its buoy; the Jenkin Buoy; and the Nore Sand and buoy. A little distance above the Nore the Medway enters the Thames at Sheerness, the Sherness Middle and Grain Spit being marked by buoys. Bearings E.S.E. and W.N.W.

Season Tickets.—(*See* GREAT WESTERN RAILWAY *and* LONDON AND SOUTH WESTERN RAILWAY.)

"Shaftesbury."—The industrial-school ship of the London School Board has been stationed at Grays since July, 1878, and is certified for 350 inmates, 70 of whom may be Roman Catholics. The boys are sent to the *Shaftesbury* by two justices, or a stipendiary magistrate in the metropolis, and are children whose cases come under the provisions of Sections 14 and 16 of the Industrial Schools Act, 1866. A child may also be sent to an industrial school under Section 12 of the "Elementary Education Act of 1876," where an attendance order has not been complied with, and where the parent satisfies the court that he has used all reasonable efforts to compel the child to attend school.

Sheerness, Kent, on the right bank, at the mouth of the river, from London about 46 miles. A station on the Sittingbourne branch of the London, Chatham, and Dover Railway; about two hours from London. The station is five minutes' walk from the steamboat-pier, and about twenty minutes' walk from the post-office. Population, 13,956. Soil, London Basin with sand. Sheerness is a fortified dockyard and garrison town, barring the mouth of the Medway, and the fortifications are of considerable importance and mount a large number of heavy guns. The dockyard is only of secondary importance, owing to the fact of its basins being too small to accommodate the large iron ships of the present time. Vessels of a smaller class are repaired and fitted, and wooden ships are occasionally built. In Sheerness Dockyard is the only naval barrack in England. It has accommodation for 1000 men. The visitor who is desirous of seeing what an English dockyard of the first class is like should take a steamer to Chatham. Admission to Sheerness Dockyard is easily obtained—the only requisite being that the name of the visitor should be inscribed in a book at the principal entrance. Casual visitors, however, not being allowed to enter the workshops, practically miss the most interesting part of the show. For more extended facilities, application should be made to the Captain-Superintendent. The older part of the town, which is in fact Sheerness proper, and which contains the dockyard, railway station, &c., is known as Bluetown, and has been supplemented of late years by three suburbs known as Miletown, Banks-town, and Marine-town, the three being generically known as Sheerness-on-Sea. It appears to have been the intention of Sir Edward Banks—who founded Banks-town, and whose private residence has since been converted into the " Royal Hotel "—and of the land societies who are responsible for the erection of Marine-town, to found a watering-place in emulation of Southend over the way. The effort, however well intended, has not been crowned with a brilliant success. There is a long and well-built sea-wall, which, as to its frontage, is trim and orderly enough; but the back of the embankment, which presents itself to the view of Marine-town, is but an untidy and shabby piece of work. The shingly beach affords good bathing. There are bathing-machines and a swimming-bath, available for gentlemen, at all times of the tide.

Mile-town contains one building of great interest to the Wesleyan connection. The chapel in Hope-street was built and used by the Rev. John Wesley, the founder of the great Wesleyan community. It is a wooden edifice, and 40 years ago was removed from Blue-town to its present site.

There is a handsome building at the corner of Trinity-road, known as the Victoria Hall, containing accommodation for concerts, theatrical, and other entertainments, and capable of seating about 1,200. The Literary Institute, with reading-room and smoking-room (admission 1*d.*), occupies a portion of the upper floor. The institute has a library of about 2,500 volumes. A similar institution, for the benefit of the garrison, is situated close to the entrance to the Royal Artillery Barracks, and is a building containing, on the ground floor, a large room for games, &c., where bagatelle-boards, dominoes, &c., are provided. At one end of this room there is a refreshment bar, at which refreshments, except intoxicating liquors, may be obtained. On the upper floor is a large reading-room, with newspapers and periodicals. This room is also fitted up as a theatre, and here theatrical representations take place, as well as concerts and penny-readings, by officers, non-commissioned officers, and men. There is a library of 1,800 volumes of history, biography, fiction, &c. There are quarters for the librarian in the building, and adjacent to it is the fives'-court, gymnasium, and quoit-ground. The whole is managed under the regulations laid down for the purpose in the Queen's Regulations and Orders for the Army.

A Freemasons' lodge meets in the Victoria-buildings. The 13th Kent Artillery Volunteers have their headquarters at Sheerness.

Steamers run daily in the summer to Chatham, Rochester, and Southend. Sheppey Cliffs are worth a visit, and there are some curious little villages in the island ; otherwise the excursionist must at present rely on the train which joins the main London, Chatham, and Dover Railway at Sittingbourne, and affords ready access to the Kentish coast, &c. The line from Higham across the Isle of Grain gives Sheerness another convenient route to London.

BANK.—London and County, High-street, Blue-town.

HOTELS. — " Fountain," Blue-town, close to pier and station ; " Royal," Banks-town.

MARKET DAY.—Saturday.

PLACES OF WORSHIP.—Dockyard Chapel, Holy Trinity, and St. Paul's (parish church) ; the Roman Catholic Church of St. Henry and St. Elizabeth, and Catholic Apostolic Church ; Baptist, Bible Christian, Congregational, Primitive Methodist, and Wesleyan Chapels.

POLICE STATION.—Railway-road, close to station.

POSTAL ARRANGEMENTS.—Post Office (money order, savings bank, telegraph, and insurance) : Head office, High-street,

Mile-town ; Branches in High-street, Blue-town, and Redan-place, Marine-town. The Blue-town and Marine-town branches also transact insurance business. Mails from London at 7 and 10.30 a.m., 7 p.m. Mails for London at 7.50 and 10.45 a.m., and 2.30, 7.20, and 8.20 p.m. On Sundays, 7 a.m. from London, and 6.10 p.m. for London.

NEAREST Bridge, Rochester ; Station and Ferry, Sheerness.

FARES to Victoria, Holborn Viaduct, and Ludgate : 1st, 8/-, 12/- ; 2nd, 6/-, 9/-; 3rd, 3/6, 6/-.

FARES to Charing Cross.—The same.

Sheerness Middle Buoy.—An 8-foot, convex-bottomed, conical buoy, made of iron, and painted black, and surmounted with staff and globe. It is situated at the edge of the Middle Ground Shoal, at the entrance to the Medway, and marks a depth of water, at low-water spring tide, of 20 feet. It is moored with 10 fathom of chain. The Sheerness Middle Buoy belongs to the Trinity House.

Shepperton, Middlesex, on the left bank, from London 30 miles, from Oxford 81½ miles, a terminus on a branch of the South Western Railway, 19 miles from Waterloo ; train takes about one hour. Flys meet the trains. Population, 1,126. Soil, gravel. A small village with some good houses and offering plenty of fishing, but calling for no description or remark. The station is an easy fifteen minutes' walk from the river, close to which are the church and the post-office.

The present church, perfectly cruciform, with tower at west end, was built, 1614, out of the débris of a former church standing over the Thames and built on piles (many wills being still extant leaving legacies to add piles to its foundation). On dit a flood of the Thames washed down the former edifice ; its only memorial is in a picture painted in 1548 by Anthony Vander Wyngrede of the Palace at Oatlands, now in the Bodleian Library, Oxford, where the church stands with spire in the distant bend of the Thames. The arches, windows, and sepulchral slabs in the present church came from the former ; the brick tower being added by the rector, L. Atterbury, brother to the well-known Bishop of Rochester, in

1710; the five bells being new in 1877. The learned Grocyn, the correspondent and friend of Erasmus, was rector in 1504, and entertained that reformer in the rectory, still standing. The rectory, a beautiful and unique oak-built house, some 400 years old, is deceptive to a casual observer, looking like a brick house, with two wings, twenty-one windows in front, and surrounded by gardens. Less than 100 years ago the oak house was covered with mathematical tiles to keep out damp, and the interior was modernised to suit modern requirements, but without altering the ground plan or original structure, which are still apparent to an architect's eye. The late squire of the village was a well-known man, William Schaw Lindsay, M.P. for Sunderland, and in early youth a cabin-boy in a Liverpool East Indiaman. His tomb is in the village cemetery. A tomb in the churchyard, nearly illegible, is very curious, dedicated to the memory of a negro and his wife by Sir Pat. Blake, Bart., of Langham, Suffolk : "Benjamin and Cotto Blake, from the Isle of Colombo. Go to Mauritania, Reader, learn duty of an Ethiopian, and know that virtue inhabiteth skins of other colours than thine own." In the churchyard, also, is that rarest of all black swans, a pretty and graceful epitaph, which well deserves quotation :

Long night succeeds thy little day,
    O! blighted blossom, can it be
That this grey stone and grassy clay
    Have closed our anxious care of thee ?

The half-formed words of liveliest thought
    That spoke a mind beyond thy years,
The song, the dance, by nature taught,
    The sunny smiles, the transient tears.

The symmetry of face and form,
    The eye with light and life replete,
The little heart so fondly warm,
    The voice so musically sweet ;

These lost to hope, in memory yet
    Around the hearts that loved thee cling,
Shadowing with long and vain regret
    The too fair promise of thy spring.

The grave is that of Margaret Love Peacock, a child of three years old, who died in 1826.

There is good fishing about Shepperton and Halliford.

HOTEL.—" The Anchor."

PLACE OF WORSHIP.—St. Nicholas.

POSTAL ARRANGEMENTS.—(The Post Office is now called Upper Shepperton). Mails from London, 7 and 11 a.m., 6.45 p.m. ; Sunday, 7 a.m. Mails for London, 8.55 a.m., 1.50, 7.15, and 8.25 p.m. ; Sunday, 10 a.m. The nearest money-order office is Shepperton. Telegraph-office at the Shepperton post-office.

NEAREST *Bridges*, up, Chertsey 1¾ mile ; down, Walton 2½ miles. *Locks*, Shepperton ; up, Chertsey 2 miles ; down, Sunbury 3½ miles. *Ferry* and *Railway Station*, Shepperton.

FARES to Waterloo : 1st, 3/-, 4/- ; and, 2/4, 3/- ; 3rd, 1/6½, 2/6.

Sheppey, Isle of, on the north coast of Kent, about 11 miles long and 4 broad, is bounded on the north and west by the Thames and Medway, and on the south by the Swale. The principal places in the island are Sheerness and Queenborough. The Sheppey oyster fishery is of considerable importance, and its headquarters are at Cheyney Rock House.

Shillingford Bridge spans the river with three stone arches, and connects Oxfordshire and Berkshire about 2½ miles above Wallingford. On the Berkshire side is the "Swan Inn," where rowing or picnic parties will find comfortable accommodation.

Shiplake, Oxfordshire, on the left bank, from London 68¾ miles, from Oxford, 42¾ miles. A station on the Henley branch of the Great Western Railway, about an hour to an hour and a half to Paddington by fast trains. Population, 586. Soil, gravel and chalk. Shiplake is a village pleasantly planted on the riverside, its prettiest portion being on the chalk hill which overhangs the river just above the lock. The church is dedicated to St. Peter and St. Paul, and was re-opened in 1870, after restoration, during which a chancel was added, and the peal of bells completed. The stained-glass windows are very ancient, having originally been in the Abbey of St. Bertin, at St. Omer. Grainger, author of the "Biographical History of England," was vicar of Shiplake, and died in 1766, while officiating at the Holy Communion. There is a fine bust of Mr. Plowden in the church over his memorial-stone. Mr. Plowden formerly lived at Shiplake Court, which was pulled down in 1801 ;

H

remains of its terraced garden sloping to the river are still to be seen near the chalk-pit. In this church Alfred Tennyson was married. The fine old deer-park and mansion called Crowsley Park, the seat of Major Baskerville, lord of the manor, and The Coppice, the seat of the Rt. Hon. Sir Robert Phillimore, are in this parish; also Holmwood, and Shiplake House. The vicarage was rebuilt by the present vicar in 1868. The Loddon, Pope's Lodona, enters the Thames just below Shiplake Lock.

PLACE OF WORSHIP.—St. Peter and St. Paul.

POSTAL ARRANGEMENTS. — Letters through Henley. Mails from London, 8 a.m. in winter, and 7.30 a.m. in summer. The letter-box at Church Lane is cleared at 6.40 p.m., and on Sundays at 11.40 a.m. ; that at Binfield Heath at 6.15 p.m., and on Sundays at 11.15 a.m. The nearest money-order, &c., office is at Henley.

NEAREST *Bridges.*—Up, Sonning, 2½ miles ; down, Henley 3¾ miles. *Locks,* Shiplake ; up, Sonning 2¼ miles ; down, Marsh 2¾ miles. *Ferries,* Wargrave and Shiplake. *Railway Station,* Shiplake.

FARES to Paddington, 1st, 6/-, 10/-; 2nd, 4/6, 7/6 ; 3rd, 2/10.

Shipping Office, 133, E. India Dock-road, established under the Board of Trade in 1851 as a medium of communication between owners and seamen, all engagements between whom in the port of London must by law be made through it. Hours, 10 a.m. to 4 p.m.

Shoebury.—A small village six miles from Southend by road, important only on account of its artillery barrack, and the big gun ranges across the Maplin Sands at Shoeburyness. Here some of the most important experiments in connection with the rapid development of modern ordnance have taken place, and here annually in August assemble the Artillery Volunteers, to go through much harder work, and to compete for much less valuable prizes, than their more fortunate and fashionable brethren of the rifle at Wimbledon. Except to those actually interested in gunnery, or as a drive on a summer afternoon from Southend, there is no reason to recommend a visit to Shoebury.

Shoebury Buoy, Middle.—An 8-foot cylinder buoy, made of iron, and painted black. It is situated about a mile and a half to the eastward of the West Shoebury Buoy, and marks 27 feet of water at low-water spring tide. It is moored with 10 fathom of chain. The Shoebury buoys belong to the Trinity House.

Shoebury Buoy, West.—An 8-foot cylinder buoy, made of iron and painted black. It is situated on the north side of Sea Reach, to the eastward of Southend Pier, on the edge of the Maplin Sands, and marks 24 feet of water at low-water spring tide. It is moored with 12 fathom of chain.

Shrimping and Cockling.—There are upwards of 100 sailing decked boats employed in trawling for shrimps in the Leigh (Essex) district, and some dozen row-boats. The row-boats are likewise employed here in the search for cockles, and line-fishing for bait for larger fish. Fish under 7 in. are liable to be seized. Each sailing-boat is generally worked by two men and a boy. There is but little whelk or mussel fishing. The visitor may see beds of these at low water round towards Southend, but they are brought from afar and laid down principally for bait, notices being posted againt their removal. The cockles are found on the flats when the tide is very low, and the fishermen know where to dig for them, as they leave a peculiar mark on the surface. Cockles are not allowed to be taken within the jurisdiction of the Conservancy until they are fit for the market —about 1¼ in. from the front of the shell to the nib athwart the back of it ; less than this are termed brood. No oyster-spat falls about Leigh, but a few oysters are laid down on private grounds. Shrimps are caught in a long bag net stretched on a beam, which when sunk scrapes the ground as the boat sails on, and compels the shrimps to enter it. These trawls are seldom down more than half-an-hour, and sometimes but a few minutes. When the trawl is raised on to the deck, the weeds are first "culled" out and the shrimps are thrown with shovels against almost upright wire sieves and of different calibres ; the larger ones are thus separated, and the very small shrimps thrown overboard—at least, they ought to be ; but many of them are killed in the trawl. In the winter time the bars of the sieves are closer together, as shrimps are always smaller in August, September, and October, and then the familiar hand-nets by wading are mostly used. The shrimping grounds extend from the mouth of the Thames nearly to Sheerness and Herne Bay, a distance of 35 miles. It is the opinion of the fishermen that the supply of shrimps, despite the tons that are daily sent up to the metropolis, is as great as ever. But it is only the West End fishmongers and the principal hotels at Leigh, Gravesend, &c., that can secure the finest and largest, some of which, the brown shrimp particularly, are of a size to astonish those who only see the shrimp on stalls or hawked about in baskets. There is an assistant river-keeper, whose duty it is to examine the nets, and if the meshes are under the proper size either to seize them or report them to the Conservancy. The Leigh men ought not to fish farther up the Thames than Hope Point. There is no whitebait fishing at Leigh, but there are dabs (flounders) and a few soles ; the bass and the grey mullet occasionally visit the mouth of the Thames, as do the shad, but in nothing like the shoals which formerly gave names to certain districts below London Bridge.

The picking of shrimps is an art alone acquired by practice. The fishmongers who thus prepare them for sauce may be seen to remove the shells of these "Undine" of the waters" with marvellous rapidity. This is done by first a pressure upon the tail with the thumb-nail, and at the same time a twist which severs the principal scale on the back ; a second movement strips the whole of the scales off the shrimp, and, presto ! the flesh is intact and free from incumbrance. This, however, can only be done when the shrimps are perfectly fresh ; if they are dry and have been twice boiled, the process is tedious, and then they should not be eaten by persons of weak stomachs.

Sonning, Berkshire, on the right bank, from London 71¼ miles, from Oxford 40¼ miles. Population, 465. Soil, gravel. A pleasantly-situated village, with an ancient brick bridge across the river, from which two delightfully dissimilar views are to be enjoyed. Looking up stream, the river which is here narrowed by islands covered with osiers and pollard willows, and shut in at the bend by the noble forest trees of Holme Park, presents the appearance of a placid lake. The contrast of colour between the bright light greens of the foreground trees, the richer tints of the grassy meadow in the middle distance, and the dark, almost sombre masses of the towering chestnuts in the background, form a picture not easily forgotten. Looking down stream, an entirely different scene presents itself. The river takes its sinuous course between low banks, its passage through the long open plain being marked here and there with pollards and osier-beds, and the background filled with the amphitheatre of wooded heights above Henley. Little indication of the character of the village is obtained from the river, but a few minutes' walk inland will disclose as pretty a little place as can well be desired, containing many excellent houses, evidently well looked after and cared for, and with good old-fashioned gardens. Sonning is not without literary associations, as the "Peter Plymley Letters" of Sydney Smith were written in a cottage in the village. The church, whose gray square embattled tower adds greatly to the charm of the up-river view from the bridge, is well worth a lengthened visit, containing as it does great wealth of interesting monuments and brasses, besides presenting to itself many notable architectural features. On the north side is a good old porch of elaborate design, over which is an image of St. Andrew ; and some curious iron clamps on the belfry door bear the old bell inscription : "*Deum laudo, vivos voco, mortuos ploro.*" The Sonning peal of bells has long been celebrated, and a curious entry in the archives of the Ancient Society of College Youths records their victory in a competition for a two-handled silver cup, the inscription on which says : "This cup, the gift of Mr. Peter Bluck, of Sonning, in the county of Berks, was adjudged to the Society of College Youths for the superior style in which they rang ten hundred and eight bob major in a contest with the Oxford and Farnham Societies, at the above parish church, on Monday, Aug. 4th, 1783." The church contains nave, chancel, and aisles ; the north chancel aisle being specially remarkable for the beautiful carving with which it is enriched. The handsome altar of recent date is also

H 2

elaborately decorated with sculpture. the font is modern, as is its lofty carved oak tabernacle covering, both probably dating from the restoration of the church in 1853. On the west wall of the south aisle is a handsome marble monument with brasses, to the memory of various members of the family of Palmer of Home Park. In the south aisle is a painted marble monument, dated 1630, to Katharine, Lady Lidcott, who kneels at a *prie-dieu*, a good specimen of this kind of work, and in striking contrast to a pretentious and conventional monument hard by, the work of R. Westmacott, jun., and erected to the memory of W. Barker, who died 1758. In a chapel divided from the south aisle by an oak screen, is a kind of mortuary chapel, almost entirely allotted to monuments of the Barker family, which is now, however, nearly wholly occupied by the organ. It also contained a ponderous slab, supported by four chubby marble angels, and surmounted by two marble pickle-jars of colossal size, the whole being in honour of one Sir Thomas Rich and his son, who died respectively 1667 and 1613. This now stands at the west end of the church under the tower. Under the east window was a very old monument (now removed to the south wall, close to the Barker monument), depicting the kneeling figures of three knights in armour, and three ladies, with a certain grotesqueness in the character of the faces. The inscription is unfortunately undecipherable, only sufficient remaining to show that it was of a poetical character. Lord Stowell is among the celebrities who are buried at Sonning. The brasses in this church comprise many full-length figures of members of the Barker family, dating from the middle of the 16th century, one of which, to Anne Staverton, daughter and "sole heire" of William Barker, who died 1585, has the following quaint inscription :

A frend vnto the widdoo, fatherles, sycke and poore,
A comforte and a svcker contynened she ever more.

Hard by is an unusually good brass in memory of Laurentius Ffyton, who is represented in armour, each corner of the brass bearing an elaborate coat of arms :

the date is 1434. In the neighbourhood is a brass to William Barker and Anne his wife, with the following quaint inscription :

Here lyeth the corps of William Barker, Esquire in bowelle of this grave
Whose dayes by all mens doome deserve a longer life to have.
You widowes wayle his losse and orphanes, wythe his lyffe
You dearly want his wysdomes skyll, whose causes are at stryffe.
Nor you allone lament, your frynde's untymely ffate,
His Ann doth morne amonge the most, who least maye misse her mate
Ann, spronge of Stowghton's stocke, an ancient progeny
She wyth her chyldren wayle this chaunce, and doleffull destenye.
Yet this bothe we and all have mostlye to rejoice
His faithe and fraudles hart hathe wonne the people's voyce
His bodie in this soile and earthlye fear doth lye,
His ffame in ayre, his ghost for ay doth yve alofte the skye.

An odd epitaph on Elizabeth Chute, a child of the tenderest years, deserves quotation :

What Beauty wold have lovely stild
What manners sweete what nature mild,
What wonder perfect all were fild
Vpon Reccord in this one child
And till the comming of the Soule
To call the flesh, we keepe ye Roule.

There are two curious tablets in the wall by the vestry door, dated 1533 and 1605; and the vestry, which is screened from the north aisle by a somewhat similar oak screen to that on the opposite side of the church, contains a fine old carved oak chair and table, the latter much resembling that in the hall of Christ's Hospital at Abingdon. There is a fine view from the top of the church tower. Sir Thomas Rich, the lord of the manor, left some years ago £20 per annum for the free instruction of forty poor boys, and they were taught in the master's cottage until the erection of the new schoolroom by the late Robert Palmer, Esq., of Holme Park.

Here is a splendid stretch of jack water, well looked after. Barbel, roach, &c., plentiful.

An omnibus runs daily between Sonning and Reading, leaving the "Peacock" Inn, Broad-street, Reading, at

8 a.m., 12 noon, and 4 p.m., returning from Sonning at 10 a.m., 2 and 7 p.m. ; the journey occupies about an hour.

HOTELS.—The "French Horn" on the Oxfordshire side, rebuilt in 1883 ; the "White Hart," on the Berkshire bank ; the "Bull," just through the churchyard. PLACE OF WORSHIP.—St. Andrew's. POLICE.—A constable lives in the village. POSTAL ARRANGEMENTS.—Post Office, five minutes from river (money order, savings bank, and telegraph office). Mails from London 7.10 a.m. and 12.15 p.m. ; Sunday, 7.10 a.m. Mails for London, 6.50 and 10.30 p.m. ; Sunday, 12.30 p.m.

NEAREST *Bridges*, Sonning ; up, Caversham, 3¼ miles ; down, Henley 6¼ miles. *Locks*, Sonning ; up, Caversham about 3 miles ; Shiplake 2½ miles. *Ferry*, Wargrave. *Railway Station*, Twyford, G.W.R.

FARES, Twyford to Padd. : 1st, 5/6, 9/3 ; 2nd, 4/2, 7/- ; 3rd, 2/9½.

Source of the Thames, The.—As is the case with many other respectable rivers, there is some little doubt as to what is the actual source of the Thames. Some authorities have regarded a river called the Churn, which has its rise at a place called Seven Springs, a short distance from Cheltenham, as the real source of the Thames ; but others, including such writers as Leland, Stow, and Camden, give the distinction to Thames Head near Cirencester. Between Thames Head and Cricklade, however, where the Churn and the stream from Thames Head amalgamate, the river is a small matter enough, and it is not advisable to take boat even at this point, as the stream, though navigable for small boats, is still very narrow—in dry seasons inconveniently so.

Southend, Essex, on the left bank at the mouth of the Thames, from London about 43 miles. A station on the London, Tilbury, and Southend Railway, about 1 hour 45 minutes by ordinary trains, and 1 hour 10 minutes by fast trains, from Fenchurch-street. The station is 5 minutes' walk from the Terrace ; flys meet the trains. Population, about 5,000. Soil, clay and gravel.

The West of London, at least, has for many years had a very erroneous idea of this pretty little town. It has been looked upon as a sort of Whitechapel-on-Sea, and comic writers have lost no opportunity of making capital out of the cockneyism and vulgarity which they have assumed to be particularly rampant in Southend. It will be a surprise, therefore, to most visitors to find a clean, quiet, well-built, well-arranged, and old-fashioned watering-place, with most of the advantages, and with comparatively few of the drawbacks to be found in many more pretentious places. It is no doubt true that Southend is a favourite place for excursionists, and that 'Arry occasionally descends upon the place in his thousands, but he confines himself for the most part to the old town, which is by the side of the river (or sea, as the natives prefer to call it), where he finds every accommodation in the way of taverns, cheap dinners, ninepenny teas, oysters in the season (which here appears to be July), the toothsome cockle, and the succulent whelk, and it is scarcely necessary to add, the domestic shrimp and "crease." 'Arry is also to be found on the pier, where, arrayed in rainbow tweeds, he delights in fishing for dabs, and endeavouring to persuade himself that the telescope which he is always eager to borrow is of the smallest assistance to him. The beach, too, is a favourite place for excursionists, and the bathing-machines are extensively patronised. That the strict rules of decency are not observed so well as could be wished, is unfortunately not peculiar to Southend. As to these matters, English arrangements are almost universally bad, and Southend is no better and no worse than its more aristocratic rivals. But the bulk of the excursionists to Southend are the children who come down in large and happy parties in charge of schoolmaster or parson, for "a day in the country," and whose enjoyment of the place, and of the unwonted fresh air—for Southend air is fresh and invigorating—is of itself a pleasure to watch. Even in the fullest and most lively part of the season, and in the very crisis of a big excursionists' day, that part of Southend on the cliff from the Royal Hotel to St. John's College, is as quiet and decorous as the Lees at Folkestone. Indeed, the front of Cliff

Town is remarkably like the Lees in the earlier days of Folkestone as a watering-place. Along the front of Royal-terrace, and extending to the sea-wall below, is the Shrubbery (admission 2d.). This pleasant and shady retreat is an exceedingly good instance of how much can be effected with a piece of waste cliff by a little expert landscape gardening. A local and enthusiastic writer thus describes the Shrubbery, not without a touch of gush : " Here are many cool grots, fairy dells, and leafy bowers, where one may enjoy the latest novel from Mudie's, or the enchanting aspect seaward, to be seen through the leafy apertures formed by the surrounding trees. During the gloaming the promenade is crowded by the *élite*, who have assembled to listen to the bewitching notes of the nightingale." This is, perhaps, too poetical a description, but there can be no doubt that the Shrubbery is a great addition to the attractions of the town, and that its views of Sheerness, the Kentish Hills, and the varying stream of traffic that ebbs and flows past Southend are both cheerful and picturesque. In addition to the Old Town and Cliff Town, Southend has two other suburbs, the Park Estate at the back of Cliff Town, and Porter's Town some little distance eastward of the railway-station. The new portions of the town are in nearly all cases well planned and carefully laid out. Prittlewell, an ancient village, of which, in fact, Southend is only a hamlet, is distant a mile and a half inland. The church at Prittlewell is large and handsome, mainly perpendicular, but containing remains of much earlier work. The tower is considered to be one of the finest in the county.

One of the great institutions of Southend is the pier, one of the longest, if not the longest in England. The tide receding for nearly a mile has necessitated the extension of the pier to a distance of a mile and a quarter. A tramway runs the entire length, and the tram-cars would be even more useful than they are if more frequent journeys were made. The fare each way is 3d. The pier toll is 1d. Southend Pier not only enjoys the distinction of being one of the longest piers extant, but affords accommodation to perhaps the smallest music-hall and stage ever seen. During the season concerts take place within its canvas walls in the afternoon and evening.

The public hall in Alexandra-street is a convenient building, seating upwards of 500, and provided with a stage and all appliances for theatrical performances.

St. Stephen's Convalescent Home, in connection with St. Stephen's, Poplar, was opened in 1876 for the accommodation of 8 or 10 respectable women or children, at a charge of 8s. to 10s. per week.

The Milton Hall Convent is a Home for poor old and infirm people and orphan and incurable children. It is supported by voluntary contributions of money and food, and is a branch of the Hammersmith Institution of the Sisters of Nazareth. A masonic lodge (Priory, 1,000) meets at the Middleton Hotel close to the station.

The country about Southend is somewhat flat, but is well wooded, and affords many good walks and drives. Leigh (*which see*), 4 miles ; Shoebury (*which see*), 5 miles ; Hadleigh, 6 miles ; and Rayleigh, 8 miles, are favourite land excursions, while steamers run *via* Sheerness, to Chatham and Rochester, a pleasant trip of about two hours. There is one drawback to Southend, and, in truth, a somewhat serious one. The service of trains is by no means all that it should be, and the arrangements generally at the squalid Fenchurch-street station are simply deplorable. The fares are certainly low, but little else can be said in favour of the line.

BANK.—Sparrow, Tuffnell, and Co.; High-street.

HOTELS.—" Royal," facing the sea ; " Hope," Old Town ; " Ship," Old Town ; " Middleton," close to railway station.

PLACES OF WORSHIP.—All Saints, Porter's Town ; St. John the Baptist (parish church); and St. Mary the Virgin, Prittlewell ; the Roman Catholic Church of Our Lady and St. Helen, Empress ; Trinity, Reformed Church of England ; and Baptist, Congregational, Independent, Methodist, and Wesleyan Chapels.

POLICE.—Station, Alexandra-street.

POSTAL ARRANGEMENTS.—Post Office (money order, savings bank, telegraph, and insurance), Alexandra-street. Mails from London, 7 and 9.15 a.m. and 6.45 p.m. Mails for London, 8.35 and 11.5 a.m., and 1.35 and 7 p.m. Sunday, 6.30 p.m. The Receiving Houses at Marine-parade,

Park-street, and Porter's Town are cleared a quarter of an hour earlier.

NEAREST *Railway, Steamboat Pier,* and *Ferry* (steamer to Sheerness in summer), Southend.

FARES to Fenchurch-street, 1st, 4/4, 7/-; 2nd, 3/- 5/-; 3rd, 2/2, 4/4.

Southern Outfall Sewer, situate at Crossness Point, about two miles across the marshes from Abbey Wood Station, North Kent line. Intending visitors will do well before taking their tickets to ascertain at what time their train will arrive, as the officials do not consider it necessary in issuing them to give any warning when the necessary change of trains at Woolwich Arsenal happens to involve a delay at that comfortable station of an hour and a half or so. Permission to view may be obtained at the Engineers' Department, Metropolitan Board of Works, Spring Gardens, S.W.

South Stoke, sometimes called Stoke Abbas, Oxfordshire, on the left bank, opposite Moulsford—a station on the Great Western Railway 48 miles from Paddington, from London 87 miles, from Oxford 24½ miles. Population (including Woodcote), 761. Soil, chiefly chalk. The Church of St. Andrew was restored and thoroughly repaired in 1858, and calls for no particular notice. The school, now under a Board, was endowed with twenty acres of land left by the Rev. Griffith Higgs, D.D., 1659, for the purpose. Among other charities are the following: Dr. Higgs also left £5 per annum for ever, in 1659, to be given annually to the poor; £3 to be given to six poor families "of South Stoke below the Hill," and £2 to six of "Woodcote." This charity is called "the doctor's gift." Augustine Knapp, in 1602, left 20s. a year for the poor. Henry Parslow, in 1675, left a great coat to one poor man of South Stoke, and to two poor men of Woodcote, to be given yearly. A sum of £300 (three per cent.) was recently left by Mr. W. Claxson, for the poor of Woodcote only.

PLACES OF WORSHIP.—St. Andrew's; and St. Leonard's, Woodcote.

POSTAL ARRANGEMENTS.—Letters through Wallingford. Mail from London, 7.30 a.m. Mail for London, 5.15 p.m. Nearest money-order, savings bank, and telegraph office, Goring; insurance, &c., Wallingford.

NEAREST *Bridges,* up, Wallingford 3¾ miles; down, Streatley, 2¼ miles. *Locks,* up, Wallingford 3½ miles; down, Cleeve 2 miles. *Ferries,* Moulsford and Little Stoke. *Railway Stations,* Goring and Moulsford, G.W.R.

FARES, Goring to Paddington, 1st, 7/10, 14/-; 2nd, 5/11, 10/6; 3rd, 3/9. Moulsford to Paddington: 1st, 8/5, 14/6; 2nd, 6/3, 11/-; 3rd, 3/11½.

Southwark Bridge has of late years been much improved by the introduction of a little colour into the painting of its ironwork arches, which were formerly all in solemn black, and had a very heavy appearance. The credit of being the handsomest iron bridge across the river rests between it and Blackfriars Bridge; and on the whole, though the latter is the more gorgeous, the former is perhaps the more striking. The length is 708 ft., or little more than half that of Waterloo. The arches, three in number, rest on stone piers; the centre arch having a span of 402 ft.—the longest ever attempted until the adoption of the tubular principle—and the two shore arches 210 ft. each. From the inconvenience of its approaches this handsome bridge has been from the first comparatively valueless.

Spit Buoy.—A 6-foot can-buoy, made of wood, and painted black. It is situated in Sea Reach, off Leigh, and inside Southend Pier to the westward. It marks 6 feet of water at low-water spring tide. It is moored with 6 fathom of chain. This buoy belongs to the Trinity House.

Staines, Middlesex, on the left bank, from Oxford 76 miles; from London 35½ miles. A station on the London and South Western Railway, about 19 miles from Waterloo; trains take about 45 minutes. The station is 10 minutes' walk from the Angel Hotel in the centre of the town; flys meet the trains. Population, about 5,000. Soil alluvial and gravel. Staines is a clean, well-built, comfortable and quiet little town, offering but few points of general interest. The river is here crossed by a handsome stone bridge of three arches, designed by Rennie. The parish church, St. Mary's, is situated near the river, at the end of Church-street, and is a modern erection of no particular interest save that the red brick tower, which was built in 1631, is the work of Inigo Jones, as is recorded on a stone let into the wall in 1791, and bearing the names of the then churchwardens, "Walter Molt and Daniel Endorb."

About a hundred yards to the left on leaving the churchyard is Duncroft, a good specimen of Elizabethan architecture, quaintly gabled and mullioned, standing in a pleasaunce remarkable for the beauty of its trees and shrubs. The house is sometimes attributed to an earlier period, and there is even a popular superstition that it was once a palace of King John. This, of course, is out of the question, although it may well be that the site was formally occupied by a royal residence. Local tradition has it that in this house or its predecessor the king slept on the night before Magna Charta was signed. There is an annual regatta of a local character under the auspices of the tradesmen of the town. A masonic lodge meets at the Angel Hotel. The 44th Company, 7th Administrative Battalion Middlesex R.V., have their headquarters in Thames-street. The Mechanics' Institute and Reading Room is in Church-street. The subscription for honorary members is £1 1s. per annum, for ordinary members 2s. per quarter, and the admission fee for casual visitors is 1d. per diem. Among the summer excitements are the daily visits of the coach, which here changes horses, on its way to and from Windsor ; but it must be confessed that the town is not strong in amusements.

Little of Staines is at present to be seen from the river, and that little is not interesting. The handsome Town Hall, the funds for the erection of which gradually accrued from a Town Hall Improvement Rate, is a great acquisition to the town itself, but unfortunately turns its back upon the river, the banks of which, except for an embanked wall and terrace at this point, still present the uninviting and untidy prospect which is so usual with Thames-side towns.

On approaching Staines from Bell Weir Lock, a channel to the left beyond the gas-works on the right bank leads to Tims's boat-house and landing-stage (ten minutes from the "Angel," via Church-street), where boats can be housed or hired, and where are kept the Royal Humane Society's drags and life-buoys. Here, also, is a ladies' swimming-bath ; subscription, 10s. per annum ; single bath,

4d. Lower down, past the bridge, is the Club landing-stage, and farther still, near the railway-bridge, is the comfortable "Packhorse Hotel," with a convenient landing-stage, excellent boat-house, and good accommodation for oarsmen. A footpath immediately opposite the "Packhorse" leads to the station (nine minutes): the High-street is distant four minutes' walk. There is also a landing-stage and boat-house at the "Swan Hotel" (the headquarters of the Staines Rowing Club) on the right bank.

The fishing at Staines is very uncertain; good takes are sometimes made, but these are the exception. Penton Hook, lower down, is a perfect trout preserve.

BANK.—Ashby and Co., High-street.

FIRE.—Brigade under Local Board : Captain, first officer, second officer, and engineer, nine gentlemen, and four working-men. Engine-house, Church-street.

HOTELS.—"Angel," "Railway," and "Packhorse" by the river.

PLACES OF WORSHIP.—St. Mary's (parish) ; St. Peter's Mission, Edghill-road ; Friends' Meeting House, and Baptist Congregational and Wesleyan Chapels.

POLICE.—Station, London-road.

POSTAL ARRANGEMENTS.—Post Office (money order, savings bank, telegraph, insurance office), High-street. Mails from London, 7 and 9.45 a.m., 4.30 and 5.45 p.m. ; Sunday, 7 a.m. Mails for London, 9.35 and 11.5 a.m., 4.30 and 8.30 p.m. ; Sunday, 7.50 p.m.

NEAREST Bridges, Staines ; up, Albert, 4¾ miles ; down, Chertsey, 3¾ miles. Locks, up, Bell Weir, 1¼ miles ; down, Penton Hook, 1½ mile. Ferry, Laleham. Railway Station, Staines.

FARES to London : 1st, 3/3, 5/- ; 2nd, 2/3, 3/6 ; 3rd, 1/7, 3/-.

Staines Rowing Club.—Subscription, 10/6. Colours, red and black. Boat-house, "Swan Hotel," near Staines Bridge (right bank).

Stanton Harcourt, a village in Oxfordshire, about two miles from Bablock Hithe Ferry, is distinguished in county history as the manor of the Harcourt family, to whom it was granted in the time of Henry I., and who resided here until late in the 17th century, when they removed to Nuneham Courtney. To students of English literature Stanton Harcourt is still more interesting as having been frequently visited by Pope, who finished the translation of the fifth book of "Homer" in the study which was allotted to his use by the Harcourt of that time—a circumstance which he recorded with a diamond on one of the panes of the window, a curious and interesting autograph still preserved at Nuneham Courtney. Of the old manor-house little now remains, except the tower, on the second floor of which Pope's study still exists, the view from it over the surrounding country being very charming. The kitchen of the old house also remains, and is almost unique, there being, it is said, but one other of the period in England. It is of enormous size, with prodigious arrangements for furnaces, but without a chimney, the smoke being allowed to escape by an ingenious arrangement of loopholes and shutters in the lofty roof. The present pretty house is built upon the site of the old lodge. The village itself is very charming, and possesses a remarkably handsome church with chancel, nave, transepts, and a fine square tower, at the north-east corner of which is a tourelle. There is excellent Norman work in the building, and some remarkably good windows, &c., of the Early English period. A fine old piscina in the chancel and the old rood screen are also interesting. On the south of the chancel is the private chapel of the Harcourt family, containing four altar tombs with recumbent figures representing distinguished members of the family, among them Sir Robert Harcourt, in plate armour and the mantle of the Garter, who died in 1490 ; another Sir Robert Harcourt, who fought at Bosworth ; George Simon, Earl Harcourt, who died in 1809 ; and Archbishop Harcourt, dated 1847. The chapel also contains a brass memorial tablet to members of the family, the list beginning with "Bernard the Dane," 876. In the south of the church is a curious marble mural monument, with half-length figures holding skulls, of Philip Harcourt and his wife, 1688, and a passable statue of Field Marshal Harcourt, 1830. Noticeable also is a large marble mural tablet with two allegorical female figures as supports.

Two well-preserved brasses will be found on the chancel floor, and in the chancel is an altar-tomb with a painted recumbent female figure ; and another, which probably also at one time had a figure under its canopy. Among the minor celebrities of Stanton Harcourt are John Hewitt and Sarah Drew, two virtuous villagers, who, just before the day fixed for their marriage, in 1717, were struck dead together by lightning. This incident greatly exercised the sentimental feelings of Lady Mary Wortley Montague and Mr. Pope. The lovers are buried in Stanton Harcourt churchyard, and on the south side of the church is a tablet bearing the following epitaph from the pen of Pope himself, whose genius would appear to have somewhat deserted him during its composi-tion :

Think not by rigorous judgment seized
    A pair so faithful could expire ;
Victims so pure Heaven saw well pleas'd,
    And snatch'd them in celestial fire.

Live well and fear no sudden fate ;
    When God calls virtue to the grave,
Alike 'tis justice soon or late,
    Mercy alike to kill and save.

Virtue unmoved can hear the call,
And face the flash that melts the ball.

Some half-mile from Stanton Harcourt are two large stones called the "Devil's Quoits," which are said, on doubtful authority, to have been set up to commemorate a great battle fought in 614 between the Britons and the Saxons under that Cynegil who was subsequently baptized by Birinus at Dorchester.

The soil of Stanton Harcourt is gravel, and the population of the village numbers between 600 and 700.

POSTAL ARRANGEMENTS.—Post Office in the village (nearest money order, savings bank, and telegraph office, Eynsham).

NEAREST *Railway Station*, Eynsham, about 3 miles (*which see*).

Steamboats.—The following particulars have been kindly furnished for our edition of 1885 by Mr. Edgar Shand, the General Manager of the London Steam-boat Co., Limited, Adelaide-buildings, London Bridge.

PRICE LIST OF BOATS FOR PRIVATE EXCURSION PARTIES. —The prices include pier dues, except at Blackwall, North Woolwich, all piers below except Rosherville Pier, Woolwich, and Teddington Lock dues.

The DOWN RIVER BOATS, from Westminster to Gravesend or Rosherville, vary in their carrying capacity from the *Alexandra*, which can take 1048 passengers, to the *Swift*, with 332. For the boats carrying over 1000 passengers, the charge for any day except Saturday, Sunday, or Monday, is £50, and on Mondays and Saturdays £55. The next class (900 passengers) £40 and £45; the next (610 to 640 passengers) £30 and £35; the next (546) £20 and £25; the next (454) £18 and £20; the next (417 to 437) £16 and £18; and the smallest (332 to 405) £14 and £15.

The boats are licensed to carry a smaller number of persons between Westminster and Southend or Sheerness, their carrying capacity and prices being as follows : 556 passengers, any day except Saturday, Sunday, or Monday, £55; Mondays and Saturdays, £60; 563, £55 and £60; 477, £45 and £50; 329 to 344, £35 and £40; 291, £25 and £30; 250, £21 and £25; 203 to 221, £18 and £20. Below 200, £17 and £18.

Between London Bridge and Clacton-on-Sea, the price on any day except Saturday, Sunday, and Monday, is, up to 439 passengers, £65, and below 300, £50.

UP RIVER BOATS.—From Chelsea or London Bridge to Gravesend or Rosherville, the prices are, for any day except Saturday, Sunday, or Monday, up to 453 passengers, £16, and on Mondays and Saturdays £18; between 351 and 372 passengers, £14 and £15; and between 322 and 345, £10 and £11.

For the same sized boats the charges are, between Chelsea or London Bridge and Woolwich, £12, £11, and £10; between London Bridge and Kew or Richmond, £14, £13, and £12; and between London Bridge and Hampton Court, £18.

SPECIAL NOTICE. — N.B. Above Gravesend, children not in arms count as adults; below that station, two children under twelve count as one adult. Parties engaging boats are informed that they will be held responsible for any fine or other penalty for which the Company may be held liable for any infringement of this notice.

No vessels will be let for excursions on Sundays, General Holidays, or days of Sailing or Rowing Matches, except by special agreement. No vessel will be allowed to leave Sheerness after 4.30 p.m.; Gravesend after 6.30 p.m. ; Woolwich or Greenwich after 7.30 p.m.; Kew after 6.30 p.m.; Hampton after 5.30 p.m.

Parties engaging a boat are also informed that tickets are not allowed to be sold on or near the piers, either before or on the day of the Excursion, nor for Rowing Matches.

ROWING MATCHES.—To accompany Match in afternoon from London to Erith with 200 passengers, £11 ; Greenwich or Woolwich to Erith only, with 200 passengers, £11. If required for excursion after Match, £12. Putney to Mortlake from London Bridge, £10 ; if the boat proceeds to Kew, £13, including landing ; or to Richmond, £14. The numbers to be limited to 200 on any one boat.

LIST OF PIERS AND PLACES AT WHICH THE COMPANY'S STEAMBOATS CALL.

Hampton Court.—For the Palace and Bushey-park.
Teddington Lock and Petersham.
Richmond.—For hill, park, and boating.
Kew.—Gardens.
Hammersmith.—Metropolitan & District Railway.
Putney.—For Fulham (Metropolitan Railway Station).
Chelsea and Cadogan.—For Exhibition.
Battersea Park.
   Do. (*Railway Pier*). — For Albert Palace and London, Brighton, and South Coast Railway.
Pimlico.—For Victoria.
Millbank.—Penitentiary.
Lambeth.—For Kennington-road, Princess-street, the Palace, and St. Thomas's Hospital.
Westminster.—For Parliament Houses, District Railway, Abbey, Parks, and Public Offices.
Charing Cross. — For Charing Cross, Regent-street, St. Martin's-lane, Pall Mall, and Oxford-street.

Waterloo,—For Somerset House, Strand, Gaiety, Lyceum, Drury-lane, Covent Garden, and Savoy Theatres.

Temple. — For Strand, Chancery-lane, Fleet-street, the Law Courts, &c.

Blackfriars Bridge.—For London, Chatham, and Dover Railway, the District Line, Aldersgate-street, Fleet-street, and Bridge-street.

St. Paul's.—For St. Paul's, Blackfriars, Ludgate-hill, Newgate-street, General Post Office, &c.

London Bridge.—For the City, Cheapside, Bank, Royal Exchange, King William-street, Thames-Street, Coal Exchange, Billingsgate, The Tower, and Company's Office, 2, Adelaide-buildings.

London Bridge (Surrey Side).—For the Borough, Guy's Hospital, London Bridge Railways, and Crystal Palace.

Cherry-gardens.—For Rotherhithe, Southwark-park, the East London Railway, &c.

The Tunnel.—For Wapping, London and St. Katharine Docks, the East London Railway for the Crystal Palace, &c.

Globe-stairs.—For Rotherhithe, Surrey Commercial-docks, &c.

Limehouse.—For Limehouse and West India-docks.

West India-dock.—Close to the dock entrance.

Commercial-dock.—For the Surrey and Commercial Docks, Deptford, &c.

Millwall.—For Millwall-docks and upper part of the Isle of Dogs.

Greenwich.—For Greenwich Naval College, the Park and Observatory, Naval Museum, Blackheath, Kidbrooke, Lee, Lewisham, &c.

Isle of Dogs.—For the Docks and North Greenwich Railway to Fenchurch-st.

Cubitt Town.—For Poplar, Mr. Samuda's Yard, and the lower part of the Isle of Dogs.

Blackwall.—For the East and West India-docks, Victoria-docks, the Blackwall Railway, and the North London Railway, for all stations on the North London District.

Charlton.— For the Dockyard, Barracks, Rotunda, Common, Wood-street, West Woolwich, Shooter's-hill, and Charlton. The Marine Society's Ship *Warspite.*

Woolwich.—For the Royal Arsenal, Barracks, East and North Woolwich, Plumstead, Artillery Barracks, and Shooter's-hill.

North Woolwich.—The boats call at this pier during the summer with passengers for the gardens.

Rosherville.—Gardens, Northfleet, New Thames Yacht Club.

Gravesend.—Town Pier, Milton, Tilbury.

Southend.—For Shoebury.

Sheerness.—For Chatham boats, Queenborough.

Clacton-on-Sea.—(Royal Hotel), Great and Little Holland.

Walton-on-Naze.—(Dorling's and Clifton Hotels), Thorpe, Weeley.

Harwich.—For Dovercourt and Felixstowe.

Ipswich.—Trains for Norwich, Yarmouth, Lowestoft, and all stations on Great Eastern Railway.

Smoking abaft the funnel or in the chief cabin is strictly prohibited ; no passengers are allowed on the bridge-boards, and passengers are particularly warned not to sit or stand on the paddle-boxes ; all dogs charged for at the same rate as passengers ; all luggage must be paid for ; refreshments are provided on board the vessels at fixed rates, according to an authorised scale, a copy of which may be seen on board ; children under three years of age are conveyed free—above three years and under twelve years, at one-half the ordinary fares, except in the 1*d.,* 2*d.,* 3*d.* fares. By the Act 25 and 26 Vict. c. 63, the company refuse to convey intoxicated passengers, and should such person attempt to go on board after his fare (if he has taken his ticket) has been offered to be returned to him, he renders himself liable to a penalty of 4*cs.*

HOURS OF STARTING.

Up.—LONDON BRIDGE, CITY AND SURREY SIDE (connecting the Brighton, Crystal Palace, South London, and

South Eastern Railways, with the Metropolitan, District, and Chatham and Dover Railways), TO CHELSEA.
—Summer, from 9 a.m. to 8 p.m. Winter, from 9 a.m. to 5 p.m., every 10 minutes.
Down.—CHELSEA TO LONDON BRIDGE.
—Summer, from 8 a.m. to 7 p.m. Winter, from 8 a.m. to 4 p.m. every 10 minutes.
Express boat at 9.5, calling at Cadogan, Battersea-park, Nine Elms, Westminster, Temple, to London-bridge.

Up.—WOOLWICH TO WESTMINSTER.—Every half hour.

Woolwich	...... At the hours and half-hours.		
Charlton	.... About	5 & 35 m. past hours.	
Blackwall	...... ,,	15 to & 15	,, ,,
Cubitt-town	.... ,,	7 to & 23	,, ,,

(In Summer, from 8 a.m. to 7 p.m. Winter, from 8 a.m. to 4 p.m.)

Greenwich	.... About hours and half-hours.		
Millwall	.... ,,	5 & 35 m. past hours.	
Commercial-dock	,,	10 & 40	,, ,,
West India-dock	,,	14 & 44	,, ,,
Limehouse	.... ,,	17 & 47	,, ,,
Globe-stairs	.... ,,	20 & 50	,, ,,
Tunnel	.... ,,	24 & 53	,, ,,
Cherry-gardens	. ,,	26 & 55	,, ,,
London-bridge	.. ,,	13 & 35	,, ,,
Blackfriars	.... ,,	8 & 41	,, ,,
Temple	.... ,,	11 & 44	,, ,,
Charing Cross	.. ,,	14 & 47	,, ,,
Westminster	.... Arrive about 17 & 50 ,,		,,

Down.—WESTMINSTER TO WOOLWICH.—Every half hour, from 8.10 a.m. to 7.40 p.m. in the Summer, and from 8.40 a.m. to 4.40 p.m. in Winter.

Westminster	....	10 & 40 m. past hours.	
Charing Cross	.. About	15 & 45	,, ,,
Temple	...... ,,	17 & 47	,, ,,
Blackfriars	...... ,,	20 & 50	,, ,,
London-bridge	.. ,,	hours and half hours.	
Cherry-gardens	.. ,,	5 & 35 m. past hours.	
Tunnel	.... ,,	8 & 38	,, ,,
Globe-stairs	.... ,,	12 & 42	,, ,,
Limehouse	...... ,,	15 & 45	,, ,,
West India-dock	,,	18 & 47	,, ,,
Commercial-dock	,,	22 & 51	,, ,,
Millwall-dock	.. ,,	27 & 56	,, ,,
Greenwich	...... ,,	hours and half hours.	
Cubitt-town	.... ,,	3 & 33 m. past hours.	
Blackwall	...... ,,	10 & 40	,, ,,
Charlton	.... ,,	17 & 47	,, ,,
Woolwich	...... Arr. about 3 & 33 ,,		,,

For all piers above Westminster passengers must change boats at London-bridge or Westminster, and at Blackfriars for the District Railway.

TABLE OF SINGLE FARES.

	Sundays	
Nine Elms and all piers between, to Waterloo	1d.	2d.
Lambeth, Westminster, Charing Cross, &c., to London-bridge ..	1d.	2d.
Lambeth, Westminster, Charing Cross, the Temple, and Blackfriars to or from Cherry-gardens and Tunnel	2d.	3d.
	Aft	Deck
Lambeth and Westminster, to or from Globe-stairs, Limehouse, and West India-dock	3d.	4d.
Lambeth and Westminster, to or from Commercial-dock, Millwall, and Greenwich	4d.	6d.
Lambeth and Westminster, to or from Cubitt Town, Blackwall, Charlton, and Woolwich	5d.	6d.

	Sundays	
Chelsea to London-bridge	2d.	4d.
Chelsea to Tunnel ..	3d.	
,, West India-dock	4d.	
,, Greenwich..	5d.	
,, Woolwich ..	6d.	

(No thro' booking Sunday or Holidays)

	Aft	Deck
London-bridge to or from Cherry-gardens or the Tunnel	1d.	2d.
London-bridge to or from Globe-stairs, Limehouse, or West India-dock	2d.	3d.
London-bridge to or from Commercial-dock, Millwall, and Greenwich	3d.	4d.
London-bridge to or from Cubitt Town, Blackwall, Charlton, and Woolwich	4d.	8d.
Cherry-gardens to or from Tunnel or Globe-stairs	1d.	2d.
Cherry-gardens or Tunnel to or from Limehouse, West India-dock, or Commercial-dock	2d.	3d.
Cherry-gardens or Tunnel to or from Millwall and Greenwich ..	3d.	4d.
Cherry-gardens or Tunnel to or from Cubitt Town, Blackwall, and Woolwich	4d.	8d.
Limehouse, West India-dock, or Commercial-dock to or from Millwall..	2d.	3d.
Limehouse, West India-dock, or Com.-dock to or from Greenwich .	3d.	4d.
Limehouse, West India-dock, or Commercial-dock to or from Cubitt Town, Blackwall, Charlton, or Woolwich.. .. — ..	4d.	8d.
Limehouse to or from West India-dock	1d.	3d.
Globe-stairs to or from Limehouse..	1d.	2d.
,, ,, Cherry-grdns.	1d.	2d.
West India-dock to or from Commercial-dock..	1d.	2d.
Millwall to or from Greenwich ..	2d.	2d.
,, ,, Blackwall, Charlton, or Woolwich	4d.	8d.
Woolwich to or from Charlton ..	1d.	2d.
Battersea Park and all piers between, to Lambeth..	1d.	2d.

Steam Launches are too often the curse of the river. Driving along at an excessive rate of speed, with an utter disregard to the comfort or necessities of anglers, oarsmen, and boating-parties, the average steam-launch engineer is an unmitigated nuisance. There are some owners who show consideration for other people, but their number, unfortunately, is very limited, and for the most part the launches are navigated with a recklessness which is simply shameful. Perhaps the worst offenders are the people who pay their £5 5s. a day for the hire of a launch, and whose idea of a holiday is the truly British notion of getting over as much ground as possible in a given time. Parties of this kind, especially after the copious lunch which is one of the features of the day's outing, stimulate the engineer to fresh exertions, and appear to enjoy themselves considerably as they contemplate the anxiety and discomfort of the occupants of the punts and rowing-ooats which are left floundering helplessly in their wash. Should there be ladies on board a boat in difficulties, their terror proportionately enhances the amusement of these steam-launch 'Arries. Unfortunately, these excursionists are not alone in their offences against courtesy and good behaviour. Too many people who ought to know very much better keep them in countenance by their selfish example. In 1883 an Act of Parliament, 46 & 47 Vict. cap. 70, was passed to make special provision with respect to steam launches navigating the Thames above Kew Bridge. Under this Act steam launches and their owners must be registered, and any owner or person in charge of any steam launch in course of navigation under steam or any other mechanical power is bound to produce the certificate of registration to any officer of the Conservators, under a penalty of 40s. for non-compliance. The fine for using a steam-launch without certificate is not less than £5 and not more than £10 for every day on which the offence is committed. The number of the launch is to be conspicuously displayed, and the owner, in default, is liable to a penalty not exceeding £5. Steam launches being navigated after sunset and before sunrise are to display, at least four feet above the hull, a bright white light behind a glass shade or slide,

upon which the registered number of the launch must be conspicuously painted in black figures, as well as a green light on the starboard side and a red light on the port side. These lights must be of such a character as to be visible on a dark night with a clear atmosphere at a distance of at least one mile, and in default of the proper carrying out of this clause the person in charge is liable to a penalty not exceeding £5. Every person who knowingly causes or permits to be concealed the registered name or number of any steam launch, while such steam launch is used for the purpose of navigating the Thames above Kew Bridge, shall be liable to a penalty not exceeding £5. If complaint is made to the Conservators as to the navigation of any registered steam launch, the owner is bound to give all information in his power as to the person who was, at any particular time, in charge of the launch, and, should he fail to do so, is liable to a penalty not exceeding £20. Section 15 is particularly deserving the attention of boating men and anglers, and runs as follows :

"Every vessel navigating the Thames shall be navigated with care and caution and at a speed and in such a manner as not to endanger the lives of persons or the safety of other vessels or moorings or cause damage to any vessel or moorings or to the banks of the Thames or other property.

"Special care and caution shall be used in navigating vessels when passing vessels of all kinds, especially those of the smaller classes and such as are employed in dredging or removing sunken vessels or other obstructions.

"If the safety of any vessel or moorings or of any persons is endangered or damage is caused thereto or to the banks of the Thames by a passing vessel, the onus shall lie upon the person in charge of such passing vessel to show that she was navigated with care and caution and at such speed and in such manner as directed by this section.

"The person in charge of any vessel who in navigating such vessel contravenes or fails to observe the provisions of this section shall for every such offence be liable to a penalty not exceeding twenty pounds."

It will thus be seen that the public has now been armed with ample powers to protect themselves, and that it will be their own fault if the Editor of the DIC-TIONARY OF THE THAMES does not find it necessary in revising the book for the season of 1885 to cancel the description of the average steam launch engineer with which this article begins.

It is understood that the owners of steam launches have formed an influential society to protect each other against possible groundless complaints, and also to keep an eye on such of their body as misbehave themselves. With the latter object the public will cordially agree, and there can be no objection to the former if it is honourably carried out.

Strangers' Home for Asiatics, Africans, and South Sea Islanders, West India Dock-road; E.

Streatley, Berkshire, on the right bank, from London 84¼ miles, from Oxford 26¾ miles. Population, 650. Soil, chalk and loam.

This beautifully-situated village lies at a bend of the river at the feet of the great chalk downs of Berkshire, and faces its twin village Goring (a station on the G.W.R., 45 miles from Paddington), with which it is connected by a long bridge (toll 1d.). It is a very convenient resting-place for boating-parties, there being excellent boat-houses at the "Swan Hotel," and possessing also rare attractions for the artist and lover of peaceful English riverside scenery.

From the bridge beautiful views are obtained in all directions, the rushing weirs and wooded hills down stream forming a remarkable contrast to the quiet rushy reach above, and, on either hand the villages nestle picturesquely in the many-tinted shade of venerable trees. At few places on the river is the combination of almost every variety of Thames scenery so striking and so pleasant as at Streatley and Goring.

The village of Streatley probably derives its name from the Roman Road, which crossed the Thames at the fords which occur here, where the river strikes the flinty beds of the chalk formation. The chalk hills of the Berkshire Downs no doubt once joined the Chilterns on the Oxfordshire side, and, forming a barrier, produced a lake extending for a great distance, until its waters, boring through the chalk, drained the upper valley of the

Thames, and, in fact, made it a river. Roman remains have been occasionally found here.

Like all the parishes bordering on the Thames, it runs back a considerable distance from the water, giving to the inhabitants all the privileges of water frontage and meadows, cornland, woodland, and higher pasturage.

The earliest notice of the place is in the cartulary of the Abbey of Abingdon, which recites a gift of land at "Stretlea," by Ina, King of Wessex, in A.D. 687.

At the time of the Conqueror, we find from Domesday Book that the manor, which had been held by the Saxon Esgar in the time of Edward the Confessor, had been transferred to the Norman follower of William, Geoffrey de Manville, and that a priest named Wibert held of him the church of the manor, together with some land and four acres of meadow worth 50s. From that time we pass to February, A.D. 1215, just four months before the signing of the Magna Charta, and we find the tithes being assigned by Herbert Pone, Bishop of Sarum; the great tithes to the monastery of Saffron Walden, the small tithes with a redecimation of the great tithes to the perpetual endowment of the Vicarage. To the Vicar was assigned at the same time one manse situate at the waterside, and about two acres of land adjoining it. Later on a small Dominican priory was attached to the church; on the site there was a house which, until the enclosure of the parish in 1817, was standing, and called the Rectory. The great tithes on the dissolution were given to the Chapter of Westminster, but afterwards in some unexplained manner found their way into lay hands, and the small remainder of them at the enclosure of the parish was commuted into land, as were the small tithes of the Vicarage.

The church seems to have been built under the direction of the same Bishop Pone who endowed it, as it has the same date and many of the features, as regards details, of the great cathedral church of Sarum. It is given generally upon no extant authority as St. Mary's, but there is better evidence to show (viz. the time at which the village feast is always held) that it should be called St. John the Baptist's. It is noticeable for a good square tower, and for the many magnificent trees which surround it, and contains some good brasses. One, with a figure of a lady in a ruff, is on the vestry wall; one in the south aisle, dated 1603, records the fact that the deceased had six sons and eleven daughters; another immediately underneath has on it two figures, and is in excellent preservation; and one at the end of the north aisle, with full-length figure of a lady, commemorates the death of Elizabeth Osbarn, 1440.

Among the notable excursions from Streatley is Basildon Park, distant about 2 miles, where there is a collection of pictures well deserving a visit. About the same distance, among the Berkshire hills, lies Aldworth, the church of which contains a remarkable collection of monuments of the De la Beche family, respecting which many odd legends are still current among the natives. A very aged yew, measuring some 28 feet round, which stands in the churchyard, and is supposed to be even older than the very ancient church itself, is among the Aldworth sights.

For the fishing, see GORING.

INNS.—"The Bull," up the village; "The Swan," on the river.

PLACE OF WORSHIP.—St. Mary's.

POLICE.—A constable lives in the village.

POSTAL ARRANGEMENTS. — Letters from Reading. Mails from London, 6.30 a.m. and noon; Sunday, 6.30 a.m. Mails for London, 9.35 a.m., 6.30 p.m. Sunday, 6.30 p.m. Nearest money order, savings bank, and telegraph office, Goring.

NEAREST *Bridge*, Streatley; up, Wallingford 6 miles; down, Whitchurch 4 miles. *Lock*, Cleeve ¾ mile; down, Whitchurch 4 miles. *Ferries*, Moulsford and Basildon. *Railway Station*, Goring, G.W.R.

FARES, Goring to Paddington: 1st, 7/10, 14/-; 2nd, 5/11, 9/6; 3rd, 3/9.

Sturgeon occasionally come up the Thames, but they were never numerous in this river. Provision was made in ancient Acts excepting them from the vulgar fate of other fish, and in the instructions to the City water-bailiffs for the time-being orders were issued that the sturgeon "was not to be secreted," and that all royal fishes taken within the jurisdiction of the Lord Mayor of London, as

namely, whales, sturgeons, porpoises, and such-like, should be made known, and the name or names of all such persons as shall take them shall be sent in to the Lord Mayor of London for the time being, The sturgeon therefore is always, when taken, sent direct to grace the table of majesty. The presence of mud (if it is *clean* mud) does not, from their hog-like habit of ploughing up the deposit of the stream, form any obstacle to their progress into fresh water, nor does the latter appear to affect them, even immediately from their presence in the sea. They have never been known to be taken by line and bait, but they often get entangled in the nets of the fishermen, which they greatly mutilate, from their amazing strength, in their efforts to escape.

The flesh of the sturgeon is looked upon with suspicion little short of aversion by some persons, but it, according to the parts submitted to the operations of the cook, may be rendered into the choicest of dishes—one portion simulating the tenderest of veal, another that of the sapid succulence of chicken, and a third establishing its reputation to a claim to most of the gastronomic virtues of the flesh of many acceptable fish in combination. The great *chefs*, Francatelli and Ude, used to aver that there were one hundred different ways of rendering sturgeon fit for an emperor; and Soyer would boast that he had added two more methods of its culinary preparation to these apparently exhaustive receipts.

Sufferance Wharves.—(*See* LEGAL QUAYS.)

Sunbury, Middlesex, on the left bank, from London 26½ miles, from Oxford 85 miles, a station on the Thames Valley branch of the South Western Railway, 16½ miles from Waterloo; the trains average about three-quarters of an hour. The station is nearly 1½ mile from the river. Population, 3,368. Soil, gravel and brick earth. A village with a long street (Thames-street) straggling untidily along the bank, with a few shops, and several excellent houses; at right angles to it, to the eastward, runs French-street, a very pleasant neighbourhood. In ancient records, Sunbury is called Sunnabyri, and Sunneberie. Lysons supposes the name to be derived from the Saxon words, *Sunna*, the sun, and *Byrie*, a town. There was a church here in the time of Edward the Confessor, then belonging to the Abbots of Westminster. It was afterwards transferred to the Bishop of London, when the following arrangements were made: The inhabitants of Sunbury had to provide money for supplying the tallow candles for the High Altar of St. Paul's, and a minor canon had to sing a musical mass (*missa cum cantu*) every day. At the end of the year, if there was any surplus in the funds to provide the candles, it was to be spent for the purchase of the vestments of the minor canon who sang the mass. The church was pulled down in the reign of George II., and another built according to the taste of that period. It was reconstructed in 1856, a new Byzantine chancel and aisles were built, the windows altered throughout, and a handsome western porch erected. The upper portion of the tower remains the same, but a plan for its future reconstruction hangs up in the tower basement, which will, it is hoped, be carried out at some future time. Several charitable bequests have been made to the church, mostly for the distribution of bread, and two for keeping the tombs, &c., in decent order. There is little of importance in the church itself, which has been decorated in the florid Salviati mosaic style. Under the south-west gallery, partly concealed, is a mural monument to Richd. Billingsley, 1682, " of St. Martin's, Wistminster, who was unhappily drowned." There is a good marble font.

Near to Sunbury is the new and pretty racecourse constructed by the Kempton Park Club, at Kempton, formerly called Kenyngton. The estate is upwards of 300 acres in extent. The mile course is nearly flat, and 30 yards wide at the narrowest point. The inner course is about 1½ mile in length; the half-mile course is straight. Races take place at frequent intervals.

Sunbury is reached from the Surrey shore by means of a ferry, which crosses the weir stream from the Ferry Hotel to the boat-houses on the lock island.

Trout are taken at the weir; dace and chub with the fly; barbel, roach, and perch are pretty plentiful.

The Thames Angling Preservation Society has a rearing pond and stream close to Sunbury Lock, where the young trout are placed from the hatching apparatus, and remain until they are sufficiently large to be placed in the Thames.

INNS.—" Ferry," " Magpie," " Weir," and " Flower Pot" near river.

PLACES OF WORSHIP.—St. Mary's; a Roman Catholic Church; and Congregational and Wesleyan Chapels.

POLICE. — Metropolitan Police-station (T Division), Thames-st.

POSTAL ARRANGEMENTS.—Post Office (money order, telegraph, and savings bank), Thames-street. Mails from London, 7 and 9 a.m., 7.30 p.m.; Sunday, 7 a.m. Mails for London, 9.10 a.m., 2.50 and 7.50 p.m.; Sunday, 8.50 a.m.

NEAREST *Bridges*; up, Walton, rather more than 1 mile; down, Hampton Court, 3¼ miles. *Locks*, Sunbury; up, Shepperton 3½ miles; down, Molesey 3 miles. *Ferry* and *Railway Station*, Sunbury.

FARES.—To Waterloo: 1st, 2/6, 3/-; 2nd, 2/-, 2/6; 3rd, 1/4, 2/3.

Surbiton.—A suburb of Kingston, has grown immensely of late years. Some of the best houses face the river, and it contains what is generally known as the villa residence in every size, and at almost all rents. It is very convenient of access from London, being on the main line of the London and South-Western Railway, and affords excellent facilities for boating, the distance between locks here being nearly five miles. Along the riverside the authorities have constructed an esplanade, with gardens, which extends from the Waterworks some distance towards Kingston, and affords a fine promenade. From the ferry opposite Raven Island, by Grove-road, nearly opposite to the railway station, is ten minutes' walk.

The headquarters of the well-known Kingston Rowing Club and Thames Sailing Club (*both of which see*) are at Surbiton, the boat-houses of the former being on Raven Island, and of the latter on the right bank, a little above the island. Five minutes from the river are the Surbiton Reading Rooms, Library, and Recreation Ground. Here, in addition to library, &c., is one of the fastest cinder-paths in England for bicycle-riding, a cricket ground, bowling green, lawn tennis, &c. The annual subscription is £1 1s. The churches are all modern.

buildings of no particular interest. There is also a Surbiton Club (entrance £2 ; subscription £5 ; election by ballot in committee : two black balls exclude).

For CAB FARES, &c., &c., *see* KING-STON.

BANKS.—London and County, Victoria-terrace ; London and Provincial, Victoria-road.

FIRE. — Surbiton Fire Brigade, St. James's-road (under control of Surbiton Improvement Commissioners) : Super-intendent and 8 members. Fire Escape Brigade : Superintendent and 3 members.

HOSPITAL.— Cottage, York Villa, Vic-toria-road. Patients are required to pay not less than 2s. 6d., or more than 10s. 6d. per week.

PLACES OF WORSHIP.—St. Mark's, Christ Church, and St. Andrew's (Chapel of Ease to St. Mark's) ; The Roman Catholic Church of the Archangel St. Raphael ; and Baptist, Congregational, Primitive Methodist, and Wesleyan Chapels.

POSTAL ARRANGEMENTS.—Post Office (money order, savings bank, and tele-graph). Mails from London, 7.30 and 9.45 a.m., 2.45, 5.45 and 8.30 p.m. Sun-day, 8 a.m. Mails for London, 7.30 and 10 a.m., 4.20 and 9 p.m. Sunday, 7 p.m.

NEAREST *Bridges* (from Messenger's Island), up, Hampton 2 miles ; down, Kingston ¾ mile. *Locks*, up, Molesey 2¼ miles ; down, Teddington 2½ miles. *Ferry* at the Island. *Railway Stations*, Surbiton and Kingston.

FARES.—From Kingston or Surbiton to Waterloo : 1st, 2/-, 2/6 ; 2nd, 1/6, 2/-; 3rd, 1/-, 1/8.

Surly Hall.—A tavern well known to all oarsmen, and especially dear to every Etonian. It is on the Berks bank, about half a mile above Boveney Lock. The house has recently been renovated, and affords reasonably good accommodation. During the summer season the Eights of the Eton Boat Club pay periodical visits to Surly, on which occasions great havoc is wrought amongst the ducks and green peas. In a meadow opposite are laid out the tables for the feast at the annual cele-bration of the birthday of George III., the 4th of June, the great event, since the abolition of Montem and Election Saturday, in the Eton boy's year.

Surrey Commercial Dock (The) is situated on the peninsula between the Lower Pool and Limehouse Reach. Dock House, 106, Fenchurch-street, E.C. The best mode of approach to the Surrey Commercial Dock System is by the Deptford-road Station of the East London Railway from Liverpool-street.

Sutton Courtney, Berkshire, on the right bank, a village at the weir just above Sutton Bridges, formerly belonged to the Abbots of Abingdon, and was given by Henry II. to Reginald Cour-tenaye. Population, about 1,100. "The Abbey" is an interesting building of the Gothic period, and formerly belonged to the Abbots of Abingdon. The Manor House dates from Edward III., and con-tains some very interesting architectural details. The Church of All Saints is a good Gothic building, with square tower, and is remarkable for the width of its nave. It has a good perpendicular screen and some fine windows of the same period. On a parvise over the south porch are the Courtenaye arms. The village contains many curious and pic-turesque cottages and farmhouses of the Elizabethan period, with carved gables and barge-boards.

POSTAL ARRANGEMENTS. — Nearest money order and telegraph office, Abing-don, Mails from London, 7.30 a.m. ; Mails for London, 7.10 p.m.

NEAREST Railway Station, Culham (*which see*).

Swan-upping.—Centuries ago swans were considered royal birds. In the reign of Edward IV. no one was permitted to keep swans who did not possess a freehold of at least five marks annual value, ex-cept the king's son, and an Act of Henry VII. condemned robbers of eggs to a year's imprisonment, and a fine at the will of the sovereign. As a mark of favour the king sometimes granted to an individual or a corporation "a game of swans," and along with it the right of a swan mark. Thus the Dyers' and the Vintners' companies have possessed, from time immemorial, the privilege of owning and marking swans. The reason why the right was granted to them was pro-bably a desire on the part of the Crown to prevent trouble arising between the Royal Swanherd and the Thames Con-servancy. The date of the granting of the privilege is not certain. Swans of a certain age not marked may be claimed by the Crown, and these birds are known as " clear-billed." The marks were changed in the year 1878, after the Society for the Prevention of Cruelty to Animals had prosecuted, unsuccessfully, the swanherds employed by the Crown and the two City companies. The marking, or " upping " as it is technically called, is effected by cutting the upper mandible of the bird, and stopping the slight bleeding with pitch. The new system of marking, which omits at least half the old number of cuts, consists of two diamonds on royal birds, two small nicks on either side of the mandible on birds belonging to the Vintners' Company, and one nick cut on the right side of birds belonging to the Dyers'. The two nicks on the Vintners' birds gave rise to the wellknown tavern sign, " The Swan with Two Necks." The process of Swan-upping is conducted with much ceremony. It takes place in July or August, when the markers of the three owners take count of all swans in the river, and mark the clearbilled birds which have reached maturity. The work is frequently watched by dignitaries of the companies from saloon steamers, and the occasion serves as no bad excuse for a picnic. A few years ago a great cry was raised by anglers and the inhabitants of the banks of the Thames, that the swans were terrible enemies to the fish, that they haunted all the spawning grounds, and swallowed the eggs till they could eat no longer. Mr. Buckland was accordingly consulted by the Lord Chamberlain on the subject; and, after his analysis, it was proved that the statements of the anglers were exaggerated, for the swans did not devour the spawn by preference, but only incidentally whilst feeding on the vegetable matter and river growths to which the spawn is frequently attached. The Crown, nevertheless, has no desire to increase the number of birds on the river, which is maintained at about 500 grown birds and cygnets, thereby limiting the total to 610, allowing 65 to the Dyers and 45 to the Vintners.

Swimming.—The races for the amateur championship of Great Britain took place, originally in the Thames, but in 1874 the *venue* was changed to Hendon. Mr. Horace Davenport was for six years

amateur champion, and on his retirement, Mr. J. P. Taylor won, and still holds, the title. The Lords and Commons', Cup, annually swum for in the Thames, from Westminster to Putney, was a challenge cup, value £30, to be held three years. It was won outright by Mr. Horace Davenport. The Challenge Cup, given by the Floating Baths' Company, course, Putney to Floating Baths, is now held by G. Bell, the halfmile amateur champion.

The following clubs, excepting the Otter, hold their principal race—the captaincy race—in the Thames :

AMATEUR.—Meet at the Fitzroy Bath, Tottenham-court-road, on Friday evening. Subscription, 10s. 6d. per annum.
ATLANTIC.—Meet at the City of London Bath, Golden-lane.
BOROUGH OF FINSBURY.—Meet at the Central Bath, St. John-street, on Tuesday and Thursday evenings.
CAMDEN.—Meet at St. Pancras Bath, Camden Town, on Thursday evening. Subscription, 1s. per month.
CYGNUS.—Meet at Addington-square Bath, Camberwell, on Tuesday and Thursday evenings. Subscription, 10s. per annum.
EAST LONDON.—Meet at Poplar Bath, East India-road, on Tuesday evening. Subscription, 1s. per month.
ILEX.—Meet at Floating Baths, Charing Cross, on Monday evening.
OTTER.—Meet at the Marylebone Baths during the season. Captaincy swum for in the Serpentine.
OXFORD (UNIVERSITY).—Oxford.
PACIFIC.—Meet at Central Bath, St. John's-street, on Monday evening.
SANDRINGHAM.—Meet at Metropolitan Bath, Shepherdess-walk, on Tuesday evening.
SOUTH LONDON.—Meet at Lambeth Bath, Westminster Bridge-road, on Wednesday evening. Subscription, 1s. per month.
SOUTH-EAST LONDON.—Meet at Victoria Bath, Peckham, on Tuesday evening. Subscription, 2s. 6d. per annum.
SURBITON.—Meet at Raven's Eyot, Surbiton, during the season.
THAMES.—Meet at Putney during the season.
WEST LONDON.—Meet at Fitzroy Bath, Tottenham-court-road, on Tuesday evening. Subscription, 2s. per quarter.

WHITEHALL.—Meet at Floating Bath, Victoria Embankment, on Tuesday evening.

ZEPHYR.—Meet at Fitzroy Bath, Tottenham-court-road, on Wednesday evening. Subscription, 2s. per quarter.

Swimming Association of Great Britain (The).—Subscription : London clubs, £1 1s. per annum ; Country clubs, 10s. 6d. per annum. H. I. Barron, hon. secretary. Headquarters : Goswell Hall, Goswell-road, London, E.C.

Taplow, Buckinghamshire, so to speak a suburb of Maidenhead—at all events to the frequenters of "The Orkney Arms"—although the village itself stands some distance from the river on the opposite bank. In the parish is Cliveden, the splendid seat of the Duke of Westminster. The house dates from 1851, two previous mansions on the same site having been destroyed by fire. The Grosvenor art treasures are not to be found at Cliveden, but the pavement of Staffordshire tiles in the entrance-hall deserves notice. It was the gift of Mr. Herbert Minton to the late Duchess of Sutherland, in gratitude for the interest and trouble she took in encouraging the potteries, and in procuring them patterns. Taplow Court, now the property of Mr. W. H. Grenfell, was entirely rebuilt in 1851 by Mr. C. P. Grenfell, M.P., under the superintendence of Mr. Burne, the architect. The collection of pictures includes a Marriage of St. Catherine, by Titian; a Holy Family, by Giulio Romano; and examples of Schiavone, Gaspard Poussin, Canaletto, Jan Steen, Van de Heyden, Reinagle, Varley, and Turner. There are some curious brasses in Taplow Church, a modern building at some distance from Taplow Court. The old parish church was close to the house, in the old churchyard, where the ancient mound and the yew tree are still to be seen. A stone cross has been erected to mark the original situation of the church. *Railway Station,* Taplow. Fares to Paddington, 1st, 4/-; 7/- ; 2nd, 3/- ; 5/3 ; 3rd, 1/10½.

Teddington, Middlesex, on the left bank, 18½ miles from London, 93 miles from Oxford, a station on the South Western Railway 13½ miles from Waterloo ; the trains average forty-five minutes ; the time occupied on the alternative route

to Ludgate is much longer. The station is about three-quarters of a mile from the "Anglers," near the weir. Population, 6,500. Soil, gravel. Teddington is a pleasant and rapidly-growing village, with no particular claim to attention except that here is the first lock on the river, and that at the western extremity of the village is Bushey Park.

The church is of no particular beauty or interest, inside or out, and is a plain brick edifice with a whitewashed interior. The churchyard is extremely well kept, and is rendered as attractive as possible with shrubs and flowers. South of the chancel is a heavy marble mural monument, in memory of Sir Orlando Bridgman, keeper of the seals to Charles II., who died in 1674. On the north wall over the reading-desk is a mural tablet with scrolls, skulls, and cherubs, which commemorates that famous actress, Peg Woffington ; or, as the inscription has it, Margaret Woffington, spinster, who died, aged 39, in 1790. In the south aisle is a conventional monument of a kneeling lamenting female figure, by Richard Westmacott, R.A., to W. T. Stretton, 1814. Let into the same wall is a brass, with male and female figures, to John Goodyere and Thomasyn, his wife. John died, as nearly as can be deciphered, in 1506. On the east wall of the south aisle a brass inscription will be found to "Ricardus Parsons Tontonensis," 1613. The John Walter of *The Times* is buried here, and there is a tablet to his memory in the church. The churches of St. Peter and St. Paul, and St. Mark, are both modern.

At Teddington is a Mutual Instruction Reading Society, under the presidency of the vicar, with circulating library of reference, lectures, classes, &c. Candidates are admitted by ballot ; the subscription is nominal. There is also a Horticultural Society, which held its eighth exhibition in 1879.

The angling below this and at the weir will repay a visit. Very large carp are caught here, and the dace are in plenty.

FIRE.—Station, Park-lane.

HOSPITAL.—Teddington and Hampton Wick Cottage, Hampton-road.

HOTELS. — "The Anglers," by the river ; "The Clarence," near the station.

PLACES OF WORSHIP. — St. Mark's Mission Church ; St. Mary's (parish church) ; SS. Peter and Paul ; Christ Church (Free Church of England) ; and a Wesleyan Chapel.

POLICE.—Station, Church-road.

POSTAL ARRANGEMENTS.—Post Office (money order, savings bank, telegraph, and insurance), High-street. Mails from London, 6.30 a.m., 2 and 7 p.m. ; Sunday, 6.30 a.m. Mails for London, 9.45 a.m., 12.45, 4.35, and 8.30 p.m. ; no despatch on Sunday.

NEAREST *Bridges*, up, Kingston about 2 miles ; down, Richmond 3 miles. *Locks*, Teddington ; up, Molesey 5 miles. *Ferry*, Twickenham. *Railway Station*, Teddington.

FARES to Waterloo : 1st, 2/-, 2/6 ; 2nd, 1/6, 2/- ; 3rd, 1/-, 1/8. To Ludgate, 1st, 2/-, 2/9 ; 2nd, 1/6, 2/3 ; 3rd, 1/2, 1/9.

Temple Yacht Club (Established 1857), Club-house, Anderton's Hotel, Fleet-street. — The officers of the club consist of a commodore, vice-commodore, rear-commodore, treasurer, and hon. secretary, who, with five members, form the committee. Election is by a ballot of members, and one black ball in four excludes. None but amateur yachtsmen are admitted members of the club. Subscription, £1 1s. The club flag is a blue burgee, with a yellow-winged horse rampant.

Tench are frequently taken in the Thames at Penton Hook, Walton, Hampton, and Kingston. The stock has of late years been largely increased between Kingston and Staines by contributions from the Home Park and Bushey Park, and from the Hampshire Avon at Ringwood.

Thames Angling Preservation Society.—(*See* FISHING.)

Thames Church Mission, Office, 31, New Bridge-street, Blackfriars, London.

Thames Ditton, Surrey, on the right bank, from London 22½ miles, from Oxford 89¼ miles. A station on the Hampton Court branch of the South Western Railway, 14 miles from Waterloo ; the trains take about 40 minutes. The station is ten minutes' walk from the river. Population, 1,900. A pretty little village in a sequestered corner opposite Hampton Court Park, very popular with punt-anglers, and, formerly to a larger extent than at present, with excursionists from London. Increased railway facilities have taken visitors farther afield, and Ditton is no longer so popular as it was in the days when Theodore Hook wrote his well-known verses in praise of its little inn. There is in truth little except the prettiness of the situation to attract visitors except the church, which contains some fine brasses, and is itself a curious building, with old oak beams, rambling galleries, and queer lights in the roof. It has chancel, nave, and south aisle, the latter added fifteen years ago, and a low square tower, with a very unassuming little wooden spire. The font is of great antiquity, as is also an old canopied stone tomb from which the figure has disappeared. The brasses, an unusually fine collection, have been removed from their original positions on the floor, and are now placed upon the walls, where they can not only be well seen, but will be protected from inevitable wear and tear. On the north wall of the chancel is the memorable brass of Robert Smythe and Katheryn his wife, who died respectively in 1539 and 1549. It contains nine kneeling figures. Underneath is a coat of arms, apparently belonging to the brass below, which is that of William Notte, and Elizabeth his wife, daughter of Robert and Katheryn Smythe. William died in 1576, and Elizabeth eleven years later. They are represented kneeling at a *prie-dieu*, with a small family of nineteen children kneeling with them. Near the canopied tomb already mentioned are some very elaborate brass coats-of-arms, with the motto " *Qve Sera Sera*," and a brass of " Eras. fforde, sone and heyre of Walter fforde, sometyme tresorer to Kynge Edward IV., and Julyan the Wyffe." The dates of their deaths are given as 1533 and 1539. Large families appear to have been fashionable in these parts at that period, as Erasmus kneels in company with six sons, and Julyan with twelve daughters. On the wall just by the vestry door are the effigies of Cuthbert Lakeden, who died 1540, John Boothe, 1548, and Julyan, " sometyme the wyef of the said Cuthbert and John," who erected this monument 1580. She died 1586, aged 77. Hard by is a brass inscription in memory of Ann Child, " the davghter of William Child, of Estsheene, in the parish of Movrclack, in the Covnty of Surrey." The date is

1607, and it may be assumed that the Movrclack is supposed to represent Mortlake. On the wall above the pulpit stairs are two large full-length figures of John Cheke, "who departed this transitorye lyfe, 1690, and Isabel, doughter of Wm. Seilearde, of London." Seven young Chekes kneel with their father, above whom is his coat-of-arms. Also by the pulpit steps are the praying figures of John Polsted (1540), and Anne Wheeler, with their four daughters, Anne, Jane, Elizabeth, and Julyan, "the which Julyan erected this monument, An. Dni. 1582, and in the 73rd yeare of her age." There are several marble tablets in the church, and a long list of charitable bequests hangs in the vestry, one of which is odd. By it W. Hatton left £20 a year to the minister, "if he be chosen by the major part of the chief inhabitants." If he were not so chosen, the benefaction was to go to the poor.

In the centre of the village is a handsome drinking fountain, newly erected at the cost and charges of the lord of the manor of Weston. Close to the railway station are almshouses founded by H. Bridges, 1720. The National Schools are aided by the interest of £1000 left by Sir Charles Sullivan, of Imber Court.

This part of the river is far too crowded in the summer season with small craft to enjoy a day's angling, but in the winter a very fair haul of roach and dace, with, perhaps, a perch or two, may reward the perseverance of the angler.

HOTEL.—"The Swan."

PLACES OF WORSHIP.—St. Nicholas; and a Congregational Chapel.

POSTAL ARRANGEMENTS.—Post-office (money order, savings bank, and telegraph). Mails from London, 7 and 10.30 a.m., 8 p.m.; Sunday, 7 a.m. Mails for London, 8.10 a.m., 2.55 and 6.55 p.m.; Sunday, 10 a.m.

NEAREST *Bridges*, up, Hampton Court 1 mile; down, Kingston 1¾ mile. *Locks*, up, Molesey about a mile; down, Teddington about 4 miles. *Railway Station*, Thames Ditton.

FARES to Waterloo, 1st, 2/-, 2/8; 2nd, 1/6, 2/-; 3rd, 1/2, 1/9.

Thames Haven Cattle Station.— Thames Haven (Essex).

Thames Haven Company, Limited, 8, London-street, E.C.—The business of this company is the landing and housing of foreign animals and the forwarding of them to the London cattle market.

Thames National Regatta.—For watermen. Was established twenty-five years ago, and remained one of the principal professional regattas of the year until 1866, when the old organisation by which it was conducted broke up. In 1868 the regatta was revived under the auspices of a committee of rowing men, under the title of the Thames Regatta. This, however, only existed for nine years, and was then elbowed out of the field by a new regatta, instituted by the railway and steamboat companies, and called the International Regatta. The International did not succeed in obtaining a sufficient amount of public support, and is already numbered with the things that were.

Thames Nautical Training College, Training-ship *Worcester*, off Greenhithe, and Office, 72, Mark-lane.—Object: To provide properly qualified officers for merchant vessels by training cadets for a seafaring life, under an able commander and schoolmaster, with efficient subordinate officers. The annual terms of the admission in the upper school for cadets from thirteen to sixteen years of age are £52 10s., and in the lower school for cadets from eleven to thirteen years of age, £47 5s., payable in advance, with a charge to each of £10 10s. per annum for uniform, medical attendance, washing, and use of school books and stationery. Youths only who are intended for the sea are entered on board the training college.

Thames Rowing Club (The) was founded in 1861 as a pleasure club only. Its headquarters were then at Simmons's. There were very few members at first, but the numbers rapidly increased, and in 1862, when club races were first started, the club numbered nearly 150. In 1877 the Thames Boathouse Company (Limited) was formed for the purpose of providing a boat and club house for the club. Money was raised by means of shares, the club and the company being kept quite distinct. The result has been the construction, at a cost of more than £3,000, of the present Thames Boat-house, on a site about 300 yards above that of the London. The club at present numbers over 400 members. The subscription for new members is £2 2s. a year, with an entrance fee of £1 11s. 6d.; A payment of £12 12s., or of £7 7s. after five years' full membership, entitles anyone to an honorary life membership. The election is by ballot in general meeting; one black ball in five excluding. Colours, red, black, and white.

Thames Sailing Club, Surbiton.—The object of the club is to encourage the sailing of small boats, especially upon the upper waters of the River Thames. The officers are commodore, vice-commodore, rear-commodore, and honorary secretary and treasurer. The committee consists of 7 members, in addition to the 4 officers. Election is by committee. Entrance fee, £1 1s.; subscription, £2 2s. Burgee white, dark blue cross, red foul anchor in centre of cross. Ensign white, dark blue cross, red foul anchor in fly.

Thames Steam Tug and Lighterage Company, Limited, City Chambers, Railway-place, E.C.; Corn Exchange, Mark-lane; London and North-Western Railway, Poplar, E.; 19, Brunswick-street, Blackwall, E.; and Northumberland Wharf, Brentford End.

Thames Tunnel.—This great, but for many years comparatively useless, work of Sir Isambard Brunel was carried under the river from Wapping (left bank) to Rotherhithe (right bank) at a cost of nearly half a million of money. For about twenty years after its completion it was one of the recognised sights of London, and a kind of mouldy and poverty-stricken bazaar established itself at the entrance of the tunnel. The pence of the sightseers and the rent of the stalls proved wholly insufficient even to pay current expenses, and in 1865 the Tunnel Company were glad to get rid of their white elephant at a loss of about half its original cost. It now belongs to the East London Railway Company.

NEAREST *Steamboat Pier*, Tunnel; *Railway Stations*, Wapping and Rotherhithe; *Omnibus Routes*, Blackwall and Rotherhithe.

Thames Valley Sailing Club (Hampton).—The object of the club is similar to that of the Thames Sailing Club. It is managed by a commodore, a vice-commodore, a rear-commodore, hon. secretary and treasurer, and a committee of five members. Election is by committee. Entrance fee, 10s. 6d.; subscription, £1 11s. 6d. Half members are also admitted at a subscription of 10s. 6d., but they, as well as the honorary members, are debarred from holding office. Burgee red, with gold foul anchor. Ensign red, with gold foul anchor in fly.

Tide Table.—High Water at London Bridge on Saturdays in 1885.

Saturday,			MORN.		AFT.	
Jan.	3	..	3 4	..	3 28	
"	10	..	8 48	..	9 24	
"	17	..	2 38	..	2 54	
"	24	..	6 54	..	7 21	
"	31	..	2 5	..	2 29	
Feb.	7	..	7 2	..	7 26	
"	14	..	1 42	..	2 2	
"	21	..	5 44	..	6 7	
"	28	..	1 3	..	1 29	
Mar.	7	..	5 43	..	6 2	
"	14	..	0 28	..	0 52	
"	21	..	4 46	..	5 6	
"	28	..	0 0	..	0 23	
April	4	..	4 40	..	4 56	
"	11	..	11 11	..	11 41	
"	18	..	3 46	..	4 8	
"	25	..	10 53	..	11 27	
May	2	..	3 40	..	3 58	
"	9	..	9 0	..	9 41	
"	16	..	2 43	..	3 6	
"	23	..	9 12	..	9 48	
"	30	..	2 43	..	3 1	
June	6	..	7 14	..	7 42	
"	13	..	1 37	..	2 1	
"	20	..	7 38	..	8 6	
"	27	..	1 49	..	2 7	
July	4	..	5 58	..	6 19	
"	11	..	0 25	..	0 52	
"	18	..	6 17	..	6 39	
"	25	..	0 44	..	1 8	
Aug.	1	..	4 56	..	5 12	
"	8	..	11 38	..	0 0	
"	15	..	5 4	..	5 23	
"	22	..	11 51	..	0 0	
"	29	..	3 58	..	4 14	
Sept.	5	..	10 7	..	10 48	
"	12	..	3 55	..	4 16	
"	19	..	9 58	..	10 39	
"	26	..	2 57	..	3 13	
Oct.	3	..	8 27	..	9 11	
"	10	..	2 51	..	3 11	
"	17	..	7 48	..	8 24	
"	24	..	1 54	..	2 11	
"	31	..	7 2	..	7 39	
Nov.	7	..	1 51	..	2 11	
"	14	..	6 14	..	6 38	
"	21	..	0 41	..	1 2	
"	28	..	5 46	..	6 24	
Dec.	5	..	0 49	..	1 11	
"	12	..	5 8	..	5 26	
"	19	..	11 37	..	0 0	
"	26	..	4 57	..	5 20	

'At the Nore high water is generally about 87 min., earlier than at London Bridge, at Gravesend about 50 min., and at Greenwich about 14 min. At Chelsea it is about 30 min., Putney 40 min., Kew 55 min., and Richmond 75 min. later.

Torpids.—*See* UNIVERSITY (OXFORD) ROWING.

Tilbury Fort is in Essex, opposite Gravesend. The original Tilbury Fort was built by Henry VIII. in 1539, and when Elizabeth's army was encamped at West Tilbury was but a small building. King Henry's Fort was considerably enlarged by Charles II., when the Dutch fleet were making themselves very officious in the Thames and Medway, There is not much to see in Tilbury Fort, the principal object of attraction being the room in the old gateway once occupied by Queen Elizabeth. At Tilbury is a station of the London, Tilbury, and Southend Railway, and a steam-ferry to Gravesend.

FARES to Fenchurch-street : 1st, 2/5, 3/9 ; 2nd, 1/9, 2/10 ; 3rd, 1/2, 2/- ; *and see* GRAVESEND.

Tilehurst.—Here are a ferry and a station of the Great Western Railway, between Caversham and Pangbourne. Here also is the new "Roebuck" Hotel, which is very well spoken of, but of which the Editor has not had personal experience.

Tower of London.—The most interesting relic of the past that can be seen to best advantage from the river is the Tower of London, situated on rising ground about half a mile below London Bridge. The most conspicuous portion of the present mass of buildings and masonry, which covers some thirteen acres of ground, is the White Tower, a quadrangular keep 90 feet high, whose four turrets have been familiar to English eyes for centuries. Some evidence exists as to the probability of a Roman fortress having occupied the present site, but it was not until 1077 that the Tower was commenced by Gundolph, monk of Bec, who afterwards became Bishop of Rochester. The keep, or White Tower, consists of three floors besides the vaults, which were formerly used as dungeons. The walls are from twelve to fifteen feet thick. Each floor contains three rooms, not counting the chambers and stairs sunk into the solid wall. The main storey was the garrison stage, held by the king's guards, and consisted of two apartments and the crypt, which was occasionally used as a prison. Above is the banqueting floor, formerly a part of the royal palace, and St. John's Chapel, the best specimen of Norman architecture extant, which occupies two storeys of the keep. Above the banqueting floor is the state floor, which contained the great council chamber, the lesser hall, and the galleries of St. John's Chapel, whence there was a passage to the royal apartments. On this floor, Richard III. condemned Hastings, and Anne Boleyn and Lord Rochford were tried. Despite the thickness of the walls and the scanty means of exit (one well-stair only allowing entrance or escape), the first prisoner immured in the White Tower broke his bondage. This was Flambard, Bishop of Durham, treasurer to the early Norman kings, who, after making his guards drunk, slid down a rope attached to a window shaft sixty-five feet from the ground. Years afterwards the same feat was attempted by Griffin, in the reign of Henry III., with less success, for the unlucky prisoner's coil broke, and Griffin lost his life on the spot. In this tower for twenty-five years lived Charles of Orleans, grandson of Charles V., and father of Louis XII., kings of France. Taken prisoner at Agincourt, he lived his mournful life until the sum of 300,000 crowns was paid for his ransom. During the period of his captivity the unfortunate prince wrote many poems, some of which are extant. Below the ground were the dungeons, one of which, called Little Ease, was the prison of Wyatt and Guy Fawkes. In the largest of the four turrets which surmount the roof was incarcerated Maud, the fair daughter of Baron Fitzwalter, who resisted till her death the disgraceful advances of King John. In the year 1663 the aspect of the keep was altered by Sir Christopher Wren. Part of the exterior was cased with flint and mortar, two of the turrets were rebuilt, and the openings were altered into Italian windows. Encircling the White Tower are the inner ward and the outer ward. The former, planned and partly built by the monk of Bec, was the original fortress, and was protected by twelve strong towers built on the wall and forming part of it. The inner ward was the royal quarter, and comprised, besides the keep, the royal rooms, the mint, the jewel-house, the wardrobe, the queen's garden, St. Peter's Church, besides quarters for the bowmen and the constable. It was, in fact, the king's castle, and the people had no right of access. The outer ward lay between the vallum, or inner wall, and the outer scarp of the ditch. It was regarded as the people's quarter, and on stated occasions the citizens claimed right of access from the king ; the object, no doubt, being to guard their right to be present in the courts of justice which sat in the tower. The King's Bench was held in the lesser hall of the keep, the Common Pleas were heard in a hall by the river, which has not survived the modern improvements.

In front of the fortress on the riverside is Tower Wharf, the work of Henry III., and one of the wonders of his reign. The earth on which it is built had to be recovered from the Thames, and the foundations were difficult to lay. The building was unfavourably regarded by the London citizens, and on two occasions the wall and the water-gate fell. The king, however, persevered, and finally completed his wharf, twelve hundred feet long, and his water-gate, better known in history as Traitor's Gate. On this wharf cannon used to be planted. Many of the smaller towers which command the wharf and the ditch are memorable for the illustrious dead who were confined therein. In the Devereux the Earl of Essex was immured ; in the Bell Tower Queen Elizabeth. In Bowyer's Tower Clarence was drowned, and in the Bloody Tower the two sons of Edward IV. were murdered. The Beauchamp Tower is perhaps the most interesting nowadays, as the building has been admirably restored, and the inscriptions on the walls have been secured from obliteration. In the north-western corner of the quadrangle is the chapel to St. Peter Ad Vincula, remarkable for the number of famous persons who have been buried beneath its stones. Anne Boleyn and Katherine Howard were interred here, and among others, Protector Somerset, and his brother, Thomas Seymour, Lady Jane Grey and her husband, and Sir Walter Raleigh. In another part of the tower is the Regalia, where the royal jewels are kept, and close by is the Horse Armoury, a collection of ancient and mediæval arms and armour exhibited on wooden figures of horses and men. The first prisoner in the tower was, as we have before remarked, Flambard, Bishop of Durham ; the last were the Cato-street Conspirators (1820). The last execution which took place there was when Lords Lovat, Kilmarnock, and Balmerino went to the block after the rebellion of 1745. A severe fire broke out in 1841, and caused much loss in buildings, stores, and arms, but the tenements which were subsequently erected were very great improvements. Nowadays the Tower serves as a Government store-house for rifles, bayonets, and military accoutrements generally. The government is vested in a constable, who is always a military officer of great repute, and a lieutenant-governor, with subordinates, and the corps of the Yeomanry of the Guard, or Beefeaters. Admission free on Mondays and Saturdays ; on other days a small fee is payable for permission to visit the Beauchamp Tower, the Regalia, the Armoury, and other objects of interest.

NEAREST *Railway Stations*, Mark-lane (Dis.) and Cannon-street (S. E.); *Omnibus Routes*, Fenchurch-street and Aldgate High-street ; *Steamboat Pier*, London Bridge.

Tower Subway.—A curious feat of engineering skill, in the shape of an iron tube seven feet in diameter driven through the bed of the Thames between Great Tower-hill (left bank) and Vine-street (right bank). The original intention was to have passengers drawn backwards and forwards in a small tram omnibus. This, however, was found unremunerative, and the rails having been taken up the tunnel has since been open as a footway. Unfortunately, however, after subtracting from its diameter the amount necessary to afford a sufficient width of platform, there is not much head-room left, and it is not advisable for any but the very briefest of Her Majesty's lieges to attempt the passage in high-heeled boots, or with a hat to which he attaches any particular value. It has, however, one admirable quality, that of having cost remarkably little in construction.

NEAREST *Steamboat Pier*, London Bridge ; *Railway Stations*, Aldgate (Metrop.) and Cannon-street (S.E.) ; *Omnibus Routes*, Aldgate High-street and Fenchurch-street.

Trinity Buoy Wharf is rather difficult of approach. The best mode of access, when available, is from the Blackwall Station, across the two entrances, Old and New, of the East India Dock, then to the left along the edge of the basin and out through the little wicket-gate into Orchard-street, at the eastern extremity of which is the gate of the Trinity House premises. When the little wicket-gate is shut, the best station is Poplar, either on the Blackwall Railway if coming from the west, or on the North London Railway if coming from the north. In the latter case pursue eastwards the East India-road, and its continuation the Barking-road, till you reach Orchard-street on the right hand just beyond the dock. In the former make your way along Brunswick-street and Naval-row into East India Dock Wall-road, following which northerly you will arrive at the junction of the East India and Barking roads, whence proceed as before. Coming from the eastward, the best station is the Barking-road on the North Woolwich Branch of the London, Tilbury, and Southend Railway, whence the route lies westerly along the Barking-road. The wharf itself is situate on the western bank of the *embouchure* of Bow Creek into Bugsby's Reach, about half-way between the entrances of the East India and Victoria Docks. At this establishment is constructed the whole of the lighting and buoying apparatus of the United Kingdom, and of the other parts of the Empire dependent upon the Trinity Board. Application to view the establishment should be made to the secretary of the Trinity House, Tower Hill ; but it is a longish day's work from any habitable part of London.

Trinity House, Tower-hill, London, E.C.—The Corporation of Trinity House of Deptford Strond, originally a voluntary association of the shipmen or mariners of England, first received its name in the charter received from King Henry VIII. in 1514, in which it is described as the " Guild or Fraternity of the most glorious and undividable Trinity of St. Clement." An Act of Elizabeth refers to the master, wardens, and assistants of the Trinity House of Deptford Strond ; and all the charters which were subsequently granted to the corporation speak of " the master, warden, and assistants of the Guild, Fraternity, or Brotherhood of the most glorious and undivided Trinity, and of St. Clement, in the parish of Deptford, in the county of Kent." The arms of the corporation, granted in 1573, are thus described in the quaint language of the heralds : " Argent, a plain cross Gules, between four ships sable, and fore and topsails up, and underneath, on a wreath of their colours, a Demi-Lion Rampant Gardant, and crowned with a crown imperial Or : or in his right paw an arming sword Argent-hilt and pomell Or, langued and armed Azure, doubled Gules. Motto, *Trinitas in Unitate.*" By the Act above mentioned the corporation received authority to erect and maintain beacons, marks, and signs of the sea, for the better navigation of the coasts of England, and from this beginning has in time grown the present magnificent organisation of lighthouses, lightships, buoys, and beacons. The affairs of the corporation were at first conducted at the hall adjoining the almshouses belonging to the brethren at Deptford, which was then the station at which outgoing ships were supplied with pilots—incoming vessels being, it is supposed, similarly accommodated at a branch station at Leigh, on the Essex coast—and when the old building became, from lapse of time, untenable, a new hall and additional almshouses were erected, in 1765, on land called the Upper Ground. This building is still in existence, but it is now only used for the distribution of alms and pensions. That part of the business of the corporation which is more closely connected with shipowners and other allied trades was first carried on Ratcliffe, then at Stepney, then in Water-lane, Tower-street, and finally, after the Water-lane premises had been twice destroyed by fire, the present commodious and handsome Trinity House on Tower-hill was built, from designs by Wyatt, in 1798. In the very early days of the corporation—*circa* 1520—when Government dockyards and arsenals were first established, the direction of the Deptford Building

Yard, with the superintendence of all Navy stores and provisions, was confided to the Trinity House, and the first master, under King Henry's charter, was Sir Thomas Spert, commander of the man-of-war *Henry Grace-a-Dieu*, and some time controller of the navy. The minutes of the corporation were partly destroyed by the fire in 1714, but Government records prove that the early Trinity Brethren reported upon ships intended to be purchased for the navy, regulated the dimensions of those to be built, and settled all questions as to their armament, stores, and crews. In 1647 Parliament dissolved the corporation, but twelve years later reconstructed the brotherhood, and their charter, renewed by James II. in 1685, still remains in force, with some supplementary provisions introduced during the present reign. It was stipulated in the charter that the members should be liable, if required, to serve the Crown at sea, being, in return, exempted from land service; and twice, at least, they rendered good service to the State under the provisions of this clause. At the time of the great mutiny at the Nore in 1797 the Elder Brethren removed all the beacons and buoys which could guide the fleet out to sea, and when a French invasion was threatened in 1803 they undertook the defence of the entrance of the Thames, manning and personally officering an efficient squadron moored below Gravesend, and making all arrangements for the removal of all buoys, &c., which might guide the hostile fleet on its way into the river. In 1836 an Act of Parliament was passed strengthening the position of the Trinity House, and giving it powers to purchase from the Crown, as well as from private proprietors, all interests in coast lights. By various Crown patents the corporation had been empowered to raise money by tolls for the maintenance of such lights and for other analogous purposes, and it was further provided that the surplus revenues should be devoted to the relief of indigent and aged mariners, their wives, widows, and orphans. By 1853 the allowance to out-pensioners out of these surplus funds amounted to £20,000, and an income of nearly half as much more, derived from properties held in trust for benevolent uses, was devoted to the maintenance of the almshouses at Deptford and Mile

End, and to other charitable purposes connected with those who go down to the sea in ships. It is not surprising that an institution having the command of such large sums of money, and entrusted with the exercise of duties of such national importance, should have received, on several occasions, very close attention, and, indeed, searching scrutiny from Parliament. Several committees of the House of Commons have been appointed to investigate the affairs and management of the Trinity House, and of special importance were those of 1732, 1822, 1834, 1845, and 1858. The attention of the committees of 1732 and 1822 was more particularly directed to the pilotage systems, while the latter investigations dealt more especially with the management of lights, buoys, and beacons. The results of the labours of these committees were, in effect, creditable to the corporation, whose powers, thus approved, became gradually extended. A fundamental change, however, occurred when Parliament, in 1853, transferred to the Board of Trade the control of the funds collected by the corporation from tolls and dues, and required the official sanction of the Board to all the public disbursements of the Trinity House. The moneys devoted to the carrying out of charitable designs were largely reduced, and, after payment of vested interests and pensions, the corporation has since been entitled to no more than the distribution of its private income, derived from funded or trust property still, as before, devoted to the support of its almshouses, to grants of relief, and to various objects for the promotion of the welfare of sailors both of the Royal Navy and of the merchant service, with a certain reserve for upholding the dignity of the corporation at its house. The court, or governing body, consisted under the charter of 1514 of master, wardens, and assistants, thirteen in all, elected annually by all the brethren. In 1604 the distinction between Elder and Younger Brethren was drawn for the first time, and in the charter of 1609 the management of affairs was entrusted to the master, wardens, assistants, and Elder Brethren, which form of government remains in force at the present day. The Elder Brethren are, naturally enough, elected from among those of the Younger

Brethren who desire the promotion. The Younger Brethren, whose number is unlimited, are admissible at the pleasure of the court, are entitled to vote at the election of master and wardens, and may look forward, as, has been said, to grow up in time to be Elder Brethren themselves. Otherwise they have no voice in the management of the affairs of the corporation. Of the governing body of thirty-one, now in process of reduction to twenty-four —master, wardens, assistants, and Elder Brethren—the greater number have been brought up to the sea and are called acting Elder Brethren, while the remainder is made up of persons of position, such as members of the Royal Family, ministers of state, distinguished naval officers, and the like, who may, perhaps, be correctly described as honorary members. Of the acting Brethren, two—one admiral and one captain — at present represent the Royal Navy, the remainder are officers of the mercantile marine. Vacancies in the court are filled up by ballot of the whole of the Elder Brethren. The objects for which the corporation was founded are described in its charters as "being to treat and conclude upon all and singular articles anywise concerning the science or art of mariners," to encourage navigation, to provide for pilotage, to relieve poor and aged mariners, to see to the ballastage of ships in the Thames, as a means of clearing and deepening the navigable channels, and most particularly to place beacons and buoys and to preserve sea marks along the coast. Among other duties the Brethren have to examine navigating lieutenants in the Royal Navy, and to sit as nautical advisers with the Judge of the High Court of Admiralty. It will thus be readily seen that the acting Brethren are not in the enjoyment of any sinecures. The official establishment consists of secretary and assistant secretary, eight senior clerks, seven assistant clerks, twelve junior clerks, and four temporary clerks. There are also an engineer, three assistants, and one draftsman, and clerk of works. Men of the highest position are always consulted on purely scientific questions, and in this department the late Professor Faraday has been succeeded by Professor Tyndall. At the head of the engineering department, which undertakes all the duties connected with the erection and main-

tenance of lighthouses, beacons, buoys, &c., is Mr. James N. Douglass, who comes of a family distinguished in the history of lighthouses, as the buildings on the Bishop Rock, Small's Rock, and the Wolf Rock will amply testify. The Trinity House has 78 lighthouses on its list, 63 of which are on shore, 11 on outlying rocks, and 4 on sands. Those on shore are of brick, stone or timber, those on rocks of granite, and those on sands on iron piles. Those above the Nore are the Northfleet, the Mucking, and the Chapman. In addition to their lighthouses on the English coast, the Trinity House has charge of two abroad, one at Heligoland and one at Gibraltar. Of lightships, the Trinity House has 38 in position and 5 in reserve : and look after, besides, some 450 buoys and 60 beacons. Six steam vessels and 7 sailing - tenders are employed in the service ; there are over 20 store-houses ; and the working-staff in all these services numbers over 800 men of all ranks. At the time of the election of H. R. H. the Duke of Edinburgh to the office of master, a memoir of the history, &c., of the corporation was written by Sir Frederick Arrow, the deputy-master, and printed for private circulation, and the writer of this article has to acknowledge his obligation to this very interesting *brochure*.

The Masters of the Trinity House during the present century have been :

1800 Right Hon. William Pitt.
1806 Earl Spencer.
1807 Duke of Portland.
1809 Marquis Camden.
1816 Earl of Liverpool.
1828 Marquis Camden.
1829 H.R.H. the Duke of Clarence (afterwards King William IV.).
1831 Marquis Camden.
1837 Duke of Wellington.
1852 H.R.H. the Prince Consort.
1862 Viscount Palmerston.
1866 H.R.H. the Duke of Edinburgh.

And see
BALLASTAGE,
BUOYS,
CHAPMAN LIGHTHOUSE,
MUCKING LIGHTHOUSE,
NORE LIGHT,
NORTHFLEET LIGHT, *and*
PILOT STATION.

Tripcock Reach, sometimes called Barking Reach, runs not quite a mile and a half from Tripcock Point (or Margaretness) to Crossness. Barking Creek is on the left (Essex) bank, at the north-west of the reach. On the other side are the Plumstead Marshes. Bearings E. by S. and W. by N.

Trip from Cricklade to Oxford.— Although scarcely any of the scenery of the Thames above Oxford is to be mentioned in the same breath with the beauties of Nuneham, of Henley, of Marlow, or of Cliveden, there is still much to attract the lover of nature who is content with quiet and pastoral landscapes, and to whom the peaceful solitude through which the greater part of the journey lies, will have a peculiar charm. It is not advisable to take boat at Cricklade. For some distance below this little Wiltshire town the stream is narrow, and in dry seasons uncomfortably shallow. Travellers, therefore, who come to Cricklade, with the intention of seeing as much of the river as possible, may be recommended to take the very pretty walk of about ten miles along the towing-path of the Thames and Severn Canal to Lechlade. Here the river proper may be said to begin. To this point boats may be sent by the Great Western Railway, or, if hired by Salter of Oxford, in the usual way in his vans. Should short journeys only be taken, the " Trout Inn," at Tadpole Bridge, may be noted as a clean little place, making up a small number of beds ; and the market-town of Bampton is only a couple of miles distant should the little inn be full. Perhaps the best course, however, is to push on at once to Eynsham, and, leaving the boat at the bridge, to sleep in the town. Excursions can then be made next day to Cumnor, Stanton Harcourt, or other interesting places in the neighbourhood, and the journey finished at Oxford the same afternoon.

LECHLADE, from Oxford about 33 miles. Half a mile after leaving Lechlade on the right is

ST. JOHN'S LOCK, with an average fall of 3 feet ; and just below it is the St. John's Bridge, with the " Trout Inn " on the left bank. For some distance below this stream is very narrow, and generally weedy ; and, after passing Buscot Church,

a couple of sharp turns bring us on the left to

BUSCOT LOCK, from Oxford 30½ miles, with an average fall of rather more than 4 feet. After passing the lock the river pursues a most tortuous course for some distance, and about a mile further down, after the first good stretch of water we have had, is Hart's Weir, which in ordinary seasons will be found open, and with little or no fall. Should the season be a dry one, a good deal of care is necessary in shooting this and the other weirs on the Upper Thames. A couple of miles lower down is the little village of Eaton Hastings ; Faringdon Hill, with its large clump of Scotch firs, being a conspicuous object on the right bank, and two miles further again is

RADCOT BRIDGE, distant from Oxford 26 miles. Approaching this bridge, the stream divides, and in anything like a dry season the right-hand channel should on no account be taken, as the navigation immediately below the bridge is awkward by reason of weeds and shoals. The next point is

OLD MAN'S BRIDGE, 25 miles from Oxford, and after about two miles of rather monotonous travelling, we come, sharp on the left, to

RUSHY LOCK, 23 miles from Oxford, with a very slight fall ; and a mile further to

TADPOLE BRIDGE, 22 miles from Oxford, with the " Trout Inn," a convenient place for luncheon, if the traveller is going from Lechlade to Eynsham in one day. Tadpole Bridge is situated in a pretty country, especially on the Berks side ; and, for some distance below, the river, which is hereabout very narrow and with many aggravatingly sharp turns, runs through a prettily wooded landscape. Rather more than a mile from Tadpole is Ten Foot Bridge, and two miles lower down are the village and ferry of Duxford. A mile or so below this there is considerable shoaling, and half a mile further an island with Poplars, where the Berks bank should be followed. After making two or three bends, beyond this point, there is a prettily wooded bank on the right, and a short mile of capital water for rowing brings us to

NEW BRIDGE, from Oxford 15 miles, which, notwithstanding its name, is of great antiquity. Convenient for refreshment is the " Rose Inn," and just above the bridge the little river Windrush falls into the Thames. Another mile brings us to the bridge where was formerly Langley's or Ridge's Weir, and hereabouts are some very good reaches and pleasant country. About 4½ miles from New Bridge is

BABLOCK HITHE FERRY, 10½ miles from Oxford, below which there is a fine stream, the scenery becoming very good, with fine bold hills and the Earl of Abingdon's woods at Wytham. After passing Skinner's Weir, rather more than 1½ mile further, the river twists and turns about a great deal, until we reach

PINKHILL LOCK, 8½ miles from Oxford, with a fall of about three feet. Round a good many corners, and rather more than a mile off, is

EYNSHAM BRIDGE, from Oxford 7 miles, and just below, round a very sharp corner, which necessitates a considerable deal of caution, is the weir. Good reaches for about three miles bring us to

KING'S WEIR, sharp on the right, the stream to the left going to the Duke's Lock, the junction with the Oxford Canal. Our route lies over King's Weir, which is provided with a roller slip. Passing presently under Godstow Bridge at the end of the cut, the ruins of Godstow Nunnery being on the right, is

GODSTOW LOCK, 3½ miles from Oxford, on leaving which a pretty view of the city is obtained. A little distance lower down is an island where a number of boats are kept for hire ; and on the right of this is Medley Weir, with a fall of about a foot. From this point the river runs past the railway and some very unæsthetic cottages to Osney Bridge, the weir on the right requiring attention. Three hundred yards further is

OSNEY LOCK. Extensive alterations are now (1885) being made here. A little further is Folly Bridge, Oxford.

Trip from Oxford to London.— Twenty years ago this delightful excursion was almost unknown except to ardent devotees of aquatics, and although at that time there were comparatively few hotels along the river-bank, there was generally very little difficulty in obtaining accommodation. Of late years the

journey has become one of the regular things to do, and in a fine season the river swarms with boats for some four months. Hotels have sprung up and have been enlarged in all directions to meet the demand; but, especially if there be ladies in the party, it will be found discreet not to trust to the chance of getting rooms at the end of the day's journey, but to write or telegraph beforehand to secure what is wanted. The drawback of this plan of course is that it binds the traveller to a fixed itinerary, and parcels the journey out into so many days, whatever may be the temptations to linger on the way or to push forward.

On the other hand, to arrive at a landing-stage about dinner-time, wet through and hungry, and with perhaps three miles and a couple of locks to the next hotel, it is, to say the least, annoying to find that some more wary wayfarers have occupied the quarters which you had hoped to obtain. In the height of the season, indeed, especially on Saturday and Sunday, considerable notice is necessary to ensure even the humblest quarters.

There are many ways of making this excursion ; perhaps the pleasantest form of conveyance is a randan skiff with two sitters, as there is thus plenty of rest and variety in the work. People who do not own suitable boats would do well to engage what they want from Mr. Salter, of Oxford, who lets boats specially for these excursions at rates which include carriage back to Oxford, thus relieving the hirer of any responsibility after he has finished his trip and deposited his boat with one of Mr. Salter's agents, from whom he will take a receipt.

It is, of course, undesirable to take much luggage in the boat. There are so many railway stations on or near the banks of the river that the heavy luggage which may be required for a lengthened stay can be forwarded from place to place without difficulty. Good waterproof rugs or sheets to protect such bags, &c., as are taken must not be omitted from the outfit. The most convenient stopping-places are Abingdon, Wallingford, Streatley, Pangbourne, Sonning, Wargrave, Henley, Medmenham, Marlow, Cookham, Maidenhead, Bray, Windsor, Staines, Chertsey, Halliford, and Hampton Court. At all of these places there is good hotel accommodation. The prices of the Thames hotels are, as a rule, fairly reasonable; although, like all similar matters, they have shown a considerable tendency to increase of late years. The fashionable places, such as Oxford, Henley, Maidenhead, and Windsor (so far, at least, as regards the two big hotels, opposite the Castle), are, of course, more expensive than the others, and may be called even high in their charges. The hotels at the other places vary but little. Generally speaking, 14s. or 15s. a day will cover the expense of bed, breakfast, lunch, dinner, and attendance. To say that the majority of Thames hotel-keepers still have fossil ideas as to the value of wines is only to say that they are human, and——hotel-keepers. It is astonishing that nobody can be induced to try the experiment of stimulating a largely-increased consumption by a system of reasonable charges. There is, undoubtedly, a fortune waiting for the sensible man who is first in the field.

So many accidents have occurred and

CLASS OF BOAT.	Tedding-ton, or lower, if agreed at time of hiring.	Eton.	Henley.	Per day after first week.	Per week, after first week.
	£. s. d.	£. s. d.	£. s. d.	s. d.	£. s. d.
Canoe, whiff, outrigged dinghey	1 10 0	1 5 0	1 0 0		
Dinghey (not outrigged), sculling boat, double canoe	2 0 0	1 15 0	1 10 0	2 6	0 10 0
Pair-oared gigs	2 10 0	2 5 0	2 0 0	3 0	0 15 0
Randan gigs	3 0 0	2 15 0	2 10 0	5 0	1 0 0
Four-oared gigs	3 10 0	3 0 0	2 10 0		
Eight-oar	5 0 0	4 10 0	4 0 0		
Larger Boats:				7 6	1 10 0
Large shallop four-oar	6 0 0	5 0 0	4 0 0		
Large four-oared gig, with side seats .. } Randan pleasure skiffs	4 0 0	3 10 0	3 0 0		
Pair-oared ,, ,, 19 feet to 20 feet, with side seats	3 10 0	3 0 0	2 15 0	5 0	1 0 0
Pair-oared pleasure skiffs, 16 feet to 18 feet, with side seats	3 0 0	2 15 0	2 10 0		
Ditto, fitted with tent cover and mattress ..	3 15 0	3 10 0	3 5 0	7 6	1 10 0
Randan, with ,, ,, ,,	5 0 0	4 10 0	4 0 0		
Tent, with ground sheet, per week, 12s. 6d. ..					
Bell tents, 15s.					

One week allowed for journey, after which extra hire will be charged, unless notice be given that the boat is done with, and where left. 2s. 6d. to be paid for care until van calls. Boat vans from Oxford to Kingston, Richmond, or Wandsworth, and back, usually every week during the summer. Gentlemen's boats carted. Competent watermen at reasonable charges. Cooking stoves and requisites for camping supplied.

continue to occur, not only to novices but to practised oarsmen familiar with the river and its vagaries, that without any desire to assume the office of mentor, or to lay down the law to people who may quite well know what they are about, a word of caution may be added here before starting on the trip. The river is safe enough for anyone who can manage a boat, but too much care cannot be observed in all boating excursions. "Sky-larking," which sacrifices almost as many lives as incautious bathing, will of course be avoided by all sensible people; but it cannot be too strongly or too often urged that a very little carelessness may produce a very great disaster, and that, although it is very easy to get into the river, it is sometimes uncommonly difficult to get out again, more especially if the scene of the accident be in a lock. Locks should always be treated with the greatest respect, both in entering, passing through, and leaving, and a wide berth should be given to all weirs, mill-streams, and lashers. Towing against a strong stream requires more care on the part of the coxswain as well as of the person on the bank than people are generally disposed to believe. A typical accident occurred

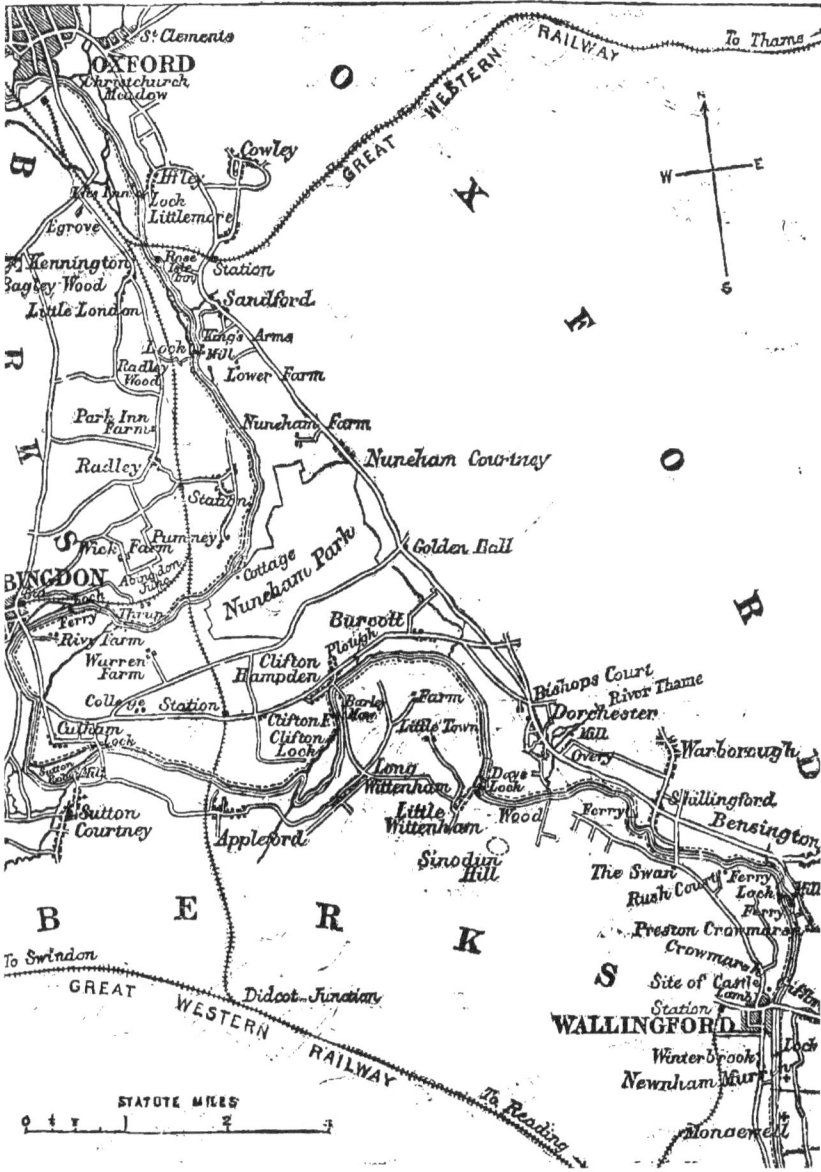

St. Clements

OXFORD

Christchurch
Meadow

RAILWAY

To Thame

GREAT WESTERN

O

Cowley

GREAT

X

Hilex
Lock
Littlemore

W ——— E

Iffley
Lock

Egrove

Kennington
Bagley Wood
Little London

Rose
Isle

Station

Sandford

F

King's Arms

O

Lock
Hill

Radley
Wood

Lower Farm

Park Inn
Farm

Nuneham Farm

Radley

Nuneham Courtney

O

Station

Pumney

Golden Ball

Wick Farm

Abingdon
Junc.

Cottage

Nuneham Park

R

BINGDON

Lock

Thrup

Burcott
Plough

Ferry

River Farm

Clifton
Hampden

Warren
Farm

Barley
Mow

Farm

Bishops Court

River Thame

College

Station

Clifton E

Little Town

Dorchester
Mill

Warborough

Cutham
Lock

Clifton
Lock

Long
Wittenham

Dove
Lock

Wood

Dover

Ferry

Wallingford

Bensington

Sutton
Courtney

Appleford

Little
Wittenham

Sinodun
Hill

The Swan

Ferry
Lock

Hill

Ferry

B E R K

Rush Cou

Preston Crowmars

Crowmarsh

To Swindon

S

Site of Castle

GREAT

Didcot Junction

WESTERN

RAILWAY

Station

WALLINGFORD

To Reading

Winterbrook

Lock

Newnham Mur

STATUTE MILES

0   ¼   ½   1   2   3

Mongewell

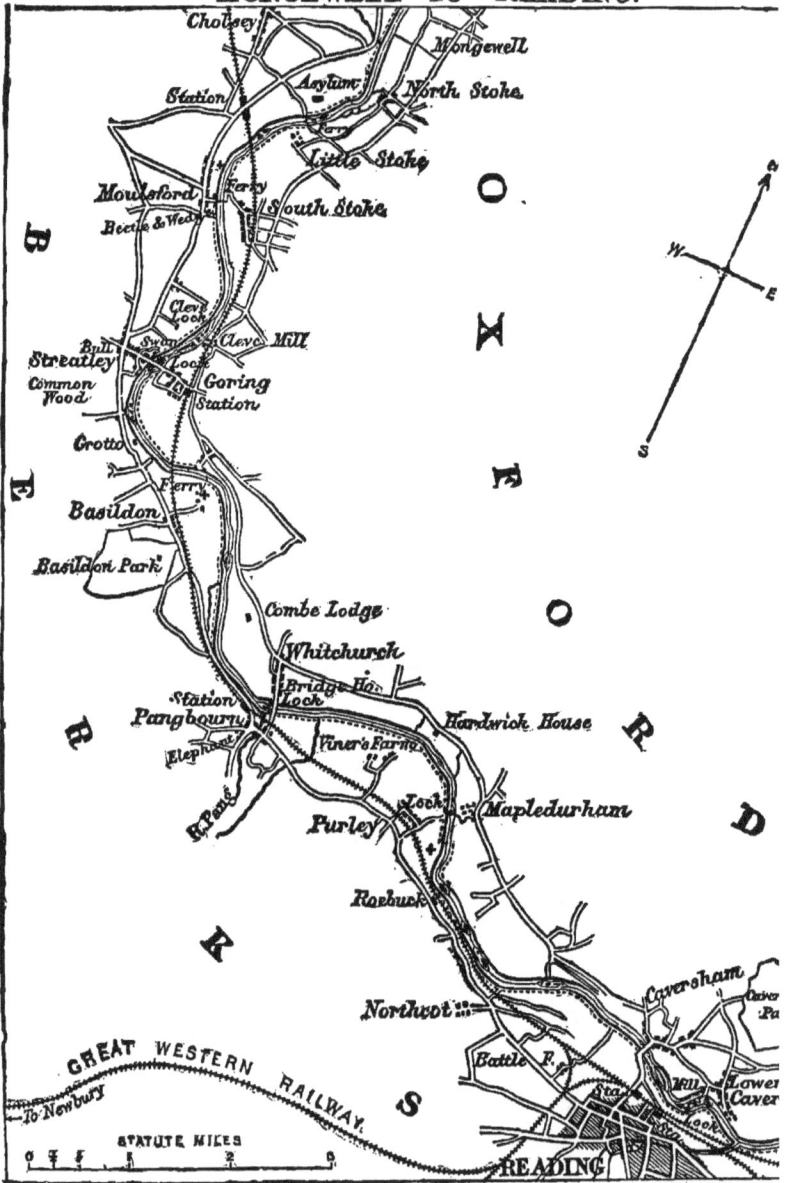

MONGEWELL TO READING.

Cholsey

Mongewell

Station Asylum North Stoke

Little Stoke

Moulsford Ferry South Stoke

Beetle & Wedge

Clere Lock

Bull Swan Clere Mill

Streatley Lock

Common Wood Goring Station

Grotto

Ferry

Basildon

Basildon Park

Combe Lodge

Whitchurch

Station Bridge Ho. Lock

Pangbourn

Elephant Viner's Farm Hardwick House

R. Pang

Lock Mapledurham

Purley

Roebuck

Northcot Caversham

Caver Pa

GREAT WESTERN RAILWAY

To Newbury Battle F. Mill Lower Caver

Lock

STATUTE MILES

READING

OXONFORD

BERKS

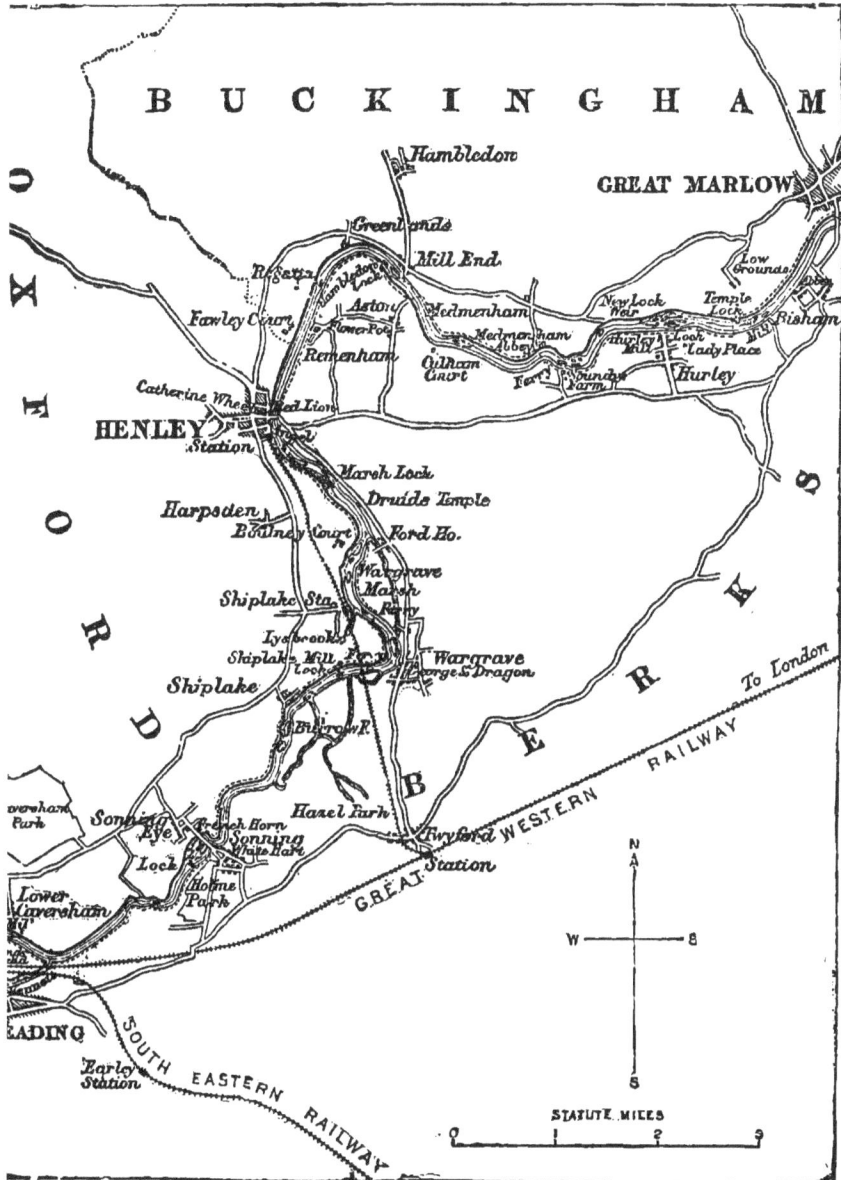

B U C K I N G H A M

Hambledon

GREAT MARLOW

Greenlands

Mill End

Low Grounds

Regatta

Aston

Medmenham

New Lock Weir

Temple Lock

Bisham

Fawley Court

Lower Pool

Medmenham Abbey

Hurley Mill

Remenham

Culham Court

Ferry

Lock

Lady Place

Catherine Whē

Red Lion

Hurley

Hurley Farm

HENLEY

Station

Marsh Lock

Druids Temple

Harpsden

Bolney Court

Ford Ho.

Wargrave Marsh

Shiplake Sta.

Ferry

Lyabrook

Shiplake Mill

Wargrave

Lock

George & Dragon

Shiplake

Burrow R.

B

E R K S

Hazel Park

To London

oreham Park

Sonning

French Horn

Twyford

RAILWAY

Eye

Sonning

WESTERN

Lock

White Hart

Lower Shiplake

Holme Park

Station

GREAT

N
W — E
S

RAILWAY

READING

SOUTH

EASTERN

Earley Station

RAILWAY

STATUTE MILES

0   1   2   3

Stanford's Geog'l Establ

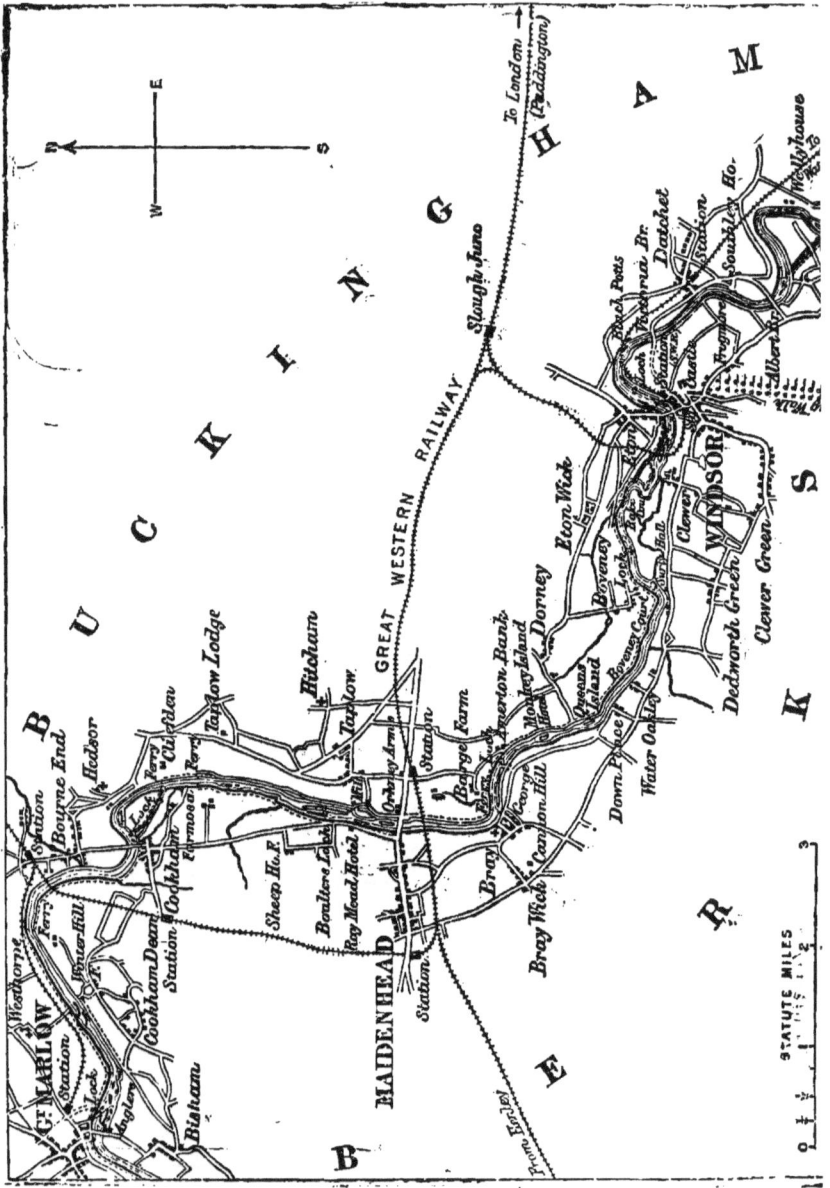

GREAT MARLOW TO DATCHET.

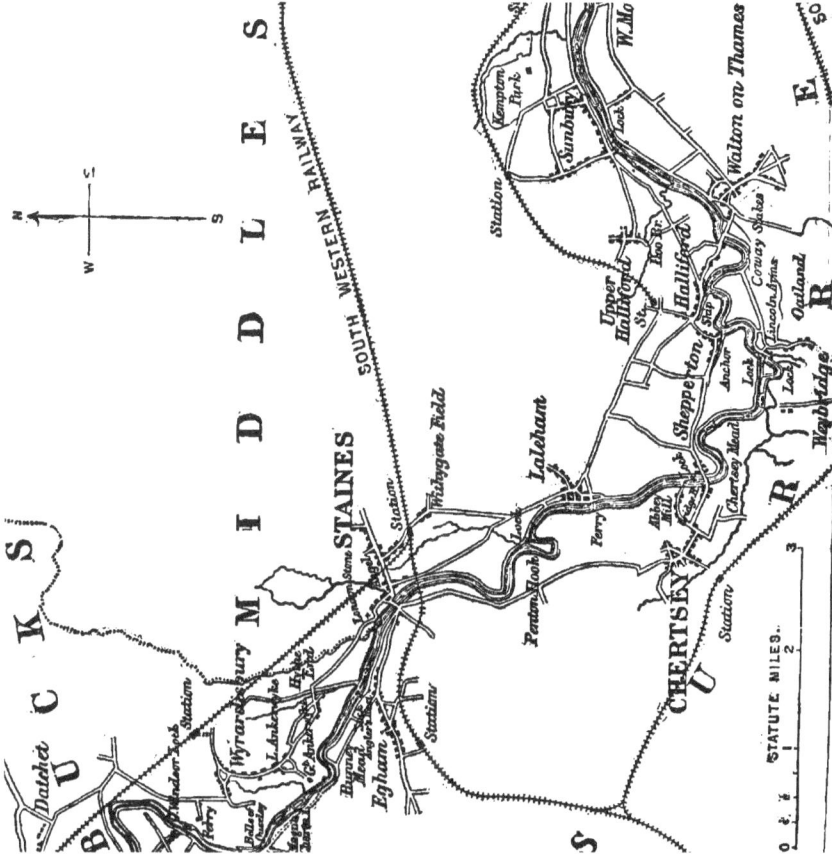

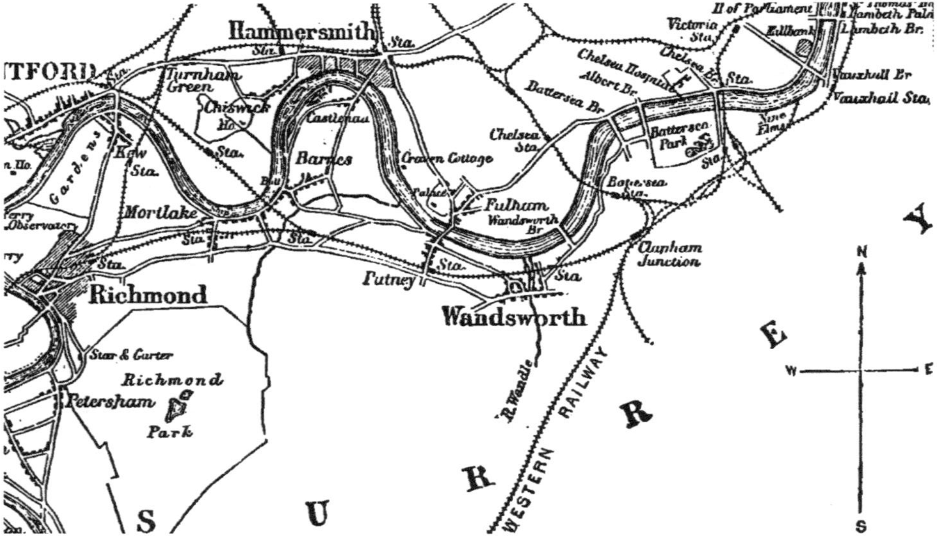
Hammersmith
Turnham Green
Chiswick Ho.
Kew Sta.
Mortlake
Barnes
Castlenau
Craven Cottage
Fulham
Wandsworth Br.
Putney
Wandsworth
Richmond
Star & Garter
Richmond Park
Petersham
Chelsea Sta.
Battersea Br.
Albert Br.
Chelsea Hospital
Chelsea Br.
Battersea Park
Battersea Sta.
Clapham Junction
Victoria Sta.
H of Parliament
Millbank
Lambeth Br.
Vauxhall Br.
Vauxhall Sta.
Nine Elms
R. Wandle
WESTERN RAILWAY
Observatory
Gardens
S U R R E Y
N
S
W
E

near The Grotto at Basildon on the bank holiday of August, 1879, when a boat, which was being towed up against a strong flood, and was steered suddenly too far into the stream, was absolutely pulled over by the tow-rope, and capsized with a loss of two lives.

OXFORD, from London Bridge about 111½ miles. The towing-path, after leaving Folly Bridge, Oxford, follows the right bank. On the left are the boat-rafts, and the barges of the various colleges moored off Christ Church Meadows, where in the winter, after a flood, there is sometimes capital skating. About three-quarters of a mile from Folly Bridge are the long bridges, across a backwater, which re-enters the Thames —in this part of its course sometimes called the Isis—half a mile below Iffley. Here is the University bathing-place. The passage is impeded by weirs, and the course of the river must accordingly be followed. Rather more than half a mile farther is the " Isis Tavern " (right bank). Here the right bank must be followed, with a careful eye on the lasher, which appears rather unexpectedly, as the weir-stream which turns Iffley Mill, and which is marked by a large Conservancy " Danger " board, is very rapid and unprotected, and

IFFLEY LOCK, average fall 2 ft. 6 in., is reached. The lock is in good condition, but the upper gates want repairing. It has a roller slip. Half a mile below Iffley is the iron bridge of the Great Western Railway, from beneath which is a very pretty view of the spires of Oxford, particularly of the tower of Magdalen College, and at the bottom of the next reach (left bank) is Rose Island (sometimes called Kennington Island, the little village of that name being on the opposite bank), with its plain but snug little inn, the " Swan." Here the river takes a sharp curve to the right, and just below the island is a rustic bridge to the Oxfordshire bank, and the tow-path just below crosses a backwater by an iron bridge. The course of the river is, however, quite plain. On the right (the mill, weir-stream, and " King's Arms Inn " are left) is

SANDFORD LOCK, average fall 7 ft., from London 108 miles 7 fur., from Oxford 2 miles 5 fur. The pools at

Sandford Lasher are very dangerous for bathing, and the obelisk that stands on the bank should warn bathers to avoid the spot. At a safe distance below are the boat-houses and bathing-places of St. Peter's College, Radley. Leaving Sandford, the woods of Nuneham Courtney form the background of the prospect, and two miles from Sandford is Nuneham Park, the seat of E. W. Harcourt, Esq., M.P. Three-quarters of a mile farther is an island, which may be passed on either side. The stream on the right is, in fact, a cut made by Earl Harcourt. The old river on the left, which is more convenient for picnic parties going to Nuneham, is slightly the shorter of the two, but care must be observed in passing under the rustic bridge at the bottom of the island, as in dry seasons the water shoals considerably. Pleasure parties land at the cottages by the bridge, where once stood a lock. For regulations, &c., see NUNEHAM COURTNEY. Along the left bank for some distance is one of those grand pieces of woodland scenery for which the Thames is so renowned. The woods extend as far as the iron railway-bridge, after passing which the spire of Abingdon church appears above the trees to the right. Rather more than a mile below the cottages at Nuneham is the fall on the left where the old and present channels diverge. Below the fall is a ferry, and the tow-path crosses to the left bank. Half a mile farther, and sharp to the left, is

ABINGDON LOCK, average fall 6 ft., from London 104¼ miles, from Oxford 7¼ miles. This is a good stone lock, with a strong stream rushing over the weir. A little farther is

ABINGDON BRIDGE, with the Nag's Head landing-place for the " Crown and Thistle," and the Anchor for the " Queen's Hotel." A quarter of a mile below the bridge (right) the river Ock and the Wilts and Berks Canal enter the river. The river here runs through flat meadows. The view of Abingdon, with the spire of St. Helen's, is very pretty. Half a mile below the Ock, the unnavigable channel which was left above Abingdon re-enters the river, and half a mile farther the river takes a very sharp turn to the left, into a long and narrow cut ; the broad stream to the right leads to the weirs of Sutton Courtney, the cut to the left, which is crossed by two small wooden bridges, leads to

CULHAM LOCK, average fall 7 ft., from London 101¾ miles, from Oxford 9¾ miles. Just below are Sutton Bridges; boats coming up must be careful to keep the right bank. Going down the next reach is the first view of Wittenham Clump, a grassy hill, crowned with a clump of trees, which is visible for many miles upward and downward, and reappears in the most unexpected places as the river winds around it. The country is flat as far as Appleford iron railway-bridge, rather more than a mile from Sutton Bridges. Below this are some pretty reaches backed by Wittenham, although the banks continue flat. A mile below Appleford Bridge is the weir to the right, and at the end of a cut to the left, which is half a mile long, and is crossed by two wooden bridges, is

CLIFTON LOCK, average fall 3 ft., from London 92 miles 7 fur., from Oxford 12 miles 5 fur. About half a mile below (coxswains coming up must be careful and keep to the right, after passing the bridge) is Clifton-Hampden, with its red brick bridge. Here the tow-path crosses to the Berks side. On the cliff to the left are the church and vicarage, embosomed in trees, which come down to the water's edge, and the view down the reach is closed by luxuriant trees backed by the soft outlines of the distant hills. As we proceed the view becomes still prettier, the middle distance being broken by an eyot with a magnificent horse-chestnut tree. A mile and a half brings us to the ferry, where the tow-path crosses, and on the left to

DAY'S LOCK, average fall 4 ft. 6 in., from London 96 miles, from Oxford 15½ miles. This is one of the most striking views, the course of the river appearing to be blocked by Wittenham Clump and Sinodun Hill. A little over a mile on the left bank is Dorchester (*which see*) with its famous abbey church, which is well worth a visit. The footpath crosses the Roman remains known as The Dyke Hills. On Sinodun Hill on the right is a fine Roman camp. Two miles below the lock is a ferry, where the tow-path crosses, and three-quarters of a mile below, after a sharp turn in the stream, is Shillingford Bridge, at the foot of which, on the right

bank, is the "Swan Inn" on the Berks shore, and where the tow-path again crosses to the left bank only to re-cross a mile farther down at the village of Bensington or Benson. Below the ferry on the right is

BENSINGTON LOCK, average fall 6 ft. 6 in., from London 92 miles, from Oxford 19½ miles. Emerging from the lock some care is necessary owing to the strong cross current to the weir, against which boats coming up should particularly guard. Below the mill-stream is a ferry, but the tow-path keeps to the Berks shore. The country from here to Wallingford is charmingly wooded. The large red brick mansion on the left bank is Howberry Park, after passing which we soon arrive at Wallingford Bridge, the landing-place for boats being on the right, a short distance above the bridge.

WALLINGFORD, from London 90¾ miles, from Oxford 20¾ miles, is a very convenient place to break the journey, and the breakfasts and ale at the "Lamb" deserve particular attention. The "Town Arms Inn" is at the foot of the bridge. The "George" and "Lamb" Hotels a few minutes' walk up the High-street. The tow-path crosses at the bridge. Half a mile below stood Wallingford Lock, a structure with little or no fall to justify its existence. It was removed in 1884. Here is a ferry where the tow-path again crosses. On the left the belfry of the tiny church at Newnham Murren peeps above the trees, and immediately below on the same side are the velvet lawns and shady groves of Mongewell House, one of the most delightful residences on the river. From this point is a fine reach about a mile in length, with flat banks, the monotony of which is relieved by some fine trees, and there is a good view of the wooded heights above Streatley. At the bottom of this reach the church tower of North Stoke appears on the left. On the opposite side a little farther down, and some distance inland, are the extensive buildings of the Berks County Lunatic Asylum at Cholsey. Here is Little Stoke Ferry, where the tow-path crosses. Half a mile brings us to the brick bridge of the Great Western Railway near Moulsford Station, just above which there is a little island, and about half a mile farther, after passing Moulsford Church, on the bank of the river, is the "Beetle and Wedge Inn" and ferry. Here the tow-path again takes the Berkshire bank, and a fine stretch of water succeeds. It is here that the trial eights of Oxford University are annually rowed. At the turn of the river is a ferry, and just below, on the right, is

CLEEVE LOCK, average fall 4 ft., from London 85½ miles, from Oxford 26 miles. There is a lovely view from here of the hills and woods above Streatley, and the succession of weirs below the lock affords a variety of charming peeps. About half a mile below, where there are a quantity of weeds and rushes, the stream divides, the right branch going to

STREATLEY, where there is good accommodation and a first-rate boat-house at the "Swan Inn." It is, however, not safe to trust getting quarters at the "Swan," without previous correspondence, as the whole house is not unfrequently let for weeks together. The cut to the left, at the diverging point, leads to

GORING LOCK, average fall 5 ft. 6 in., from London 84 miles 7 furlongs, from Oxford 26 miles 5 furlongs. Here is a favourite place for campers. After passing through the lock and under the bridge, which here crosses the river (tow-path left bank), the scene continues extremely picturesque, with bold wooded hills on either side. About a mile brings us to The Grotto (right bank), a large white house backed with fine trees and with lawns sloping to the river. Passing under the railway-bridge the beech woods on the Oxford side appear to bar the way. At the ferry, below the bridge, the tow-path crosses. Farther on to the right are Basildon church and village, and farther still, opposite the beech woods and on the brow of the hill to the right is Basildon Park. At this point a fine stretch of water runs almost in a straight line for a considerable distance ; the banks on either hand are well wooded, and the view up or down is one of the most sylvan on the river. Just before making the bend before Pangbourne Reach, is Coombe Lodge, with its beautiful park, and at the end of the chalk ridge on the right is

PANGBOURNE, from London 80¾ miles, from Oxford 30¾ miles. A stay may con-

veniently be made here, and boats left at the "Swan," close to the lasher. On the opposite side of the river is

WHITCHURCH LOCK, average fall 4 ft. This lock requires some care on entering from this side, as it is inconveniently situated in an unexpected corner with an awkward mill-stream. Below the lock a wooden bridge connects the villages of Whitchurch and Pangbourne, and at its foot is the pretty house known as Thames Bank. The tow-path keeps to right bank. From here the scenery continues very pretty, the river running through richly-wooded country. The bold range of chalk downs on the left are succeeded by the woods above Hardwick House, the seat of the Lybbe family, the best view of the house being obtained from below a little eyot, a couple of hundred yards beyond it. A long row of poplars on the left, and of chestnuts and limes on the right, in the midst of perfect views, lead to

MAPLEDURHAM LOCK, an old wooden lock, on the right, with an average fall of 5 ft., from London 78½ miles, from Oxford 33 miles. After leaving the lock there is a charming view, and a very strong cross stream usually runs through the rather narrow channel. Boats coming down should be carefully handled on leaving the lock. Below the last backwater (left bank) is Mapledurham Church, and Mapledurham House, the seat of the Blount family. Two or three hundred yards below is the ferry, where the tow-path crosses, on the right being Purley Park and Purley Hall. Half a mile farther at the ferry below the "Roebuck Hotel," at Tilehurst, the tow-path re-crosses to the right bank. From this point, for about two miles, the scenery is uninteresting, but improves a little along the last two reaches above

CAVERSHAM BRIDGE, the nearest point for Reading, with two inns, the unpretentious but very snug "White Hart" (right bank) and "Crown" (left bank). Boats can be housed at Causton's boathouse, under the bridge, and at Moss's on the left bank. About half a mile farther is

CAVERSHAM LOCK, average fall about 3 ft. 6 in., from London 74 m. 1 f., from Oxford 37 m. 3 f. This is a good brick lock, in approaching which great care is necessary. The lock cut is extremely narrow and insignificant, and follows the right bank. What appears to be the main stream on the left is in reality a very rapid and dangerous current leading to the weir. There is a Thames Conservancy notice of danger, indicating the proper route, on the point of the island. Boats going down, therefore, cannot keep too close to the right bank all the way from Caversham Bridge. Three-quarters of a mile from the lock the Kennet enters the Thames and is crossed by the Great Western Railway-bridge at its mouth. Nearly a mile farther on the river takes a sharp turn to the right, and passing an eyot we come to the woods of Holme Park, and to the umbrageous walk along the bank known as Thames Parade. The right bank should here be closely followed, as the remarks already made in regard to Caversham Lock also apply to

SONNING LOCK, a good lock of stone and wood with an average fall of 4 ft. 6 in., from London 71½ miles, from Oxford 40 miles. The floral tastes of the lock-keeper generally make Sonning Lock very bright and gay, and it is besides very prettily situated amongst trees. The short distance from the lock to

SONNING is also very pretty. At Sonning are the " White Hart " on the right bank, the " French Horn " (rebuilt in 1882, and now one of the prettiest and most convenient of the river-side hotels), up the mill-stream under the wooden bridge, on the left, and the "Bull" just through the churchyard. At Sonning Bridge the tow-path crosses. Rather more than a mile from the bridge is an island. Keep to the left bank, as the stream to the right goes to some eel-bucks. Hereabouts the river winds considerably. Approaching the white house among the trees on the hill (left bank) is an island, either side of which can be taken. On the left of the next reach is a pretty bit of wooded chalk cliff, and below is the picturesque clump of trees on Phillimore Island. On the hills on the right past the island, the house known as Wargrave Hill appears in sight ; and the house on the left bank opposite the island is known as The Coppice. Immediately below on the right is a series of lashers leading to Shiplake Lock, on the left of which is a mill-stream.

SHIPLAKE LOCK is a stone lock, average fall 5 ft. 6 in., from London 63 m. 5 f., from Oxford 42 m. 7 f., just above the junction of the Loddon, right bank, with the Thames ; and a quarter of a mile beyond this point, after the railway-bridge, is

WARGRAVE, with its well-known " George and Dragon Inn." Here is a ferry, but the tow-path remains on the left bank until another ferry, about half a mile farther, opposite Shiplake station, where it crosses to the right bank. On the hills to the right are Hennerton and Temple Combe, and on the river bank to the left opposite a number of islands is Bolney Court. Below the islands the tow-path again crosses by another ferry. On the right are the woods of Park Place, and half-way down the next reach is its pretty boat-house and fishing cottage, with its lawn and vista among the trees. The road here is carried over a bridge made by General Conway, to whom the place formerly belonged, with materials from the ruins of Reading Abbey. A long wooden bridge to the lock island leads to

MARSH LOCK in the centre, the stream past the pretty house and garden on the right running to the mill. Marsh is an antiquated specimen of a wood lock, with an average fall of from 4 ft. 6 in. to 5 ft. It is distant from London 66 miles, and from Oxford 45½ miles. There is a strong stream below the lock, and the river diverges at an island ; the left (tow-path) side should be taken by boats into ladies, the Henley bathing-sheds being on the right bank. A mile from Marsh Lock we come to

HENLEY, with abundance of hotel accommodation, and one of the most favourite resorts on the river. A handsome bridge spans the river here ; the tow-path crosses to the right bank. The next mile and a quarter down to the island with the temple is the Henley Regatta Course. At Fawley Court, the large white house on the left, opposite Remenham, is the boundary between the counties of Oxford and Bucks, and about half a mile below this island on the left is Greenlands (see HAMBLEDEN). A short half-mile farther on the right is

HAMBLEDEN LOCK, once enjoying an evil reputation, now a good brick lock and altogether much improved. It has an average fall of 4 ft., and is from London 62¾ miles, and from Oxford 48¾ miles. Half a mile beyond is a ferry, the tow-path crossing, and close by on the right is the "Flower Pot Inn," at Aston, a well-known haunt of artists. At the next bend in the river the red brick house on the right is Culham Court, and here the view up the river to the poplars and wooded hills above Hambleden is very charming. Passing Culham keep to the left bank, leaving the island known as Magpie Island on the right. Half a mile farther, on the top of the high-wooded hill on the left, is a farmhouse, on a site where has been a farm since Domesday Book was compiled. Two miles from the lock is Medmenham Abbey (*which see*), with the "Ferry Boat Hotel," a well-known and convenient place for water-parties. On the opposite bank among the trees on the top of the hill is Rose Hill ; and on the hill to the north-westward of Medmenham is Danesfield, the seat of the Scott-Murray family. At Medmenham is a ferry, and the tow-path crosses. At the island below Medmenham the left bank should be followed, as it is a shorter journey. After passing the island a charming reach is opened, with the Danesfield and Harleyford woods clothing a chalk cliff to the water's edge, the centre of the background being occupied by the long stretch of falling water at the Tumbling Bay of New Lock, carefully avoiding which, and keeping to the right bank, we enter the cut leading to

HURLEY LOCK, a wooden lock with an average fall of 3 ft. 6 in., from London 59 m. 1 f., from Oxford 52 m. 3 f. On the right bank is the village of Hurley with Lady Place, so well known in connection with Lord Lovelace in the revolution of 1688 ; and on the backwater on the Bucks side is Harleyford House, Sir W. Clayton. Nearly half a mile lower down is a ferry, at which the tow-path crosses, and a little farther on the left is

TEMPLE LOCK, much in want of repair, average fall 4 ft. 6 in.; from London 58½ miles, from Oxford 53 miles. On the right bank is Temple House, the seat of Colonel Owen Williams. Leaving the lock, and passing Temple Mills on the right, about half a mile brings us to Bisham Grange, and, a little retired from

the river, Bisham Abbey, the seat of G. Vansittart, Esq. Bisham Church is prettily situated at the water's edge on the right bank, and is well worth a visit. About half a mile farther is

MARLOW, with its graceful suspension bridge and ugly church. Marlow is a good halting-place, and there are two comfortable hotels, the "Complete Angler" on the right bank of the river, and the "Crown" at the top of the High-street, five minutes' walk. The latter is to be recommended for casual visitors, as considerable notice is generally required to ensure rooms at the "Complete Angler." Boats are taken care of by Haynes, under the bridge, and by Shaw. Three hundred yards below the bridge is

MARLOW LOCK, a wooden lock with an average fall of 5½ ft., from London 56¾ miles, from Oxford 54¾ miles. It is on the right-hand side after passing the long weir, where the navigation must be carefully attended to, as the weir on the right, and the mill-stream on the left, both closely approach the lock. Past the lock there always is a strong stream to the point. The tow-path continues on the left bank, and a fine stretch of water through a country which becomes less interesting as we leave Quarry Woods brings us to Spade Oak Ferry, rather more than two miles from Marlow Lock, where the tow-path crosses. About half a mile farther the railway crosses the river, and on the left bank is Bourne End, a favourite fishing-station. After passing the mill with the towering chimney, Hedsor, the seat of Lord Boston, becomes visible on the heights on the left bank. Another three-quarters of a mile brings us to

COOKHAM. A bridge crosses the river here, and at the "Ferry Hotel" the tow-path crosses by two ferries to the lock island, and thence to the Bucks shore under the Cliveden woods, only to re-cross by another ferry a quarter of a mile lower down. At Cookham Bridge the river diverges into several channels. On the left is the broadest stream, which is blocked by a weir at the private fishing waters of Hedsor ; the two on the right are backwaters made by Formosa Island (*which see*). The entrance to the lock is along a very narrow cut, crossed by a wooden bridge, which also crosses what is known as Odney Weir, a good bathing-place in ordinary seasons, but requiring caution when the river is flooded.

COOKHAM LOCK is the most beautifully situated on the river, just under the woods of Hedsor and Cliveden. It is of wood, and the average fall is 3 ft. 6 in. From London 52½ miles, from Oxford 59 miles. On the right is Formosa Island, and on the left the fishing cottage at Cliveden. A little below the ferry is the spring and cottage, and farther yet is a magnificent view of Cliveden, the seat of the Duke of Westminster. The mansion dates only from 1851. Two houses which previously occupied the site were burnt down, one in 1795 and one in 1849. The scenery down the next reach and past the islands is exceedingly beautiful, and is generally considered the finest on the river. The flatness of the right bank, however, somewhat detracts from its claims to be considered a perfect landscape. Not quite 2½ miles from Cookham Lock is

BOULTER'S LOCK, from London 50 m. 3 f., from Oxford 61 m. 1 f. This, a good stone lock, with an average fall of about 6 ft., is approached from above by a long narrow cut on the right. The stream on the left is dangerous, but the Conservancy danger-signal on the point of the eyot is of ample dimensions, and easily to be distinguished. Below the lock there is at all times plenty and to spare of stream for some distance. On the right bank, between here and Maidenhead Bridge, are the "Ray Mead" and "Thames" Hotels. On the island on the left is a new and handsome house of Sir Roger Palmer. Below that is the comfortable mill-house, and on the hill above, embedded in trees, is Taplow Court, the seat of W. H. Grenfell, Esq. (*which see*). Three-quarters of a mile from Boulter's Lock is Maidenhead Bridge. The ivy-covered house close to the bridge on the right is Bridge House, occupied by Lord Polling-ton, and opposite is the Guards' Club House and Skindle's well-known "Ork-ney Arms Hotel."

MAIDENHEAD, a convenient stopping-place, with two excellent hotels: Skindle's on the Taplow side of the bridge, and the "Bear" in the town. The "Ray Mead" is nearer Boulter's Lock. Below Maidenhead Bridge is the Great Western Rail-way-bridge, supposed to be the largest

brick bridge in the world, with a singular echo lurking in its enormous span, and on the left is the pretty dwelling, known as Orkney Cottage. A mile from Maiden-head is the pleasant village of Bray, where there is a convenient hotel on the river bank, and where the church and Jesus Hospital deserve more than passing attention. Rather more than a quarter of a mile on the left is

BRAY LOCK, distant from London 48¼ miles, from Oxford 63¼ miles. For many years this was a rotten and dangerous structure, but was rebuilt in 1884-5. Half a mile farther is Monkey Island (*which see*), and here for a little distance there is a good stream. After the next island, on the right, are the following houses: Down Place, Oakley Court, and The Fishery. Two miles and a half from Bray Lock, on the right bank, is Surly Hall, an inn well known to Eto-nians. About another half-mile brings us to

BOVENEY LOCK, on the left. The weir-stream is wide and strong, and when there is much water in the river, very dangerous. The lock is of wood, with an average fall of about 3 ft. 6 in., and the distance from London is 45 m. 1 f., and from Oxford 66 m. 3 f. On the right is Windsor racecourse, and three-quarters of a mile down is Athens, the bathing-place of the senior Eton boys. Opposite the point, at Upper Hope, is a backwater on the left called Cuckoo Weir, also an Eton bathing-place. A wide berth must be given to the point at the bottom of the short reach here, which is known as Lower Hope, as a sandbank has formed just under it. The creek on the right is Clewer. The Great Western Railway-bridge and the Brocas clump on the left are next passed, and we arrive at

WINDSOR on the right bank, and Eton on the left. From London 43 m. 1 f., from Oxford 68 m. 3 f. Boats can be left either at Goodman's or Parkins's, or at the "Bridge House Hotel." The river is here crossed by a stone bridge of three arches. The South Western Railway-station is close to the river, the Great Western and the "Castle" and "White Hart" Hotels a few minutes' walk up Thames-street. After passing through Windsor Bridge the right bank,

on which is the tow-path, should be kept.
The rapid and dangerous stream to the
left runs to the weir, and the neighbourhood of the Cobbler, as the long pro-
jection from the island is called, is
undesirable when there is much water in
the river. Not half a mile below Windsor
Bridge is

ROMNEY LOCK, a good stone lock
with an average fall of 5 ft. 9 in., from
London 42¾ miles, from Oxford 68¾
miles. After passing through the lock
beautiful views of Eton College, the
playing-fields, and Poet's Walk are
obtained on the left, and on the right
is Windsor Castle and the Home Park.
A quarter of a mile from the lock the
river is crossed by the railway bridge.
The house on the left immediately below
is Black Potts, the residence of the Rev.
Dr. Hornby, Provost of Eton. Farther
down is the Victoria Bridge, one of two
which cross the river at each extremity of
the park, and about a mile and a half
from Romney Lock is

DATCHET, on the left bank. Here will
be found fair accommodation for man
and boat. After the second of the royal
bridges (the Albert) is passed, the right
bank must be kept, and a long narrow
cut, crossed halfway by a wooden bridge,
leads to

OLD WINDSOR LOCK, of stone and
wood, with rather inconvenient sills. It
has an average fall of 4 ft. The distance from London is 39¼ miles, from
Oxford 71¾ miles. Shortly after passing
the lock is a ferry, but the tow-path still
continues on the right bank. Three-
quarters of a mile from the lock, in pretty
scenery, is the well-known " Bells of
Ouseley " tavern, where the stock ale
deserves attention. Half a mile farther
down Magna Charta Island, with its
cottage, is on the left, the wooded heights
of Cooper's Hill with the Indian Engineering College on the right. Below is
Ankerwycke House, and the summer-
house known as the Picnic (see PICNIC).
After Ankerwycke the scenery becomes
flat and tame, and even ugly, if such a
word can be used in connection with the
Thames anywhere. Runnymead is on
the right bank, which should be followed
to

BELL WEIR LOCK, a good stone
lock, with a fall of about 5 ft. ; from

London 36 m. 7 f., from Oxford 74 m.
5 f. Here is the " Anglers' Rest Inn."
A footpath close to the inn leads to
Egham. Half a mile below Bell Weir
Lock on the left bank is London Stone,
which formerly marked the limit of the
jurisdiction of the Conservancy. The
passage to the left is the nearest way to
Staines Church, Tims's boat-house, and
the ladies' bath. The Colne enters the
Thames on the left between Bell Weir
Lock and Staines. Two or three hundred
yards farther is Staines Bridge and the
town of

STAINES, nearly a mile from Bell Weir
Lock. On the left is the " Pack Horse
Inn," with good accommodation for
boating parties, and on the right the
" Swan," with landing-stage, &c. At
Staines the tow-path crosses to the left
bank, which should be followed on
approaching

PENTON HOOK LOCK, about 1⅜ mile
from Staines, from London 34 miles,
from Oxford 77½ miles. Care must be
taken to avoid the weir-whirl, which is
very dangerous, and insufficiently protected. There is a fall of 2 ft. 6 in.
There are plenty of trout about here.
After this lock (about half a mile) is
Laleham and the ferry. Laleham House,
the seat of the Earl of Lucan, is just
below. Still keeping to the left bank, we
next come to

CHERTSEY LOCK, with a fall of about
3 ft. ; from London 32 miles, and from
Oxford 79½ miles. A quarter of a mile
farther is Chertsey Bridge, at the foot of
which, on the right, is the Bridge House
Hotel. A wide berth should be given to
the first point below the bridge, on the
tow-path side, as the water here shoals
considerably. Hence the river winds very
much between flat banks to

SHEPPERTON LOCK, on the left, with
an average fall of 5 ft. 6 in., and is
distant from London 30 miles, from
Oxford 81½ miles. Here the Wey enters
the Thames. The tow-path crosses to
right bank. The village of Shepperton
is three-quarters of a mile from the lock
on the left, and half a mile farther is
Halliford and "Bob" Stone's popular
"Ship Hotel." On the right are extensive views of the woods above Weybridge,
Oatlands Park, and Walton. Three-
quarters of a mile below Halliford are

Coway, or Causeway Stakes, and immediately afterwards comes

WALTON BRIDGE, which consists of four arches. On the right below is Mount Felix, and the village of Walton. Half a mile on the left is a tumbling-bay, whose neighbourhood will be best avoided, and half a mile beyond this, on the right, is the cut leading to

SUNBURY LOCK. The weir to the left is very dangerous. Sunbury Lock is a good one, of stone, with a roller for pleasure-boats. From London 26 m. 3 f., from Oxford 85 m. 1 f. From the boat-house on the lock island is a ferry to Sunbury. There is some pretty scenery on the left below the lock, the right bank being very flat and dull. A strong stream known as Sunbury Race runs here. About 1½ mile below the lock is an island, either side of which may be taken. On the right are Molesey Hurst and race-course, and on the left

HAMPTON. Here is a ferry, and on the left bank, below the church, Garrick's Villa. Half a mile farther is Tagg's Island, with Hotel and boat-houses, and on the right (the weir must on no account be trifled with) is

MOLESEY LOCK. This is a wooden lock, with an average fall of 6 ft., and has a roller for pleasure-boats. It is distant from London 23 m. 3 f., from Oxford 88 m. 1 f. Below is Hampton Court Bridge, an ugly iron erection, Hampton Court being on the left, and East Molesey, with the railway-station, on the right. The tow-path here crosses to the left bank. Nearly a mile below the bridge, on the right, is Thames Ditton, with the "Swan Hotel," and Boyle Farm, the residence of the late Lord St. Leonards. At the top of the waterworks is the beginning of the Kingston Regatta Course. Passing Messenger's Island we come to Surbiton, and nearly a mile lower down to

KINGSTON BRIDGE, of five stone arches, from London 20½ miles, from Oxford 91 miles. The market-place and a railway-station are close to the bridge. From Messenger's Island to the Surbiton station is ten minutes' walk. Below Kingston Bridge is the railway-bridge. The tow-path crosses to the right bank, and the next point is

TEDDINGTON LOCK, a first-rate stone lock, on the right, with a smaller lock, as well as a roller for pleasure boats. The fall is nearly 9 ft., and the distance from London 18½ miles, from Oxford 93 miles. On the left is Teddington, and an almost uninterrupted line of villas extends along that bank as far as Twickenham. About a mile from the lock is Eel Pie Island, opposite which is Petersham, and Ham House, the seat of the Earl of Dysart, almost hidden among the trees. On the left is Orleans House, and down the river rises Richmond Hill, crowned with the famous "Star and Garter." Making the bend just below the next island is, on the right bank, the ivy-clad residence of the Duke of Buccleuch. Not quite three miles from Teddington Lock is

RICHMOND BRIDGE. Boats may be left either at Messenger's boat-house, or at Wheeler's, close to the bridge. The trip is generally concluded here, the banks of the river below this point presenting little or nothing to attract the visitor. Except, therefore, in the case of oarsmen bound for one of the metropolitan club-houses, it is recommended that the boat should finally be left at Richmond.

Trout.—The young of trout have been placed in the river literally by millions with discouraging results. Where, however, this species of salmonidæ have been introduced into the waters of a sufficient size (say of 1 lb. to 2 lb. weight) to hold their own against their many enemies, notably at Maidenhead, Cookham, and Bray, the fish have lived to propagate and give unmistakable sport to the trout fisher.

The Thames trout proper grow to an enormous size, but it is remarkable how little the artificial fly is used on this river for its capture; the common plan being by live-baiting or spinning a bleak or minnow, the heavier fish, more particularly in the commencement of the season, falling a prey to the former ignoble mode of angling.

It is, however, believed that if fly-fishing were pursued as persistently as are the practices of spinning and live-baiting, the results would show that at the end of the season as many trout would have been taken as by both the other plans put together.

With regard to pike—an acknowledged

greatly inferior fish—the identically same processes of capture are resorted to as those used for the taking of the nobler trout.

The most usual way of angling for trout is by spinning. This is done with a running line, a certain number of hooks, triangular and otherwise, whipped on to a strand of silkworm-gut, and baited with a bleak or minnow in such a manner that the tail of the fish, being slightly bent, shall, when drawn through the water, meet with sufficient resistance as to make the whole turn rapidly in the water. There is some practice required to place a fish thus effectively on these hooks, which are technically called a "flight;" some of the fishermen are great adepts at it, and it would be well for the beginner to take a few lessons from these men to render him independent of their assistance, more particularly in the commencement and therefore the best period of the season, when the fishermen are (certainly the most experienced are) pre-engaged it may be for some time previously to its opening. To this flight is fixed a bottom or trace, likewise of gut, of two feet or a yard in length, on to which are threaded, or hung in a loop beneath it, a row of shots or pipe-lead, of a weight sufficient to sink the bait to the required depth of water according to the nature and swiftness of the stream, and on this are affixed from one to three small brass swivels—preferable to steel, as they do not rust and clog their action. Thus prepared, the length of the flight being adapted to the size of the bait, it is cast rather across the stream from the reel or winch. The Nottingham winch is much to be preferred, as it does not entail the previous drawing off sufficient line for the throw, and thus prevents entanglements. When the bait is cast as far as needed, the line is wound up again with sufficient rapidity to cause the bait to gyrate in an attractive way, and the throw is repeated. In spinning in rapid currents, or from weirs, or in mill-tails, the line may be drawn in very slowly; indeed, in likely places remain almost stationary, as the action of the stream and hand in general will also hook your prey with little if any movement from the arm; a smart stroke, but not a violent one, will, however, upon your feeling the

seizure, assist to drive the hook home, particularly if it has come in contact with the bony part of the mouth. In very clear water the rod should be kept as low as possible towards the surface of the water, for if the flashing of the rod is seen it is very likely to scare your quarry. Live-bait fishing for trout, before alluded to, is unsportsmanlike, but the heaviest and most sluggish fish are mostly taken in that unscientific manner. If trout be fished for with a fly, the fly should be of a good size, as for grilse or small salmon ; and worm-fishing for Thames trout should be altogether tabooed, although many are thus caught, particularly at the bottom, when legering with a heavy lead for barbel.

Twickenham, Middlesex, on the left bank, $17\frac{1}{2}$ miles from London, 94 miles from Oxford, a station on the South-Western line $11\frac{1}{2}$ miles from Waterloo ; the trains average about half an hour. There is an alternative route to Ludgate Hill, but the journey occupies much more time than that to Waterloo. Flys meet the trains. From the station to the river is a good quarter of a mile. Population, 11,000. Soil, alluvial. Twickenham is a very long and rambling village, stretching along the road towards Bushey and Teddington for a couple of miles or so. The village, which is practically a suburb of Richmond, has been much increased by building, and along the river bank there is now an almost uninterrupted succession of houses from Richmond Bridge to Teddington Lock. The principal interest of Twickenham lies in its literary associations. It was to Twickenham that Pope came in 1715, and here in 1744 he died. For some years the villa with the gardens and grotto, which were contrived according to the grotesque taste of that period, were religiously preserved. In 1807, however, Lady Howe, who was probably not gifted with the poetic temperament, destroyed the house, and there is now little if any trace of what was left by the poet. Strawberry Hill, the seat of Horace Walpole, is still standing, and was considerably enlarged by the late Countess Waldegrave, but the sham castellated Gothic building is only noteworthy from its associations—beautiful it certainly is not. The traces of Walpole lasted longer than those of Pope, as it was not until 1842 that the great Strawberry Hill collection afforded an opportunity for a display of eloquence on the part of George Robins, the auctioneer. Twickenham or Twitnam Park once belonged to Sir Francis Bacon. Among the other distinguished persons whose names are connected with Twickenham are Lady Mary Wortley Montagu, Secretary Craggs, and Hudson and Sir Godfrey Kneller the painters. In later days Orleans House and other residences were occupied by members of the Orleans family during the Second Empire. Orleans House is now the Orleans Club (*which see*).

At St. Margaret's, Twickenham, is the Royal Naval Female School for the daughters of necessitous naval and marine officers. The offices are at 32, Sackville-street, London. On the Hampton Road is the Metropolitan and City Police Orphanage. Subscribers and donors are invited to visit the orphanage on Saturdays, between two and four. The first Wednesday in each month at the same hours is visiting-day for relatives, &c. In Whitton Lane is the Economic Museum, which has been established "with a view to impart in a manner at once scientific and entertaining that knowledge of common things which is so necessary for securing health and comfort." The museum is open for inspection and study upon Wednesdays and Saturdays from 2 to 5 p.m., on other days by appointment. All admissions are free. The Montpellier Lecture Hall, Orleans-road, has a license for music, is capable of holding 430, and can be hired for public entertainments. The Assembly Room is at the Town Hall. There is also a library and reading-room.

The church of St. Mary is a sufficiently plain, not to say morose, building of red brick, with a redeeming point in the shape of its ivy-covered embattled tower. The interior is plain in character, with oak galleries right round the walls, which are almost covered with monuments and tablets. On the south side of the south aisle is a mural tablet with coloured busts to Francis Poylton and his wife, Susan, dated 1642. Of Susan it is here recorded, "Shee yet liveth, bvt desireth with him to bee desolved and to be with Christ." Round the corner to the left, in a stone placed against the wall, is a brass of the middle of the 14th century to Ricus Burton. On the wall in the north gallery is Bishop Warburton's pyramidal monument to Pope, with a medallion bust of the poet, and the following inscription :

POETA LOQUITUR.

Heroes and kings your distance keep,
In peace let one poor poet sleep
Who never flatter'd folks like you,
Let Horace blush and Virgil too.

Kitty Clive the actress is buried in the churchyard.

BANK.—London and Provincial, King-street.

FIRE.—Brigade Station, Queen-street.

HOTELS AND INNS. — "Albany," "King's Head," "Railway Station," "White Swan," river-side.

PLACES OF WORSHIP.—Holy Trinity, St. Mary's, and St. Stephen's, East Twickenham ; and Baptist, Congregational, and Wesleyan Chapels.

POLICE.—Metropolitan (T Division) Station, London-road.

POSTAL ARRANGEMENTS.—Post Office (money order, savings bank, telegraph, and insurance), King-street. Mails from London, 6.40 and 8.45 a.m., 1.55 and 6.50 p.m. ; Sunday, 6.40 a.m. Mails for London, 9.45 a.m., 12.50, 3.25, 4.50, 9.15, and 9.30 p.m. ; Sunday, 8 p.m.

NEAREST *Bridges*, up, Kingston about 3 miles ; down, Richmond 1½ mile. *Lock*, up, Teddington 1¼ mile. *Ferry* and *Railway Station*, Twickenham.

FARES to Waterloo : 1st, 1/6, 2/4; 2nd, 1/2, 1/10 ; 3rd, -/11, 1/6. To Ludgate-hill : 1st, 1/8, 2/6 ; 2nd, 1/4, 2/- ; 3rd, 1/1, 1/9.

Twickenham Rowing Club.—Election is by ballot in committee ; one black ball in five excludes. Entrance fee, £1. 1s. ; subscription, £2 2s. Colours, dark blue with crimson horizontal stripe. In 1880 the club opened a new boat-house on Twickenham Eyot.

University Boat Race.—Not many years ago the annual eight-oared race between the Universities of Oxford and Cambridge was an event which concerned only the crews, their friends, the members of the Universities, and that small portion of the general public which took pleasure in river sports. It was a quiet, friendly

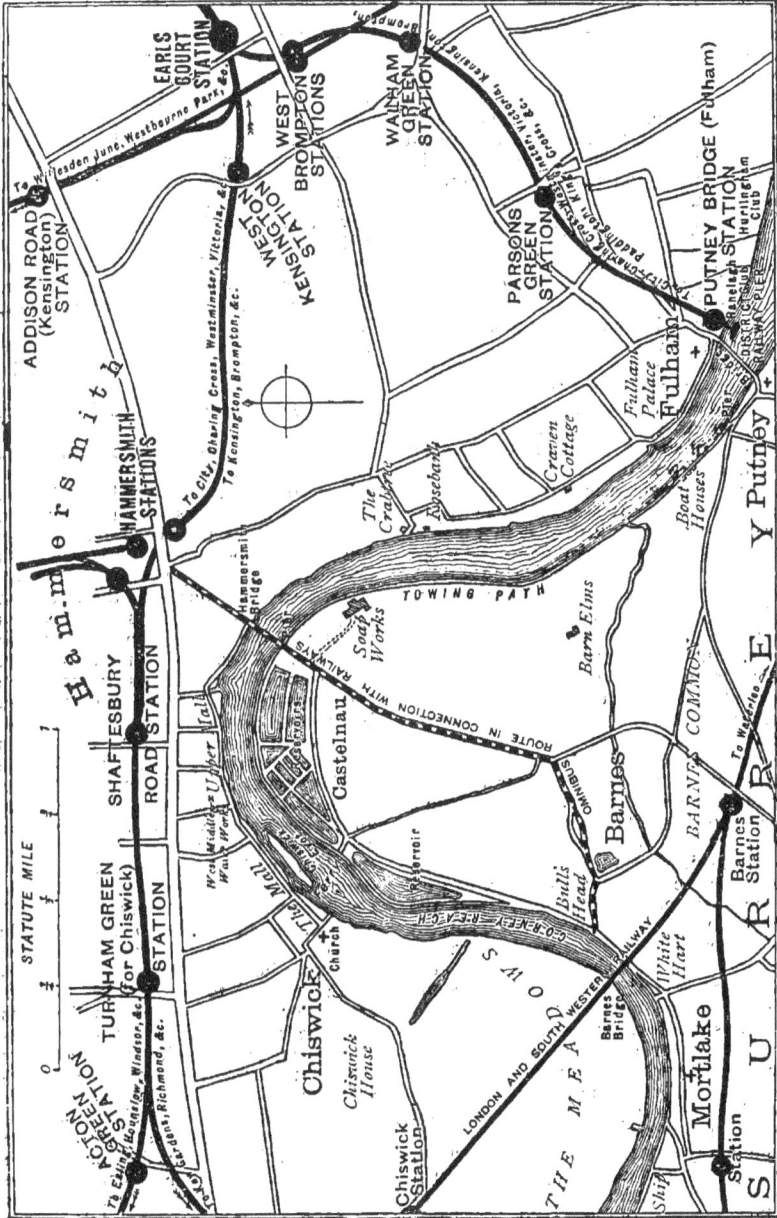

Typographic Etching Co., Sc.

sort of gathering enough in those days. The comparatively few people who watched the practice of the crews all seemed to know each other. It was a wonderful week for parsons. Past University oarsmen, their jerseys exchanged for the decorous high waistcoat, the white choker taking the place of the rowing-man's muffler, were to be met all over Putney, and about Searle's yard and the London Boat-house. The towing-path was a sort of Rialto or High 'Change, on which old friends met and renewed their youth as they talked over old times, and criticised their successors. There were but few rowing-clubs then ; the river had not become the fashion ; the professional touts and tipsters had not fastened on the boat-race ; the graphic reporter as yet was not. There was betting, of course, but it was of a modest kind, and was unaccompanied by publicity. The whole had the ring of true sport about it. It seemed indeed to be the only event that kept alive that idea of sport for its own sake which was fast fading out, if it was not already extinct, in most other contests. Of course it was all too good to last. The popularising process was not likely to spare the boat-race. First of all aquatics generally grew more in favour, and so a larger public was attracted to take an interest in the battle of the blues. Then the newspapers took the subject up, and the graphic reporter worked his will with the race and its surroundings, and the extraordinary multiplication of sporting newspapers and sporting articles in papers of all sorts, let loose any number of touts on to the towing-path. Finally the ominous announcement of "Boat-race, 5 to 4 on Oxford (taken in hundreds)," and the like began to appear in the price current of Tattersall's ; and the whole character of the race was changed. What the blue fever is now, and has been for some years, every Londoner knows well. Perhaps it is because the boat-race is the first of the spring events—as it were, the first swallow which indicates at least the possibility of a summer—perhaps it is because of the very natural readiness that exists among the masses to take advantage of any excuse for a holiday ; perhaps it is because of the sheep-like tendency of the British public of all classes to follow a leader of any kind anywhere,

that the complaint assumes so epidemic a form with every recurring spring. It is certain, at all events, that for some time before the race there is taken in it —or affected to be taken, which does just as well—an interest which has about it even something ludicrous. Every scrap of gossip about the men and their boats, their trials and their coaches, is greedily devoured. Year by year, to gratify the public taste in that direction, has the language of the industrious gentlemen who describe the practice become more and more candid, not to say personal. The faults and peculiarities of individual members of the crews are criticised in some quarters in terms which might be considered rude if applied to a favourite for the Derby, who presumably does not read the sporting papers, and which, when used in speaking of gentlemen who may perhaps have feelings to be hurt, seems to the unprejudiced mind even offensive. The gushing reporter not only attends the race itself, but disports himself on the towing-path after his peculiar and diverting fashion on practice days, and daily develops the strangest conglomeration of views on matters aquatic in the greatest possible number of words. All sorts of dodges, borrowed from some of the shabbiest tricks of the "horse-watcher's" trade, are adopted by touts, amateur and professional, to get at the time of the crews between certain points, or over the whole course. The race is betted upon as regularly as the Derby, as publicly, and as generally. Cabmen, butcher boys, and omnibus drivers sport the colours of the Universities in all directions : the dark blue of Oxford and the light blue of Cambridge fill all the hosiers' shops, and are flaunted in all sorts of indescribable company. Every publican who has a flag-staff hoists a flag to mark his preference and to show which way his crown or so has gone — unless, as is sometimes the case, he be a dispassionate person with no pecuniary interest involved, in which case he impartially displays the banners of both crews. Everybody talks about the race, and it generally happens that the more ignorant of the matter is the company the more heated is the discussion, and the more confident and dogmatic the opinions expressed. That thousands and thousands of people go down to the river on the important day who do not know one end of a boat from the other, who have no prospect of seeing anything at all, and no particular care whether they do see anything or not, is not surprising. That other thousands go, knowing perfectly well that all they are likely to see is a mere glimpse of the two crews as they dash by, perhaps separated by some boats' lengths after the real struggle is all over, is equally natural. Thousands and thousands of people go to the Derby on exactly the same principles. That 'Arry has claimed the boat-race for his own is only to say that he is there as he is everywhere, and that circumstance is not perhaps to be laid to the charge of the boat-race. But the fact is, and becomes more and more plain every year, that the boat-race is becoming vulgarised—not in the sense that it is patronised and in favour with what are called "common people," but in the sense that it has got to be the centre of most undesirable surroundings—and that its removal from metropolitan waters would not be lamented by real friends of the Universities, or lovers of genuine sport. It is not so bad as the Eton and Harrow cricket match, which has been utterly vulgarised by "society," genuine and sham, and for which there is no kind of excuse or reason. The University crews cannot meet each other on their own waters, as cricketers can play upon each other's grounds. They must have a neutral course to row upon. It is probable, before very long, that it will occur to the authorities that there are other suitable pieces of water in England besides the Putney course, and that there is no reason whatever why, if the annual *vexata quæstio* of the rowing superiority of the rival Universities is all that is to be taken into account, the race should not be rowed elsewhere. The managers of the race or their friends have shown signs of some confusion of mind on this head on more than one occasion. Protests have gone forth that it is a private match with which the public have nothing to do. The crowding of spectators to see the practice—and as many people go nowadays to Putney on a Saturday afternoon, if there be a good tide, as used to go to the race itself twenty years ago—has been complained of. The general exhibition of interest has been

deprecated. It has been intimated that all this newspaper publicity is distasteful and undesirable. In some strange way the boat devoted to the service of the general body of the press on the day of the race is always either so slow a tub as to be of little use, or else meets with some mysterious accident which deprives its occupants of any but a very distant view of the proceedings, while their more fortunate brethren, who happen to have been educated at Oxford or Cambridge, are careering gaily after the racing boats on board one of the University steamers. The independent sporting papers say that accurate information has become more and more difficult to get, and newspaper reports—except in special quarters —are, following out the private-match theory, discouraged as much as possible. But it is all to no purpose. The boat-race can never shake off its surroundings so long as it continues to be rowed at Putney. Change of air will, in all probability, shortly be found necessary to restore it to a healthy condition—a condition in which it certainly is not now.

As matters stand at present, the race is rowed annually, about the Saturday before Passion Week, between Putney and Mortlake, usually with the flood-tide, although occasionally the reverse course has been taken. The crews are generally at Putney for a fortnight or more for practice, a very much longer period of training on the tidal water being considered necessary now than was the case in the earlier years of the match. Four steamers only accompany the race : one for the umpire, one for either University, and one for the press ; and although this arrangement is decidedly an advantage from the point of view of the public safety, the spectators about Hammersmith and Barnes lose a singular sight. The charge through the bridges of the twenty steamers or so which used to be chartered to accompany the race was something to see ; but although it was magnificent it was not safe, and it was fortunate that the Conservancy regulations stopped it before some terrible accident occurred. That nothing very serious ever happened in that fleet of overcrowded, swaying, bumping, jostling boats was an annual cause for wonder ; and it became sometimes, when one was on board one of the fleet as it approached Hammersmith, matter for rather serious consideration to speculate at what particular moment the mass of spectators on the suspension-bridge would break it down and plunge with the ruins into the river. Fortunately the bridge stood long enough for the official mind to be exercised on the subject before anything happened, and it is now wisely closed during and for some time before and after the race. The best points of view are at Chiswick, on Barnes Terrace, or, best of all, perhaps, on Barnes Railway Bridge, tickets for which are to be had at Waterloo Station. Otherwise, railway travelling between London and Mortlake cannot be recommended on boat-race days—for ladies at all events.

The Universities rowed their first match over a course of two miles and a quarter at Henley, and have met 40 times over the London course, as will be seen by the subjoined table, with the result that Oxford has won 21, and Cambridge 18 races, while the race of 1877 was given by the judge as a dead heat. It is significant of the kind of influences that now prevail that this decision was productive of much discontent, and that the judge, who had officiated for a long period, was in the following year superseded. Of course all sorts of improvements have been made in the boats in which the competitors row, the introduction of outriggers in 1846 and the adoption of sliding-seats in 1873 being the most radical alterations; but it is noticeable that from some cause or another the sliding-seats, which the modern rowing-man looks upon as an absolute necessity, do not seem to have increased the pace of the boats—if the time test goes for anything, that is to say. This is the more remarkable, as rowing men appear to be agreed that a crew rowing in fixed seats would have no chance against opponents of exactly equal merit on slides. It may be that the times taken before the days of chronographs were not exactly trustworthy. However it may be explained, the fact remains.

It will be seen that success has often favoured one or other of the Universities for a series of years, only to go over to the other side for another series. The most important consecutive score is that of Oxford, from 1861 to 1869.

WINNERS OF THE UNIVERSITY BOAT RACE OVER THE METROPOLITAN COURSE.

Year.	Winner.	Course.	Time.	Won by
1836	Cambridge	W. to P.	36 m. 0 s.	1 m.
1839	Cambridge	W. to P.	31 m. 0 s.	1 m. 45 s.
1840	Cambridge	W. to P.	29 m. 30 s	¾ length.
1841	Cambridge	W. to P.	32 m. 30 s.	1 m. 4 s.
1842	Oxford	W. to P.	30 m. 45 s.	13 s.
1845	Cambridge	P. to M.	23 m. 30 s.	30 s.
1846	Cambridge	M. to P.	21 m. 5 s.	2 lengths.
1849	Cambridge	P. to M.	22 m. 0 s.	easily.
1849	Oxford	P. to M.	—	foul.
1852	Oxford	P. to M.	21 m. 36 s.	27 s.
1854	Oxford	P. to M.	25 m. 29 s.	11 strks.
1856	Cambridge	M. to P.	25 m. 50 s	½ length.
1857	Oxford	P. to M.	22 m. 35 s.	35 s.
1858	Cambridge	P. to M.	21 m. 23 s.	22 s.
1859	Oxford	P. to M.	24 m. 40 s.	Cam. snk.
1860	Cambridge	P. to M.	26 m. 5 s.	1 length.
1861	Oxford	P. to M.	23 m. 30 s.	48 s.
1862	Oxford	P. to M.	24 m. 41 s.	30 s.
1863	Oxford	M. to P.	23 m. 6 s.	43 s.
1864	Oxford	P. to M.	21 m. 40 s.	26 s.
1865	Oxford	P. to M.	21 m. 24 s.	4 lengths.
1866	Oxford	P. to M.	23 m. 35 s.	15 s.
1867	Oxford	P. to M.	22 m. 40 s.	½ length.
1868	Oxford	P. to M.	20 m. 56 s.	6 lengths.
1869	Oxford	P. to M.	20 m. 5 s.	3 lengths.
1870	Cambridge	P. to M.	22 m. 4 s.	1¼ lngth.
1871	Cambridge	P. to M.	23 m. 5 s.	1 length.
1872	Cambridge	P. to M.	21 m. 15 s.	2 lengths.
1873	Cambridge	P. to M.	19 m. 35 s.	3¼ lgths.
1874	Cambridge	P. to M.	22 m. 35 s.	3 lengths.
1875	Oxford	P. to M.	22 m. 2 s.	10 lngths.
1876	Cambridge	P. to M.	20 m. 20 s.	won easily
1877	{ Oxford } { Camb. }	P. to M.	24 m. 8 s.	dead ht.
1878	Oxford	P. to M.	22 m. 13 s.	10 lngths.
1879	Cambridge	P. to M.	21 m. 18 s.	4 lengths.
1880	Oxford	P. to M.	21 m. 23 s.	3¾ lgths.
1881	Oxford	P. to M.	21 m. 52 s.	4 lengths.
1882	Oxford	P. to M.	20 m. 12 s.	7 lengths.
1883	Oxford	P. to M.	21 m. 22 s.	3½ lgths.
1884	Cambridge	P. to M.	21 m. 38 s.	2 lengths.
1885	Oxford	P. to M	21 m. 36 s.	3 lengths.

In 1829 Oxford beat Cambridge easily over 2¼ miles at Putney, in 14 min. 30 sec. On five occasions the Universities have met in their heats for the Grand Challenge Cup at Henley with the following results:

Year.	Winner.	Time.	Won by
1845	Cambridge	8 m. 30 s.	2 lengths.
1847	Oxford	8 m. 4 s.	2 lengths.
1851	Oxford	7 m. 45 s.	6 lengths.
1853	Oxford	8 m. 3 s.	1½ foot.
1855	Cambridge	8 m. 32 s.	2½ lengths.

Also at the Thames Regatta, 1844, Oxford beat Cambridge.

This is what may be called the Morrison era, as the brothers Morrison were either in the boat or coaching during the whole, or the greater part, of that period, and finer crews than some of those which comprised such men as Darbishire, Willan, Tinné, the Morrisons, Hoare, Yarborough, Woodgate—to mention only a few names—have never been sent to Putney. Then Cambridge, who had persevered with the utmost pluck through most disheartening difficulties and defeat, learnt the proper lesson from Morrison, and the light blue once more came to the front under the auspices of Goldie. After this admirable stroke and sound judge, who did wonders for Cambridge rowing, came Rhodes, and plenty of good men have since been found to do battle at Putney for the honour of Cambridge.

Different times have been given by different authorities as the duration of the race in the last few years. In one case two of the most trustworthy are at issue as to a matter of half a minute, so there must evidently be some mistake somewhere. The times adopted in the preceding list are those given by the editor of the "Rowing Almanack," a thorough good judge of rowing, who has had many years' experience of timing races, and, being invariably careful, is presumably accurate.

In 1885 the race was rowed on the 28th of March, with the following result :

Oxford 1
Cambridge 0

The following are the names and weights of the crews :

OXFORD.

	st.	lb.
W. S. Unwin, Magdalen	10	10½
J. S. Clemons, Corpus	11	9
P. W. Taylor, Lincoln	13	6½
C. R. Carter, Corpus	13	2
H. Maclean, New	12	12
F. O. Wethered, Christ Church ..	12	6
D. H. Maclean, New	13	1½
H. Girdlestone, Magdalen (stroke)..	12	7
F. J. Humphreys, Brasenose (cox)..	8	2

CAMBRIDGE.

	st.	lb.
N. P. Symonds, Lady Margaret ..	10	8
W. K. Hardacre, Trinity Hall ..	10	8
W. H. W. Perrott, First Trinity ..	12	2½
S. Swann, Trinity Hall	13	3½
F. E. Churchill, Third Trinity ..	13	2½
E. W. Haig, Third Trinity	11	8
R. M. Coke, Trinity Hall	12	3¾
F. I. Pitman, Third Trinity (stroke)	11	11½
G. Wilson, First Trinity (cox) ..	7	11

University (Oxford) Boat Club, 1884.—TORPIDS.—Feb. 21 to Feb. 27. The following was the order of starting and finish :

FIRST DIVISION.—Order of starting : 1, Corpus ; 2, Brasenose (1); 3, New (1); 4, Magdalen ; 5, Trinity ; 6, Christ Church (1) ; 7, Keble (1) ; 8, Exeter ; 9, Pembroke ; 10, Lincoln ; 11, Worcester ; 12, Balliol.

Order of finish : 1, Corpus ; 2, Brasenose (1) ; 3, New (1) ; 4, Magdalen ; 5, Christ Church (1) ; 6, Trinity ; 7, Exeter ; 8, Keble (1) ; 9, Balliol ; 10, Queen's ; 11, Pembroke ; 12, Wadham.

SECOND DIVISION.—Order of starting : 1, University ; 2, Queen's ; 3, Christ Church (2) ; 4, Oriel ; 5, Wadham ; 6, Hertford ; 7, St. John's ; 8, Merton ; 9, St. Catherine's ; 10, Keble (2) ; 11, New (2) ; 12, Jesus ; 13, Brasenose (2).

Order of finish : 1, Lincoln ; 2, Christ Church (2) ; 3, Hertford ; 4, Worcester ; 5, St. Catherine's ; 6, Oriel ; 7, University ; 8, New (2) ; 9, Jesus ; 10, St. John's ; 11, Keble (2) ; 12, Brasenose (2) ; 13, Merton.

COLLEGE EIGHTS, May 15 to 27.

The boats started thus : Exeter, 1 ; Magdalen, 2 ; Corpus, 3 ; Brasenose, 4 ; Keble, 5 ; Pembroke, 6 ; Hertford, 7 ; New, 8 ; St. Catherine's, 9 ; Trinity, 10 ; St. John's, 11 ; Christ Church, 12 ; Lincoln, 13 ; Worcester, 14 ; University, 15 ; Balliol, 16 ; Queen's, 17 ; Wadham, 18 ; Merton, 19 ; Oriel, 20 ; Jesus, 21.

And finished in the following order : Exeter, 1 ; Corpus, 2 ; Magdalen, 3 ; Brasenose, 4 ; Keble, 5 ; Christ Church, 6 ; New, 7 ; Trinity, 8 ; Hertford, 9 ; Pembroke, 10 ; St. John's, 11 ; St. Catherine's, 12 ; Balliol, 13 ; Worcester, 14 ; Queen's, 15 ; Merton, 16 ; University, 17 ; Oriel, 18 ; Lincoln, 19 : Jesus, 20 ; Wadham, 21.

The Exeter crew, the head of the river, consisted of: G. Pinckney, L. Stock, A. S. Bengough, A. B. How, H. Walrond, W. A. B. Walter, R. A. Pinckney, W. D. B. Curry (stroke), W. E. Maynard (cox).

UNIVERSITY SCULLS, June 6.

Final Heat.

W. S. Unwin, Magdalen College, beat T. A. Brassey, Balliol College.

CHALLENGE OARS, June 11.

Final Heat.

W. S. Unwin, Magdalen, and H. J. Reade, Brasenose, beat E. L. Puxley, Brasenose, and R. S. de Havilland, Corpus.

UNIVERSITY COXSWAINLESS FOURS, Nov. 5, 6, and 7.

Magdalen beat New, Corpus, Trinity, Christ Church, and Lincoln.

TRIAL EIGHTS, December 6.

From Great Western Railway Bridge, Moulsford, to Cleeve Lock, about a mile and a half.

Balfour's Crew, 1 ; Unwin's Crew, o.

Balfour's Crew : W. Radcliffe, Magdalen ; S. H. Fothergill, New ; L. S. R. Byrne, Trinity ; F. E. Cuming, University ; J. H. Ware, B.N.C. ; C. R. Carter, Corpus ; F. O. Wethered, Christ Church ; H. Balfour, Trinity (stroke) ; W. E. Maynard, Exeter (cox).

Unwin's Crew : C. K. Bowes, Christ Church ; C. S. Clemons, Corpus : G. Trower, Keble ; R. Girdlestone, Magdalen ; G. F. Hornby, Corpus ; P. W. Taylor, Lincoln ; H. H. Walrond, Exeter ; W. S. Unwin, Magdalen (stroke) ; H. E. Bull, Magdalen (cox).

Vauxhall Bridge, an iron structure of five spans, was built in 1811-16 and connects Kennington with Pimlico. NEAREST *Railway Stations,* Vauxhall (S.W.) and Victoria (Dist., L. & B., and L. C. & D.); *Omnibus Routes,* Vauxhall Bridge-road, and Albert Embankment ; *Cab Rank,* Grosvenor-road.

Vesta Rowing Club, established in 1872. Election by ballot of members, one black ball in three to exclude. Entrance fee, 10s. ; Subscription, £1 10s. ; honorary members, 10s. 6d. Colours, crimson and black stripes oblique. Boathouse, Putney.

Victoria Bridge, Windsor, Home Park, an artistic iron bridge, connects Berks and Bucks, crossing the river to the north of the park about half a mile above Datchet.

Victoria and Albert Docks (Royal). —These Docks, which belong to the same company as the St. Katharine and London Docks, commence at the eastern extremity of Canning Town, just below the farthest point of the East India Docks. They are approached by the North Woolwich Branch of the Great Eastern Railway, and reach from Blackwall to Galleon's Reach, considerably below Woolwich— a distance of three miles in a direct line.]

Victoria Embankment, London, extends along the left bank from Westminster to Blackfriars, a distance of about a mile and a quarter, and was constructed by Sir Joseph Bazalgette, the Engineer to the Metropolitan Board of Works. The whole of the space now occupied by the Embankment was covered by water or mud, according to the state of the tide, and few London improvements have been more conducive to health and comfort. The substitution of the beautiful curve of the Embankment, majestic in its simplicity, with its massive granite walls, flourishing trees, and trim gardens, is an unspeakable improvement on the squalid foreshore, and tumble-down wharves, and backs of dingy houses which formerly abutted on the river. It is to be regretted that difficulties of approach make this noble thoroughfare less useful than it should be. At Westminster and at Charing-cross, both from Northumberland-avenue and from Whitehall-place, and at Blackfriars, the approaches are all that can be desired, and are worthy of the Embankment itself; but the streets leading from the Strand, such, for instance, as Arundel-street and Norfolk-street, are both steep and inconvenient. From Arundel-street to Blackfriars, indeed, there is no carriage way on to the Embankment. The general appearance of the Victoria Embankment is still somewhat marred by the presence here and there of unsightly buildings, which it may be hoped will ere long be removed —and probably not even the designer of the Charing-cross Railway Station would call that useful building in any way ornamental—but it is nevertheless singularly rich in architectural features. Somerset House, the Temple, the Adelphi-terrace,

OXFORD REGATTA COURSE.

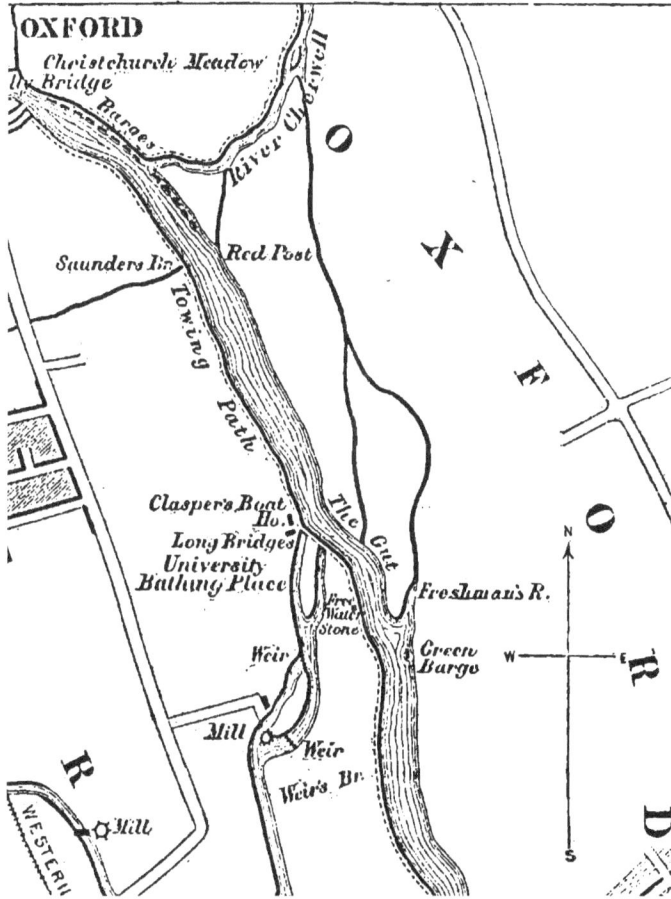

OXFORD

Christchurch Meadow
Bridge
Barges
River Cherwell
Saunders Br.
Red Post
Towing Path
Clasper's Boat Ho.
Long Bridges
University
Bathing Place
The Cut
Fresh Water Stone
Freshman's R.
Weir
Green Barge
Mill
Weir
Weir's Br.
Mill
WESTERN R.

OXFORD

N
W — E
S

the St. Stephen's Club, the School Board House, and other fine buildings, are either on or visible from the Embankment. It would seem from the numerous pedestals which the architect inserted in his design, that it was in contemplation to place an alarming number of statues along the road. Possibly this plan will eventually be carried into effect. At present the Embankment has only six statues to offer to the inspection of the critic : those of Sir James Outram at the foot of Whitehall-place ; Brunel, near Somerset House ; John Stuart Mill, near Norfolk-street ; William Tyndale, the first English Translator of the New Testament ; Robert Raikes, the originator of Sunday Schools, a short distance west of Waterloo-bridge ; and Robert Burns, near Charing Cross Bridge. In curious contrast to the modern statues is Cleopatra's Needle, which, owing to the public spirit and energy of Mr. Erasmus Wilson and Mr. John Dixon, is now a conspicuous object on the river wall at the bottom of Salisbury-street. There is a floating swimming-bath at Charing-cross, and a Thames Police-station just below Waterloo-bridge, close to which is moored the *Rainbow*, now the drill ship of the Royal Naval Artillery Volunteers.

NEAREST *Bridges*, Westminster, Waterloo, Blackfriars (all carriage-roads), Charing-cross (foot) ; *Steamboat Piers*, Westminster, Charing-cross, Waterloo, and Temple ; *Railway Stations*, Westminster (Dist.), Charing-cross (Dist. and S. E.), Temple (Dist.), Blackfriars (Dist. and L. C. & D.) ; *Omnibus Routes*, the Strand and Fleet-street.

Waldegrave Rowing Club, Twickenham.—Election in general meeting ; one black ball in five excludes. Entrance fee, £1 1s. (none for effective members of any amateur rowing club) ; subscription, £1 1s. Motto, *Semper paratus.* Colours, black and gold.

Wallingford, Berkshire, on the right bank, from London 90½ miles, from Oxford 21 miles. A station on the Great Western Railway ; from Paddington 51 miles. The time occupied by the trains varies from two to three hours. The station is about 12 minutes' walk from the river. Omnibuses meet the trains. Population, 2,972.

Wallingford, a very ancient town which, to this day, shows evident signs of having been of some importance at the time of the Roman invaders, has figured largely in the history of England. The remains of extensive fortifications, erected at the Roman period, will be found on the left on the road to the station. Shortly after the Conquest the old castle here was greatly strengthened, and figured frequently in the little wars and internecine disputes which so largely made up the domestic history of the country for the next three or four hundred years. Later on the town had again bitter experience of warfare, and suffered cruelly at the hands of Fairfax, who took it in 1646 after a long siege. Little now remains of the stronghold except a few crumbling walls and an old window enclosed in the gardens of Wallingford Castle, the seat of Mr. J. K. Hedges. Wallingford is a Parliamentary borough, with a constituency of 1,226, and is at present represented by Mr. Pandeli Ralli, a Liberal. The town is governed by a mayor, four aldermen, and twelve councillors. The principal business centre is the Market-place, where is the spacious corn-exchange and the Town Hall, supported on an arcade of somewhat squat pillars. In the council-chamber above hang some portraits of more or less merit. One of Archbishop Laud, "a munificent benefactor to this boro'," in his sixty-fourth year, dated 1635, and ascribed to Holbein, bears a remarkable resemblance to other portraits of this worthy in the neighbourhood, one in the council-chamber at Reading, the other in the Town Hall at Henley. Probably they are all copies from the same original picture. A portrait of the Hon. Mr. Justice Blackstone, recorder of the borough, 1749, presented by his grandson, the member for the town, in 1841, is apparently a modern picture, and depicts the learned judge in wig and robes. The fire-engine house is under the Town Hall. Wallingford is but a dull place, and even in its churches has but little to offer in the way of antiquities. The town once contained fourteen churches, but now has but three. The disappearance of the other eleven, and the comparative bareness of the three that remain, may, probably, be attributed to the rough handling of Fairfax's Roundheads. The church of St. Mary, in the Market-place, restored in 1854, has on its tower a mutilated tablet, supposed, by persons of lively imagination, to represent King Stephen on horseback. In the church, which has nave, chancel, and two aisles, is a tablet to the memory of Walter Bigg, alderman of the City of London, and a native of Wallingford, who died 1659, after bequeathing £10 yearly to the grammar school—this being its original endowment—and £10 annually for the relief of the poor. The worthy alderman's memorial is surmounted by a skull wreathed incongruously with laurel-leaves—why it is difficult to see. In the west end of the nave is a memorial tablet to Henry Stampe, who died in 1619, which has some curious carving and a somewhat odd inscription. In Thames-street, near the bridge, is St. Peter's, the burial-place of Mr. Justice Blackstone, which is further distinguished by a singularly hideous spire which rises from the square flint tower, and which, said to be from the design of the learned judge himself, was erected by him. Sir William is buried here, and a monument to his memory has been built into the outer part of the south wall of the church at its eastern end, on which there is the following inscription, viz. :

H S S
Kyrie Eleison.
SIR WM. BLACKSTONE, KNT.,
One of the Judges of His Majesty's Superior Courts at Westminster, who was born A. D. 1724, and died 24 Feb. 1780.

Edward Stennett, one of John Bunyan's friends, lies buried in the graveyard. In the north wall, at its eastern end, a small stone is inscribed to his memory thus : " Here lyeth the body of Mr. Edward Stennett, who died in November ye 28th, 17 5, aged 77." A chip of the stone having fallen off, the date is imperfect. The spire was finished in 1777, the church in 1769.

At the end of Thames-street is St. Leonard's Church, the handsomest of the three. It was rebuilt in 1849, has a nave, chancel, and south aisle, and affords some good specimens of later Norman architecture.

Bigg's Grammar School existed for more than 200 years, and was then in abeyance for 15 years. New schools were then established under a scheme of the Endowed Schools Commissioners, and new school buildings were opened in 1877. They are situated on the right-hand side of the road to the station, and are handsome buildings, with lofty, well ventilated and lighted school rooms, with every modern convenience. Bigg's £10 per annum is now represented by an income of £210, and the scholars comprise sixty boys and thirty-five girls. The entrance fee both for boys and girls is 10s., and the school fees per term, boys under thirteen, £1 5s., above thirteen, £1. 12s. ; and for girls under thirteen, £1, above thirteen, £1 7s. There are the usual three terms in the year. The head master receives boys, and the head mistress girls, as boarders : terms, including school-fees, £34 13s. per annum ; weekly boarders, £28 7s.

Archbishop Laud left £45 a year for apprenticing five boys, Sir Thomas Bennett £150 a year to be given to fifteen old people, and there are several similar charities.

Tusser, the author of that quaint old book, the " Five Hundred Points of Good Husbandry," was educated at Wallingford, but does not appear from his own account to have been too happy here. He says :

O painful time, for every crime,
What toosed eares ! like baited beares !
What bobbed lips ! what yerks, what nips !
What hellish toies !
What robes how bare I what colledge fare !
What bred how stale I what pennie ale !
Then Wallingford, how wert thou abhor'd
Of sillie boies !

The headquarters of the Royal Berks Horticultural Society are at Wallingford. It is the oldest society of a similar class in the county, and was established in 1831, under the direct patronage of King William IV. It was then a general Horticultural Society, but has been since 1855 a cottagers' society only. An Art Loan Exhibition and prizes for needle-work have been appended to it, with, however, separate funds.

The Free Library and Public Institute, St. Mary's-street, was founded in 1871. Subscriptions vary from 5s. to £1 1s. Visitors are admitted, and all inhabitants of the town of " ten years of age and upwards " are entitled to the free use of the public reading-room.

Favourite excursions from Wallingford are to Swyncombe, about 5 miles ; Ewelme (*which see*), 4 miles ; and Wittenham Clump and Hills, 3 miles.

BANKS. — Hedges, Wells, and Co., Market-place ; London and County, High-street.

FAIRS.—June 24, September 28.

FIRE.—Engine at Town Hall.

HOTELS. — " George," High - street ; " Lamb," High-street.

INN. —" Town Arms," by the bridge.

MARKET DAY.—Friday.

PLACES OF WORSHIP.—St. Leonard's, St. Mary's, St. Peter's ; and Baptist, Primitive Methodist, and Wesleyan Chapels.

POLICE.—Station, St. Mary's-street.

POSTAL ARRANGEMENTS.—Post Office (money order, savings bank, telegraph, and insurance), St. Martin's-street. Mails from London, 7 a.m., 1.0, 6.20, and 11 p.m. ; Sunday, 7 a.m. Mails for London, 9.15 a.m., 3.15, and 10 p.m. ; Sunday, 10 p.m.

NEAREST *Bridges*, Wallingford ; up, Shillingford 2½ miles ; down, Streatley 6 miles. *Locks*, up, Benson 1¼ mile ; down, Cleeve 5¼ miles. *Ferries*, Benson and Little Stoke. *Railway Station*, Wallingford.

FARES to Paddington : 1st, 9/5, 16/- ; 2nd, 7/-, 12/- ; 3rd, 4/3. No Sunday trains, but passengers can book to Moulsford (3 miles by road from Wallingford), where flys can be had.

Walton, Surrey, on the right bank, 28 miles from London, 83½ from Oxford. A station on the London and South Western Railway 17 miles from Waterloo, the trains averaging about three-quarters of an hour. Flys meet the trains. The station is twenty-five minutes' walk from the river ; the cab-hire is 2s. 6d. Population, 6,050. Soil, gravel. The ancient village of Walton, which lies some little way back from the river, is not without interest. In addition to Causeway or Coway Stakes (*which see*) there are various traces of the Roman occupation in the immediate neighbourhood, both at Oatlands and St. George's Hill. The latter is the site of one of the innumerable camps of Cæsar, traces of which are still visible, and it is believed by those competent to form an opinion that a still greater camp existed at Oatlands.

From St. George's Hill may be obtained one of the finest views on the river, extending over seven counties. The village, with its long straggling High-street, and, at right angles to it, Church-street, still retains an air of primitive simplicity. Here was the residence of the regicide Bradshaw, and not far off, at Ashley Park, the Lord Protector himself is said to have resided. Local tradition, never slow to minister to local self-importance, holds it an article of firm belief that in Bradshaw's house the signatures were affixed to the death-warrant of Charles. Besides Bradshaw, and Admiral Rodney, who was born in Walton, the most notorious inhabitant of the village in former times was William Lilly, the famous astrologer, who, notwithstanding his presumed study of the black art, was at one time a church-warden of the parish, and is said to have practised medicine there and in the neighbourhood with some considerable success.

The church, dedicated to St. Mary, a very ancient structure, dating probably from Saxon times. The most prominent feature is the fine old buttressed tower, but the pillars in the interior, the east window of the south aisle, and the stone-work of the windows in the north aisle, are of antiquity and will repay examination. On the north wall of the chancel hangs, framed and mounted on wood, the famous brass representing John Sellwyn, "kepper of her Matis. parke of Otelande," with his wife, five sons, and six daughters. Between Sellwyn and his wife the former is represented performing a marvellous feat. Stag-hunting in Oatlands Park with Queen Elizabeth, Sellwyn is said to have suddenly leaped from his horse to "the back of a stag, to have plunged his sword into the neck of the beast, which fell dead at the feet of the Queen," a circus-like performance which no doubt greatly gratified the virgin monarch. On the north wall of the chancel is a brass, with an excellent likeness, to the memory of J. F. Lewis, R.A., who died in 1876. On the south wall of the chancel is one of Chantrey's commonplace effigies to the memory of Christopher D'Oyley, who died in 1795. Over the door leading from the chancel to the churchyard is a mural monument, surmounted by an hour-glass and skull, to Thomas Fitts Girald and his wife, with a curious epitaph, which concludes :

Thovgh fvtvre Tymes or Malice will not Credit,
Present Trewth svbscribs to svch was their Meritt.

It bears date 1619. On a pillar by the pulpit is the confession of faith said to have been made by Queen Elizabeth, on the subject of Transubstantiation :

Christ was the worde and spake it,
He took the bread and brake it,
And what the worde doth make it,
That I beleive and take it.

In the north aisle is Roubiliac's towering monument to Richard Boyle, Lord Viscount Shannon, topped by a full-length statue of that nobleman (who, it is recorded, was a volunteer at the battle of the Boyne), and surrounded by drums, cannon, flags, and other warlike "alarums." At the feet of Boyle is a life-size woful female figure holding on to an urn. In the gallery to the south is a rambling old pew, surmounted and surrounded by iron spikes, claimed as their property by the Askews of Burwood Park. Under the monument to Fitts Girald, on the pavement facing the chancel door, is the slab placed by Elias Ashmole, in memory of Gulielmi Lillii, Astrologi Peritissimi, 1681. In the vestry is preserved the iron scold's bridle, the donor of which is said to have lost an estate through the instrumentality of a gossiping lying woman. The date of the bridle is 1632, and it bore at one time the following inscription :

Chester presents Walton with a bridle,
To curb women's tongues when they are idle.

There are a number of charities in connection with the church, the principal of which is the rent, now amounting annually to £280, of 39, Bishopsgate-street, bequeathed by Thomas Fenner in 1635.

Walton is noted for its bream hole, and is good for chub, roach, &c.

For Oatlands Park *see* WEYBRIDGE.

BANK.—Ashby & Co., Church-street.

FAIR.—Easter Monday.

FIRE.—Station, High-street (Superintendent, engineer, foreman, nine firemen).

HOTELS.—"Angler," by the river; "Duke's Head," in the village ; "Old Manor House" and "Swan," by the river.

PLACES OF WORSHIP.—St. Mary's and Wesleyan Chapel.

POLICE.—Two constables live in the village. Station, Hersham.

POSTAL ARRANGEMENTS.—Post Office (money order, savings bank, telegraph, and insurance), Bridge-street. Mails from London, 7 and 9.10 a.m., 5.45 p.m.; Sunday, 7 a.m., over counter, 7 to 10 a.m. Mails for London, 10.30 a.m., 3 and 9 p.m.; Sunday, 8 p.m.

NEAREST *Bridges*, Walton ; up, Chertsey 4½ miles ; down, Hampton Court 4½ miles. *Locks*, up, Shepperton 2½ miles ; down, Sunbury 1¼ mile. *Railway Stations*, Walton and Hersham.

FARES to Waterloo : 1st, 3/-, 4/-; 2nd, 2/-, 3/-; 3rd, 1/5, 2/6.

Wandsworth Bridge.—A new bridge crossing the river rather more than a mile below Putney, and connecting Wandsworth and the south-west with the extreme west of London, *via* Walham Green.

Wargrave, Berkshire, on the right bank, from London 68¼ miles, from Oxford 43¼ miles. Population, 1,785. Soil, gravel and chalk. A pleasant village on the road from Twyford to Henley, both stations on the Great Western Railway, in the middle of a first-rate fishing district, and highly popular amongst artists. Public evidence of the latter fact is afforded by the sign of the principal inn of the village, the "George and Dragon." Here Mr. G. D. Leslie, R.A., has depicted the terrific encounter between the saint and the reptile ; and on the other side Mr. J. E. Hodgson, A.R.A., has limned St. George, his work concluded, his spear stuck in the ground, taking his pint of beer with a thoroughly comic air of complacent content. There are many good houses in the village, especially on the river's bank, and the village, though quiet and retired, is an enjoyable place to put up at.

The church at Wargrave (St. Mary's) was originally of Norman date, but the only portion remaining of the old church is the north door. The present church is built of flint and stone, and is beautifully situated on a green amidst very fine elm-trees. The ivy-mantled square tower is of brick, and of the beginning of the 17th century ; it contains a fine peal of six bells. The interior of the church is in want of restoration. On the south wall of the church is a monumental tablet to Mr. Day, the author of "Sandford and Merton," who lived, and was killed by a fall from his horse, in Wargrave parish. The east window is a "Mary window," and was put up to the memory of a late vicar (the Rev. James Hitchings) by the parishioners. The churchyard surrounds the church, and is very pretty and extremely well kept ; in it is the Saxon font, once used in the church. In the north aisle are many tablets and monuments to members of the Ximenes family over an old oak raised pew, with some curious carvings on the side. On the north side of the chancel is a marble mural tablet to the memory of Richard Aldworth, who died in 1623, surmounted by a brig in full sail. Inside the altar-rails on the north side is a very large brass—"a token of love here placed"— to the memory of Lieutenant-Colonel Raymond White, late of the 6th or Inniskilling Dragoons, by his brother officers in 1844. There is a small but fine black oak tabernacle to the font. Among the bequests is one by Mrs. Sarah Hill, who left £1 annually to be given at Easter in new crown pieces to two boys and two girls. No boy is to have the reward who is undutiful to his parents, was ever heard to swear, to tell untruths, to steal, to break windows, or to do any kind of mischief. Any boy who would have the courage to lay claim to this reward, and could conscientiously say that he had fulfilled all the necessary conditions, must, one would think, be a lineal descendant of the exasperating Master Sandford himself.

A large school in the village for the children of the parish is generally known as Piggott's School, a certain Mr. Piggott having about a century ago left a sum of money to clothe and educate 20 boys and 20 girls, these children being now educated with the others who attend the parish school.

There is capital fishing about Wargrave and Shiplake.

HOTEL.—" The George and Dragon."

PLACE OF WORSHIP.—St. Mary's.

POSTAL ARRANGEMENTS.—Post Office (money order and savings bank). Mails from London, 7.30 a.m.; 1 p.m. ; Sunday, 7.30 a.m. Mails for London, 8.40 a.m., 7.5 p.m. ; Sunday, 10 a.m. The nearest telegraph office is Twyford.

NEAREST *Bridges*, up, Sonning 3 miles ; down, Henley 3¼ miles. *Locks*, up, Shiplake ½ mile ; down, Marsh 2¼ miles. *Ferries*, Wargrave and Shiplake. *Railway Stations*, by ferry, Shiplake ; by high-road, Twyford.

FARES from Twyford to Paddington : 1st, 5/6, 9/3 ; 2nd, 4/2, 7/- ; 3rd, 2/9½.

"Warspite."—(*See* MARINE SOCIETY.)

Waterloo Bridge, from a design by Dodd, the earliest of John Rennie's three, and also commonly considered the finest. As to this there may perhaps be a question, some critics preferring London Bridge, or even Southwark, as grander if less ornate. The perfect level, too, of the roadway in the case of Waterloo, whilst the first of all merits from a practical point of view, somewhat narrows its artistic opportunities ; whilst the uniformity of the arches is considered by some to give it too much the air of "a length out of a viaduct." In all other respects it is the handsomest bridge across the Thames : consisting of nine elliptical arches 120 ft. in span and 35 ft. in height, supported on piers 20 ft. wide at the spring of the arches, and surmounted by an open balustrade. It is not so wide as London Bridge by 11 ft., but is very nearly half as long again—1,380 ft.—without the approaches, which are on the Middlesex side 370 ft., and on the Surrey side 766 ft. in length. It was opened in great state on the second anniversary of Waterloo, 18th June, 1817. There is in existence a curious print of a design for this bridge by T. Sandby, R.A., comprising a colonnade on the top of the bridge, and a classical temple at the end.

NEAREST *Railway Station*, Temple ; *Omnibus Route*, Strand ; *Cab Rank*, Wellington-street.

Watermen's Company.—The following account of the position of the company, both from the point of view of legal enactments and of custom, which is so often stronger than law itself, is abridged from the admirable report of the Thames

Traffic Committee, lately issued. The Watermen's Company is an old guild dating from the 14th century, who for many generations had the monopoly of the navigation of the Thames under various Acts or ordinances of the Crown. By an Act of 1859, 22 and 23 Vict. c. 133, s. 2, which is the principal Act now governing the Watermen's Company, the monopoly of the freemen of the company in carrying goods for hire was put an end to. No restriction was placed on the ownership of barges so employed, but the owners were required to register them with the company. By the same Act no person is allowed to act as a waterman or a lighterman, or to ply, work, or navigate any wherry, passenger-boat, lighter, vessel, or other craft upon the river, from or to any place or vessel within the limits of the Act, i.e., between Teddington Lock and Lower Hope near Gravesend, except : 1. Freemen of the company duly licensed ; 2. Apprentices duly qualified and licensed ; under a penalty in the cases of a passenger-boat rowed for hire of £5, and in other cases under a penalty of 40s. on anyone who so works, and in the case of a barge, of £5 on the barge-owner employing him. Freedom of the company is obtained by apprenticeship of at least five years, either to a freeman or the widow of a freeman, or to a registered barge-owner employing a freeman. Registered owners of barges were also, according to the terms of the Act, to be deemed qualified to be admitted as freemen. In addition to the freedom, licenses were required. In order to obtain a lighterman's license a freeman must have served a five years' apprenticeship, be 19 years of age, and have been for two years immediately preceding his application continuously engaged in working a barge or lighter within the limits of the Act. In order to obtain a waterman's license a freeman must have served a five years' apprenticeship, be 19 years of age, and have been for two years preceding his application continuously engaged in working a boat or craft within the limits of the Act. The master of an apprentice may obtain a license for an apprentice to take sole charge of a boat or other vessel if the apprentice has worked and rowed upon the river as apprentice for two years, and passes an examination before the

Court of Watermen. An appeal lies to the Conservators of the Thames in the case of the refusal of a license. The court of the company may withdraw a license for misconduct or incompetency, subject to an appeal to the Conservators. Barges used within the limits of the Act must be registered with the company, and the names and official numbers of the barges must be painted on them. Passenger-boats plying for hire within the limits of the Act must be registered with and licensed by the company, and the number of passengers fixed by the company. The managing body of the company is a court consisting of a master, four wardens, and nineteen assistants ; they are self-elected out of the freemen of the company. The court has power to admit freemen, to grant licenses, to bind apprentices, to appoint inspectors, to fix fares for passenger-boats, and to make bye-laws for carrying the Act into effect, and for the government and regulation of lightermen and watermen. The court has also jurisdiction to hear and decide any complaint made by freemen and apprentices against each other for infraction of the Act and bye-laws, and to impose penalties. In 1860 a code of bye-laws was made by the company under this Act, and approved by the Conservators of the Thames. In 1864 an Act was passed to amend the Conservancy Act which contains the following provisions with respect to the Watermen's Company and their privileges : Persons enabled to take apprentices (i.e., freemen and registered barge-owners employing a free-man) are enabled to contract with men of 20 years of age to serve in a lighter or a steamer on the Thames ; after service of two years such men are authorised to apply for and obtain a license from the company in the same terms and with the same effect as in the case of licenses granted by the company to apprentices. By the same Act craft passing entirely through the limits of the Act, i.e., from above Teddington to places beyond Gravesend, or vice versa, and barges coming out of the Grand Junction Canal, were exempted from the obligation to employ licensed lightermen. By the same Act barges navigated from any place above Teddington were enabled to ply as far as London Bridge without employing a licensed lighterman. It is to be observed that the Act of 1859, whilst enabling any persons who had not served an apprenticeship and who were not members of the company to own barges, expressly provided for the admission of such persons to be members of the company ; that provision has not been acted on, and the chairman and secretary of the company distinctly state that the court of the company have declined to act upon it. This refusal to carry the Act into effect is important, especially when connected with the fact stated by Mr. Scovell and admitted by Mr. Williams, who is a member of the court of the company, viz., that barge-owners who are not members of the company are at a disadvantage in getting labour to work their barges. The effect of the abovementioned enactments is to create a monopoly of the navigation of barges on the Thames in favour of the freemen and apprentices of the Watermen's Company. What the precise extent and limit of that monopoly may be is doubtful. According to strict grammatical construction of certain bye-laws, the freemen of the Watermen's Company would have the monopoly of navigating the whole of the ships, English and foreign, which enter or leave the Thames. In practice the restriction to the employment of freemen is only applied to vessels which both begin and end their voyage within the limits of the Act, that is, between Teddington and Lower Hope Point, just below Gravesend. The practical effect of the monopoly, therefore, at present is, that all vessels, whether steamers, barges, or other sailing craft, which trade or ply from place to place within the above limits, must be navigated by either freemen of the company duly licensed by the company ; or by apprentices to a freeman or to a barge-owner also duly licensed by the company ; or by men who have served two years with a freeman or registered bargeowner, and are also duly licensed by the company. From this restriction are exempted : 1. Vessels going completely through the district from Teddington to beyond Gravesend, or vice versa. 2. Barges coming out of the Grand Junction Canal. 3. Barges coming from above Teddington if not going below London Bridge. 4. Barges coming from the river Lea. In order to

complete the statement of the law concerning the Watermen's Company reference must be made to the following bye-laws of the Conservators : "All barges, boats, lighters, and other light craft navigating the river shall, when under way, have at least one competent man constantly on board, for the navigation and management thereof, and all such craft of above 50 tons burden shall, when under way, have one man in addition on board, to assist in the navigation and management of the same, with the following exceptions : when being towed by a steam vessel, or when being moved to or fro between any vessels or places, a distance not exceeding 200 yards." It appears that there is a difference of opinion on the meaning of the bye-laws. The Conservators in framing them have purposely abstained from requiring the second man to be a freeman of or licensed by the company, whilst the company are of opinion that he must possess that qualification. If a complaint that the second man does not possess it is taken before the magistrates, they act, it seems, on the view taken by the Conservators, and dismiss the case ; but if it is taken before the court of the company, they inflict a fine. The owners and managers of the river passenger and excursion boats complain bitterly of the obligation to employ free watermen. They have no voice in the management of the Watermen's Company, and the examination and license of the company does not afford the least security for competency or character. They have boats which run beyond Gravesend to Sheerness and other places, and although they may have men in those boats who prove themselves competent by constantly navigating up to London Bridge, they are unable to employ those men in the boats plying above Gravesend. The report on the loss of the *Princess Alice* contains the following passage : "The court has in its judgment already severely censured George Thomas Long, the first mate of the *Princess Alice*, for irregularities connected with the look-out kept on board that vessel, and it has reason to fear that the reprehensible system which prevailed on board this ship of allowing the crew to make their own arrangements and station themselves at the wheel or look-out is not confined

to this vessel alone. It has been re-marked that all the crew of this vessel, including the captain, were London river watermen, and so also were some of the refreshment contractor's servants."
—(*And see* BARGES.)

LIST OF FEES UNDER ACT AND BYE-LAWS.

	Payable by Freemen.	By other Persons.	On Renewals by Freemen.	On Renewals by other Persons.
	£ s. d.	£ s. d.	£ s. d.	£ s. d.
Entries for binding, assignment, or freedom ..	0 1 0	0 1 0	—	—
Binding of apprentices and stamps	1 8 0	1 8 0	—	—
Assignment of apprentices and stamps	1 0 0	1 0 0	—	—
Certificate of binding, assignment, or freedom ..	0 2 6	0 2 6	—	—
Freedom of the company and stamp	2 6 0	5 0 0	or annually	0 10 0
Original registry of owner of craft and annual renewal	0 10 0	1 0 0	0 2 6	0 5 0
Copy of certificate if lost	0 5 0	0 10 0	—	—
Certificate of registry of ownership _.	0 2 6	0 2 6	—	—
Registering address	0 5 0	0 5 0	—	—
„ barge	0 1 0	0 1 0	—	—
Search as to ownership of barge	0 1 0	0 1 0	—	—
Registering mortgage, &c.	0 1 0	0 1 0	—	—
License to work as waterman or apprentice	0 2 6	—	0 2 6	—
„ lighterman	0 2 6	3 11 0	0 2 6	0 2 6
„ apprentice to waterman, lighter-man, or barge-owner	0 2 6	0 2 6	0 2 6	0 2 6
Licensing waterman's rowing boats	0 1 0	—	0 1 0	—
„ sailing boats	0 5 0	—	0 5 0	—
Registering bumboats	0 2 6	0 2 6	0 2 6	0 2 6
„ boats to be let out..	0 2 6	0 2 6	0 2 6	0 2 6
Searching registries	0 1 0	0 1 0	—	—
Book of Laws	0 2 0	0 2 0	—	—
Table of fares	0 0 1	—	—	—
Affidavits as to craft, or in verification of certificate as to age..	0 1 0	0 1 0	—	—
Affidavits in lieu of lost certificate, &c.	0 2 6	0 2 6	—	—
List of court	0 0 6	0 0 6	—	—
Summons	0 1 0	—	—	—
„ for witness	0 0 6	—	—	—
Annual payment by freemen	0 3 0	—	—	—
„ of owners of craft	0 6 0	—	—	—

Watermen's Fares.—TABLE OF RATES OR FARES, limited and fixed by the Court of Master, Wardens, and Assistants of the Company of Watermen and Lightermen of the River Thames, that every waterman is entitled to be paid for his labour, in conveying any person or persons in a passenger boat from place to place, or to or from steamers or other vessels on the river, within the limits of the said Act.

A TABLE OF RATES FOR WATERMEN from London-bridge, westward, as far as Chelsea-bridge.

Oars, 6*d*. *Sculler*, 3*d*.

From London-bridge, above the said bridge, to Southwark-bridge.

From Southwark-bridge to Blackfriars-bridge.

From Blackfriars-bridge to Waterloo-bridge.

From Waterloo-bridge to Westminster-bridge.

From Westminster-bridge to Lambeth Stairs or the Horse Ferry.

From Lambeth Stairs or the Horse Ferry to Vauxhall-bridge.

From Vauxhall-bridge to Nine Elms or opposite.

From Nine Elms or opposite to Battersea New-bridge.

From Battersea New-bridge to Swan Stairs, Chelsea, or opposite.

From Swan Stairs, Chelsea, or opposite, to Chelsea-bridge.

Oars, 1s. Sculler, 6d.

From London-bridge, above the said bridge, to Blackfriars-bridge.
From Southwark-bridge to Waterloo-bridge.
From Blackfriars-bridge to Westminster-bridge.
From Waterloo-bridge to Lambeth Stairs or the Horse Ferry.
From Westminster-bridge to Vauxhall-bridge.
From Lambeth Stairs or the Horse Ferry to Nine Elms or opposite.
From Vauxhall-bridge to Battersea New-bridge.
From Nine Elms or opposite to Swan Stairs, Chelsea, or opposite.
From Battersea New-bridge to Chelsea-bridge.

Oars, 1s. 6d. Sculler, 9d.

From London-bridge, above the said bridge, to Waterloo-bridge.
From Southwark-bridge to Westminster-bridge.
From Blackfriars-bridge to Lambeth Stairs or the Horse Ferry.
From Waterloo-bridge to Vauxhall-bridge.
From Westminster-bridge to Nine Elms or opposite.
From Lambeth Stairs or the Horse Ferry to Battersea New-bridge.
From Vauxhall-bridge to Swan Stairs, Chelsea, or opposite.
From Nine Elms or opposite to Chelsea-bridge.

Oars, 2s. Sculler, 1s.

From London-bridge, above the said bridge, to Westminster-bridge.
From Southwark-bridge to Lambeth Stairs or the Horse Ferry.
From Blackfriars-bridge to Vauxhall-bridge.
From Waterloo-bridge to Nine Elms or opposite.
From Westminster-bridge to Battersea New-bridge.
From Lambeth Stairs or the Horse Ferry to Swan Stairs, Chelsea, or opposite.
From Vauxhall-bridge to Chelsea-bridge.

Oars, 2s. 6d. Sculler, 1s. 3d.

From London-bridge, above the said bridge, to Lambeth Stairs, or the Horse Ferry.
From Southwark-bridge to Vauxhall-bridge.

From Blackfriars-bridge to Nine Elms or opposite.
From Waterloo-bridge to Battersea New-bridge.
From Westminster-bridge to Swan Stairs, Chelsea, or opposite.
From Lambeth Stairs or the Horse Ferry to Chelsea-bridge.

Oars, 3s. Sculler, 1s. 6d.

From London-bridge, above the said bridge, to Vauxhall-bridge.
From Southwark-bridge to Nine Elms, or opposite.
From Blackfriars-bridge to Battersea New-bridge.
From Waterloo-bridge to Swan Stairs, Chelsea, or opposite.
From Westminster-bridge to Chelsea-bridge.

Oars, 3s. 6d. Sculler, 1s. 9d.

From London-bridge, above the said bridge, to Nine Elms or opposite.
From Southwark-bridge to Battersea New-bridge.
From Blackfriars-bridge to Swan Stairs, Chelsea, or opposite.
From Waterloo-bridge to Chelsea-bridge.

Oars, 4s. Sculler, 2s.

From London-bridge, above the said bridge, to Battersea New-bridge.
From Southwark-bridge to Swan Stairs, Chelsea, or opposite.
From Blackfriars-bridge to Chelsea-bridge.

Oars, 4s. 6d. Sculler, 2s. 3d.

From London-bridge, above the said bridge, to Swan Stairs, Chelsea, or opposite.
From Southwark-bridge to Chelsea-bridge.

Oars, 5s. Sculler, 2s. 6d.

From London-bridge, above the said bridge, to Chelsea-bridge.

A TABLE OF RATES FOR WATERMEN from London-bridge, eastward, as far as Crawley's Wharf, Greenwich.

Oars, 6d. Sculler, 3d.

From London-bridge, below the said bridge, to Irongate or opposite.
From Irongate or opposite to Union Stairs or opposite.
From Union Stairs or opposite to Wapping Dock Stairs or opposite.

From Wapping Dock Stairs or opposite to Shadwell Dock Stairs or opposite.

From Shadwell Dock Stairs or opposite to Kidney Stairs or opposite.

From Kidney Stairs or opposite to Limehouse Hole Stairs or opposite.

From Limehouse Hole Stairs or opposite to the "Torrington Arms," Limehouse Reach, or opposite.

From the "Torrington Arms," Limehouse Reach, or opposite, to George's Stairs, Deptford, or opposite.

From George's Stairs, Deptford, or opposite, to Lower Water Gate, Deptford, or opposite.

From Lower Water Gate, Deptford, or opposite, to Crawley's Wharf, Greenwich, or opposite.

Oars, 1s. Sculler, 6d.

From London-bridge, below the said bridge, to Union Stairs or opposite.

From Irongate or opposite to Wapping Dock Stairs or opposite.

From Union Stairs or opposite to Shadwell Dock Stairs or opposite.

From Wapping Dock Stairs or opposite to Kidney Stairs or opposite.

From Shadwell Dock Stairs or opposite to Limehouse Hole Stairs or opposite.

From Kidney Stairs or opposite to the "Torrington Arms," Limehouse Reach, or opposite.

From Limehouse Hole Stairs or opposite to George's Stairs, Deptford, or opposite.

From the "Torrington Arms," Limehouse Reach, or opposite, to Lower Water Gate, Deptford, or opposite.

From George's Stairs, Deptford, or opposite, to Crawley's Wharf, Greenwich, or opposite.

Oars, 1s. 6d. Sculler, 9d.

From London-bridge, below the said bridge, to Wapping Dock Stairs or opposite.

From Irongate or opposite to Shadwell Dock Stairs or opposite.

From Union Stairs or opposite to Kidney Stairs or opposite.

From Wapping Dock Stairs or opposite to Limehouse Hole Stairs or opposite.

From Shadwell Dock Stairs or opposite to the "Torrington Arms," Limehouse Reach, or opposite.

From Kidney Stairs or opposite to George's Stairs, Deptford, or opposite.

From Limehouse Hole Stairs or opposite to Lower Water Gate, Deptford, or opposite.

From the "Torrington Arms," Limehouse Reach, or opposite, to Crawley's Wharf, Greenwich, or opposite.

Oars, 2s. Sculler, 1s.

From London-bridge, below the said bridge, to Shadwell Dock Stairs or opposite.

From Irongate or opposite to Kidney Stairs or opposite.

From Union Stairs or opposite to Limehouse Hole Stairs or opposite.

From Wapping Dock Stairs or opposite to the "Torrington Arms," Limehouse Reach, or opposite.

From Shadwell Dock Stairs or opposite to George's Stairs, Deptford, or opposite.

From Kidney Stairs or opposite to Lower Water Gate, Deptford, or opposite.

From Limehouse Hole Stairs or opposite to Crawley's Wharf, Greenwich, or opposite.

Oars, 2s. 6d. Sculler, 1s. 3d.

From London-bridge, below the said bridge, to Kidney Stairs or opposite.

From Irongate or opposite to Limehouse Hole Stairs or opposite.

From Union Stairs or opposite to the "Torrington Arms," Limehouse Reach, or opposite.

From Wapping Dock Stairs or opposite to George's Stairs, Deptford, or opposite.

From Shadwell Dock Stairs or opposite to Lower Water Gate, Deptford, or opposite.

From Kidney Stairs or opposite to Crawley's Wharf, Greenwich, or opposite.

Oars, 3s. Sculler, 1s. 6d.

From London-bridge, below the said bridge, to Limehouse Hole Stairs or opposite.

From Irongate or opposite to the "Torrington Arms," Limehouse Reach, or opposite.

From Union Stairs or opposite to George's Stairs, Deptford, or opposite.

From Wapping Dock Stairs or opposite to Lower Water Gate, Deptford, or opposite.

From Shadwell Dock Stairs or opposite to Crawley's Wharf, Greenwich, or opposite.

Oars, 3s. 6d. *Sculler*, 1s. 9d.

From London-bridge, below the said bridge, to the "Torrington Arms," Limehouse Reach, or opposite.

From Irongate or opposite to George's Stairs, Deptford, or opposite.

From Union Stairs or opposite to Lower Water Gate, Deptford, or opposite.

From Wapping Dock Stairs or opposite to Crawley's Wharf, Greenwich, or opposite.

Oars, 4s. *Sculler*, 2s.

From London-bridge, below the said bridge, to George's Stairs, Deptford, or opposite.

From Irongate or opposite to Lower Water Gate, Deptford, or opposite.

From Union Stairs or opposite to Crawley's Wharf, Greenwich, or opposite.

Oars, 4s. 6d. *Sculler*, 2s. 3d.

From London-bridge, below the said bridge, to Lower Water Gate, Deptford, or opposite.

From Irongate or opposite to Crawley's Wharf, Greenwich, or opposite.

Oars, 5s. *Sculler*, 2s. 6d.

From London-bridge, below the said bridge, to Crawley's Wharf, Greenwich, or opposite.

The stairs or landing-places at either end and on either side of the aforesaid bridges to be, for the purpose of the above fares, considered as part of the respective bridges.

From Chelsea-bridge, westward, to or towards Teddington Lock, 6d. for every half-mile for oars, and 3d. per half-mile for scullers.

From Crawley's Wharf, Greenwich, eastward, to or towards Broadness Point or Grays, 6d. for every half-mile for oars, and 4d. per half-mile for scullers.

Over the water directly, between Teddington Lock and Blackwall Stairs, and to or from steamboats, ships, or vessels moored opposite or near to any public stairs, causeway,. or plying-place within such limits, where the distance from the stairs or plying-place to the ship does not exceed the distance directly across the river (except the Sunday ferries, the fare for which · is 2d. each person), for one person, 3d.; two persons, 1½d. each ; exceeding two persons, 1d. each.

Over the water directly, at and between Blackwall Stairs and Woolwich inclusive,

and to or from steamboats, ships, or vessels moored opposite or near to any public stairs as last aforesaid, for one person, 4d.; exceeding one person, 2d. each.

To or from any steamboat, ship, or vessel, arriving at or departing· from its moorings, ·between London-bridge and Woolwich inclusive, aforesaid, with or for passengers, for one person, 4d.; exceeding one person, 3d. each.

Over the water directly, eastward of Woolwich aforesaid, as far as Broadness Point, and to or from steamboats, ships, or vessels moored opposite or near to any public stairs as aforesaid, for one person, 6d.; exceeding one person, 4d. each.

To or from steamboats, ships, or vessels above Crawley's Wharf, at a distance from the place of landing or embarking the fare, to be at and after the rates herein-before provided with respect to the distances of the several stairs between London-bridge and Crawley's Wharf aforesaid, and if below Crawley's Wharf, then at and after the rates hereinbefore provided between Crawley's Wharf and Broadness Point.

Persons taking a boat between Teddington Lock and Woolwich aforesaid, to be rowed upon, about, or up and down the river (not going directly up and down from place to place), to pay at the rate of oars 1s., and a sculler 6d., for every half-hour they respectively shall be so engaged.

Watermen detained by passengers stopping at ships, wharfs, or otherwise, to be paid for time or distance, conformably to the rates hereinbefore set forth respectively, at the option of the waterman.

The above fares in all cases to include passengers' luggage, not exceeding 56 lbs. for each person. All luggage above that weight to be paid for at or after the rate of 4d. for each 56 lbs.

A TABLE OF RATES FOR WATERMEN between Broadness Point and Grays, and Lower Hope Point, below Gravesend.

Over the water directly, and to and from any steamboat, ship, or vessel, opposite or near to any public plying-place between Broadness Point and Grays, and Lower Hope Point aforesaid, both inclusive, for one person, 1s. ; exceeding one person, 6d. each.

From the Town Quay at Gravesend, to or from Gladdish's Wharf on the west, and to and from all steamboats, ships, vessels, and places lying and being between the same, and from the Town Quay, to and from the canal entrance on the east, and to and from all steamboats, ships, vessels, and places lying and being between the same, for one person, 1*s*. ; exceeding one person, 6*d*. each.

From the Town Quay at Gravesend, westward, to or from any steamboat, ship, vessel, or place between it and the Red Lion Wharf, for one person, 1*s*. 6*d*. ; exceeding one person, each 9*d*. Northfleet Creek, 2*s*. 6*d*. ; 1*s*. 3*d*. Broadness Point or Grays, 3*s*. 6*d*. ; 1*s*. 9*d*.

From the Town Quay at Gravesend, eastward, to or from any steamboat, vessel, or place between it and Denton Mill, for one person, 1*s*. 6*d*.; exceeding one person, each 9*d*. Shorn Mead Battery, 2*s*. 6*d*. ; 1*s*. 3*d*. Coalhouse Point, 3*s*. 6*d*.; 1*s*. 9*d*. Half-way Lower Hope, 5*s*.; 2*s*. 6*d*. Lower Hope Point Battery, 6*s*. 6*d*. ; 3*s*. 3*d*.

Watermen bringing the same passengers or any of them back from any steamboat, ship, vessel, or place, to be paid only one half the fare above stated by such person or persons for the back passage.

Watermen detained by passengers stopping at steamboats, ships, wharfs, or other places, to be paid for time or distance according to the rates herein set forth respectively, at the option of the waterman.

The above fares in all cases to include passengers' luggage or baggage not exceeding 56 lbs. for each passenger. All beyond that weight to be paid for at or after the rate of 6*d*. for each 56 lbs.

For a full boat load of passengers' luggage or baggage, the same fare as for carrying eight passengers.

For half a boat load, the same fare as for carrying four passengers.

TIME FOR A PAIR OF OARS.	*s*.	*d*.
For the first hour	2	0
For the second hour	1	6
And each succeeding hour	1	0
For the day (the day to be computed from 7 o'clock in the morning to 5 o'clock in the evening, from Michaelmas Day to Lady Day, and from 6 o'clock in the morning to 6 o'clock in the evening, from Lady Day to Michaelmas Day)	12	0

Watermen's Licenses for Rowing Boats and Vessels.—Bye-laws for the regulation of boats and vessels used for carrying persons or passengers on the river Thames, between Chelsea-bridge, in the county of Middlesex, and Teddington Lock, in the counties of Middlesex and Surrey.

SCALE OF SKIFF FOR SIX PASSENGERS.

That the burthen, size, and dimensions of a skiff boat to carry six persons or passengers shall be as follows (that is to say) : The extreme length over all, 20 ft. 6 in., and not exceeding 25 ft. ; the length of the keel, 17 ft. 6 in., and not exceeding 22 ft.; the depth at the lowest part, between the main and spray rowlocks, or at the lowest part of the boat, 1 ft. 6 in.; the extreme breadth at the main thwart, at the top, and within the gunwales, 4 ft. 6 in. ; the breadth of the main thwart, at a rise of 3 in. from the keel, 3 ft. 1 in.; the breadth forward, at 4 ft. from the main thwart, and at a rise of 8 in. from the keel, 3 ft. 1 in. ; the breadth aft, at 4 ft. from the main thwart, at a rise of 4¼ in. from the keel, 3 ft. 1 in.

SCALE OF SKIFF FOR EIGHT PASSENGERS.

That the burthen, size, and dimensions of a skiff boat to carry eight persons or passengers shall be as follows (that is to say) : The extreme length over all, 24 ft., and not exceeding 27 ft. ; the length of the keel, 21 ft., and not exceeding 24 ft. ; the depth at the lowest part, between the main and spray rowlocks, or at the lowest part of the boat, 1 ft. 7 in. ; the extreme breadth at the main thwart, at the top, and within the gunwales, 4 ft. 8 in. ; the breadth at the main thwart, at a rise of 3 in. from the keel, 3 ft. 3 in. ; the breadth forward, at 4 ft. from the main thwart, and at a rise of 8 in. from the keel, 3 ft. 3 in. ; the breadth aft, at 4 ft. from the main thwart, and at a rise of 4¼ in. from the keel, 3 ft. 3 in.

SCALE OF WHERRY FOR SIX PASSENGERS.

That the burthen, size, and dimensions of a wherry boat or other vessel to carry six persons or passengers shall be as follows (that is to say) : The length of the keel, 22 ft. 6 in. ; the extreme breadth in the midships, 4 ft. 6 in. ; the depth in

K

the midships, 1 ft. 5 in. ; the breadth of the floor at thirdlands, in the midships of the state-room, 2 ft. 11 in. ; the rise of the floor at thirdlands, in the midships of the state-room, not to exceed 3½ in. ; the breadth of the floor at thirdlands, at the timber on the fore side of the backboard thwart, 2 ft. 7 in. ; the rise of the floor at thirdlands, at the timber on the fore side of the backboard thwart, not to exceed 4½ in. ; the breadth of the floor at thirdlands, at the timber on the fore side of the spray thwart, 2 ft. 1 in. ; and the rise of the floor at thirdlands, at the timber on the fore side of the spray thwart, not to exceed 7 in.

SCALE OF WHERRY FOR EIGHT PASSENGERS.

That the burthen, size, and dimensions of a wherry boat or other vessel to carry eight persons or passengers shall be as follows (that is to say) : The length of the keel, 20 ft. 6 in. ; the extreme breadth in the midships, 4 ft. 6 in. ; the depth in the midships, 1 ft. 6 in. ; the breadth of the floor at thirdlands, in the midships of the state-room, 3 ft. 1 in. ; the rise of the floor at thirdlands, in the midships of the state-room, not to exceed 2¾ in. ; the breadth of the floor at thirdlands, at the timber on the fore side of the backboard thwart, 2 ft. 9 in. ; the rise of the floor at thirdlands, at the timber on the fore side of the backboard thwart, not to exceed 4 in. ; the breadth of the floor at thirdlands, at the timber on the fore side of the spray thwart, 2 ft. 3½ in. ; and the rise of the floor at thirdlands, at the timber on the fore side of the spray thwart, not to exceed 6 in.

LUGGAGE.

That in all cases when luggage is carried by any of the persons or passengers in the boats licensed under the provisions of these bye-laws, the number of persons or passengers such boats are permitted to carry shall be reduced one respectively from the number of persons or passengers contained in such respective licenses, for every complete hundredweight of luggage so carried as aforesaid.

Waterside Church Mission, St. Andrew's, for sailors, fishermen, and emigrants. London depôt, 36, City Chambers, Railway-place, Fenchurch-street, E.C.

West Blyth Buoy.—A 16-foot conical buoy, made of iron, and painted with black and white stripes. It is situated in Sea Reach, opposite the Mucking Light, on the edge of the Blyth Sand, and marks a depth of water, at low-water spring tide, of 17 ft. It is moored with 18 fathom of chain. The three Blyth buoys were transferred to the Thames Conservancy in 1865, and have only been retransferred to the Trinity House within the present year.

West London Rowing Club, founded in 1856, and consequently one of the oldest clubs on the river. Election by ballot of members, one black ball in five excludes. Entrance fee, £1 1s. Subscription, £2 2s. for active, £1 1s. for non-active members. Members are permitted to take up life-membership on certain conditions. Colours, scarlet and white stripes. Club-house, Putney.

Westminster Bridge varies very much in appearance with the state of the tide. It is always rather a cardboardy-looking affair, but when the river is full, and the height of the structure reduced as much as possible, there is a certain grace about it. When, however, the water is low, and the flat arches are exposed at the full height of their long, lanky piers, the effect is almost mean. Except, however, for the excessive vibration arising from lightness of construction, it is one of the best, from a practical point of view, in London, the roadway being wide and the rise very slight.

Westminster School Rowing.—The present boathouse is situated at Battersea, about two hundred yards below the railway-bridge, and the boys travel thither in a steam-launch which carries them to their boats from Parliament Stairs in about half-an-hour. The Westminster colour is pink, assigned to the boys by King William IV. The crew of the first eight wear pink flannel jackets, pink caps, or straw hats with a pink ribbon. The colours of the second eight are pink and white.

West Thurrock, Essex, a long-shore parish, scattered for some three miles along the road leading from Grays to Purfleet. Population, 1,372. Soil partly marsh, partly rich and light. The church, called the Pilgrim Church, stands on the river bank at St. Clement's Reach, far

away from the nearest house. It was built soon after the murder of Thomas A'Becket, for the convenience of pilgrims to his shrine at Canterbury. It is dedicated to St. Clement, and although not large, is interesting, with some unusual architectural features, especially in the east window and in the chantry. The church greatly needs and will repay restoration.

INN.—"Old Ship."

PLACE OF WORSHIP.—St. Clement's.

POSTAL ARRANGEMENTS.—Money order office and savings bank. Mails from London, 6.50 and 10.30 a. m.; office open for delivery, 7 a.m. to 8 a.m., and 10.30 a.m. Mails to London, 8 a.m., and 4.50 p.m. Same on Sunday. Nearest telegraph station, Grays.

NEAREST *Railway Stations*, Grays Thurrock, and Purfleet (*which see for* FARES).

Weybridge, Surrey, on the right bank, about 2½ miles by road from Walton, a station on the London and South Western Railway, 19 miles from Waterloo ; the trains average about ¾ hour. The station is about a mile from the village, twenty minutes' walk from the river, and ten from the church. The Basingstoke Canal, the Bourne, and the River Wey join the Thames just below Shepperton Lock. There is but little in Weybridge to detain even the most determined sight-seer. When he has inspected the column on the green erected to the memory of the Duchess of York, the original Seven Dials stone, and has searched for the remains of an old palace of Henry VIII., the lions of Weybridge are exhausted, unless Oatlands Park, which is about midway between Walton and Weybridge, be deemed worthy of a visit. Oatlands was for a long time royal property. Henry VIII. is said to have acquired it in his usual affable manner, and after various vicissitudes the property again came into the royal hands of the late Duke of York, who built the present not very royal building known in these later days as the "Oatlands Park Hotel." The park has been cut up and sold in "lots to suit purchasers." The famous grotto, which took twenty years to construct and upon which no less than £40,000 is said to have been wasted, still exists, and is shown to visitors for a small fee. How £40,000 could have been spent in con-

structing two or three rooms and a passage of oyster-shells and cement is a mystery. The Dogs' Graveyard, in which are deposited the remains of about fifty of the Duchess's favourite companions, each with a headstone and many with epitaphs, is not now open to the general public. The church dedicated to St. James is a fine modern building of stone erected in 1847 in the pointed Gothic style. Most of the windows are filled with modern stained glass. Under the tower on the north wall will be found a monument by Chantrey to the memory of Frederica Charlotte Ulrica Katharine, Duchess of York. On the floor near the west end of the church are three brasses : one to the memory of John Wolvde, 1598 ; an inscription on brass, dated 1642, to Hvmphry Dethick, One of His Maties Gent : Vshers (Day,"' Waiter) ; and another, dated 1586, to Thomas Inwood ye Elder, which represents him with three wives, two children behind the first, and three behind the second. The churchyard is rendered pleasant by many shrubs.

In the vaults under the Catholic church of St. Charles Borromeo, King Louis Philippe, Queen Amelie, and other members of the Orleans family were buried. The only member of that family left there now is the Duchesse de Nemours.

BANK.—London & County, Church-st.

FIRE.—Station, opposite church.

HOTELS.—"Oatlands Park ;" "Hand and Spear," by the Station ; "Lincoln Arms," near the river.

PLACES OF WORSHIP.—St. James's ; St. Michael's ; and the Roman Catholic Church of St. Charles Borromeo.

POSTAL ARRANGEMENTS.—Post Office (money order, insurance, telegraph, and savings bank). Mails from London, 7 and 9.15 a.m., 5 p.m. ; Sunday, 7 a.m. Mails for London, 10.30 a.m., 3.30, 8.45, and 10 p.m.; Sunday, 8.45 and 10 p.m.

FARES to Waterloo : 1st, 3/6, 5/- ; 2nd, 2/6, 3/6; 3rd, 1/7, 2/10.

Wharfingers' Association of the Port of London (The), held at the offices of Messrs. Arkcoll and Cockell, 190, Tooley-street, Southwark, was established in 1858 to protect the interests of the wharfingers of the Port of London; to watch any measures which may be introduced into Parliament having a tendency to interfere with the free navigation of the river; and to secure for the public the free delivery of goods overside from vessels discharging cargoes in the various docks.

Whitchurch, Oxfordshire, on the left bank opposite Pangbourne, a station on the Great Western Railway, 41 miles from Paddington, to which it is united by a long wooden bridge. From London 80¾ miles, from Oxford 30¾ miles. Population, 836. Soil, chalk. A straggling village of considerable size, with a good church, with a curious wooden steeple, close to the river. The church is dedicated to St. Mary, and has been greatly restored and rebuilt, showing, however, still many signs of its early Norman character. It contains several good brasses; in the chancel on the north side is that of Roger Geary, 1450, attired in cope, &c.; and within the altar rails is that of Thomas Walich, with figures of a knight in armour, and his wife, 1420. In another part of the church is the brass in memory of Peter Winder, once curate of the parish, who died 1610, and is represented kneeling, in his robes. In the north aisle is a mural monument to Richard Lybbe, lord of the manor of Hardwick, and his wife Joanna, 1599. The two figures, both curiously painted and gilded, kneel at a *prie dieu*, he in armour, she in ruff and quaint head-dress. A most elaborate coat-of-arms and crest crown the monument. Here also is a tablet :

To Richard Lybbe, of Hardwick, Esq., and Anne Blagrave united in sacred wedlock 50 years, are here againe made one by death she yielded to yt. change Ian. 17, 1651, which he embracied Ivly 14, 1658.

EPITAPH.

He, whose Renowne, for what completeth Man, Speaks lowder, better things, then Marble can : She, whose Religious Deeds makes Hardwick's Fame Breathe as the Balme of Lybbe's Immortall Name, Are once more Ioyned within this Peacefull Bed ; Where Honour (not Arabian-Gummes) is spred, Then grudge not (Friends) who next succeed 'em must Y'are Happy, that shall mingle with such Dust.

All the windows are of stained glass, and are mostly memorials. The Powys and Gardiner families figure largely in every part of the church.

One of the most celebrated historical mansions on the river is Hardwick House in the parish of Whitchurch, about 1½ miles from the lock, and rather more than half a mile from Mapledurham.

PLACE OF WORSHIP.—St. Mary's.

POSTAL ARRANGEMENTS. — Money order office. Nearest telegraph and insurance office, Pangbourne. Mails from London, 6.40 a.m., 1.15 p.m.; for London, 1.15 and 6.40 p.m.

NEAREST *Bridges*, Pangbourne ; up, Streatley 4 miles ; down, Caversham 6¼ miles. *Locks,* Whitchurch ; up, Goring 4 miles ; down, Mapledurham 2½ miles. *Ferry,* Basildon ; *Railway Station,* Pangbourne (*which see for* FARES).

Whitebait was formerly caught much higher up the Thames than at present. The principal area of supply is now between Woolwich and Gravesend, the legal season being April to September. Dr. Günther, the eminent ichthyologist of the British Museum, pronounces whitebait to be the fry of the herring, and this opinion appears to be confirmed by strict comparative induction with the presumed parent fish. That they are not a distinct and matured species of fish is presumed to be decided from the fact that the most careful examination has never resulted in the discovery of the slightest appearance of spawn in their ovaries. The whitebait, however, as served up at table, is not entirely the young of one description of fish ; a few turns of the prong will develop quite a heterogeneous assortment, which consists of the young of herrings, sprats, pricklebacks, gobies, weevers, sand-eels, pipe-fish, white shrimps, and here and there an infant stone-loach. Dr. Buckland, in his "Familiar History of British Fishes," tells us : "The run of fish varies much. If the weather is hot and quiet for many days continuously the water gets stagnant ; but a breeze with rain sweetens the water and brings up the fish." Sprats are caught as far up as Erith after a gale of wind. The "spratty stuff" and the smig bait come up into the river first ; when the herring fry comes up the sprats fall off back into the sea. Directly the weather begins to get warm the sprats fall off. The herrings in April are beginning to come ; the little sprats are getting scarce and will return in November next as full-grown sprats. If a basket of whitebait be now examined, there will be found a large number of minute fish from an inch to an inch and a half long, perfectly transparent, with a large eye and no scales visible ; the body is covered with a few black spots ; these are the " smig herring." The scales are just beginning to appear on some of these young fish in the form of a band of silver along the edge of the abdomen. Towards the middle or end of next month the young herrings will have put on all their scales, technically called " taking scale," and the sprats will be nearly out of the river altogether. Londoners are under the idea that whitebait are necessarily very small. Large quantities, however, of these young herring are caught and thrown back into the water, the reason assigned being that they are not marketable fish, like the small " spratty stuff."

Windsor, Berkshire, on the right bank, from London 43 miles, from Oxford 68½ miles, a terminus on branches of the Great Western and South Western Railways. From Paddington 21 miles, trains taking from 35 minutes to an hour ; the Great Western Railway-station being about 8 minutes' walk from the bridge. From Waterloo the distance is 25 miles, the time occupied in transit about an hour ; the South Western Railway-station is four minutes' walk from the river. The time occupied in transit from the Mansion House by the best trains is from an hour and a quarter to an hour and a half. Flys meet the trains at both stations. Population, about 12,000. The counties of Berks and Bucks are here joined by a handsome stone bridge of three arches.

Windsor was originally called Windleshore, presumably from the numerous bends in the river hereabouts, and was given by King Edward the Confessor to the monks at Westminster. It first rose into importance when William the Conqueror, getting rid of the monks by persuading them in the gentle Norman fashion to exchange their land here for other estates in Essex, built the first castle. Being built on the side of a hill Windsor presents a very picturesque appearance from the water, and consists of several good streets, with excellent shops and numerous pleasant private residences. The principal business thoroughfares are Thames-street, leading from the

river ; High-street, a continuation of Thames-street ; Park-street, leading to the Long Walk ; the Castle-hill, Peascod-street, and Sheet-street. From Thames-street " The Hundred Steps " lead to the Castle, the main entrance of which is in Castle-hill just off the High-street, and nearly opposite the Great Western Railway-station. Since 1276 Windsor has returned members to Parliament, the number, formerly two, having been reduced in 1867 to one. The borough, which has a constituency of 2054, is now represented by R. Richardson Gardner, Esq., a Conservative. It is under the government of a mayor, six aldermen, and eighteen councillors, with a high steward—at present H.R.H. Prince Christian—recorder, treasurer, and town-clerk. There are infantry barracks in Sheet-street and Victoria-street, and cavalry barracks at Spital, some half-mile from the town. The D Company of the 1st Berkshire Volunteers have their headquarters in Church-lane. There is a theatre in Thames-street, a convenient building enough, but it is generally understood that Windsor is not what is called a good theatrical " pitch." The so-called Bachelor's Acre is a piece of land belonging to the Corporation, in which the inhabitants have the right of disporting themselves, and is the centre of rejoicings on public festivals. The Town Hall is in High-street, and is the work of Sir Christopher Wren. It is said that when the hall was finished the Corporation, doubting the strength of the floor, insisted upon its being made additionally secure by the support of stone pillars. These Sir Christopher added to please the worthy burgesses ; but being himself quite satisfied with his work as it originally stood, took very good care that the capitals of the pillars should not touch the beams, as may be seen at the present day. Thus everybody was satisfied, and as the floor has remained and supported great weights ever since with no more than a fair amount of deflection, Sir Christopher conclusively proved his case. Outside the hall on the north side is an extremely commonplace statue of that very commonplace queen, Anne the Good, for which a courtly poet has provided the following inscription :

Arte tua sculptor non est imitabilis Anna
Annæ vis similem sculpere sculpe Deam.

This is pretty strong, but is to be matched on the south side where the Statue of George of Denmark, half dressed in periwig and Roman costume, and grasping the inevitable truncheon, is declared to be dedicated *Serenissimo Georgio Principi Daniæ Heroi Omni Sæculo Venerando.* Windsor being a royal borough is a capital place for toadying of this kind, and within the precincts of the castle stands an equestrian statue of Charles II., on the pedestal of which Old Rowley is described as "best of kings," beyond which, in the way of adulation, it would be difficult to go. It was erected at the cost of Tobias Rustat, Yeoman of the Robes. The Town Hall contains some good portraits, as well as some copies, which are well worth inspection. The custodian will generally be found at any time between 11 and 1, and 3 and 6, somewhere about the premises. The pictures, mostly full-lengths, comprise George IV. in the robes of the Garter, by Sir Thomas Lawrence; George III. and Queen Charlotte, after Sir Joshua Reynolds; Queen and Prince George (with more truncheon and more armour), by Clostermann; Charles I., by "Old Stone;" Queen Mary II. and William III. (this latter a remarkably good portrait), by J. Riley; and portraits of the late Prince Consort and of her present Majesty, presented by herself. In the Council Chamber are portraits of Archbishop Laud, after Vandyck; James II., by Sir Godfrey Kneller; Prince Rupert, by D'Agar; William Pitt, by Gainsborough; James I., by Miravelt. Two very curious portraits: one of Queen Elizabeth, after Lucas de Heere; the other of Charles, Earl of Nottingham, once Constable of the Castle, and High Steward of Windsor, by Zucchero, also hang in this room. Here also is the marble bust, by the late Joseph Durham, A.R.A., of Charles Knight, who was well known in connection with Windsor, which was his native town, and which saw the beginning of his long and useful literary career. The bust is an admirable likeness. The carved oak mayoral chair taken from the old parish church, which also is in the Council Chamber, is curious.

The parish church is in the High-street, and is dedicated to St. John the Baptist. It is externally a somewhat plain building, with a large embattled square tower with pinnacles at the angles. Within it is handsome, though rather heavy in its general effect, with open chancel, nave, aisles, and galleries. The peal of bells is said to date from the time of Queen Elizabeth. The chancel is rather garishly decorated in the Salviati mosaic style, with five panels representing angels and objects symbolical of the Crucifixion, such as the crown of thorns, the soldiers' dice, the nails, hammer, St. Veronica's handkerchief, &c. The screen is surmounted by carved figures of angels, and the roofs of the chancel and apse spring from similar statues. The centre window of the apse is a memorial to the late Mrs. Ellison, and represents the visitation of the sick, &c. On the south side of the chancel facing the organ is a spacious royal pew, with a separate entrance from the churchyard, chiefly remarkable for its fine carved railings, the work of Grinling Gibbons. On the wall of the north-west vestibule are two ancient black-letter inscriptions, almost illegible, of which one appears to be to the memory of William Canon and "Elizabeth his wyfe, and all their chyldrene," and to be of the time of Henry VIII. Here also is the tomb of Chief Justice Reeve, with the busts of himself and wife, supported by two marble figures of children, the one with inverted torch, the other with a medallion representing justice. On the stairs is a large and extremely florid monument, well stocked with angels, statues, and cherubim. In the north aisle is a quaint monument without date, but apparently of the 16th century, with kneeling figures of father, mother, and children, and bearing the following inscription: "In Happie memorie of Edward Iobson and Elynor his wyfe, by whom the sayd Edward had issve vi sonnes, vidz Edward, Frances, Hvmfrie, James, William, Richard, and iiii daughters, Elizabeth, Elizabeth, Catharine, Sara." In the west gallery is a large picture representing the Last Supper, which is apparently of some importance, and may or may not possess merit; but as it is at present hung it is impossible to make anything of it except that it is of prodigious size. All Saints' Church is a chapelry of the parish church, and is situated in the Frances-road. Holy Trinity Church, near the Clarence-road,

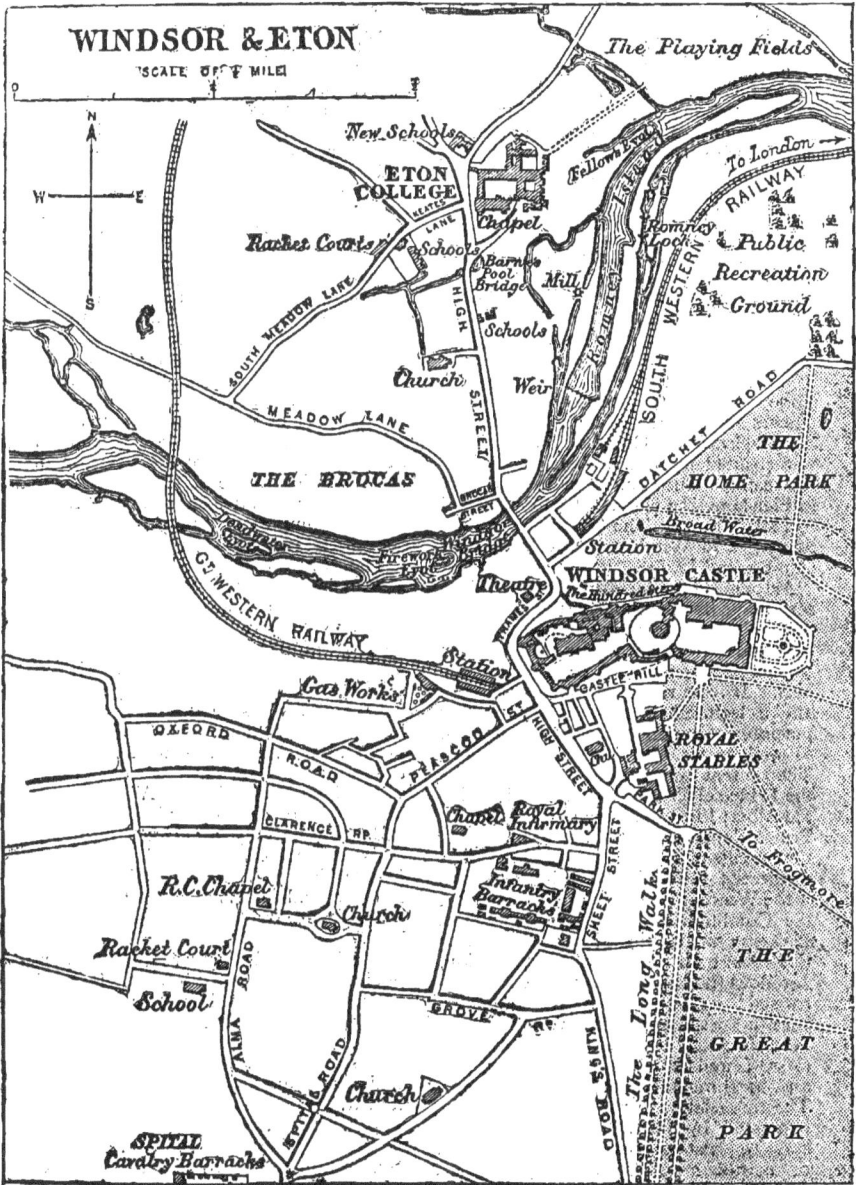

WINDSOR & ETON

SCALE OF ¼ MILE

The Playing Fields

New Schools

ETON COLLEGE

Fellows Eyot

To London

WESTERN RAILWAY

Racket Courts

KEATES LANE

Chapel

Schools

Barnes Pool Bridge

Romney Lock

Public Recreation Ground

HIGH STREET

SOUTH MEADOW LANE

Mill

Schools

MEADOW LANE

Church

Weir

SOUTH

DATCHET ROAD

THE HOME PARK

THE BROCAS

Broad Water

Station

GT. WESTERN RAILWAY

Firework

Theatre

WINDSOR CASTLE

The Hundred Steps

Station

Gas Works

CASTLE HILL

OXFORD ROAD

PEASCOD STREET

HIGH STREET

ROYAL STABLES

CLARENCE RD.

Chapel

Royal Infirmary

To Frogmore

R.C. Chapel

Church

Infantry Barracks

SHEET STREET

The Long Walk

THE

Racket Court

GROVE

GREAT

School

ALMA ROAD

SPITTAL ROAD

PARK

Church

SOUTH

SPITTAL Cavalry Barracks

Stanford's Geogl. Estabt

is the garrison church in Windsor, and contains a memorial to the Brigade of Guards, and has, on an illumination running round the entire face of the gallery, the name of every officer and man of the three battalions of Foot Guards that fell in the Crimea, 2,129 names in all. The texts which surmount the memorial were chosen and paid for by the Queen. There are also many beautiful monuments to officers of the Household Brigade, notably those to Sir Thomas Biddulph, Lord Rossmore, Sir Algernon Peyton, and Earl Ranfurley. There is also a beautiful painted window at the east end, given by the Grenadier Guards; as well as windows in the south and west by the Coldstream Guards; a very handsome stone pulpit by the Scots Guards; and a stone font by the non - commissioned officers and privates of the 2nd Battalion of the Grenadier Guards. The reredos was painted by Mrs. Robins, the wife of the rector. The Church of the Saviour, in Bier-lane, is a chapel of ease attached to Holy Trinity. The Chapel Royal, All Saints, is in Windsor Great Park, near Cumberland Lodge.

Among the public institutions of Windsor may be mentioned the Literary, Scientific, and Mechanics' Institution in Sheet-street, which was established in 1835, and now numbers nearly 200 members. It has a reading-room and library, and a lecture-hall, which is used for the purposes of gymnastic and other classes, as well as for the delivery of lectures. The present building was inaugurated by the Prince of Wales in 1880, and is called the Albert Institute, in memory of the late Prince Consort, who took great interest in the success of the institution. Intimately connected too with the Prince Consort is the Windsor Association for Improving the Condition of the Working Classes, Park-street. It is expressly stated that this is not an eleemosynary institution, nor does it purpose to relieve the distressed ; its object is to stimulate and cherish the spirit of industry, and thus to raise the social condition of the labouring classes, and it gives rewards for past and encouragement to future exertions. The association arose from a desire expressed by H.R.H. the Prince Consort to bestow some mark of favour on cottagers in and around Windsor, who were diligent in keeping their homes

tidy. The design enlarged as it grew, and eventually it embraced every kind of industrial occupation. Neat cottages ; well-cultivated gardens or allotments ; the bringing up of families honestly ; long service of labourers, artisans, or domestics, especially of young persons in their first situations, are the objects sought out and rewarded. Special notice is taken whether children have been duly sent to school ; whether payments have been made to sick clubs, savings banks, or other provident institutions ; or assistance given to poorer relatives. The association also provides encouragement for the cultivation of any honest skill or useful talent. For this purpose an exhibition is held at the meetings for garden produce of every kind, and handicraft, whether in works of taste or usefulness, executed by cottagers in their leisure hours, and prizes are awarded for the best specimens. Care is taken to secure the selection of well-deserving persons. Besides these objects the committee has at various times taken up important questions, such as allotments, model dwelling-houses, &c.

The Naval Knights of Windsor, who were endowed by Mr. Samuel Travers in 1728, inhabit a house in Datchet-lane. They are seven in number, and must be, on appointment, superannuated or disabled lieutenants of the Royal Navy. Promotion subsequent to appointment does not now, as was formerly the case, involve resignation ; and, indeed, the present knights all appear to have attained the rank of commander.

The Masonic Hall in St. Alban's-street is the work of Sir Christopher Wren, and is devoted entirely to masonic purposes. It is the freehold of the Windsor Castle Lodge, No. 771. The Etonian Lodge, No. 209, and the Windsor Castle Chapter of the Royal Arch also hold their meetings here.

The Eton and Windsor Royal Humane Society was established in 1835. Its headquarters are at the "King's Arms," Eton, and it consists of about 40 working members and about 100 honorary members with subscription of 6s. per annum. The main drags are kept in constant readiness at Mr. Norwood's, coach-builder, Eton, close to the river. Drags are also kept at various places up the river as far as Surly Hall, and down as far as Datchet, and a waterman is kept for the safety of the public during college vacation at Cuckoo Weir bathing-place.

A regatta is held here annually, when challenge and presentation prizes are offered for competition.—(*See* WINDSOR AND ETON REGATTA.) There is also a racecourse, at which meetings are held at different periods of the year. It is a flat course with a straight 6 furlongs, and is about a mile from the town, on Ray's Island, above Clewer.

Windsor offers many attractions to the excursionist. Maidenhead and Cookham with their beautiful scenery are within a convenient distance by water, and inland there is an almost endless succession of interesting and pleasant excursions from which to choose ; Ascot, Sunninghill, Winkfield, Warfield, Binfield, St. Ann's Hill, near Chertsey, are all within six or eight miles from Windsor, and are reached through a charming country. Virginia Water, which is about six miles from Windsor, and is approached through the forest, should on no account be missed. This was a favourite retreat of George IV., who caused the country on its banks to be laid out with all the resources of the landscape gardener's art. The scenery is consequently charmingly diversified, and as much as possible is made of the lake, which is upwards of a mile and a half long and of varying width. There is a good hotel here, the "Wheatsheaf."

Windsor is favoured with an abundance of freshwater fish of all kinds, and it is seldom that an angler returns without some sport, more often with a heavy bag than otherwise. Very fine trout are taken every season in the weir at the back of the "New Inn," Eton, a favourite resort of anglers. Barbel, perch, roach, and gudgeon are in abundance.

BANKS.—London and County, High-street ; Nevile Reid and Co., Thames-street.

FAIRS.—Easter Tuesday, July 5, October 24.

FIRE.—Volunteer Fire Brigade (Captain, foreman, engineer, sub-foreman, sub-engineer, hon. treasurer, hon. surgeon, hon. secretary, and twenty pioneers): Headquarters and steam fire-engine station, Acre House, Bachelor's Acre ; manual-engine station, Police-station, Sheet-street ; fire-escape station, St. Alban's-street.

HOTELS.—"Castle," High-street ; "White Hart," High-street. The comfortable and reasonable "Bridge House Hotel," though on the Eton side of the bridge, is also convenient for visitors to Windsor.

MARKET DAY.—Saturday.

PLACES OF WORSHIP.—Chapel Royal, All Saints, Windsor Great Park ; Chapel Royal, St. George's ; All Saints, Frances-road ; Holy Trinity Church ; St. John the Baptist (parish church), High-street ; St. Stephen's, Oxford-road ; and the Church of the Saviour, Bier-lane ; the Roman Catholic Church of St. Edward ; and Baptist, Congregational, Primitive Methodist, and Wesleyan Chapels.

POLICE.—Station, Sheet-street.

POSTAL ARRANGEMENTS.—Post Office (money order, savings bank, telegraph, and insurance), Park-street, just beyond the parish church. Mails from London, 7 and 10.30 a.m., 2.30 and 6.30 p.m. ; Sunday, 7 a.m. by letter carrier, over counter from 7 to 10 a.m. Mails for London, 10 and 11.10 a.m., 2.0, 4.20, and 10 p.m. ; Sunday, 10 p.m.

NEAREST *Bridges*, Windsor ; up, Maidenhead 7 miles ; down, Victoria 1½ mile. *Locks*, up, Boveney 2 miles; down, Romney ¼ mile. *Railway Stations*, Windsor (L. & S.W.R., G.W.R., and District).

FARES to Paddington or Waterloo : 1st, 3/9, 5/6 ; 2nd, 2/10, 4/3 ; 3rd, 1/11. To Mansion House, 1st, 4/4, 6/6 ; 2nd, 3/3, 5/- ; 3rd, 2/3, 4/1.

REGULATIONS FOR PUBLIC CARRIAGES.—A first-class carriage shall mean every full-sized carriage drawn by more than one horse, and constructed to carry six adult persons ; a second-class carriage shall mean every carriage drawn by one horse, and constructed to carry four adult persons. The following fares shall be charged by the drivers of all carriages :

Fares for Time, to commence from the time of leaving the stand : For every hour or any less time, 1st class, 4/ ; 2nd, 3/-. For every additional quarter of an hour or any less time, 1st, -/9 ; 2nd, -/6.

Fares for Distance, to commence from leaving the stand : For any distance not exceeding one mile, 1st, 2/- ; 2nd, 1/-. For every additional half-mile or any less distance, 1st, -/9 ; 2nd, -/6.

The above fares shall include any charge for the personal luggage of the hirer not exceeding fifty-six pounds, and where the quantity of luggage carried shall exceed such weight, the person hiring the carriage shall pay twopence for each package in excess. Any person hiring a carriage for conveyance to any distance within eight miles of the Guildhall of New Windsor shall be charged according to distance, unless at the time of the hiring he shall declare that such hiring is to be by time ; and if the passenger is brought back from the place of his destination to the place from which he started, or to some place short thereof, he shall, in addition to the fare for the outward journey, pay as the fare for the return journey half the amount chargeable in respect of the distance so travelled on the return journey. If he be carried back beyond the point of starting, he shall be charged from such point as for a new hiring. Every carriage hired for a distance may be detained to take up the fare ten minutes without any extra charge, but if kept beyond that time, the person hiring the same shall pay a proportion of the fare as allowed for time for so long as the same shall be detained. When any carriage shall be called and shall proceed to a place to take up the fare, and shall be sent away without such fare, the driver shall be entitled to demand and receive one shilling. Driver is bound to give a ticket and produce if required a copy of the bye-laws ; is also bound to have a check-string.

Windsor and Eton Amateur Regatta.—The course is under a mile, down stream, starting from Clewer Point and finishing at Goodman's Raft. Winners of the Challenge Cup, 1878, Albion R.C. ; 1879, Thames R.C. ; 1880, Eton Excelsior R.C. ; 1881, Reading R.C. ; 1882, Reading R.C. ; 1883, Eton Excelsior R.C. ; 1884, Marlow R.C. Winners of the Ruthven Challenge Cup, 1878, Eton Excelsior R.C. ; 1879, Elvington R.C. ; 1880, West London R.C. ; 1881, Cookham R.C. ; 1882, Marlow R.C. ; 1883, Maidenhead, R.C. ; 1884, Deerhurst R.C. (Eton).

RACES IN 1884.

REGATTA, Friday, August 1.
Course—From Clewer Point to Goodman's Raft.

: JUNIOR SCULLS,
    Final Heat.
R. G. Westmacotte, Eton College ...   1

SENIOR SCULLS.
F. I. Browne, Grove Park R.C.   ...   1
RUTHVEN CHALLENGE CUP.
    Final Heat.
Deerhurst R.C. (Eton): C. D. Hohler, S. Williams, W. H. Goschen, H. E. L. Puxley (stroke)   1
Kingston Junior R.C.   0
SENIOR PAIRS.
    Final Heat.
C. D. Hohler and W. H. Goschen (Eton)   1
CHALLENGE CUP FOR FOURS.
Marlow R.C. : W. T. Shaw, W. T. Porter, C. H. Yates, J. S. Kirpatrick (stroke), A. Shaw (cox) ...   1
Abney R.C.   0
Maidenhead R.C.   0

Windsor and Eton Angling Preservation Association has for its object the improvement and preservation of the fishery from the City Stone, Staines, to Monkey Island. The annual subscription is £1 1s. ; annual subscribers are also admitted at 10s. 6d. A reward of 10s. 6d. is offered " to any one who shall give sufficient information to any member of the committee of any illegal fishing, or being in unlawful possession of fish during the close season, provided that it be considered by the committee a fit case for prosecution ; and if the person so prosecuted be convicted by the magistrates, the amount shall be doubled." A reward of £1 is offered to any one capturing an otter in the water under the supervision of the association. Some thousands of recently hatched trout were presented to the association in 1878, and again in 1880, by the late Mr. F. Buckland, and placed in the Thames near Cuckoo Weir. It is satisfactory to be able to add, on the authority of Mr. Charles Layton, the hon. secretary, that "poaching is getting a thing of the past in this neighbourhood."

Windsor Castle.—To see Windsor "aright" is not quite so simple a matter as that of "Fair Melrose." Granted the moonlight, and the absence of that peculiarly diabolical kind of Scotch mist known as an " easterly haar," there is no special difficulty about seeing Melrose Abbey. There it is, beautiful enough, what there is left of it ; but no very great amount of time or exertion is required to see all that

ndsor it is far other-
)e seen are so numé-
d over such a vast
bleau itself shrinks
rhen compared with
1 appreciative eye,
withal, and some
cessary to take away
impression of the
e in Europe, dating
e antiquity, but well-
sinews trained to
stairs and traverse
ionable magnitude.
of the show be set
. All is well worth
II.'s Tower to the
f George III. But
[uite another matter.
must be explained
own to the public
of the royal family.
s, so to speak, at
d far between ; but
the hours given to
:uliar, as almost to
the Grand Steward
Constable of Wind-
:ver of those amiable
duty of making such
devolve, has been
ainst the trustees of
luseum for a puzzle
tlety of that arrange-
public are permitted
Tower on any day
:r and from 11 to 4
to see the Curfew
lust be made to the
to contemplate the
roper official at the
must be interviewed
of 1 and 3. Still
:est are open on any
)ert Chapel is open
hursday, and Friday.
ut tickets ; while St.
ay be viewed every
sday, between the
4. This is not all,
go to Windsor we
apartments. These
public, during the
n and the court, on
s, Thursdays, and
ion of tickets, to be
Library, Old Bond-
3heldon, 126, Strand,

and of Messrs. Keith, Prowse and Co., Cheapside, as well as at Collier's Library at Windsor. The private apartments can only be seen by special order granted rarely by the Lord Chamberlain. But setting that august functionary aside for a moment, let us see how we stand as members of the public. Having ascertained that the Queen and the court are absent from Windsor, we struggle to arrange a table of days. The first fact we realise is, that we had better not go to Windsor on a Saturday. On Wednesday we could see the Albert Chapel, but would be shut out of St. George's and the state apartments ; while if we went on Monday or Tuesday we should be shut out of the Albert Chapel. We therefore fall back upon Thursday or Friday, with the reflection that persons in authority might just as well have said so at once, and saved us the mental agony of working out the puzzle for ourselves. On Thursday and Friday, then, all that is visible at any time is visible—royalty always being absent—save and except the east terrace or grand parterre opposite the private apartments of the sovereign, open in her absence on Saturday and Sunday afternoons only. But the day, however happy it may be, will not be a long one, for on the longest summer day all is closed at 4 o'clock, and nothing is open before 11. Wherefore there is no need to rise at un-English hours, and the best part of the summer day is gone before we can begin to inspect Windsor Castle.

On leaving the railway-station we make for the Castle-hill entrance, not forgetting Collier's Library and the slip of yellow paper which will be required of us on passing into the state apartments, and we are moreover armed with the coveted pass for the private apartments, in which the privileged to wear the Windsor uniform, as it is called, and the happy guests invited to visit royalty, are permitted to penetrate. All the energy of Windsor officialism is directed towards the maintenance of the "privacy" coveted by royalty. During the royal residence no soul but the officers, equerries, and others on duty may venture to cross the grand quadrangle or the antechamber wherein the royal pages, as they are called, keep watch and ward over the corridor on which the private apartments open.

Beginning to see Windsor Castle sys-

WINDSOR CASTLE, STATE APARTMENTS

Upper Ward Quadrangle

East Terrace

South Terrace

North Terrace

ROUND TOWER

Castle Ditch

SCALE
0   25   50   150 FEET

Stanford's Geog.l Estab.t

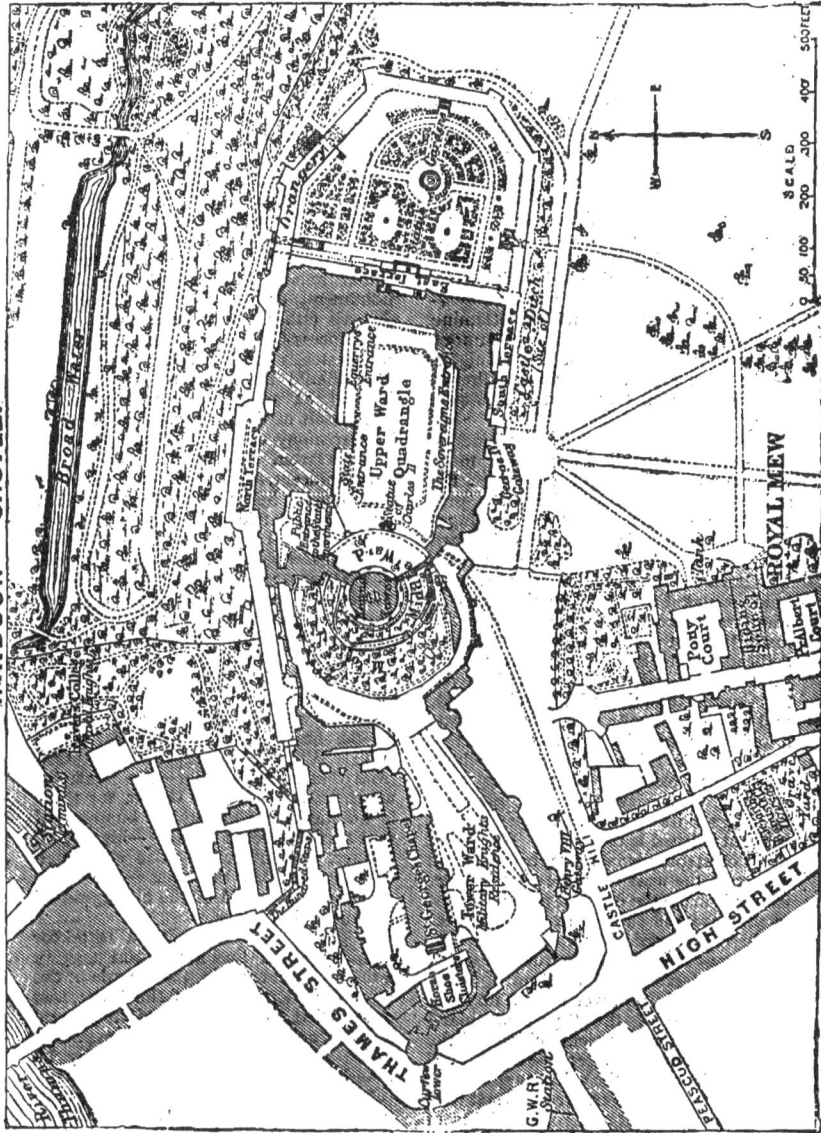

WINDSOR CASTLE.

tematically it is well to begin with the lower ward, as it is called, and attack the Winchester Tower, built by William of Wykeham, and described by him, "Hoc fecit Wykeham;" Henry III.'s Tower ; and glance at rather than inspect the Garter, the Salisbury, and the Curfew Towers. Grandly picturesque in their exterior aspect, these edifices have no minute beauties to engage the hasty sight-seer, although we cannot help showing some interest in the military knights, as they are called—the elderly gentlemen one sees about Windsor on festive occasions, in uniform with black belts as if they were all surgeons. There is, however, no time to spare, and we determine to begin with St. George's Chapel, famous as the central rallying spot of the Knights of the Garter, as the Elizabeth Church at Marburg was that of the Teutonic Knights.

It is hardly necessary for the modern sight-seer to trouble himself any more with Henry I.'s Chapel than with the ancient hill-fort, which doubtless preceded the round tower of the Plantagenets. This much is certain, that Edward III., called Edward of Windsor, who was born in the great Norman stronghold, founded a chapel on the ruins of whatever preceded it, shortly after the institution of the Order of the Garter, and dedicated it to St. George, the patron saint of that order. The chapel proved less durable than the order of knighthood, and became radically unsafe before it was a hundred years old, and was completely demolished by Edward IV., during whose reign the existing chapel was constructed. It is easy to see that, like most buildings of its class, St. George's Chapel was not finished in one reign. The grand flight of steps, for instance, by which we approach the west entrance of the nave, was only made the more durable, and the roof of the nave and choir were added respectively by Henry of Richmond and his son, to replace the wooden structure which topped the edifice of the Sun of York. Edward's walls, however, remain intact, a fine example of the "perpendicular" period. The more recent ceilings of the two last Henrys are of course more florid in style, the ribs of the columns spreading over the roof in rich tracery adorned with the blazon of dead and gone Knights of the Garter, and the "Rose en Soleil,"

the well-known cognisance of the Sun of York. The great west window at the end of the nave is a patchwork made up of odds and ends of ancient stained glass collected from various parts of the chapel, and eked out with modern work. Despite its defects, this window throws down a mass of rich hues which adds vastly to the splendour of the nave. The Beaufort Chapel has been emptied of some of its monuments, removed within a few years to Badminton, and it may be added generally that the minor chapels are only worth a hurried glance. A similar remark will apply to the Kent monument, erected in memory of the Queen's father, and to the cenotaph of the Princess Charlotte, a much-talked-of but tasteless production. Far more time should be given to the choir—devoted, as a matter of course, to the celebration of divine service, and also to the ceremony of installing the Knights of the Garter. This part of the chapel is magnificent, and loses nothing of its splendour by being of a size convenient for the eye to take in from a favourable standpoint. The stalls of the knights are on either side of the choir, and those of the sovereign and the princes of the blood-royal under the organ gallery. Over each stall, but beneath the banner, a canopy of beautiful carved work supports the sword, mantle, and crest of each knight. The banner, of course, is emblazoned with his armorial bearings, repeated with his name, style, and titles on the brass plate at the back of the stall. When death removes a knight from that sublime order—one wearer of which said, " I like the Garter, for there is no merit or confounded humbug of that sort connected with it "—his sword, banner, and other insignias are taken down saving only the brass-plate, which remains as a record of the distinguished honour he has borne.

A genial antiquary with a taste for heraldry might find a pleasant task in writing and illustrating the records of the most illustrious Order of the Garter, as exemplified in the stalls of its several knights and their curious succession of noble tenants, among whom may be found Sigismund, Emperor of Germany (Mr. Carlyle's Sigismund "super-grammaticam"); Casimir IV., King of Poland; the Duke of Buckingham (Richard III.'s

Buckingham) ; Lords Hastings, Lovel, and Stanley ; the unfortunate Earl of Surrey ; Charles V. ; Francis I.; Sir Robert Dudley (otherwise Earl of Leicester) ; and Lord Burleigh (not Mr. Tennyson's, but Queen Elizabeth's). The stall of the Sovereign glows with purple and gold. On the pedestals of the knights' stalls the life of our Saviour is represented in very rich carved work, and on those of the royal family the adventures of St. George.

On the north side of the choir, near the altar, are carved the attempt of Margaret Nicholson to assassinate George III.; the procession of that king to St. Paul's to return thanksgiving for his recovery in 1789 ; the scene in the interior of the cathedral ; and a representation of Queen Charlotte's Charity School. The stained glass windows on either side of the choir afford a rich display of colour and heraldic lore, containing the arms of the Sovereign and various Knights Companions of the Order of the Garter ; the arms of each knight are encompassed by the cognizance of the order and surmounted with his crest and coronet.

The large window over the altar is a recent addition. Its place was formerly occupied by Sir Benjamin West's "Resurrection" window ; but this work was replaced by the Albert Memorial Window, designed by Sir Gilbert Scott, and executed by Messrs. Clayton and Bell. Beneath this richly-tinted window is an alabaster reredos beautifully sculptured.

In the centre of the choir, near the eleventh stall on the Sovereign's side, is the royal vault, in which repose the remains of Henry VIII., his queen Jane Seymour, Charles I., and an infant daughter of Queen Anne. On opening the vault for the interment of the latter the other coffins were discovered, but no further research was made till 1813, when the Prince Regent caused it to be again opened, in order that a controversy as to the burying-place of Charles I. should be finally set at rest. The accuracy of the previous investigations was amply vindicated, the head and body of Charles being found in a plain leaden coffin. The skeleton only of Henry VIII. was found. Perhaps ho exhumation was ever immortalised as was that of 1813, the subject of Lord Byron's epigram entitled "Windsor Poetics," first called "The Vault," pronounced by its author too

farouche, an opinion in which the majority will probably concur.

Another noteworthy tomb in St. George's Chapel is that of Edward IV. in the north aisle. Before studying it, however, the visitor must mark the gallery or Queen's closet fitted up for the accommodation of Her Majesty when attending divine service, and also occupied by her at the marriages of the Prince of Wales and the Princess Louise (Marchioness of Lorne). Beneath this are the iron gates said to have been made by Quentin Matsys, the painter-blacksmith of Antwerp. These gates were formerly placed on the tomb of Edward IV., together with his armour and surcoat of crimson velvet embroidered with rubies, pearls, and gold ; but during the civil war the Parliamentary forces made short work of the finery, and all that is left of the tomb now is a black marble slab with Edward's name in raised brass letters. On a flat stone at the base is inscribed : "King Edward IV., and his Queen, Elizabeth Widvile." The skeleton of the king was found to justify the report of his kingly stature. The handsomest man, and incomparably the greatest warrior of his time, must have been at least six feet two in his stockings. Queen Elizabeth Widvile's remains were discovered when the present royal cemetery was constructed, together with a coffin containing the remains of Prince George, her third son. Farther on lie George, Duke of Bedford, and Mary, fifth daughter of Edward IV. The windows in the north aisle commemorate the "Sun of York," his Queen, the Rutland family, and the Hanoverian Sovereigns of the Order of the Garter.

The Albert Chapel, adjoining the east end of St. George's Chapel, was built originally by Henry of Richmond as a royal mausoleum for himself; but upon his final choice of Westminster Abbey it stood neglected until Cardinal Wolsey obtained a grant of it from Henry VIII. From that time it was called Wolsey's Tomb House, and Benedetto, a Florentine sculptor, was employed in 1524 to erect a costly monument. He was paid 4,250 ducats for that part of the design which he erected, and £380 13s. sterling was paid for gilding about half of it. It was destined never to hold the corpse of the magnificent prelate who planned it.

Charles I. is said to have intended to make of it a royal tomb-house for himself and his successors, but ship-money and the Long Parliament and Oliver Cromwell overturned this — like many other designs of the king. During the occupation of Windsor by the soldiers of the Parliament the tomb was dismantled, the images of gilt copper taken away and sold for £600. Nothing was left of the tomb but a sarcophagus of black marble. In 1805 this was used for the sepulture of Nelson in the crypt of St. Paul's.

When James II. turned towards the Church of Rome he resolved to fit up the forlorn chapel for the celebration of the rites of the ancient faith, and Verrio, whose saints and heroes "sprawl," as Pope has it, on the ceilings of the castle, went to work on its decoration; but when Romish services were held, and the Pope's nuncio received in St. George's Hall, the people arose, broke the windows, and otherwise defaced the building. For nearly a century Wolsey's Tomb House lay neglected, until George III. determined to construct a royal vault beneath it, since when the members of the royal family have been interred there. It was not, however, till after the death of the late Prince Consort that the present scheme of decoration was commenced. By the desire of the Queen this historic building was completely restored in honour of her husband. Sir Gilbert Scott was the architect, Messrs. Clayton and Bell the designers, Baron Triqueti the sculptor, and Dr. Salviati the decorator in mosaic; Miss Susan Durant, a pupil of Baron Triqueti, being the sculpturess of the marble busts on each scriptural tablet.

The roof literally blazes with the Salviati mosaics, and the light entering through the stained glass windows is enriched with gorgeous dyes. Baron Triqueti's "Pictures in Marble" cover the wall under the windows, and Messrs. Poole's marble flooring is also a fine piece of work. The general effect of the Albert Chapel, which is only 68 feet in length, and is very elegantly proportioned, is of almost overpowering richness. At the entrance to the chancel is the cenotaph. Its base is of black and gold Tuscan marble, and the sculptured figure of the late Prince Consort of the purest Carrara. The effigy of the Prince is recumbent, in the armour of a knight

of the 14th century, wearing the Order of the Garter, and in the act of sheathing his sword. The reredos is also a very finely executed work in the costliest marbles, and the communion-table is of one splendid slab. The actual place in which the body of the late Prince Consort lies is the mausoleum at Frogmore, on the left-hand side of the Long Walk at a short distance from the castle. This magnificent tomb, erected at the sole expense of the Queen, the cost amounting to £200,000, is not one of the sights of Windsor, being only thrown open on one day of the year—that of the anniversary service—and then only to a limited number of the residents of Windsor. Near the Prince's mausoleum is that of the Duchess of Kent, the Queen's mother.

After the Chapel of St. George the state apartments are the chief objects of a visitor to Windsor. These are very handsome, although the modern educated eye turns aside at times from the somewhat garish splendour of the style of the first French empire, which, with that of Louis XVI., prevails in the majority of the rooms. The paintings, however, are alone worth a visit to Windsor. In pictures the Castle is rich, and in china and costly furniture wonderfully so. There is, indeed, no finer storehouse of good and beautiful work than Windsor Castle. It is a mine from which a dozen magnificent collections might easily be quarried, and, unlike Hampton Court, contains little or no rubbish. There is thus none of the boredom in going over Windsor that one experiences in numerous show-places, where the corn is in slender proportion to the chaff.

The order in which the state apartments are usually shown commences with the Queen's Audience Chamber. Verrio has covered the ceiling with a subject oddly chosen for the time at which it was painted. Amid a wild crowd of heathen gods and goddesses very scantily clad, Catharine of Braganza, Queen of Charles II., is discovered, personified as Britannia, and proceeding in a car drawn by swans towards the temple of virtue. The contemplation of this really very gorgeous work of art raises a suspicion in the ribald mind that perhaps court painters, like Signor Verrio, were sometimes sharp satirists. She is making off, this poor ill-used queen, apparently from the English court, where she was quite out of place, attended, however, by a choice bevy of the brazen beauties of the period. She is the wrong Britannia, too. There is only one form of the wave-ruler in which the writer believes, and that is her image as impressed upon the coinage of this realm. The original Britannia was not the virtuous, ill-used queen, but the pert baggage known as La belle Stuart, afterwards married to the Earl of Richmond.

Magnificent Gobelins tapestry decorates the walls of the audience chamber. The subject is the story of Esther and Vashti. The tapestry is beautifully fresh and vivid in colour. Three somewhat remarkable pictures are hung in this room—two Honthorsts—one of the father and one of the grandfather of William III., and a picture of Mary Queen of Scots, by Janet.

The old ball-room, now called the Vandyck Room, is of handsome proportion, but is in no respect profusely decorated, unless the matchless Vandycks on the walls be considered as decorative. A lengthy critical or descriptive notice of those fine works is hardly necessary. There is the famous picture in which appear Charles I., his Queen, Henrietta Maria, and family, Charles II., and James II. Several replicas of this picture exist, some of which are certainly painted by Vandyck and his pupils. Another remarkable portrait of Charles is that in which he is seen from three points of view. It was painted for Bernini, the sculptor, and sent to him at Rome in order that he might execute the bust which was destroyed by fire at Whitehall in 1697. Bernini, on receiving the picture, is said to have been struck with the "fey" look of the face, and expressed his opinion openly that his royal client had an evil future before him. Charles was so well pleased with the bust, that he sent the sculptor a ring worth 6,000 crowns. The equestrian portrait of Charles is also in this room, and is the picture engraved by Lombart, and which was sold after the king's death for £200. After the Restoration Lombart, who after engraving it had erased the face of Charles and substituted that of Cromwell, put in the face of Charles II. and demanded 1,500 guineas for the picture. but was com-

pelled to relinquish it for 1,000. In this Vandyck Room are many other pictures by that great master—portraits of Killigrew and Carew; of Queen Henrietta Maria ; of Lady Venetia Digby ; of the second George Villiers, Duke of Buckingham, who died at Kirkby Moorside " in the worst inn's worst room ;" of the celebrated Prince de Carignan, the military commander ; of that " busy stateswoman, the Countess of Carlisle ;" of Mary, Countess of Dorset ; and of Sir Anthony Vandyck himself. In this room are some magnificent cabinets, among which is one by Gouthier of the perfect ormolu of the best period of Louis XVI., a marvel of metal work, undercut and chiselled with all the delicacy of the daintiest specimens of the goldsmith's art—a very perfect and beautiful piece of furniture, which would probably fetch £10,000 at Christie's.

The Queen's State Drawing-room, or Zuccarelli Room, contains some fine pictures by Zuccarelli and an interesting portrait of Henry, Duke of Gloucester, son of Charles I., who died at Cologne in 1660 ; as well as portraits of the three first Georges, and of Frederick, Prince of Wales—" Fred, who is dead," and of whom no more could be said in the opinion of the epigrammatist. Posterity, however, is inclined to reverse the verdict of contemporaries in the case of this prince as in that of " Butcher " Cumberland. " Fred, who was alive and now is dead," was a prince of infinitely higher culture than either his brave little father or his half-witted son. " Fred " it was who collected many of the finest pictures now at Windsor to prove that he by no means abhorred " boets and bainters " as his father did.

Lovers of Grinling Gibbons should mark in the so-called state ante-room the delightful carvings of this master. The apartment, it should be borne in mind, was in Charles II.'s time "the king's public dining-room ;" the apartment, in fact, in which the king and royal family dined—in imitation of the ceremonial observed at Versailles—before the whole court. Its original purpose explains the edible birds, beasts, and fishes which "sprawl" all over the ceiling, and the exquisite carvings by Gibbons of fish, game, flowers, and fruit.

The Waterloo Chamber has been

greatly laughed at on account of its resemblance to the cabin of a ship. It was constructed in the time of King William IV., and its peculiar shape is said to have been suggested eventually by that nautical monarch, who lay in state in its midst. It is nevertheless a fine, lofty room, looking very handsome when lit up, and occupied by the officers of the Queen's household, who dine there on grand occasions. The walls are covered with pictures, all of which are interesting either as works of art or as the representations of historic personages. A large number are by Lawrence, others by Sir Martin Arthur Shee, Sir David Wilkie, Sir W. Beechey, &c. This Waterloo Gallery forms part of a splendid series of apartments, including the Throne Room, St. George's Hall, and the Grand Reception Room. The latter is 90 ft. long, nearly as long as the Waterloo Gallery, and is splendidly furnished in the style of Louis XIV. At one end is the great green malachite vase presented to Queen Victoria by the Czar Nicholas. Beautiful tapestry adorns this sumptuous if rather overpowering apartment, and the chandeliers are as wonderful as those at Versailles.

The St. George's Hall—where the very great banquets are held—is in the so-called Gothic style, and very long and narrow. It may be called disproportionately narrow with perfect justice, for although 200 ft. long it is only 34 ft. broad. In recesses opposite the windows are portraits of the Sovereigns of England from James I. to George IV. Above wave the banners of the original companionship of the Knights of the Garter. As a show place St. George's Hall suffers from its want of proportion, and has a gloomy look when shorn of its proper decorations; but nothing can be more magnificent than this gallery on the rare occasions when a foreign crowned head is entertained at a grand banquet. Comparisons are frequently made between Fontainebleau and Windsor, but such parallels are hardly worth while making. There is, of course, a tragic interest, fresh and recent, attached to Fontainebleau and happily absent from Windsor, and there is this much to be said for the delightful French château, that it is a school of the decorative art of the last three centuries, and that its Galerie de

Henri Quatre—imitated, but, of course, longo intervallo, in the library of the Reform Club—is peerless; but on the other hand Windsor has the advantage of size and of every adjunct of splendour. Interesting and beautiful Fontainebleau cannot be made magnificent, while Windsor always can at a few days' notice. St. George's Hall, when filled with guests in toilettes and glowing uniforms; when lit up by the gay sheen of pearls and the glitter of diamonds around a table covered with that wonderful service of gold plate, which cannot be stolen because it would require a special train to carry it away, is as superb a banqueting hall as any in Europe. Then the advantage of the dark oaken lining of the room is seen. It is not intended to form a picture in itself. It is only the frame for one.

The private apartments are open to comparatively few persons. They are cut off from the public state apartments by the Grand Corridor and very badly lighted parts of the castle. The corridor is of immense length, extending round two sides of the quadrangle, and a subterranean system extends all round it for those of meaner sort, who may not be permitted to cross the sacred parallelogram. The corridor at Windsor is a marvel. It is absolutely full, throughout its five hundred and twenty feet of length, of such cabinets as drive collectors frantic, and of such old Oriental work that the Japanese Ambassadors—fine connoisseurs in such matters—stood aghast the first time they were privileged to witness them. Distributed in these cabinets and cases, all of rare workmanship, is a museum of china, Chelsea, Oriental, and Sèvres —the magnificent Sèvres collected by the "old Marquis of Hertford" for his master, King Florizel. It would be ridiculous to say that such Sèvres as can be seen in the Queen's private apartments at Windsor was ever cheap; but, considering its enormous cost of production, it went at low prices at the time the Windsor collection was formed. There is some good china at Buckingham Palace in the rooms through which Her Majesty's lieges pass before reaching the royal presence, but nothing there will give more than a very slight idea of the ceramic wealth of Windsor Castle. There is any quantity of *rose pompadour*, and *œil de perdrix, vert pomme*, and *bleu du roi* in the form of the almost priceless *vaisseaux à mât* (the cognizance of the city of Paris) and in every other shape peculiar to the best period of *pâté tendre*. Magnificent pictures hang on the wall of the corridor—choice specimens of Canaletto, Romney, Reynolds, and Gainsborough—and bronzes of faultless execution appear between the fine cabinets and superb Oriental vases. In the north corridor, fitted up as an armoury, is the wonderful tiger's head of solid gold studded with gems, taken from Tippoo Sahib at the storming of Seringapatam, and said to be worth £30,000. It is an amusing as well as valuable trophy, for as the golden tongue of the animal is seen lolling out of its mouth, it is almost impossible to resist the temptation to make it wag. It seems to weigh at least a pound, and permits itself to be wagged freely.

From the main artery of the corridor the various drawing and other rooms open out. The three drawing-rooms are all interesting. The White Drawing-room is not yellow, like that terrible trial to the complexion at Buckingham Palace, but actually white and gold in the later style of Louis XVI., with rich carvings heavily gilt standing out from the white ground. The doors of this room close without the slightest noise, and with that perfect fit which characterises the finest cabinet work. Pictures of the royal family, by Winterhalter and others, and of no particular merit, look down from the walls. Gouthier's finest cabinets are in this room, not only beautiful in their own unrivalled work, but inlaid with superb mosaics and porcelain plaques. Everything is good in the White Drawing-room except the pictures and the carpet, the latter of which is absolutely maddening with its rosebushes and hollyhocks.

The Green Drawing-room, so called from its walls of green satin, is a beautiful apartment; but its hangings and furniture are almost lost sight of in the interest excited by the celebrated service of Sèvres made for Louis XVI., which afterwards became the property of George IV. No rival exists to this famous set of Sèvres. The hue of the *bleu du roi* is perfect, and the paintings, mostly of sylvan and marine subjects, are by the "most eminent hands" ever

employed at the royal manufactory. There is little of the rich heavy gilding by which Sèvres is sometimes marked. There is, indeed, a zone of pure white between the gilt rim and the picture, which, therefore, is not toned down by its surroundings; but appears in its pristine beauty. With the exception of a couple of plates this famous service is complete. Other grand pieces of Sèvres are distributed about the Green Drawing-room, the ceramic contents of which have been valued at £200,000. This room is the most distant apartment generally visited by the Queen, except on the occasion of a state dinner in the Royal Dining-room, when the Crimson Drawing-room is crossed. On other occasions this gorgeous apartment is occupied by the ladies and gentlemen of the Queen's household. In one corner is the grand pianoforte on which Her Majesty received her first lessons.

The Royal Dining-room is very plain. Its only and too conspicuous ornament is the wine-cooler, designed by Flaxman for George IV. when Prince Regent. It is in the style of Capo di Monte porcelain, but is silver gilt. It is several feet long, and has been derisively termed the "royal font" and the "King's pap-boat."

The Rubens Room is another interesting room, used on state occasions, and contains, among other fine specimens of the great Flemish master, his own portrait; one of Helena Forman, his second wife; and the celebrated "St. Martin sharing his cloak with the Beggar." The Throne Room has also its interest as the theatre of the installations of the Knights of the Garter. Everything is of Garter blue, and the cognizance of the order meets the eye in every direction. Perhaps the most beautiful object in the room is the carved ivory throne of Indian workmanship which was exhibited in 1851.

The Queen's private sitting-room looks over the Long Walk, and is decorated with a bust of the late Prince Consort by Theed, and Landseer's picture, "The Return from Deerstalking." In the Oak Room—an octagonal apartment just over the Sovereign's entrance to the castle—in which the Queen takes luncheon and dines, there is the wonderful portrait of herself by the Baron von Angeli, probably the most realistic portrait in the world.

Windsor Park and Virginia Water are almost beyond the limit of an average visit to the royal borough, and equally beyond that of the physical power of most one-day excursionists. It is, however, possible to see all in a long summer's day by driving to Virginia Water, after seeing the Castle and the Long Walk. Anyone who can remain over night at Virginia Water should do so. The lake, albeit artificial —the work of "Butcher" Cumberland— is singularly beautiful, and will amply repay exploration. At sunset myriads of rabbits come down to feed on the sweet grass near the water's edge, and a whistle will cause a stampede affording one of the prettiest sights in the world—a welcome change to the eye weary of bright colours and cunning workmanship.

Windsor, Old, Berkshire, on the right bank, from London 38¾ miles, from Oxford 72¾ miles. Population, 1500. Soil, gravelly. A small village prettily situated in a wooded country about two miles from New Windsor. Here was a palace of Edward the Confessor, and here Earl Godwin, as the story goes, being suspected of having compassed the death of the king's brother, protested his innocence, declaring his hope that the piece of bread he was about to eat might choke him if he lied. Whether he lied or not does not certainly appear, but he was choked for all that. The palace is also reputed to have been the scene of an unseemly quarrel between Earl Tosti and his brother, Harold, resulting in one of those personal encounters which were not of unfrequent occurrence in royal circles about that period. Cumberland Lodge, the residence of their Royal Highnesses Prince and Princess Christian, and the Royal Lodge, once the summer residence of George IV., are in this parish, which also contains several other mansions of importance.

Beaumont Lodge, once the residence of Warren Hastings, is now known as St. Stanislaus's College for Catholics. It is conducted by Fathers of the Society of Jesus, and the course of studies comprises the usual branches of a mixed classical and scientific education. There is a preparatory school in the west wing for the younger boys. Terms are, for boys over ten, £60; boys under ten, £50, with certain extras. "The rector will at once resign the charge of any boy

for whose correction ordinary means are found ineffectual."

The Royal Tapestry Works here originated in the first instance in the suggestion of Mr. H. Henry, the artist from whose designs the interior of the London terminus of the Midland Railway, the Prince of Wales's pavilion at the Paris Exhibition, the Carlton Club, and Mr. Christopher Sykes's house in Hillstreet, were decorated. Mr. Henry making considerable use of tapestry in his work, and not seeing why it could not be manufactured as well in England as anywhere else, submitted the idea to the late Prince Leopold, who entirely concurred in Mr. Henry's views. Ultimately the project was laid before the Queen, and cordially approved by Her Majesty. A Crown grant of 15 acres of land was made, and in 1876-77 a committee was formed to carry the plan into execution, with Prince Leopold as president, and the Princesses Christian and Louise as vice-presidents. Many fine works have been produced under the management of M. Brignolis; and the late Mr. E. M. Ward, R.A., who took a great interest in the works, designed a series of large cartoons which were here executed in tapestry.

The church, close to the river, is dedicated to St. Peter, and was restored in 1864. Besides chancel and nave, it has a north chapel, a tower, and spire. It contains a brass and some monuments of but little interest. In the churchyard is the tomb of Mrs. Robinson the poetess, and George IV.'s ill-treated "Perdita."

INN.—"Bells of Ouseley."

PLACE OF WORSHIP.—St. Peter's.

POSTAL ARRANGEMENTS.—Post Office (money order, telegraph office, and savings bank). Mails from London, 7.30 a.m., 12.45 and 9.0 p.m. Mails for London, 10.5 a.m., 5.45 and 8.45 p.m. The wall letter-box, Ouseley Lodge, is cleared at 9.50 a.m. and 5.50 p.m.; Sunday, 10 a.m. The wall letter-box opposite the "Wheatsheaf" is cleared at 10.15 a.m. and 5.55 p.m.; Sunday, 10.25 a.m.

NEAREST *Bridges*, up, Albert 2½ miles; down, Staines 3¾ miles. *Locks*, up, Old Windsor 1 mile; down, Bell Weir 2 miles. *Ferry*, "Bells of Ouseley." *Railway Station*, across the fields, Wraysbury (one mile from "Bells of Ouseley"); by road, Datchet.

FARES to Waterloo, from Wraysbury: 1st, 3/6, 5/6; 2nd, 2/6, 3/9; 3rd, 1/9, 3/3. From Datchet (*see* DATCHET).

Wingfield Sculls.—(*See* CHAMPIONSHIP, AMATEUR.)

Woolwich Arsenal.—Three minutes' walk from the South Eastern Railway-station, and ten minutes from the steamboat pier. Visitors must be furnished with a ticket from the War Office, obtained by personal application, or by letter to the "Secretary of State for War, War Office, Pall Mall, S. W.," stating names and addresses, and declaring that they are British subjects. Visitors with tickets are admitted on Tuesday or Thursday between the hours of 10 and 11.30 a. m. and 2 till 4.30 p.m. Foreigners must have special tickets, obtained through their ambassadors in London. Strangers without passes are refused admission. The Artillery Barracks, the head-quarters of the Royal Horse and Foot Artillery, are about fifteen minutes' walk from the steamboat pier, and ten minutes from the South Eastern Railway-station. These barracks are admirably situated, facing the common where all the artillery exercises and the great reviews take place. The band of the Royal Artillery plays frequently, in the Repository Grounds or on the common, about 5 p.m., from May till October. The Rotunda, an interesting military museum, near the barracks, is open from 10 till 6 in summer, and from 10 till 4 in winter. The Royal Military Academy, where cadets are trained for the Royal Engineer and Artillery services, is situated on the common, about one mile from the arsenal. Woolwich Dockyard was formerly used for the construction of ships for the Royal Navy, but was closed in 1869, on the recommendation of a parliamentary committee. From the Woolwich steamboat pier may be seen the point of the Thames facing the Beckton Gasworks, where the steamer *Princess Alice* sank in 1878, with upwards of 600 persons, after collision with the steamer *Bywell Castle.* A "Guide to Woolwich and the Vicinity," price 2*s.*, is published by Jackson, *Kentish Independent* Office, Woolwich. From Fenchurch-street and Liverpool-street (60 min.), 1st, 1/-, 1/6; 2nd, -/9, 1/2; 3rd, -/6, -/10, for North Woolwich 1*d.* more. Chalk Farm, 1st, 1/-, 1/6;

2nd, -/8, 1/-; for North Woolwich same fares. The Arsenal from Charing-cross, 1st, 1/6, 2/6; 2nd, 1/-, 1/8; 3rd, -/10, 1/2; par., -/8. Cannon-street and London Bridge, 1st, 1/4, 2/2; 2nd, 1/-, 1/8; 3rd, -/9, 1/2; par., -/8. Trains run also to the Dockyard from these stations at same fares.

Woolwich Reach, two miles long from the bottom of Bugsby's Reach to Woolwich Ferry. On the right (Kent) bank, Woolwich, with arsenal, dockyard, &c., and training-ship *Warspite.* Opposite, North Woolwich and its gardens.

"Worcester."—(*See* THAMES NAUTICAL TRAINING COLLEGE.)

Yacht Clubs and Burgees.

ALEXANDRA, Red, with arms of county of Essex.

CORINTHIAN, Blue, laurel leaf in gold in centre.

ERITH, Red, red Maltese cross in white shield.

JUNIOR THAMES, White, blue cross through.

LONDON SAILING CLUB, Blue, yellow dolphin.

NEW THAMES, Dark Blue, with Phœnix.

NORE, Light Blue, dark blue cross through, anchor in centre.

ROYAL HARWICH, Blue, lion rampant or.

ROYAL LONDON, Blue, with crown over City arms.

ROYAL THAMES, Blue, white cross, red crown in centre.

TEMPLE YACHT CLUB, Blue, with a yellow-winged horse rampant.

THAMES SAILING CLUB, White, dark blue cross, red foul anchor centre of cross.

THAMES VALLEY SAILING CLUB, Red with foul anchor.

(For particulars *see under the respective heads.*)

Yachts (In Dock).—The charges in the London, St. Katharine's, Victoria, and East and West India Docks are as follows, the only exception being that the East and West India Docks charge a trifle less for yachts between 150 and 200 tons :

YEARLY RATES.			£	*s.*	*d.*
Under 25 tons ..	..	..	3	3	0
25 tons and under 50 tons ..		..	6	6	0
50 ,,	,,	100 ,,	12	12	0
100 ,,	,,	150 ,, ..	18	18	0
150 ,,	,,	200 ,, ..	26	5	0

Docking and undocking, per ton ..   .. 3*d.*
Rent, per week, per ton   ..   ..   .. 1*d.*

No charge less than 10*s.* Steamers charged on builder's measurement.

Yachts entering dock will be subject to yearly rates, unless notice be given within three days from date of entrance that they are to be placed on weekly rates.

Yachts on yearly rates will be charged 10*s.* per yacht in addition if the rates are not paid within one week from the date of entrance.

Yantlet Buoy.—An 11-foot can-buoy, made of wood, and painted with black and white stripes. It is situated in Sea Reach, below the Chapman, at the western extremity of the Yantlet Middle Sand, and marks a depth of water, at low-water spring-tide, of 18 feet. It is moored with 18 fathom of chain. This buoy was in 1865 transferred to the Thames Conservancy, and has only recently been re-transferred to the Trinity House.

Yantlet Creek, in Kent, on the right bank. The limit of the jurisdiction of the Thames Conservancy, an imaginary line being here drawn across the river to the Crow Stone, an obelisk on the Essex coast, about one mile westward of Southend. Yantlet Creek divides the Isle of Grain from the mainland. Opposite the entrance of the Creek, which is in a flat and marshy country, is the Yantlet middle shoal, with its black and white striped buoy. Yantlet is five and a half nautical miles westward of the Nore.

MAIDENHEAD.

THE RAY MEAD HOTEL,

Near Boulter's Lock. Proprietor, W. DEACON.

ESTABLISHED 1854.

This Hotel is situate on the Banks of the Thames, and being immediately under and facing the beautiful woods and scenery of Taplow Court and Cleveden, offers to the public the most charming situation on the River.

Pleasure Boats, Punts, Steam Launches (to carry 30) let by the Day, Week, or longer term.

PICNICS ARRANGED AND SUPPLIED.

Letters and Telegrams have prompt attention.

MOULE'S
PATENT EARTH CLOSETS

The Only Competitive Prize ever Offered was Won by

MOULE'S PATENT EARTH CLOSET COMPANY.

AT THE

INTERNATIONAL HEALTH EXHIBITION

A

GOLD MEDAL

WAS AWARDED

For the Great Efficiency of these Closets.

5a, GARRICK STREET, COVENT GARDEN, LONDON.

212

GREAT WESTERN RAILWAY.

RIVER THAMES.

THE GREAT WESTERN RAILWAY having Stations on the Banks of the River at BRENTFORD, WINDSOR, TAPLOW, MAIDENHEAD, COOKHAM, BOURNE END, GREAT MARLOW, HENLEY, READING, PANGBOURNE, GORING, MOULSFORD, WALLINGFORD, and OXFORD, affords unequalled facilities to those desirous of seeing it. The following are the arrangements :—

CHEAP DAY EXCURSIONS.

CHEAP DAY EXCURSION TICKETS are issued daily by certain specified Trains, from 1st May to the 31st October of every year, to the following places, from PADDINGTON, Royal Oak, Westbourne Park, Kensington (Addison Road), Uxbridge Road, West Brompton, Chelsea, and Battersea; from ST. MARY'S WHITECHAPEL, Aldgate, Bishopsgate, Moorgate Street, Farringdon Street, and Stations on the Metropolitan Railway between St. Mary's Whitechapel and Edgware Road inclusive ; and from HAMMERSMITH, Shepherd's Bush, Latimer Road, and Notting Hill, at the following Third Class Return Fares :—

	s.	d.		s.	d.
Windsor	2	6	Cookham		
			Bourne End		
Taplow			Great Marlow	3	6
Maidenhead }	3	0	Henley		

The fare from St. Mary's Whitechapel and Whitechapel Stations to Windsor is 2s. 8d.

Similar Tickets are also issued to WINDSOR *via* Ealing from *Stations* on the District Railway ; and to TAPLOW *and the other Stations*, *via* Earl's Court and Westbourne Park only, from Stations between Whitechapel and Earl's Court inclusive, from Kensington (High Street), and all Stations between Putney Bridge and West Brompton inclusive, at same fares.

The Trains by which these tickets are available are published on special bills, copies of which can be obtained at any of the Great Western City Offices and Stations, or at any Station on the Metropolitan or District Lines. The cheap tickets are available only on the day of issue and by the specified Trains.

CHEAP SATURDAY TO MONDAY TICKETS.

On SATURDAYS and SUNDAYS, all the year round, First and Second Class Return Tickets to WINDSOR are issued at PADDINGTON, Kensington, Uxbridge Road, and Westbourne Park ; from ALDGATE, Bishopsgate, Moorgate Street, King's Cross, and Stations on the Metropolitan Railway between Aldgate and Edgware Road inclusive ; also from Hammersmith, Shepherd's Bush, Latimer Road, and Notting Hill, available for the return journey till the Monday following, inclusive. Fares from either of the above-mentioned Stations, First Class, **4s. 6d.** ; Second Class, **3s. 6d.**

Similar Tickets are also issued from Mansion House and all Stations on the District Railway to Hammersmith inclusive, and at Kensington (High Street), West Brompton, and Walham Green by through Trains *via* Ealing, at same fares.

Similar Tickets are also issued on Saturdays only, from Victoria, Battersea, Chelsea, and West Brompton, available for return during the same period, and at the same fares.

Also on SATURDAYS and SUNDAYS, all the year round, Cheap First and Second Class Return Tickets to HENLEY are issued at PADDINGTON, Kensington, Uxbridge Road, and Westbourne Park, also from Hammersmith, Shepherd's Bush, Latimer Road, and Notting Hill, available for the return journey till the following Monday inclusive. Fares, First Class, **7s. 6d.** ; Second Class, **5s.** Also from ALDGATE,

Bishopsgate, Moorgate Street, King's Cross, and Stations on the Metropolitan Railway between Aldgate and Edgware Road inclusive, and from MANSION HOUSE, Blackfriars, Charing Cross, Victoria, and all Stations on the District Railway between Mansion House and Earl's Court inclusive. Fares, First Class, **8s.** ; Second Class, **8s. 6d.**

Similar Tickets are also issued on Saturdays only, from Victoria, Battersea, Chelsea, and West Brompton, available for return during the same period. First Class, **7s. 6d.** ; Second Class, **5s.**

These Tickets must be used on the down journey on the date of issue, but are available for the return journey by any train on Sunday or Monday.

CHEAP TICKETS FOR PICNIC AND OTHER PLEASURE PARTIES.

Between the 1st May and the 31st October of every year, First, Second, and Third Class Return Tickets, at Reduced Fares, are issued, with certain limitations, at the principal stations to *bonâ-fide* Pleasure or Picnic Parties of not less than Six First Class, or Ten Second or Third Class passengers.

The tickets are available for use on the day of issue only; they are not issued to London except in special cases, nor from London to any place more than 30 miles distant.

In order to obtain these tickets it is necessary that application should be made for them at least three clear days before the excursion is proposed to be made, and the application must specifically state that the party is exclusively a pleasure party, the probable number of the party, the class of carriage for which the tickets are required, the station from and to which the party will travel, the date of the proposed excursion, and the train selected.

CONVEYANCE OF BOATS AND CANOES.

Small Boats and Canoes that can be conveyed in a Guard's Van, and do not require the special use of a vehicle, are charged 1d. per mile, with a minimum of 2s. 6d. The minimum charge for a Collapsible Canoe is 1s.

Boats and Canoes requiring a truck or trucks are charged 3d. per mile for first truck, and 2d. per mile for each additional truck, with a minimum charge of 7s. 6d. for first truck, and 5s. for each additional truck.

When more Boats than one can be loaded safely on the same truck or trucks, the extra Boats are charged as follows :—

When belonging to the same owner, for each extra Boat 25 per cent. of the charge for the first Boat.

When not belonging to the same owner, no reduction is made.

Boats conveyed on carriage trucks, when accompanied by the crew or other men (not less than four in number), are charged two-thirds of the above rates ; in all cases by special agreement. The reduction is made only one way if the crew, or other men, accompany the Boat only one way, but is made both ways if they accompany the Boats both going and returning.

The time within which Boats may be sent to and returned from Regattas extends from a week before to a week after the Regatta.

The above rates apply from Station to Station only, and in all cases on the understanding that the owner takes all risks of loading, unloading, and carriage.

J. GRIERSON, *General Manager.*

PADDINGTON TERMINUS.

DORCHESTER.

THE WHITE HART HOTEL.

Good Accommodation for Boating Parties and Bicyclists.

DINNERS ON THE SHORTEST NOTICE.

LOUISA DEARLOVE, Proprietress.

HALLIFORD.

THE SHIP HOTEL.

This well-known Hotel, being situated on the very bank of the River, and commanding extensive views of the surrounding country, offers every comfort and the best accommodation for Picnic Parties, Anglers, River Tourists, &c. Dinners, Teas, &c., provided on the shortest notice. Wines and Spirits of the choicest qualities.

PROPRIETOR, ROBERT STONE.

KEATING'S POWDER

DESTROYS BUGS FLEAS MOTHS BEETLES

Sold in Tins 6ᵈ 1/-&2/6

NURSE EDDA'S INFANT CARMINATIVE.

THIS unequalled remedy is entirely free from any Opiates or noxious or strong acting Medicine ; its effect is instant in relieving Infants from GRIPES, WIND, COLIC, &c. It is guaranteed a simple, harmless Medicine. No one in charge of a Baby should be without it ; have it ready in the house. *Price* 1s. *per Bottle at all Chemists, or free by Parcels' Post ; same Price,* 12 *Stamps, to* THOS. KEATING, *Chemist, St. Paul's, London.*

KEATING'S WORM TABLETS.

NEARLY all children suffer from Worms ; if suspected do not wait, you can with ease cure the child ; this remedy is sure to cure ; safe to use (has no effect except on Worms). *Tins,* 1s. 1½d., *at all Chemists.*

LONDON. MR. BURR'S HOTEL.

10, 11, & 12, Queen Square, W.C.

Near the British Museum, and about half a mile from places of amusement. "I will mention where you may get a quiet resting-place. In search of that sort of thing I have, in my time, wandered into all sorts of hotels and boarding-houses ; but the rattle of the cabs along the pitch-stoned roads has ever come between me and my rest. The quietest and nicest place that I have discovered within easy reach of the sights of London is Mr. and Mrs. BURR'S, 10, 11, 12, QUEEN SQUARE, near British Museum. There is a home feeling there, and a quiet at night, which are quite refreshing."—Çà et là. First Class only. Established 25 Years. Particulars in print sent to any address. Tell the Cabman. **11, QUEEN SQUARE.**

9